Islands and Empires

COGNELLA HISTORY OF EUROPE SERIES

Islands and Empires

A History of Modern Britain

Thomas Mockaitis, Vivien Dietz, Richard Floyd, and Dana Rabin

cognella®

SAN DIEGO

Bassim Hamadeh, CEO and Publisher
David Miano, Specialist Acquisitions Editor
Michelle Piehl, Senior Project Editor
Jess Estrella, Senior Graphic Designer
Trey Soto, Licensing Specialist
Jaye Pratt, Interior Designer
Natalie Piccotti, Director of Marketing
Kassie Graves, Senior Vice President, Editorial
Jamie Giganti, Director of Academic Publishing

Cover images: Copyright © 2013 iStockphoto LP/Nikada; Copyright © 2015 iStockphoto LP/mbbirdy; U.S. Air Force, 1943; Joseph Nash, Louis Haghe, and David Roberts, Dickinsons' Comprehensive Pictures of the Great Exhibition of 1851, Dickinson, Brothers, 1852; Copyright © 2017 iStockphoto LP/justhavealook.

Printed in the United States of America.

cognella® ACADEMIC PUBLISHING
3970 Sorrento Valley Blvd., Ste. 500, San Diego, CA 92121

BRIEF CONTENTS

DETAILED CONTENTS

INTERPRETING THE BRITISH PAST

The Historian's Craft

The study of history is the study of the past. Historians identify moments of change, reconstructing the processes by which changes happened and why.

Change is inevitable, but it occurs at different paces at different times, depending on the particular forces driving it. Change, moreover, should not be mistaken for progress. Events do not unfold toward any predetermined goal; they may move forward or backward or even sideways, and observers often disagree over how to view such developments. Identifying both innovations that prompted change and continuities that resisted it, historians assess whether the changes were superficial or radical, gradual, or sudden. The examination of these processes allows historians to connect the past to the present through a study of how previous generations identified problems and how they tried to resolve them. Beyond an inventory of past peoples and their cultures, societies, difficulties, and accomplishments, an awareness and understanding of the past can provide perspective on our societies today.

SOURCES

How do we access the past? How do historians find out what happened, and how do they make sense of it? Finding answers to these questions is not easy; knowledge about the past is not available to us in a comprehensive form, nor is it ever complete, transparent, or fixed. Instead, it is produced by historians using a combination of facts and analysis.

Historians focus on *primary sources* both to find facts and to analyze their subjects. Primary sources are defined as any texts or artifacts created at the time under study. Primary sources might include official government records (e.g., census returns, laws, administrative memos, police reports), published works (e.g., books, maps, newspapers, pamphlets, sheet music), and unpublished private papers (e.g., account books, diaries, letters, family photographs). Recent historical scholarship has paid particular attention to material culture, sharing both methods and findings with the related disciplines of anthropology, archeology, and art history. It is only the imagination that limits the kinds of sources that might be examined and analyzed for the historical secrets they contain. These artifacts are the foundation of the historical accounts that the authors of this textbook used to construct a narrative of British history.

In addition to primary sources, historians rely on existing scholarship, examining books and articles written years, decades, and even centuries earlier. Such works, produced by previous historians through their own examination of primary sources, are known as *secondary sources*.

Contemporary historians use them to gain a deeper understanding of the time period under consideration, its larger context, and the particular questions they seek to answer. The discipline of history is therefore an ongoing conversation among scholars.

Argument drives the conversation. This does not mean that historians behave belligerently. To the contrary, historical thinking necessitates empathy. In order to understand the past, we must examine sources—primary and secondary—and the ideas expressed in them from the point of view of those who produced them. This process demands recognizing other positions, those of both historical subjects and fellow historians, and assessing the past on others' terms. It also requires synthesizing material from a variety of perspectives to formulate informed opinions about past issues and debates, the historical circumstances that shaped them, and their relationship to present-day concerns. The same process applies whether the historian's particular topic is a certain person, event, or set of ideas. In short, historical interpretation necessitates a shift from mastering content to analytical reasoning, and always with evidence marshalled in support of the resulting argument. So rather than an amassing of facts, the study of history relies on the combination of fact and interpretation. Historians use this combination to ask and answer questions about the past. Their interpretations are always shaped by the contemporary historical moment in which they write, produced within a framework of personal beliefs and prejudices. Point of view and perspective, and sometimes even an explicit agenda, influence how historians formulate historical questions and what evidence they choose to pursue and analyze, hence the ongoing conversation about those decisions and the arguments they inform.

Historians develop their expertise with specific geographical and chronological foci. Subspecialties like legal history, social history, women's and gender history, environmental history, medical history, the history of science, labor history, and urban history allow for thematic emphases. Historians often choose and interpret their sources with a particular theoretical approach. For example, historians use gender theory to answer questions about the different roles and status assigned to men and women in the past. A Marxist approach might be brought to bear on economic data or sources recounting how factories developed. The study of the slave trade and US slavery could draw on economic theory as well as theories that account for racialized thinking. Cultural history might involve discursive analysis or the study of everyday life. Historians meanwhile use various methodological approaches such as statistical analysis, literary analysis, or visual analysis depending on the sources they are using. Historians are not bound by any one methodological or theoretical approach; in fact, the most skilled historians combine them in order to present the most detailed, nuanced, and accurate account.

The historian Teodoro Andal Agoncillo explains it this way: "History is written by every generation. Every generation writes its own history using the same sources. The interpretations vary according to time."[1] But historical writing is not fiction. Again, we return to the centrality of evidence, primary sources produced at the time that the historian is writing about. In the course of the conversation, historians assess the merit of a work of scholarship, its strengths and weaknesses, by examining both the quality and the quantity of evidence that the author uses and the ways in which they deploy the evidence in the construction of their arguments. The term *revisionism* is often used to describe work by those who challenge a predominant historiographical interpretation. It could result from the discovery of new sources or a new analytical perspective, and if it gains support from other historians, it may emerge as the new orthodoxy.

PERIODIZATION

Historians attend to issues of timing on multiple levels: the contexts in which their historical subjects operated; in which their primary sources were produced and received; and in which their fellow practitioners researched, analyzed, and wrote. *Periodization* is another way that historians take time into account. Periodization is the division of history into discrete blocks of time; it imposes order and system to the vast expanse of historical time. An epoch or a period is usually identified as having some stable shared characteristic which varies by culture, society, and geography. These labels can seem arbitrary, and they are regularly challenged and reordered as part of the discipline of history and the ongoing scholarly conversation.

In European history time is divided into ancient, medieval, early modern, and modern history. The dates assigned to each of these periods are the subject of debate, but generally, the early modern period is said to begin with the invention of the printing press in the fifteenth century. The modern period is usually dated as beginning with the French Revolution. This book, then, opens in the early modern period, and it is those perspectives and sensibilities that populate the first few chapters. For many historians, the eighteenth century is considered a time of transition out of the early modern and into the modern. To avoid confusion in a book about modern Britain, we have referred to the eighteenth century rather than the early modern period.

A traditional set of choices explained in chapter 2 has this account of modern British history beginning in 1688, with what has been called the Glorious Revolution. As with all questions of periodization, this decision may seem arbitrary, and indeed there are other historical events that could have been chosen as the starting point for the book's narrative. The pages that follow describe developments, some violent and others peaceful, in 1707, 1714, 1760, 1783, and 1801 (to name just a few) that signaled important political transitions. A case could also be made for transformative cultural or environmental occurrences, such as a philosophical publication, a scientific discovery, or a natural disaster. But the conflict in 1688, which sent a king into exile and redefined the relationship between Crown and Parliament on the eve of the eighteenth century, was an event to which successive generations of Britons kept looking back. It offers a compelling beginning for contemplating not only modern British history but also the nature of historical perspective and the process of historical interpretation. In addition to our starting point the authors have chosen to divide the period from 1688 until the present into three parts. The first continues through "the long eighteenth century" until 1815 and the end of Britain's wars against revolutionary and Napoleonic France. The second part covers "the long nineteenth century," and the third part the period from 1914 and the outbreak of the First World War until the present.

Despite the constant debates that surround periodization, it is extremely useful to historians and students of history. It allows us to shape our understanding of the past and make thematic connections, to recognize characteristics that developed in a certain time or place and how they changed over time. Of course, the periods we have identified do not end neatly on the last day of a given century or the first day of the next one. Events and cultural preoccupations do not fall into 100-year spans that begin when the calendar shifts. Historians acknowledge the coherence of a certain set of events (like Britain's successive wars against rival France, including the War of American Independence and culminating in those following the French Revolution) with the concept of "the long eighteenth century." References to "the long nineteenth century" similarly recognize a coherence in the patterns, values, and world views of Europeans that was severed by the First World War. Each of these divisions of time is, again, the subject of conversation and sometimes heated debate. And the patterns an economic historian traces over a certain set of decades might clash with those trends documented by a women's historian of the same period. This is the stuff of historical argument: it imbues the field with vitality because the different perspectives highlight the many histories of any given time period.

HISTORIOGRAPHY

Such considerations are elements of *historiography*, the study of the writing of history and of written histories. Historiography examines the historical scholarship produced on a given topic like the Irish Famine, or in more general terms it refers to the study of trends within the discipline and among its practitioners such as the rise of social history in the 1960s, the interest in women's history and the turn to gender history in the 1970s and 1980s, and the emergence of cultural history in the 1990s. When the latter, it functions as an account of the ongoing conversation between historians on that particular subject, of how historical questions and arguments developed over time. Historiography has thus been called "the history of history."[2]

Over the last two decades the entire field of British history has changed dramatically. The emphasis has shifted from an overwhelming focus on England, to a study of the four kingdoms, England, Ireland, Scotland, and Wales of the British Isles, and the connections between their histories. This comparative approach to the well-known narrative of English history often exposes a different set of significances and their real and material consequences. Most provocatively, this approach questions the coherence of the British Isles as a unified kingdom. For example, as the study of colonialism and empire have grown, the concept of internal colonialism has been developed to describe the English desire for political, economic, and cultural control of Wales, Scotland, and Ireland. In a similar vein, the idea that Ireland was England's "first colony" strikes some American students of Irish ancestry as preposterous, again calling into question those attributes considered a shared inheritance of the British Isles.

Another important historiographical trend related to British history has been the emphasis of the entangled nature of British history with all aspects of European history. For strategic reasons Britain sometimes positioned itself as an island, separate from the European continent. This public relations myth of splendid isolation suggested that Britain avoided alliances in its foreign policy in order to prevent burdensome entanglements that would compromise its autonomy. Another myth about Britain's history is that of British exceptionalism, this one founded in England's common law tradition (as opposed to the Roman law that informed legal practices elsewhere in Europe). Although many if not most nations believe themselves to be somewhat exceptional, British exceptionalism justified numerous oppressive and violent policies related to colonial and imperialist endeavors on the grounds of Britain's constitutional monarchy and its discourse of democracy and liberty. Citing the common law tradition and later the ideology of rule of law, Britain held itself up as a beacon of equality and freedom while exploiting and subjugating other peoples and lands. Our account of British history denies both of these myths and instead argues that Britain was invested in the history of Europe and intervened to protect its interests there constantly, driving historical circumstances on the continent and across the globe. Britain's vast empire expanded exponentially in the eighteenth and throughout the nineteenth century, ranging from Ireland to India, from the Caribbean to Africa, Malaysia, and Hong Kong. The "imperial turn" in scholarship has also been quite transformational, pushing the current generation of historians to acknowledge that Britain's empire was not an accident and that it did not just "fall into Britain's lap." Instead, it was a work of determined acquisition, maintained with vigilance on the part of the government, a project in which many felt pride. The corollary of this fact is that Britain and its colonies were entangled and intertwined. The interconnections between Britain and its colonies produced an economy, a culture, and a society that was co-constituted. Highlighting Britain's relationship with the British Isles, its empire, Europe, and global events, we hope renders a deeper and more comprehensive understanding of its history.

Geography of Modern Britain

Geography played an important role in how history unfolded in the British Isles and contributed to the different economies and ways of life. Twenty-one miles from the continent of Europe, Britain is a part of Europe but has always maintained a separate identity. Two keys to British history are Britain's relationship to the sea and the channel that separates it from the continent.

The relationship between Britain and the sea changed over time. In addition to wave after wave of migrations that began in prehistoric times, and later included Romans in the first century BCE, Anglo-Saxons in the fifth century CE, Vikings in the eighth, and Norman followers of William the Conqueror in the eleventh, the sea was a highway for trade, war, and exploration. The sea also provided defense. This fact had serious consequences. Because the British felt safe, they did not feel they needed to have a large standing army during peacetime. They also developed their navy and became a maritime power. At first the sea isolated Britain from civilizations of the Mediterranean: Mesopotamia, Egypt, Greece, and Rome. But as the Atlantic replaced the Mediterranean as the center of commerce and culture, Britain moved from the periphery to the center of power and world events.

There are 5,000 British Isles dominated by two major islands, Britain (which was called Britannia by Julius Caesar) and Ireland—altogether 120,000 square miles. England is less than half this big (50,331 square miles). Wales is 7,500 square miles, Scotland 30,000, and Ireland 32,000. So when we talk about England we are talking about the southern part of the main island of the British Isles.

England is divided into two major districts. One is a Lowland area with heavy soil that covers approximately the southeastern half of England. Because of its rich soil, the majority of the population lived in the Lowlands before the Industrial Revolution. The most important of the many navigable rivers is the Thames, the site of the capital city of London established by the Romans in 200 CE. The highlands in the northwest are mountainous with many minerals and fossil fuels including coal, lead, and copper. The soil cannot be used for agriculture; instead, this area is used for grazing and sheep farming. Other important landmarks include the Lake District and the Pennine Mountains. To the west, England's 160-mile boundary with Wales took its modern form in the early sixteenth century. But it is much as it had been in since the eighth century, loosely following a series of rivers as well as Offa's Dyke, a great earthwork named for the Anglo-Saxon king of Mercia (757–796). Wales's other borders are all water, and its largest centers of population hug the coast. Medieval castles dominate Wales's rugged northwestern edge along the Irish Sea, the commercial centers of Cardiff and Swansea its southern shore along the Bristol Channel. The land itself is mostly mountainous. Wales's highest mountain range is Snowdonia in the northwest, while the lush valleys and craggy peaks of the Cambrian Mountains traverse central Wales from the northeast to the southwest. Such topography made Wales a center for mineral extraction—slate, ironstone, and coal—and an especially difficult place to cultivate crops. Its agriculture, therefore, focused on livestock farming, and the slightly more arable land on its southeastern border with England. Scotland's band of barren moorland forms another border with England, providing a partial explanation for why Scotland developed its own separate society and government. Farther north, the Scottish Lowlands include fertile soil, rolling wooded hills, sparkling streams, and a chain of lakes. The bulk of the Scottish population lives here and always has, and this is where Edinburgh

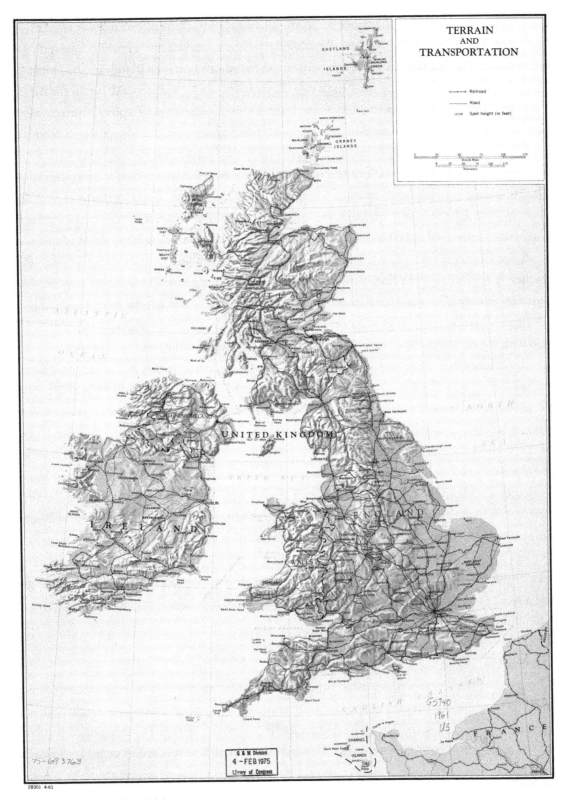

FIGURE 0.1 The British Isles.

and Glasgow are located. Still farther north are the Highlands, the traditional home of clans. It has always been difficult for even a small number of people to make a living in these inhospitable, but beautiful, surroundings. In addition to the main island, the northern islands of Shetland and Orkney and the Hebrides ring Scotland's Highlands to the north and west. Although the use of the terms *highlands* and *lowlands* is often overlaid with prejudice, the geographical differences in Scotland contributed to the development of social, political, economic, and cultural differences along with those of language, political allegiances, and religious affiliation.

Ireland's lowlands soil is rich and fertile. The island's mountainous region is along the coast. The 200-mile-long Shannon River is the longest in the British Isles. The port towns of Dublin, Cork, Wexford, Belfast, and Galway served as economic hubs and engines of commerce. Ireland is separated from England, Wales, and Scotland by the Irish Channel, which is about 50 miles at its widest point, and this distance led to the development of a unique civilization there, which was frequently oppressed by the English but never fully culturally or politically dominated. With only 18 miles between Ulster and the Kintyre Peninsula in western Scotland, Ireland and Scotland had strong ties, as reflected in linguistic borrowing and intermarriage among ruling families. Ireland also maintained commercial and political ties with the European continent.

The islands that made up the British Isles in the seventeenth century were home to diverse cultures, ethnicities, languages, religious beliefs, legal traditions, customs, and ways of life. The people who lived in each of the four kingdoms did not see themselves as having much in common with each other, let alone with those who inhabited the other kingdoms. In 1688 the population of the British Isles was 8.4 million: there were 5 million in England, 400,000 in Wales, 1 million in Scotland, and 2 million in Ireland. Most people in Wales and Ireland spoke Welsh and Irish. In Scotland's Highlands many spoke Scottish Gaelic, while Lowland Scots spoke a Germanic Scots. Although the English tried to impose English common law in Ireland and Wales, it was only partially adopted. Scotland retained its own legal system founded in Roman law. Religion, in particular, divided people in the wake of the Reformation and the proliferation of Protestant sects that followed. Religious diversity and conflict prevailed within each of the kingdoms, though the majority in England and Wales followed the Anglican Church, in Scotland the Presbyterian Church, and in Ireland the Catholic Church.

Britain in 1688

At the end of the seventeenth century, Britain stood poised on the cusp of great economic and social transformation. The preconditions of that transformation already existed and would coalesce over the next seventy years. The Revolution of 1688 preserved rights of Parliament and secured private wealth from arbitrary taxation. The majority of British people still engaged in primary food production, but farmers and agricultural laborers formed a smaller percentage of the general population than they did in other European countries. Fewer people needed to grow food meant more laborers available to work in mines and factories; growing urban centers meanwhile encouraged more efficient food production. Abundant resources, especially coal and iron ore, and a system of rivers that could be connected by canals favored the birth of industries, as did creation of a central bank and the invention of joint stock companies. The attitude toward making money, often called the entrepreneurial spirit, however, would prove to be a key factor in combining these advantages to produce the Industrial Revolution.

By the turn of the eighteenth century, attitudes and ideas had also changed, particularly on the subject of religion. A century and a half of religious conflict had finally run its course. Anglicanism was the official religion, but the authorities had little interest in enforcing conformity upon other Protestant sects who enjoyed de facto freedom of worship. Catholicism remained a marginalized religion, and in Ireland penal laws reduced the Catholic majority to an impoverished rural under-class. As the concept of civil society developed during the eighteenth century, however, religion became more a matter of private practice and less a matter of public concern. Pioneered by Sir Isaac Newton and John Locke, science and natural law became the new faith, at least for the educated. Among the aristocracy, dour Puritanism gave way to a more permissive attitude toward morality. How far down the social ladder these changes in outlook and attitudes went is hard to determine.

Identifying the broad sweep of trends and patterns unfolding in 1688 presents serious challenges. Trying to determine what life was like for ordinary people of the British Isles is even more difficult. Most people at the time either could not read and write or were only marginally literate. Even if they could have written about their lives, their accounts might have been disappointing. Records created by those with the leisure and inclination to write letters and keep diaries suggest that they probably spent less time reflecting on their circumstances than we do today. They also geared their expectations to the realities that circumscribed them. For most people quality of life meant having enough to eat (and perhaps a bit more so that they could feel comfortable rather than merely fed), a place to live, and good health. Indirect evidence suggests that by these modest standards, life was getting better for ordinary folk.

The plague occurred in Britain for the last time with the London visitation of 1665–66. People continued to suffer from other endemic diseases (smallpox, measles, typhoid, etc.), but until cholera made its way to Britain from India in the nineteenth century, no large-scale pandemics struck the islands. There were also fewer famines. With the exception of Ireland, people went hungry but rarely starved. Indeed, diet generally improved, thanks to the real treasure of the Americas, new food crops. The potato proved particularly valuable for feeding the poor. Based on evidence such as consumption of white bread (desirable because the well-off preferred it) and meat, British people probably ate better than many of their continental counterparts. Despite the general prosperity, however, great inequality and widespread poverty persisted, which in turn produced social unrest.

The long eighteenth century (1688–1815) would see Britain emerge as a preeminent power at the center of a global network of trade, commerce, and empire. It would undergo profound demographic, social and cultural change driven by interaction between Britain's overseas territories and the metropole. That interaction would shape the lives of conquered people. By the end of the period, people would be demanding political and social reform in Britain and across the empire.

IMAGE CREDIT

Fig. 0.1: Source: https://commons.wikimedia.org/wiki/File:British_Isles-_Terrain_and_transportation._4-61._LOC_75693763.jpg.

Overview, 1688-1815

The period 1688–1815 was defined by historical trends and patterns that began with the Revolution of 1688 and continued through the Napoleonic Wars. Chapter 1 analyzes the demographics of the British Isles and the nature of society. Chapter 2 examines political structures as well as the creation first of Great Britain and then of the United Kingdom. Chapter 3 situates Britain in a world-historical context, examining the series of conflicts with France known as the "second hundred years' war" and the expansion of the British empire. In chapter 4, the authors explore the beliefs, ideas, and attitudes that comprised the eighteenth-century worldview. Chapter 5 looks at political affairs, including the role of parties and patronage. The section concludes with a discussion of economic transformations (chapter 6), what has often been called the Industrial Revolution, as well as important developments in other sectors of the economy, including agriculture and transportation.

CHAPTER 1

Structures and Patterns of Everyday Life

Something remarkable happened in the middle of Britain's long eighteenth century, a period of war and revolution defined here as starting with the expulsion of King James II in the Revolution of 1688 and ending with the defeat of Napoleon at the Battle of Waterloo in 1815. Population growth, which had been static at the close of the seventeenth century and slow in the opening years of the eighteenth (there had even been, in the late 1720s and early 1740s, short periods of decline) shifted into high gear around 1750. Growth rates became both faster and more sustained. Compared to the almost 5 million inhabitants of England in 1688, there were 5.75 million in 1750, 8 million in 1794, and 10 million in 1812. England's population more than doubled during the long eighteenth century, with almost all the growth coming in the second half. Scotland also experienced unprecedented expansion after 1750, increasing from 1.2 million at midcentury to 1.6 million in 1801 and 1.8 million in 1811. Wales was and remained much more sparsely populated; London had more residents than all of Wales throughout the eighteenth century. Still, Welsh population figures inched toward 500,000 in 1780, 600,000 in 1801, and 700,000 in 1811. Nowhere else in western Europe was there comparable expansion; the relatively small island of Britain came to contain a disproportionate share of Europe's people.[1]

Counting People

As the following chapters will demonstrate, the effects of these developments in all areas of life—social, economic, imperial, and political—proved monumental. Their causes, however, were more subtle, even mysterious to contemporaries. Were declining mortality rates responsible, or was it increasing fertility? Improvement occurred in both areas. The average life expectancy in 1700 hovered somewhere between 36 and 37 years; it rose to approximately 40 over the course of the century. In particular, maternal and infant mortality decreased, with pregnancy, childbirth, and the postpartum period, though still dangerous, becoming much less so to mother and child. But the biggest change came in fertility itself; more births appear to have played a larger role—by as much as two and a half times—than any simultaneous triumphs over disease and death. Thanks to changing economic circumstances, the average English age at first marriage dropped by almost three years over the course of the long eighteenth century, from approximately 28 to 25 for men and 26 to 23 for women. Younger wives meant longer marital reproductive windows, and for married couples fertility rose, perhaps by as much as 20 percent. Meanwhile, the proportion of the population that never married declined. Despite these trends, more sex (or more reproductive sex) occurred outside of wedlock as well; the incidence of both illegitimate births and pregnant women marrying increased considerably.[2] Family construction was thus in flux in the long eighteenth century.

Of course, these figures are averages and mask important regional and socioeconomic variations. Scottish women were a little older at first marriage than their English counterparts, and the more elite a couple the greater the age difference between bride and groom. The daughters of the aristocracy tended to wed youngest of all, often to men as much as ten years their senior.[3] Moreover, counting births may obscure population increases that resulted from immigration and losses from emigration; both types of movement occurred, especially between metropole and colonies. Britain in the eighteenth century, and London in particular, was ethnically and racially diverse. Many Irish moved there in search of work, and one sign of Britain's expanding trade and empire was the presence of ten to fifteen thousand Blacks, enslaved and free, in the capital, and perhaps half that number in the provinces (especially in the port towns of Bristol and Liverpool).[4] Such qualifications are endless, reminding the historian of the danger of generalizing from particular findings; the nature of individual experience, even that of particular communities, is rarely captured in aggregate trends.

But it is striking that contemporaries were counting people too, and in wholly new ways contemplating patterns of population change. For them, it was a matter of national prosperity and, at times of war, survival, to know the number of Britons, where and with whom they lived, how much they earned, and how they were employed. Two notable examples of this frame our period. At its start, Gregory King, a herald and engraver who became one of the first economic statisticians, compiled "A Scheme of Income and Expense of the Several Families of England Calculated for Year 1688" as part of a larger project (table 1.1). He influenced others interested in such matters, including the economist Adam Smith, although King's work was not published until the early nineteenth century, in the immediate wake of the first national census. The latter, mandated by Parliament in 1800 and conducted in 1801, was repeated every decade (except during World War II) thereafter. King's table and that first census offer telling bookends for the long eighteenth century, glimpses into both the nature of British society and how contemporaries sought to understand and order it.

In 1695, King became a commissioner in charge of a new tax on baptisms, marriages, and burials, a convenient day job for someone interested in demographic data. With his "Scheme of Income and

TABLE 1.1 Gregory King's "A Scheme of Income and Expense"

NUMBER OF FAMILIES	RANKS, DEGREES, TITLES, AND QUALIFICATIONS	HEADS PER FAMILY	NUMBER OF PERSONS	YEARLY INCOME PER FAMILY
160	Temporal lords	40	6,400	2,800
26	Spiritual lords	20	520	1,300
800	Baronets	16	12,800	880
600	Knights	13	7,800	650
3,000	Esquires	10	30,000	450
12,000	Gentlemen	8	96,000	280
5,000	Persons in offices	8	40,000	240
5,000	Persons in offices	6	30,000	120
2,000	Merchants and traders by sea	8	16,000	400
8,000	Merchants and traders by sea*	6	48,000	200
10,000	Persons in the law	7	70,000	140
2,000	Clergymen	6	12,000	60
8,000	Clergymen	5	40,000	45
40,000	Freeholders	7	280,000	84
140,000	Freeholders	5	700,000	50
150,000	Farmers	5	750,000	44
16,000	Persons in sciences and liberal arts	5	80,000	60
40,000	Shopkeepers and tradesmen	4½	180,000	45
60,000	Artisans and handicrafts	4	240,000	40
5,000	Naval officers	4	20,000	80
4,000	Military officers	4	16,000	60
511,586			**2,675,520**	
50,000	Common seamen	3	150,000	20
364,000	Laboring people and out servants	3½	1,275,000	15
400,000	Cottagers and paupers	3¼	1,300,000	6.5
35,000	Common soldiers	2	70,000	14
849,000			**2,795,000**	
	Vagrants		**30,000**	
511,586	**Increasing the wealth of the kingdom**		**2,675,520**	
849,000	**Decreasing the wealth of the kingdom**		**2,825,000**	
1,360,586			**5,500,520**	

Source: Gregory King, *Two Tracts*, ed. G. E. Barnett (Baltimore: Johns Hopkins Press, 1936).

* This second category of maritime merchants is what King wrote; versions in which it appears as "Merchants and Traders by Land" are subsequent alterations, though it is possible that this is what King intended.

Expense" King sought to depict various groups' contributions to "the Wealth of Kingdom," dividing society into 26 categories that ranged from temporal lords and spiritual lords (aristocrats and bishops) to vagrants. According to King, the former, with their tiny numbers (just 186 families) and august wealth, led those who increased national prosperity. The latter, along with others whose income fell below the subsistence line, decreased it; relying on public poor relief, private charity, and other means to scrape by, the unemployed and the working poor constituted more than half of the population.

King's findings may resonate with twenty-first-century readers attuned to recent political debates about income inequality and the top 1 percent. But what about his method? The categories King employed reveal essential features of British social organization in his day. For example, he labeled social units as families, but they were in fact households, with the richest containing on average forty members—extended kin and servants as well as parents and children. Even in the middle ranks of society, households typically contained employees who were not kin. Moreover, for all of his interest in wealth creation and loss, King ranked families by status, with more affluent sea merchants listed below less affluent office holders; the type of work one did, whether one owned land, and to whom one was related mattered too, and sometimes mattered more. King therefore employed both titles and occupations to identify groups and quantify their size. Following King's lead, this chapter will explore the nature of those social rankings and how status operated.

King made his calculations during a commercial, colonial war (Nine Years War, 1688–1697), and used them in part to compare England's economy to those of its chief trade rivals. Britain was competing for foreign trade and territory with both its enemy, Catholic France, and its ally, the Protestant Netherlands; many believed that a large, employed populace was the key to victory. A century later, clergyman and political economist Thomas Robert Malthus took a gloomier view, worrying about how much the populace had increased. In his 1798 *An Essay on the Principle of Population*, Malthus warned that population growth will inevitably outstrip food supply, precipitating famine, disease, or other corrective disasters.[5] Malthus thus attributed a pending demographic catastrophe to the economic improvements and pursuit of personal happiness that led to earlier marriages and increased fertility. Malthus's work went through many editions, but as scholars critiqued his predictions, the politicians who ordered the first census had more immediate motives for counting heads. "Especially in a defensive war," Parliament declared amidst hostilities with revolutionary France (1793–1802) and fears of foreign invasion, "it must be of the highest importance to enrol and discipline the greatest possible number of men."[6] Clergymen, local officials, and schoolmasters thus gathered information in their "Parish, Township, or Place" about the number of inhabitants (distinguishing males and females, including children, and excluding men already in the armed forces), houses, and families per house. They recorded in 1801 a population of approximately 10.9 million people living in 1.8 million residences in England, Scotland, and Wales, and specified how many persons were engaged in agriculture, in trade, manufacturing, and handicrafts, and in none of these. Authorities meanwhile estimated that the population of Ireland, which in the past year had been joined to Great

Britain by an act of union, "somewhat exceeds" 4 million, a figure extrapolated from the number of Irish homes subject to a hearth tax.[7] No occupational breakdown was even attempted for Ireland, where the majority of inhabitants engaged in agriculture.

Census data collected in the localities documented each community street by street, house by house. From such documents we learn that women often headed households; in this example (figure 1.1), 46 percent of householders were women. We also see that some people lived at their place of employment; four females and one male are listed as residing at the establishment of Messrs. Pleas & Co., where perhaps one worked in trade. But even the important census distinction between households and families does little to explain the arrangements at Sarah Fernside's single-family dwelling in which resided three males and fifty-nine females, ages unknown, none of them engaged in agriculture, commerce, or industry. Was Fernside a widow? Did she never marry? Were any of the house's many inhabitants her children or siblings? Did she run a business in the house, a school for girls perhaps? The many questions invited by Sarah Fernside's census entry suggest the complexity of domestic life and gender relations in the long eighteenth century. This chapter will also explore the variety of ways in which Britons thought about and experienced gender and family—as spouses, parents, and children—in the long eighteenth century.

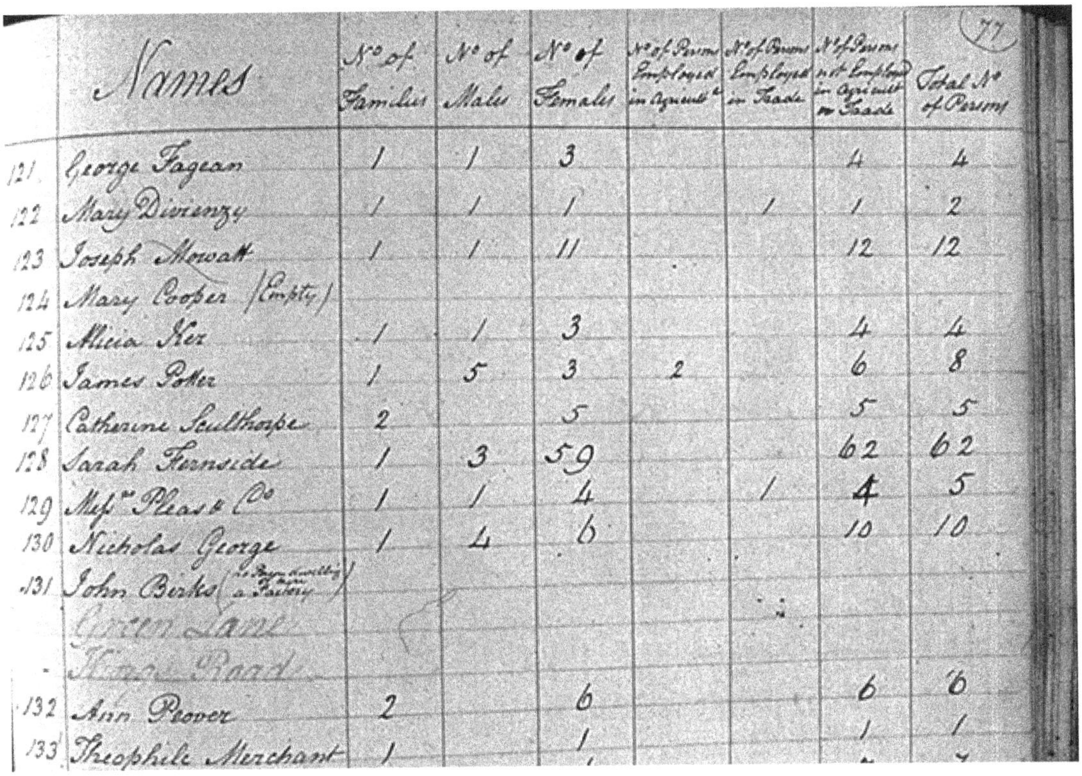

	Names	No. of Families	No. of Males	No. of Females	No. of Persons Employed in Agriculture	No. of Persons Employed in Trade	No. of Persons not Employed in Agriculture or Trade	Total No. of Persons
121	George Fagean	1	1	3			4	4
122	Mary Divenzy	1	1	1		1	1	2
123	Joseph Mowatt	1	1	11			12	12
124	Mary Cooper (Empty)							
125	Alicia Ker	1	1	3			4	4
126	James Potter	1	5	3	2		6	8
127	Catherine Sculthorpe	2		5			5	5
128	Sarah Fernside	1	3	59			62	62
129	Messrs. Pleas & Co.	1	1	4		1	4	5
130	Nicholas George	1	4	6			10	10
131	John Birks ([illegible] a Factory)							
	Green Lane							
	[illegible] Road							
132	Ann Peover	2		6			6	6
133	Theophile Merchant	1		1			1	1

FIGURE 1.1 Sample from the 1801 census returns for Essex.

Status, Patronage, and Deference

Historians of the early modern period often refer to the "Great Chain of Being" to convey how individuals living at the time might have imagined their situation in the world (figure 1.2). The great chain was an old idea, dating back to the classical philosopher Aristotle who viewed the universe as

FIGURE 1.2 Drawing of the Great Chain of Being from Didacus Valades, *Rhetorica Christiana*, 1579.

made of different forms arranged in a hierarchy from the most basic and earthly, like rocks, metal, and plants, to those considered to have more spirit, like animals, human beings, and the divine. People were organized by the amount of spirit they were considered to have, starting with kings, queens, and nobles at the top and peasants at the bottom. Within households, fathers came first, then mothers, sons, daughters, and servants. Early modern people understood this ordered and ranked universe to be divinely ordained. They believed that those individuals or societies that broke the chain through any kind of disobedience would be punished with illness, a bad harvest, earthquakes, floods, and war. We see this cultural consensus on the importance of order and anxieties about the threats to it in Shakespeare's plays when Macbeth, who murdered a king and seized the throne unlawfully, suffers paranoia and death or when elderly King Lear upends the rightful order by placing his daughter in charge of him. Things do not end well for Lear either.

Macbeth and *King Lear* date to 1605–06. A century later, gradations of social rank created a nuanced vocabulary of "orders" with which Britons were conversant. The king or queen still topped the social hierarchy and surrounded themselves at court with the titled nobility (dukes, marquises, earls, viscounts, and barons), those "temporal lords" at the pinnacle of Gregory King's model. Below these peers, as they were also called and whose prestige was based on birth and sometimes bought with wealth, were the gentry. The latter included baronets, knights, esquires, and simple gentlemen. The original baronets all bought their title; the position was created in the early seventeenth century when James I, eager to raise revenue, decided to sell a hereditary but non-noble honor for a set price. Knights were men whose title was conferred by the monarch to recognize their personal merit or as a reward for service to the Crown. Two knights represented each shire or county in the House of Commons. Below the baronets and knights, both called "Sir," were esquires, members of the higher orders of the gentry, and finally there were the simple gentlemen who occupied the lowest rung among the gentry. These were often men of distinction without any specific rank. The hierarchy was, therefore, complicated and layered. The categories themselves are not as important as the way in which the fine distinctions between them reflected the importance of rank in British society.

These men (and they were all men) staffed local government as justices of the peace and, as we shall see in chapter 2, held national political posts. The wealth of these first two "sorts"—the noble and non-noble gentlemen—was based in land ownership, which brought the highest honor and prestige. Merchants or burgesses were next in line; their commercial wealth did not garner much esteem, as King again demonstrated, but often their cash flow was much stronger than those of higher ranks whose wealth was tied up in land. Britain's population lived mostly in rural areas and the yeomen, mostly farmers who owned their land, occupied the important middling position there. At the bottom were tradesmen, husbandmen who worked small landholdings, cottagers and day laborers who had no land of their own and worked as casual labor on farms, and paupers who made up the majority of the population. Order, rank, and status shaped a person's world, their daily life, their opportunities, and their prospects. Its rigidity was a widely accepted cultural value. In 1709 Daniel Defoe, who began his life in business as a commission agent and a tile manufacturer and ended up a writer of pamphlets and later novels, described it thus:

1. The great, who live profusely
2. The rich, who live plentifully
3. The middle sort, who live well
4. The working trades, who labour hard, but feel no want
5. The country people, farmers etc. who fare indifferently
6. The poor, who fare hard
7. The miserable, that really pinch and suffer want.[8]

Defoe's model, like that of his near contemporary Gregory King, suggests a pyramid or dome-shaped society with overlapping descriptors defining the various levels. Over the course of the century the trading classes and the working poor expanded in number, but the overall picture did not change much and the prestige of landed wealth did not diminish.

Rather than a very strictly divided system in which those above and those below were separated like steps on a stairway, the gradations between each rank and status were extremely fine. Although it contradicted the idea that God had placed everyone in position on the order, some people could realistically aspire to rise in the ranks. This was especially true of the middling sorts as they were called, a name that captures the various grades and ranks below the landed elite. Even the possibility of such social mobility created tension because it challenged an older notion of an ascribed or bestowed status that did not change over one's lifetime. Here's where we see new values in the eighteenth century pulling against traditional ones, and the changes are generally attributed to the new opportunities provided by global commercial ventures related to colonization, empire, and industry, and in particular the influx of money from the slave trade. Seafaring, both on private ventures and in the navy, was an occupation that could in an exceptional case result in tremendous wealth and social success not tied to one's birth or family and not reliant on inheritance. By the end of the century, there were fortunes to be made by a lucky few in manufacturing too. Other professions—in the law, the arts, the academy, and the church—did not necessarily bring great riches, but in an increasingly urban, commercial, and literate world, their ranks expanded considerably. Of course, self-made men met resentment and hostility from aristocrats and other landed gentlemen used to unchallenged supremacy. The wealth acquired by the middling sort did not always result in successful ascension to the next rung of the social ladder. When it did, their mimicry of the very wealthy worked as a source of stability, a force against change. It became a cliché that the first thing a successful merchant would do was buy a country estate and set himself up as a member of the gentry.

The strict social order that organized people's lives in the eighteenth century constituted a moral economy balanced on patronage and deference. Patronage refers to protection or guardianship. As a behavior, it involves one's use of money or influence to affect the interests of another, often referred to as a client. Although sometimes explicitly stated, there was always an implicit understanding that the recipients would defer or yield to their superiors, so deference is the respectful acknowledgment of the authority or superiority of someone, in this case the patron. It could be genuine and reflect a sincere regard for the status, intelligence, or power of the patron, or instrumental, performed out of practical respect or regard. In the eighteenth century, patronage often referred to the bestowal of an office or a post bequeathed in the church, the army, court, or other department of state to reward a loyal follower or to appease an estranged or alienated one. These offices generated tremendous income for their holders, some of which was public money that the office holder might invest during his tenure in office.

There were, of course, many types of patronage. Sarah Churchill, who famously used her close friendship with Queen Anne to further the military and political career of her husband John, the first Duke of Marlborough, in a classic display of political patronage, was also an important patron to painters, sculptors, and architects. The arts, in general—literary, musical, as well as visual—depended on patronage. But in more commonplace spheres, middling men found themselves at the service of their superiors, providing the necessary labor as lawyers, physicians, and tradesmen that made the system work. Counting a prominent member of the local gentry among one's customers could attract new business and transform a bookseller or tailor's prospects. Keeping that important customer happy, needless to say, often required the beneficiaries of patronage to perform flattery and obsequiousness in order to maintain their positions.

Meanwhile, the relationship of aristocrats, gentry, and middling folks to those below them is often characterized as paternalist. Many have pointed to both elites' sense of *noblesse oblige* (the obligations that accompany privilege) and simple survival—they constituted, after all, an affluent minority of the population—to explain their participation in a moral economy that ensured that bread prices never rose too high in order to contain the poor and ensure their obedience. The most significant expression of the two faces of paternalism can be found in the administration of the poor law, a parish-based system of public relief. The parish, both an ecclesiastical unit and a division of a county (sometimes overlapping, sometimes with different boundaries), was the smallest unit of local government and administration. Since 1601, the Elizabethan Poor Law had compelled each parish to tax its propertied members and to appoint overseers of the poor to provide basic services for those it deemed "deserving": the involuntarily unemployed and those unable to work. The old and infirm received "indoor relief" in an almshouse; the able-bodied, if lucky, received "outdoor relief" in the form of tools and materials with which to work and, occasionally, some cash support. Orphaned or abandoned children, and those whose parents could not provide for them, became wards of the parish, placed in mandatory apprenticeships. Vagrants or those who refused to work were fined or incarcerated in houses of correction or, most commonly, driven from town, forced to wander. Because local taxes paid for poor relief, minimal and harsh as the assistance was, communities sought to limit the number of potential recipients. By the late seventeenth century, laws restricted who could settle in a community; unsettled residents who fell on hard times were removed to their home parishes, and transient pregnant women were excluded from parishes that feared the birth of another local dependent. Population growth exacerbated these pressures throughout the long eighteenth century and the poor law could not keep pace with need. In 1795–96, a time of grave economic crisis occasioned by harvest failure and war, poor Britons received more support from private charity than the poor law.[9]

The Rule of Law

The great disparities of wealth created conflict and crime, but Britain had only a small standing army and no police force. Concerns about the arbitrary exercise of military power were central to the Revolution of 1688; keeping an army at home in peacetime was discouraged in its wake. Even the bustling metropolis of London waited until the 1820s for Britain's first professional police force. How then was order maintained in the eighteenth century? The Riot Act of 1715 empowered civil authorities to order threatening gatherings of 12 or more persons to disperse. Failure to comply within an hour of a magistrate "reading the Riot Act"—the text of law had to be proclaimed verbatim—was a felony punishable by death.

The Riot Act targeted disruptive (or potentially disruptive) behavior, and its exercise often had political dimensions. But it was part of a broader, and ultimately more commonplace, use of capital statutes in the eighteenth century. Douglas Hay has argued that the maintenance of obedience and deference relied on the harsh criminal law that prescribed the death penalty for over two hundred offenses, most of them crimes against property including pickpocketing and forgery. The explosion in the number of property-related felonies punishable by death, what later came to be called the "Bloody Code," began with Waltham's Black Act passed by Parliament in 1723. Momentum for the act was quite personal, sparked by poaching in Windsor Forest and other elite properties between 1721 and 1723. To punish and stop the raids, the Black Act identified and defined more than fifty new offenses now punishable by death. Aimed at "Blacks," the gangs of poachers who blackened their faces to hide their identities, the name of the act signaled one of the new behaviors now defined as a crime punishable by death: entering the woods in any disguise.

More generally, the strength of law as a cultural and coercive force allowed those in authority to rule and maintain order.[10] In the eighteenth century the rule of law and its core principles—which proclaimed that everyone was equal before the law, that laws were to be made public, and no one was above the law—had strong ideological force. They were, in other words, a system of ideas that provided a general orientation or way of understanding the world, especially social relations. But ideologies like these are often not presented as formal arguments; they are not necessarily logical, and they often show circular reasoning. They are embedded and transmitted in everyday things such as stories, gossip, public speeches, novels, songs, and (today) movies. This was certainly the case in terms of eighteenth-century notions of the law.

Contemporaries praised Britain's rule of law. Every session of the assize court that tried felonies twice a year began with a sermon in front of a full courtroom presided over by circuit judges. Reeve Ballard, a clergyman, declaimed in a sermon on the occasion of a 1745 court session that "All Government was design'd for the benefit of the Governed, and the Laws are the Strength and Sinews of it."[11] Equality before the law was often expressed through praise for the law's impartiality. As Richard Green observed in a sermon in 1744, English society was "divided into Superiors and Inferiors," but he stipulated that in the eyes of the law all must be considered "in the Light of Equals, namely, as having all an equal Claim to Justice."[12] Contemporaries, both elites and ordinary people, touted the rule of law as their English "birthright," and many exclaimed, as Ballard did, that "in no Nation upon Earth, is there such an equal administration of Justice, as in our Nation."[13]

It was at this time that rule of law became Britain's signature ideology and a central justification for its imperial authority and superiority. Britons compared themselves favorably with their close European neighbors and rivals, the French, pointing out that nobles across the channel enjoyed special rights and privileges, including tax exemptions and special criminal procedures, written into the law. Looking farther afield, they defined the Ottoman Empire and other eastern empires as tyrannous and autocratic. Britons thus often justified their imperial claims in the eighteenth century by citing the benefits of the rule of law, which they would extend to (or impose upon) others, while politicians and the press alike celebrated their legal system's impartiality.[14] Indeed British culture and society embraced the rule of law as a superior and universal value. It is important to remember, however, that the ideology of rule of law did not emerge organically or progressively from its abstract claims; it was produced through collision both abroad in the empire and at home with those considered "outsiders" like Scots, Irish, Catholics, Africans, and Jews, who often went to court to claim the rights of Englishmen to which they believed they were entitled.

The jurist William Blackstone spoke of the rule of law as a responsibility shared among male elites. The stakes were high: order and deference depended on the appearance of "legal and effectual justice" lest magistrates incur "contempt from their inferiors" or "censure" from above.[15] The discourse of the rule of law and equality before the law resounded in the popular press, especially when a member of the elite was accused of a crime. In January 1760, Laurence Shirley, fourth Earl Ferrers, shot his steward, John Johnson. At his murder trial on April 16, Ferrers conducted his own defense: he denied responsibility for Johnson's murder, citing a history of occasional insanity. The defense failed, and he was found guilty and sentenced to death and anatomization. Ferrers was hanged at Tyburn, London's famous gallows, on May 2, 1760; the scaffold was hung in black to distinguish him as a nobleman.[16] The *London Evening Post* applauded the fact that he shared the fate of common thieves, highwaymen, and murderers proclaiming "the Execution … does Honour to this Kingdom, in respect to the impartial Administration of its Justice. In many other Countries Murder is too frequently committed with Impunity, especially when the Assassin happens to be rich or ennobled"[17] (figure 1.3).

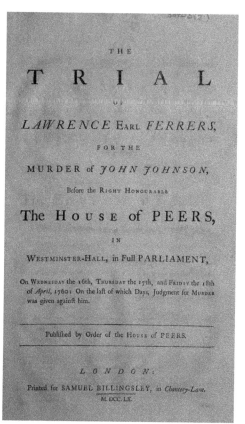

Mr JOHNSON, Steward to the Earl of Ferrers, SHOT by his Lordship at Staunton Harold, in Leicestershire.

THE

TRIAL

OF

LAWRENCE Earl *FERRERS,*

FOR THE

MURDER of *JOHN JOHNSON,*

Before the Right Honourable

The HOUSE of PEERS,

IN

WESTMINSTER-HALL, in Full PARLIAMENT,

On WEDNESDAY the 16th, THURSDAY the 17th, and FRIDAY the 18th of *April,* 1760: On the laft of which Days, Judgment for MURDER was given againft him.

Publifhed by Order of the HOUSE of PEERS.

LONDON:

Printed for SAMUEL BILLINGSLEY, in *Chancery-Lane.*
M. DCC. LX.

Earl Ferrers, as he lay in his Coffin at Surgeons hall.

FIGURE 1.3 (a) Print depicting Ferrers shooting his steward, Johnson. (b) Published account of Ferrers' trial. (c) Print depicting Ferrers' corpse at Surgeon's Hall for public display and dissection.

Slavery and the Law

Praise for the rule of law thus echoed in the ballads, songs, pamphlets, and newspapers read in coffeehouses and on London's streets. Among those influenced by the expanded discussion of rights and liberties were the enslaved. The British, world leaders in the slave trade, had by the 1780s shipped more than 1,250,000 Africans to Jamaica, Barbados, and the smaller West Indian "sugar islands" while almost 300,000 had been sold in North America.[18]

Slaveholding, although more pervasive in the colonies than the metropole, was practiced and tolerated throughout the British Empire. The first enslaved Africans were brought to England during the reign of Elizabeth I. In the eighteenth century, wealthy colonial landowners and their families who aspired to "going home" often returned to Britain with their slaves. There, enslaved persons were generally not used for field labor; most slaves in Britain worked as domestic servants, kept by their masters for convenience or as a mark of prestige. The circumstances of urban slavery, however, often allowed opportunities for escape, and many Africans self-emancipated while in London and other British cities.

James Somerset is one of the best-known enslaved people to seek the freedom, equality, rights, and privileges promised by the ideology of rule of law. Born in West Africa around 1741, Somerset was eight years old when he was bought by European slave traders and sold in Virginia to Charles Stewart. Stewart (and Somerset as part of his household) moved to Boston in 1764 and then relocated to England in 1768. On October 1, 1771, Somerset left his master's London house and refused to return. He remained at large for two months before he was captured by slave hunters and, on Stewart's orders, delivered to the custody of one John Knowles, captain of the ship *Ann and Mary*. He was brought on board, confined in irons, and bound for sale in Jamaica. Abolitionists working on Somerset's behalf, calling themselves his godparents in a striking expression of how paternalism and patronage could be used for good, publicized his situation and applied to William Murray, first earl of Mansfield and chief justice of King's Bench, for a writ of *habeas corpus*, Latin for "you have the body." The writ directs the detainer to bring his prisoner to a court at a specified time for a particular reason.[19]

Somerset's case was immediately seen as a test of the legality of slavery in England. Slaveholders campaigned for a decision that would recognize colonial laws legalizing slavery in both the colonies and the metropole while abolitionists advocated a ruling that would forbid slavery in England. Although it resulted in Somerset's discharge, Mansfield's judgment did not outlaw slavery in England. Mansfield resolved only the question of the writ of *Habeas Corpus*, disallowing the forced return of former slaves to the colonies and declaring it illegal to compel slaves to leave England.[20] But Somerset's case called attention to the tensions underlying so much of the eighteenth-century social order, tensions between, on the one hand, the universal premise of equality before the law and Britain's promise of freedom and liberty, and on the other hand the realities of empire and slavery, property and profits, hierarchy and patriarchy, patronage and deference.

Mansfield's own household further illustrates how slavery lay at the center of the imperial web that entangled the British Isles and its colonies. His grand-niece Dido Elizabeth Belle, also known as Elizabeth Dido Lindsay, lived in Mansfield's home for thirty years starting in 1761. Her mother, an African enslaved woman called Maria Belle, was taken prisoner in an attack on a Spanish vessel in the West Indies by her father, Sir John Lindsay, Mansfield's nephew and a captain in the Royal Navy (figure 1.4). After her capture, Maria was brought to England where she gave birth to Dido. Maria Belle subsequently disappeared from the historical record. Dido Belle's father had little contact with his daughter, who lived with the childless Lord and Lady Mansfield, inhabiting, as one scholar put it, a space in the household "between the family and the servants, not really fitting in with either group."[21] Belle was in charge of the dairy and the poultry yard and took her meals with the other servants, but her status as both a Black servant and a member of the family gave her access to the drawing room after dinner, famously shocking the former governor of Massachusetts, Thomas Hutchinson, when he attended a family dinner in 1779.[22] We can only speculate about the influence that this domestic situation had on Mansfield's understanding of race, slavery, and servitude, and ultimately on his Somerset decision. For her part, Dido Belle lived in an intimate familial space that reflected the very lack of separation between the colonies and the metropole. An analysis of her life reveals how her experience was shaped at the intersection of family, class, race, and gender.

FIGURE 1.4. (a) Dido Elizabeth Belle and her cousin Lady Elizabeth Murray, by David Martin, 1778. (b) Sir John Lindsay, by Nathaniel Hone. (c) William Murray, first Earl of Mansfield, by Jean-Baptiste van Loo.

Gender

Even more than it does today, gender organized the lives of groups and individuals in the early modern period. Historian Susan Kent defines gender as "the knowledge that societies formulate, the understandings that various cultures produce about sexual difference—differences in the physical, mental, moral, and emotional compositions of men and women that are ascribed to nature and that prescribe the proper roles and activities men and women are supposed to engage and enjoy."[23] In simple terms, gender describes what is not sex. It distinguishes the biological from the culturally and socially determined. Expectations about gender inform what is considered feminine and masculine and the boundaries between appropriate and transgressive behavior. But these differences of gender are not unchanging truths about the nature of a man or a woman: instead they are constructed, shaped by cultural and social norms, and change over time, shaped by historical circumstance, social and cultural mores, economic trends, and political cultures.

Eighteenth-century ideas about gender worked as an ideology. Some people conflate gender and women, but it's important to remember that gender ideology defined expectations for both men and women in the eighteenth century; masculinity and femininity shaped each other building on binary oppositions. What made one was considered the opposite of the other and vice versa. These differences were considered biological and innate, with many references to female and male nature, and were intricately connected to the social order.

Power and hierarchy were fundamental to culture and society, and enforcing the standards of feminine and masculine behavior was an instrumental way to preserve the existing social order. To exemplify and explicate the subordination of women to men cultural commentators cited the biblical story of Adam and Eve. God was said to have made Adam first and Eve later, from Adam's rib. Many pointed to Eve's sin as an example of women's uncontained nature and their need for male supervision and guidance at every turn. Women were considered more emotional than men, sexually avaricious, and appetitive. They were accused of being shallow and engaging only in gossip and frivolity. Men were considered logical, controlled, rational, and capable of deep thought, which equipped them with the ability to lead their households and the government. The split between mind and body was reflected in the cultural assumption that women were more literal, tied to the earth and to their bodies, while men could engage in abstract thought. Because of their association with the body and reproduction, women were attributed with innate knowledge of illness and healing, although this assumption changed throughout the eighteenth century as physicians professionalized and expanded their reach. As with all such essentialist generalizations and prejudices, these were full of contradictions. Manliness included fighting, dueling, hunting, drinking, and uncontrollable anger. Women's simplicity was paired with accusations of manipulative and controlling behavior.

The theory of intersectionality observes that a person's life experience is shaped by economic, social, racial, religious, ethnic, and political aspects of their identity.[24] This is certainly true of gender and social status, which combined to dictate what kind of work a person did, their level of education, their perception of their body, their clothing, and their relationships with family. In rural areas women were generally relegated to running the household: they tended the garden and the dairy, took care of the livestock, and managed the income from the sale of any extras at the market.

Men worked in the fields. Cottagers with little or no land often engaged in the textile trades, with women and children spinning wool, plaiting straw, and making lace while men operated weaving looms and knitting frames. In a more urban setting, women worked as servants or alongside their husbands running a business or artisanal workshop, with widows often continuing the enterprise after their husbands' death. But eighteenth-century Britain was a patriarchal society, and the chain of being certainly reflected that value. Within the ordered hierarchy, from the wealthiest at the apex to the poorest at the bottom, women occupied their positions alongside the men in their lives, but they were always inferior to them.

Prescriptive literature about women urged them to be virtuous, chaste, silent, modest, and pious. Men were to live by a code of honor; they were expected to ensure the financial security of their families, and they were to lead their households by making decisions and providing moral guidance. While working women always retained their physical autonomy and moved through the city or the countryside relatively freely in order to perform work as servants, midwives, or farm hands, aristocratic women were more restricted to the home, and when they ventured beyond its confines, they were allowed to visit only carefully chosen venues such as parks, music festivals, balls, churches, or chapels. They were always to be accompanied there with an appropriate chaperone charged with guarding their virtue and safety. It is important to remember, however, that this prescriptive literature existed to define societal norms, establish rules to live by, and enforce them. Often the very existence of this kind of prescriptive literature suggests the frequency of exceptions and transgressions. So while it represents an ideal, there were many who lived outside the confines of these guidelines.

A women's legal status was always dictated by the most important man in her life. Until marriage, girls were in the orbit of the most senior male member of their family or guardian, and after marriage husbands took charge. William Blackstone, a prominent eighteenth-century English jurist and legal commentator, explained that "[b]y marriage, the husband and wife are one person in law: that is, the very being or legal existence of the woman is suspended during the marriage, or at least is incorporated and consolidated into that of the husband: under whose wing, protection, and cover, she performs every thing; and is therefore called in our law-French a *feme-covert*."[25] By these rules, any property a woman brought to the marriage, or wages she earned while in it, belonged to her husband, and he could dispose of it however he saw fit. In practice, the status of *feme covert* was largely a legal fiction. Women skirted these restrictions, acting as legal agents with and without the help of their male kin in both criminal and civil courts and in business. Nevertheless, the existence of the legal category tells us a lot about gender expectations while the actions of real women reveal both their legal literacy and their desire to thwart these rules.

There are excellent examples of female rulers who defied contemporary gender expectations, each of them grappling with how a woman—be she married or single—could rule. At the start of the long eighteenth century, sisters Mary and Anne Stuart each became queen (Mary II, 1689–94, and Anne, 1702–14). Mary shared the throne with her husband as co-monarchs, but her younger sister Anne, though married, served as sole sovereign (figure 1.5). In this official regard, Anne resembled an earlier queen, Elizabeth I (1558–1603). Both also oversaw major political transformations: Elizabeth finalized the Protestant Reformation in 1559 and Anne in 1707 the treaty that united Scotland with England and Wales. (As queen of both countries, Anne technically negotiated the treaty with herself.) Yet in their personal lives, and in how they handled the matter of female rule, Elizabeth and Anne are a study in opposites. While Elizabeth, famously single, confronted the contradictions she embodied as a female monarch by claiming herself a virgin married to her people, fertility and its failure characterized Anne's reign. Of Anne's 17 pregnancies, tragically none of her children survived to succeed her and carry on the Stuart line. Elizabeth tried to control her image, portraying herself as both king and queen, famously declaring, "I may have the body of a weak and feeble woman, but I have the heart and stomach of a king."[26] Although lacking Elizabeth's charisma, Anne too threw herself into the job of being monarch, taking seriously her responsibilities as the head of the Church of England and the guardian of the constitution altered by events in 1688. At her death, Britain had emerged as a world power after success in the War of the Spanish Succession (1701–13), which dominated her entire reign.

FIGURE 1.5 Queen Anne, by Michael Dahl, 1702.

At the other end of the late eighteenth century, the French Revolution had a great impact on British ideas about government, citizenship, and subjecthood. The language of rights expanded to include working-class men, as articulated most famously by Thomas Paine in *The Rights of Man* (1791).[27] But women joined the discussion too. Mary Wollstonecraft (figure 1.6) actually beat Paine both to press and, more or less, to a compelling title, publishing in 1790 her *Vindication of the Rights of Men*.[28] Immediately before and after, she penned important treatises on women: *Thoughts on the Education of Daughters: With Reflections on Female Conduct, in the More Important Duties of Life* (1787) and the *Vindication of the Rights of Woman* (1792).[29] Wollstonecraft's argument for greater educational opportunities for women spoke directly to her concern that middle-class and elite women engaged only in trivial activity out of boredom and lack of choice. She argued that

FIGURE 1.6 Mary Wollstonecraft, by John Opie, 1797.

if women were in charge of their young children's education, they had to be better prepared to do so. Wollstonecraft is often referred to as an early feminist. Although that label is an anachronism, she certainly was a strong voice for women's rights, and her writing began a rethinking of gender norms and expectations, especially regarding women's education.

Marriage and Family

Mary Wollstonecraft's life demonstrates how individual experiences might both conform to and deviate from the demographic trends discussed. Wollstonecraft, like many other women of her day, married while pregnant. But she also married much later than most (aged 37), was already a mother (her daughter from a previous relationship, Fanny, was born out of wedlock), and died of complications just days after the new baby was born. During Wollstonecraft's brief marriage to the political philosopher William Godwin, the couple lived in adjoining houses—both parties eager to maintain a degree of independence—sometimes communicating by letter. Their daughter, Mary (who ran away at a young age with the then married poet Percy Bysshe Shelley, whom she later wed), carried on not only her mother's name but vocation; an author too, Mary Shelley published *Frankenstein* in 1818.

Wollstonecraft and Godwin's aversion to the institution of marriage derived largely from their politics; they married only to legitimate their coming child, and Godwin adopted Fanny for similar reasons. But others less radical than they questioned marriage practices as well. A century earlier, Mary Astell, another advocate for women's education, wondered in her 1700 publication, *Some Reflections upon Marriage, Occasion'd by the Duke & Duchess of Mazarine's Case*, "[H]ow comes it, may you say, that there are so few happy marriages?" Most marriages were not as bad as that of the duchess, a European aristocrat who fled to England to escape an emotionally and physically abusive husband to whom she had been joined, at age 15, in an arranged marriage. Moreover, Astell, though never married herself, was not opposed to marriage per se. A devout, conservative Anglican, she viewed it as an institution ordained by God, "the Institution of Heaven, the only Honourable way of continuing Mankind."[30] Yet Astell worried that people, and men in particular, often married for the wrong reasons—pursuing beauty, or wealth, or wit—when in fact they should be looking for the qualities they enjoyed in a friend. Once married, she observed, men mistreated their wives (though most not with the ferocity of the Duke of Mazarine), so unequal was the power between them.[31] Part of the problem lay in how difficult it was to undo an unsuccessful union, making one's choice of a partner particularly important.

In England and Wales, a divorce was granted only in cases of adultery and required a private act of Parliament, an expensive process limited to the rich and well connected. As a result, a mere 325 couples divorced in England in the almost two centuries between 1670 and 1857 (the law changed in 1858), with only four of those cases brought by women.[32] It took extraordinary, reprehensible behavior on the part of a husband for a wife to win a divorce, like the violence, drinking, and infidelity of the unstable Earl Ferrers, who two years after his wife divorced him was the last aristocrat to be hanged in England (for murder). A legal separation—"divorce from bed and board" that prohibited remarriage until the death of the estranged spouse—could be obtained by either party through ecclesiastical courts on moral grounds that included cruelty and heresy as well as adultery. This too was rare, but another aristocratic couple, Lord and Lady Grosvenor, distinguished themselves in 1770 by suing one another in church court for adultery. They separated, he paid her an annual allowance, and she remarried (by all accounts happily) within weeks of his death 32 years later. Some aggrieved husbands opted, in lieu of divorce or legal separation, to sue their wives' lovers for financial compensation in "criminal conversation" proceedings, an act that reinforced a wife's status as the property of her husband. Before seeking a separation, Lord Grosvenor had won £10,000 in damages in such a suit against the Duke of Cumberland, the king's brother.[33] The fact that men received custody of the children when couples split, yet another sign of women's subordinate status, kept even wives with means in bad marriages. Scottish arrangements proved more equitable, and divorces more numerous, over the long eighteenth century. Under Scottish law, which differed from the common law tradition that had evolved in England and been imposed on Wales, both husbands and wives could sue for divorce on grounds of desertion as well as adultery, and criminal conversation suits were not allowed. Still, there were relatively few Scottish divorce petitions, only one or two per annum from 1690 until 1770 when the number started to increase, reaching twenty-two in 1816. Historians may be struck by this "spectacular rise," but even at their height in Scotland, formal divorce proceedings remained exceptionally rare.[34]

Astell's *Reflections on Marriage* also contributed to a growing public debate over courtship and betrothal. Among the elite, for whom marriages were largely economic arrangements, means by which families secured and exchanged land, money, and status, there were two competing concerns. The first was that families bartered away their marriage-aged children for economic and social gain. The artist William Hogarth made this point in 1743–45 with *Marriage A-la-Mode*, a set of six paintings reproduced and sold as engravings that tell the too familiar story of a disastrous marriage contracted by greedy parents. In the opening panel (figure 1.7), the aptly named Earl of Squander, proud of his noble family tree but short of cash to finish building a new mansion, negotiates the marriage of his heir to the daughter of a rich merchant. The ill-matched couple look miserable (like the two yoked dogs at their feet), the hovering lawyers and bill collectors excited. Affairs, disease, murder, and suicide follow, and by the end of the series husband and wife are both dead. What Hogarth satirized, some prospective brides and grooms took steps to avoid. The next year (1744), Lady Caroline Lennox, the eldest child of the Duke and Duchess of Richmond, eloped with Henry Fox after her parents rejected his proposal. Although a political associate of the Duke of Richmond, Fox was an unsuitable match for his daughter, in age almost twenty years Caroline's senior and in social standing very much her junior, a gentleman but not a noble. Things worked out for these lovebirds; their marriage proved long and successful, and after four years Caroline was reconciled with her parents.[35] But the flurry of eloping heiresses, real or perceived, caused considerable angst and led to the passage in 1753 of Lord Hardwicke's Marriage Act. The new law required parental consent for brides and grooms under the age of 21 and that all marriages take place in an Anglican Church under precise and public procedures. In practice, however, a

FIGURE 1.7 *Marriage A-la Mode: 1. The Marriage Settlement*, by William Hogarth, 1745.

balance was struck between parental authority and personal choice. As the century wore on, upper- and middle-class children insisted on more consultation with their parents about their marriage partners and the right to refuse a choice made for them. Some historians have thus argued that the period was marked by the rise of "the companionate marriage."[36]

But these were the concerns of the rich and propertied. Among the working poor, courtship took a different form. Young people living and working away from home had more autonomy and choice in what prospects to pursue. Male and female servants slept in separate rooms, the girls often with the family's daughters or in the kitchen or attic, and the men in the barn. Courting consisted of visiting the girls' bedroom and might also include "bundling" in bed fully clothed. Marriage became possible only when a couple achieved financial independence, which accounts for the comparatively late, but also falling, age of marriage in the eighteenth century. When their relationships were considered "serious," and if marriage had been broached as a possibility, a pledge of a troth might be followed with sexual intercourse. Parish registers attest to many births seven or eight months after marriage. Illegitimacy rates rose during economic downturns when austerity led to a change of plans and marriage was no longer an option.

The percentage of the population that never married was in fact quite large. An estimated one-fifth of women never married in the long eighteenth century; in 1696, a third of the adult female population of the port town of Southampton had never married.[37] In some cases, very real unions went officially unrecognized. After the passage of Lord Hardwicke's Marriage Act, Jews and Quakers were exempt from marrying in the established Church of England, but other religious minorities, most notably Catholics, were not. Marriages performed by a Catholic priest were technically illegal in England, their offspring illegitimate.[38] The 1753 law also challenged long-standing folk customs whereby couples married themselves with such binding gestures as exchanging rings or jumping over a broom. Historians estimate that half of all marriages were of this sort around the time that the new law went into effect; in its wake, couples, especially of the lower social orders, simply chose to cohabit in "consensual unions."[39] Many of their contemporaries, however, had no partner, wedded or consensual. For women of independent means, remaining single could be a deliberate choice, a way to free themselves from a husband's control; for others, it was the difficult consequence of difficult circumstances.

Mary Astell's life story reflects both these scenarios. Her family was from the upper echelons of Newcastle's commercial community, her father the manager of a coal company. He died when she was 12, leaving the family in tight financial straits. Any money they had was invested in Mary's younger brother's education; she received no dowry and, with her widowed mother, had to move in with an aunt. When both older women died, Mary went to London at age 22 and, aided by female patrons, established herself as a writer. At various stages in her life she owned a small house, founded a charity school for girls, and lived in a patron's home. Thanks to her education and connections, she was able to provide for herself, and such experience no doubt informed her views on marriage. But the absence of a dowry, and her family's channeling its resources toward her brother, had limited her options considerably. In this regard, Astell had much in common with other daughters of the middling sort who remained single throughout their lives. Consider the case of Ellin Stout, the only daughter in a family of six children. Her oldest brother inherited the family home and farm, while each younger brother received a settlement of £100–200 and Ellin £80. In the years that followed, the family deemed her too sickly to marry, and her brothers borrowed regularly (at low or no interest) from the money that would have otherwise comprised her dowry. Yet Ellin was fit enough for a lifetime of work as an unpaid housekeeper and shop assistant for her brother William, an ironmonger and grocer, and occasional stints helping brothers Josias and Leonard in their trades as well. When Ellin died, Leonard sent his second daughter to replace her as William's housekeeper. As the Stouts' historian remarks, the labor (and in Ellin's case money) of middle-class daughters "represented a family resource that could be deployed by fathers, mothers, or brothers to supplement the family income, shore up kin connections, and free other family members for more specialized work or to attend school."[40]

For families possessing land or a business, primogeniture, the practice by which the family's main property passed to the first son (or closest, ideally male, relative), prevailed. The eldest Stout boy inherited the family farm in this way, his younger brothers using more modest cash inheritances to establish themselves in trade. Such arrangements were especially important among the nobility and gentry who comprised the top 2 or 3 percent of society, their wealth and power intricately tied to ownership of vast landed estates. These elite families' social and political position depended on the estate remaining intact, with the income derived from it (from rent, mining, and other uses) supporting younger sons, daughters, widows, and others. A legal device called entail thus operated to restrict landowners from dividing or selling the estate; it was to pass to the next generation much as it was inherited by the present one.

Such a system invited jealousy and conflict between relatives and inspired the plotlines of Jane Austen's novels. In *Sense and Sensibility*, an only son inherits his father's country house, effectively evicting his half-sisters and stepmother, despite having promised his dying father that he would care for them. In *Mansfield Park*, Edmund Bertram's plans to become a clergyman are temporarily derailed when resources intended to help establish his career are used to pay the gambling debts of his older brother and heir to the family's landed estate. Like Austen's fictional Edmund, many real-life younger sons found careers in the church, but others went farther afield, joining the military or seeking their fortunes in colonial spaces. Thomas Thistlewood was a second son of a tenant farmer, a far less august family than the Bertrams, born in Tupholme, Lincolnshire, in 1721. His schooling was followed by an apprenticeship to an English farmer and a long journey to India, past the Cape of Good Hope and Brazil, selling English goods aboard a ship that belonged to the East India Company. When he realized his prospects for land ownership or a profitable marriage in England were slim, he left for Jamaica in 1750, where he began as a plantation manager and overseer and eventually made enough money to buy land and slaves. Thistlewood's diary recounts how younger sons of modest means could achieve wealth and status overseas. It also details the brutalities of white rule and slavery in the colonies, chronicling the sadistic punishments to which he subjected those under his control and a world in which white men raped women of color with impunity. And it reveals the complicated family relationships that often resulted. Thistlewood had a son, who was called "Mulatto John," with an enslaved woman named Phibbah. His relationship with Phibbah, whom he described in his will as his "wife," lasted for more than three decades. Only upon his death, however, did Thistlewood free his enslaved partner Phibbah, and when he did, he also bequeathed to her two slaves.

Tensions over resources rocked families at the bottom of the social scale as well, perhaps even more profoundly. For an unmarried domestic servant, pregnancy and motherhood could lead directly to unemployment and homelessness, a situation that accounted for most cases of infanticide in the eighteenth century and harsh laws that made even concealing a pregnancy a capital crime. For a couple, each additional child, on the one hand, had to be fed and clothed; on the other hand, that child was soon able to contribute to the family economy with its labor, both paid and unpaid. This proved just one of many domestic balancing acts. Historian Anna Clark describes the "struggle for the breeches" whereby some working husbands and wives battled for control of wages, expenditures, and decision making.[41] Meanwhile, illness or unemployment of a family member could tip a household from marginal subsistence into abject poverty. Desertion by overwhelmed husbands and fathers was endemic.

Somewhere between 5 and 15 percent of marriages ended this way, especially at times of war when men could find employment and a new life far from home in military service.[42] Even indentured servitude in the colonies, while less glamorous, provided for some an out. Unhappy wives and mothers had fewer escape routes given the meager wages and employment opportunities available to women.

Drinking, sometimes a cause and sometimes a consequence of such tensions, did little to calm difficult family situations. In the first half of the eighteenth century, gin became the drink of the poor, especially in London. With spirits extremely cheap (gin prices fell well below those of beer and ale) and readily available (London is reported to have had seven thousand dram shops in 1730), the "gin craze" was blamed for crime, prostitution, madness, disease, and death (figure 1.8). Even if the effects of the gin craze were exaggerated by contemporaries and historians, the ravages of extreme poverty, poor

FIGURE 1.8 *Gin Lane*, by William Hogarth, 1751.

medicine, and the limited support provided by England's poor law tore families apart. Parents died, leaving an extraordinary number of orphans to be cared for by the parish or even to fend for themselves. It is sobering to contemplate both that widows headed approximately 20 percent of all households and that women were disproportionally represented among the poor.[43] In Scotland, poor women outnumbered poor men two to one.[44] Thus, while a rich widow might welcome the opportunity to manage her own and her children's affairs, something she was technically unable to do while married, a poor widow had a very different experience. She was particularly vulnerable, a situation reflected in contemporaries' recognition of a special category of crime: "widows' thefts" of food. When the economy was bad and prices high, some communities even reduced the charge from grand larceny (punishable by a heavy fine, penal servitude, or death) to petty larceny. With only a light fine, often postponed, parish officials thus avoided the burden of caring for children left behind by a single mother.[45] In her 1701 petition for pardon at the Old Bailey (London's central criminal court), Ann Hartley described herself as a "poor, indigent woman and having two small children to provide for, and no subsistence but what she was, and is, forc'd to work hard for." The records do not explain whether Hartley was widowed, abandoned, or never married. Her crime, "counterfeit[ing] herself [as] the widow of Henry Hudson, lately deceased on board His Majesty's Ship *Oxford*," in order to claim the dead seaman's wages, suggests how difficult it was for a woman alone, and especially a mother, to makes ends meet. Hartley begged the judges to "moderate the punishment due to her crime, so as she may obtain her liberty to provide for her poor children."[46]

Childhood and Adolescence

Childhood was generally divided into three phases: infancy, ages two to seven, and ages seven to twelve or fourteen. Although children's illnesses contributed to a high mortality rate, if they lived to two years old, their chances of survival were much higher. The experience of childhood depended on the child's gender and also the social class of the child's family. Historians have argued extensively about how children were treated in the past. Although earlier accounts tended to condemn many to bad parenting, accusing both fathers and mothers of being cold and violent, more recent scholarship has found a range of parental approaches that includes affection and concern as well as harsh treatment. Some historians have speculated that high infant mortality rates inhibited parents from forming strong emotional bonds with children until they survived childhood illnesses, but there is also ample evidence of the profound grief suffered and expressed by parents who lost their infants and young children. Compelling signs of parental love come from the history of London's Foundling Hospital, a charity ironically established in 1741 for the "education and maintenance of exposed and deserted young children," of which there were many. In its early days, mothers simply brought their babies (legitimate and illegitimate) to the door; after 1763, they had to petition for a baby's admission. The statements in those petitions, and the tokens departing mothers left with their children, suggest that child abandonment was a last resort for the poor, a desperate act of love—to provide for a child—when all other options had failed.[47]

At the HOSPITAL

For the Maintenance and Education of exposed and deserted Young Children in Lambs Conduit Fields.

On   ye   day of   17   at   o'Clock   there will be

Performed in the Chapel of the said Hospital, a Sacred Oratorio called

Composed by George Frederick Handel Esqr.

The Gentlemen are desired to come without Swords, and the Ladies without Hoops.

N.B. There will be no Collection. Tickets may be had of the Steward at the Hospital, at Bathos Chocolate House in St. James's Street, at Batsons Coffee House in Cornhill & at Toms Coffee House in Devereux Court at half a Guinea each.

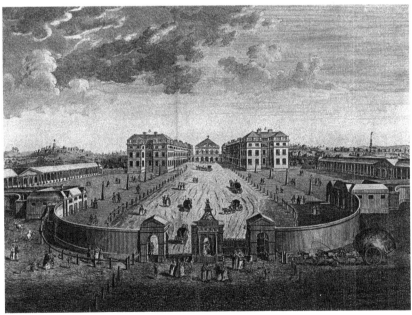

FIGURE 1.9 (a) Admission ticket for May 1750 performance of the Handel's *Messiah*, one of his annual *Messiah* benefit concerts for the Foundling Hospital performed in its chapel. (b) Foundling Hospital, 1753.

FIGURE 1.10 *The Fashionable Mamma, or the Convenience of Modern Dress*, by James Gillray, 1796.

Mothers and women generally had the responsibility for caring for the infants in the household, and most mothers breastfed their babies. While aristocratic women had often hired wet nurses for the task, by the middle of the eighteenth century wealthy women too were pressured to breastfeed (figure 1.10). In the colonies this pressure pivoted on racial hierarchies. In his abhorrently revealing *History of Jamaica*, Edward Long, a British colonial administrator, castigated white mothers in Jamaica when he described the island and the characteristics of slave society:

> Whilst I render all due praise to the Creole ladies for their many amiable qualities, impartiality forbids me to suppress what is highly to their discredit; I mean, their disdaining to suckle their own helpless offspring! They give them up to a Negroe or Mulatto wet nurse, without reflecting that her blood may be corrupted, or considering the influence which the milk may have with respect to the disposition, as well as health, of their little ones. This shameful and savage custom they borrowed from England; and, finding it relieves them from a little trouble, it has gained their general sanction. How barbarous the usage, which, to purchase a respite from that endearing employment so agreeable to the humanity of their sex, so consonant to the laws of nature, at once so honorable and delightful to a real parent, thus sacrifices the well-being of a child! The mothers in England are at least able to find some healthy labourer's wife.[48]

In fact, critics of wet nursing back in Britain levied similar arguments against the practice with an interesting class twist. Far from identifying the wet nurse as "some healthy labourer's wife," they worried that poor and uneducated women did the job—one that uniquely reconciled maternal duties with the need to earn a living—and through their milk passed along undesirable traits to their charges. In this single practice, we see how gender, race, and class intersected in the long eighteenth century and how contemporaries used them to evaluate, define, and control social relations.

In elite and middle-class families, women—mothers, aunts, grandmothers, or governesses—were in charge of children's education as well as their religious and moral direction. Seven was considered the "age of reason," which called on the intervention and guidance of fathers or male tutors. The occasion was marked by the "breeching" ceremony when boys who had been wearing the same infant "dresses" as girls were put in their first pair of pants. In the seventeenth century, reformers of the church and society known as the Puritans had emphasized their children's obedience as well as a theologically driven desire to restrain the child's will and bend it to that of the parents. These attitudes persisted in the eighteenth century as exemplified by Susanna, the mother of John Wesley, the future founder of Methodism, who wrote to her son in 1732 that "[i]n order to form the minds of children, the first thing to be done is to conquer their will and bring them to an obedient temper." In another passage, she said, "When turned a year old (and some before) they were taught to fear the rod and to cry softly."[49] In the mid-eighteenth century, however, ideas about children as "innocent and delightful playthings" took hold, and some parents took a more relaxed and affective approach revealed in the whimsical design of toys and the playful tone of children's books, which included novels about children and distillations of the scientific discoveries of Sir Isaac Newton by "Tom Telescope"[50] (figure 1.11).

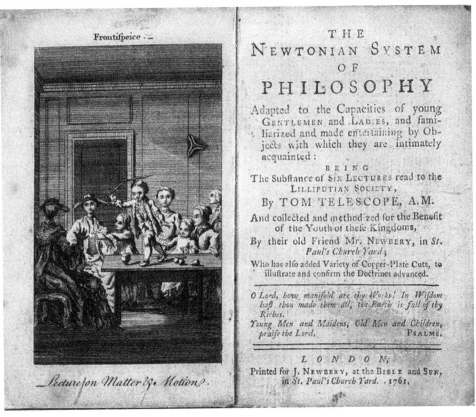

FIGURE 1.11 Fourth edition of *Tom Telescope*, a science book for children, 1770.

Formal education was reserved for boys, and the age at which it began was not set; those who lived in towns would attend schools run by the church as early as four or five while those who lived in more rural areas or in country villages began at six or seven. Students were taught to read first, with writing following by the age of eight. Because school was not mandatory and children often served the family's needs at the cost of their schooling, many in England knew how to read but not how to write. Literacy rates are difficult to determine, but historians note significant gains over the course of the long eighteenth century. Male literacy rose slowly from perhaps 10 percent in 1500, to 45 percent in 1714, to 60 percent around 1750. Women's literacy increased much more dramatically from 1 percent in 1500 to 25 percent in 1714, and to 40 percent in 1750.[51] Although those in rural areas may not have read with fluency or frequency, they probably had enough skills to consult an almanac or chapbook, a small book that might contain stories, ballads, and poems. Urban areas tended to have higher literacy rates: London led the way as a center of publishing and print culture.

John Locke's *Some Thoughts Concerning Education* (1693), a manual for an audience of gentlemen guiding male children, described a child's mind as a blank slate that could be shaped according to a mentor's wishes. This belief in the environment as formative of character and intelligence accompanied an emphasis on education in the middle and upper classes to ensure the proper moral formation of children. In wealthy families, male children would be sent away to school, where they would remain throughout their childhood and adolescence. Among the middling ranks, most boys attended day school while girls of both middling and aristocratic families were taught at home by a female relative. In addition to the basic literacy and numeracy taught to middling girls, those of the upper ranks might also learn French, drawing, and music.

Children in working families were considered part of the labor force and were expected to work alongside their parents in workshops and on farms. Daniel Defoe's *Tour Thro' the Whole Island of Great Britain*, published 1724–1726, described families he observed in Halifax "all full of Business; not a Beggar, not an idle Person to be seen." Indeed, "the Women and Children … are always busy Carding, Spinning &c. so that no Hands being unemploy'd, all can gain their Bread, even from the youngest to the ancient; hardly any thing above Four years old but its hands are sufficient to it self."[52] Defoe regarded such family labor positively, much as he did that of his fictional heroine, Moll Flanders, who as a ward of the parish (her mother a transported convict) was set to needlework at a very young age. Less rosy were the autobiographical accounts from some who labored young. John Saville, born in 1759, wrote of his own fears, and those of his father, as they lost control over his prospects:

> Until I was seven years old, I lived partly with my father and grandmother and partly in
> the Horton Workhouse. I was then bound apprentice to a man … he turned me over to
> the colliers in Delholme; on which my father said to him, 'I had rather you'd tied a stone

around his neck, and drowned him". I was a fine, growing, active lad a time. I saw some cripples in the house of my new master, and the thought came across me that I was to share the same fate with them. At first I was taught to spin worsted; but it was not long before I was taken to the Coal-pit.[53]

As early as the sixteenth century the English were known throughout Europe for sending their children off to other people's homes as servants or apprentices, to learn a craft or a profession, but Saville's experience shows how the practice had changed. A traditional apprenticeship involved a legal agreement in which the young person was bound to serve their employer, often for seven years, in the exercise of some handicraft, art, trade, or profession; the employer was reciprocally bound to instruct him. Apprenticeships generally separated female and male youths, and masters and mistresses took on the parental responsibilities of supervising the young people in their households. The number of apprenticeships offered and regulated by guilds declined throughout the seventeenth century as guilds lost their monopoly on certain kinds of production. The numbers tell the story: at the end of Elizabeth's reign in 1603, 15 percent of London's population was apprenticed; this fell to 5 percent of the capital's population by the beginning of Anne's reign in 1702. Although apprenticeship declined, many young people still entered the workforce away from home. In the eighteenth century one out of six English men and women lived part of their lives in London, where the growing middle class had an insatiable appetite for servants.

Apprentices and servants account for Britain's high geographical mobility in the eighteenth century. Although they didn't necessarily venture far, most living within 15 miles of their birthplace, young adults working as laborers or servants, often changed jobs and masters quite frequently, spending only weeks or months in any one household. Because they were away from their parents, these teenagers had more autonomy in their decisions about where to work. Although small farms continued to rely on live-in servants and skilled trades retained apprenticeship, apprenticeship as an almost universal part of the life cycle declined in the 1780s and 1790s and was replaced with piecemeal production or day labor for wages. Indeed, by the end of the long eighteenth century, more children worked and at younger ages, with little or no opportunity for school. The emerging factory sector owed much to child labor, with young workers, many starting under the age of ten, representing a disproportionate proportion of its labor force.[54]

We chose to begin this textbook about modern Britain with a survey of the social aspects of life. We did so quite consciously, because without an understanding of the experiences of all sorts of people, both as groups and as individuals, the larger trends of political, economic, and intellectual history can get lost in abstraction, focusing on the elite, the well educated, and the wealthy. It is often they who leave us written sources about their lives or their intellectual output. But theirs is the view of the minority. It is incumbent upon us to expand the lens through which we reconstruct historical experience so that many voices are heard and many experiences recounted.

IMAGE CREDITS

CHAPTER 2

Structures and Patterns of Politics

In 1788, Britons marked the one hundredth anniversary of the Revolution of 1688 with perhaps the "first organized public centennial celebration of any historical event."[1] Church bells were rung, guns fired, mementos sold, and banquets held on November 5 in recognition of William of Orange's landing in England on that day in 1688, and the subsequent departure of the "despot" King James II. Not all the revelers, however, celebrated the same things. Members of the newly founded and commemoratively named Revolution Society used the occasion to press for political reform. Meanwhile conservatives challenged any legacy of innovation, instead interpreting the Revolution of 1688 as a judicious restoration of the established political order after a period of royal misrule.[2] Such divisions grew even more intense by the time the 101st anniversary rolled around. When Richard Price (moral philosopher, dissenting clergyman, and political radical) addressed the Revolution Society in November 1789 with *A Discourse on the Love of Our Country*, France was embroiled in a revolution of its own. Inspired by the new French National Assembly and its "Declaration of the Rights of Man and of the Citizen," Price nonetheless gave much of the credit to his British forebears. Back in 1688, he explained, an "era of light and liberty was introduced among us, by which we have been made an example to other kingdoms, and became the instructors of the world."[3] Critics immediately challenged Price's proud remarks, unleashing a public debate about Britain's political past, present, and future, as well as its connection to developments across the Channel. By 1793, the nation was at war with revolutionary France (now a republic, and eventually an empire) in hostilities that would rage for over two decades. Revolution thus framed Britain's long eighteenth century, and the events of 1688 informed the political discussion throughout.

Historians, too, disagree over how to interpret the revolution that kicked James II off the throne, replacing him in 1689 with his daughter Mary and son-in-law William of Orange as the joint monarchs Mary II and William III. The traditional interpretation describes it as "bloodless," or the "Glorious Revolution," as commentators closer to the events also called it, because, they claimed, it transpired with relative speed and ease. Revisionists view it more dramatically—a major upheaval, "the first modern social and political revolution to transform the Early Modern European world" that redirected the most important spheres of public life.[4] The policies governing these changes took months to unfold, and hence revisionists both tend to drop the label "glorious" and extend the time frame, referring to the "Revolution of 1688–89." In a tidy demonstration of how historiographical orthodoxy evolves, this once alternative view now has the upper hand.

Looked at from the vantage point of Ireland, even the extended revolutionary timeframe of 1688–89 seems insufficient, for James II and his supporters continued to fight there, hoping to retake his crown, and the consequences were far from bloodless. James invaded Ireland (from his French base in exile) in March 1689, called a Parliament in Dublin, and declared himself king. Over a year later, supported by Irish and French forces, he met William III at the Battle of the Boyne (July 1, 1690). Once again, William bested his father-in-law, and once again the latter fled to France. Still, in his absence, James's Irish supporters managed to keep his cause alive for another year. Upon their surrender in 1691, approximately 14,000 Irish soldiers decamped for France and beyond. William offered Irish Catholics who remained home the opportunity to keep their land in exchange for their loyalty, but the Protestant Irish Parliament saw fit to impose on them a harsh penal code. In Scotland too, upheaval and violence continued for years, though how it played out was different still.

Revolutionary events of the late seventeenth century opened important constitutional issues concerning the relationship between Crown and Parliament, between politicians and the people, between England and Scotland, and between Great Britain and Ireland. As this chapter will show, these issues, and the tensions arising from them, dominated British political life in the long eighteenth century. Meanwhile, as other chapters will show, the revolution influenced developments far beyond the constitutional and national political realm—in the church, economy, cultural life, and imperial and foreign policy.

Succession in an Age of Revolution

James II lost the crown (two crowns actually, for he was also James VII of Scotland) three years after succeeding his brother, Charles II, as king. Their father, Charles I, had lost not only the crown but also his head, having been tried and executed in 1649 for high treason after an extended conflict that included two civil wars between royal and parliamentary forces and rebellions in Scotland and Ireland. The monarchy itself and the aristocratic House of Lords were subsequently abolished, unleashing a decade of political experimentation with various forms of republican government. In 1660, however, the old system was restored and a Stuart king returned to a reestablished throne; indeed, it was declared that Charles II had been the lawful king since the execution of his father 11 years before.

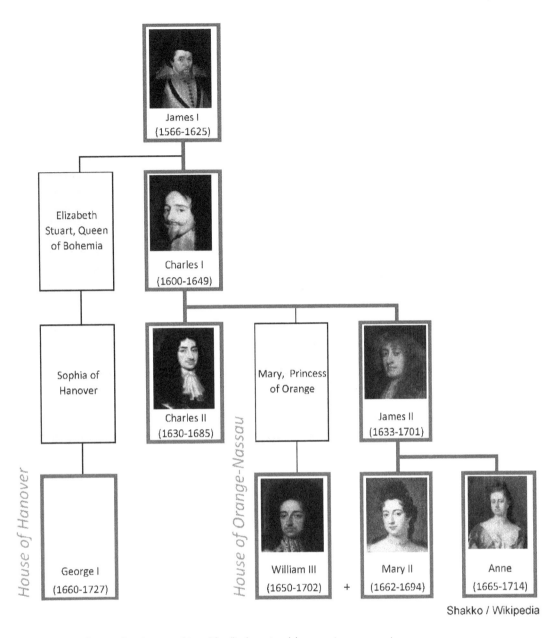

Tree diagram labels:

James I (1566-1625)

Elizabeth Stuart, Queen of Bohemia

Charles I (1600-1649)

Sophia of Hanover

Charles II (1630-1685)

Mary, Princess of Orange

James II (1633-1701)

House of Hanover

George I (1660-1727)

House of Orange-Nassau

William III (1650-1702) + Mary II (1662-1694)

Anne (1665-1714)

Shakko / Wikipedia

FIGURE 2.1 Stuart family tree (simplified) showing Hanoverian succession.

Younger brother James's succession proved more problematic. As it became clear that he was Charles II's heir (the king, though father of many, had no legitimate children eligible to rule), a political movement formed to exclude James Duke of York from the throne. James was a Roman Catholic, yet as a result of England's Protestant Reformation, the monarch served as head of the Anglican Church. How could a Catholic lead the Protestant state church, some asked? Would he seek to restore Catholicism, healing the sixteenth-century schism with Rome and forging an alliance with rival Catholic France? Those politicians who sought to exclude James, and to pursue a more aggressive policy against France, formed the Whig Party. Between 1679 and 1681, the Whigs introduced three parliamentary bills to bar James from the throne. Defending James's position, and in particular the right of hereditary succession, which they believed derived from God, were members of the Tory Party. Aided by Charles II, who convened and dismissed Parliaments in such a way as to quash the exclusion bills and augment royal power, the Tories prevailed. James became king upon his brother's death in early 1685. A failed rebellion a few months later by Charles II's illegitimate son, James Duke of Monmouth, who sought to overthrow James II, was easily suppressed. In fact, the new king deftly used the occasion to justify creating a French-style standing army to better keep the peace and protect the nation, augmenting the absolutist potential of the Crown even more.

Religion and royal power remained divisive issues throughout James II's short reign. In both spheres, critics accused him of the very abuses with which his father had been charged: popery and tyranny. But, as historian Steven Pincus argues, James II was quite forward looking, even modern, in his policies. To help Catholics, who constituted a tiny minority burdened by legal and political restrictions, James II promoted religious toleration—a rare, progressive position at the time. His former allies, the Tories, were great defenders of the Anglican establishment's religious monopoly, so James II looked for support far across the religious and political spectrum, offering similar liberties to Protestant Dissenters who, like Catholics, suffered for refusing to conform to the state church. He issued executive orders to these effects, the Declarations of Indulgence, and set about packing Parliament with those who would support his efforts legislatively. Backing all this up was James II's "newly intrusive and powerful state," manifest in not only the standing army but also an improved navy and efficient administrative, propaganda, and censorship machines.[5] When, in June of 1688, James's second wife gave birth to a son, who as a male leap-frogged over his adult half-sisters in the line of succession, some of the king's enemies became especially concerned. The two princesses, Mary and Anne, were Protestants, and their eventual ascension promised change to their father's religious and pro-French policies. But the newborn prince would be raised a Catholic and thus invited the prospect of codifying James II's innovations.

Among those enemies was Mary's husband, William of Orange, a prince and military leader of the Dutch Republic. Eager for Mary to inherit her father's crown, and to secure a united Protestant (and anti-French) commercial and foreign policy, William embraced opposition rumors that the newborn prince was an imposter, smuggled into the palace by Catholic conspirators in a warming pan. A royal inquiry showed the rumors to be false, but that hardly diminished their appeal, or the cover they offered William for invasion. In fact, William had been contemplating military action for some time, and in June received a secret letter from seven noblemen, four Whig and three Tory, inviting him to assist in their "deliverance." William's correspondents maintained that "the people are so generally dissatisfied with the present conduct of the government in relation to their religion, liberties and properties (all of which have been greatly invaded) … that your Highness may be assured there are nineteen parts of twenty of the people throughout the kingdom who are desirous for change, and who we believe would willingly contribute to it."[6] This probably overstated the opposition to James; the king had many supporters. But that some Tories, James II's original defenders in his quest to become king, were among the letter's signers, and that they predicted massive defections from England's armed forces once William landed, gave William hope of success. Once underway, his campaign unfolded more or less on cue, with military desertions and popular uprisings throughout England, as William marched toward London. Two days before Christmas, James II abandoned all efforts to negotiate with his son-in-law and escaped to France. In early 1689, a new Parliament met to decide what to do next.

Parliament traditionally met at the monarch's will. Yet in 1689, as at the Restoration in 1660, the affairs of kings were settled by a convention parliament, a body convened in the absence of a sitting sovereign. Its members came from the traditional parliamentary classes—noblemen (the hereditary peers) and bishops sitting by virtue of their titles in the House of Lords and propertied gentlemen elected to the House of Commons by other propertied men. Whigs and Tories both participated, their differences more apparent now that James II had fled. The nature of his departure, or how to describe it, was itself a contested issue. Rather than declaring James II deposed, which had radical implications that thrilled some Whigs but offended Tories, the convention parliament ultimately agreed that he had "abdicated the government." Having left the country by his own volition, or so the tale was spun, his throne was "thereby vacant." Most Tories, given their commitment to hereditary succession, championed Mary's right to succeed (she was next in line after James II and his also absent infant son), while some favored a regency in the name of the missing king or prince. But William, and his most ardent Whig supporters, sought the crown for himself. In the end, a strange, unprecedented compromise emerged— joint rulers, William III and Mary II, with executive power vested in the conquering soldier. As for subsequent successions: the surviving spouse would rule alone after either William or Mary died; Mary's children were then next in line, followed by Mary's younger sister Anne, Anne's offspring, and finally any child a widowed William might have in a subsequent marriage. An additional restriction further interrupted the rules of hereditary succession. "Whereas it hath been found by experience that it is inconsistent with the safety and welfare of this Protestant kingdom to be governed by a popish prince," the politicians concluded, Catholics (or anyone married to a Catholic) were barred from the throne.[7]

FIGURE 2.2 William III and Mary II.

These arrangements were set forth in the Declaration of Rights, a document read aloud to William and Mary in February 1689 when they were offered their joint office, and subsequently enacted in law as the Bill of Rights that December. William became sole monarch when Mary died of smallpox in 1694, and because the royal couple was childless, Queen Anne succeeded upon his death in 1702. Two years earlier, however, Anne had suffered double, tragic losses: In January 1700, her final (and probably 17th) pregnancy ended in a stillbirth, and in July her only surviving child, a son aged 11, died. The convention parliament's careful provisions for subsequent succession had, sadly, not extended far enough. Thus in 1701, Parliament returned to the task. The search for a suitable heir led, ultimately, to the family of Sophia of Hanover, an elderly German princess who descended from James I (great-grandfather of Mary and Anne) through the female line. When Sophia's son, George Lewis, Elector of Hanover, succeeded Anne in 1714, inaugurating the Hanoverian dynasty and a slew of King Georges, at least 58 candidates more closely related to the late queen had been passed over.[8] But they were either illegitimate, or like her half-brother James Francis Edward Stuart ("the warming-pan baby," now called "the Pretender" for his insistence that he was the rightful heir), Catholic. Once again, political exigency had triumphed over the strict rules of royal hereditary right, and Parliament chose a monarch and confirmed its choice in law—the 1701 Act of Settlement. This in itself was remarkable, even revolutionary, in Europe of the day.

Structure of the State

Britain does not have a written constitution; there has never been a written document that lays out the structure of the government or its obligations to its subjects. Nonetheless, legal commentators spoke in the eighteenth century of an unwritten constitution made up of acts of Parliament, law reports of court judgments, treaties, and conventions that had evolved over a long period of time. Among the documents that comprise the unwritten constitution is Magna Carta, "the Great Charter of the Liberties of England" (1215), the Petition of Right (1628), the Bill of Rights (1689), and the Act of Settlement (1701). This unwritten constitution bestowed Parliament—made up of the monarch, the House of Lords (a hereditary body), and the House of Commons (an elected body)—with "sovereign and uncontrollable authority in making, confirming, enlarging, restraining, abrogating, repealing, reviving, and expounding of laws … concerning matters of all possible denominations, ecclesiastical, or temporal, civil, military, maritime, or criminal."[9] Together, and paradoxically, written and unwritten law made up England's constitution whose "very end and scope," the English jurist William Blackstone proclaimed, was "political or civil liberty."[10]

Political or civil liberty was very much on the mind of the authors of the Bill of Rights. In addition to settling the succession, it outlined James II's particular transgressions and established means for preventing similar royal behavior in the future. It mandated, for example, that parliamentary proceedings be protected by freedom of speech and that elections to the lower house "ought to be free." The monarch could neither "levy money" (tax) nor "dispense" with or "suspend" any established law without parliamentary approval. Keeping a permanent standing army in

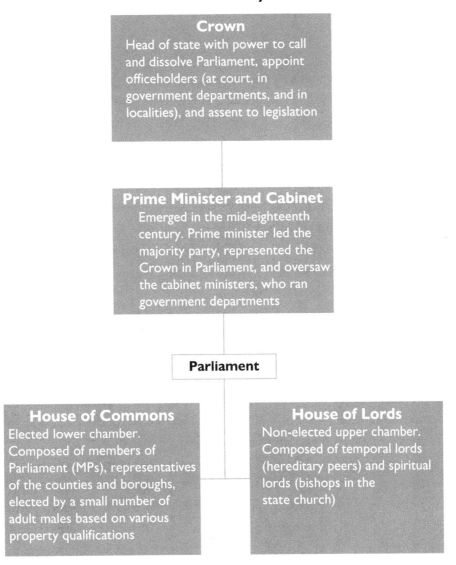

British Political System

Crown
Head of state with power to call and dissolve Parliament, appoint officeholders (at court, in government departments, and in localities), and assent to legislation

Prime Minister and Cabinet
Emerged in the mid-eighteenth century. Prime minister led the majority party, represented the Crown in Parliament, and oversaw the cabinet ministers, who ran government departments

Parliament

House of Commons
Elected lower chamber. Composed of members of Parliament (MPs), representatives of the counties and boroughs, elected by a small number of adult males based on various property qualifications

House of Lords
Non-elected upper chamber. Composed of temporal lords (hereditary peers) and spiritual lords (bishops in the state church)

FIGURE 2.3 Chart of state structure.

peacetime, like the one James II had built, now also required parliamentary consent. Some of the provisions of the Bill of Rights were new; others affirmed old practices which James II, it claimed, had violated with his "pretended powers." The combined effect was to guarantee that Parliament be a regular part of government. The Bill of Rights also decreed that Parliament meet frequently. It did not specify how frequently, perhaps because any monarch who needed to raise money (and those at war always did) would have no choice but to summon it. Marked as the long eighteenth century was by near incessant warfare, starting immediately with William III's declaration of war against France and suppression of Scottish and Irish uprisings in favor of James II, Parliament now met annually. In a round-about way, practical necessity thus guaranteed Parliament a regular and central place in the post-revolution constitutional settlement.[11]

ELECTIONS

How often elections occurred for the members of Parliament (MPs) who sat in the House of Commons was a different and politically complicated matter. Elections kept representatives attuned to the needs of their constituents. Yet when politicians, parties, and monarchs liked arrangements within Parliament, they often preferred to avoid the risk of a new election. To keep William in line in 1694, Parliament secured the Triennial Act, which mandated that a general election be held at least every three years. (William previously rejected similar bills on several occasions.) In 1716, the dominant political party at the time, the Whigs, reversed course, sponsoring the Septennial Act, which extended the permitted interval between elections to seven years (and, conveniently, the Whigs' current majority in the House of Commons for another four years). They justified the new procedure, which remained in place until 1911, on the grounds that elections were both expensive and divisive. They were right, though it could also be argued that the Septennial Act exacerbated the problem; the job of MP, with its longer tenure, was now a more valuable a prize. Even in uncontested races, where a candidate had no rival, it took an increasingly hefty purse to win. In 1689, the famous diarist and naval administrator Samuel Pepys spent almost £9 to become MP for the Essex borough of Harwich. In 1727, it cost the Viscount Perceval one hundred times that amount, a mind-boggling sum even after adjusting for inflation. More telling still, Perceval stood unopposed, and Harwich had only 32 voters for him to woo. Much of Perceval's money was probably spent eliminating potential rivals from the field.

When there was a contested election, such as that in the county of Oxfordshire in 1754, famously satirized by William Hogarth in series of paintings (figure 2.4), the money expended on food, drink, favors, and outright bribes could exceed comprehension. The Tories reportedly spent more than £20,000 in their bid to return Oxfordshire's two MPs; on the Whig side, the prime minister and King George II, who favored that party, pledged over £7,000 in government funds. After a week of polling, the presiding election officer issued a "double return," in essence declaring it a draw. It fell to the House of Commons, which also functioned as a court to resolve election disputes, to adjudicate the results. The Whig-dominated body surprised nobody when it ultimately installed both Whig candidates. For the past 44 years, Oxfordshire had been an uncontested Tory seat. By entering the field in 1754, the Whigs had broken that streak. But before the next general election, the third Duke of Marlborough, a prominent Whig aristocrat, brokered a deal with the Tories: Everyone would avoid another costly competition by splitting representation of the county, with each party advancing just one candidate for the two available posts. Marlborough put forward his younger brother Lord Charles Spencer, who in 1761 began representing Oxfordshire, uncontested again, but now a divided seat with both a Whig and a Tory MP.

FIGURE 2.4 *An Election Entertainment* and *The Polling*, by William Hogarth, 1755.

These events, considered extreme even in their day, nonetheless reveal many basic features of the eighteenth-century electoral system. Oxfordshire was one of England's 40 counties, each of which elected two MPs to the House of Commons. Its approximately 4,000 electors, like those in all English and Welsh counties (the latter returned only one MP apiece), qualified for the vote according to rules established back in the early fifteenth century. Land was the key: Voters in the English and Welsh counties possessed (but did not have to own) freehold property worth 40 shillings (or £2) a year. After the Act of Union in 1707, Scotland's counties also sent MPs to Parliament in London, but they followed much more restrictive landholding requirements for the vote.

FIGURE 2.5 Map of English and Welsh counties.

Counties were the geographic and administrative units that divided up the nation, but within them were boroughs, towns, or other settlements that had, also centuries earlier, been granted representation by royal charter. There were 203 English boroughs, most of them represented by two MPs, who were elected through a dizzying variety of franchise arrangements. Harwich was a corporation borough, meaning that only members of its council (mayor, aldermen, and the like) could vote. But in a few "open" boroughs, almost all adult male residents could. In others, electors had to contribute to the poor rates, while in what came to be known as "pocket" and "rotten" boroughs a few great landowners controlled the entire franchise. Among the latter were once important but now depopulated places that included an uninhabited cow pasture (figure 2.6) and, in a particularly notorious case, land that had fallen into the sea. Different qualifications to vote prevailed in still other types of boroughs. All told, almost a half of boroughs had an electorate under 100, yet boroughs contributed most of the House of Commons' 558 members. England, too, was disproportionately represented, with a total count of 489 MPs compared to 24 from Wales and 45 from Scotland.

The gender dimensions of all this were fascinating. In the nineteenth century, new legislation would identify electors as "male persons." But in the earlier period, no one had bothered to specify. As a result, in some borough franchises, women who met the official requirements could, technically, vote. A few apparently did in the late seventeenth century. By the eighteenth century, however, husbands exercised this right for their propertied wives, and unmarried women appointed

FIGURE 2.6 *Old Sarum*, by John Constable, 1834.

proxies.[12] Another consequence of the persistence of a system established long ago was that, due to effects of inflation and agricultural improvement since the fifteenth century, electors of lower social standing than originally intended had, especially in the counties, gained the franchise. That said, the population grew faster than the electorate in the eighteenth century, resulting in a proportional decline of voters among adult men. When William and Mary ascended the throne, 20 percent of adult men could vote; in 1754, the year of the contested Oxfordshire election, only 17 percent possessed the right.

GOVERNANCE AND OFFICES

There were property qualifications for becoming a MP as well, and because it was an unsalaried position only the very affluent could afford to serve. Some wealthy professionals—lawyers, military officers, and merchants—became MPs, but most were landed gentlemen. It was common for MPs to be the sons, younger brothers, and clients of the titled aristocrats who sat by hereditary right in the House of Lords, as was the case with Oxfordshire's Lord Spencer (younger brother of the third Duke of Marlborough). The world of parliamentary politics was thus occupied by the elite clique of propertied families at the top of the social pyramid. Among these rich power brokers (which included women, sometimes in possession of landed estates with electoral interests in their own rights, and sometimes widows overseeing affairs on behalf of minor heirs), the sort of agreement Marlborough reached with his Tory counterparts grew increasingly common. In the general election of 1761, a mere 53 constituencies had contested races. Many of the men eligible to vote, a small group to begin with, rarely had the opportunity to go to the polls. When they did, they were likely subject to the elite influences, including that of a landlord or employer, for there was no secret ballot.

FIGURE 2.7 Henrietta Godolphin, second Duchess of Marlborough.

Both chambers of Parliament, along with the monarch, ratified all legislation. Much of it was private business, bills introduced in either house on behalf of individuals or communities. In 1706, two years after his stunning victory at the Battle of Blenheim, the first Duke of Marlborough procured a private act to circumvent male-centric inheritance laws so his daughters could succeed to his English titles; upon his death, his eldest, Henrietta, became second Duchess of Marlborough *suo jure* (in her own right). Similarly, only by acts of Parliament could one obtain a divorce or permission to build a turnpike road. In public money matters, however, the House of Commons always took the lead. As the elected representative of the people, it had sole authority to initiate bills that raised taxes or appropriated funds. "The Security of our Liberties," the politician John Carteret wrote, is "not in the Laws but by the Purse being in the Hands of the People."[13] The elite House of Lords, whose members included the richest noblemen (a seat did not accompany the Duchess of Marlborough's title) and royal courtiers, thus ironically played

FIGURE 2.8 *The House of Commons, 1793–1794.* Prime Minister William Pitt the Younger addressing the house, by Karl Anton Hickel.

second fiddle to the lower chamber, exercising its veto power more than introducing legislation. It had once been the case that the monarch's chief advisers, members of the ministry (or cabinet), all sat in the House of Lords. Over the course of the eighteenth century this too changed, as ministers increasingly controlled political life from the House of Commons. The monarch could still appoint anyone to the cabinet they wished, but to be an effective minister one needed to rank among the leaders of whatever party held a parliamentary majority.

If parliamentary service did not confer income, offices—in the church, armed forces, and government departments—did. Some offices, called sinecures, even provided a salary without requiring any work. Or, if work was required, a clerk might be hired to do it, leaving the officeholder to turn a mighty profit. All offices, as well as pensions, were the Crown's to dispense, and monarchs delegated much of that responsibility, and power, to their ministers. Frederick North, second Earl of Guilford, used and explained the system well. Upon becoming prime minister in 1770, he arranged for his half-brother Brownlow North, a young clergyman, to receive a number of church posts, including that of Bishop of Lichfield and Coventry. In response to questions about so inexperienced a cleric occupying so august an office, the politician explained that "if Brownlow had to wait until he was older he might no longer have a Prime Minister for his brother." In fact, Lord North remained prime minister until 1782, by which time lucky Brownlow had been enthroned at age 40 as Bishop of Winchester, a much more prominent (and lucrative) post. That was enough. Having reached the apex of the church hierarchy, Brownlow stayed at Winchester until his death 39 years later, using his own patronage to advance the ecclesiastical careers of his sons and, in keeping with family tradition, seven-year-old grandson.[14]

Not everyone aspiring to office had a prime minister for a brother. But many MPs entered Parliament specifically to gain access to this patronage network—for oneself and for one's family and friends. Job opportunities abounded, especially in the administrative, revenue, and military sectors, which had started to grow after the Restoration but exploded in size during the wars of the long eighteenth century. The army and navy increased threefold between 1680 and 1780; at wartime, military spending represented at least two-thirds of total government expenditure. The national debt, meanwhile, which barely existed when William III began the Nine Years War, hit £16.7 million by that war's close in 1697. At end of the American War in 1783, the debt stood at £245 million, having almost doubled (from £131) over its course.[15] The American War debt was particularly disturbing. For the first time that century, there was no British victory to justify the expense; meanwhile, fears over the loss of Britain's vast, protected market in colonial North America made the magnitude of the debt appear even more ominous. The government committed itself to serious debt-redemption efforts in the mid-late 1780s, taking a big chunk out of the total owed, but the national debt shot up again during the French Wars that began in 1793.

Taxes grew too, both to meet immediate expenses and to service the interest payments on the debt, at rates and to levels that far outstripped Britain's rivals. Whether measured as shares of per capita income or commodity output, the British tax burden was at least twice as heavy as that in France. The responsibility for managing all this money fell to the Treasury, which oversaw income and expenditure, and the revenue departments, which assessed and collected taxes. This required manpower and new administrative procedures. The Excise establishment, which employed approximately 1,300 individuals in 1690, had almost 5,000 on staff in 1783; it was almost twice as big in 1783 as the *entire* fiscal administration back in 1690. New government departments and institutions were created as well, such as the Bank of England in 1694. By revealing the scope and operational efficiency of this bureaucratic juggernaut, which he dubbed "the fiscal-military state," John Brewer overturned the long-standing historical assertion that eighteenth-century Britons flexed their muscles abroad, in imperial expansion and war, while

FIGURE 2.9 The Great Hall, Bank of England, by Thomas Rowlandson, 1808.

insisting on a weak centralized state at home. Under the old model, after the Revolution of 1688–89 ended any possibility of British royal absolutism, much of the administrative work of government devolved to the localities where it was done by amateurs and volunteers. Brewer's model of a professionalized fiscal-military state acknowledges the importance of such local governance. But it also reveals the "sinews of power" that connected the localities to the central state and that transformed a small island nation into an international, imperial powerhouse.

Local administration occurred at the macro level in counties and at the micro level in parishes, the tiny, face-to-face units of ecclesiastical organization in which most Britons went about their daily lives. Each county was overseen by a lord lieutenant, an aristocrat appointed by the Crown in recognition of his local standing, whose chief duties included leading the militia. The lord lieutenant in turn dispensed other offices, such as that of justice of the peace (JP), primarily to members of the landed gentry but also to some prominent clergymen. The JP's sphere of activity involved, as the title suggests, the administration of justice, though most were not trained legal professionals. They tried offenders for the sort of petty crimes that disturbed the peace of the community and issued arrest warrants for those accused of more serious transgressions. Four times per year they met at Quarter Sessions, in which JPs from throughout the county presided over trials for noncapital criminal cases that required a jury. Defendants charged with capital crimes were remanded to the periodic Assizes, courts administered by traveling justices sent out on circuit by the Crown. In addition to their judicial duties, the JPs in Quarter Sessions oversaw a vast array of administrative matters: supervision of the poor laws, jails, and asylums; maintenance of highways, roads, and bridges; licensing of alehouses; and much more. As the population and economy expanded over the course of the century, so too did the responsibilities and numbers of JPs. Meanwhile, the people who did the actual work of collecting the poor rates, distributing poor relief, serving as constables, and inspecting the highways were drawn from the parishes in which they lived. These were not wealthy men but rather self-sufficient members of the middling ranks of local society: freeholders and farmers, clergymen, and other professionals. Technically, all this regional authority emanated top-down from the monarch. In reality, officials in the countryside, as well as the councils that functioned in urban municipalities like the county JPs, had considerable autonomy.

The overall structure of the state could neither predict nor control how political life unfolded. That was determined by the interactions between politicians—the parties they formed and the policies they pursued—and by the voice of the people. For despite the exclusion of the majority of Britons from electoral, parliamentary, and governmental responsibilities, they too participated actively in the world of eighteenth-century politics.

Creation of Great Britain

These developments had momentous effects on the political relationship between the constituent parts of the British Isles. England and Wales had a special relationship that dated back centuries and began with medieval conquest. English and Welsh kings had vied for territory in the western half of their shared island both before and after the Norman Conquest. In the late thirteenth century England's Edward I prevailed, conquering the Principality of Wales, and bestowing upon his heir the title "Prince of Wales" (a tradition that continues to this day). Yet English control of the region remained far from secure or uniform. That changed in the sixteenth century under Henry VIII, when two Acts of Union (1536 and 1543) annexed Wales to create a single state. English law and administration were extended to Wales, the English language made the official tongue in its courts. It was at this time that Wales was divided into counties that returned MPs to England's Parliament.

Edward I also successfully invaded Scotland, but in 1328, after two wars of independence, a Scottish king regained that throne. Thereafter, England and Scotland remained two separate kingdoms until 1603, when James VI of Scotland ascended to the English throne, creating a Union of Crowns. This meant that there were two crowns on the same head. James (reigned in Scotland as James VI, 1567–1625, and in England as James I, 1603–1625) first embodied this arrangement, which his Stuart descendants in turn inherited. Although James had tried to implement a more formal union, his efforts to do so in 1606, and those of his successors in 1667 and again in 1689, failed because of the general animosity between the two kingdoms. Such differences had their roots in the medieval wars of conquest and independence, and more recently in the very different paths by which the two kingdoms had navigated the Protestant Reformation. Eventually, driven by the desire to suppress Scotland's Parliament in order to eliminate its opposition and resistance to English policies, England pursued union with Scotland. Scottish independence in this regard seemed to undermine both England's domestic and imperial interests. Some in Scotland thought independence undermined their own domestic and imperial interests as well; they sought union in order to ensure Scotland's access to England's colonies and resources.

England's Revolution of 1688–89 removed not only its king, James II, but also Scotland's James VII. A Scottish convention parliament followed England's lead in offering its throne to William and Mary, but many Scots resented how this had come to pass. A small but determined minority eager to undo recent events and known as Jacobites (from "Jacobus," the Latin version of "James") took up arms in support of James, especially in the Scottish Highlands, but were defeated. In August 1691 William offered a pardon to those Highland clans that had resisted, but only if they pledged allegiance in front of a magistrate by New Year's Day. On New Year's Eve, 1691, Alasdair MacIain, the chief of the MacDonalds of Glencoe, arrived at Fort William to take his oath, but was told he would have to travel to Inveraray (70 miles away) to take it. He did so on January 6, 1692. When John Dalrymple, secretary of state, heard that MacIain was late taking the oath, he saw his opportunity to make an example of the clan in order to discipline and "tame" the others. "My Lord Argyle tells me, that Glencoe has not taken the oath, at which I rejoice. It is a great work of charity to be exact in the rooting out of that damnable sect, the worst in all the Highlands."[16] One hundred and twenty troops arrived at Glencoe on February 2 under the command of Captain Robert Campbell. They were housed by the MacDonalds and enjoyed their hospitality for 10 days. On February 12 orders arrived stipulating that they were "to fall upon the rebels, the Mac-Donalds of Glencoe, and put all to the sword under seventy"[17] (figure 2.10). The killing began at 5:00 a.m. on February 13. Alasdair MacIain was shot. Houses were set on fire. Thirty-eight MacDonalds were killed on the spot while 40 women and children died of exposure in the mountains where they sought refuge.

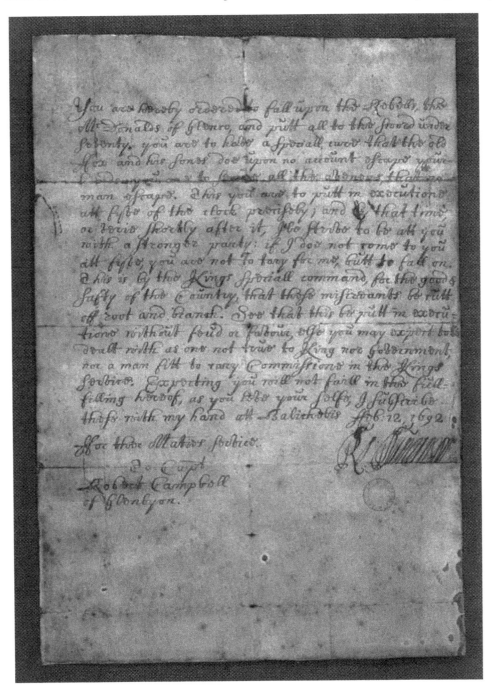

FIGURE 2.10 The order for the massacre of the MacDonalds at Glencoe, 1692.

Although the overwhelming majority of Scots were not Jacobite sympathizers, the act of terror perpetrated by the state on its own people at Glencoe fueled the animosity between Scotland and England. So did economic conflicts. On the one hand, England excluded Scotland from its colonial trade. On the other hand, Scotland pursued commercial plans which blatantly contradicted William's foreign policy. In 1695 it initiated a colonizing effort at Darien in today's Panama in Central America, a site claimed by Spain. Many in William's court believed it would interfere with the king's alliance with Spain, and William's consequent lack of support for the Darien initiative contributed to its massive failure and the death of many of the colonists. That costly disaster overseas, along with famine in 1695–99 at home, were exacerbated by English tariffs on Scotland's most profitable products: coal, salt, and linen. These protective tariffs levelled at a time of great hardship in Scotland on its exports to England contributed to an economic depression.

Most proximate to the eventual union, however, was England's 1701 Act of Settlement that named "princess Sophia and the heirs of her body" as Anne's eventual successor. The Scottish Parliament, again resentful over being inadequately consulted and having its affairs dictated by England, passed the well-named Act of Security in 1704. This Scottish law insisted that upon Anne's death its new monarch must be a Protestant descendant of Scottish kings (as Sophia and her Hanoverian heirs were) but not necessarily the English successor. Scotland, in other words, threatened to separate the two crowns unless it was better treated. England, meanwhile, did not trust Scottish promises to name a Protestant heir. Fearing it might soon face James II's son, James Francis Edward Stuart (the Pretender), enthroned as James VIII of Scotland just above its northern border, England resorted to economic blackmail with a new law of its own. Its Aliens Act of 1705 would ban the import of all Scottish staple products into England and cause all Scots to lose the privileges of Englishmen under English law, endangering any property rights they held in England, if Scotland did not agree to a union and accept the future Hanoverian Succession.

Years of difficult negotiations between commissioners representing the Parliaments in each country resulted in the Treaty of Union creating Great Britain. It stipulated free trade between England and Scotland and retained both the Scottish Kirk (Presbyterian state church) and legal system (derived from Roman law and quite different from English common law). It abolished the Scottish Parliament while expanding its counterpart in London's Westminster by creating 16 new seats for Scottish nobles in the House of Lords and 45 for Scottish MPs in the House of Commons.

Propaganda on both sides agitated for and against the union. The English writer Daniel Defoe had worked secretly as a government agent in England, gathering information on party divisions and the general political mood of the country. During the fight for the union, he vociferously defended it to the English. He later traveled to Scotland and wrote about the economic benefits that would redound there. Such effort he hoped might convince the Scots, many of whom bristled at the condescension of the English. The latter, unfortunately, often cast their participation as a civilizing mission aimed at brutish Scots, particularly Highlanders. Thus, while the English

Parliament voted quickly to approve the union, the plan faced strong opposition in the Scottish Parliament. The Scottish act finally passed with votes secured through patronage, bribery, and the promise of economic prosperity, and Anne, as queen of both nations, signed the treaty with herself. It went into effect on May 1, 1707.

FIGURE 2.11 Interestingly titled map of "The North Part of Great Britain Called Scotland," by Herbert Moll, 1714.

Political union created tense ties that often frayed as religious, cultural, and economic differences pulled the English and the Scots in opposite directions.[18] Throughout the first half-century of the union, many Scots believed that they had the worst part of the bargain, and some turned to the Jacobites, espousing support for the restitution of the Stuart dynasty. James II had died in 1701, but the movement coalesced under the leadership of his son, the Pretender. Meanwhile, in the ongoing war between Britain and France, Louis XIV liked the idea of using Scotland to stage an invasion of England. In 1708, the Pretender and some Scottish Jacobites attempted, with French help, an attack in the Firth of Forth. They lost the element of surprise when the plot was discovered, and they were met by the Royal Navy.

The Jacobite movement revived in 1715, 1719, and most dramatically in 1745, the last under the leadership of the Pretender's son, Charles Edward Stuart, in turn known as the Young Pretender. But the Jacobites never numbered more than a minority of Scots, and in the decades following the union much changed. The British government worked relentlessly, and often brutally, to weaken the cultural, social, and economic character of the Scottish Highlands and to force their integration into British commercial networks. Many Scots ascended to positions of military and administrative leadership across the British Empire. In London, they were welcomed into the highest positions of power within the cabinet and worked as advisors to the king with seemingly easy access to him. By the end of the century, the English perspective had shifted, and the Scots, once derided by their southern neighbors, were now generally seen as effective, competent, useful, and loyal.

Creation of the United Kingdom of Great Britain and Ireland

When English and Scottish negotiators plotted the union that would create Great Britain, Ireland was excluded from the talks. In the wake of that union, the newly configured nation rebuffed the Irish suggestion of a similar union with it, preferring to keep Ireland, and its Parliament, in a subservient position. Yet almost a century later, the first plan for the union between Great Britain and Ireland, proposed in the summer of 1798, was modeled on the Scottish Union of 1707. As in the Scottish case, finalizing a deal proved a long and complicated business. On July 2, 1800, the Irish Parliament voted to abolish itself; on August 1, 1800, the British Parliament passed its version of the act, and both received royal assent; and on January 1, 1801, the arrangements went into effect, creating the United Kingdom of Great Britain and Ireland.[19]

Yet the roots of Ireland's relationship with England had perhaps more in common with that of Wales than of Scotland. It extended back to the twelfth century, when Ireland was divided into several kingdoms over which a high king exercised over-lordship. Nobles and mercenaries from England crossed the Irish Sea and intruded into these affairs, making alliances with various Irish leaders and acquiring land, until in 1171 King Henry II launched an invasion of his own. Not only was Henry II the first English monarch to go to Ireland, but his successful campaign established England's claims to sovereignty there. The part of Ireland that came under direct English control—subject to English laws, enforced from an administrative center in Dublin, and settled with English colonists—became known as the Pale. Beyond the Pale, English monarchs claimed over-lordship, but the Gaelic Irish maintained their own culture and often resisted English authority.

Centuries later, in the midst of rebellion and religious conflict sparked in part by the Reformation, Henry VIII upped the ante and took the title of King of Ireland. The Lordship of Ireland thus became, in 1542, the Kingdom of Ireland, and the entire country had to obey English law. Until that time, only the "English of Ireland" sat in Ireland's Parliament, which had enacted the Act of Union, granting Henry his new royal title. Now, in an attempt to win loyalty, the Gaelic elite were admitted into the Irish Parliament, which, like the English Parliament, was comprised of a hereditary House of Lords and a House of Commons, elected according to a restricted franchise. The Irish Parliament was not, however, as free in its actions as its English counterpart (where Welsh members now also sat). Under Ponyings' Law, passed in 1495 and still in effect, all of the statutes of the Irish Parliament had to be approved by both the Irish and the English Privy Councils.

This was actually a highpoint for Ireland in its ongoing relationship with England. As we shall see in chapter 3, conditions became even harsher in the late sixteenth and seventeenth centuries, the situation culminating in the Catholic Irish rising in support of James II in 1689. The Catholic majority was ultimately excluded from Irish political life. In the eighteenth century, at about the same time that North American colonists started their rebellion, Irish nationalists also sought to sever their unequal connection with Britain; by the century's end, tensions ignited around the discourse of rights. The French Revolution in particular exacerbated political and sectarian divisions in Ireland and contributed to a cycle of violence, resistance, and reprisal. The government of revolutionary France intervened directly as well, planning invasions of Ireland as part of its war against Britain (begun in 1793) and in support of the Irish independence movement. Many British politicians concluded that the only effective way to restrain the threat of Irish insurrection, and a permanent separation, was to take full control through union.[20]

The matter became especially urgent when, in May 1798, the anticipated uprising began. Prime Minister William Pitt proposed a plan for union that included Catholic emancipation, but, acquiescing to the objections of Irish Protestant politicians eager to preserve their legal privileges and political monopoly, not to mention the pervasive anti-Catholic prejudice in Britain, that element was purged. Although doing so lost the Pitt administration any support for the bill among Ireland's Catholics, union without emancipation preserved its biggest appeal for Ireland's Protestant elite, namely their coalition with the Protestant majorities in England, Scotland, and Wales.

In so fraught a climate, the first time it came up in the Irish Parliament in January 1799, the measure failed. The government prepared for a second attempt by funding an aggressive propaganda campaign that produced and circulated pamphlets, broadsides, songs, and cartoons, flooding the publishing markets in London and Dublin. The works predictably touted the legal, economic, political, and diplomatic advantages of union.[21] But the pamphleteers commissioned by Pitt's government during this pivotal 18-month period also compared the Irish Union to marriage, promising disingenuously that a merger would strengthen each of the parties. One pamphlet written in 1799 as a letter to John Foster, who led the opposition to union in the Irish Parliament, described the two, Britain and Ireland, as "divided and distinct." The author claimed that

> union alone by consolidating the interests of both, each conceding and each embracing, can substantiate the power of either; resembling two flames, that by meeting become one, and burn the stronger and the brighter for their union. Such, Sir, would be the marriage of Great Britain and Ireland, who would then form one family living in one house, and having but one interest, with that interest directed to their common advantage.[22]

The analogy to family is a familiar trope and one that had great portability.[23] The quotation reveals the anxiety surrounding this particular relationship in 1799, gesturing at the dangerous contingencies that would result if each member of this union behaved independently, unconfined by a framework of family, shared obligations, and responsibilities. Marriage would provide this framework. Everyone at the time would have understood that according to legal theory marriage suspended a wife's independent existence: when a woman married, she became a *feme covert* and ceased to exist as a legal actor.[24] While Irish constituents may have balked at the prospect of their coverture, British prejudices against the Irish, that included spurious notions of their inherently inferior intelligence, indolence, and incivility, fueled apprehensions about union. Both sides met the prospect of union and the blended family with hostility at worst, ambivalence at best. Yet with consent from each party, the union would be accomplished, and Ireland's subordination assured.

Contemporaries often referred to the union with Scotland in 1707 when debating the union of Ireland with Great Britain. Despite the different historical circumstances surrounding these two instances of incorporation, they shared important similarities. In both the threat posed by France spurred action, and war with France formed the background of the negotiations. In both economic incentives and concerns were at the center of negotiations. In both achieving union depended on the collaboration of Indigenous advocates who cooperated with London's agents to force the union through in the face of considerable opposition. Accusations of corruption and illegitimacy tainted both. [25]

The two Acts of Union that forged first Great Britain in 1707 and then the United Kingdom of Great Britain and Ireland in 1801 rearranged political, economic, and cultural relations within the British Isles. These acts created and recreated a new state. Yet, as we have seen, the intense domestic negotiations by which three parliamentary bodies ultimately consolidated themselves into one did not take place in a vacuum. Concerns about colonial trade, international relations, and even foreign invasion inspired the idea and permeated the details of union. Meanwhile the product of union—that new and evolving state comprised of several nations—emerged in the eighteenth century as both a European and a global power. The next chapter explores that development, putting the making of Britain in a world historical context.

IMAGE CREDITS

CHAPTER 3

Britain in a World Historical Context

Britain was already an empire in the seventeenth century, controlling an array of colonies stretching around the globe. During the eighteenth century, that empire was most established in the Atlantic, where Britain held 13 colonies on the Atlantic seaboard of North America, 26 islands in the Caribbean, enclaves in Central and South America, and trading posts along the coast of West Africa. But Britain also had a notable and ever-growing presence in Asia, from which the East India Company brought valuable commodities to the British Isles. To protect its empire, Britain strove for and generally maintained naval supremacy throughout the eighteenth century.

Within the continent of Europe, Britain had two primary concerns. It sought to keep the Low Countries (modern Belgium, Luxembourg, and the Netherlands) out of the hands of any great power that might use them as a base from which to challenge British maritime interests or perhaps to invade Britain itself. It also sought to maintain a balance of power on the continent, forming or joining coalitions to check the ambition of any would-be hegemonic state. Both imperatives brought it into repeated conflict with France, the preeminent land power in Western Europe. Britain's principal rival in Europe was also its main adversary overseas, so continental wars with France invariably had a colonial dimension. Imperial, European, and domestic affairs were thus inextricably intertwined.

In the last quarter of the eighteenth century, Britain faced new ideological and political challenges in what historians now call the Atlantic Revolutions. The first upheaval came in North America, where the 13 colonies resisted British efforts to tighten control and growing unrest exploded into open rebellion and a Declaration of Independence in 1776. After eight years of fighting, in which white colonists and both enslaved and free Blacks could be found on either side, and seeking neutral middle ground, the colonies won independence. They did so not by defeating the British Army, but by persuading British politicians that the costs in blood and particularly treasure of continuing the war were not worth the benefits of winning. The French Revolution of 1789 posed a more serious threat closer to home. The ideology of "liberty, equality, and fraternity" challenged the very basis of the British political system. In response, Britain joined a series of coalitions against France from 1792 to 1815. If fear that revolutionary ideas might spread were not enough of an incentive to oppose France in the early years, the expansionist zeal of its new leader provided an even greater impetus to action once Napoleon crowned himself emperor in 1804.

Revolutionary fervor also found fertile ground throughout Europe's colonial dependencies in the last decade of the eighteenth century. A slave rebellion in France's colony of Saint-Domingue offered a peculiar, and ultimately short-lived, opportunity for British imperial expansion and protection of its slave trade. Meanwhile in Ireland, a movement combining the goals of political independence and religious equality not only rose in rebellion but invited French military aid. Revolution and colonial resistance, as much as European alliances and rivalries and the pursuit of empire, shaped Britain.

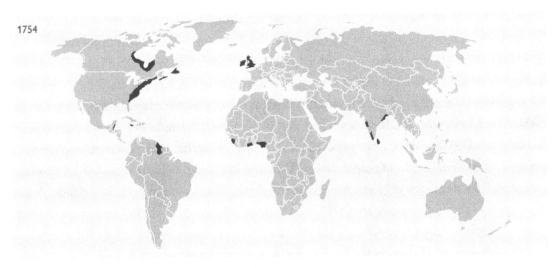

FIGURE 3.1 British Empire in mid-eighteenth century.

Nation Defined by Empire

The historian P. J. Marshall has said that Britain in the eighteenth century was "a nation defined by empire."[1] If we take this as our starting point, it is imperative to relate what we have discussed about British society and politics in chapters 1 and 2 to the global phenomenon of empire because they were inextricably linked, and, as scholarship has demonstrated, they were co-constituted.

Empire is usually defined as a territory or an aggregate of many separate states and territories ultimately under the rule of a single sovereign state. This definition of empire, which suggests a neat and cohesive whole, belies the lived reality, for empire was a messy business. Discovery and expansion always involved violence and collision. As Britons constructed their empire, Indigenous populations resisted the establishment of British rule, defying the appropriation of their land and claiming their autonomy.

Empire began close to home with England's hegemony over the British Isles consisting of Wales, Scotland, and Ireland. By the middle of the eighteenth century, it encompassed an aggregate of states and territories stretching from Gibraltar in the Mediterranean to North America, where it included colonies along the Atlantic seaboard and the West Indies, Guyana in South America, the African Gold Coast, India, and Burma. While Britain would lose the 13 North American colonies in the Treaty of Paris signed in 1783, this loss in the Atlantic World was offset by the acquisition of far-flung lands in the Pacific Ocean and expansion in South Asia. By the end of the century, the empire's reach extended to Australia and New Zealand.

Scholars have wrestled with understanding the realities of Britain's empire since John Cabot's arrival in Newfoundland in 1497. They used to distinguish between several empires. The First British Empire centered on the Atlantic World. It featured settler colonies in North America, plantation colonies in the Caribbean, and the Transatlantic Slave Trade, and it dominated the British imperial imagination until the loss of the 13 colonies. The Second British Empire, built around the East India Company's trading networks east of the Cape of Good Hope, mostly in Asia, and around Britain's exploitation of lands "discovered" (i.e., sighted and mapped for them) by Captain James Cook, was dated roughly 1783–1860. Historians now reject this nomenclature, arguing that it pays too much attention to periodization and to the notion that Britain's imperial venture changed radically as a result of the American Revolution. There were, after all, 26 colonies in North America and the Caribbean, and they operated in many similar ways, the most obvious being that labor was organized through a system of legalized raced and chattel slavery. The relentless attention historians have traditionally paid to the 13 lost colonies of North America overlooks the 13 other colonies in the Atlantic World that remained within the empire after 1783 and continued to generate profit well into the nineteenth century. Similarly, beyond the Americas, Britain had been extending and consolidating its reach in India long before the 13 colonies in North America achieved independence.

English trade with India began in the early seventeenth century. The East India Company, incorporated by royal charter on December 31, 1600, traded in cotton, silk, tea, and opium. While trade took center stage, over the course of its long presence in India Britain's political and military control of the subcontinent expanded. Britons justified their intrusions in the eighteenth century with promises to eradicate the autocratic rule of Indian princes who abused their people and did not respect the law, while in the nineteenth century they claimed a "civilizing mission" carried out by missionaries. Britain's resulting wealth was built on the destruction of local political structures and custom and the devastation of local economies.

Recent scholarship examines the phenomenon of *settler colonialism.* This term refers to the establishment of new communities in which a substantial white population removed and erased the Indigenous people and developed its own distinctive identity and sovereignty. Settler colonial societies developed in North America, Australia, New Zealand, and South Africa. Like the plantation societies created on islands in the Caribbean, which depended on slavery to produce surplus for profit, these colonies developed their own governing institutions in which white settlers had representation in their own governance. Lines of race hardened over the eighteenth century with people of color, both Indigenous people and those transported to these colonies as enslaved laborers, excluded from most positions of power and any role in governance.

Beyond settler colonies and plantation societies, imperialism included various governing schemes. The white officials of the East India Company eventually ruled nearly 200 million people in India, while the British military garrisoned strategic points such as Gibraltar. In contrast to the American colonies, where legislative bodies often exercised autonomy that defied orders from the metropole, appointed governors answerable only to London ruled Crown colonies. All these forms of governance coexisted in the eighteenth century, making the British Empire a patchwork of different types of administration and oversight. Because it always employed military and/or economic power, the system is often referred to as extractive imperialism: Britain extracted from its colonies resources it needed at home or those marketable at home and abroad.

What a long view over the sixteenth through the early nineteenth century demonstrates is that this extractive model of imperialism, one that removed resources from whatever region of the world in which it was located to increase Britain's wealth, was infinitely appetitive. The long-distance voyages of "discovery" that marked the early modern period continued in the late eighteenth century with James Cook, who explored Oceania (Australia, New Zealand, and the islands of the southwest Pacific). Driven by the desire for scientific discoveries and raw materials, Cook's three voyages between 1768 and 1780 established Britain's hold on Australia. After Britain took official possession of the eastern half of Australia in 1788, it established a penal colony there where eventually 1.2 million British immigrants, free and forced, settled. As had happened earlier in North America, the forced labor regimes imposed on the Indigenous population and the spread of disease led to the decimation of the Aborigines, their depopulation exacerbated by their forced dislocation.

The tremendous growth of the British Empire provided job opportunities and, potentially, a common purpose and national identity for those who served. The ranks of colonial administration included many men from Wales and Scotland. Britain protected its colonies with a powerful navy and a relatively small army supplemented by local levies of white colonists and Indigenous people. The army recruited rank and file soldiers from the poor and marginalized people of the British Isles. For example, Irish Catholic recruits made up 20 percent of the British army by the start of the American War, an increase of 14 percent since the 1750s.[2] Britain's maritime fleets also increased, its ships worked by a large number of mariners involved in commercial shipping and in Britain's powerful navy. Although far less diverse than merchant ships, naval crews were, according to Nicholas Frykman, "among the most cosmopolitan and multinational assemblies of workers to be found anywhere in the Atlantic World."[3] To meet the growing need of such a large number of ships during the French Wars at the end of the century, Parliament enacted the Quota Acts—laws passed in 1795 and 1796—that mandated local authorities deliver a certain number of recruits to the navy and in some cases to the army.

Sailors expressed growing alarm about impressment and the harsh conditions on board navy ships, where life was difficult, food poor, and discipline brutal. Objections to impressment appeared in newspapers and pamphlets.[4] Riots against the practice of pulling men off the streets and out of taverns and forcing them into naval service took place around England and in Canada in the 1790s.[5] The historian Nicholas Rogers has found an instance of rioters disrupting the work of press gangs in blackface, making a comparison between the life of an impressed sailor and an enslaved Black.[6] In his account of life in the navy between 1780 and 1819 William Richardson was far more explicit: "People may talk of negro slavery and the whip, but let them look nearer home, and see a poor sailor … if he complains he is … flogged with a cat, much more severe than the negro driver's whip, and if he deserts he is flogged … nearly to death."[7]

The sailors' comparison of their plight with that of enslaved Africans was not new, but it took on a particularly shrill tone in the context of the rising discourse of abolition that brought more attention to slavery and the slave trade at the end of the eighteenth century. The sailors' rhetoric referenced English liberty

FIGURE 3.2 (a) *The Press Gang*, unspecified author, scanned from *Vaisseau de Ligne, Time Life*, 1979. (b) *The Press Gang, Or English Liberty Displayed*, from *Oxford Magazine*, 1770.

and freedom in an attempt to draw a very firm boundary between the sailor's life and that of an enslaved person. The sailors claimed whiteness as a privileged legal category that entitled them to the rights of man. These assertions remind us of the dichotomy between freedom and slavery that framed so much of eighteenth-century discourse. The comparison of naval service to slavery was one that white sailors rejected, insisting that their whiteness and their service to Britain's empire entitled them to liberty and freedom.

Empire at Home and Away
TWO ISLANDS: INTERNAL COLONIALISM AND IRELAND

Ireland's people—approximately 3 million in 1700—lived in a separate kingdom with a separate parliament. Yet, it is perfectly reasonable to describe Ireland as England's first colony, and the relationship between the neighboring islands of Britain and Ireland in the eighteenth century as internal colonialism.

Establishment of the Kingdom of Ireland under Henry VIII in the 1540s, and related efforts to win the loyalty of the Irish Gaelic elite, had ended neither oppression nor resistance in Ireland. To the contrary, a new and particularly brutal phase of conquest followed. Martial government was established to enforce English law, and a policy of plantation, physically seeding Ireland with loyal English subjects, extended and institutionalized the appropriation of Irish land. Large swatches of the island were confiscated, reconstituted as plantations, and granted to English colonists. Tensions arose not only between the Gaelic Irish and the newly arrived English planters and administrators but between the "Old English" in Ireland, heirs of the medieval conquests and mostly Catholic, and the "New English" Protestants who came in the sixteenth century.

The province of Ulster, in particular, became a hotspot at the end of the sixteenth century when a rebellion started there in response to English authority. With Spanish support, the resistance spread, and England came close to losing its hold on Ireland. After nine years of war, England prevailed in 1603, and soon thereafter established its largest plantation yet, covering almost a half million acres. James VI of Scotland had recently inherited the crown of England, and Scots joined English settlers in a united Protestant effort to colonize the largely Catholic and Gaelic province. At the same time, across the Atlantic, the London Virginia Company established its plantation at Jamestown. The colonization of Ulster and the Chesapeake, and soon New England, were all part of a broader settler movement.

It was in Ulster, again, that an Irish Catholic rebellion erupted in 1641. Figuring out how to subdue it contributed to the tensions between Charles I and his English and Scottish Parliaments; when those tensions turned to civil war in 1642, the Catholic majority seized power in Ireland. After Charles I was defeated and the monarchy abolished, the reconquest of Ireland was one of the first acts of the radically Protestant commonwealth regime. Commonwealth forces under the leadership of Oliver Cromwell ruthlessly punished Irish Catholics for both their rebellion in 1641 and subsequent support of the pro-Catholic royalist cause. Military victories were accompanied by atrocities perpetuated against the civilian population: soldiers killed after they had surrendered, prisoners of war transported overseas as indentured servants, towns burned, and land confiscated. Famine and plague exacerbated the staggering loss of life. When it was over, Cromwell's forces were paid with Irish land.

The Irish rose again in support of Charles I's son, James II. They, as we have seen, refused to accept the Revolution of 1688 that removed Catholic James II from the throne and took up arms against the new Protestant monarchs, William and Mary. After William crushed Irish Catholic resistance at the Battle of the Boyne, Catholics were excluded from membership in Parliament in Ireland; they were already excluded by the Test Act in England, which passed penal laws further restricting Catholic rights. These punitive measures and the complete domination of Ireland by Protestants is referred to as the Protestant Ascendancy, which granted Ireland's wealthy Protestant landlords uncontested social, cultural, economic, and political power. Catholics were barred from holding state office, running for elected office, joining the armed forces, and practicing law. Then, in 1728, Catholics were disenfranchised too.

Statistics on landownership demonstrate the severe disparity of wealth between Catholics and Protestants that became even more drastic over the course of the eighteenth century. Catholic ownership declined from a very small 22 percent (down from 59 percent 1641) to 14 percent. To ensure that this trend continued, the Act to Prevent the Further Growth of Popery, passed in 1704, prohibited Catholics from acquiring any more land and required them to practice partible inheritance, bequeathing equitable portions to each son rather than engaging in the practice of primogeniture. If one of the heirs was Protestant, however, he received the entire inheritance. The result was the division of large Catholic estates into smaller and smaller parcels of land.

The power of the Irish Parliament declined, particularly over Britain's attempts to control Ireland's thriving woolen industry. In 1720 when the Irish appealed to the king to support their parliament's right to final jurisdiction, the British Parliament responded with the Declaratory Act for "better securing the dependency of the kingdom of Ireland on the Crown of Great Britain." The act asserted the right of Britain's parliament to make laws binding on Ireland. Forty-four years later, it imposed a similar measure on the North American colonies as they protested British efforts to tax them.

ONE NATION: SCOTLAND AND WALES

England took a similar approach to pacifying the Catholic Scottish Highlands of the north and west, which were still governed by the medieval clan system. This system was often mythologized. Talk of clans and chieftains played into popular stereotypes of English superiority and Scottish lack of civility. In reality, from the seventeenth century onward, it really makes more sense to fall back on the mundane labels of landlord and tenants than the romantic concepts of chieftain and clans. Still, the Highlands with their largely Scots-Gaelic speaking Catholic, rural population contrasted with the more urban, English-allied Scottish Lowlands. After union, this divide became especially pronounced as Lowlanders had even greater reason to look southward, and as resistance to the Hanoverian succession continued to resonate among some Highlanders. English initiatives in the Highlands were commonly imposed as punishment for their support of the Stuart claimant to the throne. In the 1720s and '30s, for example, General George Wade and his English troops engaged in building a network of roads across the Highlands as a defensive response to the Jacobite Rebellion of 1715.

Those roads also facilitated the Highland Clearances, forced evictions that cleared the land of people beginning in the middle of the eighteenth century and continuing on and off for the next century. These evictions were carried out as part of the enclosure movement to create large farms and in response to rebellion. After another, and the most threatening, Jacobite uprising in 1745–1746, the British government imposed restrictive laws on the clans to limit the power of the chiefs and undermine Gaelic culture including banning bagpipe music and clan tartans. The government also enabled new landlords to acquire land in the Highlands in order to expand capitalist agriculture there. Rural peasants were transported from inland farms or glens to coastal towns, where they engaged in occupations such as commercial fishing and processing, light manufacturing, or kelping (i.e., collecting and drying seaweed to prepare it for chemical extraction, mostly connected to soap making). Others emigrated, many of them to the Canadian Province of Nova Scotia ("new Scotland"). In the now cleared Highland glens, lucrative sheep grazing replaced arable farming. This coerced resettlement could be tremendously destructive and disruptive. In addition to the cultural and economic damage inflicted on the Highlanders, the Clearing radically changed the distribution of Scotland's growing population. At midcentury, perhaps half of the population lived north of the River Tay, and one-third lived in the Highlands or islands. By the twentieth century the Highlands population fell to a low point of a mere 4 percent.

At roughly the same time that the Highland Clearances began in the northwest of Scotland, Parliament passed a law clarifying the status of the town at its south-eastern tip. Berwick-up-on-Tweed, which sits on the English-Scottish border, had historically been contested, passing back and forth between the two nations. With the Act of Union in 1707, it became part of the English county of Northumberland. After the '15, the government built a large military barracks at this strategic spot; after the '45, Parliament reaffirmed that English, not Scottish law, applied in Berwick. It did so by creating a statutory definition of England that included England, Berwick-upon-Tweed, and Wales. As mentioned in chapter 2, Wales had been politically assimilated into England's administrative and legal structure in the sixteenth century. The Wales and Berwick Act of 1746 confirmed the even longer standing legal arrangements there as well.

It proved harder, however, to repress Welsh culture. English was the language of the government, so it was imperative for anyone who wished to pursue a profession within the civic administration or socialize among the elite to speak it. Yet the mountains provided Wales a geographical region where it could preserve its culture from English interference until the railways were built in the 1840s. The Welsh language continued to be spoken by a majority of the population. In the 1770s, 90 percent probably spoke only Welsh, but, while bilingualism increased steadily, as late as the 1880s an estimated 75 percent still preferred their native tongue.[8] That language was itself the subject of new study and pride in the eighteenth century. In 1707—the year of Scottish Union—the Welsh philologist and keeper of Oxford's Ashmolean Museum, Edward Lhuyd, published *Archaeologia Britannica*, in which he demonstrated that the Welsh language was related to Cornish, Breton, Irish, and Gaelic and that they all derived from a common language that he called Celtic. Lhuyd, who died just two years later, unfortunately missed the explosion of "Celtomania and druidomania," his discovery unleashed. In 1716, the historian Theophilus Evans published *Drych y Prif Oesoedd* (Mirror of the Early Centuries), a work that "not only rescued the national history of Wales from the condescension of English writers but also provided the reading public with a bold, rollicking version of the past in their own tongue." Still, with no cities to compare with Dublin, Edinburgh, and Glasgow, Welsh intellectuals tended to leave for England, and much of the work celebrating the Celtic past, especially its bardic and religious traditions, was undertaken by London-based Welsh cultural societies.[9]

EXTERNAL COLONIALISM AND INDIA

Internal colonialism was just one form of English expansion. The empire had expanded across the globe in the seventeenth century. Like other early modern European empires, Britain's was based on a combination of private enterprise and state ventures. Colonial trade was carried out not by a monarch, but by chartered companies. The charter was a document from the government detailing what commodities the company was allowed to trade and where and permitting it to carry out all kinds of state-like actions, such as raising a militia, making war, concluding treaties, and conquering overseas territory—as the company saw fit in pursuit of profit. This autonomy encouraged an "anything goes" mode of conducting trade. England's chartered companies formed in the seventeenth century included the Virginia Company (1606), the Massachusetts Bay Company (1629), the Hudson's Bay Company (1670), and the Royal African Company (1672). In the eighteenth century, the British Crown granted charters to the South Sea Company (1711) and the Sierra Leone Company (1792). In the nineteenth century they were joined by the New Zealand Company (1825), the South Australian Company (1835), the Royal Niger Company (1886), and the British South Africa Company (1889).

The East India Company (EIC), founded by royal charter in 1600, paid the Crown for monopoly trading rights east of the Cape of Good Hope; in other words, the company was granted the sole right to trade in Asia. It conducted most of its commercial activity in India, but it also had trading posts on the island of Sumatra and at Canton on the Chinese coast. *India* as the term was used during the eighteenth and nineteenth centuries did not correspond precisely to the modern nation of that name. It also included what are today the countries of Pakistan and Bangladesh. These territories consisted of numerous autonomous principalities, many of them nominally ruled by the Mughal emperor. The EIC's activities and influence spread far beyond trade. From its bases in Bengal, it repeatedly intervened in local disputes and extended its rule over more and more territory.

The EIC expanded its hold on the Indian subcontinent and its resources throughout the eighteenth century using any means necessary. Like most empire builders, it relied on a combination of coercion and cooptation. To accomplish these tasks, it created its own army and administrative bureaucracy—and transformed itself from a trading company into an arm of the British government, ruling a foreign territory and a foreign population. The company initially controlled trading posts along the east coast of India, but its further expansion into Bengal led to resistance by the territory's ruler. France exploited the conflict, seeking to displace Britain in the subcontinent. At the Battle of Plassey in 1757, the EIC army defeated a Bengali army supported by French troops. Then, in 1764, the EIC army defeated the Moghul emperor and the company became the preeminent power in northern India. The EIC did not, however, depose the now powerless emperor but forced him to recognize it as his protector. The EIC thus became the de facto ruler of northern India. Through a series of wars and treaties with client states, it gradually gained control of the entire subcontinent.

Although the EIC allowed Indian rulers considerable autonomy, it governed in a manner calculated to maximize profit at the expense of local people. For instance, the company redesigned the way that Indian elites related to laborers and peasants. Indian local elites had usually held hereditary rights to tribute payments from peasants, but they did not own the land occupied by those dependents. The company redefined this relationship, making the elites landowners and assigning them the task of collecting taxes from the population on their "estates." If they failed to collect the required amount, the company seized their land—a win-win proposition for the EIC that made use of Indian elites' traditional authority in new ways.

With an eye on the profits from the opium trade with China, the company insisted that Indian farmers cultivate poppies instead of food crops, which created food shortages and famine. Through their rapacious policies EIC officials became extremely wealthy, unscrupulously plundering the fortunes of the elites of the subcontinent and extracting whatever wealth they could using violence and exploiting native peoples with seemingly little supervision or oversight from the government.

The quintessential example of the avaricious company man was Warren Hastings, who served as the first governor-general of Bengal. The governor-general was the representative of the British monarch appointed to lead a given colony. Created in 1773 the governor-general had direct control of the presidency of Fort William, the EIC's base in Bengal, and he was empowered to supervise company officials elsewhere in India. Although a competent administrator—Hastings spent over

FIGURE 3.3 The trial of Warren Hastings in Westminster Hall, 1788. Walpole Library.

30 years in the service of the company taking on such issues as the reform of judicial practices and tax reform—he was very much a product of the EIC and had used the same violent and unlawful

FIGURE 3.4 Warren Hastings, governor-general of Bengal.

means in his position. In 1786 Edmund Burke initiated impeachment proceedings against Hastings, accusing him of mismanagement, malpractice, and personal corruption. The case then went to trial in the House of Lords. Although Hastings was eventually acquitted of all charges, the trial dragged on from 1787–1795. Burke led the prosecution, and the trial became a site in which to debate the role of the EIC and Britain's expanding empire. The discussion turned on the threats posed to Britain's constitution and British liberties by the EIC's exercise of "arbitrary power" in the colonies. No one advocated the interruption or termination of Britain's imperial project; instead, the discussion exposed the fiction that Britain's virtue and rule of law justified its imperial expansion.

The Hastings affair revealed the need for greater oversight of the EIC. In 1784, William Pitt the Younger passed the East India

Company Act. The act instituted a system of joint governance between the EIC and the Crown, with the Crown the dominant partner. It also created a board of governors in London to handle political affairs. The measure improved administration but did not end the exploitation of the Indian people.

Slavery and the Atlantic World

Meanwhile, across the globe other companies were involved in establishing an English, and then British, presence in the Atlantic World, including North America and the Caribbean. The first fledgling English colonies in the Americas were established in the early seventeenth century in Virginia and Bermuda. Both places found that they could grow tobacco, and by providing for the insatiable European appetite for it they secured their economic future. The West Indian colonies began as private initiatives. Bermuda and the Bahamas were settled by an enterprise that had separated from the Virginia Company while other islands like St. Kitts, Barbados, Jamaica, and Antigua were colonized by small, chartered companies. Many of these places were already claimed by Spain, and the first English colonists engaged in violent clashes to seize and defend their plantations. By the middle of the seventeenth century the English had taken control of several of the Caribbean islands that had been Spanish colonies. They established sugar plantations in Barbados and Jamaica. The mono-crop plantations of the New World in the Caribbean and the Chesapeake eventually cultivated sugar, tobacco, indigo, and cotton, thereby increasing the demand for slave labor.

The West Indian islands attracted many settlers seeking cheap land and the promise of quick profits. In the early seventeenth century the labor working these crops was provided by indentured servants. The companies promoting the settlements facilitated the immigration of hundreds and sometimes thousands of indentured servants each year. These servants from England and Ireland exchanged the cost of their passage, food, and clothing for work contracts with a four- to seven-year term at the end of which they were promised freedom and their own land. By the 1640s there were twenty-five thousand English and Scots in the West Indies. After the tobacco trade peaked in the middle of the seventeenth century, the plantation owners switched to growing sugar cane. This profitable crop made the West Indies the most valuable part of the British Empire in the early eighteenth century. Sugar was much more difficult to grow than tobacco, and it required a much larger workforce charged with arduous tasks. The supply of indentured servants no longer met the needs of the planters, who turned to importing enslaved people from Africa. The enslaved population grew rapidly, and by the 1660s there were more Black slaves than white settlers in the British West Indies.

Slaves for the West Indies and the southern colonies of North America were supplied by chartered companies, the Company of Royal Adventurers and later the Royal African Company, which established forts and other contacts along the African coast. Private investors put up vast amounts of capital to finance the trading circuit that ran from Europe to Africa to the Americas and back to Europe. In the early period textiles from India along with rum and tobacco from the Americas, and guns manufactured in England were traded for enslaved people. By the end of the eighteenth century the English were exporting an average of three hundred thousand guns to West Africa. Although the first Europeans to dominate the slave trade were Portuguese, Spanish, and Dutch, by the eighteenth century Great Britain became the world's leader. The trade was brutal, the conditions atrocious, and the treatment of Africans horrific and inhumane. Thousands of Africans died on the crowded slave ships and in their first months on the plantations. Bristol and Liverpool were the hubs of this extremely profitable trade. In the 1750s 53 slave ships a year carrying 30,000 human beings across the Atlantic Ocean left from Liverpool on one leg of the "triangle trade" that connected Britain, Africa, and the Caribbean; at the end of the century it was 80,000 to 100,000 young African men and women a year. By the 1780s more than 1.25 million Africans had been shipped to Jamaica, Barbados, and the smaller West Indian "sugar islands," and almost three hundred thousand had been sold in North America. According to the Trans-Atlantic Slave Trade Database, in the entire history of the slave trade from 1525 until 1866, 12.5 million Africans were shipped to the New World. 10.7 million survived the dreaded Middle Passage, disembarking in North America, the Caribbean, and South America. Many more than that were captured but died in transit.[10]

Wealthy West Indian planters and their families were more tied to Britain than the settlers in North America. An increasing number became absentee landlords in the eighteenth century, entrusting their plantations to overseers and returning to Britain with some of their household slaves. They established large communities in London, Bath, and Bristol; they bought landed estates in the British countryside; and they commissioned individual and family portraits that often featured their Black slaves.[11] The presence in Britain of wealthy West Indian planters and their slaves drew attention to the moral, social, and legal contradictions between the idea of equality before the law and the reality of slavery. The discomfort caused by these contradictions found expression in broadsides, newspapers, cartoons, novels, and plays in which returning planters were resented for their wealth and mocked for their social pretension. Yet however much they were ridiculed in the press, the planters established strong organizations to lobby Parliament on their behalf, proving quite adept at resisting abolitionist efforts.

West Indian planters who returned to Britain served as concrete reminders of the realities of slave ownership and the wealth created by distant slave plantations, all of it unsettling metropolitan sensibilities. They represented the inescapable fact that much of Britain's wealth was built on the slave trade and on slave labor and that, from the beginning, the government had sanctioned slavery in the colonies. In the eighteenth century the government and the Church of England accommodated and facilitated both slave holding and slave-trading in ways that expanded the practices and maximized the profits garnered.[12] It was the metropolitan demand for the products of the plantation, the same products on offer in London's markets and shops—cotton, sugar, tobacco, and indigo—that fueled the enterprise and its longevity.

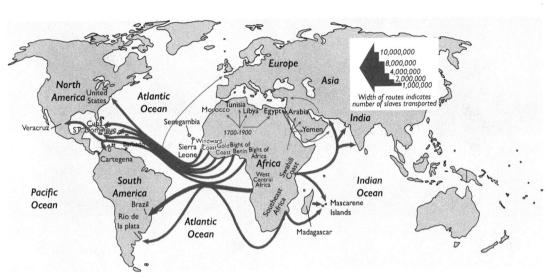

FIGURE 3.5 Slaves left Africa and reached the Americas by many routes. Although certain embarkation and disembarkation regions forged strong connections, captives from anywhere in Africa could disembark in almost any part of the Americas.

FIGURE 3.6 A view of the Roaring River Estate, Jamaica.

FIGURE 3.7 Plantation village, Jamaica, 1843.

FIGURE 3.8 Dancing scene in the West Indies, 1764–96.

European Alliances and Rivalries

During the eighteenth century two intertwined imperatives drove British foreign policy: maintaining the balance of power in Europe and defending a global empire and the commerce that it supported. The circumstances of war and diplomacy inseparably linked these goals. European wars usually had a colonial counterpart; sometimes the conflicts started in colonial territories. Victories there could be canceled out by losses in Europe and vice versa. Eighteenth-century warfare thus required a comprehensive strategy played out on many, often distant, fronts.

After 1689, the primary threat to British interests in Europe and abroad shifted dramatically. In the mid-seventeenth century that threat had come from England's commercial rival, the Netherlands (then known as the United Provinces). The two countries fought three maritime wars between 1652 and 1674 without much benefit to either. The rise of Catholic France under Louis XIV, however, reminded the two Protestant nations that they had more to fear from the common enemy than they did from one another. The Revolution of 1688, and crowning of William of Orange (Stadtholder of the Netherlands) as co-ruler of Britain, cemented the new Anglo-Dutch partnership. At the same time the decline of imperial Spain diminished the threat from that kingdom, which became a junior partner of France. These changes in the balance of power led to a series of conflicts between France and Britain that historians now describe as the "second hundred years war." Each of the wars fought between 1689 and 1815 had its own discreet causes, but all of them served the same larger purpose: to keep France from becoming the preeminent land power in Europe and to expand British commerce and empire at the expense of its continental rival.

The ascension of the Elector of Hanover to the British throne as George I in 1714 created another imperative for British foreign policy. For the next century protecting the German principality had to be factored into balance of power calculations. Hanover provided troops for the Crown, but defending it also imposed a burden on British resources. It mattered far more to the Hanoverian kings than it did to their British subjects, and over the course of the century resentment of the Hanoverian connection became a rallying point for the political opposition.

WAR OF THE SPANISH SUCCESSION

When the king of Spain died without an heir in 1700, he left his crown to the French prince Philip of Anjou, grandson of Louis XIV, who announced that the kingdoms would be unified. The prospect of the two powerful states combining under the house of Bourbon threatened to upset the balance of power in Europe. A Grand Alliance of England and Scotland (Great Britain after 1707), the Holy Roman (Austrian) Empire, the Netherlands, Portugal, and Savoy backed a rival claimant to the throne, Charles, son of the Emperor Leopold I. Savoy switched sides and joined France in 1703, and each alliance had the support of the Spanish factions that favored its candidate.

During the years of its involvement in the war (1701–1713), Britain enjoyed two great advantages. The first was a superior system of state finance. Founded in 1694, the Bank of England served as a reliable source for loans. Meanwhile, the Treasury deposited revenue in the bank and earned interest from it. Britain thus had the ability to finance wars more effectively than its adversaries. Britain's second advantage came from its general, John Churchill, later Duke of Marlborough (and ancestor of Winston Churchill). Military historians still use his victory over a Franco-Bavarian army at Blenheim on the Danube in 1704 as a premier example of eighteenth-century warfare. He went on to win a series of battles in the Spanish Netherlands (modern Belgium), but the Grand Alliance could not crack the ring of fortresses protecting France. War weariness set in at home, and Marlborough's wife Sarah, a lady-in-waiting to Queen Anne and source of the general's influence, was also falling out of favor. By 1713 it was time to negotiate a settlement.

The Peace of Utrecht represented something of a compromise but achieved Britain's primary goals. On the dynastic front, Philip of Anjou got the Spanish throne in return for renouncing all claims to that of France for himself and his descendants. The unified Bourbon threat was checked. Britain received Gibraltar and Minorca in the Mediterranean, and Newfoundland, Nova Scotia, and the territory around Hudson Bay in North America, as well as the island of St. Kitts in the Caribbean. It also received a monopoly on the slave trade with the Spanish colonies. These concessions did not, however, resolve the issue of hegemony over North America.

WAR OF THE AUSTRIAN SUCCESSION

Almost thirty years later, Britain became embroiled in another long, dynastic struggle (1740–1748), this one involving the Holy Roman (Austrian) Empire. George II, as elector of Hanover, had a stake in the imperial conflict, but also, and once again, Britain sought to preserve the European balance of power. Frederick II "the Great" of Prussia launched the war on a legal pretext for territorial gain. He opposed the Austrian heir, Maria Theresa, on the grounds that a woman could not inherit the imperial crown, but his real aim was to annex the rich imperial province of Silesia. Seeing the war as an opportunity to weaken its main continental rival, the Holy Roman (Austrian) Empire, France backed Prussia. This move predictably brought Britain in on the side of the empress. Russia, whose interests in Poland and the Baltic region clashed with those of Prussia, also supported Austria. The long, bloody, and expensive war ended with Maria Theresa keeping her throne, and Frederick taking Silesia, a development that the empress determined to reverse at the earliest available opportunity. And again, European conflict had colonial implications. In North America, Britain captured the Fortress of Louisburg on Cape Breton Island but gave it back to France in return for Madras in India. No one expected the Treaty of Aix-la-Chapelle that ended the war to last, however, as the underlying continental power struggle remained unresolved.

SEVEN YEARS WAR

The Seven Years War (1756–1763) was the first world war, a global contest among European empires with battles in India, the Caribbean, Europe, and North America. Its armies included Native Americans, enslaved Africans, Bengali princes, Filipino militiamen, and European soldiers. At stake were the imperial possessions on land as well as control of the world's oceans.

Fighting began two years earlier in 1754 when British colonial troops (including some led by Lieutenant Colonel George Washington) allied with Seneca warriors, clashed with French soldiers in the Ohio Valley. When in 1756 France and Austria, rival land powers, signed an alliance, and Russia joined them the following year, British concerns with maintaining the balance of power were raised. The empress of Austria and the tsar of Russia had a common enemy: the upstart king of Prussia. France, however, had a different motive. It hoped, forlornly as it turned out, that the new alliance would keep the peace on the continent so that it could fight a maritime war with Britain. France now considered that the British threat came not from the global empire's ability to thwart French ambitions on land, but from its dominance at sea. Britain's increasing share of world trade and its financial prowess, which allowed it to replace the Dutch Republic as the banker of Europe, rather than its army, challenged French hegemony.

Britain recognized that while the enemy remained the same, the basis of the struggle had changed. The neutrality of the Low Countries guaranteed by the Franco-Austrian alliance removed a major cause of previous wars with France. Britain now played the alliance game, not to protect the Dutch Republic and the Austrian Netherlands from France, but to prevent France devoting all its resources to the maritime and colonial struggle to come. Because Prussia would keep France engaged on the continent, Britain could not allow the kingdom to be destroyed. In 1756, it signed the Covenant of Westminster with Frederick II, agreeing that the two kingdoms should preserve peace in Germany by preventing another power attempting to alter the status quo. Britain would bankroll Prussia, which due to the nature of eighteenth-century warfare and its efficient system of taxation and recruitment could maintain an army comparable to its larger rivals. France counted on the new alliance system keeping the peace in Europe so that it could concentrate on the maritime struggle. Britain, on the other hand, counted on a continental war forcing France to divide its resources between land and sea. London's forecast proved the correct one.[13]

Although most of its European battles would be fought in Central Europe, the war started in the Mediterranean. On April 29, 1756, France besieged Minorca, which it had lost in the War of the Spanish Succession. Britain declared war in May, and the island fell to France in June. Seeing the forces ranged against him, Frederick launched a preemptive strike against Austria, invading Saxony in August. For the remainder of the war, he was in a life-and-death struggle that he should have lost. The superiority of the Prussian Army, the genius of its commander, British subsidies, the failure of his enemies to coordinate their attacks, and the timely death of the Russian Empress Elizabeth, whose successor took Russia out of the war, saved Prussia from almost certain defeat.

Britain funded her continental ally and defended Hanover. The war ended in 1763 with minor territorial adjustments in Europe: Prussia kept Silesia but returned Saxony to Austria. Hanover retained its independence. Perhaps most important, Prussia had defeated Austria and established itself as a European power.

In India, Robert Clive, an East India Company trader, led 850 European officers and 2,100 Indians to defeat a North Indian Maratha army of 50,000 supported by a small French contingent at the Battle of Plassey in 1757. After Plassey, the East India Company gained control of Calcutta. Subsequent victories drove the French out of the Bengali interior and eliminated France as a rival in the subcontinent. More significantly, Indian rulers lost their ability to resist European colonial powers.

The Seven Years War changed the balance of power around the world. Britain emerged victorious, the foremost colonial empire. Its rivals, France and Spain, lost ground. France ceded its territories in Canada, including Quebec, as well as the Newfoundland fisheries to Britain, while Spain lost Florida, gaining the Louisiana Territory west of the Mississippi in a secret deal with France. Britain returned Minorca in exchange for islands in the Caribbean the British had captured. With Britain's emergence as the dominant global empire, Indigenous forces in North America and Asia lost the ability to play the European rivals against each other.

Revolution and Resistance in the Atlantic World

AMERICAN REVOLUTION

The war for independence waged by Britain's 13 North American colonies has been enshrined in the patriotic narrative of US history. Most Americans have a very simplistic notion of what took place between the end of the Seven Years War in 1763 and the Treaty of Paris twenty years later. They envision independent-minded colonists banding together to oppose a tyrannical king and Parliament determined to tax them without their consent. Acting with singularity of purpose the colonies defeated the mightiest empire in the world and established the first modern democratic state.

The reality of the conflict is, of course, far more complex. Many people in Britain, including some members of Parliament, agreed with the American demand for greater representation. The colonists were fighting not only for their freedom, but for the right to continue enslaving people of African descent and to steal more land from Native Americans. The war never enjoyed widespread support from the colonial population. John Adams claimed that perhaps one-third of Americans supported independence, one-third remained loyal, and one-third sat on the fence. The number of fence sitters may in fact have been higher, the strength of support for the war varied with its costs and course. Many Americans who agreed with colonial demands did not wish to separate from Britain; they wanted to remain in the empire with a significant degree of autonomy. The conflict was in many respects a civil war between loyalists and patriots, and this internecine nature made it the second bloodiest war (based on per capita loss of life) in American history. The causes, conduct, and consequences of the Revolution must be understood within the context of the British Empire and the complexities of colonial and British politics.

A century and a half of living more than 3,000 miles from England inevitably set the colonies on a different path of development from the metropole. Colonial assemblies assumed the right to manage their own affairs, and a Crown preoccupied with matters at home or in other parts of the empire generally allowed them considerable latitude in doing so. While only white men of property could vote in most colonies, more of them enjoyed this privilege than did their counterparts in Great Britain. The colonists also got used to trading with whomever they pleased. Importing tea from the Dutch East India Company and sugar from the French and Spanish islands in the Caribbean technically counted as smuggling, but colonial merchants did it so openly that it became routine business practice.

The trouble began, at the end of the Seven Years War (dubbed the French and Indian War in the 13 colonies and Canada) in 1763. Britain gained undisputed control of Eastern North America with the help of colonial militias that fought side by side with British regulars to drive the French from Canada and relieve a persistent threat on the northern border of New England. Three issues, however, drove a wedge between the colonists and the metropole almost immediately: managing the native population on the frontier, paying for the defense of the colonies, and Britain's desire for improved imperial administration. Underlying British decisions lay a desire by the government in London to put management of the empire on more fiscally sound footing.

In April 1763, fearing that the British victory over the French heralded a loss of ancestral lands to American colonists, Chief Pontiac led the tribes in the Ohio Valley to attack forts and outposts on the frontier, capturing several. It took the British three years to suppress the uprising with considerable loss of life and cost to the Treasury. The British government thus decided to ban further settlement west of the Appalachian Mountains to separate colonial and native populations. To many Britons the decision seemed both prudent and humane, but it infuriated colonials eager for more land.

Closing the Ohio region to settlement was but one measure in a concerted effort to govern the empire in North America more directly and efficiently. The Crown began paying its governors, judges, and customs officials directly, removing the power of the purse, which colonial assemblies had held over them. London also sought to improve customs revenues through better oversight. The Sugar Act of 1764, which replaced the Molasses Act, actually cut the duty on imported rum from 6 to 3 pence per gallon, but unlike its predecessor, the new law was more rigorously enforced. Reasonable though such measures may have been, the colonists bitterly resented them as infringements on their rights.

If restricting settlement and governing more directly caused resentment, taxation unleashed a firestorm of discontent. Given the higher cost of colonial defense, it seemed only fair that the colonists help pay for it. Parliament in London, not colonial assemblies, passed the new taxes, and "No taxation without representation" became a rallying cry of the revolutionaries. Like most slogans it simplified a complex reality. The dispute centered on the difference between direct and virtual representation. Although returned for specific county or borough seats, British members of Parliament legislated on behalf of the country and empire as a whole. London's efforts to exercise tighter control over the colonies may also be seen as part of a larger trend toward centralization on the part of European powers seeking to rationalize administration of increasingly unwieldy empires.

In 1765, Parliament passed the first of a series of new colonial taxes. The Stamp Act required that all legal and commercial documents bear a duty stamp. Reaction to the revenue measure was swift and violent. Riots and attacks on stamp distributors rocked colonial cities, and chapters of a secret society called the Sons of Liberty sprung up everywhere. Parliament quickly realized that, not only was the Act not generating the desired revenue, but it was fueling discontent. In 1766, it repealed the Act but immediately passed the Declaratory Act, again asserting its right to tax the colonies. The Crown still needed money, which it sought to collect through a series of customs duties on glass, lead, paints, paper, and tea that passed in 1767. Parliament also created a Board of Customs Commissioners to ensure collection of the duties.

Named for Charles Townshend, the minister who proposed them, the Townshend Acts produced the same outrage as the Stamp Act. The duties led to boycotts, riots, and the infamous Boston Massacre of March 1770. The crowd included the self-emancipated, middle-aged African American sailor and rope maker, Crispus Attucks, the first of the five colonists killed. His presence demonstrates the contradictory complaints and hopes that motivated colonists to protest. As a formerly enslaved person, he was drawn to the protest by the discourse about freedom, hoping that it would apply to all enslaved people. Had Attucks lived, he would have been disappointed by the colonial resistance movement's support of slavery.

Smuggling continued. Realizing that the duties could not be collected in the face of such opposition, Parliament repealed all but the tax on tea. The king's ministers assumed, mistakenly but not unreasonably, that opposition to import duties arose because these taxes raised the price of goods. They solved that problem by allowing the British East India Company to ship tea directly to the colonies without first sending it to London. This measure so reduced costs that even with the import duty the price of tea fell dramatically, lower than even that of smuggled tea. It thus threatened the profits of smugglers like John Hancock of Boston. Patriotic principle and economic self-interest combined in a dramatic act of defiance. On the night of December 16, 1773, colonists boarded a tea ship and threw its cargo into Boston Harbor. Parliament could not ignore such a blatant challenge to royal authority and responded with a series of coercive measures dubbed "the Intolerable Acts," which took away Massachusetts's self-government and closed the port of Boston.

FIGURE 3.9 The Boston Massacre (1770) as depicted in a colored engraving by Paul Revere. Crispus Attucks bottom left. The Metropolitan Museum of Art.

FIGURE 3.10 Crispus Attucks.

London hoped that this highly focused use of coercion in response to extreme provocation would put a stop to defiance of the law. This hope quickly proved forlorn as the other colonies rallied around Massachusetts. In April 1775, colonial militias engaged British troops at Lexington and Concord, thus commencing an open rebellion against the Crown. Just over a year later on July 4, 1776, the Continental Congress declared independence from Great Britain.

If the causes of the war have been mythologized, its conduct has too. In the popular imagination, colonial militias using guerrilla tactics defeated British regulars. Nothing could be further from the truth. The Continental Congress only began to achieve success when it created a professional army. Even then, the colonists might not have won had the French not entered the war on their side in 1778. French support threatened British interests in Europe and the Caribbean, forcing Britain to divert resources to those fronts. The North American colonies soon became a secondary theater in a major war.

The American revolutionaries never faced the full might and resources of the British Empire for the simple reason that London could not afford to deploy them against them. In 1783, the government in London concluded that the cost of victory was too high. The British reasoned that the exchange of American resources for metropolitan manufactured goods would continue and the Crown would be spared the cost of governing and defending the colonies. Some observers also believed that the new republic would soon fail and return to the imperial fold. In 1783, the Treaty of Versailles ended hostilities between France, Spain, and the American revolutionaries on the one hand and Britain on the other. The 13 colonies got their independence. Britain returned Florida to Spain and ceded Senegal and Tobago, along with some territory in India, to France.

LOYALISM: CANADA AND SIERRA LEONE

Britain retained control of Canada, which had remained loyal or at least quiet during the American Revolution. The American colonists attacked Quebec during the war of independence, hoping revolutionary zeal would spread North, but the city withstood the siege and no uprising among Canadian colonists occurred. Perhaps mollified by the Quebec Act (1774), which granted them religious freedom, French Canadian Catholics had no stomach for rebellion. During and after the revolution, Canada became a refuge for American loyalists who settled in New Brunswick and Nova Scotia. White loyalists brought a large number of enslaved persons with them. But free Black loyalists also became refugees in Canada.

Britain's enemies in the 13 colonies were not the only combatants fighting for freedom. Early in the conflict in North America, the royal governor of Virginia promised emancipation to enslaved persons who ran away from their masters and took up arms for the king. Within two weeks, 300 had done so, and the Royal Ethiopian Regiment was born. A second regiment of former slaves, the Black Pioneers, was created in 1776. Three years later, fighting was not even part of the deal; the British, desperate to undermine the colonists' cause by any means, offered freedom to any enslaved person who managed to escape to British territory. The approximately 50,000 men, women, and children who accomplished this during the American War became known as Black loyalists.

Black men, of course, fought on both sides of the war. As historian David Olusoga poignantly describes, a quarter of the victorious American force at Yorktown, numbering 1,500 soldiers, were Black; among the besieged British were almost as many Black loyalists, over 1,000 soldiers, laborers, and camp followers.[14] As conditions within the British base deteriorated, many of them were abandoned, left to fend for themselves, often to be captured and returned to their masters. Those Black loyalists who survived the war with the British, victorious in their efforts to escape slavery, were nonetheless on the losing side of hostilities. They faced a bleak future in the independent United States. Eventually, some retained their freedom and were evacuated to British territory in Nova Scotia, others to Britain itself.

These were perhaps the lucky ones, but their situation remained dire. In Britain, while most white loyalists who had fled the former colonies received pensions and compensation, most Black loyalists did not. Hundreds of the latter, reports Peter Fryer, "many of them ex-servicemen, exchanged the life of a slave for that of a starving beggar on the London streets." By 1786 a resettlement plan— "to solve the problem of the black poor by dumping them overseas" in Sierra Leone on the west coast of Africa—was in the works. Recruitment proved difficult for what was an ill-planned, opportunistic operation, and the organizers, who included some prominent white abolitionists, resorted to bribery and pressure. Of the would-be settlers who eventually boarded the ships, many died in appalling conditions before even leaving port. 374 arrived in Sierra Leone in May 1787 to establish the Province of Freedom. Four years later, when the whole enterprise ended, physically as well as metaphorically in ashes, only sixty survived.

In the early planning days of this disastrous project, some had looked to Nova Scotia, rather than Sierra Leone, as a settlement site. The 3000 Black loyalists evacuated to Nova Scotia in the wake of the American War had, after all, been promised land. But in Canada too, promises remained unfulfilled. In 1790, Thomas Peters, a former slave from North Carolina and veteran of the Black Pioneers, traveled to London to complain. There the directors of the Sierra Leone Company, many of whom had organized the last venture, suggested that Peters and other Black loyalists unhappy with their lot in Nova Scotia relocate to Sierra Leone. In January 1792 over a thousand did and established a new settlement, powerfully named Freetown, on the original site. Freetown is now the capital of the Republic of Sierra Leone. Yet in 1808, in a stunning demonstration of the variety of relationships operating within the British Empire, the British government took direct control and made it a Crown colony. Extraordinary journeys, in both life experiences and miles, thus converged on the coast of Africa to forge a colony of former slaves and the descendants of slaves who had fled North America.

NEW-YORK, 21 *April* 1783.

THIS is to certify to whomsoever it may concern, that the Bearer hereof *Cato Ramsay* a Negro, resorted to the British Lines, in consequence of the Proclamations of Sir William Howe, and Sir Henry Clinton, late Commanders in Chief in America; and that the said Negro has hereby his Excellency Sir Guy Carleton's Permission to go to Nova-Scotia, or wherever else *he* may think proper. ⸺

By Order of Brigadier General Birch,

FIGURE 3.11 (a) African Nova Scotian, by Captain William Booth, 1788. (b) *Book of Negroes*, by Samuel Birch.

FRENCH REVOLUTIONARY AND NAPOLEONIC WARS

None of the wars Britain fought thus far in the eighteenth century posed an existential threat. The upheaval that began in France in 1789 was of an entirely different character. Ideologically, French republicanism threatened the very foundations of Britain's constitutional monarchy; militarily, French forces made plans to invade the British Isles. For over two decades, from 1793 to 1815, Britain engaged in a series of wars against revolutionary and Napoleonic France. These conflicts resulted in a major realignment of the European state system, marked the end of the age of limited conflict, and concluded the second hundred years' war.

The British government did not look on the first phase of the French Revolution with particular alarm. Nor did France's occupation of Nice, Frankfurt, Basel, and part of Savoy or its invasion of the Austrian Netherlands in 1792 lead immediately to war. It was the execution of Louis XVI on January 21, 1793, followed by a French declaration of war against Britain on February 1, that led it to join the First Coalition of Austria, Prussia, Spain, and the United Provinces.

Revolutionary France proved an impressive opponent. Following initial setbacks, the French government instituted the first modern draft system, the Levée en Masse, to increase the size of its army. The removal of many aristocratic officers opened military careers to talent while patriotic soldiers outperformed their adversaries. By the time the First Coalition collapsed in 1797, France had conquered the Austrian Netherlands, the Rhineland, and much of northern Italy. The British fought in the Low Countries, occupied and then abandoned Toulon, and bankrolled other coalition members, all to no avail. While Britain remained at war with France, its allies sued for peace.

The peace of 1797 did not last even a year because none of France's enemies could allow it to remain in such a strong position. In 1798, Russia joined Britain and Austria to form the Second Coalition. It fared no better than the first. The conflict saw the rise to prominence of a new French commander, Napoleon Bonaparte. Although his first venture, an invasion of Egypt in 1798, ended disastrously, Napoleon recaptured Northern Italy, which had been liberated by the Russians, after a brilliant victory over the Austrians at Marengo. A joint Anglo-Russian attempt to take back the Netherlands failed, and the two allies fell out when Britain asserted its right to search ships in the Baltic Sea. Meanwhile the domestic cost in taxation, social and economic dislocation, and political turmoil of the war—weighed heavily on the British people.

Britain's involvement in the War of the Second Coalition ended with the Peace of Amiens in 1802, but the agreement was generally regarded as just another truce. Within a year, fighting resumed. Napoleon delivered a series of devastating blows to Britain's continental allies between 1805 and 1807, defeating them at Ulm, Austerlitz, Auerstädt, Jena, Eylau, and Friedland. These victories made Napoleon master of Europe, at least on land. The emperor planned to invade Britain, but Admiral Horatio Nelson's decisive naval victory at Trafalgar on October 21, 1805, thwarted that effort. Without naval supremacy in the English Channel, an invasion stood no chance of success. The weakening of its navy also made it difficult for France to defend its colonies in the Caribbean, all of which fell to Britain by 1810.

The tide had turned. The failure of Napoleon's Continental System (a trade embargo against England), a guerrilla war in Spain, and the disastrous invasion of Russia depleted France's resources and weakened its overextended empire. Napoleon suffered a crushing defeat at Leipzig in October 1813, and the allies invaded France the following spring. They exiled Napoleon to the island of Elba, from which he returned in March 1815 before facing final defeat at Waterloo at the hands of British and Prussian forces.

Napoleon's superior generalship could not compensate for the overwhelming numbers and far greater resources of the coalition ranged against him, and Britain played a vital part in his defeat. Insularity and naval supremacy assured its safety from direct attack. Meanwhile, its financial resources enabled it to fund allies while raiding French commerce and seizing French colonies. Half a century of relative peace would follow the Congress of Vienna (1815). France and Britain would never go to war again.

FROM SAINT-DOMINGUE TO HAITI

When the French Revolution began, France, like Britain, was an imperial power. France's most valuable colony was the island of Saint-Domingue, which supplied 40 percent of the sugar sold in Europe. Production of all that sugar, as well as indigo and coffee, was done on vast plantations.

Thus, in 1789, the year the new French National Assembly declared the universal rights of man, Saint-Domingue was the world's largest single slave market and its plantations employed approximately half a million enslaved Black people. Free people of color and enslaved people on the island took note of what was happening in France. The former demanded the full rights of their free white neighbors; the latter planned and orchestrated a massive uprising that began in 1791. White plantation owners responded to these simultaneous threats by asking the British state to invade Saint-Domingue and restore "order." French planters offered to become loyal subjects of the British crown and make Saint-Domingue British if Britain would suppress the revolt. Unwilling to risk war with France, Britain refused.

Two years later, the uprising raged on under the leadership of Toussaint L'Ouverture, a former slave and brilliant general, and Britain and France were now at war. Worried that a successful slave revolution in Saint-Domingue would inspire uprisings in its own Caribbean colonies, Britain decided to invade the island. It did so in September 1793, with the support of many plantation owners. Toussaint L'Ouverture meanwhile allied with Spain. The French revolutionary government thus faced both a proslavery coalition of white plantation owners and the British military, and an antislavery coalition of Black rebels and the Spanish military.

Seeing its valuable colony slipping away, France sought an agreement with Toussaint L'Ouverture. In February 1794, the French Assembly voted to abolish slavery and finally to proclaim that the universal rights of man applied regardless of race. Toussaint L'Ouverture ended his alliance with Spain, took control of the French forces, now unified against slavery, and drove out the British invaders whom the planters had invited. This process was completed by 1798. Saint-Domingue thus remained a French colony, Toussaint L'Ouverture became its effective ruler, and Britain, fighting in defense of slavery, lost to yet another revolutionary movement. Six years later in 1804, Saint-Domingue became the independent republic of Haiti, the world's first Black-led republic and the first independent Caribbean state. National independence was the ultimate result of Saint-Domingue's revolution against slavery.

FIGURE 3.12 Toussaint L'Ouverture.

IRISH REBELLION

The revolutionary spirit of the age resonated in Ireland as well. Many Irish perceived the North American colonists as kindred spirits, fellow sufferers under British oppression. The controversial Declaratory Act, imposed on the 13 colonies in 1766, replicated that which had long limited Irish legislative autonomy. Thus, in 1782, with the North American rebels' victory in sight, the Irish Parliament took advantage of the situation to negotiate a victory of its own. Ireland's Declaratory Act of 1720 was repealed, as was Poyning's Law of 1495. The Irish Parliament now had the sole right to legislate its own domestic affairs. These efforts were led by an opposition party within the Irish Parliament, at work since the 1760s, which had taken the name "Patriots." The Patriots represented an alternative ruling elite, operating within established political channels. The example of the French Revolution, however, brought other movements, and people formerly excluded from the Irish political process, to the fore.

The 1790s saw the emergence of the United Irishmen under the leadership of Theobald Wolfe Tone, a young Protestant lawyer who promoted an Irish nationalism that would unite Catholics, Anglicans, and Protestant Dissenters.[15] Tone's campaign to promote religious toleration, republicanism, and an inclusive Ireland that would encourage reconciliation between Protestants and Catholics was extremely radical. Needless to say, it threatened the Protestant Ascendancy and the economic, political, and social power of the wealthy Protestant landowners. The United Irishmen succeeded in joining forces with the Defenders, a Catholic agrarian society that formed earlier in the eighteenth century to counter economic grievances. However, religious difference ultimately thwarted Tone's effort. Meanwhile, in 1795 Ulster loyalists created the Orange Order to defend the Ascendancy the British monarchy, and the Anglican Church. It had 30,000 members by 1797.[16]

This upheaval presented several challenges to Britain's imperial regime. Irish nationalism and separatism undermined British authority, while the political groups in Ireland confronted each other with opposing agendas and goals that portended civil war. Irish revolutionaries and reactionaries endangered Britain's imperial aspirations and weakened its war effort against France. Ireland supplied recruits for the armed forces. One in five Irish men served in the British Army between 1793 and 1815.

The 1798 rebellion broke out in Ireland in scattered uprisings concentrated in Down and Antrim in the northeast and Kildare and Wexford in the southeast. Revolutionary France had promised its support and sent troops. Wolfe Tone had been living in France since 1796, enlisting such assistance and serving in the French army himself. But weather prevented the successful landing of French troops at Bantry Bay. They finally arrived two months after the defeat of the United Irishmen by the British, who used spies and informants to infiltrate rebel ranks. The British crushed the United Irishmen with draconian measures. Rebels were slaughtered in retribution, their heads displayed on spikes.

WILLIAM THEOBALD WOLFE TONE.

FIGURE 3.13 William Theobald Wolfe Tone.

Between May and September 1798, the Irish Revolution claimed 30,000 lives and reconfigured Irish politics and history. London blamed the rebellion, at least in part, on the Protestant Irish parliament. It saw unifying the two kingdoms as "the ultimate security response by the British state to the security crisis of the 1790s."[17] The Irish Act of Union did not grant full civil rights to the Irish Catholic majority. Indeed, Catholic emancipation, which repealed the penal laws, the Disenfranchising Act, and other statutes that limited Irish Catholic freedoms, was not achieved until 1829. Ireland remained bound by political, economic, and cultural arrangements born of the contentious and often violent colonial past and affirmed in the Act of Union.

IMAGE CREDITS

CHAPTER 4

Beliefs, Ideas, Attitudes

Scholars have long depicted the eighteenth century as the Augustan Age—an ascendant period, an age of oligarchy, in which Britain took on the mantle of Rome as its empire spread. The British cast their imperial enterprise as a civilizing process, providing virtues abroad while defending against the threat of degeneration posed by interlopers from other cultures, often colonized subjects. These depictions of a homogenous Britain, one in which a shared consensus among elites and between elite and popular culture defined societal values, attitudes, and beliefs has been completely overturned by recent histories of the period. And it's easy to see why: as a dynamic, fast moving historical period during which Britain became a world power, gaining sovereignty over vast areas as geographically and culturally diverse as Quebec, Bengal, and Senegal, culture at home was not only shaped by these forces, but they shaped each other, producing an imperial culture. This period of tremendous change fractured ideas, attitudes, and beliefs in different trends and directions that reflected the multiplicity of forces, both creative and destructive, at work in British society. This chapter will explore the places in which these collisions and conversations occurred, and some of the cultural developments that ensued. We will survey the ideas, attitudes, and beliefs that developed and circulated in the eighteenth century. These will include discussions of the Enlightenment, science, art, the culture of sensibility, the rise of the novel, musical traditions, and religious belief. The chapter will end with two case studies that will demonstrate how these ideas were deployed and activated.

Places and the Public Sphere

Nowhere was the contrast between rich and poor in the eighteenth century, and the population growth that exacerbated those differences, more apparent than in the building trends of the period. The elite country house embodied the hierarchical nature of the eighteenth century and its divisions along lines of status. In contrast to the cramped quarters occupied by workers in London and the emerging manufacturing and commercial centers of the Midlands and the North, or the cottages occupied by husbandmen and women and other agricultural workers, the country house was built as a symbol of wealth and power, the site of much economic, political, social, and cultural activity in the eighteenth century. The houses were nodes of influence and privilege for large landowners who patronized local shopkeepers, appeared on grand juries, and served as justices of the peace. Their owners entertained those of similar rank, developing networks and contacts that strengthened ties among the elite. These estates were the settings of agriculture and sport, family gatherings and county balls.

To accomplish these tasks successfully, these homes projected power and authority. Many were built in the grand Palladian style popular in Britain, its North American colonies, and across Europe in the eighteenth century. Inspired by the Venetian architect Andrea Palladio who lived in the sixteenth century, the design is characterized by symmetry and perspective, carrying with it aspects of ancient Greek and Roman architecture. Queen's House in Greenwich, designed by Indigo Jones and begun in 1616, was the first English Palladian house. The style was revived after the English Civil War and developed throughout the eighteenth century. Palladian estates were built with a large central portico and prominent vertical lines on the exterior. Inside, a large entry hall and spacious living rooms showed off the ornate furnishings and knickknacks collected by

FIGURE 4.1 Clandon House, Surrey.

their owners often from around the world, tokens of empire. The bedrooms and dressing rooms were upstairs, while the kitchen and the servants' quarters were in the basement. During the later eighteenth century the "classical revival" period featured large windows that brought in an abundance of natural light supplemented by large mirrors. Examples of these "power houses" include Clandon Park in Surrey, Nostell Priory in Yorkshire, Blenheim Palace in Oxfordshire, and Holkham Hall in Norfolk.

To further enhance their prominence, the houses were often built on rising ground with plenty of space for extensive gardens and parkland. The landscape garden, also called the landscape park

FIGURE 4.2 Nostell Priory, Yorkshire.

FIGURE 4.3 Blenheim Palace.

FIGURE 4.4 Blenheim Palace Gardens.

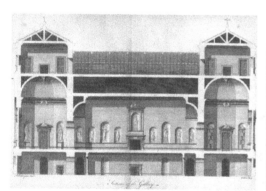

FIGURE 4.5 Holkham Hall, Norfolk, gallery. *The Seat of Thomas William Coke*, Esq, MP, by Matthew Brettingham, 1761.

FIGURE 4.6 Copper engraving, Holkham Hall, Norfolk, south elevation. *The Seat of Thomas William Coke*, Esq, MP, laid paper, by M. Booth, August 12, 1781, Norwich. F82.21.

or English garden, rejected the formal, symmetrical gardens that had been popular across Europe in the seventeenth century. Instead it presented an idealized view of nature. Rambling gardens often came right up to the doors of the house while the parks that surrounded them might include a lake, rolling lawns, groves of trees, and sometimes a re-creation of a classical temple. The effect was intentional: the house and its owners dominated, even reordered, nature.

In towns too, the wealthy embarked on dramatic building campaigns. Aristocrats transformed their urban estates into fashionable, profitable districts, producing the Georgian squares that characterize parts of London and Edinburgh to this day. The Dukes of Bedford developed London's Bloomsbury, the neighborhood in which the British Museum opened in 1759, the first publicly owned, free-entrance museum in Europe. In another example of the extractive nature of empire, by the end of the long eighteenth century the British Museum would house such international treasures as Egypt's Rosetta Stone (1802) and Greece's Parthenon marbles (1816). These powerful symbols of Britain's (and its traveling gentlemen's) expansive, acquisitive reach throughout the world are sources of great controversy today, as governments in their places of origin argue for their return. Curating the British Museum and decorating a country house had a lot in common. Less than a mile from Bloomsbury, in Grosvenor Square, one of the first posh eighteenth-century neighborhoods in London's West End, the Earl of Derby commissioned the most important architect of the day, Robert Adam, to renovate his townhouse in 1773–74. In it, Adam brought the grandeur of a country house to a confined, urban space, a physical expression of how elites divided the year between their landed estates and the London "season" of court events and Parliamentary business.

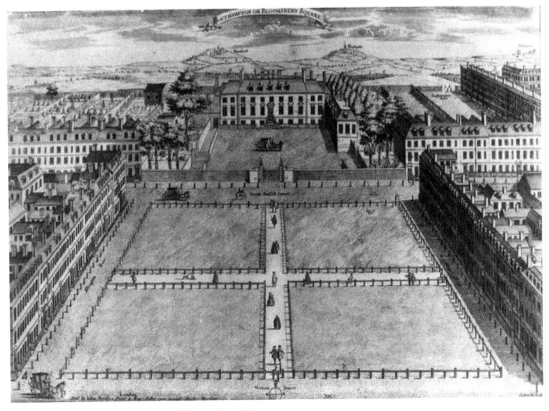

FIGURE 4.7 Southampton or Bloomsbury Square.

FIGURE 4.8 British Museum (1849).

FIGURE 4.9 Royal Crescent, Bath, England.

There were other seasons too, and whole towns built (or rebuilt) to accommodate them. Bath, in southwestern England, set the standard for resort and spa towns. The Roman baths, for which it was named, attracted those seeking cures for whatever ailed them. But it was for the social life—dances, card games, and the marriage market—that the old elite and the nouveau riche flocked to Bath. There, the master of ceremonies, Beau Nash, who was a leader of the fashion world, presided in the assembly rooms and visitors lodged in elegant residences in Queen Square and the Royal Crescent, all quintessential specimens of Georgian architecture designed by John Wood (senior and junior) and built out of locally mined "Bath stone."

At the other end of the social scale, another sort of building project was underway in the eighteenth century. As we saw in chapter 1, those supported by parish poor relief received aid in two ways: in their homes (known as outdoor relief) and in workhouses (known as indoor relief). Legislation passed in 1722 enabled parishes to build workhouses. Two thousand workhouses had

FIGURE 4.10 Roman baths, Bath, England.

been built by the 1770s and accommodated about one hundred thousand people. The residents were separated by sex. Those who could work spent their days spinning or sewing.[1] Those living in the workhouses were expected to follow a strict routine predicated on rules of moral rectitude. It was a very different world from country houses' verdant parks and Bath's gaming tables.

Meanwhile, in London's East End, home to the capital's docks, industry, and the laborers employed in them, buildings were falling down. With migrants pouring in from the countryside in unprecedented numbers in search of work and the excitement of metropolitan life, affordable housing was a rare commodity. Yet there were restrictions in some of the poorer areas to new construction. It was common therefore to build up, adding floors to the top of already old and rickety structures. It was only a matter of time before the inevitable happened. A diarist reports of being in a tavern one day when a messenger ran in. All the patrons jumped up and ran out before the messenger could deliver his news. So common, apparently, was it for buildings in the neighborhood to collapse, that everyone assumed a man in a hurry was there to warn one was starting to fall.

FIGURE 4.11 *The Cottage Door*, by Thomas Gainsborough, c. 1778.

Londoners spent a lot of time in taverns and coffee houses. The tavern was a traditional sort of establishment, but the coffee house was a relatively new and wildly popular venue. Venice welcomed the first coffee house in western Europe in 1647, and Oxford had the first English one in 1652, London later in the same year. By the turn of the century, they were common throughout London. In 1739, there were 551 in the capital, outnumbering taverns (447) and inns (207).[2] The rise of the coffee house was associated with the global movement of people, objects, and ideas and the development of a public sphere. This was especially true in London, the hub of its empire, but taverns, inns, and coffee houses were sites of the public sphere throughout the British Isles.

The public sphere, as defined by Jürgen Habermas and scholars who have followed, is an area in social life where individuals can come freely together to discuss the news, the world around them, and the problems they face. These discussions often turned to politics. This was very much an eighteenth-century development. The late seventeenth and early eighteenth century, as we have seen, saw rising literacy rates; with that came the emergence of print culture, and a fascination with stories and a hunger for news, that resulted in an explosion in the number and kinds of publications. In 1695 the lapse in the Licensing Act, by which the government had censored what got printed, allowed for the development of an independent press. The large reading audience consumed print at the growing number of circulating libraries, in chapbooks (small pamphlets), and through the thriving market in secondhand books. Coffee houses and taverns contributed to this trend, as they stocked newspapers and periodicals, each copy of which was read by (and perhaps aloud to) many customers. The public sphere was thus an important site, separate from state structures, for connecting individuals from different walks of life and for the transmission and transformation of beliefs, ideas, and attitudes.

Another site of the public sphere was the association, formal, structured organizations of people formed around a common purpose or interest. The association was also an eighteenth-century invention, and it brought people, both men and women, together for all sorts of reasons. Associations had meetings, raised awareness about issues, and produced publications. They also raised money for causes in which they believed and put on exhibitions and competitions. There were Royal Academies of Science and Music as well as Arts. Other associations were less formal, like the elite salons in London formed to share ideas, while some sprang up in response to political developments, like the Society of the Supporters of the Bill of Rights (discussed in chapter 5) and the many groups dedicated to abolition. Religious associations sponsored missionary work and education. Often these associations took the form of corresponding societies that created local, regional, national, and imperial webs of connection, articulating and transmitting ideas between city and countryside in Britain and throughout the globe. Both men and women joined and were active participants. You'll see mention of associations throughout this chapter.

Contemporaries recognized the significance of these developments. Among the most influential publications of the early eighteenth century were a pair of periodicals, *The Tatler* (1709–1711)

FIGURE 4.12 The coffeehouse politicians, 1772. Interior view of a London coffeehouse. Clients are absorbed in newspapers, in particular the *London Gazette*, and are engaged in conversation. A young woman stands in the bar at the back of the room.

and *The Spectator* (1711–1712). *The Tatler*, founded by Richard Steele, and *The Spectator*, the joint product of Steele and Joseph Addison, were what we might today call literary or cultural magazines. They contained book and theater reviews, fashion news, and essays about manners and social mores; they had a huge immediate audience, wrote specifically about and to women as well as men, and their individual issues (three per week for *The Tatler* and six for *The Spectator*) were bound and sold in volumes throughout the century. As their titles suggest, they introduced fictional persona—Mr. Spectator, for example—who witnessed and commented on the culture around them. The characters' conversations occurred in clubs and coffee houses, thus making the periodicals elements of the public sphere that were explicitly about the public sphere.

Enlightenment

One of the most pronounced intellectual and cultural trends of the long eighteenth century is the Enlightenment. Some define the Enlightenment as an attitude of mind rather than a set of shared beliefs. At its core it can be summed up as a criticism, a questioning. While some eighteenth-century commentators expressed a distrust of traditional institutions, customs, and morals, others proffered a belief in nature, individual human reason, and the perfectibility of humankind. Contemporaries would have used the word man to refer only to men although women were also participants in this movement. If there were an eighteenth-century vehicle on which to affix a bumper sticker or a slogan for this movement, it would be "Dare to Know!" which refers to the freedom to use one's own intelligence.

The movement had global origins very much shaped by European collision with the Far East and the New World and its imperial projects and colonial exploits. The reach, hold, and influence of the Enlightenment varied depending on the location. Although the French philosophers like Jean-Jacques Rousseau, Rene Descartes, Denis Diderot, and Voltaire were some of its best-known protagonists, Emmanuel Kant in today's Germany and Cesare Beccaria from Italy also participated in the exchange of ideas. In Britain, John Locke and Mary Wollstonecraft, discussed in chapter 1, were part of a long list of writers, scientists, and philosophers who contributed to the intellectual movement. The Enlightenment sparked discussions of ideal forms of governance and the promotion of freedom and liberty in contrast to absolutism and despotism. New theories circulated relating to the education of children, religious toleration, scientific knowledge, and legal reform. Many of the thinkers sought universal answers to age-old questions hoping to find new ways to approach old problems with precision and accuracy. Their writings were read, exchanged, and found their way all over the world. The movement had no set start and end dates; instead, it was a process percolating through the long eighteenth century, spanning the lifetimes of Locke, born in 1632 and Wollstonecraft, who died in 1797.

In the second half of the eighteenth century a group of Scottish thinkers, including Adam Smith, Adam Ferguson, William Roberson, Henry Home, and John Millar, developed the four stages theory, sometimes referred to as Stadial Theory. The theory narrated universal history of human progress through four stages: hunting, in which property was confined to what one person could carry, which was also called savagery; pastoralism, in which animal husbandry led to the acquisition of animal property and was described as barbarism; agricultural economies characterized by settled and landed property were deemed civilization, which was followed by contemporary European commercial society. Conveniently, contemporary Europe defined the apogee of civilization. Property and the provision of food defined each stage. This linear and universal assessment of each society has been extremely problematic. It assumes that there is only one trajectory for each society and that societies can and should be assessed as to their level of development. Europe is the adult in this model; the rest of the world falling into the category of children and adolescents in need of guidance.

Scientific experimentation and learning were important parts of the Enlightenment. In Britain in the seventeenth century several prominent thinkers began writing about the ways in which those who experiment could arrive at general laws governing the natural world, what we know today as the empirical scientific method. They proposed that careful, close, and repeated observation would reveal powerful laws that would allow human beings (they would say men) to alter and control the natural environment. The core activities of those who endeavored to participate in this project included data collection, collaboration, organization of knowledge, and the production of practical outcomes. With the Restoration of Charles II the movement took off. The Royal Society, established in November 1660 with Charles as its patron, dedicated itself to the conduct and communication of science. The state supported the society's research and innovation with the hope of big profits from an expansion of trade and technology and the ability to outflank its imperial competitors. The society's motto, *Nullius in verba* (Take nobody's word for it), encapsulates many of the Enlightenment views.

The society set lasting standards for scientific practice through its journal *Philosophical Transactions*, which established the concept of scientific priority and peer review. First appearing in 1665, the journal is the oldest continuously published science journal in the world. In the long eighteenth century alone the society published Isaac Newton's *Principia Mathematica* and Benjamin Franklin's kite experiment demonstrating the electrical nature of lightning. In the field of medicine, it published the first report in English of inoculation against disease. The society also actively encouraged scientific exploration connected to colonization and imperial expansion. Imperial expansion relied on scientific inquiry and its outcome, the collection and production of knowledge, including astronomy at the Royal Observatory at Greenwich to find a way to measure longitude and the establishment of the Royal Botanical Garden at Kew, which collected samples of the flora found in newly colonized places. Not surprisingly, the society was involved in James Cook's journey to Tahiti, which reached Australia and New Zealand. The voyage was proposed as a way to track the transit of Venus (1768–1771). Britain's scientific reorganization, its support of imperial growth and knowledge collection and production, assured the rapid industrialization that took place over the century between 1750 and 1850 and its ultimate domination of world trade.

The intellectual and cultural knowledge collection and production so typical of Enlightenment thinking resulted in the publication and circulation of Samuel Johnson's *Dictionary* (1755) and Adam Smith's *Wealth of Nations* (1776). In France, the *Encyclopedie* (1751–1780), edited by Denis Diderot and, until 1759, coedited by Jean le Rond d'Alembert, attempted to summarize all the knowledge on a given topic and to frame all knowledge in terms of natural phenomena as opposed to the supernatural or superstition. Many in Britain purchased the *Encyclopedie*, and English translations appeared almost immediately; but similar projects were underway in Britain too, among the most well-known and successful was the *Encyclopedia Britannica*, which was first published in Edinburgh between 1768 and 1771. The zeal for reform in Enlightenment circles was born of the belief that institutions that were broken could be improved and that corruption could be rooted out whether it was the monarchy, taxation, or the church. Many believed that these reforms would make a more humane and civilized society.

The movement for legal reform was set within a context that addressed ideas about governance, specifically the role of government. Francis Hutcheson, a Scottish moral philosopher, defined the object of government as "the greatest happiness of the greatest number." Many absolutist rulers, like Catherine the Great of Russia, Frederick II of Prussia, and Joseph II of Austria, considered themselves enlightened rulers and were determined to rationalize their governments. One of the institutions they sought to regularize was the legal system. In the absence of a police force, rulers had relied on dramatic, extreme, and public punishments for those caught in the act as a means of dissuading those who watched. Legal reformers criticized the harsh statutes that made up England's "Bloody Code" and supported the elimination of capital punishment. They advocated for predictable and proportional sanctions in their stead.

Lest we get carried away with this progressive rendition of the Enlightenment, let's remember that at this time lines of race hardened, the slave trade was at its busiest (more bodies were moved across the Atlantic Ocean by Europeans during the eighteenth century than at any other time during the trade), and each nation-state in Europe was implicated in this practice. And the knowledge that was gathered and produced fed imperial and colonial aspirations and endeavors. It was indeed often colonialism and trade that fueled the need to know. And everything was couched in terms of men, so the hierarchies of gender and race and rank that were used to order society were often replicated by the Enlightenment. The values of the Enlightenment are not separate from these historical phenomena; indeed they produced them. The intellectual activity of this time often reflected a European self-confidence, critical of other cultures and featuring an unfounded certainty that theirs was a unique and better way of life, the standard by which others would be judged.

Arts

The values of the Enlightenment are reflected in the cabinet of curiosities often housed in the country estates. The objects found within these cabinets were brought to Britain from around the world, yet another way in which empire always came home to Britain, remaking its tastes and sensibilities. On the large walls of these estates hung very large paintings. Britain's royals had long called on their continental connections, commissioning portraits from Dutch, German, and Flemish painters. Britain's indigenous art scene at the beginning of the eighteenth century has been called a backwater. Until the foundation of the London Royal Academy of Art in 1768, London's artists sought their training at the St. Martin's Lane Academy. Within the span of the eighteenth century, however, Britain's young elite began to travel to continental Europe, a tradition known as the Grand Tour, as part of their informal education. As with the architecture of the country homes with which we began this chapter, exposure to European art, as well as the careers of several admired and successful artists, including William Hogarth, Joshua Reynolds, Thomas Gainsborough, and J.M.W. Turner, transformed Britain by the end of the century into a more daring artistic scene, one that developed several British specialties that constituted a national style.

British high art in the eighteenth century developed at least three distinct painting styles: the conversation piece, portraits, and landscapes. The conversation piece generally depicted an informal group

FIGURE 4.13 The Graham Children, by William Hogarth, 1742.

of people captured in the midst of an ordinary scene of daily life. Families who commissioned these genre scenes sought pictures of themselves during a meal, a hunt, or a musical party. William Hogarth pioneered the conversation piece in the 1720s at the same time as the novel, a new genre discussed later, hit the presses. Portraits, while not new, were everywhere in the eighteenth century. In the words of both historian John Brewer and his subjects, Britons of means "were infatuated with 'face painting'" and commissioned portraits of themselves, friends, and relatives to mark life's diverse special events.[3]

One such event was departing on, or returning from, the Grand Tour. Those British young elites who traveled to the continent often brought home landscape paintings that inspired imitation by British painters. In 1757, Edmund Burke, an Irish lawyer, statesman, politician, and philosopher, published *A Philosophical Enquiry into the Origin of Our Ideas of the Sublime and Beautiful*. The tract roused those with time and money to travel, to tour the British countryside, Wales, the Lake District, and Scotland searching out picturesque views. The beautiful meant soft and aesthetically pleasing, while the picturesque—"in the manner of a picture"—was defined as irregular, ragged, and asymmetrical. The sublime was essentially the evocation of awe and terror. John Constable and Turner defined the distinctly British take on the landscape in two different directions: the former a realist, the latter a romantic.

Far from these effete works of art on view in the grand halls of urban and country homes of the wealthy, the satirical print, "a quintessentially British art form," circulated widely in British popular and elite culture. The golden age of the satirical print was 1780–1830 but followed from an earlier tradition of woodblocks, ballad illustrations, and broadsides, one-page posters used to advertise events or news featuring both illustrations and words. A collection of the best satirical prints would include the work of the talented and prolific William Hogarth, and later in the century, James Gillray, Thomas Rowlandson, and George Cruikshank. The popularity and currency of caricature prints illustrates the development of the public sphere and increased with the expansion of the press, Parliamentary reporting, and a growing political awareness. They spread both news and opinion among their consumers. The production and diffusion of print culture shaped perceptions of important issues in eighteenth-century society, including war, empire, governance, politics, gender, and law; the prints served as sites of conversation and debate where authors and readers could rehearse different points of view and interpretations of events while enlisting public opinion. Forerunners of today's political cartoons, these images made relentless fun of their subjects. The range of published accounts articulated anxieties and opinions; far from static, the very process of distribution made, reflected, and remade popular opinion. The number in circulation was quite modest—especially those published as broadsides—with five hundred to fifteen hundred a typical run. Those that appeared in newspapers and magazines circulated more widely; newspaper circulation grew tremendously over the second half of the eighteenth century, with annual sales increasing from 7 million in 1750 to 16 million in 1801.

Recent work argues for a much broader distribution of prints both socially and geographically. In addition to the hundreds or thousands of copies in any edition, the images circulated in London, throughout Britain, on the continent, and in the British colonies through reissues, pirated cheap copies, woodcut versions, and in broadsides and ballads; they also appeared on coins, handkerchiefs, textiles, and ceramics. Read and consumed by both men and women across the socioeconomic scale, caricatures extended political consciousness, participation, and debate in the second half of the eighteenth century and especially in the 1790s. We get an idea of the diversity of the readership, the method of delivery, and its reception in *The Caricature Shop* (1801). The mixed audience includes men and women, old and young, a person of color, rich and poor, able-bodied and disabled. The image confirms the conclusion that the prints were a part of everyday life in Georgian Britain.

Another printed source that circulated widely captured society's fascination with crime and the profits garnered by its retelling. The crime pamphlet promised "true stories" about highway robbers, petty thieves, infanticides, and murderers. Most prominent among this genre, the *Old Bailey Sessions Papers* (OBSP) began in the 1670s and featured published accounts of the cases heard at the Old Bailey, London's central criminal court. A reporter transcribed the trials, and these were published at the end of the session. The OBSP was both entertainment and news. Although the most sensational cases received more extensive coverage, when the details of the case can be confirmed, they are generally pretty accurate. The Ordinary of Newgate was the chaplain responsible for providing spiritual guidance to the prisoners in Newgate, London's prison.

FIGURE 4.14 Newgate Prison.

The chaplains wrote extensively about the lives of the convicted as they awaited execution, revealing much about the realities of the Bloody Code. These pamphlets produced in the wake of the detection, prosecution, and punishment of crime, shaped and reflected popular conceptions of the law in the eighteenth century, as well as ideas about reputation and character.[4]

Other genres of printed material multiplied in number and circulation in the eighteenth century. Newspapers and periodical literature featured the social, political, and cultural commentary from well-known figures such as Daniel Defoe, Jonathan Swift, and Joseph Addison and Richard Steele, mentioned earlier. Growing trade and commerce contributed to the expanding middling sorts who had more money to buy printed materials and more leisure time to read. Even more popular than the nonfiction writing was a new genre we know today as the novel. In the hands of writers like Daniel Defoe, Henry Fielding, Samuel Richardson, and Laurence Sterne this new literary genre became a means of exploring and interpreting the social and psychological realm of human experience. These writers delved into the relationships between men and women across the divides of class, religion, and age, giving the novel its great appeal and establishing its enduring popularity. This new genre expanded with the rise of libraries and the interest in nonreligious reading material along with the increase in the number of female readers. By the end of the century, the number of published women novelists also increased.

Novels are the very best known expression of the culture of sensibility that emerged in contemporary literature and intellectual discussion. It construed sensibility, a special and admirable susceptibility to one's own feelings and the feelings of others, as a moral faculty that would preserve humanity from the forces of secularization, industrialization, and consumerism. The culture of sensibility urged both men and women to regard the emotional component of identity and the self as integral to every person. The culture of sensibility emerged out of an interest in the origin of feelings and the belief that regulated but sincere and expressed feelings were the road to virtue. The relationship between emotion and morality preoccupied the literature of sensibility that was at its most influential and widespread from the 1740s to the 1770s. In addition to novels, philosophical essays, newspapers, sermons, and crime pamphlets also provided forums in which to ponder the place of emotion and sympathy, compassion and morality. Domestic servants played a crucial role in the spread of the culture of sensibility beyond the aristocracy and those of middling status through their increased literacy combined with their exposure to reading as part of the daily life of the household. They bought and read novels, exchanged them with the young women of the household, observed their mistresses reading privately, were present at public readings of the latest books, and overheard and engaged in discussions of these stories. This gave them intimate knowledge of the privacy of reading, the innermost thoughts and feelings of the characters who peopled these novels, and the values espoused in sentimental literature.[5]

The era of sensibility defined and dictated relationships between men and women, different classes in British society, and those considered social and racial "others," including enslaved people,

Native Americans, the poor, and the mentally ill. Given the tremendous cultural, social, economic, and political changes throughout the eighteenth century—population growth, mobility, incessant war, industrialization, and the expansion of empire—the literature of sensibility modeled these relations by showing how to respond to life's experiences through the expression of feeling. Henry Mackenzie's tremendously popular *The Man of Feeling* (1771) narrated the search for virtue through emotional expression. Harley, the protagonist, literally embodied sensibility, enacting its values as he encountered a beggar, a lunatic, and a prostitute. He sought out the places where those on the margins of society gathered, playing cards with two vagrants, visiting an insane asylum, and expressing concern for the natives of India as he questioned the morality of empire. Through direct contact with the suffering of others, Harley performed compassion, the highest emotional state, and implicitly affirmed his own superior sensibility and virtue.

The dynamic between the viewers of suffering and those they viewed necessitated some acknowledgment of the interiority of the observed. In terms of the culture of sensibility a recognition of the existence and value of the sufferer's self and the capacity for sensibility among the lower orders evolved over the course of the eighteenth century. Although some writers insisted that sensibility was a characteristic unique to the higher orders, others described it as a shared, equalizing attribute that crossed the lines of class. This acceptance of a working-class subjectivity by middle-class observers was not an act of beneficence. The acknowledgement of the feelings and the suffering of the poor affirmed the superiority of middle-class sensibility attained though contact with these suffering others.[6]

Music was another art form within and beyond print culture that shaped attitudes and transmitted ideas. The formal and elite compositions produced by Henry Purcell, who worked as a musician in the court of Charles II, included religious work as well as songs celebrating birthdays and homecomings. Purcell wrote the music for the coronation of James II. His compositions for the theater included both a demi-opera and the full-length opera, *Dido and Aeneas*. Purcell brought baroque music to England. While one can hear the Italian and French influences in his compositions, he imprinted them with his own particularly England style.[7] Beside Purcell, Georg Friedrich Handel, who immigrated to London from Brandenburg in Germany in 1710, was another eighteenth-century musician. He too worked in the royal court composing operas and oratorios, large-scale musical works for orchestra and voices, typically a narrative on a religious theme, performed without the use of costumes, scenery, or action. His instrumental compositions included the *Messiah, Water Music*, and *Music for the Royal Fireworks* celebrating the peace established in the Treaty of Aix-la-Chapelle in 1749. He attracted a middle-class audience with his more religious and morally themed works inspired by biblical stories. Both these musicians and their music celebrated England and Britain as a nation.

The ballad, which has its origins in the late Middle Ages, is a song that tells a story in popular style; most were not written down and they relied on the oral tradition for transmission. In the eighteenth century, ballads, especially broadsheet ballads, were very popular. They were usually being sung as they were sold, hawked on the streets, and they sold well. They covered a range of topics including the most important news of the day as well as the retelling of more mundane moments in everyday life. Many have social and political implications.[8] John Gay's *The Beggar's Opera*, first performed in 1728 and known as a ballad opera because many of its airs were set to popular ballad tunes, capitalized on both these elements: ballads' ubiquity and their satiric potential. And while he was at it, Gay also poked fun of a popular foreign musical import—Italian opera.

Given the tremendous military force of Britain's navy, naval ballads are some of the most important sources we have about ordinary folks and their perceptions of empire. Many of these songs capture the patriotism of the age as well as the pride the British took in their expanding empire. One of the ballads, "True Blue an old Song," proclaimed the sailors' loyalty, while the song "Hearts of Oak" declared that "Jolly Tars are our men/We always are Ready." The lyrics of the song call our attention to the bedrock of British ideology—honor, freedom, and liberty—precisely those values the sailors believed they upheld on the waves and across the globe. The mission of the military was often twinned with the protection of liberty, law, and the constitution.

Another expression of patriotism was the song "God Save the King," which would later become the British royal and national anthem. Its pronouncement of loyalty raised its popularity in September 1745 in response to the Jacobite rebellion. But the song and its lyrics were not new in 1745. (Many authors have been suggested from the Elizabethan John Bull to Henry Purcell.) The words were published in *Gentleman's Magazine* in 1745. In the same year, "God Save the King" was performed in two London theatres. In the following year Handel used it in his *Occasional Oratorio*, which retold the challenges of the Jacobite rebellion of '45. Although it was not yet the national anthem (an idea whose time had not yet come), within a year of 1745 it was played and sung when royalty appeared in public. It was sung for the first time at the coronation of George IV in 1821.

Religion

In response to the contradictions and hardships that existed in eighteenth-century culture and society, it is not surprising that one sees diverse religious and philosophical movements that grew up to try to answer the questions of the age. We can certainly count the Enlightenment and the culture of sensibility among those. While the Protestant Reformation in England, establishing an independent state church of which the monarch was head, had been motivated by the political, economic, and personal greed of Henry VIII, it was also inspired by new religious beliefs and ideas that spread throughout the British Isles. Over the course of the seventeenth century, British religion saw the development of multiple religious sects, such as the Baptists, Congregationalists, Presbyterians, and Quakers—all related to Protestantism. Referred to as Dissenters (because they dissented from the Church of England) or Nonconformists, members of all of these denominations faced prejudice and discrimination in Britain. The Scottish Kirk meanwhile developed its own reformed tradition very much influenced by Calvinism. Ireland remained Roman Catholic except for the plantations settled by English Protestants.

As the national church the Church of England was supposed to house all worship with the expectation of a uniformity of belief and practice. But from the moment of the break with Rome, England and later Britain was always confessionally divided, so there was conflict between the idea of a national church to which everyone would belong and the reality of a diversity of belief and practice that could not be housed in the Church of England. The Corporation Act (1661) barred those who had not taken the sacrament in a Church of England (Roman Catholics, Protestant Dissenters, and Jews) from serving on town corporations while the Test Act (1673) excluded non-Anglicans from military or civil office. Both were only repealed in 1828. With the passage of the Uniformity Act in 1662 which mandated adherence to the Church of England to hold any office in government or the church, Dissenters, Catholics, Jews, and Quakers were barred from Oxford and Cambridge, the training grounds for civil and church leaders. In response Dissenters established dissenting academies, schools, colleges, and seminaries that played an important part in Britain's educational system throughout the seventeenth and eighteenth centuries. The Dissenters often became the focus of resistance to the elite orthodoxies.

The Church of England in the eighteenth century generally has the reputation of being quite moribund, having lost both its authority in the lives of its congregants and their enthusiasm. Some believe that this was a consequence of the English Civil War, which had been blamed on too much religious enthusiasm. But neither was this a secular age. Religious belief was strong and religious institutions, rituals, and traditions were sought after. There is no better example of this than the phenomenon of Methodism, which grew and thrived in eighteenth-century Britain, ultimately becoming a global movement.

John Wesley (1703–1791), the founder of Methodism, was a minister of the Church of England. The name Methodists was given to his group of fellow students at Oxford, also known as the Hold Club, and referred to the methodical way in which they carried out their Christian faith. Wesley later used the term *Methodist* himself to mean the methodical pursuit of biblical holiness including bible study, prayer, communion, and acts of charity. During his lifetime Wesley crossed the length and breadth of Britain, traveling over a quarter of a million miles, mostly on horseback, delivering over forty thousand sermons.[9]

Wesley did not intend to form a new church or to break away from the Church of England. Instead he hoped to reform the church from within. His mix of methodical faith and intense belief in personal salvation attracted many among the laboring poor in newly industrial areas. These populations were often neglected by the established church. Starting in 1739 Wesley preached to huge crowds numbering in the thousands. The audiences for this outdoor "field preaching" were drawn from the working classes. He was especially popular in Wales where the Church of England had generally neglected its parishioners. He encouraged those who converted to form local societies that

FIGURE 4.15 John Wesley (1703–1791), founder of Methodism, preaching to a rapt congregation in the meeting house of Mathew Bagshaw in Nottingham, England, in 1747. From "Wycliffe to Wesley; Heroes and Martyrs of the Church in Britain," by Gregory J. Robinson, 1885, published by T. Woolmer, London.

would meet weekly in small groups, but he urged them to continue to attend their local parish church. By the late eighteenth century itinerant lay preachers led hundreds of Methodist chapels.[10]

But not everyone agreed with his ideas. Critics worried about the implications of his inclusive message and feared his popularity; especially controversial was early Methodism's allowance of female preaching (something that did not continue after Wesley's death). Wesley often faced hostility and heckling during his sermons, and he and his followers were denounced, threatened, and physically attacked. Although he wanted to remain part of the Anglican Church, the Church of England distanced itself from Wesley, his ideas, and his followers. In 1784 he set up the Yearly Conference of the People Called Methodists that became the basis of the Methodist Church. The Church fractured after Wesley's death in 1791; the different groups united into the Methodist Church of Great Britain in 1932.[11]

Meanwhile, inspired by the power of Methodism, the established church from which Methodism eventually broke, experienced an evangelical religious and spiritual revival of its own in the 1780s. The evangelical wing of the Church of England counted among its adherents prominent abolitionists William Wilberforce, later a member of Parliament who introduced bills to stop the trade, Thomas Clarkson, who expanded the cause by collecting the evidence of slavery's brutality and immorality, and Granville Sharp, a civil servant and a reformer who served as the first chairman of the Society for Effecting the Abolition of the Slave Trade. One particular congregation in the south London community of Clapham was home to the Clapham Sect, many of whom were also members of Parliament. Evangelicals in general wished to revive the church by infusing their everyday lives with Christian values and strict observance. Those of the Clapham Sect, not content with overseeing their own morality, were particularly effective at putting their beliefs to work in the world. In addition to abolition of the slave trade and slavery, they promoted missionary work at home and in the empire. Other projects included prison reform, prevention of cruelty to animals, the suspension of the game laws, and the elimination of the lottery. Quite socially conservative, theirs was a paternalistic view of the social order.

One site of connection between the Methodists and Evangelicals was the abolitionist movement. Between 1735 and 1737 John Wesley and his brother Charles visited the British colony of Georgia. Wesley served as an Anglican rector while in Georgia, spreading his teachings to the American colonies. It was in Georgia that Wesley witnessed the brutality of raced and chattel slavery. Although he was moved by the injustice of slavery, it was not until the dramatic details of the Somerset case in 1771–72 (discussed in chapter 1) seized his attention again that he became involved in the abolitionist movement, which was beginning to gain momentum. Moved by Somerset's self-emancipation and called to action by the Evangelical abolitionist Granville Sharp and the Philadelphia Quaker Anthony Benezet, Wesley wrote *Thoughts on Slavery* in 1774, attacking the slave trade and calling for a boycott on slave-produced sugar and rum. In 1787 he expressed his support for the Society for the Effecting Abolition of the Slave Trade, an interdenominational association established that year. In 1788, Wesley preached an antislavery sermon in Bristol, one of the most active slave trading ports.

Contrary to what we might expect, views on slavery did not simply correspond to views on race. The ideology of white racism did rationalize slavery, but there were also white racists who opposed the slave trade and slavery on the grounds that it was cruel to lesser creatures, or that it brought whites and Blacks into close physical proximity and led to racial mixing. Such people so fully supported segregation that they proposed schemes to ship those of African descent to Africa and spoke of this as a "return" of these people, even if the people had never been to Africa. Sharp and Wilberforce supported these initiatives. In 1792 they and the Clapham Sect founded the colony of Sierra Leone. Their vision was to resettle former slaves there as an effort to remove them from Britain. As mentioned in chapter 3, Sierra Leone was colonized in 1787 by freed slaves arriving from England; other groups followed from Nova Scotia (1792) and Jamaica (1800). The Clapham Sect continued to recruit for the colony and manage it until it became a Crown colony in 1808.

In addition to Dissenters, Methodists, and Evangelicals, Britain's population included Roman Catholics, Muslims, and Jews. By the eighteenth century many in England were convinced that Protestantism ensured their liberties, freedoms, and rights. Despite the reality of poverty in Britain, high taxes, and the harsh Bloody Code, Britons believed that their Protestantism made them "richer in every sense than other peoples."[12] They associated Catholicism, in particular, with religious superstition, but also with an elaborated set of oppressive traditions that translated into fundamental unfreedoms, including absolutism, tyranny, and slavery.

Legal restrictions on Roman Catholics in Britain date, as we have seen, back to the Henrician Reformation. After the Revolution of 1688, further legislation constrained Catholics. The preamble of "An Act for the further preventing the growth of popery" explained in 1698 that "there has been of late a much greater Resort into this Kingdom than formerly of Popish Bishops Priests and Jesuits and they do very openly and in insolent Manner affront the Laws and daily endeavor to pervert His Majesty's naturally borne Subjects." The language of the statute blamed "treasonable and execrable Designs and Conspiracies against His majesty's Person and Government and the Established religion" on the "Neglect of the due Execution of the Laws already in Force." The Act rewarded anyone who caught a Catholic priest "saying Mass or of exercising any other Part of the Office or Function of a Popish Bishop or Priest" with £100 and barred Catholic priests from opening schools. Among its harsh measures it prohibited Catholics from sitting in Parliament, purchasing land, or holding civil or military offices. Catholics could not inherit property or practice their religion freely.[13] In Ireland the Roman Catholic majority could not vote in Parliamentary elections and Catholic landowners could be readily dispossessed of their land by their Protestant relatives.

Despite the legal restrictions, elite opinions about Catholics shifted toward toleration in the second half of the century, certainly after the Seven Years War and Quiberon Bay in 1759.[14] This move to toleration was not the relentless unidirectional march to toleration and eventual Catholic Emancipation that some scholars of the Enlightenment have asserted.[15] Instead of the spread of liberal values, military necessity and imperial needs—recruitment and security—forced the expansion of Catholic rights, always a site of struggle and contestation.[16]

There were about eight thousand Jewish people in England in the eighteenth century. Many were poor peddlers, but some were very involved in Britain's imperial expansion and London's financial and commercial activity, including foreign trade, luxury goods, the insurance industry, and public borrowing. Jewish financiers held stock in the Bank of England, traded in the money market, and advised the government on its financial policies: they, like other participants in the world of credit and finance, owned the national debt, and they actively participated in selling it to the public.[17] Over the course of the eighteenth century, as Britain's military expanded, Jewish merchants provisioned soldiers with supplies and the government with loans to fund the wars. Jewish financiers also imported bullion, fundamental to international trade. They traded commodities from all over the world. Jewish traders were active in importing and re-exporting different commodities and exporting British goods. Their global commercial networks made them international brokers around the world. Jewish merchants actively promoted trade in sites all over the empire, including India, the Caribbean, North America, and South America.

In exchange for their loyalty and their economic contributions, Jews argued for the rights of Englishmen. Specifically, they wanted to be able to be naturalized without having to take

Communion or affirm their membership in the Church of England. The Jewish Naturalization Bill was introduced in the House of Lords in April 1753 and passed in the House of Commons in May. The purpose of this legislation was not the general acceptance of Jews into Britain; naturalization would still require the passage of a private act of Parliament, which would be in the reach of only a few of the wealthiest among England's Jewish population. Although it met with little initial dispute inside or outside of Parliament, the act elicited a tremendous popular furor immediately after its passage, and it was debated in pamphlets and prints, sermons, petitions, and newspaper coverage. In November 1753, immediately after Parliament reconvened, the Act was repealed.[18]

The Muslim presence in England dates back to the sixteenth century. King Henry VIII's break with the Church of Rome and his daughter Elizabeth's excommunication by Pope Pius V in 1570 left her isolated from European monarchs but free to trade with Muslim partners in Morocco as well as the Ottoman and Persian Empires. Elizabeth responded by creating economic, commercial, and political alliances with these Islamic states. These ties brought Muslim diplomats to London in the sixteenth century, and they were followed by merchants, translators, musicians, servants, and sex workers. Early written accounts refer to them as moors, Indians, Negroes, and Turks. In the eighteenth century, Muslims were recruited from the Indian subcontinent to work for the British East India Company. Arriving in British ports, they struggled to find housing because the shipping companies did not provide accommodation. They spent their time in Britain waiting months to find a ship returning to India.

Ideas in Action: Abolition and the Rights of Man

How did the ideas of the Enlightenment, sensibility, evangelicalism, and science translate into the lives of eighteenth-century Britons? The discussions of governance and governing fostered by the Enlightenment produced the language of rights, most famously for the nascent United States in the Declaration of Independence, which states life, liberty, and the pursuit of happiness as the basic rights of man, which meant men only. Yet there was not widespread anxiety about Britain's participation, complicity, and leadership of the slave trade or the huge profits flooding the kingdom from plantations in the Caribbean until quite late in the century. Some scholars have argued that the loss of the American colonies may in fact have been interpreted by some Britons as God's punishment for the complicity of Britain and its empire in both the slave trade and slavery. The tremendous shift in sensibility about slavery in the late eighteenth century and the momentum that gathered against the practice and for abolition does demand an historical explanation. But one is left with the fact that Christian doctrine had not caused an abolitionist groundswell in four hundred years, so why in the ninth decade of the eighteenth century? Although the moral imperative against the commodification of Black bodies and the inhumane treatment of enslaved people of color was strong in some abolitionist circles and may explain individual motives, some historians point to slavery's expense and the constant battle to justify it as possible reasons for the rising tide of abolitionism.

One event that focused attention on the slave trade was the crime of the slave ship *Zong*. In November 1781, the ship was headed to Jamaica with 442 enslaved on board. As they neared their destination, the captain, Luke Collingwood, discovered that they were quite a ways off course and their supply of drinking water would run out days before they reached their destination. With many of those enslaved quite ravaged by illness, as was typical of slave ships, and 10 days more of the voyage, the crew pushed 54 women and children through the cabin windows into the sea. Two days later, they threw 42 men overboard and another 38 Africans perished after that.

The murder of 134 enslaved Africans would probably not have garnered any public outcry had the story ended there. But the Gregson syndicate who owned and operated the *Zong* sued their insurers for the loss of their cargo claiming money damages for the people, regarded as property, their employees had killed. Although the first court ruling found for the merchants, the insurance company insisted on a new trial in 1783. The publicity brought slavery and the trade to the attention of many Britons, setting off an outcry of disgust. Like the Somerset case of 1772, the *Zong* put the details of the slave trade and the commodification of human beings in the unavoidable sight line of the British public.

Among the earliest and most committed abolitionists in Britain were the Quakers. George Fox had founded the Religious Society of Friends in the 1650s on the basis of his belief that there is something "of God in every person." This simple statement was radical because it threatened to overthrow all existing hierarchies of race, gender, religion, and status. Although he originally had no intention of breaking with the established church, Fox and his fellow believers were soon branded as revolutionary and their beliefs condemned. They were called Quakers by their detractors who used the name to refer to the trance-like state that they entered during their silent meetings. George Fox taught that every person could reach God themselves—"God in every man"—and that they needed no church, priest, or ritual to do so. This included women, who spoke in Quaker worship as equals to men. Because of the egalitarian implications of this claim about the worth and dignity of every person, Quakers experienced a great deal of oppressive treatment at the hands of the English and then British government. Thousands were imprisoned for their refusal to doff their hats to anyone, including their social superiors, their refusal to swear oaths, and their attendance at banned Quaker meetings.

Consistent with these beliefs the Quakers were leading proponents of religious toleration and thrived in the Caribbean as early as the seventeenth century, where they fled from English persecution. Ironically the religious toleration Quakers found in the Caribbean, specifically in Barbados, also meant that they were tremendously successful as planters, merchants, and office holders, 80 percent of whom owned and traded enslaved people. When George Fox visited Barbados in 1671, he encouraged his slaveholding followers to convert their slaves and welcome them into the Society of Friends even though most British slaveholders did not do so fearing the injunction against enslaving fellow Christians. In the case of Quakers and their slaves, the doctrinal requirement to see every human being as a human being collided with and contradicted slavery's dehumanizing ethos.

Although white abolitionists, men and women, Quakers, Evangelicals, Methodists and others, did a lot to end the slave trade, it was the resistance and self-emancipation of enslaved people that led the way and sustained the cause. Rebellion, resistance, and revolution in the case of Haiti, abolitionist writings by people of color, including Phillis Wheatley and Frederick Douglass in the American colonies, later the United States, and Olaudah Equiano and Ignatius Sanchez in Britain, sparked the movement and were ultimately responsible for its success.

A freed slave and abolitionist activist, Equiano worked with Granville Sharp, a member of the Clapham Sect and the leader of the antislavery campaign who had championed James Somerset in 1771–72 (as discussed in chapter 1) to bring attention to the case of the *Zong*. The abolitionist cause gained momentum in the wake of the *Zong* massacre. Despite their prominence among slave owners, the Quakers had been active in the antislavery campaign petitioning Parliament in 1783. A second petition by the inhabitants of Bridgwater in Somerset was sent to Parliament in 1785. Although both these efforts were met with a muted response, starting in 1787 a rising discourse of abolition brought more attention to slavery and the slave trade and put plantation owners on the defensive. The Society for Effecting the Abolition of the Slave Trade mobilized British antislavery sentiment. With a network of local contacts throughout Britain, the Society's London Committee spread its message using pamphlets, books, images, and artefacts. Thomas Clarkson and Olauda Equiano both traveled throughout Britain spreading the abolitionist message, organizing committees, distributing published material, facilitating efforts at the local level, and connecting them to London's Committee.

One of the legal means by which the abolitionists pressured Parliament was through mass petitioning. There were two nationwide petition campaigns, one in 1788 and one in 1792. In the first, over one hundred petitions against the slave trade were presented to the House of Commons in a three-month period. In 1792, on the heels of the sugar boycott described below, 519 petitions were presented. The signatures came from a diversity of regions, and in 1792 every English county was represented along with Scotland and Wales.

The results of the petitioning campaign were mixed. William Wilberforce, who led the campaign in the Commons, hoped that the petitions would result in a vote to end the trade. And in 1792 the House voted 230–85 for gradual abolition. Hundreds of thousands of people signed petitions calling for the abolition of the slave trade. In Manchester, 20 percent of the city's population signed pro-abolitionist petitions. In addition to a demonstration of the outcry against the trade and the success of abolition as a movement, the campaign demonstrated how, in the eighteenth century, the petition had become an important legal mechanism to mobilize public opinion, and for the public to mobilize Parliamentary action.

In his 1791 "Address to the People of Great Britain, on the Propriety of Abstaining from West India Sugar and Rum," William Fox, the radical abolitionist pamphleteer, called for a sugar boycott. White women were especially active in the abolitionist movement, and many of them took up the call to organize the sugar boycott to express their outrage. The sugar boycott was one of the first political causes in which British women participated so publicly. Many of the conversations over sugar and slavery took place over the tea table. This was no coincidence. Although both sugar and tea had once been delicacies that only the wealthy could afford, by the end of the century, they were a foundational part of the English diet. Tea leaves were an Asian import that became a mass consumer item in Europe, especially in England. Before 1700, there was little consumption of tea in England, yet by the 1740s the East India Company was importing 2 million pounds of tea from China. By 1800, it was importing over 20 million pounds. This tea habit of the British was not confined to the metropole. Tea was increasingly popular among the Anglo settlers in the British colonies, which is why the English state sought to place a tax on tea imports to the American colonies and why that tax was so bitterly resented. This dispute culminated in the Boston Tea Party of 1773. The sugar boycott thus had an array of cultural and political, as well as economic, implications.

Material culture often leaves us clues about attitudes and beliefs in the past, and physical objects can be extremely important for historians to study and analyze. One such object is a teapot made by Josiah Wedgwood in 1760, which was decorated with an abolitionist poem: "Health to the sick/Honor to the brave/Success to the lover/and Freedom to the slave." In addition to abolitionist teapots, there were pitchers, bowls, cups, and saucers. Women were at the forefront of the consumer revolution of the eighteenth century, and they had tremendous buying power. Their tastes drove design and reveal their preoccupations and concerns.

In the midst of discussions of governance and representativeness, women often referred to their moral virtue to demonstrate that they deserved a place in politics and to justify an expanded role in governance. Like the American colonists before them, they compared their lack of political rights to enslaved people. Their involvement in the abolitionist movement gave British women a means of performing their sensibility, their civility, their virtue, and philanthropy. Furthermore, their involvement in such a serious issue allowed them to present themselves as the opposite of frivolous and superficial beings who cared only for the latest fashions and impoverished their husbands with their uncontrolled spending.

When Fox called for the sugar boycott, women participated in many different ways. They advocated boycott in pamphlets, poetry, and fiction. They formed antislavery societies and collected signatures for antislavery petitions. When one "Humanus" wrote to the *Newcastle Courant* a year after Fox had published his pamphlet, he explained that during his recent absence from home, "the females in [his] family" had read the Fox pamphlet: "On my return, I was surprised to find that they had entirely left off the use of Sugar, and banished it from the tea table."[19] While the boycott didn't end the slave trade—the British Parliament did not outlaw the trade until 1807 and slavery was not ended until 1833—historians estimate that three hundred thousand people stopped eating sugar and that sales dropped by a third to a half. Some vendors advertised that their sugar had been produced by freemen and the sale of sugar from India (which also had abysmal labor practices) rose tenfold in two years.

Wedgwood also produced an antislavery medallion with a Black man on one knee asking, "Am I not a man and a brother?" The medallion was designed for the Society for Effecting the Abolition of the Slave Trade. It was smaller than a quarter and was used to raise awareness of the abolitionist cause both in England and in the United States. The image was used in jewelry for men and women; it also appeared on women's hairpins and bracelets. Wedgwood was raised in a family of Dissenters, associated personally and professionally with the leading scientists of his day, and active in a number of important commercial and manufacturing organizations. A close friend of abolitionist Thomas Clarkson, he was also a part of a community of business and civic leaders committed to ending the transatlantic slave trade. In his early teapot and later medallion, we see various intellectual, cultural, religious, and associational currents of the eighteenth century being put into physical service of the cause of abolition and circulated in the public sphere.

But the political mobilization of so many people was perceived as a potential threat in the 1790s. The convergence of the French Revolution and the abolitionist campaign led some to advocate the termination of all such activity as a harbinger of radicalism that could destabilize Britain's government and way of life. No doubt some protagonists of the slave trade deliberately raised the alarm to prevent the House of Commons from taking any action that would circumscribe the slave trade or slavery. In 1793, the year Britain went to war against revolutionary France, the Commons refused to engage with the subject of the slave trade and by its silence effectively reversed the resolutions made the previous year.

But there was no stopping the debate about rights, government, and representation. During the French Revolution a lengthy debate between Edmund Burke, Thomas Paine, and many others, including Mary Wollstonecraft, continued the discussion. Their lengthy exchanges about the meaning of the Revolution brought into stark view the contradictions that made up the Enlightenment and the eighteenth century. For Britons, the debate about the meaning of the French Revolution centered on questions of rights, representation, nation, law, and empire. Never limited to politicians and intellectuals, the debate between these two men and their ideas about government and its power and authority permeated English culture and society in the 1790s, providing each side a deep well of rhetoric on which to draw. Paine's *Rights of Man* responded directly to Burke's *Reflections on the Revolution in France* and referenced Burke throughout. Other authors quickly penned their own responses, and within a year of each pamphlet's publication almost a hundred printed pamphlets had appeared. By 1793, an anthology featured extracts from each work as well as the opinions of leading writers and commentators. The London Corresponding Society (1792–1799) and the Society for Constitutional Information (founded in 1780), organizations dedicated to democratic ideals, the promotion of Parliamentary reform, and the distribution of information about politics, collaborated in their efforts to make Paine's work cheaply available. Sales of these published works were brisk, and the pricing meant the works circulated to a broad readership. The number of Paine's pamphlets in circulation by 1793 reached a quarter of a million, a half a million by the end of the decade. His readers included sailors and soldiers, who as we have seen equated impressment with slavery. According to Horace Walpole in a letter to Mary Berry dated July 21, 1791, "[V]ast numbers of Paine's pamphlet [*The Rights of Man*, Part I] were distributed both to regiments and ships," although he also admitted that they "were given up voluntarily to the officers" when requested.[20]

Burke, who decades earlier had written about the sublime and the beautiful, published the *Reflections* to refute the radical philosopher and dissenting preacher Richard Price (mentioned in chapter 3) and his contention that "by the principles of the [French] Revolution the people of England have acquired three fundamental rights … 1. To choose our own governors, 2. To cashier them for misconduct, 3. To frame a government for ourselves."[21] In contrast Burke insisted that the preservation of "[g]ood order is the foundation of all good things … the people, without being servile, must be tractable and obedient. The magistrate must have his reverence, the laws their authority."[22] Burke reiterated the virtue and necessity of subordination throughout the *Reflections*. Property ownership bestowed power and authority while the growing discourse of equality and inalienable rights threatened every aspect of life.[23]

Repudiating the need for Parliamentary reform, Burke warned that "when antient opinions and rules of life are taken away, … we have no compass to govern us."[24] For Burke, law upheld hierarchy, inheritance, and an aristocratic order secured in "the Revolution of 1688, made to preserve our antient indisputable laws and liberties, and that antient constitution of government which is our only security for law and liberty."[25]

In response to Burke's axiom that Parliament in 1688 changed things forever, making further political reforms unnecessary, Paine pronounced that the capacity to participate in this process derived from "the illuminating and divine principle of the equal rights of man," and "the unity of man … that men are all of one degree, and consequently that all men are born equal, and with equal natural right."[26] These equal rights bestowed responsibilities and "place[d] him in a close connection with all his duties."[27]

Paine asserted that "a Nation has at all times an inherent indefeasible right to abolish any form of Government it finds inconvenient, and establish such as accords with its interest, disposition, and happiness." Within the nation "[e]very citizen is a member of the sovereignty, and, as such, can acknowledge no personal subjection; and his obedience can be only to the laws."[28] The law provided the connection between the individual and his political participation because when confronted with bad laws, "it is a duty which every man owes to society to point them out. When

FIGURE 4.16 Medallion, jasperware, Josiah Wedgwood's Etruria Factory, Staffordshire, England, 1787–1800.

FIGURE 4.17 Official symbol of the British Anti-Slavery Society.

those defects, and the means of remedying them are generally seen by a nation, that nation will reform its government or its constitution in the one case, as the government repealed or reformed the law in the other."[29] These prescriptions for men as the agents of change stand in stark opposition to Burke's instructions about continuity, stability, and hierarchy.

This chapter has surveyed some of the artistic, cultural, and religious trends and movements in eighteenth-century Britain. Over the course of the century, the public sphere expanded tremendously. The movement of goods and people, so much a part of Britain's empire, facilitated an expanded network of cultural communication and circulation that included contact between colony and metropole: sometimes London was the source, sometimes the receiver, and often the web of imperial entanglement bypassed London altogether, vibrantly connecting colonies and colonists.

IMAGE CREDITS

Fig. 4.6: Source: https://commons.wikimedia.org/wiki/File:Holkham_Saloon_Section.jpg.

Fig. 4.7: Source: https://commons.wikimedia.org/wiki/File:%27Southampton_or_Bloomsbury_Square%27,_London,_c1725.jpg.

Fig. 4.8: Copyright © by H. Adlard after F. Mackenzie / Wellcome Collection (CC BY 4.0) at https://commons.wikimedia.org/wiki/File:The_British_Museum;_the_entrance_facade_as_built._Engraving_Wellcome_V0013532.jpg.

Fig. 4.9: Source: https://commons.wikimedia.org/wiki/File:Royal.crescent.aerial.bath.arp.jpg.

Fig. 4.10: Copyright © by David Iliff (CC BY-SA 3.0) at https://commons.wikimedia.org/wiki/File:Roman_Baths_in_Bath_Spa,_England_-_July_2006.jpg.

Fig. 4.11: Thomas Gainsborough, "The Cottage Door," 1778.

Fig. 4.12: Source: https://commons.wikimedia.org/wiki/File:The_Coffee_House_Politicians_(BM_1868,0808.13254_1).jpg.

Fig. 4.13: Source: https://commons.wikimedia.org/w/index.php?curid=152865.

Fig. 4.14: Copyright © by Walter Besant / Wellcome Collection (CC BY 4.0) at https://commons.wikimedia.org/wiki/File:Newgate_Prison,_Inner_Court,_18th_century._Wellcome_L0001330.jpg.

Fig. 4.15: William Haven Daniels, The Illustrated History of Methodism: In Great Britain and America from the Days of the Wesleys to the Present Time, p. 234, Phillips & Hunt, 1879.

Fig. 4.16: Source: https://commons.wikimedia.org/w/index.php?curid=81729450.

Fig. 4.17: Source: https://commons.wikimedia.org/wiki/File:Official_medallion_of_the_British_Anti-Slavery_Society_(1795).jpg.

CHAPTER 5

People, Parties, and Patronage

Modern party politics, in particular the two-party system, began to take shape in the political struggles at the dawn of the long eighteenth century. The Whig and Tory Parties emerged, as we have seen, during the Exclusion Crisis. Their rivalry was still going strong in the wake of the Napoleonic Wars, when George III, now old and sick, was king and his son, the future George IV, served as regent. Both parties had outlasted the Stuart dynasty and were keeping pace with the long-lived Hanoverians. What the parties stood for, however, whom they attracted and how they exercised power, had varied considerably in the intervening years.

Rage of Party

Party power tended to shift slowly in the House of Lords. Once a "temporal lord" inherited a peerage, a seat in the upper chamber was his for life. For the "spiritual lords," the privilege came with a job, but bishoprics were few in number and turnover rare. Monarchs could create new peers and did so to reward wealthy subjects and loyal friends; this happened most often in celebration of a royal coronation. If it was done en masse and for explicitly partisan reasons, however, as in January 1712 when a Tory ministry convinced Queen Anne to ennoble 12 of their own to help pass legislation floundering in the House of Lords, the backlash could be fierce. The "jury," as the 12 were contemptuously called, were the last group so crassly elevated to alter a parliamentary majority, though threats of repeating the practice continued to prove politically expedient.

The House of Commons, by contrast, was very different. There, parties' fates could, and did, turn on a single election. This was especially true in the decades following the Revolution of 1688–89, when "the rage of party" prevailed. The Triennial Act of 1694 had mandated a new election at least every three years; in practice, slightly shorter intervals became the norm. Political unrest drove voters to the polls twice in 1701 and again in 1702—three general elections in 19 months!—the attendant campaigns fueling public debate. So did the burgeoning press, freed from state censorship in 1695 when the Licensing Act regulating it elapsed. Politics were reported in newspapers, dissected in pamphlets, set to tunes in ballads, lampooned in cartoons, and advertised on fans, playing cards, buttons, punch bowls, teapots, and the like. Most importantly, they were discussed in the public sphere of streets, clubs, coffeehouses, and taverns where all this print culture was consumed and shared.

The Spectator, an immensely popular daily London publication, both reproduced and critiqued the world of public conversation. One of its recurring topics was "this party rage," so pervasive as to afflict even "the fair sex." On June 7, 1711, *The Spectator* no. 81 decried behavior at the opera, where "two parties of very fine women" sat in "opposite side boxes, and seemed drawn up in a kind of battle array one against another." The scene cleverly evoked seating arrangements in the House of Commons and identified the two camps of opera-goers as Whig and Tory, but the women it describes take their partisanship to a whole new level, "patching"—applying fashionable beauty spots—to the left or right side of their faces to signal political affiliation. For "Rosalinda, a famous Whig partisan," a "very beautiful mole on the Tory part of her forehead … being very conspicuous, has occasioned many mistakes, and given an handle to her enemies to misrepresent her face."[1] What political realities gave rise to such satire?

A prescient politician had warned in 1689, as the convention parliament went about its work, "Fear of Popery has united; when it is over, we shall divide again."[2] Religion, ironically, contributed to those subsequent divisions. In May 1689, the convention parliament thanked Protestant Dissenters, who had resisted James II despite his promises of religious toleration, with a Toleration Act of its own. More limited than what James had attempted, the 1689 law exempted Protestant Dissenters from compulsory worship in the Anglican Church and permitted dissenting chapels and schools. Dissenters were still excluded from Parliament, government office, and town corporations under the Test and Corporation Acts, as were Catholics, who received no accommodations under the Toleration Act. But freedom of worship for nonconforming Protestants boosted their numbers, as people flocked to newly licensed dissenting meeting houses. Whigs embraced such developments; Tories, stricter defenders of the Anglican establishment, did not. Tories were especially concerned about the practice of occasional conformity, whereby a Protestant Dissenter could obtain political office by attending Anglican services once a year in token compliance with the Test and Corporation Acts. Such tensions came to a political head in 1709 when the conservative Anglican clergyman Henry Sacheverell preached a sermon (100,000 copies of which he published and sold) against "false brethren in Church and state," condemning the Revolution of 1688–89 on its November 5th anniversary. The Whig-dominated House of Commons impeached Sacheverell, making him the popular hero, even martyr, of the "Church in Danger" cause. As his long trial unfolded in the House of Lords, pro-Sacheverell crowds rioted in the streets of London, ripping pews and pulpits out of dissenting meeting houses and burning some down; and though Sacheverell was convicted, when word of his surprisingly light sentence spread, supporters celebrated with bonfires throughout the land.[3] The Whig government fell over the affair.

Tories won the resulting general election by a landslide. Having campaigned in support of Sacheverell and the Anglican establishment and for peace, they passed a law against occasional conformity in 1711 and the Treaty of Utrecht that ended the War of Spanish Succession (1702–13) in 1713. In that war, as in the last, Tories favored a "blue water" strategy of naval engagements in the colonies, while the Whigs promoted costlier land campaigns on the continent. As military expenditure, the national debt, and the demand for revenue all soared, Parliament enacted a host of indirect customs and excise duties. But the land tax, renewed annually to fund the debt, placed a unique and direct burden on landed gentlemen at a time of agricultural depression. They came to resent the wars, from which they saw others—merchants, manufacturers, and the state's creditors—benefitting at little personal cost. Landed gentlemen, of course, dominated both parties, but the individuals most involved in commerce and finance tended to lean Whig and support the massive military establishment and interventionist policies associated with William and continued under Anne.

The War of Spanish Succession also rubbed salt in the old wounds of hereditary succession. Just three months after the Act of Settlement of 1701 had decreed an eventual Hanoverian Succession, rejecting the claims of James Francis Edward Stuart, his father James II died. France's Louis XIV recognized the exiled prince as James III, the rightful king, all but guaranteeing William's entrance in the continental conflict already underway. The overwhelming majority of Tories embraced the call to war against France much as they had the Act of Settlement—as a necessary evil safeguarding Protestantism and the legacy of 1688–89. A small few, however, identified with James III and the Jacobite cause. In this climate, William III died in March 1702 and Queen Anne led the nation in war. In this climate, as we have seen, Scotland and England forged the political union that created Great Britain. In this climate, the rage of party flourished. And in this climate, Tories ended the War of Spanish Succession in 1713 in a manner that frustrated both Whigs and the heir to the throne, George, Elector of Hanover. A year later, the accession of George I transformed British political life in wholly new ways.

FIGURE 5.1 James Francis Edward Stuart, c. 1703.

Hanoverians, Jacobites, and Everyone Else

George arrived in London to mixed reviews. Cheering crowds lined the streets to welcome his carriage. Yet, as an anonymous poem addressed to the late Queen Anne suggests, there was a lot of grumbling too:

FIGURE 5.2 Medallion celebrating George I's accession (with "Saxon Steed" running from Hanover to Britain), 1714.

Behold he comes to make thy people groan,
And with their curses to ascend thy throne;
A clod-pate, base, inhuman, jealous Fool,
The jest of Europe, and the faction's tool.
Heav'n never heard of such a right Divine,
Nor Earth e'er saw a successor like thine:
For if in sense or politicks you fail'd,
'Twas when his lousy long succession you entail'd.[4]

This nasty ditty was a Tory creation. The controlling faction about which it complained was Whig. After four years out of political favor, the Whigs now had a staunch ally on the throne: a 54-year-old German prince with poor command of the English language, an aloof manner, and an ex-wife he had imprisoned for life back home. Meanwhile, he brought with him to Britain his mistress, scores of German advisers, and his grown son and heir, who in turn had a son and heir. The Hanoverian succession looked "long," and to Tories "lousy," indeed.

Even before the Tories ended the War of Spanish Succession, in which Hanover was an enthusiastic partner, George was predisposed against them. He worried about Tory sympathy for "a right Divine" (inviolable hereditary succession) and potential support for the Pretender. After Anne died, some Tory politicians refused to pledge loyalty and serve the new king. He reciprocated by dismissing others from central and local government offices. Voters, too, turned against Tories in a highly contested general election in January 1715, reversing the majority in the House of Commons. Now desperate, a tiny Jacobite clique of Tories offered to help the Pretender prepare an invasion.

Some pro-Jacobite rioting had occurred in English towns on George's coronation day and after the Whigs' electoral victory. To discourage and contain such disturbances, an "Act for preventing tumults and riotous assemblies, and for the more speedy and effectual punishing the rioters"—more popularly known as the Riot Act—went into effect in August 1715. But the Jacobite rebellion that began in September was a coordinated military affair. Its leader was John Erskine, the Earl of Mar, a Scottish politician who had supported the Hanoverian Succession but then found himself among those purged from office. Mar responded by coordinating an initially successful Jacobite occupation of northern Scotland. In contrast to the invasions of 1689 and 1708, the '15, as it is known, was launched in Britain. Along with Scots, disgruntled over union and succession, were English forces, many of them Catholic, from Lancashire. Mar met government troops led by the Duke of Argyll at the Battle of Sheriffmuir on November 13. Mar had more men, Argyll more military experience. The battle ended inconclusively, but it halted Mar's march south and prevented the Scottish Jacobites from meeting up with their English counterparts. Although the rebellion continued for two months, it never regained momentum. James arrived too late (figure 5.3) and ended up just leading his supporters to France.

Despite Mar's political motivation, the '15 was a mostly Catholic affair. When it was over and the Lord High Steward sentenced its noble leaders to death, he conceded to Catholics "One Temptation, and that a great one, to engage you in this Treason." Of the other insurgents, he exclaimed, "But then, good God! how must those Protestants be covered with Confusion, who entered into the same Measures." Few Protestants, Tories included, in fact rebelled. Moreover, as the Lord High Steward reminded the condemned lords, "the whole Body of the Commons of Great Britain, by their Representatives," regardless of party, joined in the impeachment proceedings and "are your Accusers."[5]

FIGURE 5.3 James Francis Edward Stuart landing at Peterhead.

Even so, it took a while for the Tories to rid themselves of the taint of Jacobitism, and thanks to the new Septennial Act, they did not have another electoral opportunity until 1722. Whigs tried to make the most of the situation. But internal divisions plagued them too, and the royal family had an uncanny way, both in its policies and its personalities, of exacerbating those tensions. One group of Whigs disapproved of George I's foreign policy, complaining that it over-prioritized the interests of Hanover, where the British king still spent a lot of time. This faction's leaders resigned in protest from ministerial office in 1717, joining the Tories in opposition. They also found a patron in George, Prince of Wales, who, eager for his turn on the throne, was not on the best terms with his father. These emotional, even primal areas of conflict—connection to the homeland and father-son rivalry—would persist, marking successive generations of Hanoverian kings and the politicians who served them. But when a speculative investment bubble, known as the South Sea Bubble, burst in 1720, throwing the economy and government into crisis, both "families," royal and Whig, understood it was time to kiss and make up.

At the heart of the South Sea Bubble (also discussed in chapter 6) was a chartered monopoly, the South Sea Company, established in 1711 to trade in South America. The South Sea Company never actually did much trading, but in 1719 it negotiated with the government to purchase a considerable chunk of the national debt that was in private hands in exchange for shares of company stock. To attract investors, company directors inflated tales of potential profits and manipulated shares. A speculative mania ensued. Share prices soared as eager investors, big and small, bought their way into the scheme.[6] Politicians and members of the royal family, who had both bought and been bribed with shares, were caught up in the greed and corruption when the bubble burst, share prices plummeted, and the company collapsed in an atmosphere of public hysteria. The Whig ministry that had endorsed the plan was compromised. But the opposition Whigs, marginalized from the center of power in recent years, were spared. Their leaders took advantage of the crisis to reconcile with the Whig establishment. One in particular, Sir Robert Walpole, brokered a solution to stabilize public confidence, the markets, and the national debt. A year later, when death and retirement thinned the upper ranks of government, George I appointed Walpole as First Lord of the Treasury and Chancellor of the Exchequer. But Walpole took office less as a reformer than a fixer; his ascendancy derived in large part from his ability protect the powerful and extricate the economy from their South Sea Company entanglements.

Politics of Patronage

Walpole would lead the Whigs for two decades (1721–42), during the course of which he fashioned the office of "prime minister." Political historians long called this "the age of Walpole" or "the age of political stability." The labels represent two sides of the same argument: Walpole's mastery of both court and parliamentary politics created stability by consolidating power in a Whig machine that exercised one-party rule. But in Walpole's day, his critics described the political system managed by Robert (a.k.a. "Robin") Walpole as the "Robinocracy." Their pun reveals the vibrancy of the political opposition to Walpole and the Whigs, opposition that thrived within Parliament and beyond it walls. The period, like that of the rage of party, experienced fierce, engaged, and often witty public debate. Current historical scholarship thus acknowledges the important elements of Walpole's tenure but treads lightly regarding claims of Whig supremacy and resulting political stability.

George II, like his father, preferred Whigs to Tories; there was little doubt when he ascended the throne in 1727 that he would appoint a Whig ministry. Who got the plum posts, however, was up for grabs, and Walpole was not the new king's favorite. At first, it looked like he might be replaced. Two things helped tip the scale in Walpole's favor—his friendship with George II's wife, Queen Caroline, and his persuading Parliament to grant the royal household its biggest annual income to date—and after that George II never wavered. To hold onto his office in 1727, Walpole thus exploited personal relationships, used legislative policy and "the power of the purse" to a strategic end, and demonstrated exceptional skill in parliamentary management. These were hallmarks of his approach to most political situations. They also reflected his unusual decision back in 1721, when first appointed head of the Treasury and Chancellor of the Exchequer, to remain in the House of Commons as a member of Parliament (MP) for Norfolk, rather than proceed to the House of Lords. Only when he fell from power in 1742 did Walpole accept a peerage, becoming Earl of Orford within days of relinquishing the seals of office. The speed with which he embraced that privilege at the end of his ministerial career highlights the significance of his rejecting it at the beginning.

These arrangements made good sense. The House of Commons, as we have seen, had primary legislative responsibility over fiscal affairs. The Treasury, meanwhile, managed the government's actual income and expenditure. From his perch in the Commons, Walpole oversaw the Treasury's business by introducing bills, directing debate, and influencing MPs to vote with him. Similarly, he finessed Whig Party electoral interests in the lower house. Walpole "cajoled, convinced and persuaded," putting "an enormous amount of time and effort in these personal appeals, often to very good effect."[7] And he was rewarded. As First Lord of the Treasury and Chancellor of the Exchequer, he was the chief dispenser of offices, sinecures, and real jobs in the fiscal departments of the expanding state. Both Georges, meanwhile, gave Walpole considerable influence over patronage in the military, the church, and at court. The 1701 Act of Settlement had excluded "placemen," government officeholders, from the House of Commons in an attempt to limit corruption and royal influence. Those restrictions were repealed under Queen Anne. Thereafter, the number of placemen grew, especially under Walpole. At the peak of his power, one-third of all MPs were placemen, and Walpole used his presence in the Commons to cultivate them and keep them in line. He thus extended and systematized patronage practices in ways at once efficient and corrupt. In the process, he emerged as the prime minister, the most influential of the many ministers in the king's cabinet. He had created, not just for himself but for the British political system, a new government position.

Walpole also became rich in office. While he liked to present himself as a simple country squire, chomping on apples in the Commons, he expended £1,500 per annum on wine and £15 per night on candles at his Norfolk estate where he entertained guests lavishly. Three evenings of candlelight there cost roughly the same as a year's worth of food, shelter, and clothing for a poor working family. Meanwhile, Walpole bestowed on his son Horace several sinecures, two of them even before Horace came of age.[8] The state, one might say, helped pay young Horace's allowance—to the order of thousands of pounds per year! Such arrangements, though by no means unique to Walpole, became sources of great complaint. Hence the jokes about the "Robinocracy," with its suggestion of institutionalized robbery, and the enthusiastic response to John Gay's *The Beggar's Opera*, the smash hit of the 1728 London theater season. Gay satirized Italian opera and London society in his "Newgate pastoral," set in not only Newgate Prison but the capital's brothels, taverns, and thieves' dens. Audiences quickly recognized Walpole in several of its characters—the highwayman Macheath, the receiver of stolen goods Peachum, and Peachum's well-named minion Robin of Bagshot (alias Bob Booty).

Ironically, Walpole's larger political agenda was to avoid conflict, and in particular the issues that had recently divided Parliament and the nation: religion and war. Whigs at midcentury cultivated the middle-ground in matters of faith, permitting Protestant Dissenters to circumvent the Test and Corporation Acts through occasional conformity (no longer prohibited) but refusing to dismantle the acts. Equally strategic was Walpole's policy of peace, which coincided with George II's accession and the end of hostilities with Spain in 1727. War avoidance, a somewhat un-Whiggish approach, allowed for reductions in the land tax that so irked Tories and landowners in general. It played well to the concerns of the 40-shilling freehold voters in the counties but alienated urban constituencies and those involved in trade. In the long run, it inspired a popular protest movement.

Even peacetime government costs money. To compensate for the lower land tax—the assessment rate fell by three-quarters, to its lowest level in history, between 1727 and 1732—Walpole used funds originally earmarked for debt redemption and experimented with indirect taxes. In 1733 he tried to convert some customs duties (on wine and tobacco) into excise duties. The goal was to reduce smuggling and improve revenue yields on already taxed goods; the result was a coordinated petitioning campaign, led by merchants, tradesmen, and shopkeepers, against an extension of the hated, intrusive excise administration. Walpole withdrew his plan rather than suffer defeat in Parliament, where his political enemies were making inroads among his usual supporters. In anti-excise victory celebrations over the next days, Walpole was burnt in effigy; in the general election the following year, the Whigs lost contests in some of the more populous, urban constituencies, and Walpole's majority in the House of Commons declined.

It proved a strategy worth repeating. In 1738–39, the trading community, frustrated by the government's failure to protect British interests in South America, turned a merchant of dubious repute into an unlikely hero. Captain Robert Jenkins had years earlier run afoul of the Spanish, who boarded his ship in the West Indies and, as punishment for his trespass, cut off his ear, or so he claimed. Jenkins and his ear (reportedly kept pickled in a jar) became the subject of West Indian merchants' petitioning campaign for war against Spain. A delegation of 13 aristocratic women meanwhile forced their way into the closed gallery of the House of Lords and expressed their opposition to Walpole's foreign policy. Led by the Duchess of Queensbury, who had been banned a decade earlier from court after petitioning the king on behalf of *The Beggar's Opera* author John Gay, the ladies interrupted the debate "and showed marks of dislike, not only by smiles and winks … but by noisy laughs and apparent contempts."[9] Again, Walpole succumbed to pressure in Parliament, as Tories and opposition Whigs aligned against him. The War of Jenkins' Ear thus began in October 1739. That engagement produced a more deserving seaman hero, Vice Admiral Edward James Vernon, the victor of the Battle of Porto Bello (November 1739). Over the next few years, Vernon and Porto Bello were celebrated in prints, poems, and ballads (figure 5.4), and merchants and tradesmen organized anniversary celebrations of both the battle and the admiral's birthday. Vernon's fans drew compelling comparisons between his valor and military achievements and the prime minister's corruption

FIGURE 5.4 Representations of Admiral Vernon and his victory at Porto Bello, including a painting by Peter Monamy, c. 1740.

and half-hearted pursuit of the war, which had taken a turn for the worse.[10] Another disappointing general election in 1741 ended Walpole's time at the helm of the ship of state.

Historians use the term *out-of-doors* to describe the popular agitation that contributed to Walpole's resignation in 1742. What was happening in the streets and in the petitioning campaigns brought momentum to the parliamentary proceedings in which some Whigs, frustrated by Walpole's stranglehold on power, found common cause with Tories. When the dust settled, Walpolean Whigs, the "old corps," were still in control. But for the first time in years, the ministry included a Tory, and it did so against the king's wishes. An even more "broad bottomed" coalition followed, and though it proved short-lived, its very existence suggested that the political landscape was shifting.

Another change came with the defeat in 1746 of a Jacobite uprising led by the next generation's exiled Stuart prince, Charles Edward Stuart (the Young Pretender) in support of the claims of his father (the Old Pretender). Charles Edward was the Jacobites' last best hope. The charismatic prince arrived in Scotland in July 1745 with only a very small force and little money or guns, but he secured the support of the Clan of Cameron and declared the Scottish Union abolished. His army, which took Edinburgh easily, and then marched into England with its sights on London, posed a serious threat. As they moved south, Charles Edward promised his followers that English subjects would join their cause along the route and that French military aid was on its way. He was wrong. The Jacobites made it to within 140 miles of London before they panicked, having garnered virtually no support in England, and turned northward. They won a final victory at Falkirk in January 1746 but were then soundly defeated at the Battle of Culloden near Inverness on April 16. Culloden was the last battle fought on British soil. The government responded to the '45, as the rebellion came to be called, with repression of Scots and Jacobites. Charles Edward barely escaped to the continent in September after being pursued for months. Eighty rebels were executed, and many others were driven into exile. Jacobitism did not disappear after Culloden, but it would never again shake the Hanoverian Succession to its core. In fact, a large number of former Jacobites were to be found serving the Hanoverians in a military capacity abroad within a relatively short time.

The Whigs, however, were to have a succession crisis of their own. From 1743 until his death in 1754, Henry Pelham served as First Lord of the Treasury and hence, effectively, as prime minister. Pelham represented the "old corps" Whigs, and in many respects his ministries resembled Walpole's. Like Walpole, he had the support of the king, and a good command of the House of Commons. His own brother, the first Duke of Newcastle, even held the same office of secretary of state in both administrations. Newcastle also excelled at managing the patronage machine, a task which Pelham, who was the more policy-minded, was happy to delegate. When Pelham died, Newcastle's influence and long tenure in office recommended him for his brother's position as First Lord of the Treasury. But as a duke, Newcastle sat in the House of Lords and could not exercise the direct control over the Commons that had proven so useful to both Walpole and Pelham. Could an aristocrat lead the government? The matter would not even have been a question at the start of the century.

Newcastle ultimately kept the premiership. Ministerial leadership in the Commons was awarded to Henry Fox, a protégé of Walpole's and since 1746, two years after he famously eloped with the daughter of the Duke of Richmond, secretary at war. His rival for the post was William Pitt, an opposition Whig and outstanding parliamentary orator (Fox was no slouch in debate either) who held the office of paymaster of the forces. But the king abhorred Pitt, a self-styled "patriot" and outspoken critic of foreign policy that privileged Hanover's continental interests over Britain's imperial ones. Passed over for the leadership post in the Commons, Pitt took to its floor to deliver fiery speeches decrying French incursions into British territory in North America and India and touting himself as the politician most able to find a solution. He challenged his own party's leadership and foreign policy, reaching across the aisle to the Tories and out-of-doors to the people. The Seven Years War began in 1756 but losses mounted quickly, driving Newcastle and Fox out of office. By June 1757, a new "broad-bottomed" leadership team was in place—with Newcastle again as Lord of the Treasury and Pitt now as secretary of state—to set about managing and, eventually, winning the war. In the course of that endeavor, George II died and his grandson became George III, the first Hanoverian king born in Britain. Like Pitt, the 22-year-old king had been on bad terms with George II and resented his royal predecessors' obsession with their German homeland. George III instead "gloried in the name of Briton," as he famously declared at the time. The ensuing rivalry between patriot king and patriot minister would shake up politics at midcentury.

Politics of Patriotism and Protest

One might well have expected George III and Pitt to make a great team. Pitt built his political career on challenging the "old corps" Whigs who had dominated political life under George II and forging alliances with Tories. The new king, similarly enthralled by the prospect of political housecleaning, had, as Prince of Wales, provided crucial support to Pitt as the latter fought his way to power in the early stages of the Seven Years War. Once on the throne, George awarded symbolic yet important appointments to Tories, welcoming a few to court as gentlemen of the bedchamber and installing others in prominent county posts. His most telling appointment, however, was that of his former tutor, the Scottish aristocrat John Stuart, the third Earl of Bute, to his cabinet. Bute's ministerial post represented more than the king's preference to promote some political "outsiders," be they Tory or Scottish or simply not "old corps." It was the practical expression of a governing philosophy, one that Bute had inculcated in the new king back when he served as George's teacher. Together, they hoped to assert monarchical independence, to reclaim control over patronage and policy, ceded by George I and II to the Whigs, back for the Crown. They saw it as ending corruption; their critics accused them of a power grab reminiscent of royal abuses of the last century. Both sides unleashed great propaganda machines, their mutual enmity transforming the public political debate.

This all played out against the backdrop of the Seven Years War. Pitt resigned from the cabinet in 1761 when his war plans were overruled, Newcastle in 1762 for similar reasons, and in early 1763

FIGURE 5.5 (a) William Pitt the Elder, by William Hoare, 1754. (b) Coronation portrait of George III, by Allan Ramsay, 1762. (c) John Stuart, third Earl of Bute, by Joshua Reynolds, 1773.

George purged their remaining supporters from office in a move they dramatically decried as the "Massacre of the Pelhamite Innocents." As the Pitt–Newcastle coalition lost its hold of the ministry and the war, Bute's grew. New to ministerial politics in 1760, he was already secretary of state by early 1761 and First Lord of the Treasury (and effectively prime minister) by 1762. In 1763, he too resigned, but only after bringing to an equally quick close the Seven Years War, which Pitt and the British forces in India and North America had stunningly, but very expensively, turned from defeat to triumph. Bute ended Pitt's war, but Pitt and his friends meanwhile ended Bute's ministerial career. Latching onto Bute's political inexperience, they suggested that his ascendancy came from some nefarious influence the "favorite" (a label with ominous historical associations) exerted over the young king and his mother, with whom they suggested Bute was having an affair. Anti-Scottish prejudice was whipped up too. Bute, an earnest family man whose passion was botany, was deeply shaken by the personal attacks (even though his camp gave as good as it got) and left office.

He remained, however, a close adviser to the king and the assaults continued, most notably from John Wilkes, an outspoken businessman, journalist, politician (MP since 1757), and libertine. The vehicle for Wilkes's campaign against Bute was his newspaper, *North Briton* (started in response to the pro-Bute *Briton*). On April 23, 1763, in issue no. 45, he upped the ante, aiming his criticism at George III and a speech the king had delivered in Parliament praising the recent peace treaty. Wilkes denounced the terms of treaty, declaring any praise for it a blatant lie, and by implication the king a liar for having uttered such praise. The alternative explanation, that the king was duped by his minister, was equally unflattering: "A despotic minister will always endeavor to dazzle the prince with high flown ideas of the prerogative and honour of the Crown," Wilkes bemoaned. "I wish as much any man in the kingdom to see the honour of the Crown maintained in a manner truly becoming

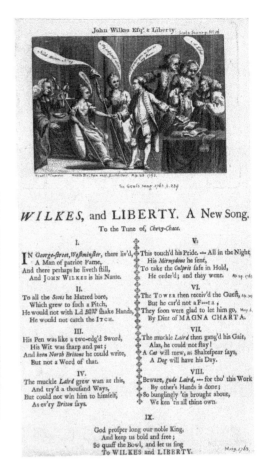

FIGURE 5.6 "Wilkes and Liberty":
(a) caricature of Wilkes by William Hogarth,
1763, (b) and (c) celebrations of Wilkes.

Royalty. I lament to see it sunk even to prostitution."[11] The government ordered Wilkes arrested with a general warrant on grounds of seditious libel; he counter-sued for his immediate release, citing immunity from such prosecution as an MP. Wilkes announced at the trial that his case would "teach ministers of arbitrary principles that the liberty of an English subject is not to be sported away with impunity, in this cruel and despotic manner."[12] He won: "Wilkes and Liberty!" became a triumphant slogan across London (figure 5.6). To strip Wilkes of his parliamentary immunity and proceed with the seditious libel charge, the government next accused him of blasphemy for an obscene, anticlerical poem he coauthored. The House of Commons duly expelled him from its membership on moral grounds, but Wilkes had already fled to France.

It is difficult to talk about political parties in the old way during this period. Various Whig factions scrambled for power, and ministries turned over with astonishing speed between Bute's resignation in 1763 and George III's appointment of Lord North as prime minister in 1770. Successive groups of Whigs both led the government and the opposition. The problem was to find politicians simultaneously acceptable to the king and effective in the House of Commons. All ministries, however, were hampered by Wilkes, the genie that Pitt's struggles with Bute had unleashed from its bottle, for Wilkes broadened the political debate. What had begun as a critique of Bute and particular policies had morphed into one against royal prerogative and a state that trampled on its citizens' rights. This would become the mantra of political protest—from Wilkes and his supporters when he eventually returned home, and from North American colonists frustrated by taxes and other measures to which they were subject. The first salvo of the American conflict, like the Wilkes conflict, had its roots in the recovery from the Seven Years War and invoked the language of the Bill of Rights.

The ministry of George Grenville (1763–65), responsible for Wilkes's arrest and parliamentary expulsion, also passed the Stamp Act of 1765 that transformed relations with North America. Grenville had been an opposition Whig for the past decade, upset like the king, Bute, and so many others by the cost of the war. Concern extended, beyond the sheer magnitude of the debt, to how the burden of defending the colonies was disproportionally borne by British taxpayers over colonial ones. The Stamp Act's duties on newspapers, dice, and legal documents would not go far in rectifying these problems, but they demonstrated parliamentary authority to tax and legislate for the colonies, bypassing the colonial assemblies, and establishing a precedent for future impositions. Grenville preemptively asserted when introducing the bill, "The Parliament of Great Britain virtually represents the whole Kingdom."[13] He was out of office, however, by the time news of colonial resistance reached Britain, leaving it to the next ministry to respond to cries of "No taxation without representation," violence (especially in Boston, where the Sons of Liberty organized), and a united colonial petitioning campaign and boycott of British trade coordinated by the Stamp Act Congress. Merchants and manufacturers in Britain also petitioned in support of their colonial trading partners and in defense of their now suffering business. The new prime minister, the Marquis of Rockingham (1765–66), secured repeal in 1766, aided by Pitt's outspoken opposition to the Stamp Act and the principles underlying it (figure 5.7). But the government simultaneously passed the Declaratory Act, which decreed, in statutory form, Parliament's power to legislate for the colonies "in all cases whatsoever." This pattern—Parliament repealing a hated tax while maintaining its right to have imposed it—would repeat in coming years. After the Townshend Acts, customs duties levied in colonial ports in 1767, unleashed another round of colonial violence and nonimportation agreements, their impositions on glass, paint, lead, and paper were all

FIGURE 5.7 *The Repeal, Or the Funeral of Miss Ame-Stamp*, by Benjamin Wilson, 1766.

removed (1770). One duty, on tea, was left in place, another provocative reminder of Parliament's legislative sovereignty. That decision would, fatefully, contribute to the Boston Tea Party in 1773 and more generally to colonial assertions of the rights of freeborn Englishmen.

As the opposition to the Townshend Acts gathered speed, John Wilkes returned home. Rather than slipping quietly into the country, the cautious approach for an "outlaw" with charges still pending against him, Wilkes stood in the general election of 1768 as candidate for Middlesex, the populous county that included London. His plan to shroud himself again with parliamentary immunity depended on his popularity among the urban voters of Middlesex, perhaps the most democratic of all constituencies, and the protection of his old ally William Pitt, now Earl of Chatham and head of yet another in the revolving cycle of ministries. The former delivered, electing the hero of 1763 on his old platform of "Wilkes and Liberty." The latter did not. Wilkes was arrested on the old charges before the session began, and on May 10, 1768, Parliament's opening day, troops opened fire on a group of his supporters protesting his imprisonment. Seven died, more were injured, and Wilkes published from jail an attack on the government for the "Massacre at St. George's Field." These events resulted in his second expulsion from the House of Commons. A new election was called for Middlesex, Wilkes stood and won again, and was expelled again. And again. Finally, after the fourth contest, the House of Commons seated Wilkes's defeated opponent, a man whom the majority of Middlesex voters had rejected. Freeholders of Middlesex petitioned in 1769 in defense of their electoral rights (the issue was now much bigger than Wilkes and his rights) and petitions followed from other constituencies. Some even suggested that the king dissolve the current Parliament.

In Wilkes's more immediate defense, business- and professional men, and even some country gentlemen, founded the Society of Supporters of the Bill of Rights in 1769. It was originally chartered to pay Wilkes's debts but unleashed a nationwide popular political movement. It was anti-aristocratic and civil libertarian. It also advocated parliamentary reform: the right of a constituency to send to Parliament anyone they wanted, more frequent elections, and more equal representation. Colonists in North America contributed to the society's Wilkes defense fund. They also toasted him (with mugs and punch bowls bearing his image), and the Sons of Liberty corresponded with him. The town of Wilkes-Barre, Pennsylvania, was even named in honor of Wilkes and an MP who had spoken passionately against the Stamp Act.

Questions of representation thus played out on both sides of the Atlantic, focusing respectively on colonial taxation and parliamentary reform and reinforcing one another in meaningful ways. The Middlesex petitioners' demands went unmet, and Wilkes remained in jail until 1770. Yet when he returned to Parliament in 1774, finally as MP for Middlesex, he spoke in defense of the American colonists' cause. The ministry was now securely in the hands of Lord North, a Whig who steered a middle course through the factional upheavals of the 1760s and won the support of the king. In 1773 North sought to improve management of affairs in both India and North America. The Regulating Act of that year reformed the administrative structure of the East India Company, the government increasing its oversight of the company that controlled ever larger swaths of the subcontinent. Of particular interest to the EIC was its tea trade, and with the Tea Act (1773) North reduced the duties on tea re-exported from Britain to the colonies. In effect, this lightened the customs burden of the old Townshend duty, but it also challenged the extensive colonial protest market in smuggled tea and provided yet another demonstration of Parliament's much-resented legislative powers. Bostonians responded with a dramatic demonstration of their own, dumping a shipment of newly arrived tea into the harbor on December 16, 1773, prompting in turn North's quick passage of the four Coercive Acts of 1774. Though the new measures targeted Bostonians—closing Boston's port and moving the

A New Method of MACARONY MAKING, as practised at BOSTON.

FIGURE 5.8 *A New Method of Macarony Making, as Practiced in Boston*, 1774. Print depicts the January 1774 tarring and feathering of customs officer John Malcolm by Bostonians, whose hats celebrate Wilkes and the Sons of Liberty.

customs house to Salem, enhancing the powers of the Massachusetts governor at the expensive of its assembly, permitting trials of Massachusetts citizens outside the colony, and increasing opportunities for billeting British troops there—the threat was felt throughout the colonies. The continental congress that convened in Philadelphia in September 1774 demanded the immediate repeal of the Coercive Acts and the removal of British troops from Boston, arguing that it was illegal for the Crown to maintain troops in a colony without the colonial assembly's consent.

In Britain, too, many were horrified by both the harshness of the measures and how they inflamed an already tense situation. In January 1775, Chatham ended his speech in the House of Lords in favor of troop withdrawal from Boston by declaring that when America's "inherent, constitutional rights are invaded, those rights she has an equitable claim to the full enjoyment of, by the fundamental laws of the English constitution, and ingrafted on the constitution by the unalterable laws of nature; then I own myself an AMERICAN; and feeling myself as such, shall, to the verge of my life, vindicate her rights." Other Americans, he warned, could be found in "every Whig," in Ireland "to a man," and in the multitudes of "Englishmen" soon to awaken to colonists' cries.[14] Protestant Dissenters, still smarting under the restrictions of the Test Act, certainly had reasons to identify with their co-religionists in the colonies, as did businessmen with their trading partners. Thus, even after shots were fired in Lexington and Concord, and a war for independence underway, many in Britain took the rebels' side. But many did not. "Interested as we are in this contest," a London newspaper editor confessed in a moment of professional confusion, "it indeed little becomes us to be dogmatical and decided in our opinions in this matter, when the public, even on this side of the water, is so much divided."[15] On the other side of the water, there was division too, with notable loyalist support in the colonies. Among the most enthusiastic defenders of the Crown in North America were, as we have seen, thousands of enslaved persons, the so-called Black loyalists, to whom Britain offered freedom from their colonial masters in exchange for military service. In November 1775, Virginia's royal governor, Lord Dunmore, issued the following declaration, a clear invitation to slaves to run away: "I do hereby further declare all indented Servants, Negroes, or others, (appertaining to Rebels,) free that are able and willing to bear Arms, they joining His MAJESTY'S Troops as soon as may be, for the more speedily reducing this Colony to a proper Sense of their Duty, to His MAJESTY'S Crown and Dignity." In so many respects, it was a civil war (figure 5.9).

FIGURE 5.9 Depiction of loyalist troops in the American Revolution, including a Black loyalist.

Like Lord Dunmore, the North ministry sought to exchange freedoms for loyalty. Keenly aware of the need for troops and the demands of security in its global outposts, the government made modest overtures to Catholics to better integrate them in the project of empire. In 1774, as things were heating up in the 13 colonies, the Quebec Act granted toleration to Catholics in that formerly French territory. Four years later, the Catholic Relief Act of 1778 addressed injustices closer to home, removing three particularly harsh, and never enforced, laws against Catholics (one of which made being a Catholic priest a felony). Both were enlightened and strategic policies, but both sparked Protestant outrage. In Britain, the Protestant Association, founded by the charismatic Lord George Gordon, organized a repeal campaign. A crowd of 40,000 to 50,000 marched to Parliament on June 2, 1780, to present a petition, signed by 120,000, begging for the repeal of the Catholic Relief Act. When the House of Commons voted overwhelmingly (6 to 192) to deny the petitioners' request, some attacked a nearby Catholic chapel. Six days followed of what contemporaries described as "universal anarchy ... approaching desolation." The looting and destruction included attacks on Catholic chapels and homes throughout the city, the breaking of Newgate and four other prisons and the release of their inmates (figure 5.10), and an attempt to destroy the Bank of England. It took 10,000 troops and the imposition of martial law in London to quell

FIGURE 5.10 Depiction of the attack on Newgate, June 7, 1780.

the disturbances. Over 300 people, and possibly as many as 1,000, died in the violence. Of the 450 rioters arrested, 160 people were brought to trial, 62 were sentenced to death, and 26 were hanged. The Gordon Riots, as they were known, revealed the depth of anti-Catholic feeling that persisted long after elimination of the Jacobite threat. Catholic France's recent entrance into the American War perhaps contributed to the situation, as did the challenges to British identity caused by its expanding empire and the war itself—the very issues that had inspired the Catholic Relief Act in the first place. Meanwhile, the government's response to the rioting—the use of troops and martial law in the metropolis—inflamed old fears of arbitrary royal power and a standing army at home. It was a lose-lose situation.

In 1779, the same year that Gordon founded the Protestant Association, some country gentlemen initiated a very different "plan of association" to combat the corruption and poor leadership they blamed for the war's mounting costs and losses. The association movement, modeled after the Yorkshire Association established by clergyman and landowner Christopher Wyvill, demanded "economical reform," the reduction of inefficient government spending. Their concerns resembled the Tory critique of costly wars at the start of the century. By now indirect excise taxes had replaced the land tax as the go-to wartime revenue source, placing a disproportionate burden on consumers and the poor. But the landowning associationists nonetheless worried that they, and all taxpayers, were underwriting the patronage system through which others were profiting from the war. They also sought parliamentary reform, of a kind that would give more weight to voices like theirs, by redistributing seats in the House of Commons to increase county representation (and reduce the influence of placemen and pocket boroughs) and mandating more frequent elections. Breaking the Septennial Act in order to encourage MPs' accountability to their constituents was, typically, a radical demand. Country gentlemen were now advocating it, too, and using their clout as wealthy electors to try to implement it. Association members refused to vote for any candidates who did not pledge to support the movement's platform in the Commons.

This "back-bench" revolt, coupled with the persistent demands from opposition Whigs to end the war, made it hard to push on after the British surrender at Yorktown in October 1781. "Oh God, it is all over," North conceded, perhaps a tiny bit relieved, upon learning of the Yorktown defeat.[16] Three months later, Henry Conway, a retired general and outspoken Whig critic of the war, sought to make it official. On February 12, 1782, Conway proposed, in the House of Commons, to cease hostilities. Many such motions had been made before, but Conway's succeeded with a majority of 19 votes. After 12 years as prime minister, over half of them embroiled in the American War, North resigned, leaving George III furious over both losses. Others would negotiate the terms of the peace settlement and the recovery to follow, though it was unclear for a while just who that would be. Three ministries followed in the next year and half. The one appointed by George III in an apparent act of desperation at Christmastime 1783 would last for a couple decades.

After Revolution in North America

Britain had lost battles in the eighteenth century, but losing a war, and one against upstart rebels, was an unprecedented and uncomfortable experience. Spending an also unprecedented amount of money in the process made it even more uncomfortable. And surrendering a vast, protected market to an uncertain commercial future was downright terrifying. It would be over a year until the Peace of Paris was signed. In the meantime, domestic housekeeping became the order of the day, and the new ministry, assembled in March 1782, embraced the spirit of economical reform articulated by the association movement.

The new prime minister, the Marquis of Rockingham, last held that office in 1765 when he had repealed the Stamp Act. George III did not like him then, and Rockingham's consistent opposition to the war had not endeared him to the king in the intervening years. But Rockingham now commanded a parliamentary majority and, as North reminded the king upon tendering his resignation, George therefore had to work with him. Representing the Rockingham ministry in the Commons was Charles James Fox, son of Henry Fox, and even more abhorred by the king than Rockingham, again for his support of the American cause but also for his way of expressing it—with brilliance, exuberance, and extravagance. Fox, for example, made a habit of dressing in the buff and blue colors of George Washington's army. Fox was a stunning orator and a willing risk-taker, who had lost £140,000 at the London gaming tables by the age of 25 and was destined to lose a lot more. He was, in other words, a dangerous politician and he had already taken direct aim at George III and the monarchy over what he perceived as the undue influence of the Crown. Fox's political philosophy had been greatly influenced by another member of the Rockingham circle, indeed its intellectual leader, the Anglo-Irish writer and MP Edmund Burke. What this group liked about economical reform, even more than its fiscal responsibility, was that its attack on patronage and placemen undermined royal power. Their reform agenda was transforming government when, three months into his ministry, Rockingham died.

The other branch of the Whig opposition were the Chathamites, heirs to Pitt, who had died in 1778 after collapsing in the House of Lords, fittingly on the occasion of an early motion to conclude the war. While the Rockinghams embraced their Whig identity, the Chathamites, like the great "patriot minister," distanced themselves from it, preferring to operate above party. This made their leader, the Earl of Shelburne, more amenable to the king, and he followed Rockingham as prime minister and finished negotiating the peace. But with Fox and North challenging the Shelburne ministry from either side, it fell in 1783. A peculiar, and clearly self-serving Fox–North coalition—the king's enemy and the king's friend—replaced it.

Fox continued his crusading reform work, inspired by Burke, this time taking on the august power of the East India Company. Their East India Bill would wrest governance in India from the chartered trading company, establishing instead a board of political appointees for fixed terms.

But an attempt to end one form of corruption reeked of another, for the proposed commissioners were all Whigs, even Fox–North friends, who would obtain control of the EIC's enormous vast patronage powers. The king seized on the hypocrisy to threaten and cajole the House of Lords to reject the bill that had just cleared the Commons. The next day, the king replaced Fox and North, on the basis of their legislative failure, with William Pitt the Younger.

The implications were many. Pitt was first elected MP in 1781, at the age of 21; now he was appointed prime minister at the ripe age of 24. He had some ministerial experience, having served as Chancellor of the Exchequer in Shelburne's brief ministry, but his great appeal to the king was in fact his relative inexperience. Pitt had not been in Parliament for most of the American War; he had not agitated against it nor participated in the factional infighting over it. His father had of course opposed the war, but Pitt cloaked himself more in the mantle of Chatham's independence than his opposition. In policy and temperament, the younger Pitt was actually a closer heir to Wyvill; he refused, for example, the sinecures that typically came with his new office (despite being a financially strapped younger son), and he endorsed an association-style program of modest parliamentary reform (which failed in Parliament). Moreover, though Pitt and the king publicly denied it, George III had consulted Pitt before engineering his coup in the Lords. The whole affair, Fox would complain, violated the rights of the Commons and added new charges to his critique of royal corruption and abuse. Fox was making a radical argument: The king did not have an absolute right to choose his ministers, but that the choice rested in the Commons, and by extension in the electorate. Fox and Pitt were now in direct competition for control of the Commons, just as their two fathers had been following Pelham's death in the 1750s. In the battle of the sons, the Pitt family again prevailed, but Fox went on to perfect the politics of opposition, and their rivalry would redefine party identity and behavior for decades (figure 5.11).

For Pitt's ministry to succeed on purely practical grounds, he needed to command a majority in the House of Commons, but the Fox–North coalition still possessed that. The king thus dissolved Parliament in March 1784 and called a general election, three years before the Septennial Act would have required a new one. The election was, in effect, a referendum on Pitt versus Fox, or more precisely Pitt and George versus Fox. The king and his chosen minister used the extensive government patronage system, its money, safe seats, and talented election managers. But the decisive action took place in the larger, more open constituencies where government influence held less sway. There, Fox's allies, many of them incumbents, fell, their defeat so associated with him that they became known as "Fox's martyrs." Fox's enemies had cast him as Oliver Cromwell, the seventeenth-century MP who had led the victorious army against Charles I, oversaw the abolition of the monarchy, and became lord protector of the republic that followed. "Mr. Fox wants to get the better of the King and be the lord protector," one election commentator reported.[17] That, coupled with recent accusations of Fox's power grab for the patronage of the East India Company, did his party in. Pitt, despite his alliance with the king, appeared to many the anti-corruption reformer.

FIGURE 5.11 (a) Charles James Fox, by Joshua Reynolds, 1782. (b) William Pitt the Younger, by George Romney, 1783.

Yet candidate Fox was reelected in the London borough of Westminster, a crowded, open district that, as home to Parliament and the royal court, had a highly politicized electorate. There he countered the negative elements of the Cromwell charge, offering himself instead as the "champion of the people," and enlisted the help of the "Women of Westminster" to make his case to the voters. Chief among his numerous and mostly elite "female canvassers" was Fox's friend Georgiana, fifth Duchess of Devonshire. Much has been made of the duchess's involvement, both by contemporaries and historians. Her mixing with the urban, male electorate was satirized in prints that depicted her kissing butchers or lifting her skirt for eager cobblers to examine her feet, and there were hints in others of a sexual relationship with the candidate (figure 5.12). Historians have also emphasized the "transgressive nature" of her behavior: how she was not canvassing for a family member, the most common role for women in electoral politics; how she neglected traditional domestic duties to campaign for Fox; and how Westminster was so unusual a constituency that what happened there would not be repeated elsewhere. Recent scholarship suggests, however, that Fox deliberately employed the "Women of Westminster" in his campaign to demonstrate that he was committed to the interests of the people. His propagandists emphasized female sensibility and virtue, suggesting that women's disenfranchisement guaranteed their political independence and disinterestedness. They were, in other words, the antithesis of one immersed in the business of East India Company patronage. The duchess and her associates, though unable to vote at the polls, thus voted in the public sphere in a way that lifted a tarnished candidate.[18]

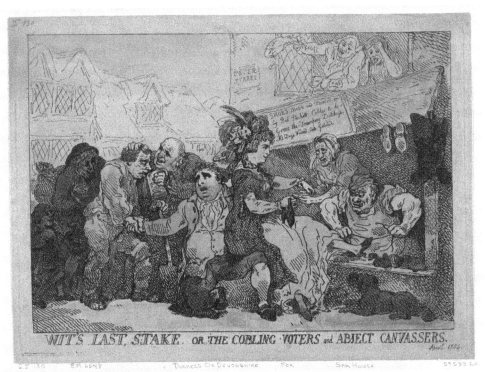

FIGURE 5.12 (a) Georgiana Cavendish, fifth Duchess of Devonshire, by Thomas Gainsborough, 1783. (b) *The Chairing of Fox*, by W. Holland, 1784. (c) *Wit's Last Stake*, by Thomas Rowlandson, 1784.

So did some other, more numerous but less prominent, female residents of London. Pitt had recently proposed an annual tax on anyone who employed a "maid servant." It seemed an uncontroversial new levy; the government argued that employing a servant was a luxury, so the tax would fall lightly and voluntarily on the rich, and there was already the precedent of a similar duty on male servants. But, in fact, relatively humble urban households employed servants, and a maid-of-all-work was far less a luxury than a male servant. Worried that the tax threatened their livelihoods, female servants cried out against it, and Fox the opposition candidate took up their cause. In 1778, the House of Commons had ended the longstanding practice of allowing women to observe its debates from the visitors' gallery, restricting women's political access in a real and a symbolic way. Just six years later and in the very same London borough, "gender was constructed" in the Westminster election "as a difference that was part of, or even essential to, the proper functioning of the electoral system. While women had played a role in electoral politics long before this period, the election called forth an explosion of interest in the political function of women, as individuals and as a group, in the rebuilding of a truly public sphere for Britain."[19] We saw similar developments in the involvement of women in the abolition movement (discussed in chapter 4) that emerged at roughly the same time.

That project of "the rebuilding of a truly public sphere" was as much a part of the postwar recovery in the 1780s as rebuilding the economy. The latter was the special preoccupation of the new administration of Pitt the Younger. While trade with North America rebounded fully and quickly, fiscal recovery took a bit more work. In 1783, the national debt was £238 million and growing; even in peacetime, spending exceeded income. It was a circular problem, for much of the expenditure went to paying the interest on the debt. In 1784, the annual cost of servicing the debt was £9 million. Pitt's administration committed itself to reversing the trend by raising revenue, ideally in ways that did not impede economic growth, and earmarking some new sources specifically for debt redemption. Administrative reforms and anti-smuggling policies (such as lowering duties as a disincentive for fraud) increased yields on existing taxes. When new revenue sources were needed, Pitt supplemented the already heavy excise and customs duties with annual license fees on luxuries goods and services with inelastic demand. In terms of the debt, he established a "sinking fund" in 1786, an inviolable source of revenue that could only be used for liquidating the debt. Walpole and Pelham both had sinking funds but eventually raided them. Thanks to a decade of peace, Pitt's started to chip away at the debt. More broadly, he experimented in ways to promote economic growth. His administration created new government boards dedicated to trade and agriculture and negotiated free trade treaties with a number of European nations. In many of these ways, Pitt proved a disciple Adam Smith, author of *Wealth of Nations* (1776). Smith in turn held the post of commissioner of Scottish Customs from 1778 until his death in 1790, thus serving the Pitt administration in his last years.

Pitt's economic policies were classically liberal. In the social and political spheres as well, he supported a number of reform causes, including moderate parliamentary reform, in the 1780s. Yet the rivalry in which he was engaged with Fox defined Pitt as the politician on the right. Both men had arisen within the Whig Party, and as they campaigned in the general election of 1784 both probably would have identified themselves as Whig (or at least the inheritors of Whig principles and politicians). But so complete was Pitt's electoral victory that year, and so full-throated Fox's opposition to the partnership of Pitt and the king, that thereafter they functioned as the leaders of two opposing parties. Fox's group kept the title Whig and emphasized its oppositional traditions dating back to the late seventeenth-century critique of an over-mighty Crown. Pitt, meanwhile, emphasized his loyalty to king and country and won over the Tory backbench. Though he would eschew this title too, he emerged over time as the leader of a remodeled Tory party.

The Whig opposition, with no immediate chance of gaining power, allied itself with the Prince of Wales, heir to the throne and, in true Hanoverian fashion, at odds with his father. Kings-in-waiting had cultivated alternative court cliques throughout the eighteenth century, offering the promise of power to political friends once on the throne. George III's eldest son was no exception. Indeed, his profligate ways (he had a penchant for actresses, architecture, clothes, gambling, and partying) made him especially vulnerable to friends in Parliament who might take his side in fights with George III and the ministry over money. He also needed cover for his illegal, not-so-secret marriage in 1785 to a Catholic widow and commoner, Maria Fitzherbert. Royal father and son could not have been more dissimilar in style and temperament; in contrast to the prince, the king was a devoted husband and father of 15 (two died in infancy), sober in his personal dealings, and obsessed with farming. While the caricaturists depicted the king as simple, somewhat doltish "Farmer George," they had even more fun depicting the decadent, drunk, and indebted Prince of Wales, often in disarray after a busy night out (figure 5.13). Similar contrasts were made between prime minister and leader of the opposition. Pitt, like Fox, was an outstanding parliamentary orator and heavy drinker, but there the similarities ended. Pitt was by varying accounts cold or shy, a workaholic, and life-long bachelor. One of the reasons George III despised Fox back in 1781–83 was that flamboyant politician's careful cultivation of the then-20-year-old prince. Those dynamics only intensified

FIGURE 5.13 Caricature of Prince of Wales (future King George IV), by James Gillray, 1792.

as the prince grew into a bored, spoiled, and power-hungry middle-aged man and Fox's position in opposition grew more entrenched.

This interplay between family and party tensions exploded in a political crisis in the autumn of 1788 when George III, who suffered from the then undiagnosed condition of porphyria, had an acute attack, which contemporaries understood as madness. This was not the first time it happened, nor would it be the last—the king's symptoms returned in 1801, 1804, and 1811—but in 1788 the need to declare a regent to rule on behalf of the incapacitated king threatened the political status quo. The Prince of Wales and his Foxite supporters were thrilled by the prospect of a regency and did everything they could to grant the prince, as regent, unlimited royal powers. Pitt's ministry sought both to limit the terms of the regency and to delay its enactment. Three months of parliamentary wrangling ensued in which Fox, the great critic of monarchical authority, ironically defended the prince's hereditary right to rule without restrictions, and Pitt argued for parliamentary oversight. George III's recovery in February 1789 preempted the Regency Bill's vote in the House of Lords, and the king and his ministry, the prince and the opposition, returned to business as usual. A few months later, revolution in France would upend British political life in more lasting ways.

After Revolution in France

Britons were already thinking about revolution when one started in France in 1789. Not only had the one hundredth anniversary of William's landing in England been celebrated in November 1788, making the timing of the Regency Crisis especially poignant, but particular groups organized to push for additional reforms, to continue what they claimed to be the unfinished business of the settlement of 1689. Dissenters led the way, calling for the repeal of the Test and Corporation Acts, though without any immediate success. Abolitionists had reason to be more optimistic. It is probably no coincidence that the first piece of abolition legislation was passed in 1788, the Dolben Act, which regulated the inhumane conditions onboard slave ships, making them a tiny bit—but just a tiny bit—less horrific. Pitt and Fox, in a rare show of bipartisanship, both supported the Dolben Act. It is intriguing to ponder what might have happened to these reform agendas, as well as Pitt's free trade program, had the French Revolution not intervened and, by 1793, returned Britain to war against its great enemy of the eighteenth century.

At first, Britons watched events in France with interest and from a distance. There was some smug satisfaction that Frenchmen were at last copying Britain by embracing a constitutional monarchy and challenging the authority of the Catholic Church. Perhaps even more exciting was the fact that Britain's chief commercial and imperial rival was now otherwise engaged, distracted by events at home. But as the violence mounted across the Channel, as Parisians stormed the Bastille and released its prisoners, reminding many of the terrible events of the Gordon Riots less than a decade ago, responses intensified. A public debate unfolded in print, begun by Edmund Burke, now making his famous journey from

Whig opposition to Tory conservatism (that culminated in a tearful goodbye to his old friend and ally Fox on the floor of the Commons as Burke switched benches). Mary Wollstonecraft and Tom Paine responded to Burke, and others to them, as Britons—rich and poor, male and female, enfranchised and disenfranchised, urban and provincial, English and Irish (and Scottish and Welsh, for revolution meant different things in different parts of the British Isles)—debated the meaning of events in France and the future of Britain. That war of ideas was discussed in chapter 4. Here we will explore the political fallout.

Fox's response to the storming of the Bastille was characteristically enthusiastic: "How much the greatest event it is that ever happened in the world, and how much the best!"[20] He and a small group of Whig politicians subsequently participated in a new type of anniversary celebration: Bastille Day parties on July 14. In Birmingham, on the second anniversary in 1791, approximately 90 people gathered for such a banquet at the Royal Hotel. Protesters gathered too, outside the hotel, and attacked the diners as they departed. They then burned down the hotel before heading to the New Meeting

FIGURE 5.14 Caricature of Edmund Burke, Marie Antoinette, and Burke's *Reflections on the Revolution in France*, 1790.

Chapel, where the scientist and dissenting clergyman, Joseph Priestley, an attendee at the Bastille-day dinner, served as minister. Rioters set fire to Priestley's chapel and other dissenting churches in town. Priestley and his family escaped their home just in time; it too was burned and looted, its library and collection of scientific instruments destroyed. The Birmingham rioters, who included members of loyalist "Church and King" clubs, had received support from local magistrates. In response to the night's destruction, George III wrote to one of his cabinet ministers, "I cannot but feel better pleased that Priestley is the sufferer for the doctrines he and his party have instilled."[21] The rioting, meanwhile, continued in Birmingham for three more days.

Others took a more defensive approach. In 1792, a lawyer named John Reeves founded the Association for Preserving Liberty and Property Against Republicans and Levelers. Soon there were over 2,000 such organizations, more succinctly known as Reeves societies. The republicans and levelers about whom they worried included members of the corresponding societies, radical political organizations which also had a network throughout Britain, the most famous of which was the London Corresponding Society (LCS). Founded in a London tavern in January 1792 by shoemaker Thomas Hardy and a handful of friends, the LCS declared that "the number of our Members be unlimited." Anyone (or any male) could join who paid one penny per week, dues low enough to allow the participation of tradesmen and artisans like Hardy, and pledged support to the proposition that "the welfare of these kingdoms require that every adult person, in possession of his reason, and not incapacitated by crimes, should have a vote for a Member of Parliament."[22] Tom Paine's call for universal male suffrage, articulated with such force in his *Rights of Man*, found expression in a new kind of political association organized exclusively by working people.

In this heated climate, the government sought to close the discussion down. In May 1792, the king issued the Royal Proclamation Against Seditious Writings and Publications. While this had some effect on the dissemination of texts like Paine's, it did not stop the political work of the corresponding societies that the government now feared, without any evidence, would make common cause with the Jacobins in control of events in France. After the execution of Louis XVI in January 1793, and the declaration of war between Britain and France in February, the government began arresting radical leaders at home. Some were apprehended at a national convention of corresponding societies in Edinburgh and then transported to Australia where they could cause less trouble. Thomas Hardy was arrested in his home in London on charges of high treason in May 1794, his papers confiscated for examination by a special parliamentary committee. He and other London radicals were subsequently acquitted by a London jury that rejected the government's alleged connection between reform and rebellion. After that, the government changed the laws with the "Two Acts," or "Gagging Acts," of 1795. First, the Seditious Meetings Act outlawed public gatherings of more than 50 people, stopping the big outdoor meetings the LCS was holding that year at Copenhagen House. Second, the Treason Law tightened the definition of that crime so that future juries would not find it so easy to acquit the likes of Thomas Hardy (figure 5.15). Government spies, meanwhile, were used to report on radicals and assist in the implementation of these laws. Fox, for his part, complained that under this state of affairs, merely proposing modest parliamentary reform, as he had done in 1792, could place one on the wrong side of a treason charge. Pitt, once a moderate reformer, was accused of his own "reign of terror."

The government was truly concerned about Jacobins at home in Britain, but also in Ireland, who might aid a French invasion. But more immediately, it worried about the sort of domestic disturbances caused by frustration and want. The great economic dislocation of war—unemployment, military mobilization, economic shortages—coincided with several disastrous harvests in the mid-1790s. Food prices skyrocketed; the cost of bread, the mainstay of the poor, seemed to double overnight. The meetings at Copenhagen House were as much to complain about food prices as to demand parliamentary reform. Also on the agenda was taxation as the wartime tax burden climbed to an extraordinary 35 percent (of both commodity output and per capita income) by the end of the wars. In 1795, Pitt's government tried to kill two birds with one stone by imposing a luxury tax on the use of hair powder. If rich society members cared enough about their wigs to pay the tax, the state would have a bit more money to wage its war; if they chose to avoid the duty and stop pouring starch on their heads, the poor would have more (or cheaper) bread. Either solution would be an improvement to the current situation. The hair powder tax, alas, did not end up helping much, but Britain's first direct income tax, a progressive measure with a graduated payment scale, did. Such a tax was the sort

FIGURE 5.15 Satirical depiction of the Two Acts, 1795.

of measure that the wealthy in Parliament had studiously avoided imposing on themselves for the entire eighteenth century, instead letting the excise burden, felt most heavily by the poor, grow and grow. But in 1799, they accepted Pitt's income tax as a temporary wartime measure.

The first year of the new century also welcomed Britain's first census, implemented, as noted in chapter 1, to assess the nation's human resources—the men and women needed to keep the military, voluntary defense forces, and economy going at a time of national crisis. As Linda Colley has pointed out, the government was as masterful at mobilizing the British people as it was at suppressing radicalism and dissent. Votes were still out of the reach of the many, but everyone was welcome, and armed, as citizen soldiers in defense of the state, and most everyone heeded the patriotic call (figure 5.16). The consequences of this experience would have profound effects on the political process and reform movement after the return to peace in 1815. By that point, Pitt and Fox would both be dead. George III would be permanently incapacitated by his illness, and the Prince of Wales would now be an experienced regent for the king. Prince George would

Supplementary-Militia, turning out for Twenty-Days Amusement. ____ 'The French Invade us, hay?____ damme who's afraid?'

FIGURE 5.16 Satire of wartime mobilization, by James Gillray, 1796.

also be estranged from his wife (having been forced to abandon Mrs. Fitzherbert and, in 1795, to marry his cousin Caroline of Brunswick in exchange for payment of his debts) and about to subject Britain to a sordid divorce case to keep her from becoming its queen. This strange event would connect the domestic life of royalty and the interests of radical reformers in a way both reminiscent of, and so very different from, the stories surrounding the warming pan baby that helped kick James II off the throne.

IMAGE CREDITS

Fig. 5.4b: Source: https://commons.wikimedia.org/wiki/File:Dish_with_Capture_of_Portobello_by_Admiral_Vernon,_November_20%E2%80%9321,_1739_MET_DP-1143-002.jpg.

Fig. 5.4c: Source: https://commons.wikimedia.org/wiki/File:The_Honble._Edwd._Vernon_Esq._Vice_Admiral_of_ye_Blue_and_Commander_in_Chief_of_His_Majesty%27s_fleet_in_ye_West_Indies_(NYPL_b12349151-423996).tiff.

Fig. 5.5a: Source: https://commons.wikimedia.org/wiki/File:William_Pitt,_1st_Earl_of_Chatham_by_William_Hoare.jpg.

Fig. 5.5b: Source: https://commons.wikimedia.org/wiki/File:Allan_Ramsay_-_King_George_III_in_coronation_robes_-_Google_Art_Project.jpg.

Fig. 5.5c: Source: https://commons.wikimedia.org/wiki/File:3rd_Earl_of_Bute_by_Sir_Joshua_Reynolds.jpg.

Fig. 5.6a: Source: https://commons.wikimedia.org/wiki/File:William_Hogarth_-_John_Wilkes,_Esq.png.

Fig. 5.6b: Source: https://commons.wikimedia.org/wiki/File:John_Wilkes_Esqr._%26_Liberty_(BM_1868,0808.4320).jpg.

Fig. 5.6c: Source: https://museum.wales/media/10116/DA004588_01.jpg.

Fig. 5.7: Source: https://www.loc.gov/pictures/item/2006678564/.

Fig. 5.8: Source: https://www.loc.gov/pictures/item/2004673300/.

Fig. 5.9: Source: https://commons.wikimedia.org/wiki/File:Soldiers_at_the_siege_of_Yorktown_(1781),_by_Jean-Baptiste-Antoine_DeVerger.png.

Fig. 5.10: Source: https://collections.britishart.yale.edu/catalog/tms:22863.

Fig. 5.11a: Source: https://commons.wikimedia.org/wiki/File:Charles_James_Fox00.jpg.

Fig. 5.11b: Source: https://commons.wikimedia.org/wiki/File:George-Romney-xx-William-Pitt-the-Younger-xx-Tate-Britain.jpg.

Fig. 5.12a: Source: https://commons.wikimedia.org/wiki/File:Thomas_Gainsboroguh_Georgiana_Duchess_of_Devonshire_1783.jpg.

Fig. 5.12b: Source: https://commons.wikimedia.org/wiki/File:The_chairing_of_Fox_(BM_1868,0808.5238).jpg.

Fig. 5.12c: Source: https://commons.wikimedia.org/wiki/File:Wit%27s_Last_Stake,_or_the_Cobbling_Voters_and_Abject_Canvassers_MET_DP871763.jpg.

Fig. 5.13: Source: https://commons.wikimedia.org/wiki/File:A-voluptuary.jpg.

Fig. 5.14: Source: https://www.loc.gov/item/2004669854/.

Fig. 5.15: Source: https://commons.wikimedia.org/wiki/File:A_free_born_Englishman!_(BM_1935,0522.12.3).jpg.

Fig. 5.16: Source: https://commons.wikimedia.org/wiki/File:Supplementary-militia,_turning-out_for_twenty-days_amusement_by_James_Gillray.jpg.

CHAPTER 6

Economic Transformations

Discussions of the economic transformations of the long eighteenth century tend to invoke the word *revolution*. For all the sectors of the economy addressed in this chapter, historians have championed a revolution—the agricultural revolution, the financial revolution, the transport revolution, the consumer revolution, and the Industrial Revolution. There have been debates about their relationship to one another. Was an agricultural revolution, which produced more food using less labor, a precondition to industrialization? Did changing consumer tastes and preferences, and new advertising and marketing strategies, inspire innovation in manufacturing techniques and products, or did demand follow supply? More fundamentally, historians have challenged what defines an economic revolution. How high should rates of growth soar? Do increasing outputs have to be universal, or can they be concentrated in particular regions or products? And what should be done with the fact that many of the "revolutionary" developments of the eighteenth century had roots in earlier times. The identity and meaning of the economic revolutions of the eighteenth century have proved more contentious even than the political ones.

Most thorny of all is the Industrial Revolution. This was once the gold standard by which all other economic revolutions were judged. Indeed, the others tended to be seen as either preconditions (agriculture, finance, transport) or consequences (consumption) of the industrial changes that transformed Britain in the long eighteenth century. But then some economic historians challenged the very idea of an industrial revolution, suggesting that the experiences of a few industries (cotton and coal in particular) had obscured the fact that most manufacturing continued well into the nineteenth century in much the same way as before. Factories and new technology, it was argued, were the exception, not the rule; the biggest changes in most sectors were the application of more labor and capital. Moreover, annual rates of growth were slower than previously thought, and any transformation that occurred must be sought in the entire century rather than in a "take-off" period after 1760. The biggest changes, in fact, occurred in the first half of the nineteenth century. For the earlier period, a new term, the "industrious revolution," was even coined. It suggested that, starting in the seventeenth century, new foreign goods—tea, coffee, and china, for example—stimulated new demands, which in turn stimulated new economic behavior. Households that had previously been self-sustaining, producing for their own needs, now produced for the market in order to make money to purchase the new goods.

All this debate did not "dethrone" the notion of an industrial revolution, but it perhaps removed the capital I and R. As the historian Emma Griffin concluded in a review of the competing arguments, by the year 2000, "while most [scholars] agreed that a revolution had taken place, none could agree over exactly what it was."[1] The following chapter embraces such creative disagreements, for industry, but also for the other economic sectors under review. It aims to explore conflicting and overlapping developments, describing transformations but, as much as possible, avoiding too-neat labels that simplify the complexity of the past.

Agriculture

As Britain returned to peace after the long Napoleonic Wars, "the single most spectacular measure" enacted by Parliament concerned grain.[2] The Corn Law of 1815, which prohibited the importation of foreign wheat until domestic prices reached an average price of 80s. per quarter, artificially preserved the high prices that had marked the wartime food economy. This was not the first such statute; corn laws dated back to the Middle Ages, and one had been enacted in 1804. But this one came, stunningly, at a time when the government was embracing free trade, removing protections in other spheres of the economy. Landowners and farmers had sought the measure, which the government defended on the grounds that it would guarantee domestic production when prices were low, thereby preventing any possibility of shortage, starvation, and the civil unrest that tended to accompany them. Yet the passage of the act occasioned civil unrest. Troops secured Parliament as demonstrators protested in London against the new legislation which would, as the poet Byron lamented, "make a malady of peace."[3] The journalist and orator Henry Hunt was blunter still, declaring it for "the benefit and aggrandizement of a few rapacious landholders … at the cruel expense of the hitherto greatly oppressed community."[4] Radicals like Hunt seized on the corn laws as a potent symbol of the corruption of a political system in which legislative bodies dominated by landlords catered to their own interests. The price of bread would join the rights of man in fueling the parliamentary reform movement until the corn laws' repeal in 1846.

If the corn laws dominated political debate for much of the nineteenth century, their passage reveal many of the economic tensions of the preceding one. Fluctuating agricultural prices—low early in the eighteenth century, especially during the "agricultural depression" of the second quarter, and rising steadily thereafter—contributed to changes in agricultural practice. The enclosure of open fields, growth in farm size, diversification of crops, and transformation of labor patterns, all of which began before 1700, intensified in the eighteenth century as British farming became an ever more capitalist enterprise. Agricultural productivity, already high compared to most of continental Europe, increased as a result. Parliament assisted in these developments. So too did the press, as farming manuals, almanacs, and journals proved runaway best-sellers. But the imperatives of old customs and new markets often clashed, pitting landowners against the landless, producers against consumers, and community commitments against individual profits. The Corn Law of 1815 was a remarkable example of both old and new agricultural forces at work in British economic life, and the passions it inspired were a sign of how much was at stake.

Historians once argued that a revolution in agricultural practices resulted in increased efficiency and higher yields in the eighteenth century, which in turn fed a growing, urbanizing population, releasing laborers from the land to work in towns and industry. Recent studies have questioned the chronology and causality of this interpretation. As early as 1700, only 48 percent of the English and Welsh workforce was employed in agriculture, and urbanization and the demand for manufactured goods perhaps inspired increases in agricultural output rather than the other way around.[5] This was even more the case in Scotland where industrialization and urbanization started later but proceeded faster. "The voracious demands for food and raw materials of the urban and industrial areas helped to revolutionise agriculture and rural society throughout Scotland."[6]

In Scotland, bad weather led to harvest failure and, ultimately, famine in the 1690s. Contemporary references to the "seven ill years" or the "lean years" did not do justice to the economic and humanitarian disaster in which Scotland's population declined by approximately 15 percent due to death and emigration. The fateful Darien Scheme in Panama was promoted in response to this crisis, which also inspired Scottish settlement in Northern Ireland and North America. In England, commentators warned of hungry "wandering Scots 'dropping dead in the streets.'"[7] Subsistence production continued in Scotland well into the eighteenth century, with only a quarter of farmers producing for the market in the early decades (and violent protests erupting when they exported grain), but subsistence crises became a thing of the past.[8] That was not the case in Ireland, where the terrible effects of harvest failures in the 1720s prompted over 3,000 people to leave for North America. The "Great Frost" of 1740–41 was even more catastrophic; starvation and disease are thought to have claimed one-eighth of Ireland's population in just a year and half.[9] Yet in England, grain surpluses prevailed in the first half of the century. Despite there being more mouths to feed, England exported grain, earning the appellation "the granary of Europe." At home, the price of bread fell, and the distilling of spirits, especially gin, increased—both signs of a glut in grain.[10] It was at this time that the process of enclosure, by which open fields, commons, and waste lands were converted to discrete units for private use, entered a new and important phase. When grain prices were low, enclosure's advocates argued that it encouraged diversification away from cereals and toward "scientific" livestock breeding; when grain prices rebounded after 1750, that it encouraged efficient and profitable cultivation.

Under traditional landholding arrangements, individuals owned or rented land within three village fields that were farmed in rotation—one devoted to wheat or rye, one to other crops, and one left fallow. The community decided what to grow on the active fields, and everyone's animals grazed on the fallow. Pasturing also occurred on uncultivated commons, where villagers might also collect firewood or berries. The wastes were generally less productive common land, where similar activities took place and landless laborers could cultivate small plots and even build cottages. The latter was sometimes done with the encouragement of the parish officers, who granted the poor allotments on the village wastes.[11] Enclosure eradicated this system of communal cultivation, pasturing, and access to waste land. Individual owners exchanged their scattered strips in the open fields and rights to the commons for consolidated larger parcels, which they enclosed with fences and hedges, freeing them (or their tenants) to manage the land as each saw fit.

Enclosure had been going on for centuries. By 1700, 71 percent of English land had been enclosed; 13 percent of the remaining open fields, commons, and wastes would be fenced in over the course of the eighteenth century, and a little over 11 percent in the nineteenth. Most of this activity occurred between 1760 and 1820, first in the Midlands and then in the south, and reflected, in part, a change in procedures. Formerly, all affected landowners had to agree to enclose; it was a unanimous decision of the propertied of a community. After 1740, however, most enclosure

FIGURE 6.1 View of field enclosure boundaries.

proceeded by a private act of Parliament, to which only 75–80 percent of landowners had to consent. Small landowners, unable to afford the cost of fence building or the loss of community grazing rights, might oppose enclosure. Once overruled by larger landowners, they often sold their stake in the formerly open fields to those same rich neighbors.

Meanwhile, villagers with rights to the commons were compensated if—and this was tricky—they could provide legal proof. But most residents who had come to rely on the commons, and especially the poor who relied on the wastes, lost vital resources. Even Arthur Young, agricultural writer, first secretary of the Board of Agriculture (established in 1793) and tireless champion of agricultural "improvement," acknowledged the problem. "By nineteen out of twenty Enclosure bills the poor are injured and most grossly," Young confessed. "The poor in these parishes may say with truth, 'Parliament may be tender of property; all I know is, I had a cow, and an Act of Parliament has taken it from me.'"[12] Loss of a cow was serious business. A cottager could earn approximately £4 per year from raising a cow on the commons, and probably another £4 from the other activities (raising sheep, pigs, and poultry and collecting fuel) typically undertaken there.[13] Imagine, therefore, the human toll of a system by which not 19 or 20 acts, as Young contemplated in one locality, but over 3,000 acts enclosed almost 4.5 million acres of open fields and commons across the country; another 2,172 acts, focusing on commons and waste, placed 2,307,350 more acres in private hands.[14] To streamline the system, Parliament, which was indeed "tender" to property and the demands of the propertied, passed a general Enclosure Act in 1801.[15]

The actual work of enclosing did not always proceed smoothly. In late July 1765, the *Northampton Mercury* published the following ad: "*This is to give NOTICE to all Gentlemen Gamesters and Well-Wishers to the Cause now in Hand*, That there will be a FOOT-BALL PLAY in the Fields of Haddon" on August 1st and 2nd for "a Prize of considerable Value." Would-be participants were to assemble at any of Haddon's taverns between ten o'clock and noon. A week later, the *Mercury* reported that the footballers "soon after meeting formed themselves into a tumultuous Mob, and pulled up and burnt the Fences designed for the Inclosure of that Field" until order was restored by "a Party of General Mordaunt's Dragoons."[16] The Haddon fence breaking was clearly a well-planned affair in support of an anti-enclosure "*Cause now in Hand.*" It represented what historian E. P. Thompson famously called "the moral economy of the crowd," efforts on the part of ordinary men and women to assert their customary rights—in this case to reclaim commons—in the face of enclosing landowners' newly articulated and legally enforced property rights.[17] A similar sense of the moral economy emboldened poor women and children to continue gleaning, gathering the stray shafts of wheat that remained after the harvest. Gleaning had been permitted on open fields, and it, like gathering wood on the commons or waste, provided an important supplement to the domestic economy of the poor. Gleaning on enclosed lands, however, was deemed trespass and theft, as a controversial court case declared in 1788, and the loss of another customary right became the source of considerable personal hardship and public debate.[18]

In the Scottish Lowlands, enclosure had a similar reach and also inspired resistance. The "levelers revolt" in the southwestern region of Galloway began in 1724 in protest against early enclosures that created large private tracts of pasture for cattle being raised for the English market. But the practice continued, and between 1760 and 1790 enclosed fields transformed the topography of the Lowland zone. In the Highlands, agricultural "improvement" had an explicit political edge, more brutal even than the parliamentary process of enclosure. As discussed in chapter 3, entire communities were evicted in the Highland Clearances after the '45, part of the British government's punishment of Jacobite sympathizers, over 800 of whom were transported to the colonies. Seized land was turned over to "gentleman farmers" for enlightened cultivation, most notably profitable sheep farming, and the eradication of "feudal" agricultural techniques to weaken the Highland clans.[19]

In all these cases, large farms run by tenant farmers rather than owner-occupiers became the norm. The combination of these two elements—farm size and type of farmer—distinguished British agriculture in the eighteenth century. The average farm size in the south Midlands of England in 1700, already large, was 70 acres. Eighteenth-century enclosure efforts, particularly active in that region, resulted in typical south Midlands farms of 145 acres by 1800. By contrast, at least a third of Irish farms were under 50 acres, and many of the bigger ones were owned by absentee landlords. On the continent, farms were even smaller, with French farms averaging 30 acres throughout the period and well into the nineteenth century. Meanwhile, in Europe, peasant owners tended to work their own land; two-thirds of French farming was done in this manner. In England, however, 85 percent of farmland was managed by rent-paying tenants, who in turn hired agricultural laborers. This three-tier model, of landowner (who paid for long-term improvements like fences and roads), tenant-farmer (who paid for livestock, crops, and short-term improvements like draining and fertilizing), and wage worker, became the hallmark of British capitalist agriculture.[20] Scotland followed suit in the second half of the eighteenth century. The cottars, who had traditionally sustained themselves on small bits of land in exchange for seasonal work on larger farms and represented as much as a third of rural Scottish society, "virtually disappeared."[21] Within Britain, Wales's agricultural system remained the least capitalist and most resembled continental Europe.[22] In part for this reason, female-headed farms persisted in Wales to a degree not seen elsewhere in Britain. In the Welsh region of Caernarvonshire, approximately 18 percent of farmers listed in estate rental books in 1750, and 14 percent of all land taxpayers in 1800 were women.[23] Yet in Wales too, processes of deforestation and enclosure, begun in the sixteenth and seventeenth centuries, continued, and the second half of the eighteenth century saw the creation of local agricultural societies that encouraged experimentation with new farming methods.[24]

These developments had, everywhere, profound effects on the living and working conditions of agricultural laborers. Traditionally, farm work had been done in family units, with any additional labor coming from agricultural servants, young men and women hired on annual contracts who lived as part of the household. As landownership and use patterns changed, and fewer workers were needed per acre due to better efficiency, hiring practices changed too; day jobs or short-term seasonal contracts, such as for the harvest, replaced agricultural service. Steady employment thus became elusive at the same time as access to commons and waste declined. In this world of a tight agricultural labor market, women lost out to men. The overall result was that agricultural workers were increasingly adult men hired on a daily basis.

Few of the celebrated agricultural "innovations" of the eighteenth century were new. Most, like enclosure, had been tried before. But in the eighteenth century, they became established and, thanks to writers like Arthur Young, their use soon spread. The turnip offers a case in point. Though the aristocratic Whig politician Charles Townshend was credited with introducing the plant, earning him the nickname "Turnip Townshend," turnips were already in use in his native Norfolk. Unlike grains, turnips were compact and could be stored for long periods of time, providing a reliable food source for livestock that otherwise had to be slaughtered over the winter. This allowed herds to grow, and more animals meant more manure, which in turn meant better fertilized soil. Meanwhile, cultivating clover and other nitrogen-fixing legumes, also in use since the seventeenth century, proved a far more efficient way to revitalize land than letting it lay fallow. The famed "Norfolk rotation"—planting wheat/turnips/barley/clover in succession—kept soil fertile and in constant use. It provided better nutrition for animals as well as making them better food sources for people. The amount of land devoted to growing turnips and clover thus increased by a factor of five between 1700 and 1850, while the amount left fallow declined. Selective animal breeding meanwhile produced some sheep that grew faster, and others that produced more milk. While enclosure did not make all of this possible, enclosed villages tended to cultivate turnips and clover, and experiment in selective animal breeding, more than open field villages.

Much has been made of Irish agriculture's failure to embrace the cultivation—indeed the cult—of turnips and clover. Arthur Young, reporting in 1780 about a recent tour of Ireland, declared with equal parts confidence and criticism that "in the management of arable ground, the Irish are five centuries behind the best cultivated of the English counties." Yet Irish farmers were neither stubborn nor ignorant in their reluctance to follow English examples. Clover and other enriching grasses grew naturally in Ireland and thus did not require expensive planting there. Meanwhile the potato served a similar, even superior, purpose to the turnip. Not only were potatoes fodder for livestock, but they fed people too; richer (per acre of cultivation) in calories and vitamins than grain, potatoes became a healthy staple in the diet of the Irish poor. Thanks in part to the potato, starting in the 1770s Ireland fed a growing population while simultaneously exporting grain to England. This only stopped in the 1840s when the disastrous Irish potato famine hit. By that time, however, Ireland had been exporting one-third of its grain output and thereby feeding one-tenth of the English population.[25] And, ironically, when high grain prices led to fears of famine in Britain in 1795, the Board of Agriculture, on which Young served, published an encouraging pamphlet entitled "Hints Respecting the Culture and Use of Potatoes."[26]

Concerns about grain exports, imports, and prices were, as we have seen, at the heart of the Corn Law of 1815. While that legislation set a minimum price level, regulating importation on behalf of producers, there were much older policies that established price ceilings, levels above which the cost of bread could not or should not rise. Such consumer-friendly practices dated back centuries and were part of the customary rights that constituted the "moral economy." Magistrates traditionally oversaw the sale of grain and bread, regulating markets in ways that guaranteed the "just price." With the rise of capitalist agriculture, such paternalist practices fell by the wayside. Yet at times of acute distress, when bad harvests and high prices threatened subsistence, and some farmers and forestallers withheld produce from market until prices rose even more, consumers took action in ways much akin to the enclosure protests. They forced sales and set prices, sometimes demanding that magistrates assist. These bread "riots," as the authorities called them, were often (though by no means always) peaceful, and women, who did the family marketing, participated in and sometimes led them. In these conflicts, as in the passage of enclosure acts, we can glimpse how issues of food production and sale were as much political as economic in the long eighteenth century.

The Political Economy of Empire: Practice and Theory

Britain's financial revolution created what John Brewer has called the fiscal-military state, widening economic, financial, and commercial networks across the globe.[27] The components of this process included the establishment of the Bank of England, the growth of the national debt, commodity markets and colonial possessions, and Britain's involvement in the slave trade.[28] Fiscal innovations expanded the availability of short-term loans that funded new industries like fire insurance, partnership banks, and trading companies and improved infrastructure with new canals and roads. They created "a whole range of securities in which mercantile and financial houses could safely invest" or disinvest.[29] Long-term public borrowing created an alternate revenue stream for the government and compensated for the shortfalls of taxes that, though relatively high, did not bring in enough money to pay for the ships and men necessary for the almost constant conduct of war over the long eighteenth century. In addition to the Bank of England, London housed the Royal Exchange and Lloyd's Insurance Market, the sites and products of the financial revolution.

The commercial expansion of Britain and its empire is a hallmark of the eighteenth century. British trade extended across the globe to India, China, Japan, Africa and the Americas. But the British were not alone in these endeavors. Fierce competition for trade raged between Britain and the European empires of France, the Netherlands, Spain, and Portugal. Empire was key to the growth of trade in Britain. After the union with Scotland in 1707, free trade was established with

Scotland, which, like the North American and Caribbean colonies, became a market for English manufactured goods. Ireland too was envisioned as a market for English goods. Britain was also a very active trading partner in the Indian Ocean world.

In England, exports rose from £6.4 million in 1711 to £7.5 million in 1721, £8.4 million in 1731, and £9.1 million in 1741, mostly due to an increase in manufacturing output. Exports of iron and steel rose from 16,770 tons in 1765–74 to 30,717 in 1795–1804, and as the empire grew in the eighteenth century so too did trade within it. Most commerce was conducted with Europe at the start of the eighteenth century, but by 1797 North America and the Caribbean took center stage as Britain's trading partners: The "New World" received a full 57 percent of British exports and supplied 32 percent of Britain's imports. Britain's trade was four times that of France.[30]

Trade with the colonies in North America and the Caribbean took off after the settlement of Virginia in 1607 and Barbados in 1625. Lured by the promise of plentiful work and the prospect of cheap land, 350,000 people crossed the Atlantic from England in the seventeenth century. In 1686 these colonies shipped over £1 million of goods to London, a hub that then shipped them out again to markets throughout Britain and Europe. Imports from the colonies included sugar, tobacco, and tropical groceries; exports to the colonies included woolen textiles. By the mid-eighteenth century the textiles sold in North America diversified to include linen and cotton fabrics. Metalware and hardware were also exported to the colonies, which were restricted in what they could manufacture.

What came to be called the triangular slave trade supplied unfree African labor to work the tobacco, rice, and sugar plantations in the Atlantic colonies. In 1698, the Royal African Company lost its monopoly, and private merchant houses funded the trade. Britain became the leader of the world slave trade with Jamaica the empire's largest and wealthiest slave colony. Textiles, metalware, food, and re-exported goods filled the slave ships on the way to Africa where they were traded and bartered for enslaved people. The routes were rarely triangular though: complicated trade paths moved between colonies and to and from Europe. Liverpool and Bristol were busy slave ports, the sites of slave auctions. The slave trade stimulated British manufacturing production by the derived demand for goods such as plantation utensils and clothing needed for enslaved laborers.[31]

As the trade hub of a global empire, London also housed its financial center. There was no stock exchange building in the seventeenth century, and shares were traded at two coffee shops in central London: Garraway's and Jonathan's, the latter named after its owner Jonathan Miles, who opened it in 1680. The business took off and by 1690 London housed at least 100 companies selling stocks. The financial market formed another imperial network of information, commerce, and confidence, and the value of stocks rose and fell according to the reports exchanged in gossip, news, and speculation. Boys were paid to collect news at the docks or from the houses of wealthy merchants and to bring back whatever intelligence they could find.

The stock market was tremendously important to the growth of the British Empire as it provided the capital necessary for imperial expansion. Despite regulations put in place in 1697, the nature of the venture inevitably led to unscrupulous practices such as the rigging of markets and the use of insider information. Ironically, the profits from trade with Europe and domestic markets far exceeded trade with Africa, Asia, or the Americas, but commercial interaction with distant and seemingly exotic imperial partners lured many investors who sought to participate. The South Sea Bubble of 1720 was the first stock market crash, prompted by the promise of profits from imperial trade with new markets, especially with Spain's South American colonies.

Robert Harley, a Tory leader, founded the South Sea Company in 1711 to rival the Bank of England, which he saw as the political arm of the Whigs. An act of Parliament granted the company a monopoly to conduct England's trade with Spain's South Sea colonies in the West Indies and South America. The promise of profits from trade in the Americas led eager investors to demand shares. Many envisioned the profits coming from the *asiento de negros*, which was the right to traffic in African slaves and to exchange them with the Spaniards in South America for payment in gold. Britain's conquest of Jamaica in 1655 provided a convenient stopover point in the long and arduous journey from Africa on the way to the final destination in the mines of Peru. In addition to transporting the enslaved, the *asiento* ships were used to smuggle profitable textiles and other manufactured goods. Slaving was the key to this prosperous trade with South America.

These trading opportunities envisioned by the company's founders never materialized. In the Peace of Utrecht (1713), the company secured a contract to transport and sell annually in Spanish America 4,800 *piezas de Indias*, a unit of the slave trade, equivalent to an adult slave of a certain height with no visible physical defects. The same contract also allowed the company to send one ship a year to trade with the Spanish colonies. This was to be the wedge into the Spanish colonial market. The company contracted with the Royal African Company to supply slaves; 13,000 enslaved persons were transported by the company's ships between 1713 and 1718. The horrors that awaited those who reached the Americas were compounded by the inhumane conditions and high mortality rates on the crowded ships.

When Britain's relationship with Spain weakened in 1718, the trade came to a stop. With Parliament's approval the company's directors shifted their focus almost immediately to high finance: the refinancing of Britain's huge war debt. False stories of the company's success resulted in the buying frenzy discussed in chapter 5. In January 1720, the price stood at £128, in March it reached £330, and in June it hit £1,050 a share. The directors held stock worth far more than the company's earning power, and just before the public realized it, many sold their shares. The crash hit in September. By December the stock was valued at £128 again. Banks failed when they could not collect loans on inflated company stock. Hard currency was scarce. Houses stood half built and abandoned. Other companies were caught up in the speculative bubble before it burst. Thousands of investors in Britain were ruined.

FIGURE 6.2 South Sea Bubble playing cards. Ace of Diamonds depicts a Welshman traveling to London to buy company stock.

FIGURE 6.3 Jack of Hearts suggests the relationship between a female investor's stock and marital prospects.

Although the crash had devastating consequences for investors, the Bank of England averted a systemic threat by underwriting the South Sea Company's scam, restoring Britain's financial stability. Overseas trade continued to expand in the 1720s and 1730s, albeit more slowly as financiers found other ways to raise capital. Fire destroyed Jonathan's coffee shop in 1748, but it was rebuilt and first renamed Stock Exchange and then Stock Subscription Room. It was officially designated as the London Stock Exchange in 1801 and soon became the city's most important financial institution.

The economic theories underlying these developments were part of the Enlightenment's project of knowledge production discussed in chapter 4. As Britain's financial revolution unfolded, commentators debated the role of the state and the relationship between the generation of wealth, morality, and virtue. Theories about the economy varied widely during this period. In the sixteenth and seventeenth centuries many believed that what came to be known as mercantilism held the key to economic prosperity. The system depended on maintaining a high level of bullion. Barring discovery of new mineral deposits, one country could increase its share of precious metal only at the expense of others. A nation acquired bullion by maintaining a favorable balance of trade with each of its trading partners. If the value of British exports to France, for example, exceeded the value of French exports to Britain, France had to make up the difference in gold or silver. In other words, mercantilism valued accumulation and equated wealth and money. The accumulation of money was accomplished through encouraging exports, especially of manufactured goods, discouraging imports, and granting monopolies.

The belief that trade generates wealth and is stimulated by the accumulation of profits envisioned a closed system of exchange and encouraged government intervention in regulating the economy by means of protectionism. Ideally a colony should provide raw materials for and purchase finished goods from the metropole. Since finished products always cost more than the materials from which they are made, this approach would increase the national wealth. One attempt to regulate colonial trade was the passage of the Navigation Acts in 1651 and 1660 to promote English (later British) self-sufficiency by restricting colonial trade and decreasing dependence on imported goods. The acts stipulated that all trade was to be conducted in British ships, staffed by British mariners, trading between British ports and those within the empire. Thus, East India Company tea would have to be shipped via London before it went to the colonies. This legislation constricted intercolonial trade and led to a great deal of smuggling and resentment, especially in the North American colonies.

The state intervention in the economy, encouraged and built into the philosophy of mercantilism, was quite anathema to advocates of free trade. Adam Smith articulated the theoretical basis of free trade in his 1776 publication *Inquiry into the Nature and Causes of the Wealth of Nations*. Discouraging the popular government policies regulating markets, setting prices, and prosecuting speculators, Smith posited that individual pursuit of self-interest would create wealth through an "invisible hand." According to Smith "the sovereign has only three duties to attend to … the duty of protecting the society from violence and invasion … the duty of protecting, as far as possible, every member of the society from the injustice and oppression of every other member of it, or the duty of establishing an exact administration of justice, and the duty of erecting and maintaining certain public works and certain public institutions." Unlike the mercantilists who urged their rulers to protect markets and restrict imports, Smith wrote that the greatest facilitator of domestic production was "to grant the most perfect freedom of trade to the artificers, manufacturers and merchants of all other nations."[32]

Recent scholars have pointed out that Smith and the other contemporary critics of mercantilism grossly oversimplified the world economy of the eighteenth century. These historians challenge the idea that a "mercantilist consensus" dominated politics. While some eighteenth-century economists and politicians believed in zero-sum economics based on acquisition of gold and silver, others took a more expansive view. Human labor, they argued, not bullion, produced wealth. Increased production and expanding markets, not conquest of territory, made a nation rich. In their conception of trade and commerce, new wealth could be created almost indefinitely. Given the lower cost of labor in the 13 North American colonies, it made sense to manufacture some things there. There was, therefore, no clear dichotomy between the metropole and its colonies.[33]

If no single theory governed eighteenth-century political economy, the practice of trade and commerce was also more complex than previously imagined. Historians once divided imperial commerce into legal trade and illegal smuggling. They explained the flouting of mercantilist regulations as "salutary neglect," the inability of the Crown to enforce the law due to its preoccupation with events in Europe. This simplistic division of the global economy into lawful and lawless sectors does not work because the same merchants, middlemen, and carriers might simultaneously engage in both, often with the tacit acceptance or even active complicity of customs officials. The imperial economy consisted of "a complex, multilateral trading system,"[34] including companies, banks, individual merchants, and kinship networks. A contemporary account by one New Yorker in 1762 illustrates how the system worked: "Our importation of dry goods from England is so vastly great, that we are obliged to betake ourselves to all possible arts to make remittances to the British merchants," he wrote. "It is for this purpose we import cotton from St. Thomas's and Surinam; lime-juice and wood from Curacoa [sic]."[35]

Imperial pathways carried goods and ideas across the globe; the tremendous growth of the British Empire and its economy also moved people to Britain as well as away from it. In response an intermittent debate unfolded in the press and in Parliament about the place of foreigners seeking to settle in Britain, their rights, and whether the government ought to pursue policies that encouraged or discouraged immigration. The kinds of arguments that took place reflected the difference of opinion between advocates of mercantilism and free trade. In the late seventeenth century and into the beginning of the eighteenth there had been several moments when populationists urged the government to encourage immigration, believing it would increase prosperity. Some argued that more liberal immigration policies would decrease the price of labor and promote freer trade. Others claimed national wealth depended on a growing population. The opponents of naturalization were those who supported mercantilist policies and included anyone who represented or had a stake in monopolies, city corporations, and guilds, foremost among these, the Corporation of London.

The empire featured in multifaceted ways in these arguments. The writer John Toland, who supported naturalization, argued for the need to replace English people "who yearly go to the Plantations, and in the service of the East India Company; not to speak of our Armies, Fleets, or Adventurers." Others proposed that new immigrants move to less settled areas in the British Isles. This internal colonization would serve "for breaking up and cultivating those desert, yet not barren grounds, of which there is still but too great a quantity in Scotland and Ireland ... under the name of Heaths, Moors, Bogs, Fens, and Commons."[36]

The subject emerged again in the midcentury after the War of Austrian Succession. The war's expense had increased the national debt by more than £30 million and an inconclusive peace did not seem to resolve the imperial disputes and rivalries, particularly with France, that had caused the war in the first place. Social and economic dislocation, the demobilization of 80,000 sailors and soldiers, unemployment, and crime in the postwar period exacerbated panic in the city of London. Populationists proffered a solution to the widespread unemployment and increasingly visible poverty, arguing that encouraging immigration would rebuild England's strength after the war and expand commerce.[37]

Domestic Markets

Britain re-exported many of the goods it imported. Tobacco grown in North America's Chesapeake, for example, was sent throughout Europe after landing at the ports of Glasgow and London. But a lot of tobacco stayed in Britain too. It is estimated that 25 percent of the population used tobacco by 1670 and that annual per capita consumption reached approximately 2 pounds in the first half of the eighteenth century. Tobacco was Britain's "first mass consumer import," though soon to be outpaced by tea, sugar, and more.[38] Such foreign goods, as well as domestically produced food and manufactures, found markets in a society being reshaped by developments in transportation, communication, and urbanization. Commodities and people were on the move in eighteenth-century Britain.

The cost and speed of transportation can either inhibit or encourage economic activity. In the eighteenth century, falling costs and rising speeds accomplished the latter. When it came to moving people, stagecoaches traveled an average of 1.96 miles per hour in 1700, with slightly faster trips in the summer and slower ones in the winter. By midcentury, the average journey speed had increased slightly to 2.26 miles per hour. But by 1820, on the eve of the railway era, stagecoach travel rates had tripled to 7.96 miles per hour with seasonal differences getting smaller.[39] What this meant for travelers is that the journey from Bath to London, which took approximately 50 hours in 1700, could be made in 1800 in only 16 hours. Even more dramatically, the almost 11-day trek from Edinburgh to London fell to a mere two and a half days over the course of the century.[40] Fares (never low) increased slightly, but after adjusting for inflation it appears that faster trips were achieved at little or no additional passenger expense. Thanks to better roads, a clergyman publishing on the subject in 1767 observed that "the carriage of grain, coal, merchandise, etc., is in general conducted with little more than half the number of horses with which it formerly was."[41] Goods in fact cost 40 percent less (in real terms) to move on roads at the end of the century than at the beginning, and freight transport by water was cheaper still.[42] Parliament was again in the thick of it all. Much as enclosure legislation reshaped the agricultural landscape, private acts of Parliament redrew the national map, granting individuals and groups the right to build roads, extend rivers, and dig canals. Throughout Britain, transport routes appeared where none had existed before. The economic theorist Adam Smith approved. "Good roads, canals and navigable rivers," he declared, "are the greatest of all improvements."[43]

Since Tudor times, road maintenance was handled locally, with parish rates collected and parish labor used to maintain roads within parish lines. This system faltered in the face of growing traffic, and an additional approach, experimented with in the late seventeenth century, was embraced in the eighteenth. Turnpike trusts, authorized by acts of Parliament to purchase land, build and maintain roads, and charge tolls became the rage. This new pay-to-travel model had its critics; turnpike gates, like enclosure fences, were sometimes attacked. In 1735, Parliament classified turnpike destruction a capital crime, thereby protecting the system it simultaneously extended with 25 new turnpike acts that decade. The arrangement was apparently here to stay: The century's two busiest turnpike-construction decades, the 1750s and 1760s, saw the passage of 170 such laws apiece and the creation of a national network of roads, and tollbooths continue to populate highways today. In Scotland, state involvement with road building was even greater. In addition to turnpikes, which proliferated after 1790, military roads, built in the Highlands in response to Jacobite disturbances in the early eighteenth century, were modernized by a government commission established in 1803. Keeping pace with all the new roads were new vehicles—bigger wagons for freight and faster, more comfortable coaches for passengers. Professional carriers emerged to serve both metropolitan and provincial markets, traveling on set schedules and contracting with innkeepers along the way for meals and overnight stops.[44]

Nonetheless, moving goods on roads cost four or five times what it did to ship them by river, and Britain was blessed with many navigable rivers. London, though inland, was a port city—indeed, it was Britain's largest port—thanks to the tidal Thames River, which connected it to the sea. The Severn, flowing from Wales through the Midlands to Bristol, was also a major trade route. But rivers did not go everywhere and often followed circuitous paths. In response, parliamentary legislation granted "river navigation companies" legal authority to reroute, widen, and even extend several rivers, an undertaking that typically involved huge investments of capital, seizure of land, and eventually levying tolls. Navigable river routes almost doubled as a result, from 850 to 1,600 miles in the period 1690–1750.[45]

Canal projects, more complicated engineering feats that often required creating reservoirs and locks and diverting water long distances, became popular in the second half of the century, culminating in "canal mania" in the 1790s. While it required eight horses to pull a 6-ton wagon by road, a single horse on a canal tow-path could manage a 25-ton barge. Canals therefore provided easy transport for heavy materials like coal. Over half the canal acts passed by Parliament by the year 1803 served collieries; the first of this class, opened by the Duke of Bridgewater in 1761, carried coal from the mines on his Worsley estate to the nearby manufacturing center of Manchester (figure 6.4). Coal-rich Wales mobilized to construct four major canals in the 1790s. Where canals were built, coal production increased, prices declined, and profits soared. On the other end of the spectrum of goods, fragile ceramics also fared better traveling by water than bumpy road, and the 93-mile Grand Trunk Canal, which linked the Mersey and Trent Rivers, ran conveniently through the pottery region of Staffordshire. Commercial centers with no navigable waterways, like Birmingham, hub of small metalware production, found canals particularly useful; building began on its first canal in 1768, overseen by the director of the Bridgewater project. Much of the construction had occurred on the duke's own land with his own money, but more often land was acquired by canal companies, incorporated entities in which local parties typically bought expensive shares. So potentially fraught were negotiations between companies and landowners that Parliament's canal acts called for the establishment of juries to determine proper compensation when mutual agreement failed. The total cost of land, construction, and maintenance of canals reached £8 million in 1795 and £20 million in 1815. Canal building represented the biggest infrastructure project of the day and one of the most profitable investments.[46]

All such developments in transportation facilitated better communication. The towns of Norwich and Bristol were home to the first provincial newspapers, founded in 1701 and 1702, respectively. By 1785, there were 45 such periodicals printed in 34 towns, and for much of the century Newcastle

FIGURE 6.4 Bridgewater Canal.

supported three papers simultaneously in print. The provincial press reported on local events, but it also reprinted "intelligence"—political, military, social, and financial news—from London. Copies of metropolitan newspapers were rushed to the provinces where local publishers, often duplicating items verbatim, kept residents abreast of events unfolding in the larger world. London's booksellers, manufacturers, and shopkeepers in turn hawked their wares in advertisements in provincial newspapers, sparking corollary trade in goods. Meanwhile, the postal service, founded in the seventeenth century, was reformed to take advantage of the new transport routes. No longer did all mail, regardless of origin and destination, have to travel via London, thus speeding delivery times.[47]

Equally mobile, it seems, were people. In an era of rapid population growth, not all communities changed at the same rate: the number of inhabitants expanded astronomically in some but stagnated and sometimes shrank in others. This can be seen at the county level, where over the last four decades of the eighteenth century the population of largely agricultural counties grew much more slowly than the national rate of 37.4 percent. Counties with considerable industry, however, vastly exceeded the average national growth rate with Lancashire, center of cotton textile production, leading the pack with a population that doubled in size in those four decades. Scotland and Wales experienced similar internal variations in growth. Such differences, demographers have concluded, are best explained by patterns of urbanization.[48]

In 1700, when approximately 17 percent of England's population lived in towns with at least 5,000 residents, over two-thirds of the town dwellers clustered in London. The capital's population increased steadily throughout the eighteenth century at rates consistent with national population growth. Yet by 1800, as much as 27 percent of the national population lived in towns. A great surge in urban living thus occurred beyond London, especially in the Midlands and the north. The population of Manchester, in the county of Lancashire, increased tenfold over the century, to a population of 89,000 in 1800. Norwich, in the eastern county of Norfolk, had since medieval times been England's second city. By 1800 it was eclipsed in size not only by Manchester but also by Birmingham, Leeds, Liverpool, and Sheffield, all of which had under 10,000 residents back in 1700 when Norwich boasted 30,000. By 1820, Britain had six cities with more than 100,000 inhabitants: London and Manchester, but also Birmingham, Edinburgh, Glasgow, and Liverpool. The presence of two Scottish centers on this list is significant, for Scotland experienced even more dramatic urbanization than England in the eighteenth century. In 1700, its capital Edinburgh had only 30,000 residents, and Glasgow 15,000. As late as 1775, still only 12 percent of Scots lived in towns with 5,000 residents or more. Yet by 1800, Scotland had caught up with England, with 27 percent of its population concentrated in urban areas and, strikingly, the majority of this growth coming in just one decade, 1790–1800. The trajectory continued. Glasgow grew faster than any other western European town of its size in the first three decades of the nineteenth century.[49]

Elsewhere in the British Isles, the story proved quite different. Wales too had its towns, and several grew in the eighteenth century, especially those that served as centers for particular economic activities. In the south, copper manufacturing spurred Swansea's expansion; in the north, Carmarthen sported both an active port and the Welsh printing industry. Still, the census of 1801 revealed that, at the dawn of the nineteenth century, not even 15 percent of the Welsh people lived in towns with 1,000 residents or more. In the next census, in 1811, only four Welsh towns had populations of over 5,000. This would soon change, with Wales becoming a profoundly urban place as the nineteenth century progressed, but at the end of the Napoleonic Wars it hovered on the cusp of this dramatic development.[50] Across the Irish Sea, Ireland too remained predominantly rural. Dublin was the extraordinary exception that proved the rule: It tripled in size over the eighteenth century, from 60,000 to 180,000 residents. Some northern cities also showed impressive growth—Belfast went from approximately 13,000 to 18,000 residents in the short period 1782–91—but Irish urbanization did not keep pace with the expansion of its general population.[51]

Given the crowding, poor sanitation, and contagion that characterized urban life, cities experienced higher than average mortality rates. Increasing fertility offset this a bit, but the growth in eighteenth-century Britain's urban populations came overwhelming from migration. People, quite simply, were moving in droves to cities and towns.[52] Goods flowed in too—food to feed the urban populace and building materials with which to house them. But most of the teeming cities were, like London, centers of commerce and manufacturing from which commodities were sent across Britain and the world. The combination of new goods—both foreign and domestic (some of the latter, like calicoes and ceramics, imitations of Indian and Chinese "exotics")—and concentration of people turned towns into shopping centers (figure 6.5). Josiah Wedgwood's pottery works were in Staffordshire, but in 1774 he opened a London showroom to display and sell his pieces. Londoners would browse, a wholly new way of shopping, buying Wedgwood's "Queen's Ware," creamware named to capitalize on the patronage of his royal customers Queen Charlotte and Catherine the Great of Russia. Advertising, celebrity endorsements, and the power of social emulation were all deployed to shape consumer demand. Not just the big towns, but small ones too sported booksellers, chandlers, mercers, drapers, and the like. Tax records suggest that in 1759 the ratio of people to shops in England and Wales was 43:1. Even at rural markets and fairs, where most of the goods were agricultural, ceramics and glassware were sold.[53] Mail-order business, thanks not only to newspaper advertisements and improved transportation but also to the proliferation of merchandise catalogues and retail warehouses, proved brisk. Peddlers and hawkers were sophisticated salespeople, enticing consumers with the latest fashions and offering credit.

Moralists debated these developments at the time. Was the pursuit of "luxury" goods a virtue, stimulating the economy, or a vice? Should such items be taxed? And what was to be made of women's roles as consumers? Did their "feminine nature" lead them in a dangerous pursuit of fashion (figure 6.6)? More recently, historians have debated how far the craze to consume, and the more fundamental ability to purchase new products, extended down the social scale. Especially at times of rising grain prices, the majority of the population had no choice but to focus its

FIGURE 6.5 A London shop, *The Repository of Arts, Literature, Commerce, Manufactures, Fashions and Politics,* 1809.

purchasing power on food and other necessities. When buying new durable items, they tended to "trade up" on basic goods—replacing, for example, wooden plates with earthenware ones. Still, a

FIGURE 6.6 Linen market, Dominica, by Agostino Brunias, c. 1780.

thriving secondhand market in clothing and the omnipresence of pawnbroker shops suggest how intimately everyone was involved in the world of buying and selling. And in the second half of the century, poor laborers often owned some of the new fashionable items of the day, a clock, or a mirror, or a teapot.[54] In 1757, the political economist Joseph Massie divided society into the following four groups: "Labouring Families," "Families which Drink Tea or Coffee Occasionally," "Families which Drink Tea or Coffee in the Morning," and "Families which Drink Tea, Coffee, or Chocolate, Morning and Afternoon."[55] He was perhaps wrong about laboring families, some of whom had apparently started to drink tea at least "occasionally." He also employed these categories in an attack on the sugar lobby, "that Rapacious Monopoly." Whatever Massie's motivations, however, and whether perfectly accurate or not, his schema provides a stunning illustration of how central domestic markets and consumption patterns, especially of new goods like tea, coffee, and chocolate, were in the eighteenth century.

Manufacturing

Industrialization in Britain in the eighteenth century was a process—gradual, inconsistent, and haphazard. By 1800 British manufacturing accounted for 25 percent of national income. The three industries that thrived most dramatically in the eighteenth century were coal, iron, and textiles. Coal and iron provided the equipment and infrastructure. Textiles made up over 50 percent of exports by value in 1750 and over 60 percent by 1800.

FIGURE 6.7 *An Iron Forge*, by Joseph Wright of Derby, 1772.

The transition from work done largely or exclusively by hand or with animals to work done with machinery necessitated raw materials and technologies of production. The raw material was coal. Indeed, coal fueled Britain's industrialization, specifically the stationary steam engine and the railway locomotive and the mass production of iron, which rose 200 percent between 1788 and 1806. With huge reserves of accessible coal in Northumberland, Durham, north and south Wales, central Scotland, Yorkshire, Lancashire, Cumbria, the Midlands, and Kent, the output of British mines rose to 3 million tons by 1700 and kept growing. Coal output doubled in the second half of the eighteenth century, reaching 15 million tons by 1800, aided by steam pumps, attached to James Watt's steam engine (developed sporadically from 1763 to 1775), to reach deeper seams. Water was the best way to convey these huge amounts, prompting, as we have seen, the construction of the canal network. The technical expertise of coal viewers, managers of the large collieries, combined with the capital provided by large landowners, often from agricultural rents, paid for these expensive enterprises. Whole families provided the hard labor required for coal mining: In the pits male miners hewed the coal with picks while women and children hauled the coal to the surface. Working conditions were difficult, unhealthy, and dangerous.

Wales was particularly engaged in, and affected by, the coal industry. As early as 1688, coal represented approximately 90 percent of all Welsh exports. This, combined with the discovery of iron and copper deposits, generated considerable wealth and made Wales by the 1730s "the greatest metallurgical centre in the world."[56] The development was by no means easy or smooth. Much of the Welsh population was forced to transition from a subsistent agrarian society to an industrial one, a process that accelerated at the end of the century, and farming became a more capitalist venture as it did elsewhere in Britain. Mining advocates also urged wealthy Welsh landowners to invest in local industrial enterprises rather than, as one interestingly put it, choosing "to rummage the East and West Indies for Money."[57] This reference to distant commercial ventures is a fruitful reminder of how interconnected all elements of the imperial economy were. Copper and brassware produced in Wales found a thriving market among slave traders on the coast of Africa, and some Welsh, like other Britons, profited from slave plantations.[58]

Another important raw material was cotton, which was mass produced on slave plantations in North America. Demand for cotton rose domestically. Once spun, dyed, and woven, cotton fabric was colorful, printable, and cheap—not to mention more comfortable and more easily washed than Britain's woolens—and became an item of mass consumption. In the colonies, the slave owners who produced so much of the raw material in turn bought cheap, imported British-made cotton clothing for their enslaved laborers. This incredible global demand resulted in cotton replacing wool as England's specialty, and cotton textile production became a centerpiece of Scottish industry as well. Cotton was adaptable to the fly shuttle loom, first introduced by John Kay in the 1730s, and in particular James Hargreave's spinning jenny invented in 1764 and Richard Arkwright's water-powered spinning frame built in 1770. The fly shuttle allowed a single weaver to weave much wider fabrics; once mechanized, automatic machine looms sped the hand process and halved the work force. The spinning jenny allowed much faster production of cloth because just one worker operated eight or more spools (this rose to 120 spools as technology advanced). The thread made by the spinning jenny was not very strong, but Arkwright's water-powered spinning frame produced much stronger thread, solving that problem. The technological breakthroughs associated with cotton spread eventually to other textiles, including wool and linen. Factories sprang up in Derbyshire and Lancashire in the 1760s, and Scotland in the 1780s. Cotton accounted for very little of the textile industry in 1750; in 1810 it made up 39 percent.

The process of mass production began early. Between 1600 and 1750, in the absence of factories, manufacturing often took place in the countryside. Those with capital wanted to avoid the highly regulated labor markets in the cities, which had been controlled by the guilds, and rural areas were closer to the raw materials necessary for production. The various terms *cottage industry*, *outwork system*, *domestic system*, or the *putting out system* all refer to a form of mass production that preceded the factory. Instead of housing all workers under one roof, this arrangement took place in the homes of those who produced the items. Investors would buy the raw materials and deliver them to the homes in the countryside where the workers would make the materials into whatever commodity was being sold: shirts, pants, shoes, boots, hosiery, hardware. Merchant/manufacturers would then supply these items to domestic and international markets.

As raw materials and capital poured in throughout the eighteenth century, this domestic or putting out system spread, continuing well into the nineteenth century and entailing quite a lot of coordination and communication. Agents known as "puttersout," "bagmen," and "foggers" acted like today's managers. The workers usually owned their own equipment, but if it was a very complicated machine like the knitting frame, they might rent it; they usually worked at home, but if space was an issue, some rented space and tools in a nearby shop. The goods produced were simple and inexpensive, made by workers who received little training and needed little or no experience to be hired. The work was generally unskilled and monotonous, and for that reason it was thought appropriate for women, the elderly, and children. These were family businesses, and everyone in a household took part in the work. The big difference from the factory was the pacing: workers had more control when working in their own homes. Relationships with the investors who paid for the work were often fraught: when the price of raw materials rose or sales of finished goods slumped, wages could fall unpredictably and cottage workers had little recourse. The work force was so spread out that coordinated resistance was difficult to organize. Investor capitalists often preferred the cottage industry to building a factory so that they did not have to invest money in a building and expensive machinery. With a rising population and more commercialized agriculture, the supply of cheap unemployed or underemployed labor was plentiful.

The rise of the factory then, took place slowly, over three generations, in piecemeal fashion. The first industry transformed was the textile industry. Cotton led the way, and wool, linen, and silk lagged behind. Although the spinning of cotton began to be housed in factories by the last quarter of the eighteenth century, factories did not spring up across all industry and production. Instead, a lot of manufacturing continued to take place in the domestic system. For example, in the textile industry powerful machines driven by steam introduced in the 1770s sped spinning, producing thread faster and cheaper than ever before. But no similar technology existed for weaving, so between 1780 and 1830 the number of domestic handloom weavers, weaving in a traditional method, shot up to try to keep pace with the thread. The factory and the putting out system of domestic production coexisted in many other industries and regions until the second half of the nineteenth century, especially in shoes, boots, clothing, and some hardware like nail making.

Much of this chapter has addressed the activities of investors, inventors, and writers, people who employed ideas and capital and the political system to transform all sectors of the economy. It is equally important to consider the people on whose backs these changes were borne, the manual laborers, paid and unpaid, of Britain and its empire. As we have seen, fewer workers were needed in the agricultural sector in the eighteenth century, where opportunities for female employment decreased. Meanwhile, the growing population redistributed itself as people flocked to cities and towns, finding employment in manufacturing, commerce, and service. The nature of work—its availability, hours, venue, safety, compensation, and so much more—was in flux in every sector. Not surprisingly, just as historians have debated the timing and magnitude of the economic transformations of the long eighteenth century, they have debated their social consequences. Did workers' standard of living improve or decline?

There seems to be consensus that in the second half of the eighteenth century real wages stagnated or slipped a bit. Adult height, an indicator of nutrition, health, and working conditions, followed a similar path. In the first half of the nineteenth century, heights fell even more, while real wages are thought to have increased a little (though on this last point there is less scholarly agreement). These trends of course mask great varieties in experience based on gender, geography, and occupational sector. But they also suggest that the "improvement," to use the buzzword of the day, that marked the British economy in the long eighteenth century was not enjoyed by all, or even most, of its workers.[59] A tangible expression of this dislocation came between 1811 and 1813 when "Luddites" purposefully smashed new textile machines in protest against the mechanization that was displacing more traditional weaving methods (figure 6.8). The Luddites' resistance, at once symbolic and desperate, could not stop unwelcome

FIGURE 6.8 Luddites.

changes to the pace—sped up and intensified—and distribution of manufacturing work. Their concerns, however, were clear.

Finally, one must always look for imperial relationships in British history. During the seventeenth and eighteenth centuries Bengal had been the center of production of the world's most desirable fabrics. Demand was especially high for its fine muslins, described to be as light as "woven air." Muslin was produced so cheaply that some cloth manufacturers in Britain were said to have conspired to cut off the fingers of Bengali weavers and break their looms. Between 1760 and 1820, importation of muslin to Britain was ended by British imposition of high duties that increased prices so much they could not compete with the flood of cheap cotton fabric produced in Britain's mills. India still grew cotton, but Bengal was no longer the center of spinning and weaving. Its weavers suffered tremendous poverty and unemployment. India subsequently became an exporter of raw materials like cotton, jute, coal, opium, rice, spices, and tea rather than manufactured goods.

IMAGE CREDITS

PART ONE

Retrospective

O n February 14, 1814, the British cellist Bartholomew Johnson died at the age of 103. His life spanned most of the long eighteenth century, so he undoubtedly experienced or at least observed many of the changes that occurred during that era. As a child, Johnson would have worn clothes made of handwoven cloth using homespun thread. By the end of his life, he was purchasing garments of fabric woven on power looms.

Born in an overwhelmingly rural England, he lived most of his adult life in London, watching its population swell from around 700,000 in 1750 to well over a million at the time of his death, the most poignant example of increasing urbanization. Like many musicians, he served as a "town wait" or watchman, patrolling the streets at night while playing his instrument as he walked his beat in the era before established police forces. He took the job, no doubt, to supplement his income from performing, which suggests he did not earn enough to be among the one in twenty British men who could vote.

Whether he realized it or not, Mr. Johnson participated in a global economy. He drank East India company tea sweetened with Caribbean sugar and filled his pipe with tobacco grown in the colony (later state) of Virginia. He ate cod caught off the coast of Newfoundland and seasoned his food with spices from Persia, Arabia, and India. If he deposited his money in the Bank of England, it was invested in companies doing business around the globe. He probably gave little thought to the enslaved Africans who harvested the products he enjoyed.

Like most Britons of his age, he was not affected directly by the long series of wars fought with France, though he probably resented being taxed to pay for them. Perhaps his orchestra was among the first to play "God Save the King," written in 1744. If they did, the lyrics may or may not have stirred patriotic feeling in him. Perhaps the American Revolution inspired him to hope for political reform. Maybe the French Revolution frightened him with its violence. He may have been too busy making a living to give either event much thought.

Bartholomew Johnson kept no diary, wrote no memoir, and left no letters for historians to study. We have no way of knowing what he felt about the world in which he lived. He may have come to the end of his long life reflecting with pride on Britain's primacy of place in European and international affairs, or perhaps he viewed such matters with indifference. If he were at all observant, he could not have helped but notice how his country had changed during the course of his lifetime, though in some fundamental ways it remained as it had been in his youth. His great grandchildren would, however, live in world unrecognizable to him. Their story belongs to the next era in British history.

PART TWO

Overview, 1815-1914

The period from the end of the Napoleonic Wars (1815) to the start of World War I (1914) not only saw enormous change but an increase in the pace of change itself. Chapter 7 discusses the dramatic growth in population, evolving gender roles, and the altered structure of society that accompanied the Industrial Revolution and urbanization. Chapter 8 situates the United Kingdom within a world historical context, examining the continued evolution of the empire and its impact on both Britons and colonial subjects. As chapter 9 explains, uncertain times produced both anxiety and a quest for certainty. Chapter 10 examines political and social reform efforts, emphasizing both agency from below and adaptation and resistance from above. This section concludes with an analysis of economic change (chapter 11) and its impact on the quality of British life.

CHAPTER 7

Structures and Patterns of Everyday Life

When George III died in 1820, his eldest son finally claimed the crown he had long coveted. George IV's wife, Caroline of Brunswick, was also eager to claim her crown, something her estranged husband vowed to prevent. Her return from exile and his parliamentary divorce proceedings against her, with the aptly named Pains and Penalties Bill, was the final stage of a most dysfunctional royal marriage marked by hatred, separation, adultery, official investigations, and scurrilous attacks in the press. Caroline's situation could not have been more extreme. Yet

many agreed when she proclaimed, "My own sex are more particularly interested in my triumph over my enemies. If my matrimonial rights are illegally annulled, theirs eventually may be rendered less secure." Thousands of British women identified with the queen, sending petitions in a nationwide campaign in her defense, like that signed by 17,642 "married ladies of London."[1] Men supported Caroline too. In fact, only male names graced the address from Newcastle-upon-Tyne. There, an angry woman complained of her exclusion—arguing that "it was a woman's cause"—and in an impressive display of maternal authority championed her queen and cause by compelling her five sons to sign.[2] The Queen Caroline Affair offered a dramatic start to a century in which legal reform, government policy, and shifting notions

FIGURE 7.1 Queen Caroline, by James Lonsdale, c. 1820.

of domesticity and gender relations redefined patriarchal power in ways that both strengthened and undermined it. The institutions of marriage and family were at the center of political, economic, social, and cultural debates.

Three Lives

Caroline and George had not met before their betrothal in 1795. Upon marrying things only got worse. They produced an heir, Princess Charlotte, in just nine months, and with that duty conveniently fulfilled they separated for the remainder of their unhappy marriage. From the very beginning, the public took Caroline's side. The Prince of Wales's profligate spending and womanizing, long satirized in the press and which their marriage was meant to remedy, continued, now inciting even more criticism. George, meanwhile, accused Caroline of similar behavior, launching in 1806 an official inquiry, the Delicate Investigation, into allegations that she had given birth to an illegitimate child. Though cleared of that specific charge, Caroline's situation became particularly difficult when, in 1811, George became regent with the onset of his father's final and permanent bout of illness. Excluded from life at court, Caroline agreed to leave the country in exchange for an annual allowance. George was especially eager to send Caroline abroad because their now-grown daughter, Charlotte, showed signs of resisting her father, under whose supervision she remained, and supporting her mother. Princess Charlotte would go on to refuse the husband her father chose for her, finally winning his consent to marry the prince of her choice. When Charlotte died in 1817 after delivering a stillborn son, George declined to notify his estranged wife; living in Italy, Caroline learned by chance of her tragic loss from a messenger bringing the news to the pope. What George did communicate was his desire to sever completely their connection, which began with investigations into Caroline's alleged adulterous relationship with her Italian companion. When George became king and Caroline returned to Britain, there were processions and meetings, in addition to those addresses (over 800), in her defense. The government worried about popular insurrection as Caroline joined forces with both the parliamentary opposition and radicals in a campaign against royal corruption and, interestingly, marital mistreatment. "All classes will ever find in me a sincere friend to their liberties, and a zealous advocate of their rights," she provocatively declared.[3] The king's bill passed narrowly in the House of Lords but had no chance of success in the House of Commons. Three weeks after George's coronation, Caroline died as she had always been—his estranged wife.

"In defending Queen Caroline's rights as an abused wife," historian Anna Clark asserts, "radicals were admitting that the rights of women were a political issue."[4] This was a profound development in circles that had promoted the "rights of man" in gendered, not universal, terms. Soon thereafter another Caroline, unhappily married to another George, used her difficult circumstances to lobby for legislative relief for mistreated wives and mothers. Caroline

Sheridan, from a well-connected but impoverished family (her grandfather had been a prominent playwright and politician, her father a colonial administrator who died when she was eight), was pressured at a young age to marry George Norton, a Tory MP. She subsequently established herself as a poet, magazine editor, and society hostess, earning money and aiding her husband's political career. He, meanwhile, subjected her to physical and emotional abuse. When she left him in 1836, he took her earnings and their three young sons; as husband, he had legal right to his wife's property and children. He refused her a divorce—only a husband could initiate such proceedings—but accused her of an affair with her friend Lord Melbourne, the prime minister, whom he attempted to blackmail and then sued for what the law delicately called "criminal conversation." George Norton lost that case, but Caroline Norton was humiliated by the proceedings. She also

FIGURE 7.2 Caroline Norton, by George Hayter, 1832.

retaliated. Privately, she followed the time-honored example of estranged wives by racking up huge bills chargeable to her husband; if her income was his, then so were her debts. Publicly, Caroline Norton campaigned for reforms that, over the course of the century, changed the legal landscape for married women.

In 1837, Norton published *Observations on the Natural Claim of a Mother to the Custody of Her Children as Affected by the Common Law Right of the Father.* The title's gendered juxtaposition of natural and legal rights went to the heart of her campaign, which included more pamphlets and a successful parliamentary bill. The Custody of Infants Act of 1839 permitted a mother, not guilty of adultery, to petition the courts for custody of children aged seven and under and for access to older children. Norton, ironically, could not benefit from this legislative triumph, for her husband had taken their sons to Scotland, where English civil law did not apply. Undeterred, she next contributed to the mounting campaign for divorce law reform. In 1854, Norton offered a graphic account of the spousal abuse she had suffered in a pamphlet describing the laws pertaining to women, and in 1855, as legislation was pending, she published *A Letter to the Queen on Lord Chancellor Cranworth's Marriage and Divorce Bill.* The subsequent Matrimonial Causes Act of 1857 moved divorce proceedings to civil courts. A husband's adultery alone remained insufficient grounds for divorce, thus perpetuating gender inequality, for a wife's adultery was actionable. But a wife could now sue for divorce on the grounds of "cruelty," which was understood as extreme physical abuse. This remained expensive and inconvenient, but less so than before when divorce required annulment in an ecclesiastical court or a private act of Parliament. Middle-class couples now had the possibility of terminating dysfunctional marriages, and 300 petitions were filed in the first year.

Shifting gender relations affected the working classes as well. In 1836, the year Norton left her husband and lost access to her children, she also published a poem entitled *A Voice from the Factories*. In it, like so many of her other publications, Norton urged political action, this time on behalf of children who "labour all day long for others' gain." While she condemned all forms of child employment, asserting that childhood should be a time of "prayer slumber fondness smiles—and hours of rosy mirth," Norton took particular aim at the plight of juvenile "factory slaves."[5] Just a little earlier, Ellen Johnston was born in Glasgow. A published poet who signed her verses "The Factory Girl" and was "crowned the Queen of Song,"[6] Johnston began work as a power-loom weaver at the age of 11, held factory jobs throughout her life, endured poor health and poverty, and is thought to have died in a workhouse when she was 39. But she hardly considered herself a "factory slave." On the contrary, Johnston celebrated in her poetry her working life and the freedom it gave her. Johnston left the home of an abusive stepfather at the age of 16. After her first love abandoned her, she wrote, "another soon offered me his heart—without the form of legal protection—and in a thoughtless moment I accepted him as my friend and protector." That relationship did not last either, but it made her an unwed mother. Embracing what "the world falsely calls a woman's shame," Johnston celebrated her daughter Mary's birth. With her own mother she then established a female household: Johnston earned money while her mother cared for Mary.[7] "It was an increasingly common way of doing things by the middle of the nineteenth century," explains historian Emma Griffin. "With family close by to take care of her child and wages that were good enough to support herself, her child and her mother, Ellen did not have to rely upon a husband. She made choices that simply had not existed to women a century earlier."[8]

Ellen Johnston's experiences could not have been more different than those of Caroline Norton or Queen Caroline. Yet she shared much in common with them beyond a poetic calling or

AUTOBIOGRAPHY,

POEMS AND SONGS

OF

ELLEN JOHNSTON,

THE 'FACTORY GIRL.'

GLASGOW:
WILLIAM LOVE, 40 ST ENOCH SQUARE,
MDCCCLXVII.

FIGURE 7.3 Title page of Ellen Johnston's 1867 published collection. (It received awards of £5 from Queen Victoria and £50 from Prime Minister Benjamin Disraeli. A second edition was published in 1869.)

the title "queen." All three were mothers; all three lived without husbands; and all three were in the public eye, sometimes shamed and sometimes praised. In their remarkable stories, moreover, we can glimpse important developments of the nineteenth century, developments that affected opportunities for men and women, attitudes toward children, and the practice of family life.

Counting People

Many of those nineteenth-century developments had roots in the eighteenth. Demographic change offers a perfect example. After the population of England and Wales doubled in the eighteenth century, it doubled again in the first half of the nineteenth and then kept right on going. The census of 1801 recorded 8.5 million inhabitants in England and Wales, that of 1901 approximately 32.5 million.[9] Scotland's population expanded at almost the same pace, nearly doubling between 1800, when it was 1.6 million, and 1871. By 1911 it had reached 4.75 million.

These overall figures encompass details that reveal a lot about social, economic, and regional differences and their impact on reproduction and family formation. Glasgow's population, for example, expanded in the 1830s, the decade of Elizabeth Johnston's childhood there, at a stunning annual rate of 3 percent. But Glasgow's crude death rate (number of deaths per 1,000 people in a year) grew too, as crowding and industry increased, from almost 25 in the early 1820s to almost 40 in the late 1840s. Other manufacturing centers endured extremely high mortality rates. Approximately half of the children in Manchester, Sheffield, and Leeds died in the 1840s before reaching the age of five. In rural areas where cottage industry prevailed, death rates increased in the early nineteenth century, bucking aggregate national trends of decline. The effects of location on life expectancy were detectable even within a few city blocks. In 1841, residents of Liverpool's poor working districts suffered a mortality rate 54 percent higher than their wealthier neighbors living in the best parts of town.[10]

Nowhere did the decade of the 1840s prove more deadly than in Ireland. The central event of the history of nineteenth-century Ireland was the blight of the potato crop that began in 1845 and the consequent period of famine that lasted at least a half-decade. The longer-term origins of the disaster, however, lay in the unprecedented spike in population, even more dramatic than those in Scotland, England, and Wales, that had been underway since the island's previous major potato blight in 1740–41. Ireland's population stood around 4 or 5 million in the 1790s and, despite the loss of some 1.5 million emigrants between 1815 and 1845, mostly from the more developed regions of Leinster and Ulster, rose to about 8.2 million by 1841. On the eve of the famine, Ireland's population may have grown by a further 300,000.

Ireland was overwhelmingly rural and, for the most part, poor. Three out of five families lived in structures with dirt floors and mud walls, but owing to inexpensive access to turf, used for heating and cooking, and especially to the potato, the population probably experienced higher living standards than many parts of contemporary Europe.

FIGURE 7.4 *An Irish Peasant Family Discovering the Blight of Their Store,* by Daniel MacDonald, c. 1847.

The blight affecting the European potato crop originated in North America and arrived in Ireland in the summer of 1845, destroying perhaps one-third of the crop. It recurred in 1846, and the destruction was total (figure 7.4). Potatoes had been an important component of the diets of most Irish families, and over a third of the population, or more than 3 million people—especially in the west and southwest—subsisted almost entirely on potatoes. The intensity of disruption makes it impossible to deal precisely, but in round figures, nearly a million were dead within a few years, and more than a million had emigrated. Emigration continued, decade after decade, into the twentieth century. Ireland never again approached its 1841 population, and only in the second half of the twentieth century did it reach late eighteenth-century levels.

Most of those who died in Ireland in the late 1840s were victims of disease rather than starvation, although often the diseases they suffered were direct consequences of malnutrition. Severe underconsumption of protein or calories led to marasmus or emaciation, especially in children; and infection, as well as inadequate levels of albumin or protein, led to edema. Potatoes are a source of vitamin C, and their removal from the diet resulted in epidemics of scurvy in Ireland. These conditions produced cases of chronic diarrhea or respiratory infections, which in turn spread dysentery or "fever" (i.e., typhus). Inevitably, populations facing such pressures were dirtier and prone to lice and other parasitic infections, often resulting in recurring (or relapsing) fever, marked by episodes of vomiting. Cholera visited the land in 1849. Contagious infection intensified, as hunger and famine pushed families in search of support or assistance elsewhere.

Migration proved a lasting consequence of the Irish potato blight and famine. Within Ireland itself there was a big shift in population from west to east. Remote regions of Munster and Connacht were virtually de-populated as families or individuals resettled in and around Dublin or elsewhere near the east coast. Still greater numbers made the passage to Britain (usually via Liverpool or Glasgow), from which most continued on to the United States, where today more than one American in ten self-identifies as having Irish ancestry.[11]

Yet many of the Irish men, women, and children fleeing starvation and disease stayed in Britain. They were the latest, but by no means the last, migrants to cross the Irish Sea to settle there. Irish communities could be found in many of Britain's growing urban centers in the eighteenth century, and during the wars against revolutionary and Napoleonic France the number of new arrivals increased. After 1801, "these settlers were," as historian Donald MacRaild reminds us, "migrants *within*, not emigrants *into*, the United Kingdom." The Act of Union, however, failed to keep Britons from treating them as "aliens" and "outsiders."[12] Irish settlers were rarely welcomed; more commonly, they faced ethnic, religious, and other prejudices, and by the 1830s government officials complained of their growing presence. The famine of the 1840s dramatically increased both the number of Irish migrants and the tensions surrounding their residence in Britain. In 1851, over 7 percent of Scotland's population had been born in Ireland, as had nearly 3 percent of the inhabitants of England and Wales.[13] In 1901, the Irish community in Britain (those born in Ireland and their Britain-born children and grandchildren) probably exceeded 2 million.[14]

Scotland's experience of the potato famine extended beyond the arrival of Irish migrants. Its own recent population growth owed much to the introduction of the potato, and as in Ireland, the potato blight of 1845 changed everything. Famine was most severe in the remote northern Highlands and western islands, where blight destroyed the population's main source of subsistence. The most prudent response was often migration, but not simply from the interior to the coasts; erstwhile Scottish peasants and crofters more often turned to overseas transportation. The chief destination was Canada, which was relatively close and therefore relatively inexpensive—and where Scottish diasporic communities had been established for a few generations—but others resettled in the United States and elsewhere, and as far away as Australia. Landlords were increasingly involved in the process, and this involvement could range from eviction to cancellation of rent arrears to partial assistance to full-paid transportation.

Despite these patterns of famine and relocation, and in contrast to Ireland across the same period, Scotland's population continued to expand, as did population elsewhere in Britain. In fact, the extraordinary rate of growth in England and Wales only started to slow a bit toward the end of the century. The 1871 census revealed a gender imbalance there that skewed female, and the proportion of "surplus women," as they were called, thereafter expanded. For this and other reasons, including personal choice, a considerable number of women remained single; in the late nineteenth century, an estimated 12 percent of all women in their 40s had never married. Meanwhile, there was less illegitimacy. Married women, too, were having fewer children. In contrast to the eighteenth century, when a drop in the age at first marriage expanded marital fertility, in the second half of the nineteenth century couples apparently engaged in family planning. Given the costs of higher education and the launching of (male) careers, many professional families concentrated resources on fewer children. In the north London community of Hampstead, an affluent suburb with a railway station providing easy access to the city, the average maternal birth rate fell by 30 percent between 1880 and 1900. Among wage laborers, women's employment opportunities seem to have influenced the number of children. Smaller than average families prevailed in communities where women might find paid work outside the home (in textile mills, for example), and larger families where such possibilities had all but disappeared (in agriculture and mining).[15]

Very different dynamics prevailed among enslaved peoples in the British Caribbean. There, mortality rates were astronomically high and birth rates low; historians speak of depletion rates, the degree to which the former exceeded the latter, on the islands. Slaveholders, responsible for these deadly conditions, found it most profitable to rely on the transatlantic slave trade to replenish the unfree workforce on their plantations, which skewed male by design. Britain's abolition of the slave trade in 1807 contributed to the reversal of these trends. Not only did enslaved women start to outnumber enslaved men after 1800, but slaveowners embraced pronatalist practices with the hope of increasing birth and infant survival rates. In this context, colonial administrations introduced a new type of census, one that counted and registered enslaved peoples, and in 1819 Parliament established the Registry of Colonial Slaves in London.[16] The British state sought to monitor both evasions of the slave trade ban and changing demographic conditions in its wake.[17]

Abolitionists used this data too. They had hoped that ending the trade would, in the long term, starve the slave system of vital workers and, in the short term, improve conditions on plantations in an attempt to prolong lives. Registration numbers dispelled the latter prospect. Poor birth and mortality figures revealed slaveholders' efforts to keep production levels and profits up by exacting more and harder labor from fewer workers. Domestic life was affected too, as enslaved mothers were forced to wean their children earlier, and families were separated with greater frequency. In Britain, this activated a new phase of the abolition movement; in the West Indies, enslaved people resisted in both small and dramatic ways. Ultimately, a two-week slave rebellion in Jamaica in 1831–32, in which 60,000 of the island's 300,000 enslaved people probably participated, convinced the British political establishment to abolish slavery. Over the centuries, more than 2 million Africans had been transported against their will to the British West Indies. Survivors of the Middle Passage and their descendants in these islands numbered approximately 800,000 when emancipation was announced in 1833.[18]

Identities and Ideologies

Among free Britons, socioeconomic circumstances influenced the personal experience of demographic change. In addressing this, historians of nineteenth-century Britain, like the people they study, often invoke the language of class. For in the late eighteenth or early nineteenth centuries, references to "the middling sort" gave way to "the middle class," and "laborers" or "working people" to "the working class." Historians have sought to explain the making of these classes, the means by which groups and individuals forged a collective identity based on shared experiences and ideas or, as Karl Marx and Friedrich Engels famously described it, class consciousness. Not surprisingly, there is considerable disagreement about when exactly this happened, and even the degree to which it occurred—whether the language of class necessarily indicated the existence of class. For like the underlying economic and social changes, the processes of class formation were gradual not sudden, uneven rather than uniform. Potentially confusing subdivisions emerged—the upper middle and lower middle classes, for example—with members of each carefully trying to distinguish themselves from those nipping at their heels. And competing identities of gender, race, locality, and nationality both cut across class lines and challenged its primacy as a category of social organization and analysis. Nonetheless, the old hierarchical way of conceiving society gave way to new "shapes in society."[19]

Discussions of class were often political. As will be shown in chapter 10, the upper class passed a parliamentary reform act in 1832 that enfranchised middle-class men but not those of the working class. Political exclusion thus had much to do with the formation of middle- and working-class identity and expressions of, and concerns about, class conflict. Later in the century when some working men, but by no means all, could vote, the Independent Labour Party (ILP, founded 1893) emerged from the trade union and socialist movements specifically to represent the interests of the working class in Parliament.

Contemporary commentators on class, moreover, understood it in economic terms. What mattered was not merely how much one earned but how one earned it. In the early nineteenth century, the upper class was largely a landed class, composed of the aristocracy and gentry who possessed large estates and derived their income from rent, though many of these same individuals were heavily involved in finance and commerce. It was a group, some historians have argued, increasingly defined by "gentlemanly capitalism," a connection between landed interests and the trading markets of the City of London, the commercial center at the heart of the metropolis. By the end of the century, given the extraordinary riches derived from imperialism and the collapse of agricultural prices, the basis of upper-class wealth had shifted somewhat to business, but profits made there were still used to purchase land and often rewarded with aristocratic titles and honors. Things proved even more complicated in the middle class, where professionals charged fees, government employees, clerks, and managers earned salaries, and businessmen generated profits. What distinguished this cohort from the economic activities of the upper class were their more modest returns and personal involvement in the actual work. But within the middle class too, considerable income differentials prevailed between, say, successful industrialists and small shopkeepers. Finally, manual laborers, skilled and unskilled, who worked primarily for others for wages, comprised the working class and the vast majority of Britons.

Given all these internal differences, what bound each class together, or at least led contemporaries to view society in terms of a tripartite class model? There were cultural characteristics members of particular classes shared, most dramatically at the end of the nineteenth century. It has been famously suggested, for example, that passions for football, fish and chips, and the music hall helped to forge a national working-class culture that transcended regional differences. Meanwhile, a devotion to volunteerism, to philanthropic public works, connected members of the middle class. Equally important, however, was that which separated the classes from one another—an "us vs. them" worldview. In this regard, the behavior of the middle class proved key. The ability to employ at least one domestic servant and to educate sons beyond the elementary school level distinguished the middle class from those below it. When members of the upper echelons of the working class made their way into the lower middle class, it was often due to educational opportunities, be they academic or vocational. And when members of the lower middle class were unable to afford servants, they ensured at least that married women did not engage in wage labor. A complementary emphasis on domestic life led middle-class families to distinguish themselves from the more libertine upper-class lifestyle they disdained. They instead championed hard work, respectability, fidelity, and sobriety, traits that conveniently supported their often family-based economic enterprises. How the home was ordered thus became a marker of class.

Such notions of domesticity informed all aspects of life. This was especially the case during the French Revolution which, despite its radical politics, the expansion of rights, and proposed suffrage for women, unleashed a discourse about family and domestic life that had at its core some extremely conservative ideas about women. French revolutionaries charged mothers with educating their children and instilling in them the ideals of citizenship and morality. In Britain, Mary Wollstonecraft's writings justified better educational opportunities for women so that they could impart those values most effectively and accurately in their capacity as mothers. This twining of women and the home was not new, but the British middle and upper classes embraced it with particular zeal in the decades that followed. The home became fetishized in the ideology of separate spheres that dominated in the nineteenth century.

According to the ideology of separate spheres, women's responsibility was to marry and have children. They were assigned a devotion and commitment to the domestic sphere because enough Britons (male and female) believed that women's natures—which they defined as passive, submissive, emotional, honorable, and nonrational—were best suited to reproduction and the home. To step into her role as "angel of the house," the guardian of virtue in the household, a woman was supposed to be a virgin before marriage with no sexual experience and little experience of the world beyond her childhood home. The home was the site of religion, faith, and discipline. This was particularly the ethos of the middle-class home which, as we have seen, touted its respectability in contrast to both aristocratic households known for wild living and little (or no) work ethic and those unkempt, disorderly homes of the working classes.

The peace and tranquility of the domestic sphere served as a refuge for men who inhabited the public sphere. Men's work outside the home was portrayed as a driven, aggressive struggle that sapped their strength. The stress of the harsh economic world could lead to temptations, intemperance, and sloth. These included extramarital sex. In contrast to his wife's purity, the double standard meant that husbands could indulge in extramarital sex without too many negative consequences. The home called them back to personal responsibility, duty, and productivity. A moral panic in the middle of the nineteenth century brought the double standard into public discourse. Critics of the status quo called for men to adhere to their marital vows, while the slogan "Votes for Women, Chastity for Men" was coined.

The biggest contradiction to the gender hierarchy represented by the ideology of separate spheres was Queen Victoria, who ascended the throne in 1837. Women were defined as the "weaker" sex, both physically and intellectually. Their subordination to male authority meant that they were always supposed to fall under the supervision of a male relation, be it a husband, father, or brother. Men held the positions of power in the economic, political, and social realms. Yet the queen was at the head of it all, the social and symbolic superior to every one of her subjects. To smooth that glaring contradiction, Victoria vigorously embraced motherhood and domesticity. She married Prince Albert soon after she became queen and started a family immediately, giving birth to nine children between 1840 and 1857. She cultivated the image of her family as the model British family, strategically bringing the children to official ceremonial functions.

FIGURE 7.5 The Royal Family (Queen Victoria, Prince Albert, and nine children), 1857.

At the other end of the social spectrum, working-class women rarely had the luxury of subscribing to notions of the domestic sphere. Poor women had always worked outside the home, and the nineteenth century was no exception. Despite the fact that their economic situation excluded them from the ideology of separate spheres, they were shaped and diminished by it because they could never measure up to this ideal. Working-class men suffered too, for they often relied on the wages their wives earned or were unable to support their families at all.

Whatever the middle-class complaints about elite homelife, their most virulent critiques pointed in the opposite direction, toward the urban poor. In this context Irish migrants were treated with particular disdain, viewed as a corrupting influence in Britain's crowded cities. "Debased alike by ignorance and pauperism," wrote James Phillips Kay in the midst of a deadly cholera epidemic in Manchester in the early 1830s, the Irish "have discovered, with the savage, what is the minimum of the means of life, upon which existence may be prolonged." In other words, they had mastered survival in the face of want, but according to Kay this was a dangerous, not admirable, accomplishment. Using the language of infection, Kay, a physician, complained that "the contagious example of ignorance and a barbarous disregard of forethought and economy, exhibited by the Irish, spread" to "the labourers of this country."[20] A decade later, Friedrich Engels expressed similar concerns in his landmark *The Condition of the Working Class in England*, published in 1845. Devoting an entire chapter to "Irish Immigration," Engels declared that the Irish, settling in industrial areas, "there form the lowest class of the population." Like Kay, he believed the Irish had "grown up almost without civilization," drawing particular (and repeated) attention to their "filth and drunkenness." Not only did Irish migrants "bring all their brutal habits" into working-class communities, but Engels also worried that they competed with the native-born for jobs and drove down wages.[21] Such invective predated the potato famine. During and after that cataclysmic event, as Irish migration intensified, so did the attacks—verbal and physical. Critics and champions of the working class, and British workers themselves, regarded the Irish as "other," blaming them unjustly for the worst elements of industrial society.[22]

This discourse of barbarism versus civilization reveals more than economic and urban conflicts. Long histories of religious animosity and colonial racism, the experiences of brutal conquest and then an unequal union, shaped derogatory stereotypes of the Irish. A culture of anti-Irishness thrived in nineteenth-century Britain that complicated relations between the two islands and "separated Irish from Irish, Protestant from Catholic, English from Irish."[23]

Colonial connections, past and present, brought other peoples to Britain in the nineteenth century. Many, like the Indian seamen known as Lascars, were temporary residents rather than settlers. Lascars' employment, mostly on East India Company ships, transported them (literally) to Britain; once there, they lived in appalling conditions in barracks, workhouses, or on the streets. Eight died in London of exposure or starvation during the winter of 1856–57. The coroner was hardly surprised; he had conducted inquests for at least 40 Indian seamen in recent years.[24] Other

South Asians pursued far better prospects in Britain, some seeking educational and business opportunities or to take the Indian civil service exam. Perhaps the most prominent was Dadabhai Naoroji, a professor of mathematics and natural philosophy from Bombay, who went to Liverpool in 1855 as a partner of the first Indian business to establish a branch in Britain. In the next few years, Naoroji opened his own business, became a professor of Gujarati (his native language) at University College London, led organizations to promote Anglo-Indian understanding, and, after losing an election in 1886, became in 1892 Britain's first Asian MP. Naoroji won by a margin of just three votes in the London constituency of the Central Finsbury, after a campaign in which opponents exploited racial and religious prejudices and described him as a "fire-worshipper." Moving frequently between South Asia and the British Isles, Naoroji also held important Indian political offices and was a founding

FIGURE 7.6 Dadabhai Naoroji, c. 1889.

member of the Indian National Congress (1885). In fact, it was to promote Indian interests that he became a British MP. His first speech in the House of Commons challenged British involvement in India, a theme at the heart of his publication, *Poverty of India* (1878), that decried the drain of wealth from India to Britain. By the turn of the century, however, a new generation of Indian students and intellectuals rejected Naoroji's moderation in favor of a more radical independence movement.[25]

The North American colonies' war of independence, as we have seen, brought Black loyalists, who exchanged support for the Crown for their freedom, to Britain. Now in the nineteenth century, and especially after 1850, fugitives from slavery in the United States fled to Britain. Like the free African Americans who came, often as abolitionists, students, and entertainers, these refugees were mostly men. According to historian David Olusoga, those who "found work … became black Victorians, mostly marrying white British women, their descendants disappearing into the background population after a couple of generations, as had the children and grandchildren of the black Georgians. The less fortunate slipped into the world of the Victorian streets."[26] There they joined the Lascars, the Irish, and the native-born poor in the overcrowded "slums" of late nineteenth-century Britain.

Family and the Law

With the Infant Custody Act of 1839 and Matrimonial Causes Act of 1857, Parliament had started to dismantle the system of coverture by which, as Caroline Norton had explained in 1855, "a married woman in England *has no legal existence:* her being is absorbed in that of her husband."[27] The Married Women's Property Acts of 1870 and 1882 addressed the financial side of this arrangement. The first act granted married women control of money they earned and inherited; the second allowed married women to own and control any property in their own right. These reforms were clearly driven by the experiences of women in the upper and middle classes. Preserving one's separate property in marriage, like the ability to leave a violent marriage, was a luxury most working-class women did not enjoy at a time when employment opportunities and wages for women lagged considerably behind those for men.

A second Matrimonial Causes Act passed in 1878, however, extended protections to physically abused wives who could not afford a formal divorce; they might instead apply to a magistrate for legal separation and a maintenance order against their husbands' wages. By 1886, desertion was also recognized as grounds for such magisterial action. The state, meanwhile, reached into the domestic lives of working-class families in other ways. Throughout the nineteenth century, legislative initiatives concerning poor relief, working conditions, and elementary education helped shape ideas about the proper duties of working-class husbands and wives, parents and children. Beyond the ideological realm, these new laws profoundly influenced many of the day-to-day patterns of domestic arrangements.

The New Poor Law of 1834 was an attempt to update poor relief in response to the overwhelming population growth, mobility, urbanization, and poverty of the early nineteenth century. Old practices, dating back to Elizabethan times, simply proved inadequate in the face of new realities. But the New Poor Law was also a cornerstone of larger state projects both to centralize government operations, creating a new bureaucracy of administrators and inspectors, and to "improve" the behavior of its most numerous, needy, and potentially disruptive subjects. The New Poor Law mandated that all relief move "indoors" to workhouses. The underlying principle was "less eligibility"—deliberately making assistance unpleasant (worse than conditions outside the workhouse) to encourage self-sufficiency. The underlying assumption, that most cases of poverty could be overcome merely by thrift and hard work, was both mistaken and cruel. Everything about workhouse life, from food, clothing, and haircuts to hours of work and sleep, were strictly regulated, inviting comparisons to prison life.

Families entered workhouses together—no longer could one or two members enter to relieve the economic burden on all—only to be separated within. The new facilities divided men and women (regardless of marital status), parents and children (figure 7.7). The hope was to prevent reproduction, physically in the workhouse and psychologically outside it, and thus limit expansion of the "pauper population." The New Poor Law's controversial "bastardy clause," absolving unmarried fathers of responsibility for illegitimate children, had a similar goal. Formerly, parish officials pressured unmarried pregnant women to name their babies' fathers, who were in turn pressured to provide either financial assistance or marriage. But these old practices were thought to encourage premarital sex and hence more babies. After 1834, unmarried fathers were let off the hook while

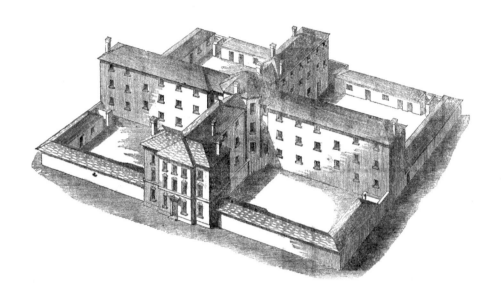

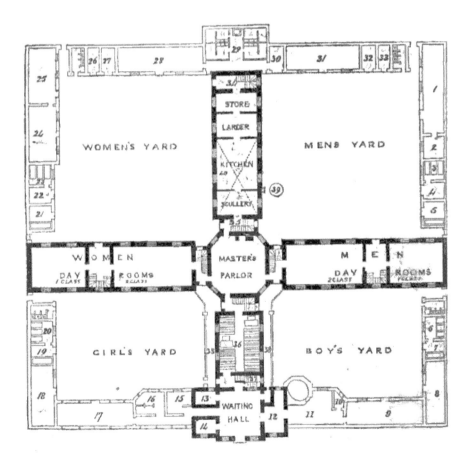

FIGURE 7.7 Plans for a New Poor Law workhouse, 1835.

unmarried mothers, in the words of a contemporary critic, were "branded ... with the epithet of W—e!"[28] The paradoxical result consigned more women and their children to the workhouse. Yet aside from such treatment of unmarried mothers, the New Poor Law administration tended to conceive of applicants in male terms—as "able-bodied" patriarchs who failed to fulfill their duty as the family "breadwinner" and whose efforts and earnings must therefore increase. Family security, it came to be believed, depended on the adult male wage.

Theory and practice of course diverged. Outdoor relief continued; after 15 years under the new system, only 12 percent of paupers receiving assistance were confined to workhouses. Among the largest categories of recipients, moreover, were mothers of legitimate children (abandoned wives and widows) and elderly women.[29] Finally, the breadwinner wage proved elusive. Many more married women contributed by necessity to their household economy with wage labor in the nineteenth century than contemporaries thought.[30] Their labor, however, was devalued and hence poorly paid.

Among wage-earning women, those engaged in the fast-growing textile and coal industries were affected by another body of laws, the factory acts, that limited the hours and conditions of labor. The earliest factory acts focused on child labor. Working at very young ages was hardly new. Children had always worked on farms, in cottage industries, and family businesses, sometimes for wages but often unpaid. Moreover, parish apprenticeship had long been a system by which abandoned, orphaned, and poor children were provided for by the community—fed, housed, educated, and trained with a skill. Usually, placements were local. But as numbers and costs spiraled in the decades preceding the New Poor Law, some overwhelmed parishes sent their pauper children to work far away, "batch apprenticing" them to the new cotton factories. An "overlooker" at a flax mill in Dundee reported how Edinburgh's orphans were sent to work in his mill, usually at the age of six or seven, for terms of three or four years. So brutal were the conditions, in which "excessive working" (typically to 10:00 or 11:00 at night) was "accompanied by excessive beating," that some young workers ran away.[31] Poor parents who did not want their children relocated to such places found they had no choice; resistance could lead to the termination of relief for the entire family. The New Poor Law ultimately ended parish and batch apprenticeship but not child labor. In fact, child labor was, in the words of historian Jane Humphries, "reinvented and propagated in the crucible of industrialization." Small bodies and unskilled workers met well the needs of certain new production processes. Beyond the factories, too, children engaged in full-time employment. For, as we have seen, as changes in the adult labor market privileged male workers and the notion of a male breadwinner, women's earning power declined. When fathers died, went to war, could not earn enough, or simply did not exist, children had no choice but to work. They did so to help feed the rest of their family, and in the period of 1800 to 1830 they did so at younger ages and greater numbers than in preceding or succeeding times.[32]

The factory acts were part of the effort to stop this trend. The first, passed in 1819, banned the employment in cotton mills of children under the age of nine and limited the workday to

12 hours through age 16. But the law had no teeth; some children continued to work 15-hour days or more. Michael Sadler MP complained to the Commons in March 1832 about how "the overworking of these children … occasions a weariness and lethargy, which it is impossible always to resist; hence, drowsy and exhausted, the poor creatures fall too often among the machinery" where "their muscles are lacerated, their bones broken, or their limbs torn off." Some are "killed upon the spot." The lucky ones are beaten awake, "beaten upon their face, arms, and bosoms—beaten in your free market of labour, as you term it, like slaves."[33]

The timing of Sadler's analogy is important: three months after the rebellion in Jamaica and three months before the introduction of the Slavery Abolition Bill in Parliament. Yet the abolition law that finally passed in 1833 did not end all unfree labor in the empire. Territories controlled by the East India Company were excluded from the act. Where it went into effect, the state compensated 46,000 slave owners for the loss of their "property"; the £20 million they were paid constituted almost half of all government expenditure that year. Meanwhile, the men, women, and children who had lived and labored in brutal bondage received no reparations. To the contrary, "they were compelled to pay some of the cost of their own manumission," now ordered to serve involuntary "apprenticeships" for their masters without pay for four or six years. In this way, it was argued, again on behalf of plantation owners, formerly enslaved people could obtain "the skills required for full freedom."[34]

Some of the reforms Sadler sought for juvenile workers in Britain were enacted that same year. The new Factory Act of 1833 shortened mill children's workday, required their part-time education, and established government inspectors to oversee enforcement. Attention turned next to coal mines, in which government investigators reported, young haulers were "chained, belted, harnessed like dogs in a go-cart, black, saturated with wet, and more than half-naked—crawling on their hands and feet—they present an appearance indescribably disgusting and unnatural"[35] (figure 7.8). Again, reformers resorted to allusions of bound labor and the language of race to argue their case. The resulting Mines Act of 1842 prohibited males under age 10 and all females from working below ground. More reforms followed, and in 1847 a 10-hour day was mandated in textile mills for both children aged 13–18 and women.

The Ten Hour Act, as it was known, established important precedents for later legislation. Women workers were treated differently than men yet identically to children, thus infantilizing them with gender-specific protections. It was also argued that women's factory work endangered not only their health, but their entire family by rendering them bad, or at least absent, wives and mothers. The law's sponsor, quoting government health reports, decried "the 'constant and unwholesome toil' of mothers, who are compelled to leave their offspring 'long days alone to breathe sickly vapours soothed by opiates.'" The "house and children of a laboring man can only be kept clean and healthy by the assiduous labour of a well-trained industrious wife," and "this is overlooked in Lancashire, where the woman is often engaged in labour from home" and children are dying.

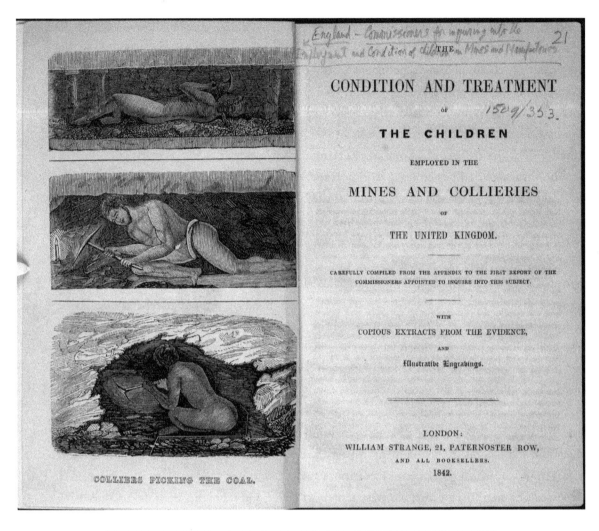

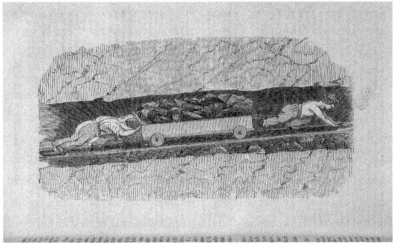

FIGURE 7.8 Report on children in the coal mines, 1842.

He therefore begged Parliament to "sanction at once the restriction which I propose with regard to females, in order to stop this frightful state of things."[36]

Many economic sectors remained unregulated in terms of the hours of female labor, and many women workers were neither wives nor mothers. Nonetheless, the factory and mine acts, like the New Poor Law, codified the notion that a woman's, and especially a mother's, proper place was in the home. This was not merely an elite ideal, the concept of separate spheres, forced by legislators on working-class families. Many laboring people, and indeed much of the trade union movement, supported legislation that restricted competition from poorly paid women workers for jobs that might otherwise go to better compensated men. The combined result was to reinforce the idea of the breadwinner wage and to undermine women's opportunities within both the family and the workplace.

The early child labor laws were industry specific; many sectors that employed children were untouched by such legislation. Yet by the end of the century, education reform had ordered young children out of the full-time labor market. The Education Act of 1870 established local boards to ensure that elementary schools were available throughout England and Wales. School boards could require parents to enroll their children, but most failed to exercise this authority. Only in 1880 did full-time education for children aged five to ten become mandatory. (In Scotland, compulsory education to age 13 began in 1872.) Still, many children fell through the cracks. Going to school required shoes and clean clothes; it also required a family to forego a child's earnings or vital domestic labor; and unless there was a free school nearby, in England and Wales it required the payment of fees until 1891. Such assaults on scant family resources kept many young children from school or juggling education with part-time employment. For older children secondary education was not compulsory. Yet like the New Poor Law and factory acts, the education acts forced families to reorganize domestic arrangements. The calculus of what raising children cost, and what they might in turn contribute to the family economy, shifted. Families, meanwhile, were monitored and, if they failed to comply, disciplined by government officials who were increasingly involved in the interlocking realms of poor relief, labor, and education. Particular aspects of private life had, for the less fortunate at least, become matters of public policy.

Childhood and Education

Victorian Britain was "a nation of children." Persons under the age of 15 constituted over a third of the population throughout the second half of the nineteenth century.[37] This had considerable cultural implications. Children became both subject and market for literature. Like Caroline Norton, many writers addressed the problem of child labor. Elizabeth Barrett Browning penned her poem *The Cry of the Children* (1843) in response to a Children's Employment Commission report. Charles Dickens, whose education was interrupted at age 11 when his father was imprisoned for debt and young Charles went to work in a blacking factory, drew on these experiences in *Oliver Twist.* On a happier note, fantastical stories appeared about and for children. Lewis Carroll's *Alice in Wonderland* (1865) is the most famous, but the genre dated back to the 1830s, when entertaining texts began competing with strictly educational and morally didactic ones. By century's end, there was a whole subgenre of periodicals dedicated to children, and a flourishing rivalry between "improving literature" and "penny dreadfuls." The former included the Religious Tract Society's *Boy's Own Paper* and the latter *The Boys of England*, a cheap magazine of adventure stories with a circulation of 250,000 in 1871. The Religious Tract Society meanwhile targeted young female readers with *The Girl's Own Paper*.[38] Painters too embraced child subjects, most notably John Everett Millais, who entertained his youngest models with fairy tales, chocolates, dolls, and books.[39] His *Cherry Ripe* (1879) and *Bubbles* (1886) became icons when the Pears Soap Company featured them in advertising campaigns (figure 7.9). Soap companies also competed for customers by including coupons for free dolls and games in their packages, expanding the burgeoning toy market to those who might not otherwise afford them.[40] About the same time, cycling became a "craze" that cut across class and gender lines; poorer kids shared secondhand bicycles, while affluent ones joined biking clubs, of which there were 2,000 by 1900.[41]

FIGURE 7.9 *Cherry Ripe* (1879) and *Bubbles* (1886), by John Everett Millais.

That said, little demarcated class divisions more clearly than childhood experience. Child mortality rates, as we have seen, demonstrated this; so did the height of those who survived to adolescence and adulthood. In 1880, a 13-year-old working-class boy was on average 4.2 inches shorter than upper-class boys of the same age. For 13-year-old girls, the height gap was even greater. Upper-class girls towered on average 5.5 inches above girls from the working class.[42] The high carbohydrate diets of the poor did not provide much nutrition.

Not only food but experience shaped differing conceptions of childhood for the various classes. Child laborers worked alongside adults in often dangerous environments, while more affluent children remained in the age-specific cocoons of nursery and school. The Factory and Education Acts sought to redefine childhood for the working class, to prolong it by keeping youngsters out of the workplace, and eventually in school, until age 10 or 13. After that, however, young people of the working class were effectively adults. Thus social reformers such as the journalist Henry Mayhew, who undertook a massive study of London poverty at midcentury, acknowledged that childhood ended on metropolitan streets by age 15.[43]

Expectations for the progeny of more affluent families were radically different. Some late nineteenth-century medical theorists, reflecting the practices of middle- and upper-class families, described childhood as reaching well into the twenties, and perhaps as far as age 30.[44] The sons of such families, tucked away at boarding school and university until starting careers, remained dependents much longer. So too did their sisters, who stayed home until marriage. The law set the age of majority at 21, but the actual transition came much earlier for those at the bottom of the social scale and much later for those at the top.

Class was especially important when it came to education. Educational opportunities were uneven, although overall they did increase significantly over the course of the nineteenth century. Improvements in education are reflected in rapidly rising rates of literacy. Consider, for example, the fact that 97 percent of those who wed in England and Wales in 1901 could sign their names in a marriage register. By contrast, in 1840, only half of all brides and approximately two-thirds of their grooms had managed to do so. North of the border, over 99 percent of Scots were able to sign marriage registers in 1901.[45] Scottish literacy rates had consistently surpassed those in England and Wales thanks to traditions within the (Presbyterian) Church of Scotland, which encouraged universal education. A national system of parish schools was available to all Scottish children regardless of sex or class; legislation compelled the affluent of each community to provide a school building and pay a teacher. Poor children might not attend for a host of reasons, most notably the need to work, but those who did were exposed to a wider, richer curriculum, sometimes including Greek and Latin, than their counterparts usually encountered in England and Wales.[46]

Because reading tended to be taught before writing, those marriage register figures probably underestimate how many Britons could read. Coal worker William Hewitt, for example, told the Children's Employment Commission in 1842 that he "went to day-school afore [he] worked in the pit." Hewitt could "read (very well) and write but very little," though to supplement the latter he was "learning in a copy-book at home."[47] Other teenage miners' testimony reveals the range of experience within the working class. John Watson reported that he knew his alphabet but "cannot write at all." He had attended school for a year before starting in the mines at age six, "and could read the Bible then." He had subsequently "forgotten everything." Yet Isaac Tipton, who began mining work at age seven, was a voracious reader. In addition to the Bible and the standard instructional text *Reading Made Easy*, Tipton read song books and swashbuckling tales of Robin Hood and the notorious eighteenth-century criminals Dick Turpin and Jack Sheppard. His eclectic reading did not stop there: "I have read a bit of Robinson Crusoe. I have read about pigs and cows dying of distemper."[48]

Before compulsory elementary education, learning opportunities for working-class children were uneven, as were the results. Many poorer Britons received a degree of education through Sunday schools. These schools were especially convenient, for Sunday was the only day wage laborers had off from work. They were also inexpensive to run—teachers volunteered, and church space was available after services—and charged low or no fees. But the primary goal of Sunday schools was religious instruction. Thus eight-year-old Sarah Gooder, who worked as a trapper in the Gawber coal pit, starting most days by 4:00 a.m. and working until 5:30 p.m., reported in 1842: "I go to Sunday-schools and read Reading made Easy. … They teach me to pray."[49] Some Sunday schools also taught writing and arithmetic, but many congregations thought it inappropriate to study anything but reading, by which they meant reading the Bible, on the Sabbath. Historians estimate that over a million children went to Sunday schools in the early 1830s, and contemporaries reported that children were "regular in their attendance."[50]

Full-time educational opportunities beyond Scotland, with its parish schools, were piecemeal and took place in day schools established on a voluntary basis. The funding needed to build a day school in England and Wales came from either affluent members of the local community or religiously affiliated philanthropic organizations committed to promoting education. Day schools tended to be large operations in which teachers instructed the older children, who in turn shared what they had learned with the younger ones. They also required full-time attendance and usually charged higher fees than Sunday schools, making them inaccessible to children who had to work. In some communities, especially urban centers, a different model of day school emerged in response to these problems. Private ventures, called "adventure schools" and often run out of teachers' homes, would let fee-paying students come and go as family and work pressures dictated. Before compulsory education, such initiatives offered a flexible, small-scale alternative to the two extremes of Sunday and day schools.[51]

For most of the century, therefore, working-class education was catch-as-catch-can. Sarah Gooder sadly told government investigators, "I would rather be at school than in the pit," while William Hewitt worked in his copy book and Isaac Tipton expanded his eclectic reading list in off-hours at home. They probably pursued learning without any hope that it would bring social or occupational advancement. The notion only gained currency in the latter part of the century. By then politicians had also embraced new ideas about educating "the masses," for as parliamentary reform extended the vote to some working men it seemed prudent that electors be literate.[52]

Educational opportunities for middle- and upper-class children were radically different. Mothers and governesses might teach all children in the home until they were six or seven, but thereafter boys were enrolled in school, typically private and fee-paying, with university-educated teachers who prepared them with an eye to attending university. Most common were the grammar schools. The sons of the upper class, however, and increasingly those of the higher reaches the middle class, were sent to prestigious boarding schools, only to come home (for the next 15 years or so) on holidays. The writer Robert Graves, born in 1895, described how being shipped off to boarding school transformed childhood: "School life becomes the reality, and home life the illusion. In England, parents of the governing classes virtually lose all intimate touch with their [male] children from about the age of eight."[53] This was not a happy state of affairs for Graves, who was miserable at most of the schools he attended.

The "public" boarding schools were, despite their name, exclusive private institutions. Eton, Harrow, Winchester, and Graves's Charterhouse were among the oldest and most famous, but such institutions multiplied in the nineteenth century. Public schools had a distinctive culture and cultivated a set of values and social relationships that became characteristic of the British ruling class. Sports were emphasized, especially cricket, football, boxing, and later rugby, which took its name from a school where, in 1823, a student ignored the rules of football, picked up the ball and ran with it, and in the process invented a new game. Thomas Arnold arrived as headmaster at Rugby five years later and initiated a series of reforms that focused on character building and transformed public school life throughout Britain. His priorities: "First religious and moral principle, second gentlemanly conduct, third academic ability." Chapel and games were more important than studies, which emphasized the classics (memorization of Greek and Latin).

In the small world of public schools, the sons of the elite lived within their own sharply graded hierarchy based on age. Students oversaw dormitory and social life, with the older ones serving as "prefects" and younger ones "fagging," serving as their elders' personal servants. Less affluent boys and those eager to study (Graves was both) were especially tormented. Wealthy industrialists and professionals increasingly sent sons to the old public schools, as well as founding similar institutions of their own. In the opinion of these fathers, boarding school offered "a crash course in manliness," far away from the maternal influences of home.[54] But the lower-middle class mostly sent its sons to local, private secondary schools. Focusing more on math and science, the secondary schools were deemed "modern" and prepared boys for the world of business, which they usually entered between age 16 and 18. Some secondary schools also sent students to university, where student life continued until age 21.[55]

The medieval universities of Oxford and Cambridge represented the pinnacle of education. An "Oxbridge" student would meet weekly with his tutor, but lecture attendance was optional. What mattered were the examinations that came at the end of three or four years and conferred a degree. Some students, especially those from the aristocracy, did not stay for the examinations. For them, attending Oxbridge was, like the Grand Tour, a rite of passage, a place to make contacts and mature. For others, university training provided entrance into the civil service and particular professions. Scotland and Ireland also had old and outstanding universities, but Oxbridge's monopoly on higher education in England only started to wane with the founding of new institutions catering to different types of students. University College London (UCL) opened in 1826 as a secular alternative to religiously affiliated Oxford and Cambridge. Three years later, King's College London was founded just a few blocks away, an Anglican response in the metropolis to UCL. Industrial and commercial cities like Manchester, Birmingham, Bristol, and Leeds saw the creation of "red brick universities," so called for their architectural style, new civic institutions focusing on practical training in fields like engineering and medicine. And in 1895, Fabian socialists established the London School of Economics; its goal was the betterment of society, and it first opened as a night school to bring higher education to the working class. University education was thus transformed during the nineteenth century, and the state became increasingly involved in funding and overseeing it. Still, on the eve of World War I, only 1 percent of young people attended university.

Gender affected education as profoundly as class. Working-class families often privileged boys' education over that of girls, keeping daughters at home to help with housework and child-minding while sending sons, as best they could, to school. When girls did attend school, their studies included sex-specific skills like sewing. Among the middle and upper classes, when boys left the home for school, most girls stayed put, studying with tutors or, more commonly, governesses. Some middle-class girls eventually went to private day schools, which differed considerably from those their brothers attended. Typically run by women, girls' schools focused on modern languages, French in particular, rather than classics, and on such "accomplishments" as music, art, and dancing. The basic academic subjects were covered too, for the purpose of girls' education was to prepare them for motherhood and being their own children's first teacher. If a girl ultimately went to boarding school, it was at an older age than boys and for the purpose of "finishing." With little expectation to prepare girls for a career, less was invested in their education in terms of both family money and study time.

Yet the educational landscape started to change for middle-class girls in the second half of the century. New types of schools were founded in response to the "surplus woman problem" and the more general recognition that some daughters would never become wives and mothers. Working as a teacher or governess was the most viable way for them to support themselves (the 1851 census revealed that 25,000 women were thus employed) and they needed training. The first women's teacher colleges were established in London in the late 1840s, right as Charlotte

Bronte's novel about a governess, *Jane Eyre*, hit the stands. Meanwhile, innovative day and boarding schools for girls sought to replicate the grammar and public school curriculums, some even with the hope of preparing girls for university. Advocates for women's higher education had, on the one hand, to make the case for women's academic ability while, on the other, reassuring the public that advanced studies would not "unsex" young ladies.[56] The difficult balance was in time achieved. The first women's colleges, Newnham and Girton, were founded at Cambridge in the early 1870s; similar institutions followed at Oxford and elsewhere. But the beneficiaries of these developments remained the exception rather than the rule. In 1900, Oxford and Cambridge each had in its student population fewer than 300 women but well over 2,500 men. For a long while, young female scholars could only attend lectures chaperoned; without escorts, critics worried, their presence would distract the young men. Women eventually won the right to take final exams and often outperformed their male peers, but they could not

FIGURE 7.10 Illustration from John Barr's short story, *The Governess; Or the Missing Pencilcase*, c. 1875.

receive degrees at Oxford until after World War I and at Cambridge until after World War II. Elsewhere, women stormed the ivory tower more completely. The University of London granted degrees to women starting in 1882, and Scottish universities treated male and female students equally as of 1892.[57]

Home and Neighborhood

At the heart of debates about employment and education were, as we have seen, concerns about gender roles within the family. Regardless of class, managing the household was woman's work; and regardless of class, managing the household was difficult work. In working-class families, it fell to wives. One appreciative son, Thomas Okey, remembered his mother's lot this way: "[A]ll the work of the house, the nursing and care of the children in health and sickness, the providing, the preparation, and the cooking of the food, the making and repairing of the clothing, and the hardest of all, the balancing of the domestic budget, fell on her."[58] Two years before Okey's birth in 1852, the General Board of Health had calculated that the back-breaking labor of carting water from the communal outside tap each week, as much as 500 pounds for a laboring family, took the equivalent of two days' of work.[59] And this was a mere prelude to the cooking and washing for which it was needed. Children would help, but not if they were young, at work, or at school. Yet Okey considered balancing the budget "the hardest of all" his mother's many responsibilities. A working-class family's well-being depended on the matriarch's ability to stretch limited resources—to shop for food and pawn possessions wisely, swap favors with neighbors, send children out to work, seek charitable assistance, and take on additional paid labor herself. This daily calculus became especially pressing when accident, sickness, unemployment, desertion, or death, of any wage-earner but especially a male breadwinner, struck.

Husbands' long workdays and leisure hours at the pub or club kept many away from home. Moreover, men typically retained a third to a half of their income for their own personal use on beer, tobacco, clothes, and the like. By contrast, everything a wife earned, and most children's income, contributed to household expenses. This arrangement was replicated in the allocation of food. The main breadwinner ate the least bread. Husbands and fathers enjoyed the most varied and extensive meals, which might include protein-rich fish and meat, and a special chair by the fire in which to consume them. Children's dietary needs came next, while wives and mothers tended to feed themselves last. When the daughter of a dock worker spied a pan full of bacon bones at a playmate's house, she proposed a game she tellingly called "Mothers and Fathers." Assuming the paternal role, the little girl claimed the biggest bone in recognition of a "hard day's work." Real life confirmed child's play. When London's dockers struck for better wages in 1889, the union strike fund established to help feed them during the difficult weeks of protest made no provision for their starving wives and children, whose only recourse was private charity.[60]

"Overall," historian Shani D'Cruze concludes, "self-deprivation was the chief means that working-class wives used to make ends meet." The combined effects of poor nutrition and unremitting, hard physical labor also meant that they experienced particularly poor health. Repeated pregnancy and childbirth exacerbated the situation, and maternal mortality rates remained high. When in 1911 the government introduced the National Insurance Act, a social security plan that included health insurance for industrial workers, it added a maternity benefit for participants' wives; in 1918 the Maternal and Child Welfare Act ordered local governments to employ "health visitors." But while infant mortality rates declined, maternal mortality increased for a while longer.[61]

Working-class families lived in extremely close quarters. Children often shared beds or slept on pallets in the kitchen, and there was scant privacy within the household. The social worker Helen Bosanquet attributed "improvident" marriage, "the curse of the poor," to such overcrowding. "Family life, which is carried on in one or two rooms, is bad enough when the family still consists of children; as they grow up to be young men and women it becomes intolerable," she wrote in 1890s. "Too often marriage is accepted as the only way to escape from conditions that have become unbearable." The results were even smaller, ill-equipped households.[62]

Outside of the house, too, privacy was rare, especially in cities. Neighbors shared not only water taps but outhouses, clotheslines, and childcare (figure 7.11). In such an environment, how one kept one's home was a crucial marker of "decency" and "respectability." Great effort went into such thankless, repetitive tasks as keeping the front curtain a pristine white in a home fueled by a sooty coal fire. Ironically, the better off the family, the more work there was to do—more rooms to clean, rugs to beat, dishes to wash, and clothes to mend. But the absence of such work could be worse. John Overs wrote of how unhappy his wife, formerly a servant in a middle-class household, was to be "cooped up in a single room, ... where by contrasting her former profusion with her present penury, she takes to fretting, gossiping, and gin."[63] Mrs. Overs was now mistress of her own home, but it did not meet her expec-

FIGURE 7.11 A street in Glasgow. *Close, No. 118, High Street*, by Thomas Annan, 1868.

tations for domestic respectability. Appearances of a different sort mattered too. A striking memory from one man's childhood was how his mother, unable to afford the fixings for a proper Sunday dinner, would "rattle the dishes" at dinnertime so that the neighbors would not know.[64] Neighbors could hear more than rattling dishes. Domestic violence was common, especially between spouses fighting over limited economic resources. It is estimated that in any London working-class neighborhood at midcentury, 10-20 men were convicted annually of assaulting their partners, a situation fueled by rampant alcohol abuse.[65] Wives too sometimes struck the first blow, and working-class mothers did not think twice about disciplining children with corporal punishment.

Although conflict was common within working-class families, so was companionship and cooperation. A resident of one of London's new apartment buildings recorded in 1889 how some men might go out at night "but the majority simply stay home with the wife and children." One "family man" in particular enjoyed playing with his sons and "putting them to bed."[66] It took the pooling of resources—money, labor, and love—to achieve and maintain a respectable lifestyle. When a spouse died, remarriage often followed soon; widows sought a breadwinner, widowers a household manager. Long-term cohabitation without marriage remained common too. At the start of World War I, thousands of unmarried "wives" claimed separation benefits when their "husbands" became soldiers.[67] And while most homes contained just two generations, the support of extended family could prove invaluable. Consider Ellen Johnston, "The Factory Girl" poet. Ellen's father moved to America when she was a child. Mrs. Johnston, unwilling to make the trip, took Ellen to live with her own parents. Years later, assuming her husband dead (though he was not), she remarried. Ellen's stepfather sexually abused her, and in response to Ellen running away, her mother beat her. Yet when Ellen had a daughter of her own, she set up house with her mother. In Ellen's domestic arrangements, we glimpse a reliance on kin that transcended the daily struggles of family life.

The same concerns—work, privacy, respectability, conflict, and love—played out in middle- and upper-class households, albeit in different ways. Wife and mother again managed the house, but also employed domestic servants. The presence of servants, their type and number, was as good an indicator of social standing as income. A lower middle-class home might have one "maid of all work," a more securely middle-class household two or three servants, while running an upper-class one required legions of paid help. Robert Graves remembered figuring out as a child the gaping divide between those who served and were served:

> The servants were trained to call us children 'Master Robert,' 'Miss Rosaleen,' and 'Miss Clarissa,' but I had not recognized these as titles of respect. I had thought of 'Master' and 'Miss' merely as vocative prefixes for addressing other people's children; but now I found that the servants were the lower classes, and that we were 'ourselves.'[68]

Within the working class, domestic service represented the largest female occupation—approximately one-quarter of all laboring women at midcentury, who worked (as many as 18 hours per day) and lived in others' homes.[69] Within the middle and upper classes, dependence on domestic service helped elevate wives and mothers to "angels of the house."

This is not to say that elite wives did not work. Their responsibilities were numerous, but rarely did they involve cooking and hauling water. Instead, they planned meals, oversaw shopping and cleaning, assisted husbands in their careers, engaged in philanthropy, and protected family connections, reputation, and capital. Sisters and daughters with small or no dowries often shared these responsibilities with the matriarch or assumed them in her absence, serving as "a second, junior 'angel' in the house" or even housekeepers for relatives.[70] Unmarried women also joined the swelling ranks of nurses, nannies, and governesses employed in strangers' homes, for affluent mothers did little of the physical, labor-intensive work of childrearing. Such arrangements, however, did not diminish the importance of motherhood. As we have seen, it increased in this period. Whereas earlier conduct manuals addressed parenting advice to fathers, in the nineteenth century they were overwhelming directed toward mothers. A mother's authority, which now extended beyond infancy through childhood, contributed to the changes in the child custody laws that began with Caroline Norton. When additional custody reform was under consideration in 1884, the *Glasgow News* challenged traditional, absolute paternal rights on the grounds that "in principle and in fact the training of the mother is in nine cases out of ten the foundation of character."[71]

Women managed the domestic sphere, but they were also active participants in public realms. In fact, the most common criticisms of maternal behavior expressed concern that they focused too much on worldly duties and pleasures. By the same token, the middle-class *pater familias* were very involved in domestic life, their role in the family central to their masculine identity. The historian John Tosh has challenged the cliché of the physically absent and emotionally remote Victorian father, pointing out that many actually worked at home; clergymen, for whom a vicarage usually came with the church, did, and so too farmers and many shopkeepers and professionals. The majority, however, commuted to work, short distances by foot or longer ones by train, tram, or omnibus with the rise of suburbia. Yet they spent a striking, perhaps unprecedented, amount of their leisure time at home. A foreign visitor remarked with a hint of amusement in 1862 that such men liked to be "home at six in the evening" in the company of "an agreeable faithful wife, tea, four or five children clambering over their knees, and respectful servants."[72] The children, however, would soon return to the nursery; servants would wash tea things in basement kitchens and sleep in the attic; women would inhabit the parlor; and men would retreat to office or den. Middle- and upper-class homes, for all their familial togetherness, were hierarchical, segregated spaces, no longer centers of collaborative labor and production.[73]

The expectation that wives be "agreeable faithful," much as servants were "respectful," reflected the unequal balance of power between spouses. Custody and divorce reform, as we have seen, addressed this somewhat. But given that most troubled couples did not separate, more revealing was the fact that only in 1884 did husbands lose the legal authority to send their wives to jail for refusing them sex. Imprisonment at home was permitted under such circumstances for a while longer. When the latter was prohibited in 1891, the *Times* announced that "one fine morning last month marriage in England was suddenly abolished."[74] Conservative *Times* readers had little to fear. Although a government commission recommended in 1911 dropping the divorce double standard (a wife's adultery was sufficient grounds for divorce but a husband's was not), it remained on the books until 1923.

Liberation, where it was achieved, thus often took cultural rather than legal forms. Dual emblems of *fin de siècle* female emancipation were bikes and bloomers, the pantaloons women wore while cycling, for women, as well as children, embraced the bicycle craze. The word *bloomers* had actually been coined in the 1850s when an American named Amelia Jenks Bloomer urged women to adopt "rational dress" in lieu of the corsets and petticoats of the day. Bloomer's costume did not catch on, but the resurrection of the term in the 1890s for the controversial cycling outfit highlights the long history of nineteenth-century activism that culminated in the "New Woman."

In 1858, the *English Women's Journal*, a monthly magazine dedicated to promoting women's employment and other opportunities, opened offices in London at 19 Langham Place. With this was born the Langham Place Group, an informal association of women that petitioned for women artists' admittance to the Royal Academy School, provided apprenticeships and technical training for women, and campaigned for women's rights. Two of the journal's editors, Barbara Bodichon and Emily Davies, founded Girton College at Cambridge. Beyond education and journalism, group members entered professions and politics, including Davies' friends, the Garrett sisters. Elizabeth Garrett Anderson became Britain's first female physician/surgeon, school board member, and mayor, all before women could vote in parliamentary elections; she also founded a medical school and a hospital she staffed with women. Millicent Garrett Fawcett became the president of the National Union of Women's Suffrage Societies. Many of the "Ladies of Langham Place," as they were known, came from an interconnected world of upper middle-class families with traditions in academe, political reform, and religious dissent. Bodichon, for example, was a Unitarian, daughter of a Whig politician and milliner who never married, and granddaughter of an abolitionist. While most women did not have their opportunities, the feminists of Langham Place argued for education and employment, and thus economic independence, for women in general. The expansion of "white-collar" jobs in schools, offices, and retail in the second half of the nineteenth century made this increasingly viable for middle-class daughters.

One of the most commented on new careers for middle-class women was in nursing, a line of work with formerly disreputable associations. Bodichon's cousin Florence Nightingale, from a more conventional branch of the family, rebelled against her upbringing to train professionally as a nurse. During the Crimean War, she famously led a group of 38 nurses to the battlefield to care for sick and wounded soldiers at the British military hospital in Scutari, and there began her lifelong commitment to sanitary and hospital reform. One applicant for Nightingale's nursing party was Mary Seacole, a mixed-raced Jamaican healer with considerable experience. Rebuffed by Nightingale's company—"Did these ladies shrink from accepting my aid because my blood flowed beneath a somewhat duskier skin than theirs," Seacole asked in her autobiography—and by the military establishment, Seacole took herself to the Crimea. Near Balaklava, she established a store and a hotel, providing supplies through the former and medical care at the latter. "Always in attendance near the battle-field to aid the wounded," a correspondent reported, Seacole returned to Britain after the war a hero but bankrupt. Military officials organized a fund-raising pageant in her honor, and she was at the time as famous as Nightingale. But whereas Nightingale became the stuff of myth, at once the nurturing "lady with the lamp" and a feminist legend, Seacole was, until recently, largely forgotten.[75] The prejudice that had excluded Seacole from Nightingale's corps also excluded her from the history books (figure 7.12).

FIGURE 7.12 Depictions of Florence Nightingale and Mary Seacole in the Crimea. While Nightingale is romanticized as "An Angel of Mercy" (1855), Seacole is depicted as a "*Vivandière*" or canteen keeper (1857).

Nightingale was 34 and Seacole 50 when they went to the Crimea in the 1850s. In 1894, the novelist Sarah Grand coined the term "New Woman" for a new type who "proclaimed for herself what was wrong with Home-is-the-Woman's-Sphere, and prescribed the remedy."[76] The New Woman became a cultural icon; artistic representations often included, along with the bikes and bloomers, short hair and cigarettes. Most evident in elite feminist circles, subscribers to the ideal could also be found working in offices and factories. In marriages, they sought control over their own bodies and reproduction, though this by no means precluded maternity. Grand, for one, believed motherhood was a woman's national duty. Her views reflect a larger shift in ideas about motherhood from the moral and religious focus of the nineteenth century to the social, scientific, and nationalist ones of the early twentieth century. The story of this shift, and the underlying demographic, legal, economic, educational, and cultural developments, is the story of the changing structures and patterns of everyday life.

IMAGE CREDITS

Fig. 7.4: Source: https://commons.wikimedia.org/wiki/File:An_Irish_Peasant_Family_Discovering_the_Blight_of_their_Store_by_Daniel_MacDonald.jpg.

Fig. 7.5: Source: https://commons.wikimedia.org/wiki/File:Queen_Victoria_Prince_Albert_and_their_nine_children.JPG.

Fig. 7.6: Source: https://commons.wikimedia.org/wiki/File:Dadabhai_Naoroji_1889.jpg.

Fig. 7.7a: Source: https://commons.wikimedia.org/wiki/File:Sampson_Kempthorne_workhouse_design_for_300_paupers.jpg.

Fig. 7.7b: Source: https://commons.wikimedia.org/wiki/File:Sampson_Kempthorne_workhouse_design_for_300_paupers,_plan_view.jpg.

Fig. 7.8a: William Strange, The Condition and Treatment of the Children employed in the Mines and Colliers of the United Kingdom, 1842.

Fig. 7.8b: William Strange, The Condition and Treatment of the Children employed in the Mines and Colliers of the United Kingdom, 1842.

Fig. 7.9a: John Everett Millais, "Cherry Ripe," 1879.

Fig. 7.9b: John Everett Millais, "Bubbles," 1886.

Fig. 7.10: John Barr, The Governess; or, the Missing Pencilcase, 1875.

Fig. 7.11: Source: https://commons.wikimedia.org/wiki/File:Close_No._118_High_Street_(-6)_LACMA_M.2008.40.98.6.jpg.

Fig. 7.12a: Copyright © by Tomkins after Butterworth / Wellcome Collection (CC BY 4.0) at https://commons.wikimedia.org/wiki/File:Coloured_mezzotint;_Florence_Nightingale,_Wellcome_L0019661.jpg.

Fig. 7.12b: Source: https://commons.wikimedia.org/wiki/File:MarySeacole_Punch.jpg.

CHAPTER 8

Britain in a World Historical Context

After being at war with France for a generation, Britain enjoyed almost a century of relative peace in Europe. From 1815 to 1914, the United Kingdom engaged in no major conflict with another European power. But this state of affairs, celebrated as a rather triumphal and self-congratulatory *Pax Britannica*, belied the violence, oppression, and almost constant military campaigns waged throughout the world on behalf of the expansion and maintenance of Britain's empire.

In chapter 3, we offered a general and capacious definition of empire as a group of states or ethnic groups governed though a range of methods and with varying degrees of centralization by a single sovereign power. In the nineteenth century, as the geographical extent of Britain's empire grew, the nature of its empire evolved. In this chapter, we will take a closer look at how empire works and examine three of empire's visible results: Empire extracts resources (natural, human, and capital), empire invites resistance, and empire produces knowledge about race and gender in order to control subject peoples.

For most of the nineteenth century, the British empire expanded steadily, sometimes in response to deliberate policy promulgated in London, sometimes as a result of local circumstances, often as a combination of both. A patchwork quilt of colonies acquired in an ad hoc manner, though by no means as an inadvertent or haphazard afterthought, and governed loosely through a variety of arrangements, spanned the globe. Attitudes and ideas formed in the eighteenth century, such as stadial theory, evolved into theories of empire in the nineteenth, such as social Darwinism and "the White man's burden." Beliefs about British national identity shaped and were shaped by the acquisition and management of colonies. Most English, Scottish, Welsh, and Irish residents of the British Isles probably took a great deal of pride in the empire, which provided employment and opportunities for advancement. Those engaged in industry, trade, and commerce viewed the empire as an important source of raw materials as well as markets for their goods. Meanwhile, the colonies became home, both temporary and permanent, to soldiers, missionaries, civil servants, scientists, and teachers. In this regard, colonies had the added benefit of absorbing the British Isles' increasing population. Perhaps most importantly, the large number of impoverished men and women excluded from educational and economic advancement by Britain's rigid class hierarchy, and viewed by authorities as a constant threat to the stability of metropolitan society, looked to greater opportunity in one of the colonies.

Britain remained engaged with continental Europe but had no cause for concern over the balance of power for most of the century. As the twentieth century approached, the unification of Germany, completed in 1871, and the emergence of the United States as a world power, recalibrated relationships within Europe and threatened Britain's global dominance. An elaborate system of alliances kept an uneasy peace. In the early twentieth century, however, competition and tensions among the European powers, and the exhaustion of territories for colonial acquisition, all contributed to the outbreak of World War I. Meanwhile, long-brewing independence movements among colonized subjects resounded with anticolonial rhetoric and action.

Throughout the nineteenth century, domestic political and social policies concerning the British Isles were informed by and in turn influenced Britain's empire. As the electorate expanded, public opinion and partisan politics played a greater role in both spheres. No matter where British voters stood on issues such as the expansion of the franchise, the state's role in health care, education, welfare, and the relationship between subjecthood and citizenship, the empire shaped British policy.

Empire Extracts

Britain's imperial domination of its colonial holdings was driven by the expansion of capitalism, the quest for profits, and the unquenchable thirst for raw materials. It justified brutality and ruthlessness with the cry of free trade, a fiction that championed Britain's commitment to maintaining access to open markets. In fact, British imperial policy in the nineteenth century reveals a determined effort to organize the world and its colonial holdings to facilitate the dominance of British manufacturing, shipping, and finance.

Far from curtailing colonial ventures, the British continued to expand their empire in the decades following the American Revolution. Their motives for doing so varied by region. The Congress of Vienna, which marked the end of the long wars against revolutionary and Napoleonic France, confirmed Britain's control of Malta (seized in 1800) and the Ionian Islands (1806). Along with Gibraltar (ceded to Britain in 1713), they gave Britain strategic control of much of the Mediterranean Sea, while Cape Colony (captured from the Dutch in 1806) provided a major transit point on the route to India. Economic incentives lay behind expansion along the coast of Africa and the Caribbean. In 1807, Sierra Leone and Gambia in West Africa became Crown colonies.

Britain also gained islands in the Caribbean and Guyana on the coast of South America, which furthered the profits from sugar cane. In the early nineteenth century, the British empire thus had three centers of gravity. The Caribbean produced large quantities of sugar cane while India provided cotton and spices. The string of outposts along the coast of Africa and across the Indian Ocean served as what came to be called "inns on the road to India," way stations for ships plying their trade between India and Britain.

The emphasis on controlling sea lanes and securing markets did not preclude imperial expansion, but the growth often occurred along the edges of existing colonies, usually as a result of local initiative. The East India Company (EIC) steadily increased its holdings in South Asia. It took control of coastal areas of Ceylon (modern Sri Lanka) in 1796 and occupied the interior kingdom of Kandy in 1815. On the Indian subcontinent the company acquired Sindh (1843) and Punjab (1849) on the Northwest Frontier and Burma (1826 and 1852). The need for greater revenue to maintain its private army and pay its other expenses encouraged the EIC to conquer more of the

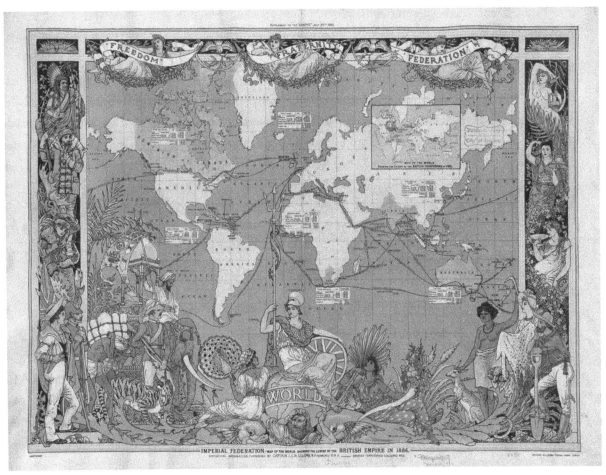

FIGURE 8.1 Map of the British Empire in 1886 reflecting racist perceptions of Indigenous peoples.

subcontinent. Expansion thus set in a motion a vicious cycle. The more the company squeezed local rulers and people for revenue, the more soldiers it needed to control them. More soldiers required more money and hence further conquest.[1] British colonies in Australia, New Zealand, and Canada steadily expanded, as did enclaves in Africa. Growth came at the expense of Indigenous people, whom the British killed, forcibly removed, or subjugated, and whose land they appropriated.

SUGAR AND LABOR

The abolition of slavery in the British Empire in 1833 presented plantation owners with a need for labor. When former slaves left the plantation complexes in pursuit of their own farms, plantation owners persuaded the colonial governments in the British Caribbean to pay for the importation of a large number of indentured laborers from India. The EIC and other government agents recruited Indians, often poor and in debt, and sent them not only to the Caribbean islands but also to Malaya, Mauritius, Burma, Australia, New Zealand, and South Africa. Indenture contracts bound laborers to a plantation for three to five years and, generally made entry into a colony contingent on working at a specific job, barred workers from changing jobs, and prohibited demands for improved wages or working conditions.

When this program of importing labor from India ended in 1917, some 150,000 Indians had been imported to Trinidad, for example, which at that point had a population of less than half a million. As cheap labor, Indian indentured workers drove down wages of the former enslaved people. The surge in British cotton production during the Industrial Revolution and Britain's destruction of India's textile industry (discussed in chapter 6) had created unemployed laborers desperate for work. Even before the abolition of slavery, these laborers had been sent, usually forcibly, to other British colonies. But they became especially important after abolition. In the Caribbean in the years after emancipation, the colonial government and landowners conspired to create an overabundance of labor in order to drive down labor costs. As a result, the Caribbean islands today are overpopulated, with heavy out-migration.

OPIUM, GOLD, AND DIAMONDS

The desire to impose free trade on reluctant trading partners and to extract profit from newly created or expanded markets led to wars with China in 1839–42 and again in 1856–60. While Britain justified the wars as protecting free trade, China opposed the flooding of its cities with opium, loss of sovereignty, and the control of foreign intervention.

As discussed in chapter 6, the consumption of tea in the British Isles increased tremendously in the eighteenth century. Until the mid-nineteenth century, most of Britain's tea came from China, along with silks and porcelain. To pay for these imports, the EIC shipped Indian opium to China. The Chinese state restricted foreign trade to the port city of Canton, which the traders were allowed to visit only during certain, specified periods each year. They could only trade with a small group of licensed Chinese merchants called the Cohong.

Opium is an addictive drug made from poppies. Initially, opium smoking was adopted in China as an occasional indulgence for China's upper classes, such as ceremonial court officials, government clerks, or military officers in quiet posts. Gradually it spread to more and more of the elite, and their rate of use increased. In 1807, Chinese state officials debated whether to ban it. Advocates of a ban argued that opium addiction was setting a bad example for the common people and ruining the morale of soldiers and state officials. Advocates of legalized opium argued that if it were outlawed, government officials who were opium users could be easily blackmailed by threats to expose their habit. Supporters of legalized opium won the debate.

Around 1818, a cheaper and much more potent form of opium was developed, and its use spread quickly. In 1815, the amount of opium imported into China was sufficient to support about 125,000 addicts, but by 1839, China was importing enough opium to supply at least 10 million addicts.[2] Most of the new Chinese users were poor. Opium has greater adverse effect on poor users than it does on rich ones. If an addict has a good diet, opium's harmful effects are quite gradual. But if an addict is poor, and the purchase of the drug cuts into the purchase of food, then the harmful effects are quick and severe. Chinese society suffered immensely from this expanded trade.

Britain too had opium addicts, especially in London and other port cities that handled imperial traffic. But opium was not a controlled substance. It was readily available without a prescription at pharmacies and markets in urban and rural areas throughout Britain that also sold cocaine and even arsenic. Laudanum, alcohol mixed with 10 percent opium, was recommended for a wide range of ailments including coughs, menstrual cramps, and crying babies.

In China, however, the extent of use, the debilitating effect of the drug on the population and the trade's depletion of hard currency eventually prompted a severe crackdown. In March 1839 Chinese state officials confiscated 20,000 chests of opium, dumping them in the ocean. In response to what it considered an attack on British subjects and their property, Britain declared war. Superior organization and military technology, particularly a decisive advantage in warships, made the outcome inevitable. The Treaty of Nanking (1842), which ended the conflict, reveals that the British wanted more than just unrestricted sale of opium. The Chinese ceded Hong Kong to Britain, opened four more treaty ports to trade, and were forced to pay reparations for the opium they had destroyed. The EIC was allowed to continue the opium trade. Supported by France, Britain fought the Second Opium War (1857–1859) to enforce the terms of the treaty and further open China to Western economic activity. Over the next four decades, China became a site of ever increasing drug addiction. By 1900, there were as many as 40 million addicts in a population of 400 million. Widespread addiction contributed greatly to the instability of the Chinese state in the early twentieth century, when the imperial government fell.

FIGURE 8.2 British ships attacking a Chinese battery on the Pearl River during the first Opium War, 1841. From *Narrative of a Voyage Round the World*, performed in Her Majesty's ship Sulphur, during the Years 1836-1842, Including Details of the Naval Operations in China, from December 1840 to November 1841, by Captain Sir Edward Belcher, RN.

FIGURE 8.3 The Kimberley Mine: an open pit and underground diamond mine in Kimberley, South Africa.

Extractive imperial activity intensified in the second half of the nineteenth century when gold was discovered in Australia in 1851, South Africa in 1886, and in Canada in 1896. In Africa during the 1880s, chartered companies such as the Royal Niger Company, the British East Africa Company, and the British South Africa Company drove imperial expansion. These privatized efforts were far cheaper for the British state than establishing direct rule. Tropical colonies provided rubber, palm oil, cotton, coffee, tea, sugar, cocoa, and minerals such as petroleum, tin, copper, diamonds, and gold. In South Africa, the discovery of diamonds in 1867 was followed by a gold rush in the 1880s. South Africa absorbed large numbers of white immigrants drawn to get-rich schemes. Although few became wealthy, they were paid at better rates than the Indigenous Black workers whose exploitation fueled the gold and diamond rushes.

Settler Colonialism

"Settlement colonies," later dubbed "White Dominions," absorbed Britain's increasing population, discussed in chapter 7. Settler colonies experienced dramatic growth during the nineteenth century. Australia had a European settler population of just over 5,000 in 1800. By midcentury 405,000 inhabitants of European descent lived in the continent's colonies. Fifty years later the number had jumped to almost 3.8 million. During the twenty years between 1841 and 1861, the English-speaking population of Canada more than doubled, rising from approximately 480,000 to almost 1.4 million. British settlements in New Zealand grew at a similar rate, but until diamonds and gold were discovered in the late nineteenth century, South Africa's white population grew more slowly.

In her "Typology of Colonialism," historian Nancy Shoemaker defines settler colonialism as the phenomenon in which "large numbers of settlers claim land and become the majority. Employing a 'logic of elimination,' … they attempt to engineer the disappearance of the original inhabitants everywhere except in nostalgia."[3] After the loss of the 13 North American colonies, Canada, Australia, South Africa, and New Zealand became Britain's primary settler colonies. As white populations increased in these places, they demanded representative government and local rule. Beginning with the Australian Colonies Government Act of 1850, the British government granted to its Australian colonies limited autonomy, which developed into independence as members of a British Commonwealth federation in 1901. The British North America Act of 1867 created the Dominion of Canada as a self-governing federation of Ontario, Quebec, New Brunswick, and Nova Scotia under the British Crown. New Zealand became a dominion in 1907. In 1910, the British created the Union of South Africa, combining its colonies with the former Boer republics of Transvaal and the Orange Free State into a single dominion.

The British also justified expansion with the specious argument first proposed by John Locke that Indigenous people did not use the land to its fullest potential, with potential defined as profit. Other British propaganda asserted that colonists were occupying largely vacant land and that Indigenous people should either be "civilized" and absorbed into the settler communities or forcibly relocated.

In the territories that would become Canada, disease had decimated First Nations (native Canadians) during the seventeenth and eighteenth centuries. After Britain gained control of Canada in 1763, it used a series of treaties that gradually forced First Nations onto reservations. The British North America Act gave white settlers autonomy, which they soon used to further curtail native rights. The 1876 Indian Act limited native self-government. The goal of this and subsequent legislation was complete assimilation. First Nations children were forced to attend church-run residential schools where many died of disease and others suffered physical and sexual abuse. Mass graves of these victims began to be uncovered in 2021. Duncan Campbell Scott, deputy superintendent general of Indian Affairs described this genocidal policy in 1920: "Our objective is to continue until there is not an Indian that has not been absorbed into the body politic."[4]

The Aboriginal inhabitants of Australia suffered an even worse fate. Estimates of the pre-colonization Aboriginal population range from 300,000 to over 1 million. The 1920 census identified only fifty-eight thousand "full-blood" Aboriginal people left in all of Australia, a decline of 80–96 percent. Disease, especially smallpox, accounted for the greatest loss of life, but Aborigines also suffered violence at the hands of White settlers. White men spread venereal disease through rape and prostitution of Aborigine women, leaving many of those it did not kill sterile. As many as thirty thousand Aborigines, including women and children, may have been murdered by settlers.[5] Most were shot, but some were also poisoned. The remaining Aborigines suffered discrimination and could not vote in national elections until 1962.

The Maori of New Zealand fared no better than the Aborigines of Australia. Approximately ninety thousand Maori lived in New Zealand when the British arrived in 1769; by 1890, their population had declined to thirty-nine thousand.[6] As in North America and Australia, European diseases, to which the Indigenous people had no resistance, killed the most people, but thousands also died in a series of wars fought between 1840 and 1881 over New Zealand's northern island. Some British intellectuals believed the extinction of Indigenous people a necessary and inevitable consequence of colonization. One scientist considered the demise of the Maori "scarcely subject for much regret. They are dying out in a quick, easy way, and are being supplanted by a superior race."[7] Colonists bought land whenever they could, but when the Maori were unwilling to sell, the British resorted to violence. As in Canada, the increasing autonomy granted to New Zealand's white population accelerated the genocidal policy.

Indigenous people also died in colonial wars. Britain acquired most of its Victorian empire through conquest. The British army fought Pashtuns on the Northwest Frontier of India, the Ashanti in West Africa, and the Zulus in South Africa. These brutal wars devastated the Indigenous populations. The British often punished entire communities to force their surrender. C. E. Caldwell, whose *Small Wars: Their Principles and Practice* became the handbook of colonial warfare, observed unapologetically that in such conflicts "war assumes an aspect which may shock the humanitarian."[8] Rudyard Kipling, a strong advocate of Britain's civilizing mission, encapsulated

FIGURE 8.4 Maori village.

the destructive, genocidal, and extractive attributes of imperialism in describing how soldiers behaved toward those they fought:

> They will feed their horse on the standing crop, their men on the garnered grain,

> The thatch of the byres will serve their fires when all the cattle are slain.[9]

The British advantage in firepower could produce great slaughter. At Omdurman, Sudan, in 1898, an Anglo-Egyptian Army killed 10,000 Dervishes for the loss of 48 of their own men, using artillery, machine guns, and magazine rifles against an enemy mostly equipped with swords and spears. The British even fired dum dum (expanding) bullets outlawed for "civilized" warfare between white adversaries in Europe.[10]

Ireland

Ireland occupied a unique and often uncomfortable position in the nineteenth century political/ imperial system. On the one hand, it was an integral part of the United Kingdom, joined to Great Britain by the Act of Union in 1801. Irish peers sat in the House of Lords, and Ireland elected members of Parliament to the House of Commons. On the other hand, Ireland had some striking characteristics in common with Britain's overseas colonies.

The British ruling classes governed Ireland much as they did their imperial possessions in Africa and Asia. Union did not terminate the office of the Lord Lieutenant of Ireland (also known as the governor general or viceroy), a British government appointee who, with the Chief Secretary of Ireland, oversaw the executive branch. At the beginning of the nineteenth century, an Anglo-Irish Ascendancy, the beneficiary of centuries of conquest and settlement and comprising less than 10 percent of the population, ruled a majority Catholic peasant population that possessed no vote and few political rights. Legislation in 1829 (granting Catholics the right to sit in Parliament) and 1832 (rearranging the franchise) reformed the constitution such that one-seventh of English men could now vote, but in Ireland, only one-twentieth of the male population could do so.[11] For the remainder of the century the British government resisted Irish demands for home rule, the grant of local autonomy similar to that afforded Canada, Australia, South Africa, and New Zealand. Religious and racial prejudice, and demographics, had much to do with this. Many Protestant Britons feared that an autonomous Ireland with a majority Catholic population would allow the Catholic Church to control Irish politics. Moreover, British elites often viewed Irish Catholics with the same mixture of disdain and paternalism that they felt for their non-white colonial subjects. They considered that these "natives" could be "improved" to a point but would not be ready for self-government, let alone independence, for a considerable time. Successive administrations in London thus concentrated on improving living conditions for Irish farmers through land reform and tenant rights while, as will be discussed in chapter 10, home rule bills failed in 1886 and 1893. Only in the early twentieth century did the British government concede to Irish demands for autonomy, though World War I would delay the implementation of the Home Rule bill passed in 1911.

The consequences of this unequal relationship were manifest in all aspects of Irish life. In 1831, for example, modernizers introduced a national system of primary education in Ireland in an effort to end religious segregation and proselytizing in schools. All instruction in the new schools, however, occurred in English; the Irish language, Irish literature, and Irish history had no place in the new curriculum designed for Irish children. Nationalists like the journalist Charles Gavin Duffy, founder of the *Nation*, complained

FIGURE 8.5 Drawing of the potato famine.

that "the state 'deliberately starved or suppressed' Irish culture."[12] Accusations of starvation and suppression would soon extend far beyond cultural affairs. The British government's handling of the Irish famine in the late 1840s "demonstrated," in the words of historian Christine Kinealy, "that Ireland was a not an equal partner within the United Kingdom and that the needs of the Irish were of less importance than those of the people in the metropole."[13]

The government's initial response to the famine, in the fall of 1845, was to purchase £100,000 of grain from North America for resale in Ireland. Bad weather slowed delivery, and the grain did not arrive until February 1846. In March, the government instituted a public works scheme to assist famine victims in buying the imported food. At its height, the scheme employed 700,000 men for such projects as building roads and canals. Still, horrific conditions prevailed in Ireland; workers often died of starvation before getting paid the weekly wages with which to buy the imported food. Criticism of the public works project, including concerns that its elaborate bureaucracy violated the rules of free trade, led to its abandonment in January 1847. In its place, the Soup Kitchens Act directly fed over 3 million that spring and summer. By October 1847, the authorities reckoned the soup kitchen scheme had done its job, and it too closed shop. Indeed, only a few months later, in January 1848, an "official" account of the Irish famine was published, suggesting it was a thing of the past. Perhaps most cruelly of all, the government did not close Irish ports to food exports. Through much of the famine, profit-seeking merchants shipped foodstuffs from Ireland to England.

Compared to other mid-nineteenth-century expenditures, British government expenditure on famine relief in Ireland was paltry. In the 1830s, £20 million had been paid to West Indian planters in "compensation" for abolition. In the 1850s, the Crimean War cost £70 million. In the decade in between, the government apportioned less than £10 million to relief in Ireland, and nearly all of it had been spent by 1847. Subsequent relief measures placed the financial burden on Irish taxpayers. It was all a question of priorities, and Ireland was not a high one. Such official stinginess contrasts markedly with private charity. Queen Victoria contributed £2,500 and called for churches to raise money for famine relief. A national day of fasting led to the collection of £171,533.[14] Ideology contributed to the government's relative inaction. Free-trade economics, the writings of Thomas Malthus (who argued that famine relief meant more people to reproduce and, thus, more famine), and "providentialism" (the belief that God had sent the famine to reform Irish society) convinced many in Parliament that "interfering" with natural law would only make things worse in the long run.[15]

The famine left an indelible mark on Irish national consciousness. The sight of food being taken from Ireland, often in convoys with armed guards, as its people starved was an evocative and emotive image the government would never live down—and subsequent Irish nationalists would never forget. In the *Last Conquest of Ireland*, published in 1860, John Mitchel accused the British government of genocide: "The Almighty, indeed, sent the potato blight, but the English made the famine."[16]

Some Irish nationalists were thus more than ready to follow the example of French revolutionaries who, in February 1848, toppled another monarchy to create the Second French Republic. Just as the French Revolution of 1789 had inspired the United Irishmen to rebel in 1798, current events in France radicalized some Irish nationalists who had formerly focused on repealing the Act of Union. An uprising in the summer of 1848 to establish an Irish republic was quickly put down, but ideas of Irish independence were not. Republicans and home rule advocates represented competing elements of the nationalist movement for the rest of the century. The former, in the minority, tried their hand at rebellion again in 1867, while the latter sought a more limited, legislative approach to self-government, one less threatening to the idea and practice of empire. Finally, it is important to note that among the millions who packed up and left Ireland, emigrating before, during, and after the famine, were many who settled in neither the metropole nor the United States but in the far-flung reaches of the British Empire.

Governing the Empire

Like the English, Scottish, and Welsh, Irish men and women also populated the empire as desperate and hopeful settlers and as employees of the imperial project, soldiers in particular. The empire grew tremendously in the nineteenth century, and by the start of the twentieth Britain administered 47 territories of which only 12 were self-governing. In addition to encompassing a huge population of 400 million, the empire spanned different languages, cultures, religions, and ethnicities. The endurance of the empire for so long indicates that it was created intentionally not by happenstance.

The collection of colonies should not be thought of as a modern corporation whose components and subsidiaries fit neatly into an organizational chart. Rather, it resembled a patchwork quilt with pieces of different shades and shapes. The British governed through a series of local ad hoc arrangements made according to broad guidelines. As often as some colonial officials were allowed latitude in the performance of their duties and enjoyed that autonomy, others pleaded for guidance from British authorities at home and were ignored or neglected. At other times London and colonial authorities clashed, with local authorities completely contradicting instructions from the Colonial Office. The first Colonial Office (1768–1800) was established to take care of the American colonies. In 1800, it was renamed the War and Colonial Office. The name reflects the way in which territory was acquired and the constant resistance Britain's imperial conquest faced. In 1854, the War and Colonial Office was divided into the War Office and a new Colonial Office. Of course, British authorities treated colonies with a majority of white settlers who were deemed worthy of more autonomy or what was called "responsible government" differently than territories inhabited primarily by people of color. The contrast between the self-government that was developing in settler colonies like Canada, Australia, South Africa, and New Zealand and other dependencies became more visible when, in the nineteenth century, the empire expanded and non-settler colonies like India, Burma, Kenya, and Egypt became more typical. As Britain's power increased, conquest and autocratic rule did as well. British populations in non-settler colonies were quite small and isolated. In the nineteenth century the Colonial Office staff posted in the colonies numbered only 6000 for the entire empire, and the majority of Britons in non-settler colonies were civil servants and soldiers. Mixing with Indigenous populations was discouraged, and British officials and their families tended to live in their own enclaves.[17]

Strategies of rule varied, but we can discern certain patterns and tools of oppression used by the British. British courts arbitrated cases in which Britons were involved, ensuring they received favorable treatment. The British trained colonial elites all over the world and drew them into hierarchies of governance. Meanwhile, technology in the form of infrastructure such as roads, railways, and telegraph wires enabled the movement of troops and the surveillance of Indigenous populations. Heavily militarized police ensured that order was restored when it was disrupted. Violence, in a variety of forms, was always an instrument of British rule to compel obedience and put down rebellion.

Empire Invites Resistance

Indigenous resistance to colonization was constant. The perpetual wars mentioned throughout this chapter are just some examples of the conflict, defiance, and opposition that met British expansion across the globe. Although the British usually won because of their superior technology, resistance affected changes in British policy. In Jamaica, the slave uprising of 1831, known as the Baptist War, shifted British policy away from gradual emancipation through the apprenticeship program to a more immediate emancipation. Uprisings in Ceylon in the 1840s, in Sarawak in the 1850s, and in the Malay Archipelago in the 1850s and 60s expressed dissatisfaction with British domination and rule.[18]

THE INDIAN UPRISING

From 1857 to 1858, the EIC faced widespread resistance to its rule in several provinces. The British at the time called it the "Indian Mutiny," but Indian nationalists and most historians refer to it as the "Indian Uprising" or the "Indian Rebellion." Although the trouble began with a mutiny in some regiments of the EIC Army, resistance involved much more than disaffection among soldiers. The conflict, which occurred in a limited area in the north, would change the nature of British rule in all South Asia.

In 1856, the army introduced the new Model 1853 Lee-Enfield rifled musket. The gun fired a lead bullet wrapped with gunpowder in a paper cartridge. To load the musket, the solider had to bite the cartridge open, pour its content down the muzzle, and ram the paper wadding home. To facilitate ramming, the cartridges had to be greased. A rumor spread that that grease was a mixture of cow and pig fat. Biting it would violate the religious proscriptions of both Hindus and Muslims. While the offending cartridges were in fact never issued to Indian soldiers, the controversy brought to a head decades of Indian resentment of, and resistance to, British disrespect, disregard, and destruction of Indigenous cultural and religious life. Missionary activity showed little regard for local practices and customs; the imposition of an English legal system had destroyed Indigenous procedures; and land policy had alienated both soldiers and civilians. In such a climate, rumors of the offensive use of sacred (cow) and prohibited (pig) animal fat, and fears of forced conversions, proved compelling. Widespread discontent fueled support for the uprising across caste and religious lines and outside the army.

The EIC had an army of 311,000 native troops commanded by 5,362 British officers. The regular British army had 40,000 soldiers deployed throughout South Asia, reinforced by another 56,000 after the uprising began. Approximately 100,000 Indian troops mutinied, 70,000 of them from the company's Bengal Army. Several northern princes along with their armies supported the mutineers, who also raised civilian levies.[19] The majority of Indian troops remained loyal to the EIC, but British rule in South Asia was destabilized.

The rebellion took more than a year to suppress, and its pattern of violence revealed the nature and extent of discontent. The worst atrocity occurred at Cawnpore, where, following a long siege, mutineers massacred a British garrison after it had surrendered, including approximately 200 women and children. Insurgents also attacked the administrative apparatus of the East India Company. They destroyed the bank in Delhi and burned its records. They attacked indigo dye factories on British-owned plantations. They also burned government records and murdered Indians who collaborated with the British. To prevent British officials, particularly the military officers, from communicating with one another, insurgents destroyed telegraph lines.[20]

British retribution was swift and terrible. Troops carried out summary executions of prisoners and suspected rebels. They hanged some and burned others alive. British soldiers lashed sepoys to the muzzles of cannon and blew them to bits. Before hanging suspected insurgents captured at Cawnpore, British soldiers forced them to lick blood from the floor of the room in which women and children had been murdered. Despite their outrage at the treatment of British women, however, EIC and regular soldiers did not spare Indian ones. Approximately 800,000 Indians died as a result of the mutiny and the ensuing famine it caused, along with 6,000 Britons (one in seven of the 40,000 who lived in South Asia).[21]

FIGURE 8.6 Executing prisoners during the Indian uprising.

Racism underlay the ferocity of the British response. White soldiers used derogatory and dehumanizing language to describe the insurgents they killed.[22] At the same time that the uprising intensified animosity toward South Asians, it refined the British racial hierarchy. In combatting mutineers, the army relied heavily on Gurkhas from Nepal and Sikhs from the Punjab. This reliance encouraged the belief that subjugated peoples could be divided into martial or "manly" and non-manly races.[23] Sikhs, who comprised 1 percent of the population of India, contributed 20 percent of the soldiers in the British Indian Army.[24]

The British were appalled by the show of resistance and considered Indians ungrateful for the gift of "civilization" bestowed upon them. They also blamed the EIC for mismanaging its territory in the interest of profit. The uprising thus had a profound effect on British rule in India. Passed in 1858, the Government of India Act transferred oversight of the subcontinent from the EIC to a newly created India Office in London overseen by a new cabinet minister, the Secretary of State for India. A viceroy would govern India on behalf of the British government, assisted by an Indian civil service. The British also nationalized the EIC Army. Indian soldiers could no longer serve as artillerymen, and heterogeneous religious units replaced homogenous ones.

Queen Victoria followed passage of the Government of India Act with a royal proclamation affirming that Britain would honor all treaties with South Asian princes made by the EIC. The proclamation also contained an unambiguous statement of religious tolerance:

> Firmly relying ourselves on the truth of Christianity, and acknowledging with gratitude the solace of religion, we disclaim alike the right and desire to impose our convictions on any of our subjects. We declare it to be our royal will and pleasure that none be in anywise favoured, none molested or disquieted, by reason of their religious faith or observances, but that all alike shall enjoy the equal and impartial protection of the law; and we do strictly charge and enjoin all those who may be in authority under us that they abstain from all interference with the religious belief or worship of any of our subjects on pain of our highest displeasure.[25]

The queen was not embracing pluralism but making a pragmatic concession that benefited imperialism. Missionary activity had fueled the discontent that led to the rebellion, and this proclamation severely limited it in the future.

In the eyes of Britons, the Indian Rebellion confirmed their belief that darker skinned peoples either could not govern themselves or would require a long period of British tutelage before they might be trusted with autonomy. A royal governor, high commissioner, or in the case of India a viceroy, led the administration, assisted by local British officials known as District Officers or Collectors (a reference to their tax-collecting function). The British, however, did train and educate, a class of provincial civil servants to assist them and coopted local plenipotentiaries wherever possible.

FIGURE 8.7 Morant Bay Rebellion, 1865.

FIGURE 8.8 Paul Bogle.

REBELLION IN JAMAICA

The Morant Bay Rebellion that broke out in Jamaica in 1865, less than a decade after the Indian Rebellion, sparked one of the most brutal imperial crackdowns in the nineteenth century. Its reverberations in the metropole unleashed a debate about imperial rule and resulted in the reversal of the trend to self-determination and self-rule.

Despite the abolition of slavery in Jamaica in 1838, the Jamaican Assembly was still dominated by wealthy white plantation owners. Property qualifications were relatively low, so many Blacks in Jamaica could vote. Although Black Jamaicans elected some wealthy Black and mixed-race landowners to the Assembly, some politicians of color were just as dismissive of the demands of former slaves for land redistribution as white assemblymen and helped block any proposals for progressive change. Frustrations among the majority of Black Jamaicans who were poor and owned no land rose in response to the Assembly's lack of interest in the fate of the Black, formerly enslaved majority.

In April 1865 Black Jamaicans petitioned Queen Victoria, explaining their frustration about the limited possibilities to acquire their own land. The condescending response from the British Colonial Office advised the petitioners to work harder to ensure the productivity of the plantation economy. Only then could wages rise. In August, Paul Bogle, a Baptist deacon and political activist, led his followers on a 50-mile march from Stony Gut to Spanish Town, Jamaica's capital, demanding a better court system. The Governor, Edward John Eyre, refused to meet with them. On October 7 of the same year Bogle and his supporters marched again, this time to the Morant Bay courthouse where they protested peacefully. A few days later, on October 11, Bogle and 400 supporters returned to Morant Bay. They stole weapons from a police station and confronted a volunteer militia; 25 people were killed in the fighting and 31 others were injured. Attacks spread to nearby areas.

Like other colonial officials, Eyre made his career moving from one imperial outpost to another. He had been a settler in Australia, lieutenant governor of New Zealand and St. Vincent in the West Indies, and acting governor of the Leeward Islands before posting to Jamaica. Experienced and confident, he declared martial law, unleashing brutal repression by British forces who included Black soldiers of the First West India Regiment under white officers, white soldiers from Newcastle in St. Andrew, and even some Maroons (descendants of escaped slaves). Like the Indian Sepoys, Jamaican soldiers of color could be found on both sides. Government troops killed 439 Black and mixed-race Jamaicans, whipped many more men and women, and burned down 1,000 homes. George William Gordon, a wealthy mixed-race member of the Jamaican Assembly who supported the cause of the protesters and was a critic of Eyre, was arrested, convicted on weak evidence, and hanged on October 23. Bogle was captured the following day.[26]

News of the rebellion and Eyre's brutal repression split British opinion at home. Some, among them John Stuart Mill, pressed the government to prosecute Eyre for use of excessive force. Eyre's defenders included Thomas Carlyle and Charles Dickens, who compared the rebellions in India and Jamaica and justified Eyre's ruthlessness with racist portrayals of Black men in need of British rule to impose order and defend the virtue of white women. Eyre was recalled to England in July 1866. In June 1868 a grand jury declined to indict him for murder, and he was found not liable in a civil case brought against him in the 1870s. Eyre was thus both commended for crushing the rebellion and censured for his excessive brutality. Although his professional career ended, he lived until 1901 on the pension he received as a colonial officer.

With Eyre's guidance, Jamaica's white population concluded that rather than sharing power with a Black majority they would relinquish self-rule. Jamaica's two hundred-year-old House of Assembly and its Legislative Council abolished themselves, and the island became a Crown colony governed from London in January 1866. As in India, the heavy hand of the British state imposed itself more directly in Jamaica in the wake of the uprising. Administration improved, the colonial government invested in infrastructure, and some land was made available to former enslaved people. However, these measures were taken to improve the economic output of the island and prevent further rebellion, not to further the economic or political interests of the island's Black population.

Empire and the Creation of Knowledge

From the late eighteenth century, belief in the superiority of the English constitution and the Protestant faith served as a justification for colonialism.[27] When Thomas Babington Macaulay, a historian, essayist, politician, and member of Parliament for a few years, wrote in 1835 that "[a] single shelf of a good European library was worth the whole native literature of India and Arabia,"[28] he did so confident in British cultural preeminence even though he could not read Sanskrit or Arabic. Others who oversaw and commented on Britain's empire shared Macaulay's views.

Christian missionaries also lived and worked in the empire. Although at first they saw their charge as disciplining white settler populations on the frontiers, their focus by the late eighteenth century shifted to non-settler colonies. They sought to convert Indigenous populations in the

West Indies, Africa, India, southeast Asia, and China. They built schools and hospitals, bringing what they considered "civilization" to "heathen lands." Although missionaries improved the material conditions for many, their disrespect for local custom and culture divided those who converted from those who did not.

Undergirding the efforts of colonial administrators and missionaries were new ideas and academic disciplines. The study of human cultures that began during the eighteenth century was amplified in the nineteenth century. Emerging scientific disciplines like anthropology, geography, medicine, and linguistics catalogued physical and cultural difference, constructing systematic theories that classified racial and gendered hierarchies in which non-European people and women were always below white men. In the wake of the publication of Charles Darwin's *Origins of Species* in 1859 (discussed at great length in chapter 9), these differences were mapped onto theories of empire justifying British domination, authority, and superiority based on the purported inferiority of African, Indian, Aboriginal, or Middle Eastern men and all women. Late Victorian Britons believed that they were not only more civilized than these other peoples but biologically superior to them as well. Nature dictated that the strong should rule the week: Those with lighter skin were considered superior. Social Darwinists like Herbert Spencer and Houston Stewart Chamberlin did not merely divide humanity into two groups (whites and people of color); they created a spectrum of superiority based on skin pigmentation with themselves at the top and Africans at the bottom.

Social Darwinism affected British gender norms, in particular masculinity, as men took on different traits that conformed with the superior, white male roles in which they were cast. While the liberal vision of empire before the Indian Rebellion considered white male colonial administrators, soldiers, missionaries, merchants, and settlers as Christian gentlemen, beneficent and giving, bestowing civilization and free trade on child-like people, prevailing views during the second half of the century prescribed a different set of attributes. *Muscular Christianity*, a term whose origins have been traced to the novels of Charles Kingsley and Thomas Hughes published in the 1850s, called for men to perform an aggressive, powerful, and racially superior masculinity suited to conquering subhuman, animal-like savages and subduing them with authoritarian government.

As Britain's empire and colonial administrative structure expanded, women joined their husbands, fathers, brothers, sons, and cousins, even in non-settler imperial locations. White women came to the colonies to keep house for their husbands. They might also arrive as governesses for the white children who now populated the homes of colonial officials. In their roles as the guardians of motherhood, religion, and home, they ensured that imperial ideology, including the racial and cultural superiority of white people, was both taught and learned. White British women in India had greater independence than they did at home and were freer of Victorian social and gender norms. Single as well as married white women traveled to the empire to work as missionaries, educators, nurses, and, by the end of the century, doctors. In addition to physical mobility, they enjoyed greater social mobility and power, especially over colonial subjects. Meanwhile Indigenous women and families were torn apart by the empire's extractive economies. African men, whose work in colonial mines took them to isolated areas far from home, created alternate domestic lives with local women. The British saw these arrangements and indeed any sexual relationships whose patterns differed from bourgeois Western norms as prostitution, which they considered "a routine part of [Indigenous] life, and living evidence of native disorder."[29]

Yet prostitution was, paradoxically, a routine part of white colonial life as well. "Colonial officials," Philippa Levine argues, "recognized the preponderantly masculine forms in which their work was cast and argued strenuously that without prostitution, life in the colonies would be morally and physically dangerous." They considered male sexuality "an aggressive, active force, itself vital to colonial conquest." Brothels were not only legitimized but classified (into three categories) and racialized throughout the empire. First-class brothels were reserved for a white male clientele, their female sex workers either white Europeans or Indigenous women allowed to serve white men only.[30] In 1864, the Cantonment Act established a brothel (and accompanying hospital to treat sexually transmitted diseases) for every British regiment in India. Approximately 15 Indian women worked in each of these brothels to which the soldiers of the regiment had exclusive, protected access.

Racism may have been the key element in the imperial worldview, but it was not the only one. Social status also mattered. Those who governed the empire sought to replicate among colonial peoples the British class system with its fine gradations based on rank and office.[31] They coopted and even strengthened local elites, preferring to rule through them wherever possible. Another way of justifying British rule was framed as a condescending obligation to civilize and Christianize their subjects. Rudyard Kipling best articulated this notion in his famous 1899 poem "The White Man's Burden." Written as advice to US President William McKinley, who had just conquered the Philippines during the Spanish American War, the poem proclaims the obligation of imperialists to improve the lot of their subjects.

By the end of the nineteenth century, Britain's confidence was shaken by global anticolonial movements and the rise of the United States and Germany as military and industrial rivals. In contrast to Macaulay's confident dismissal of all eastern learning, Kipling's poem describes the burden of civilization falling on white Europeans who must sacrifice for the good of their subjects: "send forth the best ye breed–/Go bind your sons to exile/To serve your captives' need." The self-assurance and conviction of the Christian masculinity of midcentury was supplanted by a tone of overwhelming exhaustion.

Imperialism was still tremendously popular at home. A series of adventure books by G. H. Henty and H. Rider Haggard celebrated imperialism and the values that underlay it. The Conservative Prime Minister Benjamin Disraeli, who led the government twice in 1868 and again from 1874 to 1880, promoted a concept of "Tory democracy" that included pride in the monarchy and the empire. Disraeli's policy of "new imperialism" was simply the old imperialism ramped up to gain more votes as the electorate in Britain expanded. The production of knowledge and its propagation

"THE WHITE MAN'S BURDEN."

FIGURE 8.9 Satirical interpretation of "The White Man's Burden," the U.S. follows Britain's example, by Victor Gillam, 1899.

of theories of dominance served to justify the costs of empire and maintain the hierarchies of race, gender, and class in the colonies and in the metropole.

British Foreign Policy, 1815–1870

After the Napoleonic Wars, British foreign policy concentrated on ensuring access to markets and protecting trade routes. While in theory this "era of free trade" represented a departure from the rigid mercantilism of the past, British colonies still traded primarily with each other and with the metropole, supplying British factories with raw materials and buying their products. All this affected Britain's relationship with its allies and rivals, those countries, empires, and regions of the globe with which it was not involved in a direct colonial relationship.

THE CONTINENT, 1815–1870

The agreements engineered by the Congress of Vienna sought, as far as possible, to restore the prewar status quo. Throughout Europe, lands were returned, divided, and united. Austria, for example, got back most of its territory in Italy but lost the Austrian Netherlands, which combined with the United Provinces to form the Kingdom of the Netherlands. Meanwhile, Austria, Prussia, and Russia repartitioned Poland, and a German Confederation under Austrian leadership replaced the Holy Roman Empire. These and numerous other adjustments redrew the map of Europe while preserving the prewar balance of power.

Britain involved itself directly in continental affairs only when events affected its interests. That happened in 1830 when Flanders and Wallonia rebelled against the Netherlands. To prevent others' intervention, Britain orchestrated an international conference that created the neutral and independent kingdom of Belgium. Better a weak neutral state control this strategic location than a continental rival.

No matter how much it disliked the autocratic regimes in Eastern and Central Europe, Britain supported the equally autocratic Ottoman Turkish Empire against Russia. During the nineteenth century, Russia expanded into the Caucuses and Central Asia and had designs on the Balkans and Istanbul, the Ottoman capital linking the Black Sea and Mediterranean. These moves brought Russia into potential conflict with Britain in several areas. Afghanistan became a buffer zone between the two empires, and Persia (modern Iran) another hotspot as Britain sought to keep Russia away from the Persian Gulf and the Middle East.

OTTOMAN EMPIRE

Britain was not, however, the Ottoman Empire's unconditional ally. Ottoman rule faced serious challenges from independence movements among its subject peoples, which Britain sometimes supported. For example, when the Greek War of Independence began in 1821, Greek nationalists elicited sympathy from classically educated Britons who saw Greece as the cradle of civilization. The London Philhellenic Committee helped the revolutionaries raise war funds, while the poet Lord Byron sold his estate Rochdale Manor in support of the cause and famously traveled to Greece to fight. Byron died, of disease rather than wounds, preparing to lead an expedition against the Ottomans in 1824. A few years later, the government followed its citizen's example, albeit for less romantic reasons. The decision of France and Russia to intervene required Britain to become involved if only to have a say in the final settlement. In 1827, the three allies destroyed the Turkish fleet at the battle of Navarino in support of Greek independence. Elsewhere, Britain walked a fine line between supporting rebellion and supporting its ally. It acquiesced to the successful revolt of Mohammed Ali Pasha, the self-proclaimed Khedive of Egypt in 1805, but prevented him gaining control of Syria and declaring independence from the Ottoman Empire in 1840.

Britain's support of the "sick man of Europe," as the Ottoman Empire came to be called, was most pronounced after Russia demanded in 1853 the right to protect Orthodox Christian interests within the Ottoman Empire. The Turks refused, and the two empires broke off diplomatic relations. When Britain sent warships to the northern Aegean as a precaution, Russian troops occupied the provinces of Moldavia and Wallachia in what is today Romania. The Ottomans threatened war if the Russians did not withdraw, which the latter refused to do. Hostilities began in October. Initial Russian success against the Ottoman navy in the Black Sea led France and Britain to demand that Russia confine its fleet to the port of Sevastopol in the Crimea. When it did not comply, they declared war on Russia in March 1854.

The Crimean War was a short, limited, desultory affair. After Russia withdrew from Moldavia and Wallachia in July 1854, hostilities shifted to the Crimea where the allies besieged Sevastopol with its naval base, which fell in September 1855. When the war ended, things reverted pretty much to how they were before: Russia returned all its captured territory, demilitarized the Black Sea, and relinquished its claim as protector of Orthodox Christians within the Ottoman Empire. Moldavia and Wallachia unified into what would become Romania.

While Britain achieved its objectives, it had hardly won an impressive victory. The two most enduring British symbols associated with the Crimean War—"the charge of the Light Brigade" and "the lady with the lamp"—are reminders of its tragic, avoidable loss of life. Alfred, Lord Tennyson immortalized the former in his poem about a cavalry unit assigned to remove captured Russians guns at the Battle of Balaclava. Due to miscommunication in the chain of command, the light brigade charged straight into an entrenched enemy artillery battery with disastrous consequences. Meanwhile Florence Nightingale, on whom another poet, Henry Wadsworth Longfellow, bestowed the saccharine lamp epithet, drew attention to the appalling conditions of the hospital at Scutari, where soldiers died in great numbers from disease. As the first conflict covered by an independent war correspondent, William Howard Russell of *The Times* (London), the Crimean War made a lasting impression on the popular imagination. A generation of schoolboys played with lead soldiers in Crimean War garb. Yet the war, and its press coverage, also revealed the deplorable state of the British Army, especially its logistics and medical care. Many of the political and administrative reforms of the following decades can be traced to the British establishment's gross failure in the Crimea.

UNITED STATES

The independence of the 13 American colonies in 1783 did not end British involvement in North America. The British still controlled Canada, which would expand westward in step with the United States. Their long common border presented a continuing source of potential conflict. Fortunately, for both parties, they resolved their differences diplomatically. The Webster–Ashburton Treaty of 1842 established the northern boundary of Maine, and the Oregon Treaty of 1846 set the 49th parallel as the northwest boundary between the two countries.

The United States and Britain faced another crisis during the American Civil War. The Union blockade of the Southern states cut off vital cotton supplies to Britain's cloth industry. Mills closed amid what became known as the "cotton famine," and unemployment and hunger soared in Lancashire and other centers of the British cotton industry. The illegal seizure of two Confederate diplomats from the British ship RMS *Trent* in November 1861 further strained relations between the two countries. The Confederacy hoped Britain would at least recognize its independence and perhaps intervene on its behalf. President Abraham Lincoln defused the Trent Affair by releasing the two diplomats and formally disavowing the actions of the US naval captain who had captured them. By issuing the Emancipation Proclamation in September 1862, Lincoln turned the conflict from a war between the states into a humanitarian crusade to end slavery. Having outlawed slavery in its empire in 1833, Britain could hardly back the slave-holding Southern states. Particularly compelling, however, was the response of the unemployed cotton operatives. In December 1862, a public meeting in Manchester pledged its support for emancipation and the Union cause in what the local newspaper called an "Address from Working Men to President Lincoln."[32] The United States reciprocated by sending three relief ships filled with food, purchased by public subscription, in support of Britain's struggling cotton manufacturing communities. The workers' "decisive utterances," declared Lincoln, represented "an instance of sublime Christian heroism which has not been surpassed in any age or in any country."[33] While some of the loss of American cotton was ultimately offset by imports from India and Egypt, extraordinary exchanges like that between Manchester's workers and the president of the United States contributed to friendly Anglo-American relations.

In fact, more emigrants from the British Isles went to the United States than to all British colonies combined. Of the nearly 8 million people who left the British Isles from the 1850s through the 1890s, two-thirds immigrated to the United States. From the 1840s to the 1920s, Ireland alone sent approximately 4.5 million people. A common language, abundant land, and considerable opportunity made the young republic an attractive destination for Britons seeking a new beginning.

LATIN AMERICA

Britain held several islands in the Caribbean, British Honduras (modern Belize) in Central America, and British Guyana on the northeast coast of South America. Beyond these colonies it had close economic ties with the newly independent states of the former Spanish and Portuguese empires. Some historians argue that these countries belonged to Britain's "informal empire," territories it did not colonize but could control through economic leverage. Others have challenged this view, arguing that Britain and its South American partners engaged in mutually beneficial commerce. In either case, South America figured prominently in Britain's vast commercial network.

Although they had gained independence during the first quarter of the nineteenth century, the former Spanish and Portuguese colonies did not become important trading partners until midcentury. Britain's relationship with Argentina, Chile, and Brazil was dominated more by commerce than trade. The oligarchs who ran these countries needed capital, which British bankers provided. They paid for the loans by selling Britain agricultural products and natural resources. Argentina serviced its debt by supplying Britain with wheat and cattle, Brazil with coffee and rubber, and Chile with copper and nitrates. The need to maintain creditworthiness became so important that London bankers could influence economic domestic policy in each of these countries. The inability to restructure debt or float new loans could be ruinous, as Peru discovered when it defaulted on loans from City of London bankers in 1876. With such economic leverage Britain had no need to intervene directly. It stayed out of conflicts such as the 1879 War of the Pacific between Chile and Peru.

Britain's Empire, 1875–1914

Britain's economic position in the world began to change in the 1870s, which affected its approach to imperialism.[34] Between the repeal of the Corn Laws in 1846 and the global recession of 1873 Britain had an enormous competitive advantage in world trade. The United States and the developed countries of Western Europe needed British capital goods such as steam engines and machinery to industrialize. Once they had industrialized, however, these nations adopted protectionist policies. They also exported goods to Britain's trading partners, sometimes underselling British producers.

Structural weaknesses in the British economy exacerbated problems created by the decline of trade. Britain had geared its economy for export, which made sense when the world bought its goods. Once other nations adopted protectionism, however, this emphasis became a serious weakness. The new industrial nations had more developed domestic markets, making them less vulnerable to tariffs. Moreover, Britain's factories were older, smaller and less efficient than those of its competitors, who enjoyed an edge in newer industries such as chemicals. To make matters worse, British agriculture could not keep pace with the island nation's growing population. After 1870, Britain could no longer feed itself. These disadvantages were cumulative but not immediately apparent. The decline in foreign markets and the need to import food produced a trade deficit around the turn of the twentieth century. Because of the so-called invisible trade (insurance premiums and return on foreign investments), however, Britain managed to maintain a favorable balance of payments. This income not only hid the trade deficit, it also discouraged efforts to address structural weaknesses in the domestic economy.

Changing economic conditions had imperial consequences. France, the United States, Italy, Belgium, Portugal, and Germany attributed Britain's prosperity to its empire and resolved to acquire or expand their own colonial holdings. Britain was not going to be outdone, and so in a tragic and immoral competition during the last quarter of the nineteenth century, known as the Scramble for Africa, the European powers carved up what remained of the continent. In the face of these challenges Britain assumed formal control over areas it had previously been content to influence. In some cases, these colonial decisions were based on broad strategic considerations, both geopolitical and economic. In other instances, Britain responded to real or imagined threats from its imperial rivals. Sometimes the action of local officials led to decisions in the Colonial Office. In virtually all cases, the security of India often drove imperial policy. Britain's aggressive pursuit of its self-interest and its struggle to stay ahead of its competitors resulted in the expansion of the empire.

The occupation of Egypt in 1882 provides an example of how a complex combination of factors led Britain to replace influence with formal control. Egypt had gained de facto independence from the Ottoman Empire under Mohammad Ali in the early nineteenth century. Britain supported the Sultanate against the upstart Pasha when he sought to expand his territory. Egypt became a major supplier of cotton to British mills, especially when the American Civil War cut off supplies from the southern United States.

British interest in Egypt increased with the construction of the Suez Canal (1859–1869) by the Frenchman Ferdinand de Lesseps. Creation of a shortened route to India under French control threatened British access and position. To secure its interests in the region in 1875, Disraeli purchased almost half the shares in the Suez Canal Company from the bankrupt Khedive of Egypt. The following year France and Britain established dual control over Egyptian finances. This arrangement spared Britain the cost of occupying Egypt while at the same time preventing France from doing so.

In 1881 an Egyptian Army officer, Urabi Pasha, staged a revolt against the Khedive and sought to end foreign interference in his country. British warships dispatched to the port of Alexandria provoked riots; the ships responded by bombarding the city. In September 1882, British troops defeated an Egyptian Army at Tel al Kebir and occupied Egypt. Britain established de facto colonial rule over the country, creating a formal protectorate in 1914 at the outbreak of World War I. Control of Egypt secured the Suez Canal and limited French influence in the country.

The occupation of Egypt eventually led to the occupation of Sudan. Disraeli's rival, the Liberal Prime Minister William Ewart Gladstone, had planned to evacuate the region, but in 1884, a Sudanese religious leader known as the Mahdi besieged Major General Charles George Gordon in Khartoum, which he had been sent to evacuate. The city fell before a relief expedition reached it in 1885, and Gordon was killed. In 1898, an Anglo-Egyptian Army defeated Sudanese forces at Omdurman. The following year the territory became part of the Anglo-Egyptian Sudan under control of the British governor general in Cairo.

Meanwhile, imperial competition among the European states became so intense that German Chancellor Otto von Bismarck convened the Berlin Conference in 1884 to reconcile conflicting colonial claims. An agreement reached in 1885 declared the Congo and Niger basins open to free trade and demarcated lines separating colonial claims. Over the next decade and a half France gained a swath of territory known as French Equatorial Africa, extending from Lake Chad southeast to the Atlantic coast, and another tract known as French West Africa, running from the Atlantic eastward across the Sahel. Together these territories encompassed the modern countries of Chad, Cameroon, Congo Brazzaville, Gabon, Niger, Mali, and Senegal. The Congo became a fiefdom of the Belgian King Leopold II. Britain gained control of Nigeria, an expanded Gold Coast, Kenya, Uganda, British Somaliland, and Rhodesia (modern Zimbabwe). Germany acquired Cameroon, German Southwest Africa (modern Namibia), and Tanganyika (modern Tanzania). By the turn of the twentieth century only a handful of independent African states remained (see figure 8.10).

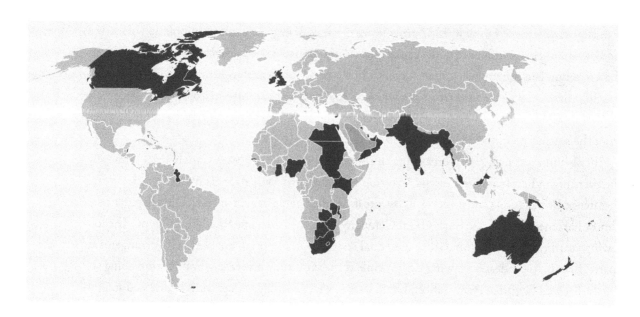

FIGURE 8.10 Map of the British Empire in 1914.

The pattern established in Africa recurred in Asia, where a combination of local and international circumstances combined to encourage the transition from informal to formal control. British merchants and the Indian government had been gradually expanding involvement in Burma, diminishing the sovereignty of the Burmese government. Britain had fought one war with Burma over border issues (1824–1826). A second conflict occurred in 1852, when the King of Burma fined two British captains for murder. A third war broke out in 1885 over a fine levied on the British-owned Bombay Burmah [sic] Trading Company and a subsequent British demand to control Burmese foreign affairs. Competition with France, ensconced in Indochina, and the threat posed by the possibility of extended French colonial control in Southeast Asia, drove Britain's imperial policy. Burma became a province of British India in 1886. In similar manner, Britain gained control of the four principal Malay States: Perak and Selangor in 1874; Negri Sembilan and Pahang in 1888. These territories formed the Federated Malay States in 1896. Across the South China Sea, Britain established protectorates over North Borneo (1882) and Brunei (1888).

In the South Pacific Britain expanded its empire primarily in response to German interest in the area. Concerned about German claims on the island, the governor of the Australian province of Queensland occupied southeast New Guinea in 1883. The following year, the British government declared this area, the protectorate of British New Guinea, just days after Germany claimed the northeastern corner of the island. The Dutch had occupied Western New Guinea since 1872. The British divided control of the Solomon Islands with Germany in 1899. They also proclaimed a protectorate over the Gilbert and Ellice Islands in 1892 and made them a colony in 1916. Fiji had been a British colony since 1874.

British Foreign Policy, 1870–1914

THE CONTINENT, 1870–1894

The unification of Germany, completed in 1871, profoundly altered the balance of power in Europe while its annexation of Alsace-Lorraine increased the likelihood of a future war with France. Seeking to recover the lost provinces but unable to beat Germany on its own, France worked to create an anti-German coalition. Germany in turn sought to isolate France. At first Berlin proved more successful. It joined with Austria-Hungary and Russia to form the Three Emperors' League in 1873. In 1879, a formal treaty with Vienna created the Dual Alliance, which became the Triple Alliance when Italy joined in 1882. Since Great Britain had no interest in continental entanglements, France stood alone.

Britain continued its policy of containing Russian expansion, particularly as it threatened British interests in the Mediterranean. That strategic imperative had led in the 1850s to its involvement in the Crimean War. In 1877, Russia invaded the Balkans again, this time allied with Serbia and in support of a Bulgarian rebellion against Ottoman rule. Russia's victory, and the terms of the resulting peace treaty, troubled Britain enough to encourage cooperation with Germany. Britain emerged from the resulting Congress of Berlin (1878), which revised the peace treaty, in possession of Cyprus, a base from which it could safeguard its interests in the eastern Mediterranean, including the northern entrance to the Suez Canal.

Neither Anglo-German cooperation nor the German alliance advantage lasted, and France eventually found an ally. In 1894, France and Russia signed a treaty guaranteeing mutual support in the event of war. The same year William Le Queux published *The Great War in England in 1897*. The novel depicts an invasion of the British Isles by a Franco-Russian coalition. The work accurately reflected the historic animosity between Britain and its continental rivals. Nine years later, the same author published a second imaginary work, *The Invasion of 1910*, but this time the invaders were German. In little more than a decade Britain's centuries-old enemies had been replaced by a newly created nation. This sea change in popular perceptions reflected an epic diplomatic shift.

CHANGING CIRCUMSTANCES, 1894–1914

During the two decades prior to World War I, a series of developments threatened the United Kingdom's primacy in world affairs. On the continent, as we have seen, German unification and French fears of German hegemony had led to the creation of rival alliance systems. Farther afield, a colonial conflict in South Africa revealed the poor state of the British army. While Britain preferred to retain its diplomatic independence, the German desire for colonies and commitment to building up its navy led many in government to question the wisdom of non-alignment. Within the British empire and even the British Isles themselves, crises over independence threatened to turn violent.

The nineteenth century closed in tension. In 1898, a British expeditionary force advancing up the Nile encountered a French mapping expedition at Fashoda in the Sudan. Both sides claimed the territory. The two colonial rivals resolved the matter diplomatically, but it revealed continuing deep distrust between them. The next year, Britain went to war with the Orange Free State and the Transvaal, two republics governed by white settlers of Dutch descent known as Boers (a term derived from the Dutch/Afrikaner word for farmer). That struggle, a legacy of Britain's colonial past, defined, in important ways, its future. It also brought Britain into conflict with Germany.

ANGLO-BOER WAR

In South Africa, the Boers had migrated inland from the British Cape Colony in the Great Trek (1835–1846), hoping to establish their own independent homeland. They settled the Transvaal and the Orange Free State, which became independent republics. However, British incursions motivated by a desire to control the mineral resources of the republics led to the First Boer War (1880–1881) and the Second Boer War (1899–1902).

The Boers won independence from Britain in 1884. Discovery of gold in the Transvaal in 1886, however, attracted British miners. The Boers refused to grant these "uitlanders" (foreigners) or the African majority equal rights. Tensions rose following an abortive raid by a British paramilitary force from Cape Colony in 1895 and British agitation for the uitlander vote in 1899. When the Boers refused the latter, Britain built up its forces on the border between the two countries. The Transvaal, backed by the Orange Free State, sent an ultimatum demanding withdrawal of British troops. Britain refused and war broke out in October.

Britain's army had not faced a comparably equipped enemy since the Crimean War. The more recent experiences of colonial warfare left it unprepared for opponents wielding artillery and modern magazine rifles. Boer forces inflicted several defeats on the British and besieged their garrisons at Mafeking and Ladysmith. The arrival of reinforcements from Britain, Canada, Australia, and New Zealand turned the tide by early 1900. Rather than accept British terms, many Boers adopted guerrilla warfare, conducting hit-and-run attacks in rural areas.

To prevent them aiding guerrillas, the British forced Boer civilians along with many Africans into concentration camps. Poor food, lack of medical attention, and unsanitary conditions led to the deaths of 28,000 Boer women and children and 20,000 Africans.[35] They then burned farms and destroyed anything of value to the insurgents. As a military tactic, scorched earth and concentration camps worked, although they led to widespread criticism of the British government. The British did not defeat the last of the Boer guerrillas until May 1902 when the remaining Boer fighters accepted British terms. The former republics became crown colonies in 1910 and merged with Natal and Cape Colony to form the Union of South Africa, as an autonomous dominion. Although many of them aided and even fought for the British, the African majority did not have the right to vote in the new country.

FIGURE 8.11 Gandhi (second row center) with stretcher bearers, Boer War.

The war cost the treasury more than £200 million. The British needed 500,000 troops to defeat 88,000 Boer soldiers. and had to use draconian methods to suppress the guerrillas. In its destructiveness and blurring of the distinction between combatant and noncombatant, the conflict foreshadowed the two world wars.

ANGLO-GERMAN COMPETITION

The Boer army had purchased weapons from Germany. The Kaiser, moreover, had voiced support for the Boer republics, and a company of German volunteers even fought for them.[36] These moves angered politicians in London, but Germany's desire to challenge Britain on the high seas proved far more worrying.

British naval strategy rested on the two-power standard: the Royal Navy must be superior to the navies of any two rival nations combined. A revolution in naval architecture during the first decade of the twentieth century made maintaining that superiority difficult. In the race to build new warships, everyone was (in theory at least) starting from scratch. Britain took an early lead. HMS *Dreadnought*, launched in 1906, made every battleship in the world obsolete. Propelled by steam turbines, it was faster than any vessel of comparable size. It also carried ten 12 inch-diameter guns and the latest range-finding equipment. Germany's 1906 and 1908 naval budgets responded to the *Dreadnought* challenge by allocating large sums to build comparable warships. As an island

FIGURE 8.12 HMS *Dreadnought.*

nation, Britain could still spend more on its navy than Germany, which needed a large army to defend its land borders. Britain thus maintained decisive naval superiority, but the arms race fueled British fear and resentment of Germany.

DIPLOMATIC REALIGNMENT

Germany's colonial ambitions also alarmed Britain. The Kaiser insisted on his nation's "place in the sun." With few areas of Africa and Asia left unconquered, Germany could only expand at the expense of the other imperial powers. This situation reminded Britain of the dangers of isolationism, encouraging it to reconsider potential alliances. So too did Russian interest in the Far East. To check Russia, Britain allied with Japan in 1902. The two nations recognized each other's interests in China and Korea. Each agreed to remain neutral should the other go to war with a third party but to provide military support should it fight more than one power.

Britain also sought better relations with France. In 1904, the two countries resolved their differences over North Africa. Britain promised not to interfere with French interests in Morocco, and France made the same promise concerning British interests in Egypt. During the next decade, this narrow colonial agreement evolved into an informal alliance known as the Entente Cordiale (literally, a "cordial understanding"). German efforts to challenge France during the First Moroccan Crisis (1905–1906), when the Kaiser encouraged Moroccan opposition to the French protectorate, led to further Anglo-French cooperation. The two nations agreed to joint military planning. Following the Second Moroccan Crisis (1912), in which Germany responded to an increase in French troops in the kingdom by sending a gunboat to the Moroccan port of Agadir, Britain agreed to protect France's Atlantic coast so that the bulk of the French fleet could be deployed to the Mediterranean.

Neither of these military arrangements amounted to a commitment to fight, but they created the understandable expectation by the French that Britain would back them in a war with Germany. Unaware of the arrangements, Germany had good reason to believe Britain would remain neutral. Because it would have provoked widespread opposition, Prime Minister Herbert Asquith and Foreign Secretary Edward Grey kept the details of the military agreements from several cabinet ministers, Parliament, and the British people. The entente thus introduced a dangerous ambiguity into a delicately balanced alliance system.

FIGURE 8.13 European alliance system, 1914.

The entente also led to rapprochement with France's ally Russia. In 1907, Britain and Russia reached an agreement over Persia that recognized a Russian zone of influence in the northern third of the country, a British zone in the southern third, and a nominally independent area in the center. Like the entente with France, the Anglo-Russian agreement, while making no mention of Germany, removed a major impediment to further cooperation in the event of a European conflict. Historians thus consider the 1907 accord as laying the foundation for what would become the Triple Entente.

NATIONALISM GROWS IN INDIA

The British envisioned their colonies evolving to the point where they could be governed by an Indigenous class of British-educated civil servants. Technically competent but sufficiently deferential, these "babus" (an Indian term of respect akin to "sir" used to designate civil servants) could be counted on to improve the welfare of their own people while safeguarding British economic and political interests. They sent the best of these candidates to England for education with the assumption that at Oxford or Cambridge the young men would learn to appreciate the superiority of British ways. What law students like Mahatma Gandhi really learned, however, was that they were not and never could be British. The color bar could not be crossed. The road to freedom lay not through English literature, law, and culture, but through their own history.

Resistance took the form of political organization and nationalist movements in the late nineteenth century. Founded in 1885, the Indian National Congress (INC, known as the Congress) sought to represent the political aspirations of the country as a whole, transcending ethnic and religious differences the British had exploited. In 1906, the INC called for self-government of all of India. In that same year conflicts between Muslims and Hindus, undoubtedly stoked by the British, led to the formation of the All-India Muslim League. In the early twentieth, activists in India called for *Swaraj* (self-government), and used tactics similar to those employed by suffragettes to achieve it. They boycotted British manufactured goods and engaged in violent action that included bombings and assassination attempts. Colonial officials in India responded with a pattern of small concessions to some political representation followed by repression that inevitably stoked anticolonial militancy. The outbreak of World War I and its impact on India further strengthened nationalist sentiment even as colonial troops fought for Britain.

IRELAND

While diplomats, administrators, and soldiers rearranged Britain's imperial and foreign relationships around the globe in the early years of the twentieth century, politicians renegotiated the union that connected Britain and Ireland. First passed by the House of Commons in 1912, Irish home rule was to become law in 1914. That two-year delay, however, allowed a crisis to brew in Ireland.

Horrified at the prospect of being governed by a Catholic majority, 237,368 Ulster Protestant men signed the "Solemn League and Covenant," declaring their refusal to accept the authority of an Irish parliament. "A Declaration of Support" for the covenant was signed by 234,046 Protestant women.[37] The Unionists, as they called themselves, were prepared to oppose home rule with force. They created the paramilitary Ulster Volunteer Force and declared "Ulster will fight, and Ulster will be right!"

Belligerence by northern Protestants ultimately played into the hands of radical Catholic nationalists. Committed to an independent republic, these nationalists had formed the Sinn Fein (Gaelic for "ourselves alone") Party in 1905. The party initially enjoyed little support, but it offered an alternative to the Irish National Party, which advocated for home rule. Now, in response to the threat posed by the Ulster Volunteer Force, republicans and home rulers joined forces to form the Irish Volunteers in 1913.

With two opposing paramilitaries arming themselves for confrontation, Ireland faced a serious threat of violence. To make matters worse, several British army officers at Curragh Camp near Dublin declared they would resign rather than compel Ulster Unionists to submit to home rule. In an attempt to defuse the situation, the government amended home rule to exclude Ulster for a period of six years, but agreement as to which counties would be included had yet to be reached. Only the outbreak of the First World War averted the crisis. With the approval of the Irish National Party, Parliament suspended implementation of home rule for the duration of the war, which most expected to be short. When the government finally instituted it in the fall of 1918, home rule no longer satisfied the aspirations of most Irish Catholic men and women.

IMAGE CREDITS

CHAPTER 9

Certitude and Anxiety in an Era of Rapid Change

The first "world's fair" took place in London in 1851, the brainchild of Queen Victoria's husband Albert. This was an important episode in the development of industrialization, urbanization, the domestication of industry; the technologies that made international travel faster, cheaper, and more common; and the expansion of empire. The Crystal Palace, where the Great Exhibition of the Works of Industry and All Nations was held, was also an important space designed by the architect Joseph Paxton, a site and structure that physically embodied the cultural implications of economic and political change. For people of the day, each element of the Crystal Palace was significant. This purpose-built glass construction built in a London park was supported by a cast-iron frame large enough to house a stand of elm trees. The building's iron girders were a new industrial product that made it possible to build in strikingly new ways. Glass for the first time was available in large quantities in Britain due to increased international trade; and the building of the Crystal Palace over the trees represented the human ability to control nature through industrial means.

Inside the Crystal Palace was an exhibition of products brought together from all over the world intended to encourage international trade, especially within the British Empire. The display was over 10 miles long with one hundred thousand objects and over fifteen thousand contributors. As the host, Britain had the most space to show off a wide range of industrial machines, including a massive hydraulic press, a steam hammer, an adding machine, printing presses, textile machines, folding pianos, and "tangible ink" that would produce raised characters on paper to aid the blind. Elegant carriages, early bicycles known as velocipedes, and giant railway locomotives reflected the technological advances in transportation. Just off the grounds of the exhibit in the Knightsbridge cavalry barracks were Prince Albert's exhibition model dwellings designed by the architect Henry Roberts. They were there to draw attention to the crisis in housing for the poor. These two storied brick houses modeled a respectable, modest, solid alternative to the old, crowded, unsanitary housing generally available to the working classes.

This was an exhibition. It was never meant to be a showroom for selling directly to consumers. Expensive and heavy equipment made up the majority of the items on display most suitable for purchase by factories or businesses. However, the organizers of the exhibition wanted to make some profit running it, so they opened it to the public. From May 1 to 23 the price of admission was £3 for men and £2 for women. On May 24 the price was dropped to a shilling a head so as to be accessible to all. The exhibition drew tremendous crowds, including the wealthiest aristocrats, middle-class professionals, factory workers, cottagers and other agricultural workers, and school-children. Saturday mornings were reserved for those with limited mobility or other disabilities. The exhibition drew visitors from all over the British Isles who took advantage of special train fares and travel packages on offer to encourage attendance.

The exhibition's organizers were worried about admitting so much of the public, rich and poor alike, into the same space at the same time. Given the labor unrest of the early nineteenth

FIGURE 9.1 The transept façade of the original Crystal Palace.

century, they worried about vandalism of the machinery. However, the organizers soon realized that their fears were unfounded. The exhibition was open for six months, and during that time over 6 million people attended. The exhibition made a profit of £186,000. Admission tickets to the Crystal Palace were one of the first mass consumer items in British history, and the Crystal Palace exhibition revealed that—as consumers—the masses were generally not antagonistic to industrial capitalism. In fact, they were fascinated by the exhibition and would gladly live in the model dwellings on display or buy those products appropriate for themselves, their families, or their homes.

The Crystal Palace exhibition exemplified the democratic nature of consumption. Looking is free and at the Crystal Palace looking was all that could be done with

FIGURE 9.2 1851 Medal Crystal Palace World Expo, London.

PLAN OF THE CRYSTAL PALACE

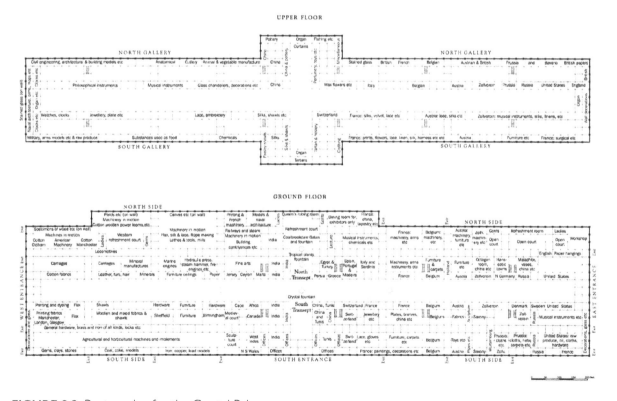

FIGURE 9.3 Paxton plan for the Crystal Palace.

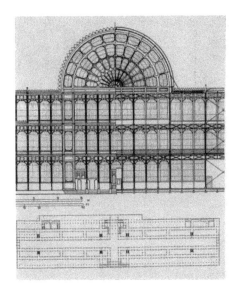

FIGURE 9.4 Partial front (left) and rear (right) elevations of the Crystal Palace.

most of the items, so everyone could consume equally. Beyond the consumer culture that it heralded, the Crystal Palace exhibition reflects the acceptance of industrialization and the shared appreciation for the beauty of industry and its innovation. As a showcase of domestic and international trade, the exhibition encapsulated the movement of people, things, and ideas throughout complex global trade and travel networks. A symbol of Britain's confidence and self-assurance, the vision of Britain as the pinnacle of civilization, the absolute conviction about the righteousness of the colonizing mission and the imperial project was offset by the organizers' hesitation about visitors from different classes rubbing shoulders.[1] These conflicting threads in the story of the exhibition capture the themes of certitude and anxiety that frame this chapter.

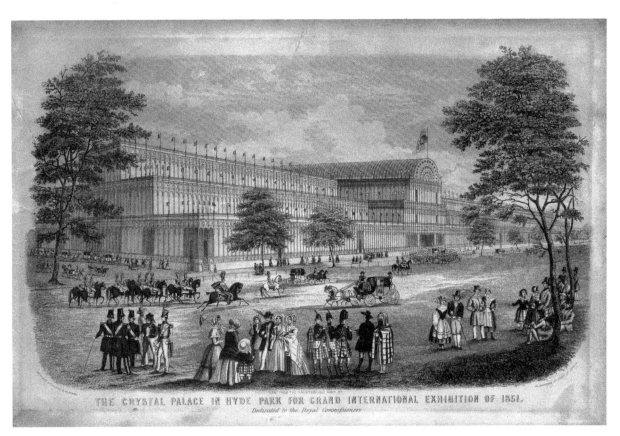

THE CRYSTAL PALACE IN HYDE PARK FOR GRAND INTERNATIONAL EXHIBITION OF 1851.
Dedicated to the Royal Commissioners

FIGURE 9.5 View from the Knightsbridge Road of the Crystal Palace in Hyde Park for the Grand International Exhibition of 1851.

FIGURE 9.6 Crystal Palace interior, Great Exhibit, 1851.

Faith and Skepticism

The dynamic economy and the tremendous changes in ideas about governance and the reach of democracy, began in the eighteenth century, became more intense as a result of the French Revolution, and culminated with the Great Reform Bill of 1832. Many believed that British society and culture was at risk of losing its way and forgetting its values. The emphasis on reason during the Enlightenment and the search for natural rather than supernatural explanations called into question the place of religion. Britain's religiously diverse and confessionally divided character now seemed to coexist with agnostics and atheists and people who found their moral, emotional, and political direction outside organized religion or any religion at all.

One conservative response to such potentially destabilizing ways of thinking and their radical implications began at Oxford's Oriel College in the 1830s when a group of clergy who were also scholars spoke out against what they saw as the secularization of the Church of England. The leaders of the movement, among them John Henry Newman, a cleric of the Church of England who eventually converted to Roman Catholicism, and clergymen Richard Hurrell Fourde, William

Palmer, John Keble, and Edward Pusey, asked whether the Church of England was an arm of the state, beholden to and shaped by the forces of secular politics, or whether the church was an ordinance of God. They called for reform and renewal through a return to the catholic—in the sense of all embracing—doctrines of the early Church fathers. They expounded their theology in *Tracts for the Times* published between 1833 and 1841. Their supporters, known as Tractarians, considered the doctrinal authority of the catholic church absolute, by which they meant faithful to the teachings of the early and undivided Church of Rome. They asserted that even during the Protestant Reformation those who remained in the Church of England considered it a catholic church and that their movement for reform was not an innovation but simply a return to this original position.

The Oxford movement's history is a history of controversy and conflict, most often with the Anglican Evangelicals who emphasized personal conversion and biblical faith, stressed the Protestant origins of the Church of England, and de-emphasized the sacraments and liturgical worship. While some of the Oxford movement's leaders, like Newman, eventually left the Church of England and joined the Roman Catholic Church, other remained within the Church of England. They worked to realize their vision of the Church by increasing the use of ceremony and ritual in church worship and establishing Anglican monastic communities for both men and women. They also promoted a better educated clergy focused on the pastoral care of their congregants instead of more worldly activity. Young priests inspired by Tractarian theology dedicated themselves to serving the poor in slum churches and ministering to the sick and the dying.

The importance of symbol and decoration went along with a revival of interest in church architecture. The Gothic revival of the mid-nineteenth century was driven by philosophers and social critics rather than architects. Literature by Sir Walter Scott, author of *Ivanhoe* and other works focusing on a swashbuckling version of the past, and the castles and abbeys that showed up in landscape paintings, cultivated a sense of nostalgia for the medieval period as a more spiritual and pious age. The English architect, designer, artist, and critic A. W. Pugin and the leading art critic of the time, philosopher and social thinker John Ruskin, believed that the gothic architecture of the medieval period represented the best combination of spiritual values and artistic creation and that the style of building might revitalize religious devotion. Ruskin went so far as to claim that only materials available during the Middle Ages should be used in gothic buildings. Some leaders of the Oxford movement and those who wished to reinvigorate what they considered waning spiritual and moral standards believed that only the gothic style was suitable to churches because they believed that the quality of medieval craftsmanship reflected the morally superior way of life in the medieval world. Ironically perhaps the best known gothic buildings of this period are the Houses of Parliament, political rather than religious, rebuilt after a fire destroyed the old buildings in 1834.

FIGURE 9.7 St. Pancras Railway Station, designed in 1868 by Sir William Henry Barlow. The redbrick structure is far from a pure representation of gothic architecture but, rather, a monumental Victorian structure that borrowed liberally from the gothic aesthetic.

In contrast with the leaders of the Oxford movement who strove to weave religious belief and ritual into their daily lives, the secularists or atheists who opposed established Christianity sought to formulate a set of moral values and practices not grounded in theology. The secularist movement had its origins in Thomas Paine's *The Age of Reason* (1794). Paine drew on the Enlightenment's rejection of supernatural events like the creation as described in Genesis. Instead he and his secular followers attempted to establish a new religion based on nature. In the nineteenth century Richard Carlile revived the movement, followed by Robert Owen, a prominent early socialist, and Charles Southwell who was a leader of the Chartist movement.

Later in the century George Jacob Holyoake established a journal called *The Reasoner* in which he espoused toleration for infidels, greater democracy, and the rights of the working classes. John Stuart Mill too urged the toleration of "blasphemous" opinions. Charles Bradlaugh established the National Secular Society in 1866.

The issue of religious toleration of course had been discussed vigorously during the Enlightenment, but restrictions on anyone who did not belong to the Church of England persisted. The expansion of rights in the late eighteenth century still did not result in full toleration of Catholics who were subjected to the parliamentary oath, which prevented them from becoming members of Parliament. In 1828 the repeal of the Test and Corporation Acts opened the door for Catholic emancipation in 1829. Despite the ultimate success of emancipation, it is important to remember that not everyone was onboard with its liberal inclusiveness. Anti-Catholic prejudice never disappeared, often amplified by and echoed in anti-Irish sentiment.

Other than the fear of violence from an increasingly oppressed Ireland, what were the intellectual trends that led to emancipation? Secularism and atheism promoted an acceptance of a diversity of beliefs. In the mid-nineteenth century the intellectual trend in historical criticism of the Bible and the study of comparative religions, which began in Germany but soon influenced thinkers in Britain, contributed to a growing sense among scholars that holy texts have a life of their own and that textual analysis could reveal more about the historical context in which they were produced. Moreover, scholars stressed that the texts conveyed universally shared values. Historical criticism is a branch of criticism that investigates the origins of ancient texts in order to understand "the world behind the text." The method involves an examination of the texts to check their authenticity and to establish their probable authorship, comparing them with other contemporaneous sources and with external evidence provided by archaeology or other disciplines. Motives, tendencies, interests, and presuppositions are all taken into account; vocabulary and style are scrutinized for consistency. These discoveries were often controversial because they frequently challenged traditional explanations or origin stories. In the process of uncovering inaccuracies or contradictions within these writings, the sacred nature of the texts might be called into question or diminished.

As discussed in part I, Britain had always been religiously diverse. In addition to Catholics and the proliferation of Protestant confessions in the seventeenth century, the eighteenth century saw the growth and expansion of Methodism. Non-Christians had always lived in Britain, and those included Muslims and Jews. Sailors from China and Hindus from south Asia brought with them their religious traditions. The existence and toleration of many different faiths eroded the idea that Britain's was an exclusively Christian society.

Jewish life thrived in Britain throughout the seventeenth and eighteenth centuries. In 1850 there were thirty-five thousand Jews in Britain, and by 1881 that number had almost doubled to sixty thousand. The increase was the result of migration to Britain from Germany, Holland, and Poland.

Jews received formal emancipation only in 1858. Again we see the long reach of the Enlightenment, the ideals of the American and French Revolutions, and the emancipation of Catholics in 1829. Those who advocated emancipation for the Jewish community argued that there could be no civic equality if political and social barriers were imposed on Jews because legal limits would negate "natural rights" and destabilize the civic equality. If the state existed in order to protect the natural rights of man, then it followed that everyone should have a right to all the liberties and advantages of citizens, no matter their color, race, or religious creed.[2]

Muslims too lived in Britain starting in the sixteenth century. They were among the sailors recruited in India to work for the East India Company. When Britain opened the Suez Canal in 1869, another wave of Muslim immigration, mostly from Yemen, followed. Many of those who came worked on ships and settled in port cities like Cardiff, Liverpool, South Shields, Hull, and London. The first mosque in Britain was built in Cardiff in 1860. Later waves of immigrants from Muslim parts of the world would be made up of students seeking enrollment in Britain's universities. The British Empire in 1911 had a Muslim population of 94 million. In Britain there were ten thousand Muslims in the first quarter of the twentieth century.

FIGURE 9.8 Benjamin Disraeli by Cornelius Jabez Hughes, 1878. Disraeli was born into a Jewish family. His family converted to Christianity when he was a child.

Muslims in Britain in the nineteenth century faced discrimination. Yet other cultural forces worked to promote toleration. Queen Victoria and Prince Albert were both Orientalists. They were impressed by the Islamic world and championed its languages, cultures, and artwork. Yet as implied by the term, often the representation of Asia and the Middle East was stereotyped and embodied a colonialist attitude endemic in Britain. Many believed that civilization in the east had stopped developing, stunted by despotic rule. British Orientalists held up their society as superior, touting the expansion of democracy as proof. The Great Exhibition in 1851 fostered Orientalism. The products on exhibit promoted the idea of the "Orient" as an entity that could be consumed through a set of objects created through its craft traditions. The India exhibit centered on a howdah adorning a life-sized stuffed elephant; the Chinese exhibit included many huge porcelain vases, Turkish rugs surrounded the Turkey exhibit, and one of the most popular exhibits, the Kohinoor diamond valued at between £1 and £2 million, embodied the riches of India, later known as the jewel in the Crown of Britain's empire.

In light of the contrast drawn between east and west, the imperial project was presented as Britain's responsibility to civilize, educate, and Christianize these backward places and people.

Christian missionaries took this responsibility seriously and traveled and lived throughout the world converting non-Christian populations all over Britain's empire. But their aspirations went beyond religious conversion and included insistent calls for the imposition of Western values and behaviors and the removal of customs, practices, and beliefs considered barbaric or primitive. Through a network of missionary schools and working in close consultation with colonial governments, they instituted radical social reforms that changed every aspect of Indigenous life affecting dress, language, sexual practice, and belief systems.

In the Orientalist movement in art and literature one sees how the "East"—present-day Turkey, Greece, the Middle East, and North Africa—captured the imagination of authors and painters who tried to represent the allure of the exotic. One of the most famous was *The Book of the Thousand Nights and a Night*, an English translation of *One Thousand and One Nights* (better known as the *Arabian Nights*), a collection of Middle Eastern and south Asian stories and folktales compiled in Arabic between the eighth and the thirteenth centuries. The British explorer Richard Francis Burton translated them, his knowledge of Arabic very much a part of the Orientalist phenomenon in Britain and across the West.

In a hostile challenge to the Orientalist practice of exoticizing the East while mastering its languages, Thomas Babington Macaulay's tract "Minute on Education," published in 1835, advocated an abrupt shift in educational policy in India. Trained as a lawyer, Macaulay served as the member of Parliament (MP) for Leeds. He composed his opinion on education during his service in India on the Supreme Council of India. Arguing that "the dialects commonly spoken among the natives of this part of India contain neither literary nor scientific information, and are moreover so poor and rude," and that "the intellectual improvement of those classes of the people who have the means of pursuing higher studies can at present be affected only by means of some language not vernacular amongst them," he declared that "English is better

FIGURE 9.9 *A Lady Receiving Visitors (The Reception)*, by John Frederick Lewis, 1873. The house in this scene was based on Lewis's own house in Cairo.

worth knowing." Although he admitted that he had "no knowledge of either Sanscrit [sic] or Arabic," he declared that he had "never found one [Orientalist scholar] … who could deny that a single shelf of a good European library was worth the whole native literature of India and Arabia." The self-satisfaction that echoes through the document captures the certainty of those who subscribed to British imperial ideology and justified the imperial reach as a generous act of charity that would lead to the improvement of the colonized.[3]

During the nineteenth century the "conversion phenomenon" featured several prominent conversions to Islam. While earlier converts might have left Britain and settled away from the British gaze, those who converted in the late nineteenth century converted in Britain, or if they converted while they were traveling abroad, they returned to Britain to continue their lives. The widespread belief in the superiority of British civilization existed beside Britain's religious pluralism and the growing alternatives to organized religion. Again the contradictions created an unsettling tension between supreme confidence and uncertainty.

FIGURE 9.10 Woking Mosque, now known as Shah Jahan Mosque, published in *Building News and Engineering Journal*, 1889.

Old Ideas

The intellectual history of the nineteenth century was as dynamic as its economic, political, and social history. Not all the developments were new, and they didn't change with the calendar. A set of ideas that circulated in the eighteenth century and persisted into the nineteenth was Romanticism, a movement in the arts and in literature that lasted into the 1840s. Its adherents emphasized the importance of inspiration, spontaneity, emotion, subjectivity, and the individual. The movement was a reaction to the hyper-rational Enlightenment ethos of the "age of reason" and a rejection of the value placed on balance, restraint, harmony, calm, and order. Artistic expression was understood as personal, a product of feeling; the artist a tortured genius in a materialistic world. Escape appealed to the Romantics who embraced the exotic, often representing the ideas of the East and contributing to Orientalism. British Romantics included poets Lord Byron, Percy Bysshe Shelley, and John Keats, novelist Sir Walter Scott, and the painters William Blake, J. M. W. Turner, and John Constable (discussed in chapter 2).

Many of the intellectual trends of the nineteenth century developed as a way of building on or in opposition to utilitarianism. The movement, summarized with the phrase "the greatest happiness of the greatest number," rests on the guiding principle that actions are neither right nor wrong but should rather be judged by their consequences. This generally secular framework posited that all of humankind is governed by the pursuit of pleasure and the avoidance of pain, that actions should be assessed on the basis of their effects, and that government or society should be set up to maximize the happiness of the population. This movement arose in the late eighteenth century and is associated with Jeremy Bentham. One of Bentham's followers, James Mill, followed its teachings religiously and tried to raise his son, John Stuart Mill, strictly according to utilitarian principles. Bentham and Mill were motivated to implement their utilitarian values by the desire for legal and social reform.

Those who lived by utilitarian principles believed that the only reason for morality is to make life better by increasing the amount of good or happiness in things and decreasing pain and unhappiness. They rebuffed moral codes or systems that included commands or taboos based on custom, tradition, or orders given by leaders or supernatural beings. They averred that the only way to assess a true or justified morality was to calculate its positive contribution to human beings or other living creatures. Needless to say, their way of thinking completely rejected traditional hierarchies of class and potentially upended hierarchies of gender and race. Certainly established church hierarchies and teachings had very little perch in this way of thinking and approaching lived experience.

New Ideas

The year 1859, in the same decade as the Great Exhibition at Crystal Palace, saw the publication of three works that define the attitudes and beliefs of the Victorian era: John Stuart Mill's *On Liberty*, Charles Darwin's *On the Origins of Species*, and Samuel Smiles's *Self-Help*. They each capture the self-satisfied smugness so typical of the Victorian era that often belied a great sense of uncertainty and anxiety. Each of these writings reflected the values of the time and inspired the self-righteous justification for and maintaining Britain's empire. They each were constitutive of scientific and cultural racism, reinscribing racial hierarchies that buttressed condescending theories of a benign imperialism and colonialism.

The liberalism that settled into the British upper and middle classes by the 1830s rested on bourgeois values best articulated by the Scottish author Samuel Smiles. Smiles wrote a series of books, including *Self-Help* (1859), *Character* (1871), *Thrift* (1875), and *Duty* (1880). A pioneer in the genre of that name, *Self-Help* sold a quarter of a million copies in Britain and became a best seller in Italy and Japan. Smiles explained that "the spirit of self-help is the root of all genuine growth in the individual; and exhibited in the lives of many, it constitutes the true source of national vigor and strength. Help from without is often enfeebling in its effects, but help from within invariably invigorates."[4] In other words, self-improvement and self-reliance will lead to genuine progress while any kind of dependence or state intervention could result in degeneration and weakness. The nationalism embedded in the quotation neatly ties the individual to a larger project while excluding those who cannot or do not adopt the recommended lifestyle.

Smiles addressed a large audience in his writings. Indeed the capacity for improvement that Smiles described pertained to those from every and any socioeconomic group, making class mobility a strong corollary and result of his prescription for self-help. According to Smiles, "Riches and rank have no necessary connection with genuine gentlemanly qualities."[5] He held that life was a struggle and that striving was the best quality to live by. He believed that aristocrats were lazy and useless, and he warned that it was more difficult to learn hard work than to achieve success if one came from humble origins. He advocated universal education and a massive expansion of the franchise.

Smiles encapsulated an emergent consensus among the middle class that espoused a belief in meritocracy, individualism, free trade, and respectability. These middle-class values coalesced around a derision of the supposed inherent debauchery of the aristocracy and the lazy, uncontained immorality of the poor. The title of this chapter is certitude and anxiety—and indeed these middle-class values reflect both the self-satisfied superiority of the middle class and their inherent insecurity about whether they really had arrived and could justify their position in society. Underlying the arrogance lurks a doubt about whether these were legitimate grounds on which male property owners had achieved their economic success, the franchise, and the right to participate in representative democracy.

John Stuart Mill's *On Liberty* defined liberal thought in the nineteenth century. Mill's idea of liberty rests on the assumption that all of humanity shares values that include the promotion of knowledge, discovery, new ideas, the arts, and the expansion of science. These, for Mill, distinguished a good life. In addition to publishing *On Liberty*, Mill wrote *The Principles of Political Economy* (1848), *Considerations of Representative Government* (1861), and *Utilitarianism* (1863). In his "The Negro Question" (1850) he urged the inclusion of former slaves in the political nation, and in "The Subjection of Women" (1869) he presented the arguments for the inclusion of women voters in the Reform Bill of 1867. His attempt to include women in the Reform Bill failed. Mill served as an MP from 1865 to 1868.

In *On Liberty* he argued that democracy does not guarantee personal freedom because a rule by majority might curtail the liberty of the minority who stand in opposition. "The will of the people, moreover, practically means the will of the most numerous or the most active part of the people; the majority, or those who succeed in making themselves accepted as the majority … [they] may desire to oppress a part of their number; and precautions are as much needed against this as against any other abuse of power."[6] Mill argued that the only legitimate reason to limit liberty was to save people from harm. He defined three different harms: by default, omission, and accident. Mill cautioned that when liberty is capacious and unrestricted, false opinions will circulate. These false opinions were, according to Mill, both good and important. Mill explained that:

> the peculiar evil of silencing the expression of an opinion is, that it is robbing the human race; posterity as well as the existing generation; those who dissent from the opinion, still more than those who hold it. If the opinion is right, they are deprived of the opportunity of exchanging error for truth: if wrong, they lose, what is almost as great a benefit, the clearer perception and livelier impression of truth, produced by its collision with error.[7]

In other words, contrary, nonconformist opinions must be allowed because their expression promotes greater liberty and ultimately serves to strengthen the side of truth and democracy.

In the same year that Samuel Smiles advocated self-help and *On Liberty* wrestled with the nature of freedom, Charles Darwin, the naturalist, published *The Origin of Species*. During his time as the ship's naturalist on the HMS *Beagle* from 1831 to 1836, he collected and compared specimens found along the coast of South America and on islands where the ship stopped, most famously the Galapagos. Based on those findings Darwin postulated that those species born with characteristics that suited their environment would have greater reproductive success, thereby ensuring the survival of those advantageous characteristics. Those lacking these traits would not succeed as well. This theory of natural selection held that those with advantages would compete more successfully to find a mate and that their offspring would be more likely to survive. Eventually Darwin's ideas, specifically the theory of natural selection, would form the basis of the theory of evolution.

In *Origin of Species* Darwin theorized that the number of different species was not fixed, but rather that it changed over time. Through natural selection those best adapted to their environment survived and reproduced those more successful attributes. Darwin speculated that random mutations, very small differences between animals in the same species, gave some members of the species an advantage others did not have. These might include a longer trunk for some elephants that then were able to reach food that was out of reach of the others. The important thing to remember is that these mutations were random and the differences among the animals Darwin observed that made some more fit to survive were arbitrary. Competition for resources is pervasive in nature, with insufficient food for all of the offspring who inevitably compete with each other to survive. Those who live to reproduce pass along their characteristics. No individual can control their mutation or what advantage or disadvantage they would gain from it. This model explained change as the result of alterations caused by chance and attributed none of it to God or any other larger controlling force. Biblical accounts of creation simply could not be reconciled with this new theory. The theory of a self-evolving process destabilized religious explanations of creation and called into question many religious and moral premises.

As controversial as Darwin's theories were in the world of science and religion, when they were adapted by thinkers and commentators into a set of beliefs known as Social Darwinism, they had an even bigger impact. Social Darwinism is the theory that the laws of natural selection Darwin identified applied to human individuals, groups, and races in the way they did in plants and animals in nature. According to the theory the weak were diminished and the development of their cultures was curtailed; without competition from the weak, strong cultures inevitably grew stronger and more powerful in their influence over those weaker than them. Those who subscribed to the theory believed that life in human society mirrored the animal kingdom's "survival of the fittest" (a phrase coined by Herbert Spencer, a British philosopher and scientist) on an individual level, a colossal misunderstanding of Darwin's theory.

Darwin's theory almost immediately was taken up by cultural theorists who adopted it to explain social phenomena. Spencer's phrase "survival of the fittest" described what he considered the competition of the modernizing world in which only the strongest would succeed. By the late nineteenth century the ideological associations of Darwin's theory were applied to the social order on a global scale. This was a new iteration of Stadial Theory developed in the eighteenth-century Scottish enlightenment (discussed in chapter 4). Applied to human beings and to cultures and societies, the theory of evolution implied a progressive narrative in which each culture or society was placed on the same continuum. Those more evolved or developed were considered more fit and successful. In this comparison Britain again put itself at the head of the line as the model of progress and the goal to which all should strive. In the meantime, before they achieved "success," Britain would guide them either directly through colonial rule or indirectly with an imperial presence.

Social Darwinism shaped attitudes toward race, poverty, nature, history, and society. It carried a great deal of weight because of its emergence from and association with science. It also seemed relevant and consistent with *laissez faire* economics and the embedded belief in progress. For some it confirmed the status quo and stressed a deterministic outlook and a more passive role for government. It was used to dissuade those who believed in a more interventionist state by arguing that nothing should interfere with "natural" processes. This secular version of the providentialism that had been so popular in the seventeenth century encouraged unrestricted competition. It explained the inequalities of wealth: those who had more were deemed of superior abilities. Their success spoke to their inherently better set of morals such as thrift and industriousness. The poor, on the other hand, were less fit and ought not to be helped. But Social Darwinism appealed to those of all political persuasions, even those who did not consider themselves conservative, and it sometimes inspired contradictory policy. For example, in the twentieth century, for those who subscribed to the growing movement in eugenics, it was a call to action encouraging interference in nature's process to hasten a certain end or ensure an outcome. Liberals like John Stuart Mill found the theory an affirmation of their goals for the slow and steady expansion of liberal democracy.

Social Darwinism hardened conservative attitudes about race and poverty by insisting that these social traits were biologically determined and that those who were Irish, Jewish, Black, or poor were inferior to the middle and upper classes, gentiles, and whites. There was no better justification for the and maintenance of Britain's empire than Darwin's theory of natural selection when it had been repackaged as Social Darwinism. It rationalized imperialism and colonialism. The liberal explanation of empire espoused by Mill and others expected that with time, education, and Christianization the imperial mission would be abandoned because the populations deemed less civilized would grow into self-governance. In contrast Social Darwinists insisted on the authoritarian governance of those people deemed inferior by people of Nordic or Germanic backgrounds—from whom many white Britons traced their descent—considered to be biologically and culturally superior.

These ideas were powerful. They shaped policy and they had very real consequences. One example comes from India in the aftermath of the Indian Rebellion of 1857. The British considered the state of the Indian subcontinent undeveloped and attributed that to its "despotic" rulers. The combination of the Indian Rebellion of 1857 and Social Darwinism changed that narrative for good. While the rebels were ultimately unsuccessful, their ability to hold out against the British for 18 months was a shock to the British and ultimately remade the British attitude to imperialism. The Indian rebellion and Jamaica's Morant Bay rebellion in 1865 sent reverberations through British culture and society, undermining its self-confidence. They also restructured the empire itself. In the case of India the EIC was abolished in 1858 and India became a Crown colony directly under the authority of the Crown. In Jamaica, the white majority was so threatened by the fight for rights among former slaves and the thought that people of color would serve in the legislature, that the Jamaican House of Assembly and the Legislative Council abolished themselves and put the colony under the direct authority of the Colonial Office. The British certitude that reminds us of the theme of this chapter was shaken and replaced with doubt. In terms of colonial policy, Britain abandoned its liberal views and deemed its colonial subjects ungrateful and irrational. Rather than seeing Indians or Black Jamaicans as younger versions of themselves (i.e., Stadial Theory), the British now defined them as totally different, savages in need of strict supervision.

Socialism

Socialism was yet another new set of ideas that took hold in the nineteenth century. The word itself emerged in the 1830s, but its ideas and the movements it spawned reappeared throughout the nineteenth century in response to the problems of industrial capitalism and the huge gap that existed between the relatively small number of the wealthy and the large number of the poor. In its simplest definition, socialism is a political and economic theory of social organization that advocates that the means of production, distribution, and exchange should be owned and regulated by the community as a whole. Robert Owen, a Welsh social reformer, has been credited as the founder of British socialism associated with "utopian socialism." In contrast, Karl Marx and Friedrich Engels used British industry as the laboratory for developing their ideas about what they considered their more scientifically and historically grounded "scientific socialism."

Owen observed industrial conditions firsthand. He began his work life as a draper's apprentice and then became a cotton spinner. As the manager of cotton mills in New Lanark, he experimented with improving living conditions and educational opportunities for factory workers: he established the New Institution for the Formation of Character and the Infant School, and he opened a company store that strictly supervised the sale of alcohol. Despite his critique of unrestrained capitalism, its greed and inefficiency, he was steeped in British middle-class paternalistic values and tried to instill order, cleanliness, temperance, and thrift in his workers. Owen became a leader in the trade union movement in the 1830s, but he was frustrated with the resistance the unions faced from factory owners. He was critical of Chartism, the working-class movement for parliamentary reform discussed in chapter 10, which he considered not radical enough for the kinds of social transformations he believed were necessary.

Owen became convinced that only the formation of "co-operative communities," or villages to house the poor and the unemployed, would solve the problems of competition; he devoted his life to founding such communities. Through the Association of All Classes of All Nations (AACAN), Owen and his followers raised money to buy land in rural areas or to buy or rent buildings in urban areas. Although the most well known is in New Harmony, Indiana (established in 1824), there were urban cooperatives in Spa Fields, London (1821–1824), in rural Orbiston near Glasgow, Lanarkshire (1826–1827), at Ralahine, County Cork (1831–1833), and Queenwood, Hampshire (1839–1845). The rural communities Owen envisioned would be largely self-contained and agricultural, numbering between five hundred and three thousand people, where property would be held in common. Promising cradle-to-grave care for members, the AACAN branches, housed in "halls of science," held lectures, teas, and dances for members, providing work and material support along with social and cultural events. Although Owen was convinced that the competition between human labor and the labor of machinery was the cause of stress, the plans for his cooperatives all included and relied on modern machinery.

Owen also dedicated himself to secularism and denounced all religion. According to Owen, human beings were naturally good and their success and development would be assured by the removal of evil. He believed that environmental factors shaped human character and that individuals had very little control or responsibility for their destinies. He considered education fundamental to the formation of a rational and humane character. The right kind of education would provide a stable and healthy environment that nurtured both the physical and psychological needs of the child. Corporal punishment was not allowed and child labor was restricted.

Karl Marx and Friedrich Engels were political activists and social theorists who also espoused modern socialist thought. Although they both were born in what is today's Germany, they relocated

FIGURE 9.11 An engraving by F. Bate, published by AACAN in 1838, of Robert Owen's short-lived utopian community New Harmony, Indiana.

FIGURE 9.12 The village of New Lanark.

to England in the wake of the unsuccessful democratic revolutions that swept the continent in 1848. In England, they collaborated in their work and writing. Engels was the son of a wealthy family, a partner in the family's cotton business. Based on his observations of workers and factory life, he wrote *The Condition of the Working Class in England* (1845), mentioned in chapter 7, with regard to attitudes toward the influence of the Irish poor on the English working class. In the book Engels described the poverty of the working classes and the conditions at the factory in order to understand the role of workers in the emergent capitalist system. Like Owen, Engels too saw the culprit as the atomization of workers and its result: competition with other workers instead of alliances with them. In London, Marx made a living writing newspaper articles, but he also relied on financial support from Engels. Marx spent most of his time in the British Library writing *Contributions to a Critique of Political Economy* (1859), *Capital* (vol. 1, 1867), and *The Civil War in France* (1871). In his books, Marx developed his analysis of the history, politics, and economics of capitalist soci-

FIGURE 9.13 Friedrich Engels.

ety. Engels worked tirelessly to translate and publish the books he and Marx had written. When socialism took off in the late nineteenth century and became a mass movement, Marx and Engels's works served to inspire and educate a new generation of socialists.

In his attempts to discover a framework for understanding the movement and development of history, Marx identified material conditions as the central elements of historical and social development and class struggle as history's driver. For Marx and Engels, socialism was the next step in the struggle for a more democratic world. Although that was true for many socialists, those who focused on the problems caused by industrialization and suggested social and economic reorganization rather than talking in terms of class struggle were more successful in convincing capitalists and industrialists to join them (or at least to talk with them) because their political agenda didn't seem quite as radical. The early socialists sought to reorganize industrial society with a more collectivist, commercial, and egalitarian ethos, but they were quite vague about the mechanism by which this new society would come into being. Marx and Engels identified that mechanism as revolution. They addressed contemporary political concerns. As compelling as their theory became, and although socialist ideas had been discussed for a long time, Marx and Engels did not have an opportunity in their lifetimes to participate in the mass socialist movement that gathered significant support in the 1880s. Marx died in 1883 and Engels in 1895. It was only in 1889 that socialist parties across Europe founded the Socialist International and allied with the trade union movement to play a much larger role in politics.

A member of that younger generation that followed Marx and Engels was the English designer, craftsman, poet, and socialist William Morris, who combined a love of design, aesthetics, and craftsmanship with his commitment to socialist ideals. He was a member of the Pre-Raphaelite Brotherhood, a secret society of young artists founded in 1848. They opposed the Royal Academy's promotion of what they considered an unimaginative and artificial historical painting style, in particular the "ideal" as defined by the paintings of the High Renaissance. They preferred what they considered the more direct, uncomplicated, and naïve style in which nature was portrayed in the works produced before those of the sixteenth-century Italian painter Raphael. They dedicated themselves to moral seriousness and sincerity they found lacking in other painters of their day. Although the "Brotherhood" was active for only five years, it exercised quite an influence on painting and the decorative arts. Morris's designs of furniture, fabrics, stained glass, and wallpaper inspired the Arts and Crafts movement in Britain. Morris believed in handmade artistic and artisan production very much at odds with the era's veneration for industry, machinery, and mechanization. His attitude showed early in his life. Apparently during a family trip to London in 1851, Morris, who was 16 years old, refused to enter the Great Exhibition at Crystal Palace because the aesthetic clashed with his sense of taste. Morris summarized his philosophy when he said, "Have nothing in your houses that you do not know to be useful or believe to be beautiful." Morris channeled his resistance to the restrictive nature of contemporary bourgeois society by embracing a belief in the self-justifying value of the beautiful against the requirement that art carry a moral or didactic message. In the hands of William Morris, the commitment to the beautiful became a militant aesthetic and a political crusade against the ugliness and exploitations so typical of late nineteenth-century British society.

FIGURE 9.14 Fruit design, by William Morris.

FIGURE 9.15 Flower design, by William Morris.

Morris was inspired to try to find an alternative to the prevailing industrial system. He blamed the atomization and the dehumanization of factory work for the divisions in modern society and the unbridgeable gap between the poor and the wealthy. Parliament's paltry efforts to intervene in the problems faced by so many impoverished workers left him quite disillusioned. In 1884, he founded the Socialist League. He frequently spoke on street corners and joined in marches.

Another group founded in 1884 as socialism was taking off in the late nineteenth century was the Fabian Society. Its goal was the formation of a democratic socialist state in Britain. Named for the Roman general Quintus Fabius Maximus Verrucosus, known as Cunctator, who defeated Hannibal using patience and indirect attacks rather than pitched battles, the society distanced itself from the discourse of revolution and instead touted respectability as its stance, persistence as its method, and evolution or gradualism as its model for change. Drawing middle-class intellectuals as members—including the social reformers Annie Besant, Sidney Webb, and Beatrice Potter Webb, and the playwright George Bernard Shaw—the focus was on teaching. Through meetings, lectures, conferences, and discussion groups the Fabians conveyed the message of the inevitable "gradual substitution of organized co-operation for the anarchy of the competitive struggle." They stressed both the peaceful and constitutional nature of this change. For them, the "economic side of the democratic ideal is, in fact Socialism."[8] In the service of better educational opportunities they founded the London School of Economics (LSE) in 1895; in 1922 they chose the beaver as their mascot for its hard-working, industrious, and sociable characteristics, all traits to which LSE students aspired.

The Fabians believed that increasing the state's intervention would address social problems caused by the inequities of capitalism. They undertook research projects concerning colonial questions and questions of war and peace and published their findings in pamphlets and books. The best known of these, *Fabian Essays in Socialism* (1889), outlined their program for reform. The essays were edited by Sydney Webb, who, along with his wife Beatrice, actively promoted collectivist social reform in the late nineteenth and into the early twentieth century. Seeing themselves as professional experts, the Webbs and other Fabians took positions in political parties and organizations in the hopes of influencing policy. Although they tried to extend their influence in the liberal and conservative parties, they didn't have much luck. They eventually joined forces with other

FIGURE 9.16 Beatrice and Sidney Webb.

socialist groups and labor unions in the Labour Representation Committee, which became the Labour Party in 1906. Given their small numbers, it is important to note that the Fabians had a profound influence on the development of socialism in Britain.

Anxious Imperialism, Degenerate Bodies, and Resistant Gender Roles

The resistance to Britain's imperial reach throughout the empire, from the Opium Wars in Qing China to the New Zealand wars of 1845–1872 to the Indian Uprising of 1857 to the Jamaican Rebellion of 1865 at Morant Bay, shook Britain's hold on its colonies and called into question the ideological foundations of empire. Some asserted that the rebellions in midcentury proved, justified, and necessitated Britain's hold on its colonies. This tension coexisted with the rapid growth of empire throughout the final decades of the nineteenth century and may have prompted Benjamin Disraeli's decision in 1876 to declare Queen Victoria queen-empress. This largely empty political title signified both the underlying insecurity of Britain's hold on India and signaled an attempt to tie together the large, diverse, and ramshackle cultures, languages, religions, and people in Britain's global holdings.

By the end of the century, the fear of losing ground was even more evident. The Queen's Diamond Jubilee in June 1897 celebrated sixty years on the throne. Over six days this performance of excess, dubbed by Joseph Chamberlain "a Festival of the British Empire," featured speeches, parties, processions, foreign dignitaries, elaborate decorations, and a thanksgiving service at St. Paul's Cathedral. These elaborate celebrations masked a fear of deterioration signaled by internal conflict—emerging from the activism of trade unions, feminism, suffragettes, Jewish immigration, Irish nationalism, socialism, poverty, and disease—exacerbated by the external threats posed by the German navy, the economic competition of both the United States and Germany, and what Edwardian Britons perceived as their ungrateful and rebellious colonies.[9]

Concern for the nation, its vigor, its bodies, their health, and the imperial project underlay the Contagious Diseases Acts (CDA; 1864, 1866, 1869), laws enacted to combat the rampant spread of venereal disease in the armed forces. The first CDA concerned port and garrison towns; they were subsequently extended to areas without military establishments to protect civilian populations. The focus of the CDAs were "common prostitutes" who were identified by plainclothes police-men, subjected to invasive medical examinations, and, if infected, remanded to "lock hospitals" (for as long as a year) and regular reexamination thereafter. Any woman could be targeted; if she refused "voluntary" examination, she had to convince a magistrate of her "virtue." In the process, poor women were registered, and an activity (sex work) in which they might occasionally engage out of economic necessity became their identity (prostitute). By the late 1860s, their predicament was the focus of a national repeal effort undertaken by various organizations. Ultimately, the most dedicated and effective group was the Ladies National Association for the Repeal of the

Contagious Diseases Acts (LNA). On New Year's Day 1870, it published "The Ladies' Protest against the Contagious Diseases Acts" in the *Daily News*. Signed by 124 prominent women, the protest charged that the CDAs violated women's constitutional rights, "punish[ing] the sex who are the victims of a vice, and leave unpunished the sex who are the main cause, both of the vice and of its dreaded consequences." Men's sexual appetites, in other words, were responsible for prostitution, but men enacted laws that penalized "fallen" women for it. There were no examinations or forced treatment of the sailors, soldiers, or civilians who paid for sex.[10] Mobilized against this "double standard" (its term!), the LNA had 57 branches by 1871. It campaigned to influence opinion and politics on the national level and mobilized resistance movements on the local level. In 1883 it celebrated the CDAs' suspension, in 1886 their repeal.

The concern with sexual disease was not restricted to the metropole. By the middle of the nineteenth century schemes to control the spread of sexually transmitted diseases (STDs) in the military existed throughout the empire. The British colonial government imposed the Contagious Disease Acts in India and other British colonies. Although some Indian women were banned from working in or near military towns known as cantonments in an attempt to regulate prostitution and curb venereal disease, the fear of homosexuality in the military led to the promotion of prostitution. In India the Cantonment Acts, passed in 1864, established brothels to service the men in each regiment. The sex workers were subject to the CDA, which had a much wider scope in India than in Britain and enforced frequent mandatory examinations of sex workers for STDs of which they alone were assumed the source. After the repeal of the CDA in Britain, the LNA turned its attention to the empire where the laws were eventually repealed. White women pointed to their active role in the LNA and the CDA's repeal abroad as evidence of their political experience, justifying their role in imperial politics in the service of rescuing Indian women of color to further the civilizational mission of empire.

The wars to maintain Britain's colonial holdings, suppress colonial rebellions, and extend its imperial holdings in Africa resulted in a tremendous need for conscripted men to serve in the growing military forces. When the government recruited for the long-lasting and brutal Anglo Boer War 1899–1902, they found that a third of the potential recruits did not meet physical military standards. The men who tried to enlist were small and short; they had weak lungs, heart problems, and bad teeth, feeding fears of "race degeneration." When military and parliamentary committees investigated the reasons for the widespread physical weakness, they ignored the poverty, overcrowding, unsanitary conditions, poor diet, and disease (discussed in chapter 7) so typical of the English working-class experience and instead blamed working-class mothers for the physical decline. The fear of degeneration and national decline motivated Colonel Robert Baden-Powell to write his bestselling book *Scouting for Boys*. Published in 1908, the book was an extraordinary success, instructing its young readers to be "loyal to the King … his parents, his country, and his employers," "to be useful," and to "obey orders of his parents."[11] The book promised to train the right kind of men and reinscribe traditional hierarchies of gender, class, and race in addition to affirming Britain's global superiority.

Not all men and women aspired to conform to these hierarchies. Resisting the ideology of separate spheres and drawing on the radical messages of the French Revolution, many women demanded more of a voice in representative politics. From the middle of the nineteenth century, women sought access to education. As we saw in chapter 7, girls began to enter the universities in the 1860s. Oxford and Cambridge had women's colleges while more liberal Scottish universities accepted women into coeducational classrooms. Starting in 1878 London University did so as well. Men at first dominated the adult education movement, but later the extension movement attracted many women.

Other women resisted the domestic sphere by accepting its values completely. Their belief in women's superior virtue led them to extend themselves outside the home through charity work. Women joined thousands of societies designed to help the poor and working members of society. Charity was considered an extension of "the flow of maternal love." Middle and upper class women joined the social and moral reform movements, working tirelessly to inspect prisons, asylums, and workhouses and to demand that Parliament intervene to ameliorate conditions in all of them. They visited the poor and the sick in their homes; they ran or supervised primary schools; and they became leaders of the temperance movement, working to limit the consumption of alcohol. The women involved in charity work made speeches and wrote editorials criticizing the industrial order and demanding an improvement in working conditions. Although men were also involved in these efforts and they often administered the charitable organizations, women were in the majority. Their charity work brought middle-class women into the public sphere. Undaunted by the disapproval of those who believed their work outside the home would eviscerate their angelic nature and unsex them, women demanded more of a voice in politics and representative democracy as a means of affecting larger societal reforms.

Thus far we have spoken only about heteronormative sexualities—men and women involved in relationships with the opposite sex. What about homosexuality in nineteenth-century Britain? Prior to the nineteenth century, sodomy, a word that referred to any kind of sexual relationship between men, had been the focus of legal and moral censure. It was in the nineteenth century that those who expressed same-sex desire or acted on it were considered a separate category of person. Attitudes toward homosexuality hardened over the course of the century. Although in the early decades of the century some argued for decriminalizing sexual relations between men, with Jeremy Bentham advocating homosexual sex as a way to inhibit population growth, by the end of the century Freud taught that homosexuality was a form of arrested development. Legislation against sodomy increased after 1870.

The Irish writer, novelist, poet, playwright, and celebrity Oscar Wilde spent two years in jail for "committing acts of gross indecency with male persons." Wilde's celebrity was based on his acerbic tongue, his wit, and his flamboyant dress. He enjoyed resisting Victorian values. As a proponent of the aesthetic movement, he, like Morris, believed in the self-sufficiency of art, its independence of moral, political, or any but aesthetic considerations. Wilde aligned himself with the Aesthetics when he asserted, "There is no such thing as a moral or an immoral book. Books are well written or badly written."[12] Among his more famous works are his play *The Importance of Being Earnest* (1895) and his novel *The Picture of Dorian Gray* (1890). Wilde married and had two sons, but he was also gay. In 1891, he began an affair with Lord Alfred Douglas, an aristocrat 16 years younger than he. Four years later, in February 1895 Douglas's father, the Marquess of Queensbury found out about the relationship. He was furious. He left a calling card for Wilde with the porter at the private Albermorale Club. The card read simply: "For Oscar Wilde, posing somdomite [sic]." In response to this public offense, Wilde felt he had to press charges. His attorney applied for a warrant: Queensbury was arrested and charged with libel. The trial began on April 3 at the Old Bailey, London's central criminal court. Despite Wilde's denials, Queensbury's lawyer promised a compelling case for Wilde's homosexual relationships, with plenty of evidence from former lovers willing to testify. Wilde's attorney convinced him to withdraw from the libel prosecution and plead guilty to the charge of "posing."

So began the first trial of Oscar Wilde on April 26. He was prosecuted under the Labouchere Amendment, section 11 of the Criminal Law Amendment Act, passed in 1885. The jury deliberated for three hours and could not reach a verdict on most of the charges. On May 7, Wilde was released on bail for three weeks of freedom. Wilde's second trial ended much more decisively: he was convicted of almost all the charges. Wilde served two years in prison. When he was released, he traveled throughout Europe before he died on November 30, 1900.[13]

The harsh attitudes toward homosexuality and society's dictates that the only acceptable masculinity was housed in a marriage with a woman meant that many men led double lives. Just as married heterosexual men had many female partners, so too did their homosexual counterparts. In both cases, male privilege allowed for physical autonomy and freedom while their wives often suffered humiliation and loneliness trapped in these marriages by economic dependence and the difficulty of obtaining a divorce. Although there were very loving marriages between men and women in the nineteenth century, for many women the sexual double standard and the ideology of separate spheres meant that they found their deepest relationships with other women.

FIGURE 9.17 Oscar Wilde.

Feminism and the Fight for Suffrage

The fight for the equality of women espoused by Mary Wollstonecraft in the late eighteenth century grew in the course of the nineteenth century into the feminist movement. Women's knowledge of political activism and organizing was honed in the abolitionist movement we discussed in chapter 4. In the mid-nineteenth century John Stuart Mill and Harriet Taylor advocated for the same political and legal rights for women as for men. Although there were many strains and subgroups among feminists, they shared the belief that women faced systematic social, political, and economic disadvantages and that the corrective lay in political activism. We've seen in chapter 7 how British feminists in the nineteenth century fought for the legal protection of women's property and equal access to education and employment, but the most heated campaign was for women's suffrage.

In their fight for the vote, white upper- and middle-class women did not question hierarchies of class and race. Their argument for the vote reflects the influence of Social Darwinism. They believed that they had earned the vote through their political activism and their philanthropy and charity work. Most did not consider British working-class women eligible, nor did they include Indian and African women in the empire as their compatriots. Quite the contrary, they made an argument from contrast for their own exceptionality. The suffrage movement is most closely associated with Emmeline Pankhurst and her daughters, Christabel and Sylvia, who led the fight for the vote from the end of the nineteenth century until 1928. Emmeline Pankhurst died a few weeks after the passage of The Representation of People Act, which granted women the vote.

The fight for women's suffrage had begun in 1866 before the Second Reform Act of 1867. A group of women gathered fifteen hundred signatures on a petition for universal suffrage and delivered it to John Stuart Mill and Henry Fawcett, two MPs who then drafted an amendment to the Reform Act that would have granted universal suffrage. The amendment failed 196 to 73. In response, several suffrage groups formed across Britain. They united in 1897 to form the National Union of Women's Suffrage Societies (NUWSS). These suffragists believed they would achieve their goal through peaceful and constitutional means using respectable strategies. They used petitions, posters, leaflets, and public meetings to argue and educate, and by 1914 their membership had grown to fifty-four thousand. Their constituents were mostly middle-class white women, although there were some working-class women among their ranks.

Frustrated with the repeated failure of these peaceful tactics, Emmeline Pankhurst and her daughters established the Women's Social and Political Union (WSPU) in Manchester in 1903. The WSPU expanded its membership to include working-class women. They recruited from the factories focusing on the vote as a single issue and the key to social reform. Later that decade they adopted more militant tactics, taking direct action by disrupting meetings, heckling Cabinet members and confronting MPs and the police, smashing windows, setting fires to mailboxes, and chaining themselves to railings. Their militancy earned them the name *suffragettes*. When they were arrested, the women would go on hunger strikes and endure painful forced feedings. In a speech she delivered in 1913, Emmeline Pankhurst explained her tactics, saying that "[n]othing ever has been got out of the British Parliament without something very nearly approaching a revolution." She cited the violence before each of the reform bills of 1832 and 1867, which prompted, finally, the expansion of the franchise to more working-class men. She went on to explain that "[m]en got the vote because they were and would be violent" but that women who had held peaceful meetings and passed resolutions "did not get it because they were constitutional and law-abiding." She went on to assert that "the only justification for violence, the only justification for damage to property, the only justification for risk to the comfort of other human beings is the fact that you have tried all other available means and have failed to secure justice."[14]

Emmaline and Christabel prioritized the vote for women as the key to further social and economic reforms. Emmaline spoke of those who fought for the vote as "the fortunate women, the women who have drawn prizes in the lucky bag of life, in the shape of good fathers, good husbands and good brothers." She explained that she was "fighting ... for the sake of others more helpless."[15] Emmaline and Christabel defined theirs as a middle-class movement. Sylvia Pankhurst disagreed with her mother and her sister. Although she too worked for the vote, as a socialist she hoped to combine her socialism and her feminism, to work with political parties sympathetic to socialism and labor and reach out to working-class women and men. Sylvia believed that freedom from poverty ought to be the first priority of any liberation movement. Sylvia was also a committed

FIGURE 9.18 The Pankhursts: Emmeline, Christabel, and Sylvia.

pacifist, and when the WSPU turned to violence, she opposed their use of militant tactics. Sylvia was expelled from the WSPU in 1914. She founded the East London Federation of Suffragettes and published a working-class women's paper, the *Woman's Dreadnought*.

With the outbreak of World War I in 1914, the suffragettes and the suffragists ceased the campaign for the vote. The government released all suffragettes who were in prison. Emmaline encouraged her supporters to "fight for their country as they fought for the vote." After the war in 1918, women over 30 gained the right to vote in England and in Ireland; all adult women were enfranchised in 1928.

IMAGE CREDITS

CHAPTER 10

Repression and Reform

Emmeline Pankhurst's remarkable 1913 speech in defense of suffragette violence, titled "Why We Are Militant," challenged far more than law and order or property. It challenged a way of thinking about the preceding century, and in particular about the three parliamentary reform acts—of 1832, 1867, and 1884—that had extended the franchise so that, by the end of the century, most men could vote.

Speaking to an American audience and invoking memories of the North American colonists' own revolution, Pankhurst declared her homeland "the most conservative country on earth." "You need something dynamic in order to force legislation through the House of Commons; in fact, the whole machinery of government in England may almost be said to be an elaborate arrangement for not doing anything." The first Reform Act, she explained, was only enacted in 1832 "after the practice of arson on so large a scale that half of the city of Bristol was burned down on a single night." Pankhurst likewise attributed the Reform Act of 1867 to "rioting" and "the fear of more rioting and violence." In 1884, threats alone sufficed to secure additional reform.[1]

This is not the way the story of parliamentary reform was typically told in Pankhurst's day, or by successive generations of historians. The more established narrative emphasized Britain's remarkable ability to avoid violence and revolution of the sort that rocked France, not only in 1789 but also in 1830 and 1848. The spring of 1848 in fact became known as the Springtime of the Peoples, as revolutionaries toppled regimes and demanded new constitutions across continental Europe. Not so in Britain. Change came there neither on barricades nor with a new constitution; it arrived through parliamentary initiative and incremental revisions of the existing constitution. Alterations to the system of representation and expansion of the franchise, along with a host of other reforms, unfolded gradually over a century. Compromise and accommodation expanded the political nation, bringing in new groups as the ruling elites deemed it safe to do so. In short, the elements of constitutional monarchy remained, but relations between the constituent parts had shifted. The power of the Crown and aristocracy decreased as that of the commons increased. At the end of the nineteenth century, a small elite still governed the country, but it was far more accountable to the people.

The heroes of this story were members of the upper middle class who demanded parliamentary reform, and were its first beneficiaries, and the landed elite who welcomed them into the club. Thus, the explanation of British political stability lay in the nature of British society, particularly the openness of its ruling class. Britain in the late early nineteenth century had what historian Harold Perkins described in the 1970s as an open aristocracy.[2] British aristocrats certainly preferred landed wealth, but they did not turn their noses up at trade. In France, younger sons of nobles had to enter the "respectable professions," the church and the military. Their counterparts in Britain had a third option, industry and commerce; the noble father often bankrolled the entrepreneurial son. And, as was the case in the eighteenth century and before, British aristocrats and gentry married their children to those of wealthy businessmen; rising men of commerce and industry gained status while landowners got much-needed infusions of cash. The openness of the British aristocracy gave the new men of industrial wealth a stake in the system rather than making them its implacable foes. In time, moreover, this hybrid elite decided the terms by which men of the lower middle class and eventually the working class could be welcomed into the franchise and even the House of Commons.

Key to this account was the voluntary nature of reform, which the ruling classes embraced, albeit slowly and occasionally with bad grace. The fear caused by revolutionary violence in France ushered in an era of British reaction lasting almost a decade after Napoleon's final defeat in 1815. When the demand for change became too great to resist, the government granted it by degrees. The Reform Act of 1832 redrew the electoral map and expanded the franchise to include the upper middle class. The Reform Act of 1867 gave the vote to the rest of the middle class and the highest tier of the working class, the so-called "aristocracy of labour." Parliament instituted the secret ballot in 1872, the Reform Act of 1884 lowered the requirements for voting even further, and a bill passed the following year created roughly equal electoral districts. This gradual expansion of the political nation staved off the more radical demands of the working-class movement known as Chartism, which disrupted Britain in the 1830s and 1840s.

Yet, as Pankhurst suggested, it was perhaps not so easy and happy a process. Chartism did not merely lose, but it was suppressed, its leaders repeatedly arrested. Moreover, its roots stretched way back to the political radicalism of the 1790s, and a popular reform movement persisted throughout the war years and the domestic repression that followed peace in 1815. At times of particular hardship and frustration, there were, as Pankhurst noted, threats and violence. The disenfranchised demanded change, and once working men achieved the vote, organized labor organized a new political party in its own name and interest. Meanwhile, women and the Irish challenged their continuing dependent status, and throughout the empire, as we have seen, independence movements arose that profoundly affected the politics of the metropole. Parliament did far more than Pankhurst acknowledged, but the celebrated stability of the nineteenth century was also a convenient cover for a period seething with uncertainty, conflict, and change.

The Return to Peace

The French Revolution, and the wars that followed, cast a long shadow on British political life. During the global struggle with France, the British government clamped down on calls for reform. As noted in chapter 5, the administration of William Pitt the Younger passed a number of repressive measures designed to prevent popular political movements. These included not only the "Two Acts" of 1795—the Seditious Meetings Act and the Treasonable Practices Act—but also the suspension of habeas corpus (1794), additional taxes on printed matter (1797), and the Combination Acts (1799 and 1800). The last measures effectively outlawed union activity, indicating that the British establishment considered collective bargaining and demands for political change two sides of the same coin. On the connection between economic and political grievances, reformers would agree.

When peace finally came in 1815, it did little to change this state of affairs. The stamp duty on newspapers had reached 4 pence per copy as the government deliberately sought to price them beyond the means of working-class readers. Such tactics, however, inspired William Cobbett, publisher of the *Political Register,* a weekly newspaper that called out government corruption and called for reform, to find an ingenious loophole. Starting in 1816, Cobbett reprinted articles from his recent editions in pamphlet form. Not technically "news"—due to both format and timing—his pamphlet sold tax-free for only 2 pence per copy. A government member declared it "Twopenny Trash," an insult its producer proudly embraced. *Cobbett's Weekly Political Pamphlet* soon gained a circulation of 40,000 (sometimes with as many as 10 readers per copy), becoming the main publication of the working class, thanks in part to Cobbett's equally creative distribution scheme of recruiting shopkeepers as sales agents. As one government informant wrote, "Every cobbler shop is supplied, and women who never talk on politics are now warm for Cobbett." Even children "purchased and read" it.[3] In 1817, Cobbett fled to the United States upon learning of plans to arrest him for sedition. His newspaper and pamphlet continued nonetheless to champion the cause of reform.

Cobbett was one activist in a diverse network of reformers who hoped that the end of the Napoleonic Wars would allow long deferred grievances to be addressed. But there were new irritants as well. A postwar recession, made worse by the demobilization of tens of thousands of soldiers seeking work, and rising food prices caused by bad harvests, resulted in economic desperation for many. Merchants responded by importing foreign grain. British farmers, meanwhile, clamored for protection, and Parliament complied. The Corn Law Act of 1815, discussed in chapter 6, forbade import of grain until the price of domestic cereal rose to a set price. The high cost of food combined with unemployment produced hardship and hunger, petitions and riots. Radicals sought both the repeal of the corn laws and the introduction of universal suffrage. Instead, the Tory government, led since 1812 by Robert Jenkinson, Earl of Liverpool, instituted new versions of old laws. In 1817, a Seditious Meetings Act, Treasonable Practices Act, and Suspension of Habeas Corpus Act reaffirmed wartime emergency measures in the absence of a foreign enemy but amidst fears of domestic insurrection. The home secretary, Lord Sidmouth, defended governmental actions this way: "An organised system has been established in every quarter, under the semblance of demanding parliamentary reform, but many of them, I am convinced, have that specious pretext in their mouths only, but revolution and rebellion in their hearts."[4]

The new Seditious Meetings Act expired in the summer of 1818, and on August 16, 1819, a rally took place in St. Peter's Field, Manchester. More than 60,000 people gathered to hear Henry Hunt, popularly known as "Orator Hunt," speak in favor of democracy, universal suffrage, and the socioeconomic benefits they would bring. The gathering was one of many such events, a product of the "system" about which the home secretary had complained, but also an effort to promote in 1819 peaceful "mass platform" meetings. Preparations on both sides were thus extraordinary. The Home Office had, for months, encouraged the local authorities to quell radicalism "either by the law or the sword." An arrest warrant was now issued against Hunt and several of his associates, that "little Gang of evil Spirits."[5] Meanwhile, Hunt invited the people of Manchester with a special appeal: "Come, then, my friends, to the Meeting on Monday, armed with no other weapon but that of a self-approving conscience; determined not to suffer yourselves to be irritated or excited, by any means whatsoever, to commit any breach of the public peace."[6] Attendees practiced disciplined marching in order to demonstrate their respectability as they processed to the field; they arrived on the 16th in great parades, some from towns miles away, accompanied by musical bands, banners, and children. But as Hunt addressed the gathering, the city magistrates instructed the local yeomanry, mobilized to preserve order, to execute the warrant. Perceiving that the yeomanry were meeting resistance, the authorities then ordered a detachment of regular cavalry to break up the crowd. The latter charged with sabres drawn. In the ensuing melee, the troopers killed 17 people and injured approximately 650. Most of the victims—who included at least 100 women and some children—were either trampled by horses or struck by swords. The official report lists among the dead an infant "Rode over by the Cavalry," and men who suffered horribly, but poetically, paired fates: John Ashworth was "Sabred and trampled on," Thomas Buckley was "Sabred and stabbed," and William Dawson was "Sabred and crushed."[7]

Widespread public outcry followed the incident, popularly dubbed the "Peterloo Massacre," a chilling parody of Britain's great victory at Waterloo four years before. There too the vanquished lay in a field of blood; but at Waterloo, the slain were Napoleon's enemy troops not British civilians (figure 10.1). Robert Poole, a recent historian of Peterloo, describes it as "the bloodiest political

FIGURE 10.1 Peterloo Massacre.

event of the nineteenth century on English soil."[8] An official inquiry investigated, but Parliament ultimately responded with more repressive measures. The Six Acts of 1819 had a familiar ring. They included a new Seditious Meetings Act and an additional stamp duty imposed on newspapers. The Blasphemous and Seditious Libels Act empowered magistrates to confiscate suspect materials, and the Misdemeanors Act expedited prosecution of the accused. The Training Prevention and Arms Seizures Acts meanwhile sought to prevent paramilitary activity and the sort of peaceful drilling exercises that had preceded Peterloo.

Peterloo meanwhile inspired some of those seeking reform to even greater radicalism, even insurrection. In what came to be called the Cato Street Conspiracy of 1820, a small group of radicals planned to murder the prime minister and cabinet at a formal dinner, not realizing that one of their number was a government agent and the announced dinner a trap. Five of the conspirators

FIGURE 10.2 Early Peeler (1850s).

were hanged and five others transported. Among the executed was William Davidson, a Jamaican-born cabinet maker (his father was the island's attorney general, his mother a Black woman), who joined a radical reading group after Peterloo. Another, Arthur Thistlewood, had long been on the government's list of dangerous revolutionaries. In 1816, Thistlewood had participated in another failed insurrection plan, in 1817 he challenged Home Secretary Sidmouth to a duel, and in 1819 he helped organize mass protest meetings in response to Peterloo.

By the mid-1820s, though, fears of revolution appeared to be waning. The Combination Acts were finally repealed in 1824, a year after a new, more moderate Tory home secretary, Robert Peel, abolished the death penalty for over 180 crimes. Peel's interest in legal reform would continue throughout the decade. He reduced the power of amateur magistrates, the sort of people who were in charge at Peterloo, and replaced them, at least in urban areas, with paid professional judges. Peel's conviction that eighteenth-century methods of law enforcement and social control were ill suited for the nineteenth century's teeming cities found ultimate expression in the Metropolitan Police Act of 1829, which created, in London, Britain's first professional police force. The new officers, known as "Peelers" or "Bobby's boys" (shortened to Bobbies, as they are still called today), were paid state employees and often of relatively humble origin. Their power, interestingly, was of more concern to the elites who had overseen the old judicial system than the populace they policed. A decade and a half after Waterloo, with its victor, the Duke of Wellington, now serving as prime minister, some modest reform—non-parliamentary reform—seemed to be on the agenda.

Decade of Reform

As we saw in part I, the constitutional contradictions of slavery and Catholic exclusion made a lie of the ideology of rule of law; meanwhile the state did nothing to ameliorate massive rural poverty, the devastation of rapid urbanization, and the dislocation of the Industrial Revolution. Yet resistance to the repressive measures taken by the British government to stem the impact of the French Revolution and prevent a similar conflagration in Britain eventually extracted some hesitant half measures of reform. The 1830s saw a spate of political concessions grudgingly enacted by Britain's elites who tried to prevent a social revolution while limiting the toll on their affluence and power. The forced nature of these reforms resulted in what some have dubbed, both with and without irony, an "administrative revolution."

ABOLITION

The 1807 act outlawing the slave trade, which came after an interruption of the abolition movement by the French and Haitian Revolutions and in the middle of the war against Napoleonic France, was a conservative compromise in response to a revolutionary era. British diplomats ironically secured treaties with 120 countries banning the trade even as the empire grew in Africa, the Middle East, and Asia.

Planters in the Caribbean resisted both full abolition of the institution of slavery and the "amelioration" schemes advocated by those who believed slavery could be fixed with better conditions. Meanwhile, and more significantly, the enslaved did not wait for freedom to be handed down as a gift. They demanded freedom and created opportunities to resist, escape, buy their freedom or negotiate for it. Fugitive slaves formed maroon societies, communities of self-emancipated slaves who lived together in remote areas and used guerrilla warfare to fight for and preserve their autonomy from plantations, slave owners, and slave catchers. Enslaved women used the courts where they could to bring lawsuits; these lawsuits were particularly relevant for women demanding their own freedom from masters who might have promised freedom to them or to the children they had with slave owners. Enslaved men joined the imperial army in exchange for promises of freedom. Three slave rebellions in the British Caribbean in Barbados (1816), Demerara (1823), and Jamaica (1831) and the demands for immediate, universal emancipation culminated in 1833 when Parliament passed an emancipation act that abolished slavery on August 1, 1834. But even this abolition was not complete. To palliate slave owners and provide the labor necessitated by the monocrop plantation culture, Parliament replaced slavery with an apprenticeship system that required slaves to work for their former masters for six more years, later reduced to four. The system never really worked, and apprenticeship was abandoned in 1838.

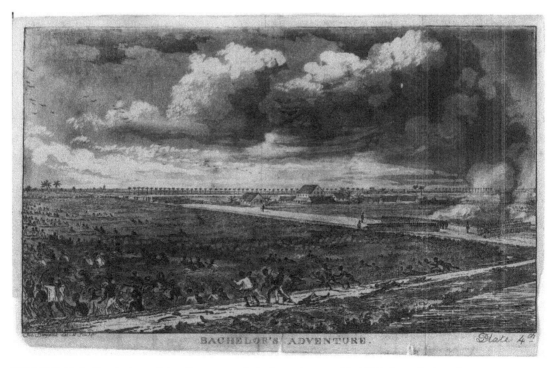

FIGURE 10.3 Depiction of the Demerara Rebellion, August 18, 1823, from Joshua Bryant, *Account of the Insurrection of the Negro Slaves in the Colony of Demerara*, 1823.

Faced with the need for labor, a refusal to redistribute land and resources, and the departure of former slaves from the plantation complexes in pursuit of their own farms, plantation owners persuaded the colonial governments in the British Caribbean to pay for the importation of a large number of indentured laborers from India (discussed in chapter 8). These persons, often poor and in debt, were bound to plantations for a seven-year, renewable term of labor. Sadly, the abolition of slavery generated another form of coerced labor to ensure the profits of plantation monocrop culture. Britain's promise of equality and liberty would extend throughout the nineteenth century to white British men at the expense of women at home and abroad and colonial people of color.

CATHOLIC EMANCIPATION

The Test and Corporation Acts were passed in the seventeenth century to prevent non-Anglicans from holding public office. Their repeal in 1828, long the goal of Protestant Dissenters, also paved the way for removing the additional restrictions that barred Catholics from political life. Although Pitt the Younger had wanted to include emancipation in the Act of Union with Ireland, he had failed on this front. A quarter century later, English prejudice against the Irish and anti-Catholicism remained potent, and conservative Tories and many Anglican clerics opposed emancipation. The Irish politician Daniel O'Connell's foundation in 1823 of the Catholic Association, with the express purpose of emancipation, caused concern not only because of its singular focus on Catholic suffrage but also because it renewed cries for political reform among other groups excluded from full rights. O'Connell mobilized a broad Irish coalition uniting those of different socio-economic backgrounds and interests under the banner of their Gaelic Catholic identity.

The Commons had twice passed an emancipation bill (1821 and 1825), only to have it defeated by the Lords. When a cabinet post became vacant in 1828, the new appointee as president of the Board of Trade, Vesey Fitzgerald, had to stand for reelection before taking office. Since he represented County Clare in Ireland, he would have to run for that seat. O'Connell decided to oppose him. O'Connell won decisively, but as a devout Catholic he was unable to take his seat. The Tory government would have to bar him from office or emancipate the Catholics. Violence in Ireland might ensue if the government denied O'Connell his seat.

Parliament passed the Roman Catholic Relief Act in 1829. Catholics could now hold office, but to weaken their growing power in Ireland, the act also raised the property requirement for voting in the Irish counties from 40 shillings to £10 (a 400 percent increase), disenfranchising many of the voters who had elected O'Connell.

Although the process of emancipation described here afforded Catholics equal political, civil, and legal status, it by no means guaranteed full social and economic opportunities and did not remove cultural and political barriers in society as a whole. Civil equality for Protestant

Dissenters/Nonconformists and atheists followed after Catholic emancipation, but the new oaths of loyalty taken upon admission to Parliament necessitated a recognition of one's Christian faith. Consequently, Jewish suffrage was not achieved until 1858. The abolition of the University Test Acts, which finally enabled Catholics, Jews, and Nonconformists to earn all degrees (except divinity) at Oxford, Cambridge, and Durham, came only in 1871.

THE REFORM ACT OF 1832

Calls for parliamentary reform by the middle classes who took credit for Britain's growth and prosperity intensified with the success of O'Connell's campaign for Catholic emancipation. The House of Commons consisted of 658 English, Welsh, Scottish and Irish members of Parliament (MPs), 486 of them representing English constituencies. Counties (known as shires) and towns (known as boroughs) had two representatives each. Six other MPs represented universities. Districts varied widely in population and voting requirements. As noted in part I, this medieval system had not been adjusted for the vast population shifts of the intervening centuries. Thus by 1801, densely populated counties had the same representation as sparsely inhabited ones. Moreover, emerging industrial cities, whose populations had begun reaching into tens or even hundreds of thousands, had no MPs, while medieval centers of population that had subsequently dwindled into tiny villages, had two representatives in Parliament. Some districts had almost no inhabitants at all. So-called rotten boroughs had so few voters that powerful magnates could appoint their MPs: Old Sarum, which had been a bustling medieval town, had three houses and just seven voters while the village of Dunwich still had an MP even though it had fallen into the sea. Others were known as "pocket boroughs" because their representation was effectively in the pocket of dominant landlords.

Voting requirements were as inconsistent as electoral districts. A fifteenth-century act had entitled property owners whose land netted 40 shillings worth of rent to vote. In the eighteenth century, Parliament adjusted the requirement to replace rent with tax assessment. Anyone owning land with an assessed annual value of 40 shillings could vote. These laws excluded the tenant farmers and agricultural laborers who made up the bulk of the rural population. In the boroughs, voting depended on the byzantine terms of the medieval borough charter. Since voters in every constituency had to sign a poll book indicating their vote, elections were hardly free and fair. Landlords and employers could—and frequently did—dictate how people voted.

The Tories won the general election of 1830, but when Wellington made clear he would not support parliamentary reform, moderate members of his own party who recognized the necessity of some measure brought down his government and supported the Whigs, who had long advocated reform. Expectations for change in the country had by then reached a fever pitch. In the manufacturing city of Birmingham, Thomas Attwood's establishment of the Birmingham Political Union

FIGURE 10.4 House of Commons before reform.

(BPU) in December 1829, modeled on O'Connell's single-issue campaign, had brought together middle-class businessmen like himself and the newly emergent working classes into an organized and vigorous peaceful campaign to extend the franchise and redistribute parliamentary representation. Elsewhere, the threat of violence loomed if Parliament delayed much longer. Nonetheless, it would take almost two tumultuous years for reformers to overcome the combined resistance of the "ultra-Tories" in the Commons, the Tory majority of the House of Lords, and the Crown.

On March 31, 1831, Lord John Russell finally introduced the Whigs' bill to the Commons. It passed its second reading by a single vote but failed in its third reading. Prime Minister Charles Grey, second Earl Grey, asked for a dissolution of Parliament and made the ensuing election a referendum on reform. The Whigs returned with a 135-seat majority committed to passing the bill, which made it through the Commons during the summer only to be defeated by the Lords in September. Riots broke out in in major cities including Bristol, Nottingham, Derby, Worcester, and Bath. Meetings of the BPU drew as many as

15,000 people and generated hundreds of petitions. The Commons passed a slightly amended bill in December, only to see it defeated in the Lords the following May. A run on gold and fear of the government's bankruptcy, epitomized by the slogan "to stop the Duke," referring to the Tory Wellington in the House of Lords, "go for Gold," added to the disruption. Presaging the words of Emmeline Pankhurst that began this chapter, unrest in the country and incidents of chaos and violence intensified to the point where even the king had to accept the inevitability of reform. William IV threatened to create enough new Whig peers to pass the bill in the upper house. Rather than face such humiliation, enough Tory lords absented themselves to let the bill finally pass. It became law with royal assent on June 7, 1832.

The act addressed the two glaring problems of the national political system: representation and the franchise. It swept away rotten and pocket boroughs and transferred seats to the growing cities. The 56 smallest English boroughs lost their seats, and the next 30 smallest were reduced to one MP each. The act created 130 new seats, most of which went to the largest towns. The Reform Act of 1832 also regularized voting requirements. The 40-shilling freeholders in the counties retained their right to vote, but they were joined by £10 copyhold owners and long-term renters with £10 leases. The act also standardized the borough franchise, allowing those who paid £10 in rent to vote.

The terms of the act are easier to explain than its full implications. While reform eliminated the worst abuses of the old system, it hardly amounted to the broad democratic change many radicals wanted. Despite the reapportionment of seats and the elimination of many rotten and pocket boroughs, districts remained unequal. Notably, rural areas continued to be over-represented. The number of voters increased from an estimated 400,000 to a definite (i.e., formally registered) 650,000, but even after reform, only about 18 percent of the adult male population could vote.

Furthermore, with no secret ballot to protect them, voters could still face intimidation by their landlords or employers. The landed interest continued to dominate the House of Lords and play a disproportionate role in the Commons. The act did not open a floodgate of further reform. Once allowed a share in power, the wealthy men of commerce and industry became as committed to preserving the new status quo as the gentry had been to preserving the old one. Over three decades would pass before Parliament would further expand the franchise, and half a century before it would establish roughly equal electoral districts. On the other hand, the Reform Act of 1832 rested on two progressive premises: the idea that electoral districts should to some extent reflect population distribution and the idea that the franchise could be expanded.

Although since its passage Whig historians have offered a romanticized interpretation, ranking the "Great Reform Act," as many called it, as a milestone in the evolution of British democracy, the limited scope of the Reform Act of 1832 set the country up for a century of continued struggle in which the wealthy hung on to power and those without fought to gain it.

FIGURE 10.5 Reformed House of Commons.

ADMINISTRATIVE REFORM

The Reform Act of 1832 did nothing to address the inequities of British society and culture, the massive poverty, and the exploitation of the new industrial work force. Atrocious work that children were doing in factories caused outrage among reform-minded members of the middle class, many of them women involved with charity work and philanthropy in the 1830s that resulted in the passage of several factory acts (discussed in chapter 7). Reformers investigating working conditions gathered information that resulted in the Factory Act of 1833 prohibiting children under the age of nine to work in textile mills and restricting the hours of everyone under 18. Other reforms followed including the Mines Act of 1842 barring all women and boys under 13 from work in the mines and the Ten Hours Act in 1847 regulating the textile industry. Unlike earlier Factory Acts of 1802 and 1819, these were designed with an enforcement apparatus to ensure supervision. They established a professional inspectorate to ensure compliance.

Administrative oversight also characterized the New Poor Law (also discussed in chapter 7). Passed in 1834, it replaced the parish relief system instituted under Elizabeth I with a central supervision of poor relief. Influenced by Benthamite utilitarian ideas, the New Poor Law reflected an ethos of self-improvement that blamed poverty on the dependence of the laboring poor on outdoor relief. Now relief, at least for those fit to work, should be given in workhouses where conditions would be as uncomfortable and demeaning as possible. The goal was to reduce the number of people eligible for relief and to force the able-bodied into poorly paid work. The Poor Law Board was established to implement all this.

To radical reformers, the New Poor Law symbolized the ruthlessness and harshness of capitalist industry. And when economic downturns hit, the workhouses could not even keep up with the number of unemployed. Yet, ironically, the New Poor Law developed the model of national administrative networks and expanded government intervention eventually used to combat the worst effects of the industrial revolution. The Public Health Act of 1848 also established a central board, though local ones remained voluntary except in communities with particularly high death rates. Finally, two decades later, the farther reaching, compulsory Sanitary Act of 1866 required local authorities to provide water, sewers, and street cleaning.

On the political front, the Reform Act of 1832 left all women and those men who did not own sufficient property outside the halls of power. Mary Smith, from Standmore, Yorkshire, sought a partial solution in August 1832. Claiming that "she & other spinsters" should, as taxpayers, "have a voice in the election of Members," hers was the first female suffrage petition ever presented to Parliament. Smith's advocacy for propertied *femmes sole*—women without husbands to represent their interests—met only laughter in the House of Commons, but some excluded men were more generously accommodated.[9] Parliament placated the disenfranchised men of the middle class with a much-needed local reform. The Municipal Corporations Act of 1835 rationalized town government and put it in the hands of local taxpayers. Prior this reform, local corporations created by royal charters, many dating to the Middle Ages, governed boroughs, and wealthy elites controlled many corporations, which were elected by very narrow franchises. In 180 boroughs, only members of the local corporation could vote. Some emerging industrial cities had no corporations at all. Since corporations provided local services such as water and sanitation and set rates (local property taxes), control of these bodies mattered a great deal.

The Municipal Corporations Act replaced exclusive corporations with elected borough councils. All male rate payers who were residents for at least three years could vote in the annual council elections. Councils would elect the mayor and alderman. The act required each borough to have a paid clerk and treasurer and to establish a police force. Towns without councils could apply for incorporation. Middle-class and even some working-class men left out of the Reform Act of 1832 could now have a say in local affairs, which historically has meant more to people than a say in national politics. It would not be until 1894 that women, married and single, could vote in elections for borough councils.

Post-1832 Reform Movements

It had been hoped (by some) and feared (by others) that the Reform Act of 1832 would usher in a new era. As we have seen, however, the new arrangement proved relatively modest. In England

and Wales, roughly one man in five over the age of 21 could now vote, and separate acts for Scotland and Ireland resulted in even more restricted franchises. Representation in the House of Commons shifted, transferring more weight to populous urban and industrial centers, and away from depopulated boroughs, but.the composition of the men sitting in Parliament hardly changed. Unsurprisingly, therefore, Parliament's outlook and sympathies, and the legislation it promoted and secured, did not differ drastically from those of the pre-reform years.

Those who believed that further and different reform was in order recognized that the impetus would have to come from outside Parliament. To this end, two noteworthy pressure groups emerged in the second half of the 1830s: Chartism and the Anti-Corn Law League.

CHARTISM

Members of the working class believed they were not getting a fair deal. This was especially disappointing given their contributions to the reform cause in general and the passage of the 1832 law in particular. A petition presented to Parliament in 1839 articulated the frustration this way:

> It was the fond expectation of the people that a remedy for the greater part, if not the whole, of their grievances, would be found in the Reform Act of 1832.
>
> They were taught to regard that Act as a wise means to a worthy end; as the machinery of an improved legislation, when the will of the masses would be at length potential.
>
> They have been bitterly and basely deceived. …
>
> The Reform Act has effected a transfer of power from one domineering faction to another, and left the people as helpless as before.
>
> Our slavery has been exchanged for an apprenticeship to liberty, which has aggravated the painful feeling of our social degradation, by adding to it the sickening of still deferred hope.[10]

This powerful statement, including yet another example of the way white Britons misappropriated the language of slavery and abolition in their quests for reform, accompanied the first national petition of the Chartist movement, signed by 1,283,000 supporters. Its signature sheets, arranged end to end, stretched for almost 3 miles and, when rolled up, formed a bundle 4 feet in a diameter.

Chartism's origins are associated with the 1836 formation of the London Working Men's Association (LWMA), though its roots extend back much further. One of the LWMA's founding members, the tailor Francis Place, had been a leader of the London Corresponding Society in the 1790s; another, the cabinet maker William Lovett, was a union activist. In 1837, the LWMA joined with Radical MPs to produce "The Six Points of the People's Charter" that gave the movement its name.

Chartism aspired, as one future leader declared, to put workers "at the top instead of the bottom of society—or rather that there should be no bottom or top at all."[11] This would be achieved through the six points. The first three—universal male suffrage, secret ballot, and equal electoral districts—focused on voting rights. All men, regardless of income, education, and region, should have equal representation in Parliament and be able to exercise their electoral choice privately. The second three points—abolition of property requirements for MPs, provision of salaries for MPs, and annual elections—focused on the composition of the House of Commons. If the Chartists prevailed, no longer could only rich men stand for election or afford to serve, and constituents could regularly vote out those who failed them.

Likeminded groups began associating with the LWMA, and a National Charter Association (NCA), formed in 1840, had by 1842 over 400 branches and 50,000 fee-paying members. It is important to emphasize the British, rather than merely English composition of Chartism, for there were branches in Scotland, Wales, and Ireland. Moreover, though the LWMA, as its name suggests, did not welcome women, the NCA did. In one local group with 500 members in 1839, 300 were men and 200 women. Where gender was taken into account when tabulating signatures on the first national petition, women tended to number around a quarter of the petitioners. Large Chartist organizations often had women's sections, and according to historian Anna Clark, "Chartist women organized themselves." She counts over 150 "flourishing female Chartist associations" in England and 23 in Scotland. When the People's Charter was first drafted, there was talk of including female—and hence truly universal—suffrage among its points. That idea was ultimately vetoed because, according to Lovett, some members feared that such a radical proposal "might retard the suffrage of men." Female Chartists thus campaigned mostly for the political rights of their husbands, brothers, and sons. But at least one male colleague declared that "the women were the better men," more militant in their commitment. When 50 Chartists were arrested during demonstrations in Mansfield in 1839, only one was armed: Elizabeth Cresswell, a framework knitter, carrying a loaded revolver.[12]

Chartist groups differed in their approaches. Some branches also advanced local, socioeconomic aims, and disagreement emerged over how and when the six points could be achieved. Those known as *moral* force Chartists preferred discussion or persuasion, relying on orderly demonstrations, pamphlets, and the like. Law abiding, they recognized that achievement of the six points might be the patient work of several years and six separate legislative initiatives. Others demanded immediate results. These *physical* force Chartists advocated violence, in some cases modeling themselves on French revolutionaries of the 1790s. Most leaders of the national movement leaned toward moral force agitation, but inevitably the physical force contingent got—and continue to

FIGURE 10.6 Chartist meeting.

get—a disproportionate share of attention. Chartist divisions thus prefigured those that would splinter the suffrage cause between constitutional suffragists and Pankhurst's suffragettes.

There were three peaks of Chartist activity—in 1838–1839, 1842, and 1848—all culminating in mass petitions to Parliament. An unimpressed House of Commons rejected a motion to even consider the first charter by a vote of 235 to 46. Over the next year, 500 Chartists were arrested on rumors of a national rising. The second charter was twice the size of the first: It included over 3.25 million signatures and stretched, when unrolled, over 6 miles. It too was rejected by Parliament. In 1848, there was, however, a whiff of possibility the air. A new revolution in France had just (and again) toppled the monarchy there, and rulers throughout Europe were scared. Sensing their time might have finally arrived, Chartists organized a third petition and a national convention. Perhaps as many as 100,000 attended the meeting at Kennington Common in South London, from which a procession was planned to march the petition to Westminster. The authorities responded with laws prohibiting more than 10 people from presenting a parliamentary petition and redefining sedition. Meanwhile, government buildings were sandbagged, cannons moved into central London, bridges across the Thames closed and guarded by soldiers, and thousands of special constables deputized.

FIGURE 10.7 Chartist meeting, London, 1848.

Under such conditions, Chartist leaders canceled the procession and delivered the petition to the House of Commons in three cabs, only for it, like its predecessors, to be rejected. Over the next few months, frustration sparked violence in some Chartist circles, and the government seized the opportunity to suppress the movement.

Those last few events had dire consequences for William Cuffay, the chairman of the Chartist committee tasked with organizing the immense procession to carry the petition across the Thames to Parliament. Incensed when the procession was called off, Cuffay blamed the movement's leaders for falling into a government trap. Four months later, he too was trapped when a government agent exposed the plot of a Chartist uprising in London. Cuffay was arrested and charged with "levying war against the queen." Convicted on the disputed testimony of two police spies, Cuffay, the Britain-born grandson of an African sold into slavery on the Caribbean island of St. Kitts, was transported at the age of 61 to Van Diemen's Land (now Tasmania) on a prison ship.[13]

It is important to note that all three peaks of Chartist agitation coincided with periods of commercial depression and general economic downturn, resulting in unemployment and falling wages. When the

FIGURE 10.8 William Cuffay, Chartist leader.

economic cycle revived, interest subsided. Contemporaries and historians have thus debated whether economics or politics drove the movement. But the commitment of radicals like William Cuffay to the cause is impossible to dismiss. Despite its immediate failure, five Chartist points ultimately became law. Property qualifications for MPs were eliminated in 1858, a secret ballot was introduced in 1872, constituencies were further standardized in 1867 and 1884, salaries were introduced for MPs in 1911, and universal suffrage was achieved in 1918 for men and 1928 for women. That it took almost a century to achieve these modest goals demonstrates just how resistant the political elite were to inclusion and constitutional change.

THE ANTI-CORN LAW LEAGUE

Among the things that had initially raised Chartists' hopes of success in 1848 was the repeal of the corn laws in 1846. Those protective tariffs that kept the price of bread high, creating hardship for poor consumers and profits for the landed interest, had been chief among working-class complaints for thirty years! Might their repeal signal a new moment for reform?

Overturning the corn laws had been the goal of another extra-parliamentary movement born in the late 1830s: the Anti-Corn Law League. As with Chartism, various like-minded groups coalesced in 1838 to bring about a national organization. Yet there was much that differentiated the two movements. Members of the Anti-Corn Law League were middle-class beneficiaries of the Reform Act of 1832, businessmen who now possessed the vote. Their complaints were with policy, and one policy in particular, not with representation and the constitution. The league advanced numerous claims, tangible and abstract, in favor of repeal of the corn laws. Once bread prices fell, they argued, workers' real wages would rise, and Britain's consuming class would expand. This would benefit other industries, spurring the economy overall. Furthermore, if Britain demonstrated a genuine commitment to free markets and let in foreign foodstuffs without restriction, overseas competitors might import more British manufactured goods. Even if that did not come to pass, the league insisted, unrestricted competition was a good thing and would prompt British farmers to experiment and innovate.

The league staged mass meetings, indoors and out, where audiences numbering in the thousands were schooled to the iniquities of the corn laws and the blessings of free trade. Tea parties and bazaars, designed to appeal to middle-class ladies, raised as much as £100,000, the proceeds from which funded the crowd-pleasing lecturers and campaigners. The league also made good use of the Penny Post, introduced in 1840, to distribute a weekly newspaper, *The Anti-Bread Tax Circular*, and other free trade literature. Finally, emulating the Chartists, the Anti-Corn Law League petitioned Parliament, where the landed interests that continued to dominate squelched its petitions too.

FIGURE 10.9 A meeting of the Anti-Corn Law League in Exeter Hall in 1846.

The league thus adjusted its strategy, taking on the actual composition of the House of Commons. Whenever there was an election—no matter the constituency, no matter the circumstances—the Anti-Corn Law League backed a candidate. In close contests, the league even dipped into its coffers to secure the vote for non-electors who promised, if enfranchised, to support repeal candidates. That is, they bought property or other qualifications for certain men to help them meet the suffrage qualification. At the same time, the league reviewed voter registration rolls scrupulously to disenfranchise, often on technicalities, unsympathetic voters. This resulted in a handful of striking electoral victories. Still, by 1845, only around a dozen MPs stood on the Anti-Corn Law League platform. This was less than 2 percent of the Commons, although others, who did not self-identify as leaguers but supported free trade, increased the impact of the movement. It was enough to pressure the government and even obstruct the day-to-day business of Parliament. The Anti-Corn Law League thus kept its single goal—complete repeal—in the public eye.

When repeal finally came in 1846, however, the Anti-Corn Law League was not directly instrumental. Other factors, especially the Irish potato famine, prompted the Conservative Party (formerly the Tory Party) prime minister, Robert Peel, to push unexpectedly to overturn the corn laws. The government had been slow to recognize the magnitude of the Irish crisis. In November 1845, Lord John Russell, leader of the Whig Party, made a bipartisan appeal, writing that "the present state of the country, in regard to its supply of food, cannot be viewed without apprehension. Forethought and bold precaution may avert any serious evils; indecision and procrastination may produce a state of suffering which it is frightful to contemplate." Russell indicated that Whigs would support Peel if he moved to repeal the corn laws. "Let us, then, unite to put an end to a system which has been proved to be the blight of commerce, the bane of agriculture, the source of bitter divisions among classes, the causes of penury, fever, mortality, and crime among the people."[14]

Six months later, Peel introduced a bill for full repeal. He explained to the House on May 15, 1846, "I do not rest my support of this bill merely upon the temporary ground of scarcity in Ireland, but I believe that scarcity left no alternative to us but to undertake the consideration of this question."[15] The measure passed that day—with essential support from Whigs and Radicals, but at the cost of splitting Conservatives. Only 112 Conservative MPs voted for repeal; 241 opposed it. Peel, victorious in his measure, had lost control of his party and resigned the next month. Those Conservatives who sided with the government and defended repeal were known for a while as Peelites. By 1859, however, they had largely coalesced with former Whigs, to emerge as the Liberal Party that would dominate the direction of so much in Britain for the next half-century.

Reform Acts of 1867 and 1884–1885

As discussed in chapter 8, the rebellions that swept the British Empire in the 1850s and '60s, from the Indian Rebellion to the "Black War" in Australia, the ongoing Maori Wars in today's New Zealand, and Jamaica's Morant Bay Rebellion, reverberated in London. White men in the settler colonies had achieved universal manhood suffrage while working-class men in Britain still faced the steep property qualifications defined by the Reform Act of 1832. Yet the subsequent expansion of the franchise in Britain, achieved in 1867, owed much to the process of whiteness that working-class men enjoyed at the expense of persons of color throughout the empire. In comparison to what imperialists portrayed as the brutish, uncivilized, disorderly colonial others in Ireland, India, Canada, Australia, and South Africa, white working-class British men were heralded as stalwart defenders of discipline, home, and family. In order to solidify British control of the empire, working-class men became citizens.

In the 1860s in Britain, recession, unemployment, and soaring prices increased privation and sharpened working-class demands for change. The growth of cities since 1832 made underrepresentation of urban districts more glaring. The growing political consciousness of the working class led to the establishment of the Reform League with its 400 branches in 1865 to fight for universal manhood suffrage and the ballot. In collaboration with the more moderate middle-class Reform Union and parliamentary representatives who included William Gladstone and John Bright, it put the expansion of the franchise again at the forefront of the political scene.

The Whigs, increasingly referred to as Liberals by this point, favored redistribution of seats to urban centers and wished to expand the urban franchise, but opposed extending suffrage to agricultural laborers, who could be swayed to vote Conservative. The Conservatives, meanwhile, wanted to expand the rural franchise but not the urban. Neither party favored household suffrage or the secret ballot, and both had a considerable number of members opposed to any expansion of the franchise. Several reform bills proposed between 1851 and 1866 floundered. One measure that did pass removed the property qualification for MPs in 1858. Despite this achievement of a Chartist demand, MPs still received no pay and had to live in London at their own expense when Parliament was in session. It thus remained the case that only men of considerable wealth could afford to serve.

A Liberal victory in the election of 1865, followed by the death of the party's leader Lord Palmerston (who had not been eager for reform), created the expectation that the Liberals would finally pass a reform bill. Led by John Russell, now in his second stint as prime minister, they proposed lowering the household franchise from £10 to £7. The bill's main proponent, William Gladstone, advocated for the expansion of the franchise to working-class men as the heads of British households. This paternalistic stance on reform was not shared by some of his fellow Liberals who feared mass democracy and preferred a gradualist approach in which men of thrift who had internalized middle-class values "earned" the vote. Gladstone's measure was defeated by a Conservative-led coalition that included members of his own party.

The bill's defeat met with a massive demonstration of working people in Hyde Park. Meanwhile, having lost their signature measure, Lord Russell's government resigned and the Conservatives formed a government with Lord Derby as prime minister and Benjamin Disraeli, the chancellor of the exchequer, as majority leader in the Commons. Though Conservatives had just voted against parliamentary reform, the prospect of succeeding where the Liberals had failed was a compelling incentive to offer a bill of their own. Ultimately, the Conservatives passed a reform bill by out-flanking the Liberals on the left, offering more sweeping changes than their counterparts. The Reform Act of 1867 gave the vote to all male borough householders as well as to those paying £10 in annual rent. These changes enfranchised the better off members of the working class in the towns and also smallholders and agricultural tenants in the counties, adding approximately 1.5 million voters to the roles. The act also abolished four more rotten boroughs and reduced another 45 with fewer than 10,000 voters to one seat each. Seats were redistributed to the growing cities.

As Catherine Hall has demonstrated, race, empire, and gender form the context of the Reform Act of 1867. The working class was often denigrated using analogies to colonial populations of color. Opponents of expanding the franchise appealed to long-established hierarchies of class and race to bolster their position. Advocates of manhood suffrage responded by portraying working-class white men as responsible patriarchal providers.[16] The extension of suffrage to working-class men granted them citizenship and incorporated white men into Disraeli's new imperial project. The vote ensured that rather than being at odds with the government, they would be more invested in imperial matters overseas and supportive of government measures taken to expand the empire and increase British control of it.

The Second Reform Act doubled the number of eligible male voters. As discussed in chapter 9, John Stuart Mill introduced an amendment to the 1867 bill that would have replaced the word *man* with *person* in order to include women in the expansion of the franchise. The motion was defeated, one of the only expansionist amendments rejected as Conservatives sought to win Liberal and Radical supporters of their bill.

The next phase of the story of universal manhood suffrage came in 1884 when the Liberals argued that the householder franchise, which had been given to the boroughs in 1867, should be extended to the counties to enfranchise all tenants and most agricultural laborers. Gladstone, now prime minister, had opposed such a measure in 1867, believing it would merely create more Conservative voters. His Liberal Party's introduction of the secret ballot in 1884, however, gave agricultural workers some protection from electoral influence and economic retaliation by landlords and employers. For that reason, the Conservatives now opposed it.

The bill cleared the Commons in June 1884, only to be shot down by the Lords, supported by Queen Victoria. In response, Gladstone warned that socialism, gaining traction on the continent and at home, would spread farther in Britain if the Lords blocked the bill. His lengthy memo to the queen on the need for the reform contained the thinly veiled threat of an expanded peerage to force through the bill. A compromise with the Conservatives averted the crisis: The Lords would pass the bill if Gladstone agreed to follow it with a redistribution act that put county electoral districts on a par with urban ones.

The Representation of the People Act of 1884 (also known as the Third Reform Act) extended the borough franchise to the counties. All male householders and lodgers who paid £10 a year in rent received the vote. More than 60 percent of the adult male population over the age of 21 could now vote. Gladstone kept his bargain by passing the Redistribution of Seats Act in 1885. Towns with populations of less than 15,000—79 in all—lost their seats; another 36 with 15–50,000 people were reduced to single-seat constituencies. For the most part, the United Kingdom now had proportional representation based on roughly equal electoral districts. Two anomalies, however, preserved elite privilege: university seats and plural voting by wealthy Britons with multiple dwellings in different locations.

Irish Home Rule

The next year, 1886, Gladstone introduced what became known as the First Irish Home Rule Bill. The Home Rule campaign occupies an anomalous place among nineteenth-century reform efforts and must be understood in a variety of contexts: Irish, British, and imperial.

Home Rule was first and foremost an Irish nationalist movement, part of a century-long process by which Irish Catholics strived for self-government. As we have seen, a minority of Irish nationalists sought immediate and complete independence, and in 1848 some had even attempted rebellion. In the early 1850s, 40 Irish MPs formed the Irish Independence Party. As it broke up over internal divisions in 1858, the Fenians, or Irish Republican Brotherhood, coalesced in Ireland and North America with more radical intent. Committed to overturning British rule, in 1867 some Fenians undertook a campaign of violence in England, which included attacking a police van in Manchester and a prison in London to free jailed compatriots. Their acts, and the British response, inflamed fear and anger on all sides. Yet as the dust settled on both Fenian violence and the Second Reform Act of 1867, the Home Rule Party (or Home Rule League) emerged in 1873 as a new advocate for the more popular, moderate, and constitutional pursuit of self-government in which the majority of Irish nationalists had long been engaged.

Home Rule began, not as demand for something new, but as a call to restore something that had been lost. Ireland, as discussed elsewhere, had its own Parliament in the eighteenth century. The Act of Union that created the United Kingdom of Great Britain and Ireland in 1801 abolished the Irish Parliament in Dublin while adding Irish seats to the UK Parliament in London. The Catholic majority had no love for the combined, oppressive Protestant-led institution, but Catholic emancipation changed the equation somewhat. Irish nationalists could elect representatives to advocate for Home Rule. As the franchise expanded over the course of the nineteenth century, that bloc of voters grew in size. The Home Rule movement was thus also a British parliamentary force, one which could install or topple a ministry. Once the Home Rule Party, renamed the Irish Parliamentary Party in 1882, became powerful enough to affect the balance of power at Westminster, it could demand that Home Rule be considered. For the Liberal Party in particular, managing the bloc of Irish MPs became as much a priority as how to govern Ireland.

Finally, Home Rule was an imperial issue, consistent with the process of devolution by which Britain granted autonomy to its settler colonies. However, the Protestant majority in the northern Irish province of Ulster, as well as Protestant landlords in the south, feared being governed by a Parliament dominated by Catholics. For these heirs to centuries of British conquest and settlement, Home Rule was tantamount to what they derogatorily called "Rome Rule," and they resisted it fiercely.

Meanwhile, the tenant farmers, who made up the bulk of the Irish population, wanted practical changes that would improve their lives. For them, political reform, and occasional violent action (destruction of property and intimidation), were means to achieve fair rents and protection from eviction. British governments responded with a combination of limited reform and coercion. For example, the Gladstone government's Land Act of 1870, which provided some relief to tenants, was followed by the revealingly named Protection of Life and Property in Certain Parts of Ireland Act of 1871. Other coercion acts banned unlawful assembly, boycotting, and conspiracy to prevent payment of rents. In such a climate, Home Rule seemed the best way to ensure needed reform.

FIGURE 10.10 Family evicted during Irish Land War.

The Home Rule Party grew into a particularly formidable force under Charles Stewart Parnell, who became its leader in 1880. Parnell's success lay in his ability to combine political action for Home Rule with grassroots agitation for land reform. As president of the Irish National Land League, founded in 1879, Parnell controlled agrarian campaigns for the "three F's:" fair rent, fixity of tenure (limiting eviction), and free sale (compensating tenants for improvements they made to rented land). When Parnell opposed in 1881 a second land act, which fell short of guaranteeing fair rent, Gladstone had him imprisoned in Dublin's Kilmainham jail. In response, Parnell and other Irish leaders issued a "No-Rent Manifesto." Violent resistance to eviction and destruction of property accompanied the rent strike. In the face of unrest, Gladstone reached an agreement with Parnell. In the "Kilmainham Treaty," Parnell agreed to withdraw the manifesto and end criminal activity in return for an improved land act.

Parnell and his associates won "the Land War," as the agrarian agitation was called, but Home Rule remained elusive. The situation changed dramatically with the general election of 1885, the first since the Reform Act of 1884 more than doubled the Irish electorate. Half of Irish men were now eligible to vote, and the Irish Parliamentary Party increased its representation in the House of Commons from 63 to 85 seats. Parnell had enough MPs to give either the Liberals or the Conservatives a majority. His price would be Home Rule.

Once Gladstone announced that he would support Home Rule, the Irish Parliamentary Party backed his Liberal Party, enabling it to form a government in February 1886. Gladstone, however, had not paid sufficient attention to the will of his own supporters. When he put forward the first Home Rule Bill, it was defeated 341 to 311. Ninety-three Liberal MPs, who would henceforth be known as "Liberal Unionists," voted with the Conservatives to defeat the bill. Gladstone's government fell. The defectors, moreover, never returned; the consequences for the Liberal Party would be long-lasting. Meanwhile, scandal engulfed Parnell when his lover's husband named him a co-respondent in their divorce proceedings. The scandal led to a leadership crisis within the Irish Parliamentary Party. Home Rule was the real victim of all the infighting.

Gladstone's motives in supporting Home Rule have been the subject of historical debate. He clearly knew that even if a bill passed in the Commons, the Lords would veto it, which is exactly what happened when the second Home Rule Bill won in the lower house in 1893. This has led some to speculate that Gladstone's real goal was to tie the Irish MPs firmly to the Liberal Party. Whatever his motives, Home Rule would have to wait until the House of Lords lost its veto power.

Under new rules established by the Parliament Act of 1911, the House of Lords could delay but not veto bills passed by the Commons. Thus armed, a Liberal government introduced a Home Rule Bill once again. The Commons passed it, in 1912 and 1913, only to have it defeated both times in the Lords. But when the Commons passed Home Rule again in May 1914, the Lords defeated it for the last time. Pursuant to the terms of the Parliament Act, the bill automatically went to the king for his signature and became law. This carefully executed constitutional scheme was undone, however, by the time it took to transact. By the spring of 1914, Ireland was consumed by unrest, and by the end of the summer Europe would be at war.

Independent Labour Party

On March 14, 1884, police locked the gates of Highgate Cemetery as thousands flocked there to pay their respects at the grave of Karl Marx on the one-year anniversary of his death. Marx, who did not have much of a following in Britain during his lifetime, was suddenly quite popular thanks to recent publications that translated and summarized his works. "Something is buzzing," declared Tom Mann, a new disciple who had left school at the age of nine to work as a miner and subsequently apprenticed as an engineer.[17] That something, as discussed in chapter 9, inspired the founding of the Social Democratic Federation, the Socialist League, and the Fabian Society—all in 1884! The Third Reform Act, also of 1884, thus passed at a busy moment in political life.

The next decade would prove equally busy. While Liberals and Conservatives competed for the support of recently enfranchised working-class voters—something they had done since the Second Reform Act of 1867, fueling the rivalry between the two parties—a new party, the Independent Labour Party (ILP), was founded in 1893 to address specifically workers' interests. Union activism had also been "buzzing" in the 1880s. Indeed, Mann, who would serve as general secretary of the ILP, first made a name for himself as an organizer of the London Dockers' Strike of 1889 and leader of a broader movement known as New Unionism (to be discussed in chapter 11). Socialism and unionism combined, sometimes easily and sometimes contentiously, to create a force that would challenge the established parties and transform political culture.

Around the time of the passage of the Second Reform Act, local trade unions of primarily "skilled" workers had formed a national organization, the Trades Union Congress (TUC). In 1868 it began holding annual conferences, and in 1871 it created a parliamentary committee to promote union-friendly legislation. Originally, the Liberal Party had welcomed working-class electoral candidates in predominantly working-class districts. Such MPs, of whom there were 11 in 1880, were known as Lib-Labs. But Lib-Labism was not to the liking of some union leaders eager to promote proposals addressing labor grievances that did not win Liberal Party approval. This was the position of Keir Hardie, a Scottish miner, union organizer, and journalist, who concluded that the Liberal Party

FIGURE 10.11 Election poster, 1895, depicting Keir Hardie in his unconventional parliamentary outfit.

was more interested in workers' votes than needs. Hardie therefore ran for Parliament in 1888 as an independent candidate. He lost, but the experience inspired the founding that year of the Scottish Labour Party. In 1892, Hardie ran again, recruited by activists in the working-class English constituency of West Ham, and won. When the new parliamentary session opened, Hardie showed up, not in the black frock coat, silk top hat, and starched wing collar worn by all MPs, including Lib-Labs, but in a tweed suit, cap, and kerchief tied around his neck. Hardie's attire caused quite a stir and signaled a challenge to the traditional order.

By 1892, there were 30 divisions of the Scottish Labour Party, and everywhere in Britain unions and socialist societies proliferated. In 1893, leaders from various groups, including Hardie, met at a conference in Bradford to create an "umbrella organization." Unity and self-definition proved tricky. Was it to be a socialist or a labor party? The name Socialist Labour Party was rejected in favor of Independent Labour Party, as organizers wanted to downplay ideology and appeal directly to workers' practical concerns. Still, the new party was understood to have a "socialist programme but without a socialist title." That platform included progressive redistributive taxation, unemployment and disability insurance, collective ownership of the means of production, and free education through university. One observer distinguished the ILP from Lib-Labism this way: "It recognized the theory of class war." It also welcomed women. A socialist schoolteacher named Katharine Conway was on the organizing committee that founded the ILP.[18]

Not surprisingly, the number of Lib-Lab MPs declined as working men chose to run as Labour candidates. Hardie, who chaired the ILP, was gradually joined in the Commons by other ILP members. In 1903, Liberals, out of power since 1895, made a somewhat desperate deal with the ILP. The Liberal Party would not offer a candidate in any constituency where a Labour candidate stood for election. In exchange, the ILP would recognize the Liberal Party as the leader of a new coalition to out-muscle Conservatives. Two separate parties thus allied, but ILP MPs remained independent labor representatives.

In the general election of 1905, the ILP won 29 seats. All but one of its MPs were manual workers—miners, shipwrights, engineers. Hardie was their leader, and their pact with the Liberal Party gave it the majority it needed to form a government.

When Hardie first took his seat in the House of Commons in 1892, as a Scot representing the London constituency of West Ham, he was joined by another groundbreaking MP: Dadabhai Naoroji (discussed in chapter 7), an Indian representing the London constituency of Central Finsbury. Unlike Hardie, Naoroji ran as a Liberal. Like Hardie, Naoroji helped found a new political party, the Indian National Congress (INC) in 1885.

Naoroji's becoming the first Indian MP was, in a way, foretold by

FIGURE 10.12 Labour leader Keir Hardie addressing crowd in Trafalgar Square, 1908.

the first non-Indian president of the INC, George Yule. Yule's predecessors at the helm of the INC were a Hindu, a Parsi (Naoroji), and a Muslim. He, by contrast, was a Scottish merchant and head of a Calcutta-based trading company, who had moved to India in 1875 and formerly served as sheriff of Calcutta. Yet, as Yule declared in his presidential address to the Fourth Congress in Allahabad:

> There are many thousands of Hindu, Mohammedan, Eurasian, Parsee and other gentlemen in the country who, if they were to transfer their persons to England for twelve months or more and pay certain rates, would be qualified to enjoy all the rights and privileges of British subjects. If you and I go to England we are qualified. If we return to India our character changes, and we are not qualified. In England we should be trusted citizens. In India well, the charitably-minded among our opponents say that we are incipient traitors! (Loud and prolonged cheers and laughter.)[19]

The peculiarly overlapping lives of Hardie, Naoroji, and Yule reveal how much, and how little, political affairs had changed in Britain and its empire. At the end of the nineteenth century, men of property still governed the United Kingdom, though in the wake of the Third Reform Act things were far more democratic than before, with approximately 60 percent of adult males able to vote. Such gains were not equally distributed. In England and Wales in 1885, two in three men could vote; in Scotland three in five; and in Ireland only one in two. In some of Britain's colonies, as Yule complained, political rights were far more restricted.

Meanwhile, the annual meetings of the Indian National Congress, like the annual conferences of the Trades Union Congress and later the Independent Labour Party, suggest the degree to which the nature of party organization had changed. The nineteenth century witnessed both the transformation of old parties, the Whigs and Tories who eventually realigned as Liberals and Conservatives, and the creation of new parties, some broad-based and others highly specialized. Grassroots organizations with platforms, known as "manifestos," now competed for the newly enfranchised voters. These structures were, ironically, often copied from extra-parliamentary organizations like the Chartists whose very purpose was to reform the political establishment, opening it up to the excluded majority.

The Chartists, as we have seen, included women in their ranks but ultimately not in their suffrage demands. Nor were women enfranchised in any of the nineteenth-century parliamentary reform acts that slowly enfranchised more men. Starting in 1869, women in England and Wales could participate in municipal elections for local government offices on the same terms (meaning with the same property qualifications) as men, though three years later a court ruling limited this to widows and unmarried women. Scottish women gained municipal voting rights in 1882, and Irish women in 1898. School board elections were meanwhile opened to women, who participated as both voters and candidates from 1870 onward. Finally, the Local Government Act of 1894 allowed married and single women with property to vote in elections for county and borough councils. By the end of the century women comprised almost 14 percent of the municipal electorate in England and Wales, and many served not just on school boards but as guardians of the Poor Law.[20] The parliamentary franchise, however, remained elusive.

Emmeline Pankhurst and her daughters founded the Women's Social and Political Union (WSPU) in 1903, the same year that the ILP made its election-winning pact with the Liberal Party. The WSPU supported the ILP, and like the ILP looked forward to a partnership with Liberals. That hope, however, soon crumbled. Two WSPU members, Christabel Pankhurst and Annie Kenney, a cotton mill worker who co-founded the WSPU's first London branch, were thrown out of a Liberal Party meeting in Manchester in 1905, arrested and imprisoned for heckling (charged with assault and obstruction) after urging that "Votes for Women" be added to the Liberal Party platform. It was around this time that the WSPU embraced militant action and its other slogan, "Deeds not Words."

FIGURE 10.13 Annie Kenney and Christabel Pankhurst.

IMAGE CREDITS

Fig. 10.1: Source: https://commons.wikimedia.org/wiki/File:Peterloo_massacre_dreadful_scene_at_Manchester.jpg.

Fig. 10.2: Source: https://commons.wikimedia.org/wiki/File:A_%22Peeler%22_of_the_Metropolitan_Police_Service_in_the_1850s.jpg.

Fig. 10.3: Source: https://commons.wikimedia.org/wiki/File:Plate_4_Bachelor%27s_Adventure.jpg.

Fig. 10.4: Source: https://commons.wikimedia.org/wiki/File:House_of_Commons_Microcosm.jpg.

Fig. 10.5: Source: https://commons.wikimedia.org/wiki/File:The_House_of_Commons,_1833_by_Sir_George_Hayter.jpg.

Fig. 10.6: Source: https://commons.wikimedia.org/wiki/File:Chartists-UK-1840.jpg.

Fig. 10.7: Source: https://commons.wikimedia.org/wiki/File:Chartist_meeting_on_Kennington_Common_by_William_Edward_Kilburn_1848_-_restoration1.jpg.

Fig. 10.8: Source: https://commons.wikimedia.org/wiki/File:William_Cuffay.jpg.

Fig. 10.9: Source: https://commons.wikimedia.org/wiki/File:1846_-_Anti-Corn_Law_League_Meeting.jpg.

Fig. 10.10: Source: https://commons.wikimedia.org/wiki/File:Family_evicted_by_their_landlord_during_the_Irish_Land_War_c1879.jpg.

Fig. 10.11: Source: https://en.wikipedia.org/wiki/File:Hardie_elect.jpg.

Fig. 10.12: Source: https://commons.wikimedia.org/wiki/File:Keir_Hardie,_Trafalgar_Square,_1908.jpg.

Fig. 10.13: Source: https://commons.wikimedia.org/wiki/File:Annie_Kenney_and_Christabel_Pankhurst.jpg.

CHAPTER 11

Economy, Industrialization, and Quality of Life

In most places and for most of history, men and women stayed in the same general vicinity they had been born and grown up in and would have noticed rather little change, even across a long lifetime. The patterns and activities of day-to-day life, dictated in part by the rhythms of the seasons, would remain, from a twenty-first-century perspective, remarkably constant. Inflation was rare, and prices and wages changed very little from decade to decade. Many goods and services were negotiated by barter rather than cash exchange. Birth rates tended to be high, but populations were stable, owing to correspondingly high death rates. Any one of the "positive" Malthusian checks (famine, disease, warfare, or repression) could abruptly interrupt this picture of overall stasis in population, but always in a downward, and never an upward, direction. This experience of general stability and continuity had begun to change in the British Isles in the second half of the eighteenth century and would all but disappear between the years 1815 and 1914.

Railways in the Nineteenth Century

At the start of the nineteenth century, traveling any great distance overland was difficult and expensive—and therefore rare. The fastest way to move around goods, people, information, or ideas remained no faster than the fastest horse. Under best circumstances, this was unlikely to exceed one hundred miles per day. Consequently, most people's lives were highly circumscribed, with obvious ramifications for commerce and economics. With few exceptions, organization was at local or regional levels and, changes brought about by agricultural revolutions in the late seventeenth and eighteenth centuries notwithstanding, something not much beyond subsistence remained the most realistic and prudent economy.

As we saw in chapters 6 and 8, the development of Britain's system of canals across the previous two or three generations somewhat improved the situation. Canals made it possible to transport goods that were too heavy or too bulky, or otherwise impractical (e.g., fragile ceramics), for people or for pack animals. But canals had limitations of their own. Once constructed, they were difficult and expensive to maintain, they were prone to leakage, they could freeze over in the winter, and they were slow, generally moving around 2 to 4 mph.

The big change in the nineteenth century was the development and expansion of Britain's railways. The basic premise of a railway was explained by Newton's laws of motion and had been worked out by practical observation long beforehand: Once in motion, smooth wheels rolling over a smooth surface meet very little resistance or friction. This made it possible to move very heavy loads, on a gentle downhill slope, with little to no effort. The first railways (or railroads) in Britain were used in the coalfields of Northumberland. They were, simply, ways (or roads) on rails, and the earliest ones ran on wooden wheels engaging wooden rails. Open carts were laden with heavy loads of coal at the pitheads and then rolled downhill to the wharfs, where they would bump gently against a buffer and come to a stop. Empty carts were then light enough they could be pulled back uphill by horses.

Like canals, railways had their limitations. Once laid, rails were fixed, and it was difficult, although not impossible, to move them. Rolling wagons on rails was a relatively slow business, and loaded wagons were incapable of even the slightest uphill gradient. They also could not safely negotiate any significant downhill slope. Railway construction required expert design and craftsmanship, and to manufacture and fit together such smooth wheels and rails required fairly sophisticated precision instrumentation. The undertaking was expensive, but the payoff was in the immense loads that could be hauled. Even primitive railways were unmatched in the ability to move heavy, bulky solids over short, relatively flat distances. The next step was to line up several wagons in a train and transfer their motive force, from gravity and horsepower, to steam locomotion.

Obviously other places in Europe faced the challenge of efficiently moving heavy, bulky goods, but various chance factors coincided to give Britain an important leg up in the development of railways at the turn of the nineteenth century. The growth in population and the growing importance of industrialization increased demands for coal, and as mines were dug deeper, flooding became more of a problem. Pumping water from a shaft is a fairly straightforward procedure, although the scale of the operation and the vast quantities of water subjected the moving parts to considerable wear and tear. Breakdowns and other technical difficulties were common occurrences, requiring regular repairs and improvisation. Typically around a coal mine there emerged a culture of self-taught workers who understood how engines worked and learned to innovate and experiment by practical tinkering.

The idea of harnessing steam energy as a means of motive force was not new; it had been used as a fuel source to power boats on still waters or against currents since the 1780s, although more as a curiosity than as a practical means of locomotion. The earliest steam engines used on railways were stationary. They were immense machines at either end of a line and capable of pulling a train of wagons by winding up strong chains or cables. Following this design, the line connecting two stations had to be nearly straight and, therefore, fairly short. The trick for a truly versatile steam powered train of wagons was self-locomotion, which required miniaturization. Soon tinkerers were at work attempting to design an engine that was strong enough to pull a train but small enough that it could be mounted on wheels without collapsing on itself or crushing the rails beneath it.

Various innovators addressed the problem, borrowing from and adapting each other's ideas, and designs were gradually more efficient. Britain's—and the world's—first major line was the Stockton and Darlington Railway (S&DR), completed in 1825 and connecting a distance of 26 miles. The design of the first engine to run it, *Locomotion No. 1*, was primitive by the standards of only a few years later; among other things, boiler inefficiencies brought the train to a complete stop fairly frequently, while the engine picked up steam, and it was capable of an average speed of only 2 mph. (This was considerably slower than a horse, of course, so the first passenger trains on the S&DR were pulled by horses rather than steam locomotion.) What mattered, though, was that *Locomotion No. 1* proved a train of laden wagons could be powered by steam; it was economical and capable of pulling several tons.

Only 5 years later, the Liverpool and Manchester Railway (L&MR) operated exclusively by steam (figure 11.1). It connected the 35 miles separating Liverpool, a major Atlantic seaport and center of world trade (later in the century it was nicknamed "the second city of the empire"), and Manchester, the most important city in the Lancashire cotton belt. Stephenson's *Rocket*, the first engine to run the line, sustained average speeds of 20 mph.

In scarcely a generation, the railways had changed the landscape, literally and figuratively, of Britain and British society. A few hundred miles of rail in around 1830 grew to nearly 7,000 by the 1850s, and every major city and port was connected, with multiple lines in and out of London. Branches off mainlines connected previously isolated and insignificant villages, bringing to them the news and the products of the empire and beyond. Remote regions, especially in the north of Scotland, which once it had taken weeks to reach, could now be brought in contact

FIGURE 11.1 A painting of the inaugural journey of the Liverpool and Manchester Railway, by A. B. Clayton.

with London in under a day-and-a-half. (Of course, when these lines were judged obsolete and no longer economical in the 1960s, these same places were cut off and left more isolated than they had been since the eighteenth century.) Migration became more common, since it was now possible to maintain physical contact with family or friends left behind. The activity of the L&MR, along which ran raw materials and finished products at thitherto unimaginable speeds, was only the most dramatic example of what was replicated in smaller, but cumulatively as significant, ways a thousand times over. Travel times and fares reduced dramatically, enabling middle- and upper-class men to live far from where they worked. Schedules were so reliable and predictable that it became necessary for Parliament to institute a single timetable, Greenwich Mean Time (GMT), across all of Great Britain and, after 1916, Ireland.

The spread of the railways across Britain facilitated regional, national, and international trade but also spurred on commercial activity at intensely local levels. It was increasingly worth the effort to transport goods or passengers to the nearest branch line stations, from where they could connect to the wider world, and vice versa. Therefore, far from sounding a death knell, the nineteenth-century railways served as a massive shot in the arm to the business of carts and wagons and personal conveyances, to say nothing of the demand for and care of horses and related "traditional" trades of shoeing, smithing, saddle and harness making, and so on.

The railways also created a vast array of new jobs. In addition to stimulating coal extraction and steel production, there was a demand for navvies, surveyors, engineers, and mechanics, as well as engine drivers, conductors and guards, and firemen. Stations needed stationmasters, porters, secretaries, telegraph (and eventually telephone) operators, and more. A midcentury census reported that over 45,000 were employed directly in the business of the railways (as laborers, officers, clerks, etc.), and 20 years later the figure had nearly quadrupled; 20 years earlier, most of these occupations had not existed.

Most of the initiative for constructing British railways, as well as most of the investment, was in private hands. The sheer scope of the undertaking, however, and the capital involved, made it inevitable that government would become increasingly involved. There were practical matters of legislating rights-of-way since a line of any significant length was bound to cross the property of multiple owners. Many recognized the railways' stimulating effect on trade and commerce and welcomed their arrival. Others were less sanguine about the obviously transformative effects of the railways; they complained they were eyesores, that noisy engines would frighten livestock, or that flying embers could set aflame fields or woods. Such concerns raised questions of compulsory purchase (i.e., eminent domain), the settling of which required time-consuming acts of Parliament.

Another area that resulted in government involvement was the cost of fares. The first trains were designed with the freighting of bulk goods in mind, but very quickly there was interest in moving people too, and almost immediately the L&MR was carrying 1,200 passengers daily. This prompted parliamentary regulation: In 1842 the Board of Trade began certifying the safety of lines before they could operate, and, in 1844, commercial passenger lines were required to run so-called parliamentary trains—where fares were capped at a penny per mile—in each direction at least once a day. This gave rise, among other things, to domestic tourism, as even families of modest means could afford a day trip to the seaside or London. The arrangement to transport one hundred fifty thousand visitors by train to the Great Exhibition in 1851 was a landmark event in the history of commercial tourism, and before long sports teams (and their supporters) could travel to away games and return the same day, thus fostering a deepening sense of British, rather than more provincial, identity.

Telegraph lines usually ran alongside railway lines, and most stations doubled as telegraph dispatch offices. (The telephone was invented in the 1870s but for some decades was not a serious contender for the simple reliability of pulsating dots and dashes.) This made possible near-instantaneous communication across Britain and connected parts of the globe, introducing modern journalistic practices set to a modern journalistic pace. There was a premium on speed, and with news carried on wire services, which were prone to disruption midway through a dispatch, the "inverted pyramid" style of reporting supplanted earlier styles—more linear, more narrative—of journalistic prose. On a more mundane level, but one that had greater direct impact on more people, the Royal Mail had taken a contract with the railways to carry the mail by trains in 1838, and standardization of rates under the Penny Post in 1840 stimulated communication in the British Isles and beyond. In the second half of the nineteenth century, railway stations became hubs of activity and information, much as the church, the village green, or the public house had been for centuries earlier.

A train cannot operate on a grade of more than 2 percent, and ideally not more than 1 percent. In nineteenth-century Britain, the goal was typically under one-twentieth of 1 percent, or a change in elevation of less than 2 feet, 8 inches for every mile of track. Such precise technical specifications called for sophisticated and finely tuned measuring equipment in the hands of highly skilled surveyors, as well as colossal feats of blasting, boring, tunneling, bridging, grading, and embanking. The lasting and permanent physical change brought about by the railways, including switchbacks and shunting yards visible by balloon or, in the twentieth century and beyond, aircraft or satellite, was every bit as profound as the pyramids of Egypt or the Great Wall of China. But whereas those endeavors were the work of generations or centuries, Britain's network of railways was largely completed in a couple decades.

Industrialization and Urbanization: The "Standard-of-Living" Debate in the Nineteenth Century

The other hallmark features of nineteenth-century Britain, and even of modern Britain more generally, are the related phenomena of industrialization and urbanization. While we can say without controversy that the transformative effects of the railways were positive, it is not possible to pass such sanguine judgment on the growth of factories and cities. On one hand, there were the splendor, ingenuity, and undoubted productive capacity embodied in the Crystal Palace (figure 11.2); on another, there were the slums, vice, and misery of Manchester or London, described by Engels or Mayhew. It was a question that was debated in the nineteenth century by contemporaries who witnessed—and experienced—the changes firsthand, and continues to absorb historians more than 150 years later; simply put, and on balance, were the effects of industrialization and urbanization good or bad?

These discussions often go under the shorthand of the "standard-of-living" debate, and compelling evidence can support either argument. The champions of these changes (called optimists), who emphasize positive effects, tend to bolster their position with hard facts and numbers (e.g., improved wages, productivity, caloric intake, etc.). The critics (called pessimists), who insist on negative change, fall back on lurid and hair-raising descriptions of squalor, exploitation, and inequality. Each type of evidence is evocative—and, on its own, seems unassailable. But each has shortcomings. Industrialization and urbanization in nineteenth-century Britain created dramatically new conditions, and those who engage in the debate implicitly deal in questions of change over time. But when considering these phenomena before the nineteenth century, there is rarely

FIGURE 11.2 Interior of the Crystal Palace.

a valid point of comparison for the before picture: The statistically minded optimist is left reconstructing negative evidence, while the anecdote-compiling pessimist must contend with the view, nearly universal any time before the nineteenth century, that "the poor are always with us." In other words, the undoubted privation and misery of the East End or a provincial mill town, before the nineteenth century, would have passed without comment or condemnation—as, indeed, it often continued to do in Britain's rural districts for a couple generations longer. But eighteenth-century ideas of enlightenment and liberalism taught that economics—or life—need not be a zero-sum game, and in the nineteenth century the unacceptable plight of the laboring poor, who were increasing numerically if not proportionately, became striking.

Negative Consequences of Industrialization

Changes in methods of production that were tentatively introduced in the eighteenth century intensified across the nineteenth century and had far-reaching social and economic consequences. At the risk of generalization, pre-industrialized workers were compensated in proportion to the finished product. At the level of individual craftsmen or artisans—say, shoemakers—they were paid for each pair of shoes they produced. Under the proto-industrial "putting-out system," a master usually paid individual workers on completion of each step in the process of producing woolen textiles. There was an incentive for speedy production (and a shoemaker who never completed a shoe or a spinner who spun no yarn would not be paid or find future employment)—but by and large workers set their own pace and worked at their own rhythm.

This capricious approach could no longer work in a factory setting. Adam Smith's dream of the efficiency brought about through the division of labor in his model pin-making factory (*Wealth of Nations*, book I, chapter 1) was not realized until the end of the nineteenth century, but it was true that factory manufacturing intensified alienation between labor and finished production. In practice, workers were increasingly paid not for the products of their labor, but rather for their time spent laboring. Under these circumstances, factory owners who had sunk vast amounts of capital into premises, the latest machinery, raw materials, and so on, aimed to maximize profit through long hours, multiple shifts, and, faced with very few regulations, ruthless practices.

The new atmosphere of factory production called for, quite literally, new rhythms of work. Factory hands were expected to work hard and conform to a uniform pace. Breaks for rest or nourishment were infrequent—unless, that is, they were demanded by a breakdown or some other limitation of the machinery itself. The notion of machines as the servants of workers was turned on its head, and it was operatives who were forced to accommodate the whims and foibles of the machines. Employers were eager to squeeze out as much productivity as possible, and the idea of the "tyranny of the clock" is apt when applied to the routine of mill towns in nineteenth-century Britain. Hours were long and unrelenting, leaving a post early was unheard of, and fines were imposed, with repeat offenders facing permanent dismissal for tardiness or any infraction that interrupted the fixed pattern of a shift. Obviously such a regimen left no room for the informal approach to labor that had led, in previous centuries, to the adoption of "Saint Monday," or the convention whereby workers did not return from their Sabbath rest until Tuesday. Now every hour counted—toward an employee's hourly wage and an employer's bottom line.

It would be grossly misleading to look for a "golden past" before the indignities of industrialization, in which masters and their apprentices or assistants (as well as their respective families) shared a common outlook and were on the same side of most issues, celebrating common triumphs and lamenting mutual setbacks. Into the nineteenth century, changing social dynamics pushed further apart the interests of masters and their men (and women). Good times were still good for all, but downturns were experienced very differently and, after each phase of bust (which seemed increasingly commonplace in a globalizing economy), alienation between employer and employee intensified. (Moreover, whereas in the past economic slumps had local, tangible causes, such as drought, now it must have seemed to laborers as though they were pawns to the abstruse and obscure forces of world markets.)

The masters of men in Manchester and other burgeoning mill towns were rejected as, and repudiated the label of, gentlemen. They preferred instead the distinction of being new men, or even simply men. This affected the structure and expectations of society in countless ways. To take one example, for nearly a century, "reading the Riot Act" (chapters 1 and 5) had often been enough to maintain social and public order. Its provisions extended a measure of lenient permissiveness, lasting up to one hour, to unruly and potentially disruptive and antisocial assemblages. After that period of grace, local constables—JPs, constables, and so on, in collusion with militia or whatever ruffians they could summon—were indemnified against any consequences, including loss of life, that occurred in the dispersal of the crowd. The system was chaotic and anarchic, albeit it the sort of chaos and anarchy that preserved existing social hierarchies—but it was also flexible. It had worked in face-to-face communities with multivalent relationships between and across social orders but could not transition to the rigidity of the factory floor where there were masters and men.

The scale and efficiency of nineteenth-century factory production, operating in an international context, was without precedent and generated vast amounts of wealth. Certainly some of this reached the pockets of the workers who labored in the factories of industrializing Britain, but, contrary to the free trade canard of the day, the rising economic tide did not lift all boats equally. Those who were already rich had the potential to become phenomenally so, while most others benefitted only slightly. The inequality gap widened, leading to very different outlooks and lifestyles in respect to where people lived, what they ate, and how they died.

The Dark Side of City Living

Smith was also wrong about the "universal opulence" he predicted in his idealized "well-governed society." If conditions at work were hard, often they were no better at what passed as homes for hundreds of thousands of workers and their families. Contemporaries agreed, whether we turn to Marx's associate and collaborator, Friedrich Engels, in his description of Manchester in *The Condition of the Working Class in England* in 1845, or the presumably more balanced accounts from parliamentary reports into conditions in provincial towns produced the same year. Workers' families lived in jerrybuilt tenements or back-to-back housing that lacked gas for lighting, privies, taps, or indeed, indoor plumbing. If corners could be cut in construction, they were—with no concern for occupants' comfort or safety. Consequently it was common to find windows or doors that failed to open or shut properly or chimneys that smoked. Often structures lacked cellars or adequate foundations and so gradually sank into soft ground (figure 11.3).

Disease was rife in the new cities of nineteenth-century Britain. Plague had not been a major public health concern since the first half of the eighteenth century, and thanks to the growing availability and acceptance of inoculation, smallpox was no longer the perennial scourge it had once been. But the spread of contagious sickness was exacerbated by overcrowding, and vectors could be any combination of conditions of urban squalor. To take only two examples, cholera (a new disease to Europe in the nineteenth century) was carried in dirty water, and tuberculosis (TB) resulted from poor ventilation.

FIGURE 11.3 A group of children at Crumpsall Workhouse, 1895–1897.

Typhus had been a problem for centuries, but in the past had been mostly associated with periods of famine and poor diet: Sustained undernourishment leaves individuals—and populations—vulnerable to opportunistic infections they might otherwise be able to ward off. These had, of course, been recurrent, if irregular, conditions for much of the period before the 1820s. Afterward, however, typhus was more increasingly associated simply with urban living, and especially with urban poverty. It was, in the estimation of contemporary authorities, "that unerring index of destitution" in nineteenth-century Britain.

Another group particularly susceptible to sickness in British cities of the nineteenth century were children. The viral disease polio was associated with young people to such an extent that, before the twentieth century, it was called simply "infantile paralysis." Instances of other conditions among children, whose immune systems had not developed resistance, were so commonplace they were routinely classified under the generic label of childhood diseases: chickenpox, measles, mumps, scarlet fever, pertussis, diphtheria, whooping cough, and more. Today such conditions are relatively unserious. We typically inoculate young children against many of these diseases, and modern medicine (analgesics, antipyretics, etc.) can treat the symptoms of others. In the nineteenth century, the same diseases killed significant numbers of children regularly. Edwin Chadwick, a public health official, reckoned in 1841 that, among the urban working classes, roughly half of all newborns died in their first year; across the wider population, the figure was estimated at one in three.

One of the achievements associated with Britain's rapid urbanization in the nineteenth century was its ability to keep pace with food production and distribution. After all, a growing population, with a diminishing proportion engaged in growing food, would prove a serious challenge for other contemporary societies. But the "Hungry Forties" in Britain were only that: hungry—and not starving, as they were in other parts of Europe. Great Britain, by contrast, had known no starvation, or fear of starvation since the years just after the Napoleonic Wars. It is no coincidence that this last dangerous period was at the cusp of the dawn of the railways and the ability to move foodstuffs around cheaply and efficiently. The repeal of the Corn Law a generation or so later initially seemed to have positive effects on British diets, since farmers turned increasingly to orchards, garden farming, dairy, and meat production, which meant a more varied, and typically more wholesome, diet than chiefly cereals and grains. (The formula of "more varied" certainly did not apply to Ireland, of course, where agricultural and transportation remained, for decades to come, medieval—and where the populace subsisted for the better part on potatoes.) But standards of sanitation and commercial ethics did not always keep pace with the efficiency of production and distribution. A Sanitation Committee presented its findings to Parliament in 1855 and reported that food available in towns and cities was regularly adulterated with non-foodstuffs, sometimes harmful to humans. What passed as milk was typically diluted with water up to 50 percent and, before routine pasteurization or adequate refrigeration, was a common vector for bovine TB.

So while workers in British cities undoubtedly consumed more calories, vitamins, and essential elements across the nineteenth century, it also likely that much of what they consumed was rancid, rotten, or contaminated.

The Role of Classical Liberalism

The intensity of the privation and disorder of urban life was owing in part to the spirit of liberalism that inspired so much in Britain in the decades following the Reform Act of 1832 (figure 11.4).

FIGURE 11.4 Cover of *The Economist*, 1846.

Municipal reform had followed in 1835, but it took some time for local government to modernize, and many towns and cities were left for decades without codes or inspectors or regulators. Such unincorporated entities were unable to issue licenses or enforce standards. The building trade was a veritable free-for-all and, with renters having no authority to which they could appeal, landlords gouged rents relentlessly. Roads were not paved, public spaces were not lighted, and sewage was not drained until the latter part of the century. Most new towns and cities even lacked a police force before the second half of the nineteenth century, so there was nothing separating lawlessness and disorder from the calling out of the militia. Granted, families might be able to live further out from inner cities, if lodging were available and affordable, but that was bound to add travel time to a long day—and of course they were not paid for it. The more plausible alternative was to live close to work, in cramped and dirty quarters, never really leaving behind the noise and smell and pollution of the factory.

This ethos of limited government prevailed for much of the period of rapid growth and had its greatest impact in liberal circles. Therefore, it is unsurprising that a Conservative prime minister, Benjamin Disraeli, took the lead in addressing—and, to a certain extent, redressing—some of the worst conditions. As Disraeli put it in 1874: "Pure air, pure water, the inspection of unhealthy habitations, the adulterations of food … [:] the first consideration of a Minister [of state] should be the health of the people."[1] Contemporary critics accused the prime minister of a cynical ploy to win the electoral support of the numerically dominant working classes who, increasingly after 1867, had an important role in deciding the fates of governments. (The Second Reform Bill had been designed for much the same purpose: to boost the electoral fortunes of the Conservative Party—although they lost the 1868 general election.) There is probably an element of truth to this, and certainly Disraeli never missed a chance to score electoral points. But his concerns for the poor and for working-class conditions, as an expression of what might be called "Tory paternalism," were genuine. Years earlier, in 1845, he had introduced to his reading public what Thomas Carlyle had called the "condition of England question" in his novel *Sybil*. Its subtitle, tellingly, was *The Two Nations*, and in book II, chapter 2, Disraeli explained what this meant for contemporary Britain:

> [There were t]wo nations … between whom there [wa]s no intercourse and no sympathy; [they were] as ignorant of each other's habits, thoughts, and feelings, as if they were dwellers in different zones, or inhabitants of different planets; who [we]re formed by a different breeding, [we]re fed by a different food, [we]re ordered by different manners, and [we]re not governed by the same laws: the rich and the poor.[2]

As prime minister, Disraeli led his government in fixing some of the problems that faced the urban working classes. The Public Health Act (1875) enforced local authorities to purify water supplies, drain sewers, and appoint overseers to supervise these improvements. The implementation of the Sale of Food and Drug Act (1875) corrected some of the problems of adulteration and contamination that had been discovered by a Sanitation Committee. (The committee, it should be noted, had met 20 years earlier—but having reported under the auspices of a Liberal government, had in the interim, predictably, done nothing.)

For all their improvements, the Public Health and Sale of Food and Drug Acts were the exceptions to the rule, and for much of the nineteenth century, the tenets of classical liberalism persisted. The exception that proved the rule was the Poor Law Amendment Act (generally known as the New Poor Law; see chapter 7). The measure might appear an ambitious and comprehensive overhaul of more than 200 years of legislation concerning paupers. In fact, its purpose was perfectly in step with the limited outlook of a liberal government. It was designed to cut costs and decrease the size of government and, of course, government spending. And to that extent, the New Poor Law was a success. Taking at reductive face value the biblical authority that "the poor are always with us" (Matthew 26:11), British liberals of the nineteenth century frowned on virtually all oversight or intervention.

Efforts to Uplift the Poor

In the context of such a spirit of limited government, much of what passed to alleviate or improve the plight of the urban poor fell to private charitable interests. The established church, Roman Catholic until the sixteenth century and various shades of Protestant thereafter, had always taken a prominent role—a basic tenet of the faith was that whatever was done to the poorest and weakest was done to Jesus himself—and even the lines drawn up by the 1834 Poor Law Amendment Act reflected the old parish divisions of the medieval church. But the increase in population since the late eighteenth century, and the scope of distress that faced Britain in the nineteenth century, especially in the overcrowded neighborhoods of its towns and cities, exceeded the capacity of the established church, and even the bigger nonconformist sects, to provide much help. Some evidence also suggests that the liberal ethos of the age, prioritizing as it did the individual, prompted main-line Protestants (not including most Methodist groups) to forsake charitable efforts and leave the down and out to their own devices.

Most Methodist groups rejected this outlook, and it was as an extension of the mission to the East End of London that Catherine and William Booth founded the Salvation Army in the 1860s. The aim was to bring spiritual and physical succor to the destitute, and they were especially concerned to meet the needs of the poorest of the poor, whom William Booth called the "submerged tenth" (i.e., an underclass permanently excluded from organized religion [the Salvation Army excepted, of course], influence, education, opportunity, or—broadly put—society itself). The Booths shocked the previously complacent middle-class public by comparing, unfavorably, the depth of poverty found in British inner cities to conditions of those living in parts of Africa.

Charles Booth (no relation to William or Catherine) was a wealthy shipbuilder, originally from Liverpool, who had read pamphlets and accounts decrying the horrors of London's East End— but did not buy it. So Booth hired teams of investigators to visit and interview nearly every poor household in London. Their efforts confirmed the grinding poverty of William Booth's "submerged tenth." In fact, in the East End, it was more like a "submerged third" and, across a broader swathe of the metropolis, around 30 percent lived in varying degrees of poverty (figure 11.5). Booth's findings, published in a multivolume *Life and Labour of the People of London* (1891–1903), had especial impact because, rather than simply bemoaning awful conditions, they provided detailed comparisons of the circumstances across different neighborhoods, grounded in hard statistics. He identified specific problems, raising the hope that they could be resolved by specific, targeted solutions. Accordingly, policymakers and reformers had concrete starting points for goal-oriented programs to tackle the problems of urban squalor.

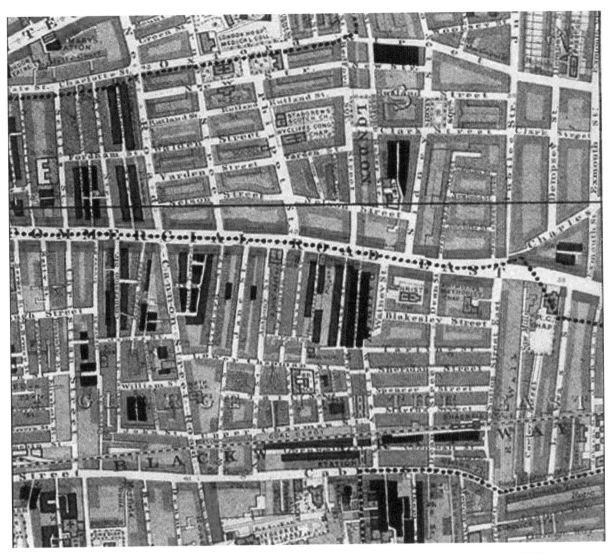

FIGURE 11.5 Part of Charles Booth's poverty map showing Commercial Road in Whitechapel 1889. The red areas are "well-to-do," and black areas are the "lowest class ... occasional labourers, street sellers, loafers, criminals and semi-criminals."

Charles Booth's massive work attracted the notice of Seebohm Rowntree, a Quaker and philanthropist and a scion to one of the biggest employers in York. Rowntree accepted Booth's account, but northern prejudice made him skeptical such horrors could exist outside the dregs of London. To test the hypothesis, Rowntree, like Booth, dispatched teams of investigators into the working-class neighborhoods of York and published their findings in *Poverty, A Study in Town Life* (1901). What they found was that conditions in York, where nearly 30 percent lived in poverty, were not very different from in London.

Rowntree's work was important because it applied systematic principles to define poverty through a "standard of physical efficiency": a sliding scale that set the bare minimum required to pay for rent and fuel, provide an adequate and nutritious diet, and, averaged across a year, cover other anticipated expenses (e.g., repaired or replaced clothing or shoes). Put another way, Rowntree defined, or explained in measurable terms, what it meant to be poor. But the standard of physical efficiency did not allow for any extras (toys, hair ribbons, tobacco, bus or rail fare, etc.), nor did it leave anything left over for saving, so any added expense or any slip in income (e.g., loss of work or a sick or injured wage earner) could spell catastrophe. Moreover, Rowntree's investigations showed that many households failed to meet the standard of physical efficiency and so found themselves, week after week, sliding deeper toward the depth of the "submerged tenth" (or third) of York. This overall picture, that working families often could not meet the costs they needed for basic necessities (or to sustain physical efficiency), was borne out on many points by the *Report of the Royal Commission on Labour*, submitted in 1895.

Rowntree was also important for having identified a cycle in which working-class individuals were likely, across a single lifetime, to rise above and sink below the standard of physical efficiency—and therefore fall in and out of poverty. In its most predictable pattern, working-class individuals were likely to be born in large families to struggling parents—and to be poor. Entering their teenage years, they earned wages in their own right and contributed to the family income—and they were not poor. Poverty returned with marriage and a new growing family, until the next generation started work and left home. And toward the end of life, when the chief wage earner was too old or frail to continue working, poverty set in as a final and permanent condition. The system was stacked against them, with predictable potholes, and urban working-class life was likely to begin and end below the standard of physical efficiency.

This emphasis on earnings, expenses, and a cycle of poverty contradicted the paternalistic liberal outlook of self-improvement and self-help. Rather than something that was "always with us," to be deplored by upright Victorians, poverty was not the fault of the indolent or incontinent working classes. Nor was there a single or monolithic cause to poverty, to yield before a single and comprehensive solution. Instead, poverty was generally owed to any one or more of several related factors that boiled down to not enough money to meet basic expenses. This challenged many Victorian orthodoxies.

The Positive Side of Factory Work

If conditions could be so bad in British towns and cities across the nineteenth century, the question must be asked: Why were they such popular destinations? For they undoubtedly were: The 1851 census showed that slightly more than half the UK population was urban, and the number of town and city dwellers grew in the decades that followed. Clearly natural increase was not the deciding factor since towns and cities often were unhygienic death traps. Yet fresh waves of migrants from the countryside kept coming.

Towns and cities were centers of productivity and generated wealth at a rate that had been unfathomable only a generation earlier. Even if the wealth were spread unevenly, and even if one-third were in some measure of distress, over two-thirds were not. The rapid growth of nineteenth-century Britain lent itself to disruption and instability, but it remained the richest society the world had known. For many, those odds were worth the gamble.

Factory labor in the nineteenth century meant long hours and strict discipline, but wages were paid regularly, in cash, and shifts were not subject to the uncertainty of weather or seasonal ups and downs. And for many (i.e., adult males, who, in senior positions as overseers or machine operatives) wages were particularly competitive. A common misconception links factory labor to low levels of skill and correspondingly low rates of pay, but in nineteenth-century Britain, the opposite was true. Factory operatives were skilled workers in important trades; far from being menial drudges, they were valuable, and valued, labor, commanding a premium wage. (Their predecessors, under the putting-out system, had not been hearty and independent yeoman craftsmen with prized skills; this is part of the mythic "golden age" narrative of the pre-industrial past.)

Women in factories performed different jobs from men, and were paid less, but still were paid more than their peers who worked in domestic service, as laundresses, cleaners, or in other fields open to women. Because there were relatively few regulations in nineteenth-century liberal Britain, factories also employed children, often starting around the age of nine. Children, like women, did not operate machinery; their work was unskilled (and their wages reflected this), but they were important, and cheap, sources of menial labor around the factory floor. Into their teenage years, boys could begin to train for lucrative positions as machine operators, and girls could move into better paid jobs performed by older women.

The availability of work for women and even children, as well as men, was a big factor that pulled families from rural backgrounds to the mill towns of industrial Britain. To be sure, there had always been work in the countryside. But much of this was not well paid, and in some cases compensation was not in regular cash wages. Therefore, the move from a rural district to a mill town could mean the difference of, on one hand, a single chief breadwinner and, on another, four or five or six reliable sources of cash income. The attendant expenses of urban living notwithstanding, this was bound to have a big impact on a family's living standards and even allow the possibility of modest savings.

King Cotton and Other Industrial Triumphs

The most important manufactured product throughout the nineteenth century was cotton. The production of cotton textiles in the British Isles had begun with humble origins in the second half of the eighteenth century, and as late as the 1770s, when non-cotton textiles (mostly wool) accounted for over a quarter of manufactured products, cotton amounted to a mere 1 percent. But the consumer market quickly realized that, especially in a supply-and-demand economy with growing transport and communications opportunities, cotton had a lot to offer. It produces a fabric that is lightweight yet strong and easy to tailor and clean. In a globalized economy, it had real possibilities, and the take-off of cotton textiles rivals that of the railways in the same period.

The undertaking was truly global. Cotton was grown in the nineteenth century in India, Egypt, and elsewhere, but the premium product, with the longest fibers capable of being spun into strong threads and woven into the desirable Sea Island cotton, was especially suited to the climate of the American Deep South. There it was planted, cared for, harvested, and cleaned by nearly 2 million Black slaves, over 40 percent of the enslaved population of the United States, originally of African descent. From interior plantations, the cleaned raw cotton was moved in bulk—often by rail, depending indirectly on British innovation and sometimes directly on British capital investment—to ports such as Charleston, Savannah, Mobile, and New Orleans. Some of it crossed the Atlantic for manufacturing districts in France or in the German states, but the majority was bound for Liverpool, and from there, by rail, to Manchester and its vicinity. Processed cotton textiles were then distributed (again, by rail) across the UK or, via Liverpool, to the British Empire and the wider world. It was a global, globalizing interest that turned on a British axis of Liverpool and Manchester, with spokes reaching to the Americas, Europe, Africa, and Asia.

By 1861, there were over 2,500 cotton factories operating in Lancashire, employing 430,000 hands, a majority of whom were women. The activity of these mills led directly to the employment (as dockers or stevedores who handled the raw cotton and the finished product, retailers, merchants, etc.) of at least as many more again. Add to this the hundreds of cotton mills outside Lancashire, and easily 1 million relied on cotton for their livelihoods. Taking into account dependents, *The Economist* reckoned that, of an English and Welsh population of 20 million, one in five was supported by the cotton business.

Seventy-five percent of the cotton produced in Lancashire was grown in the American South, and during the Civil War, the Union blockade of the rebelling states put hundreds of thousands out of work in the UK. The impact rippled widely through other sectors of the economy, affecting the livelihoods of at least a couple million Britons, as unprecedented numbers turned to soup kitchens and other types of relief (figure 11.6). Contemporaries called it the Lancashire Cotton Famine, and its impact on world trade made it a defining moment in the history of globalization.[3]

Despite the evident importance of cotton in the years 1815–1914, often it is the heavy side of industry—in the earlier period, trains and the rails they ran on; at the turn of the nineteenth and twentieth centuries, dreadnaught battleships—that captures the imagination. They provide for iconic moments such as Philip James de Loutherbourg's *Coalbrookdale by Night*, 1801 (figure 11.7) or the photograph of Isambard Kingdom Brunel striking a pose before the massive chains of his *S.S. Great Eastern* in 1857 (figure 11.8). But it is no coincidence that, when we think of British industrialization in the nineteenth century, instead of Birmingham or Bradford, we think of Manchester, nicknamed by contemporaries "Cottonopolis" and identified by Engels as "the first manufacturing city of the world"⁴—for no subsequent industrial and commercial expansion would have been possible had it not been for cotton laying the groundwork. The secret behind Britain's expanding commerce and manufacturing was not measured in the hundreds of tons of steel produced or the millions of tons of coal extracted. These things mattered, of course, but they came later. It started with the billions of pounds of imported raw cotton manufactured into billions of yards of exported cloth woven in its mills.

FIGURE 11.6 An 1862 newspaper illustration showing people queueing for food and coal tickets at a district Provident Society office.

FIGURE 11.7 Coalbrookdale by Night.

FIGURE 11.8 Isambard Kingdom Brunel.

The importance of cotton is easy to understand when approached from the perspective of the consumer. Products of heavy industry such as trains could only be bought by the phenomenally wealthy (typically consolidated financial interests), and military hardware was commissioned only by the government drawing on the collective purse of millions of taxpayers. The sums of money involved were immense, but the buyers were necessarily few in number. Cotton was different. It was so simple and so cheap that working-class families could afford it. Since urban and industrial workers were paid cash wages, they could buy finished cloth, and since several members of a family might bring in cash, a household's spending ability was boosted, contributing to a national cash flow. To be sure, manufacturers' profit margins were small, but since there were always more laborers than anything else, the consumer base was tremendous.

Thus, the industrial working classes were a key component to British wealth and stability across the nineteenth century. They were the shock troops of expansion, both as producers and as consumers. For all the attention given to overseas markets—the zero-sum game outlook of mercantilist orthodoxies dies hard—the success of Britain's expanding commerce and manufacturing was domestic. It was producing, selling, *and buying* that did it.

Efficient mechanized production of cotton, a basic necessity with broad and constant demand, provided the capital British entrepreneurs needed to expand other industrial endeavors. British coal output increased every year of the nineteenth century, from 11 million tons to over 225 million tons, or an increased output of 1950 percent. By the twentieth century, over one-quarter was being exported. British steel production increased every decade between 1870 and World War I, from 300,000 tons to 6.5 million tons, or an increase of more than 2000 percent per decade. British cotton production also increased across every decade of the nineteenth century, including the 1860s. In the 1810s, Britain processed under 100 million pounds of raw cotton; in the 1910s, the figure had risen to over 1.86 billion pounds. Between 1801 and 1821, Britain exported an average of less than 115 million yards of cotton textiles per decade; this had grown to over 5.5 billion yards, or an increase approaching 5000 percent, a hundred years later.[5]

Despite all this productivity, much of which plainly rested on a commitment to liberal economics, there are ways in which Britain fell victim to its own success in the decades leading up to World War I. Many in Britain were genuine enthusiasts of free trade, and successive governments faithfully practiced what they preached. The Conservative government of Sir Robert Peel famously repealed the corn laws in 1846 and, as Liberal chancellor of the exchequer in the 1850s and 60s, William Gladstone systematically removed most remaining tariffs. As *The Economist* newspaper commented in 1876, on the centenary of Adam Smith's *Wealth of Nations*:

The fetters in which pre-existing laws bound our commerce, have been removed, and the result is that we possess the greatest, the most stable, and the most lucrative commerce which the world has ever seen.[6]

British capital investment built the railways that made the grain fields of North America and central and eastern Europe—whose imports they did not tax—accessible. Following Smith's prudent maxim "never to … make at home what it will cost … more to make than to buy," Britain absorbed the cheaper and more abundant raw materials, and ultimately the finished products, of Germany and the United States. As a result, the end of the nineteenth century and the start of the twentieth century is often portrayed as a period of economic downturn, and even depression, in Britain.

But this gloomy picture requires some qualification. After all, real wages for working families steadily grew for almost every period across the second half of the nineteenth century and, at the start of the twentieth century, were more than double what they had been half a century earlier.[7] There was no serious industrial slump before 1914, and exports did not fall off sharply. On the contrary, in most cases industrial production continued to rise, as did export levels. The export of that old standby, cotton, increased regularly, as did British exports of coal, helped, in both cases, by an expanding empire and growing world population. Likewise, the steel industry expanded into the early twentieth century. Iron was the only heavy industry to decline across the period, but that was only because it had been supplanted by the superiority of steel.

Persistence of Rural Life

Factories and rapidly growing towns and cities were novel phenomena in Britain across the nineteenth century and, as such, garnered considerable attention. Memorable examples are provided in much of the literature of the day. Most of the novels of Charles Dickens are generally set in London, although one of them, *Hard Times*, takes place in Coketown, a fictitious amalgam of probably Manchester and Preston. Even the novels of Anthony Trollope and George Eliot, which often are set away from city or factory, and seem to deal with more "traditional" themes, nevertheless do so consciously in the context of the "new" looming prominently in the background (figure 11.9). Elizabeth Gaskell juxtaposed these differences explicitly in the title of her novel *North and South*. Set in Milton (i.e., "Mill-Town," a very loosely disguised version of Manchester), the novel develops and explores a series of stark distinctions between the newer, modern, industrial city of the nineteenth-century North and the older, tradition, agricultural countryside of the South.

FIGURE 11.9 George Eliot (Marian Evans), portrait by Frederick William Burton, 1864.

These and other literary works were popular in their day, influencing attitudes to complex phenomena. Because they are still read—and, increasingly, dramatized for television or film—today, they continue to color perceptions of the period. Among other things, many nineteenth-century writers tended to valorize a bucolic, pastoral, and idyllic past, before the coming of the railways and the growth of towns and factories. They also imply, especially from the perspective of posterity, a mighty juggernaut—a steam engine might be the more apt analogy—rolling relentlessly over the rural world it supplanted. The case of the Corn Laws could be taken as exemplary. They were designed to promote the economic advantage of rural interests which, in the first half of the nineteenth century, dominated Parliament. Their repeal was recognized, rightly or wrongly, as a defeat for that interest, and a victory for factory owners in towns and cities—and five years later the Census first reported Britain's urban majority. But the simplistic equation of modernity with cities and industrialization in nineteenth-century Britain, while a primitive countryside dwindled into obscurity, downplays the tenacity of a rural lifestyle.

Rather than ushering in an unremitting trajectory of rural decline, the growth of British cities across the nineteenth century stimulated and energized rural interests and activity. An obvious place to look is in the growth and production of food. Notwithstanding the fact Britain was increasingly feeding itself from overseas, there were only a few foodstuffs (i.e., grains and cereals) that were regularly imported. It remained most practical to consume milk, meat, and most seasonal fruits and vegetables from home, and the growing population—quadrupling between 1815 and 1914, and for more than half that time clustered in towns and cities—depended on the ability of the countryside to support them. Urban expansion also facilitated the growth of village economies by stimulating demand for agricultural or otherwise rural products. The building trade required timber, bricks, and stone, as well as lead for plumbing, sand and limestone for glazing, and ever-increasing amounts of coal. The raw materials for all these products were found in the countryside and were moved, from country to city, by trains.

It is obvious a simple narrative of rural decline fails to tell the whole story of Britain in the nineteenth century, and it is misleading to imagine a mass exodus from farmers' fields to factory floors. Economic historians reckon that 51 percent of the British workforce was engaged in the industrial sector in 1851, but defining or assigning employment categories is a notoriously vague undertaking: The 1851 Census shows that only 6 percent of workers had jobs in factories, and most of these would have worked in limited, relatively small-scale ventures, employing fewer than a hundred hands. These were hardly the "dark Satanic mills" described in Blake's poem and could even be seen as sort of halfway houses between the putting-out system and the factories of the twentieth and twenty-first centuries. The overwhelming majority of workers classed as "industrial" were clearly doing something other than factory work, and the single greatest occupation listed in the 1851 Census, accounting for close to one-quarter of the workforce, was "[a]gricultural labourer, farm servant, [or] shepherd." Many of the patterns and rhythms of rural life persisted, and employment and activities associated with the countryside remained familiar well into the second half of the nineteenth century. They depended on, but otherwise remained very remote from, London or Manchester.

But even with these qualifications, the changes brought about in where people lived and how they earned livings were striking, and the patterns intensified, especially in respect to agriculture. By 1901, Britain's agricultural sector had more than halved from its level half a century earlier, to 9.1 percent. Ten years later, it was down to a mere 8.6 percent. The big change in the industrial sector, on the other hand, had already taken place by the mid-nineteenth century: From 51 percent in 1851, it crept up only to 52 percent in 1911, and thereafter it actually entered decline. (Nowhere else in Europe experienced decline in its industrial sector until the 1980s.)

Looking beyond this period, however, and into the twentieth century, the change that would have more lasting significance than the supplanting of industry for agriculture, and that had already begun between 1815 and 1914, was the inexorable rise of the service (or "tertiary") sector of the economy. This shift reflects not so much a rise or fall of cities or the countryside, as the steady and sure ascendency of the middle classes. Britain's middle classes grew steadily—in size, influence, prominence, and combined wealth—throughout the nineteenth and twentieth centuries. Perhaps the most striking demonstration of this fact before World War I is the growth of the servant class since every middle-class establishment needed its servants. According to the 1851 Census, domestic service was the second most prolific occupational category, and over 1 million workers, close to nine in ten of whom were girls or young women, were employed as household servants. By the turn of the twentieth century, one British girl in three was employed as a *slavey*—a term that speaks volumes about the arduousness of the tasks performed by those in domestic service, to say nothing of how their employers regarded them. Britain's servant class grew until World War I and, looking to the service sector generally, the "tertiary" category accounted for 40 percent of Britain's economy in 1910. The socioeconomic story of Britain in the twentieth century had already begun in the nineteenth century: It was a story of the rise of the middle classes and of defining individual as employers or as employees.

IMAGE CREDITS

Fig. 11.7: Source: https://commons.wikimedia.org/wiki/File:Philipp_Jakob_Loutherbourg_d._J._002.jpg.

Fig. 11.8: Source: https://commons.wikimedia.org/wiki/File:Robert_Howlett_(Isambard_Kingdom_Brunel_Standing_Before_the_Launching_Chains_of_the_Great_Eastern),_The_Metropolitan_Museum_of_Art_(cropped).jpg.

Fig. 11.9: Source: https://commons.wikimedia.org/wiki/File:George_Eliot_7.jpg.

PART TWO

Retrospective

On April 4, 1903, Margaret Anne Neve (nee Harvey) died on Guernsey, a British island off the coast of France. Born in 1792, she lived across three centuries and witnessed unprecedented change. As a child she may have lived in fear of invasion by Napoleonic France, but as an adult she enjoyed the long era of peace and prosperity between the battle of Waterloo and the outbreak of World War I. Born in the age of sailing ships and horse-drawn carriages, she departed a world dominated by steam ships and locomotives. She might have seen the first automobile produced in Britain in 1892 but died just before mass production made these vehicles widely available.

Her father had made a fortune in shipping, which gave her the opportunity to attend school in Bristol and later Brussels, where she became fluent in French and Italian and conversant in German and Spanish. She could also read koine Greek, the language of the *New Testament*. She married in 1823 and spent 25 years in London. During this period she saw the capitol transformed into a megalopolis at the center of world trade and commerce. Following the death of her husband, Neve returned to Guernsey. She had no children. Neve lived on the island for the remainder of her life, first with her mother and then her sister, with whom she traveled extensively throughout Europe. She knew the essayist Charles Lamb, the writer and philanthropist Hannah More, and the historian and politician Thomas Babington Macaulay.

Far better educated that most men, even those from prosperous families, she did not have opportunities commensurate with her intellect and ability. If Neve resented the inferior status to which society confined her, she left no record of her feelings. No surviving diary or letters record her observations about the political reforms of the nineteenth century, which expanded the franchise to working-class men but not to upper-class women. Founded in the year Neve died to advocate for female suffrage, the Women's Social and Political Union arrived too late to affect her life. In the eyes of British society, her most significant accomplishment was her tremendous longevity. She witnessed an incredible span of history, which, had she been given the opportunities afforded men, she might have influenced more directly. The status of women would improve dramatically in the twentieth century, although the struggle for gender equality continues to the present.[1]

Overview, 1914-2021

Contemporary Britain begins with the First World War. The era can be divided into two periods, one of violent conflict, including the two world wars (discussed in chapter 12), stretching from 1914 to 1945, followed by one of relative stability but profound change, lasting until the present. Chapter 13 examines the social and economic upheaval of the interwar period, including the post–World War I recession, the rise of the Labour Party, and the Great Depression. Chapter 14 covers the era of decolonization and diplomatic realignment as the United Kingdom sought to maintain its international status despite waning military power. Chapter 15 takes up economic and social change as postwar austerity gave way to an era of prosperity followed by challenges that persist to the present. The section concludes with a discussion of art, culture, and ideas in chapter 16.

CHAPTER 12

Britain in the Era of World Conflict

I n 1910, the journalist and future Noble Peace Prize laureate Norman Angell published *The Great Illusion.* "The general proposition embodied in this book," he confidently concluded, is "that the world has passed out of that stage of development in which it is possible for one civilized group to advance its well-being by the military domination of another."[1] Industrialized nations, he argued, had become so economically interdependent as to make the cost of war so unacceptably high that no rational leader would engage in it. Angell clearly understood that modern armaments would make war incredibly destructive, but he grossly underestimated the capacity of states and individuals to engage in irrational behavior.

Far from being an age of unprecedented peace and prosperity, the twentieth century (especially its first fifty years) proved to be the bloodiest in human history. For the United Kingdom, the two world wars and the period of instability between them contributed to the precipitous decline of British economic strength and military power. They also heightened demands of subject peoples for freedom from the empire and of British men and women for a better quality of life.

The Great War

The arms race and the alliance system made a European war more likely, but they did not make it inevitable. The assassination on June 28, 1914, of Archduke Franz Ferdinand, heir-apparent to the thrones of the Austro-Hungarian Empire, produced outrage and the expectation that Serbia must be punished, but in the following weeks a deceptive calm returned. Once Vienna delivered its ultimatum to Serbia on July 23, however, events spiraled rapidly out of control. Austria-Hungary declared war on Serbia five days later. Russia backed its ally, which precipitated Germany to declare war on Russia, drawing in Russia's ally France.

Amid this maelstrom, London remained uncommitted. On July 30, Germany tried to secure British neutrality, which Grey refused to guarantee. For its part, Germany refused to assure the foreign secretary that it would respect the neutrality of Belgium, which might be used as a route for invading France. The British Cabinet met on July 31 to discuss the situation. They authorized Grey to demand from both France and Germany a promise that they would honor the 1839 treaty guaranteeing Belgian neutrality but not to warn Germany explicitly that such a violation would bring Britain into the war on the side of France. Paris complied but Berlin demurred because its strategy called for attacking France through Belgium. On August 4, German forces invaded the small kingdom. When London protested, German chancellor Theobald Bethmann-Hollweg dismissed the neutrality treaty as "a scrap of paper." The United Kingdom declared war on Germany the same day.

HOME BEFORE THE LEAVES FALL

The soldiers who marched off to war in August 1914 believed the conflict would be short. That belief and the fact that European nations had not fought one another for 40 years helps explain the nationalistic euphoria that swept the belligerent nations. British officers wondered whether they should pack dress uniforms for Christmas in Berlin. Most people thought the war would be over before the autumn leaves fell.

Technological and social changes occurring over the previous half century would soon obliterate the short-war illusion. Magazine rifles, machine guns, high-explosive shells, smokeless powder, and barbed wire would make warfare more lethal than ever before. Free, compulsory public education had imbued citizens with patriotic fervor and xenophobia. Conscription produced mass armies that could be transported and supplied by vast railroad networks. These changes meant that the Great War would not be won by decisive battles but by a long, grinding struggle of attrition, costly in blood and treasure.

Compared with the major land powers, though, Britain had a very small professional army in 1914. It numbered approximately 247,000 officers and men and was supported by a territorial reserve force that could be mobilized for a total strength of approximately 975,000. By comparison, Germany had a standing army of 700,000, which expanded to 3.8 million by mobilizing reserves within a week. France had roughly the same number of regulars, but with its smaller population could mobilize only 2.9 million.

If Britain had a small army in 1914, its navy ruled the waves. Despite an aggressive building program Germany never matched the Royal Navy in battleships and cruisers. With its decisive advantage in surface vessels, the United Kingdom could keep the German navy bottled up in port and impose a blockade on merchant shipping to starve Germany of vital resources. In response Germany concentrated on building submarines with which to interdict British shipping to the same end.

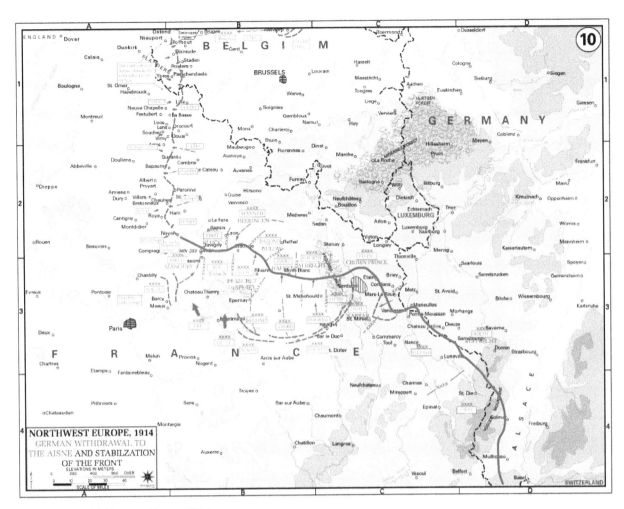

FIGURE 12.1 Western Front, 1914.

The German invasion plan nearly succeeded, but the allies halted it in front of Paris. As 1914 drew to a close, the belligerents were exhausted and deadlocked on every front. A line of trenches ran from the English Channel in Belgium to the Swiss border. Similar lines ran from the Baltic Sea to the Carpathian Mountains. The size of armies, the terrain on which they operated, and the weapons they used created stalemate.

FROM EUROPEAN TO WORLD WAR

The expeditionary force deployed to France in August 1914 consisted almost entirely of long-service professional soldiers recruited in the British Isles. The British Expeditionary Force (BEF) suffered appalling casualties, and by December the Western front had frozen into a trench deadlock that would not be broken for four bloody years. To continue the war, the British government had no choice but to tap into the vast manpower of the empire. Nearly 3 million colonial and commonwealth

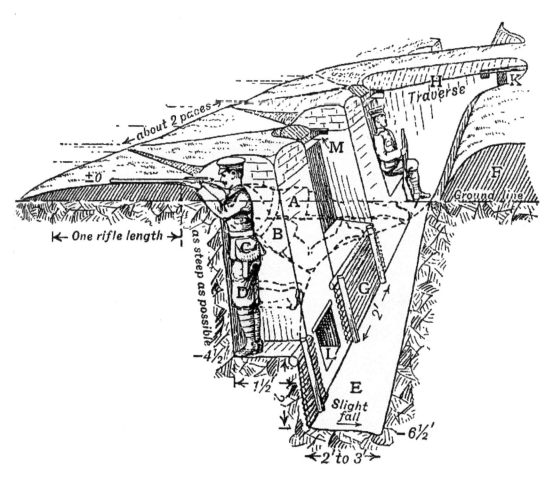

FIGURE 12.2 Trench construction diagram.

troops answered the call to fight for the king-emperor. Tens of thousands more were conscripted as laborers. The war could not have been won without the efforts of the peoples of the empire, and the experience of fighting it made a lasting impression on their societies.

In late September and early October 1914, two divisions of Sepoys (Indian soldiers) landed in Marseilles and were rushed to the front to fill the gaps in the BEF's dwindling ranks. These 24,000 men were the first installment of a South Asian contingent that would number 1.5 million, more than 600,000 of them combatants. British India (comprising modern India, Pakistan, Bangladesh, Burma, and Sri Lanka) made the largest contribution of colonial or dominion troops to the war effort. Necessity compelled the British government to overcome its extreme reluctance to let people of color kill white Europeans. Only 140,000 Indians served on the Western front, most deployed during the desperate days of late 1914. As the British opened theaters in the Middle East, however, they relied heavily on Indian troops. These forces made up the bulk of the soldiers who fought in Mesopotamia (modern Iraq) and contributed substantially to the Sinai and Palestine campaigns. Three thousand joined the ill-fated Gallipoli expedition, and more than half of those died. Indian soldiers also served in East Africa, helping to secure Germany's colonies.

The dominions also contributed substantial numbers of troops. More than 300,000 white Australians and 100,000 white New Zealanders deployed overseas during the Great War. Combined into the Australian–New Zealand Army Corps (ANZAC), these soldiers fought at Gallipoli, in Mesopotamia and Palestine, and on the Western Front. More than 600,000 Canadians crossed the Atlantic to fight on the Western Front. At Vimy Ridge in 1917, they went into battle for the first time as a truly Canadian army commanded by their own officers. White South African forces pursued Lieutenant Colonel (later general) Paul von Lettow-Vorbeck throughout East Africa. Thousands of Africans, whom neither the British nor white South Africans would arm, served as bearers and provided other logistic support for this campaign. The British coerced many of these laborers to support the war effort.[2]

Other colonial troops fought in the Great War. The King's African Forces, recruited from Britain's East African colonies, reached a peak strength of more than 30,000. By 1917, they bore the brunt of the fighting against German forces in East Africa. Caribbean colonies contributed 15,000 recruits, most of whom served in the West India Regiment or the British West Indies Regiment. They fought in France, Italy, and the Middle East. The dominions and colonies also contributed labor to the war effort.

The vast majority of dominion and colonial troops volunteered for service. Some did so out of a sense of duty. Others saw recruitment as an opportunity for financial gain. Mahatma Gandhi encouraged Indians to enlist, although he might have been motivated by political expediency as much as loyalty to the empire. "If we would improve our status through the help and cooperation of the British," he wrote, "it was our duty to win their help by standing by them in their hour of need."[3] Only Canada resorted to conscription in 1917, and instituting it produced a violent backlash in Quebec that required deployment of troops and led to the deaths of four civilians.[4]

With a few exceptions, colonial troops did not suffer disproportionately to British or White dominion soldiers, but they were subject to racial discrimination. While white troops from Australia, New Zealand, Canada, and South Africa served under their own officers, colonial contingents were commanded by British officers. Colonial units deployed to Europe were often segregated, particularly in areas where they might interact with civilians. Indian soldiers on leave in London were taken on guided tours, while their white counterparts could roam freely, and wounded colonial troops were confined to hospital precincts out of concern that they would fraternize with white nurses.[5]

How precisely the experience of the Great War effected the peoples of the empire is difficult to determine. Identity formation among the dominions and colonies predated the war and would have continued regardless of the 1914–1918 conflict, but it is hard to imagine that the tremendous contribution soldiers from all over the empire made in the Great War could not have accelerated their demands for greater autonomy if not outright independence. Australians still celebrate

ANZAC day every April 25, commemorating the date their soldiers went ashore at Gallipoli. The idea that this single campaign forged Australian national consciousness, however, has been debunked. Nonetheless, the event was scripted into the mythology of Australian national consciousness, so it clearly made an impression.

Indian nationalism predates the Great War but changed in its nature and increased in its intensity following the conflict. Four years of senseless slaughter exploded the myth of the superiority of Western civilization.[6] Amid the war's growing unpopularity the Secretary of State for India made a vague promise of self-government in July 1917. "The policy of His Majesty's Government, with which the Government of India are in complete accord," he declared, "is that of the increasing association of Indians in every branch of the administration and the gradual development of self-governing institutions with a view to the progressive realisation of responsible Government in India as an integral part of the British Empire. They have decided that substantial steps in this direction should be taken as soon as possible."[7] The statement became part of a 1918 report on the Indian Constitution, which in turn led to the 1919 Government of India Act. These measures fell far short of nationalist expectations and led Gandhi to adopt his noncooperation strategy.[8]

THE COURSE OF WAR

By the end of 1914, it became clear to the keenest observers, including Secretary of State for War Lord Herbert Kitchener and Chancellor of the Exchequer David Lloyd George (who became prime minister in 1916), that the war would be a long battle of attrition. Britain tried to knock Turkey out of the war, but the Dardanelles campaign failed, and operations in Mesopotamia and Palestine achieved success only belatedly with no effect on the Western Front. For four long years British and French forces hammered away at the German lines in France and Belgium hoping to break through ever more sophisticated systems of trenches defended by barbed wire, concrete bunkers, and machine guns and backed by increasing numbers of artillery pieces.

Of all the engagements of the Great war, the Battle of the Somme epitomizes the nature of trench warfare and the extent of the carnage. On July 1, 1916, British soldiers formed up shoulder-to-shoulder four ranks deep and walked across no man's land. Alerted by a five-day artillery bombardment and other preparations for the offensive, the Germans had sheltered deep underground. They emerged from their bunkers, set up machine guns, and mowed the British down like grass. Twenty thousand men died in one day. Despite this appalling loss, General Douglas Haig continued the offensive for four and half months. His army suffered 420,000 casualties for no strategic gain.

Superior resources and population ultimately decided the issue. By the beginning of 1917, the belligerents faced serious manpower shortages. The British blockade continued to strangle the Central Powers while Britain kept its lifeline to America and its colonies open. Germany declared unrestricted submarine warfare in an effort to starve Britain into submission. The move led the

FIGURE 12.3 British trench on the Somme.

United States to enter the war on the allied side. American naval power tipped the balance in favor of Britain in the U-boat war, and the promise of new reserves of manpower along with the collapse of its allies convinced Germany it could not win.

THE HUMAN FACE OF WAR

During the Great War, the United Kingdom mobilized approximately 6 million men, about 14 percent of its 1914 population. Contrary to popular belief, the death toll was comparable to that of other wars. Slightly more than 700,000 men, 11.5 percent of those deployed, died.[9] Nonetheless, no war in modern history has left such an indelible impression on the consciousness of the British people. Never before had so many men been mobilized nor so many died. The human dimension of the war can easily be lost in the sheer magnitude of the slaughter. Fortunately, the participants produced a wealth of material documenting their experience.

In August 1914, 20-year-old Vera Brittain viewed the outbreak of hostilities with all the enthusiasm of her generation, expecting it to be a brief, heroic interlude on the road to adult life. She had every reason to be optimistic. She had just matriculated at Oxford University and fallen in love with the young poet Roland Leighton, who volunteered to fight along with her brother Edward and their friend Victor Richardson (the "three musketeers," as they called themselves). When the troops failed to come home "before the leaves fell," Brittain took a leave of absence from university and became a Volunteer Aid Detachment (VAD) nurse. Her experience caring for wounded soldiers, including German prisoners, gave her keen insights into the war, which she shared in her memoir, *A Testament of Youth*.

The war brought Brittain plenty of heartache but also a strange sense of liberation. She lost her fiancé just before Christmas 1915. Richardson died in June 1917, and her beloved brother was killed on the Italian front in June 1918, five months before the end of the war. Being a nurse, however, gave her a broader range of experience than she could have imagined growing up in her comfortable but confining middle-class home. She reflected on how liberating it felt to move about London unescorted, since no one had the energy or inclination to enforce Victorian proprieties. "It is quite thrilling to be an unprotected female and feel that no one in your immediate surroundings is particularly concerned with what happens to you so long as you don't give them any bother," she confided in Roland. "After years of sheltered gentility," she wrote, "I certainly did feel that whatever the disadvantages of my present occupation I was at least seeing life."

Her memoir offers one of the most insightful looks at the Great War from those who experienced it firsthand, what came to be called "the lost generation." She reflected bitterly that what she called the "voracious trinity" of "God, king, and country," for whom she and others were asked to sacrifice so much, had taken from her so many of those she had loved. Although far more articulate than most contemporary women, she captured the sense of loss, helplessness, and futility so many of them must have felt. News of the armistice brought her neither joy nor peace of mind. "I realized, with all that full realization meant, how completely everything that had hitherto made up my life had vanished," she reflected. "The war was over; a new age was beginning; but the dead were dead and would never return."[10]

Robert Graves was just 19 when war broke out. Like Vera Brittain, he had grown up in a comfortable middle-class home that provided him a good education. He had graduated Charterhouse School and been accepted to St. John's College, Oxford, but delayed matriculating until the end of the war. He enlisted in August 1914, taking a commission as a second lieutenant in the Royal Welch Fusiliers. Like the rest of his generation, he expected the war to be over in a few months and considered it a mild inconvenience that would delay his entry into university by no more than a term.

Graves saw combat on the Western Front, nearly dying of wounds he received at the Battle of the Somme. After recovering, he spent most of the remainder of the war stationed in England. Suffering from what today would be diagnosed as post-traumatic stress disorder, Graves wrote

Goodbye to All That in an effort to exorcise the ghosts of the Great War, which continued to haunt him. His memoir captures themes common to all those who wrote about the conflict. Motivated by patriotism to enlist, he soon realized the futility of the conflict and described the misery of trench warfare in vivid detail. Survival rather than heroism became the goal. "The best way of lasting the war out," he concluded, "was to get wounded." Being wounded at night in a quiet sector, he cynically calculated, gave one the best chance of receiving a "blighty," a wound serious enough to get a soldier sent home without doing him lasting harm.

Like Vera Brittain Graves found that devotion to "God, king and country" had become meaningless, but loyalty to his regiment kept him in the fight. As the war progressed, Graves witnessed the growing gulf between the trenches and the home front. He could not understand the animosity civilians felt toward the enemy. "England felt strange to us returned soldiers," he reflected on his feelings during leave. "We could not understand the war madness that ran about everywhere." Graves considered the Germans he fought to be men like himself, victims of the same cataclysm. At the end of his time at home he "felt glad to be sent up to the trenches."[11]

Brittain and Graves came from privileged backgrounds, atypical of most who served in the Great War. The vast majority of the 5 million British men who put on a uniform and the more than 3 million women who worked on the home front came from the working classes. Most lacked the education, income, and leisure time to write memoirs. Privileged though their backgrounds were, however, Graves and Brittain shared the same experiences as their contemporaries. Trench warfare was just as miserable and dangerous for subalterns from elite schools as it was for privates from the slums of Manchester or Birmingham. VAD nurses from middle-class homes did the same exhausting, dirty work as their less privileged sisters.

While ordinary people did not publish memoirs, they did write letters, many of which have been preserved in archives. These letters are as noteworthy for what they omit as for what they say. They do not extol the virtues of dying for God, king, and country. Most do not even discuss the causes of the war or British objectives in fighting it. Instead, they capture the experience of service. Despite the natural inclination of soldiers to spare loved ones the horrors of war, some men did describe trench life in vivid detail, although they avoided graphic portrayals of suffering and death. "Life in the trenches is not a picnic, either we have about four or five days out of them and eight or nine in them," one soldier wrote. "When we are out supposed to be resting, we have to go on working parties, digging etc., then wherever we are, we are always under shell fire, so it's not much rest after all."[12] "My goodness what a reception the Huns had in store for us, they simply swept the ground with machine gun fire and shrapnel," another soldier wrote to his mother. "Poor old 'C' coy caught it hot. … It was found impossible to make any advance in our quarter, so I dug myself in and awaited events. It was horrible suspense, as I seemed to be the only man untouched, all around me, and being personally acquainted with each man, made matters worse; in fact, it's all wrong to call them men, as they were mostly mere boys."[13]

Under such conditions, men focused on creature comforts they might ordinarily have taken for granted. A bath, a hot meal, clean clothes, and respite from the front figure prominently in the letters of ordinary soldiers. "At present we are living very well indeed, with bacon and kidneys for breakfast, steaks and vegetables for dinner, jam and honey etc. for tea and bread and cheese and pickles for supper," one man wrote from France in 1915. "Not bad for "active service,"[14] Another described a bit of recreation: "Had a game of football about two weeks ago with R.G.A. Battery, the pitch being a serious drawback. I think it was a cabbage patch. Still, we managed to get a good game in and most important of all, won. The weather here has on the whole been very good just lately only getting an occasional day's rain."[15]

Sometimes the writers blended memoires of past pleasures with descriptions of current horrors. "I would give a quid for a pint of beer down the club," one soldier wrote. "The fighting just lately has been terrible. Our shells knock the enemy all ways and the sight in the trenches that we take is awful," he continued. "We wear our respirators because of the awful smell of the dead. I'll never get the sight out of my eyes, and it will be an everlasting nightmare. If I am spared to come home, I'll be able to tell you all about it, but I cannot possibly write as words fail me. I can't describe things."[16]

Above all, soldiers' letters reveal their incredible capacity to endure suffering. "While in the trenches last week John and I were up to our knees in water and got our gum boots half full. The line is a bit quiet lately and only now and again do we get a shelling, but one gets used to it."[17] The war was not some heroic adventure in which to prove one's manhood, but a harrowing experience to be gotten through with what the British call "cracking on."

THE HOME FRONT: POLITICAL AND ECONOMIC IMPACT

In the United Kingdom, as in other belligerent nations, ceremonial "domestic truces" put an end to the internal quarrels between political factions or social orders that had marked the prewar days. In Ireland both nationalist and loyalist leaders urged volunteers to enlist. Trade unions, with the exception of coal miners, pledged not to strike and, in return for support of the war effort, the government agreed to consult labor leaders about wages and conditions. The Women's Social and Political Union (WSPU) stopped its campaigns of civil disobedience on behalf of the suffragette movement.

Britain also took measures to prepare the home front for war. The furthest reaching legislative response to World War I was the Defense of the Realm Act (DORA) passed through Parliament the first week of fighting and periodically strengthened thereafter. The measure gave the government wide authority in requisitioning property and resources and directing labor and industry. More notoriously from a latter-day perspective (most contemporaries did not object), DORA allowed for strict censorship of the press, promoted domestic spying, and implemented trials by military courts for civilians who had violated laws passed specifically for matters of national safety. A shell shortage in 1915 prompted first the Munitions Act (1915) and then the creation of a wartime cabinet portfolio of Ministry of Munitions. The government limited the profits of munitions makers and, to produce weapons of war more efficiently, dictated specifications and requirements. In other words, the government told the industry how to do its business and set the price the government was willing to pay for munitions. The Corn Production Act (1917) paid subsidies to farmers to ensure production and encouraged the plowing up of land that had lain fallow for years. Domestic food production increased by 50 percent within a year, but there was still a shortage, so in 1918 a new Food Ministry promoted voluntary rationing. This proved inadequate, and rationing of sugar, butter, margarine, jam, tea, and bacon was made mandatory. The government also limited pub hours, intervened in rail transport, and took a hand at regulating rents and prices. It even created Daylight Saving Time, or what in the UK is called Summer Time, to save energy used for lighting. The government increased taxes to fund the war effort. Between 1914 and 1918, the maximum income tax rose from 9d. in the pound to 6s. As there were 12 pence to the shilling, this worked out to a 700 percent increase.

These truces were temporary accommodations "for the duration" only. Other changes had more lasting effects. DORA was replaced in 1920 by an Emergency Powers Act, which was implemented intermittently during the interwar years (and beyond) and laid the groundwork for most of the defense regulations of World War II. The size of state bureaucracy shrank after November 1918 but remained double what it had been in August 1914. Quite simply, a change in how the British public viewed involvement and intervention by the state occurred. People realized that a government capable of mobilizing the economy, resources, and population to manufacture military equipment could with equal effectiveness build new homes and schools, deliver health care and provide food, and modernize infrastructure. Full delivery of such services would have to wait until after another world war, but important tentative steps were taken as early as 1919, with the creation of a permanent Ministry of Health.

Such levels of state involvement, of course, were incompatible with the ideals of laissez faire economics and individual liberty that had dominated British thinking in the nineteenth century. Notwithstanding the legislative steps taken in the previous decade by the governments of Campbell-Bannerman and Asquith, distinguishing themselves as *new* liberals as opposed to *classical* liberals (see chapter 13), even this level of intervention was not sufficient to fight a major war. In 1916, Asquith was replaced by the much more hands-on David Lloyd George, and the resulting government reshuffle brought on board a number of Conservatives and Labourites in what was a genuine wartime coalition.

Women had been an important part of factory labor since the mid-nineteenth century, but more British women found work in factories between 1914 and 1918, and the industries that employed them and the tasks they were assigned expanded. Many did dangerous work in shell factories, where they were killed in explosions or suffered long-term health effects from TNT poisoning.

FIGURE 12.4 Munitionettes machining shell cases in the New Gun Factory, Woolwich Arsenal, London, World War I.

FIGURE 12.5 Women's Land Army farm workers in Hertfordshire, 1917.

Probably the more striking change to contemporaries, and one that was lasting, was the rise of the "business girl," as women moved into clerical and secretarial posts. These were positions that, before the war, had been almost exclusively men's work. After the war, and with a few exceptions, they were increasingly regarded as women's work. Another new sight—although, again, for the most part a wartime expedient—were the 80,000 uniformed women who served directly in the armed forces, albeit in noncombat roles.

Manual laborers worked hard under wartime conditions but also reaped significant benefits, labor opportunities and pay. Indeed, compared to the middle classes and those living on fixed incomes, the economic standing of the working classes actually rose. Government and management assumed these changes would be temporary. Organized labor saw things differently and, although (once again) it would take another world war before relations clarified, the chord of a more assertive voice for labor, demanding a necessary, productive, and permanent place in economic deliberations and planning, had been struck during World War I.

THE HOME FRONT: SOCIAL AND PERSONAL IMPACT

For the first time in modern history, British civilians faced attack at home. Germany launched air raids on the British Isles beginning in 1914 and, in a foretaste of World War II, terrorized inhabitants in London even took to sleeping in Tube stations. In fact, Zeppelins (hydrogen-borne dirigibles) armed with bombs were slow and clumsy: They tended to blow off course, and their size and slow speed made them vulnerable to anti-aircraft measures. Gotha C.IV twin-engine bombers were bigger threats, although the Imperial German Army Air Service had not learned to deploy them to maximum effect by the war's end. Altogether, fewer than 1,500 civilians were killed in Britain as a result of direct attack, but compared to World War II, destruction of domestic infrastructure was virtually nonexistent.

British military casualties, on the other hand, were greater between 1914 and 1918 than between 1939 and 1945. Nearly 1 man in 10 between the ages of 20 and 45 was killed and, of these, the vast majority were 20 to 24. Unlike other wars, families of wealth and social status suffered disproportionately. About one in five Oxford graduates of military age was killed, and about one in five sons of peers. To find a comparable killing off of British aristocrats would require going back to the Wars of the Roses. Asquith confided to a friend that the death of his son, Raymond, had destroyed all his pride in the past and all his hopes for the future, and future Conservative prime minister Andrew Bonar Law lost two sons in rapid succession. High ranking officers also suffered casualties: Over 6 percent of serving British generals were killed in action, died of wounds, or died as a result active-service causes, and nearly 12 percent were wounded or taken prisoner. They accounted for 0.3 percent of Victoria

 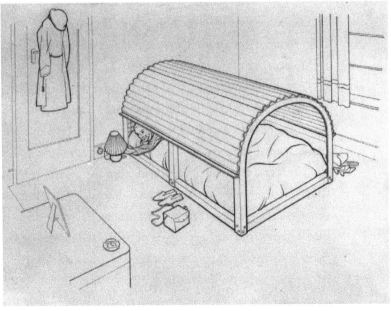

FIGURE 12.6 (a) World War I poster: Recruitment and fear of Zeppelins. (b) World War II indoor air raid shelter.

Cross (VC) medals awarded during the war. Junior officers were hit even harder, owing to the convention of their leading men "over the top," often into concentrated machinegun fire.

Writing only a few weeks before the war's end, Asquith's daughter-in-law, Cynthia, observed that peace, when it arrived, would be an odd and unfamiliar phenomenon. So many inconveniences and hardships were only temporary, and regular patterns of life would be ultimately reestablished. But everyone must "at last fully recognise that the dead are not only dead for the duration of the war."[18] In the judgment of noted military historian John Keegan, "Psychic wounds of such depth are not healed with the first dulling of memory. They fester in the collective consciousness, and the national consciousness of the British … , in the aftermath of 1918, rebelled at the thought of a repetition of such suffering."[19] This attitude accounts in part for the widespread popularity of non-involvement and appeasement of dictators in the 1930s.

THE PEACE SETTLEMENT

The Armistice of November 11, 1918, stopped the fighting but did not formally end the war. Germany had agreed to withdraw across the Rhine and negotiate a settlement based on US president Woodrow Wilson's Fourteen Points. The newly created German republic had every reason to expect fair treatment at the peace table. It would be bitterly disappointed. The British kept their blockade in place, causing starvation in Germany but assuring compliance with allied terms.

Germany lost just over 14 percent of its territory. It returned Alsace-Lorraine to France and gave the Sudetenland to the new state of Czechoslovakia. It ceded a corridor of land leading to the free city of Danzig to a reconstituted Poland. The allies also forced Germany to compensate them for the cost of the war. Destruction of the German navy eliminated a threat that had encouraged Britain to go to war in the first place. The Austro-Hungarian Empire was also broken up, and Italy received Trentino, South Tyrol, and the port of Trieste. To add insult to injury, Germany had to accept full moral responsibility for the war.

A few enlightened individuals, most notably British economist John Maynard Keynes, recognized that these harsh terms would harm not only Germany but the rest of Europe and, possibly, the entire world. His call for reducing reparations and reintegrating Germany into the international economy as soon as possible, however, fell on deaf ears. The vindictive nature of the Versailles settlement stemmed from the nature of the war and how the allies had motivated their people to fight it. For Britons, defending Belgium went only so far as a *cause célèbre*. The senseless slaughter on the Somme and at Passchendaele had to be justified by turning the war into a great crusade, a struggle of civilization against barbarism. Poster art inspired patriotism, and atrocity stories demonized Germans as "terrible Huns." Having loosed the demon of nationalism, the politicians had to appease it. They might have realized that the best solution to a terrible war was a restorative peace, but the people they represented demanded that Germany be made to pay for the terrible losses in blood and treasure.

The Interwar Period
EXPANDING THE EMPIRE

The British Empire reached its broadest extent in 1920 with the acquisition of German colonies in Africa and the Pacific and Ottoman territory in the Middle East. It covered just under a quarter of the earth's land surface, and about the same percentage of the earth's people lived under the Union Jack. Despite this expansion, however, the empire was weaker than it had been before the war. Territories like the Mandate of Palestine proved expensive to govern but conferred no commensurate advantage. Nationalist movements had been developing before the war and in some areas intensified afterward.

INDEPENDENCE FOR IRELAND

The outbreak of war had halted the implementation of Home Rule, which otherwise would have gone into effect before the end of 1914. Notwithstanding, the leader of the Irish Parliamentary Party, John Redmond, supported the war effort and agreed to delay implementation until the end of hostilities. Most Catholic nationalists agreed that cooperation not conflict was the surest route to Home Rule, a view that Gandhi shared for India. Despite the fact the government never applied conscription to Ireland, over 200,000 men volunteered, and 35,000 died—a higher percentage of fatalities than the United Kingdom average.

However, not everyone in Ireland accepted the logic of wartime loyalty. Some were especially struck by the incompatibility of Britain's claim to be defending the freedom of "small nations" abroad while denying it to Ireland. The old Fenian maxim that "England's extremity is Ireland's opportunity" struck a renewed chord, especially given the resistance in Ulster. Some nationalist in the south even favored seeking help from the Kaiser.

The ultranationalist element in the Irish Volunteers (sometimes referred to as the anti-Redmond volunteers) planned for an uprising. Sir Roger Casement traveled to Germany on their behalf and tried to recruit Irish prisoners of war (POWs) to fight for the cause. That effort failed but he successfully negotiated for the transportation of 20,000 rifles, 10 machine guns, and sufficient ammunition to the south coast of Ireland. Casement also wanted, but was unable to secure, artillery pieces and at least a handful of German advisors. As it turned out, the shipment of arms and ammunition was intercepted by the Royal Navy on April 21, 1916, and Casement himself arrested shortly after he landed.

Plans for an uprising in Dublin went ahead all the same, and on April 24, Easter Monday, the revolutionaries seized the General Post Office and other buildings, proclaimed in poetic and prophetic language establishment of an independent Irish republic, and appointed themselves its provisional government. Three groups were involved: the Irish Republican Brotherhood or IRB (originally the Fenians), the anti-Redmond Volunteers, and the (socialist) Irish Citizen Army. Although they had different visions of the future, they agreed on the need to secure independence immediately by force. Confined primarily to Dublin, the rising caused considerable destruction but had no chance of success. The British suppressed it in less than a week with the approval of most Irish men and women.

The government's handling of the aftermath of the Easter Rising cost it that popular goodwill. The army and police killed 66 insurgents during the fighting and wounded more than 2,000 others, most of whom were innocent civilians. The executions that followed stretched over several weeks and alienated the general public. Fifteen leaders of the insurrection were shot following summary trials by a military tribunal which permitted no defense (a violation of Crown law), and Casement

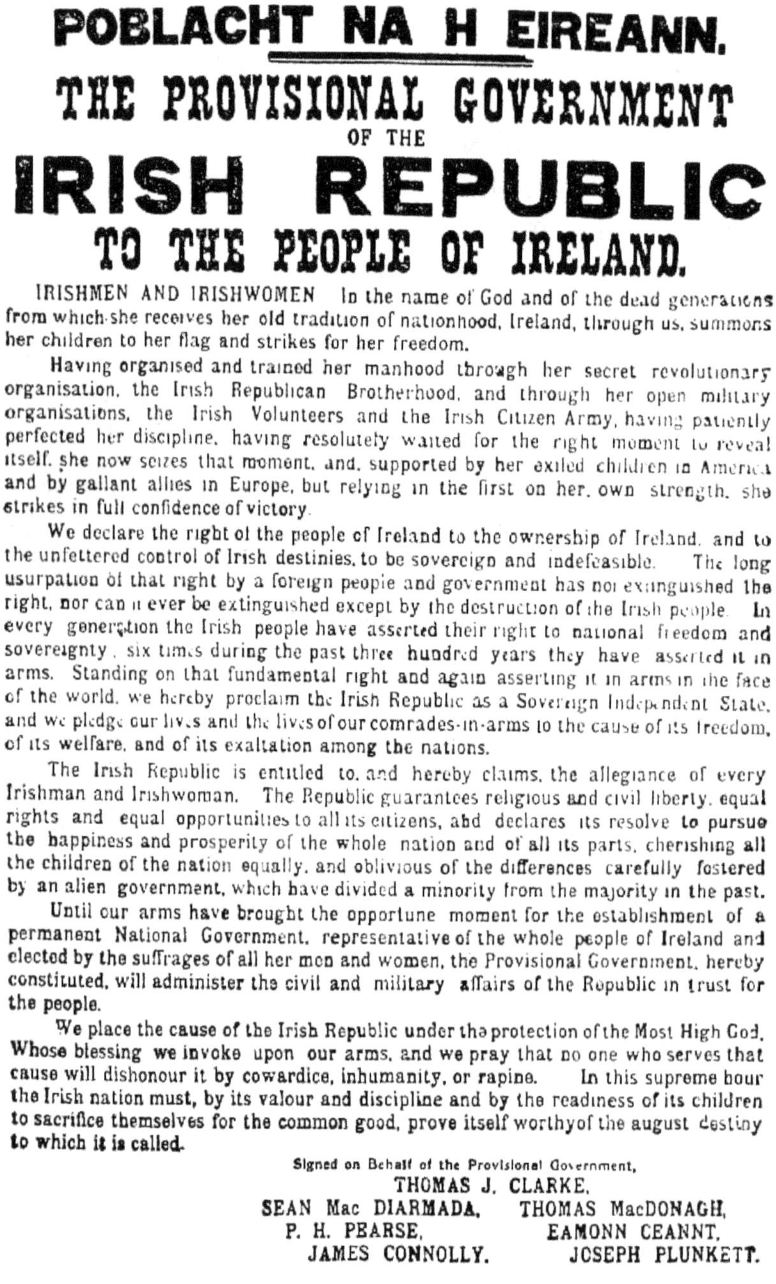

POBLACHT NA H EIREANN.
THE PROVISIONAL GOVERNMENT
OF THE
IRISH REPUBLIC
TO THE PEOPLE OF IRELAND.

IRISHMEN AND IRISHWOMEN   In the name of God and of the dead generations from which she receives her old tradition of nationhood, Ireland, through us, summons her children to her flag and strikes for her freedom.

Having organised and trained her manhood through her secret revolutionary organisation, the Irish Republican Brotherhood, and through her open military organisations, the Irish Volunteers and the Irish Citizen Army, having patiently perfected her discipline, having resolutely waited for the right moment to reveal itself, she now seizes that moment, and, supported by her exiled children in America and by gallant allies in Europe, but relying in the first on her own strength, she strikes in full confidence of victory.

We declare the right of the people of Ireland to the ownership of Ireland, and to the unfettered control of Irish destinies, to be sovereign and indefeasible.   The long usurpation of that right by a foreign people and government has not extinguished the right, nor can it ever be extinguished except by the destruction of the Irish people.   In every generation the Irish people have asserted their right to national freedom and sovereignty; six times during the past three hundred years they have asserted it in arms. Standing on that fundamental right and again asserting it in arms in the face of the world, we hereby proclaim the Irish Republic as a Sovereign Independent State, and we pledge our lives and the lives of our comrades-in-arms to the cause of its freedom, of its welfare, and of its exaltation among the nations.

The Irish Republic is entitled to, and hereby claims, the allegiance of every Irishman and Irishwoman.   The Republic guarantees religious and civil liberty, equal rights and equal opportunities to all its citizens, and declares its resolve to pursue the happiness and prosperity of the whole nation and of all its parts, cherishing all the children of the nation equally, and oblivious of the differences carefully fostered by an alien government, which have divided a minority from the majority in the past.

Until our arms have brought the opportune moment for the establishment of a permanent National Government, representative of the whole people of Ireland and elected by the suffrages of all her men and women, the Provisional Government, hereby constituted, will administer the civil and military affairs of the Republic in trust for the people.

We place the cause of the Irish Republic under the protection of the Most High God, Whose blessing we invoke upon our arms, and we pray that no one who serves that cause will dishonour it by cowardice, inhumanity, or rapine.   In this supreme hour the Irish nation must, by its valour and discipline and by the readiness of its children to sacrifice themselves for the common good, prove itself worthy of the august destiny to which it is called.

Signed on Behalf of the Provisional Government,
THOMAS J. CLARKE,
SEAN Mac DIARMADA,   THOMAS MacDONAGH,
P. H. PEARSE,   EAMONN CEANNT,
JAMES CONNOLLY.   JOSEPH PLUNKETT.

FIGURE 12.7 Proclamation of Irish republic, 1916.

was hanged a few months later. Even though the vast majority of Irish Catholics remained loyal, the government applied marshal law throughout the south. Anger at the revolutionaries turned to resentment of the British government.

A hopeless rebellion became a *cause célèbre* and its leaders became martyrs. Dissatisfaction with British rule in Ireland hardened into hatred and, in the words of the poet W. B. Yeats, "a terrible beauty [was] born."[20] The government considered the immediate implementation of Home Rule an emergency palliative response, but it was too late. The gesture was regarded as a sign of weakness rather than magnanimity and suggested that violence, not politics, was the way forward. Sinn Féin won 73 seats in the 1918 UK general election, the once-mighty Irish National Party only 7. Sinn Féin MPs refused to take their seats in Westminster and declared themselves the elected representatives of the Dáil Éireann, the parliament of the new republic. The Irish Republican Brotherhood became the Irish Republican Army (IRA), which conducted a successful insurgency. The Anglo-Irish War (known in Ireland as the War of Independence) ended with a treaty in 1921. The revolutionaries had to settle for the Irish Free State and commonwealth membership rather than complete independence. This compromise sparked a bitter civil war that ended in victory of the Free State Army over the IRA in 1923.

REDRAWING THE MAP OF THE MIDDLE EAST

Europeans were not the only ones attracted to President Wilson's promise of "self-determination of peoples." Prince Faisal, son of Hussein the Sharif of Mecca, came to Versailles to argue for the rights of Arabs whom the British had liberated from Ottoman Turkish rule. Two members of the Arab Bureau, a section of Britain's Cairo Intelligence Department, Thomas Edward (T. E.) Lawrence, who had helped lead the Arab Revolt, and Gertrude Bell, who would advocate for Feisal becoming king of Iraq, supported him.

The Arab delegation faced a formidable obstacle. In 1916, Britain, France, and Russia had secretly agreed to carve colonies out of the Ottoman Middle East. Named for the British and French diplomats who initialed the original memorandum, the Sykes–Picot Agreement gave territory to each Entente member and designated other areas as "protectorates." The agreement underwent modification during the war and as a result of the peace conference. Russia's claim to territory ended with the Bolshevik Revolution, and French and British territorial claims had to be adjusted.

At the end of the day, the redrawn map reflected colonial interest with little regard paid to the wishes of those who lived in the region. France gained control of what is today Syria and Lebanon; Britain received territory encompassing modern Iraq, Israel/Palestine, and Jordan. Both nations received these territories, not as colonies, but as "mandates" of the newly created League of Nations. The league required the administrating power to develop the region in the interest of local people and submit annual progress reports.

In administering its mandates, Britain faced complications created by conflicting promises it had made during the war. In 1915, Hussein ibn Ali, the sharif of Mecca, had corresponded with

Sir Henry McMahon, British High Commissioner in Egypt, setting conditions for an Arab Revolt against Ottoman Turkish rule. The British agreed in principle to creation of an Arab state with undetermined boundaries provided that the revolt succeeded.

Two years later, British Foreign Secretary Sir Arthur Balfour sent a letter to Lord Rothschild declaring that "His Majesty's government view with favor the creation of a homeland for the Jewish people in Palestine." Balfour added the caveat that "it being clearly understood that nothing shall be done that may prejudice the civil and religious rights of non-Jewish communities in Palestine." Both the motive for making this declaration and its meaning have been the subject of intense debate. As with the Hussein-McMahon correspondence, it made a vague promise, deliberately using the term *homeland* instead of *state* and without explaining what "homeland" meant.

After the war the British made some effort to honor their conflicting promises. Hussein's son Faisal captured Damascus and proclaimed himself king, but the French ousted him. Hussein's other son Abdullah became emir of Transjordan, which became the Kingdom of Jordan, which he ruled until his death in 1952. The mandate of Palestine contained a clause calling for the creation of a Jewish agency to facilitate immigration into Palestine.

The setup of Palestine led to conflict. Although Zionist immigrants during the 1920s occupied legally purchased, often marginal land, their presence sparked resentment, which led to intermittent violence, most notably the Hebron riots during which Palestinian Arabs killed 67 Jews. As long as immigration numbers were low, the violence remained localized and sporadic. When the Nazis took power in Germany in 1933, however, immigration into Palestine increased dramatically. As a result, a full-scale Arab revolt against British rule broke out in 1936 and lasted until 1939. The British suppressed it but also promised to limit further Jewish immigration, a decision that merely deferred the crisis until after the Second World War.

In June 1920, Sunni and Shia Arabs in the Tigris-Euphrates Valley revolted against British rule. The British deployed more than one hundred thousand troops to suppress the uprising, which took the lives of 876 British and Indian soldiers and more than eight thousand insurgents and civilians and cost the treasury more than £40 million.[21] On March 21, Colonial Secretary Winston Churchill convened a conference in Cairo to put administration of Mesopotamia on a firmer, less costly footing. The meeting created modern Iraq and made Faisal its king. The redrawn map created a country with a Shi'a majority ruled by a Sunni minority and the region's Kurdish population living in four different countries. Iraq became independent when the League of Nations mandate expired in 1932. The legacy of instability caused by redrawing the map of the Middle East persists to the present.

NATIONALISM AND RESISTANCE IN SOUTH ASIA

Despite the tremendous contribution India made to the war effort, the British did not reward its sacrifices. Instead of "self-government," the 1919 Government of India Act granted *responsible government*, a paternalistic term that implied South Asians had not yet reached the point at which they could govern themselves. The act created a system of dyarchy, dividing authority between the central and provincial governments, established an all-India legislature, and expanded the franchise. However, British provincial governors-general could veto acts passed by partially elected local assemblies, and the viceroy could override acts of the national legislative assembly. The Indian National Congress objected to the act, which fell short of its demand for independence.[22]

Fearing militant activity by radical nationalists, the British government past the newly Anarchical and Revolutionary Crimes Act, commonly known as the Rowlett Act for the author of the report upon which it was based. The act continued measures promulgated under the emergency regulations of the war years, including suspension of habeas corpus and limitation of jury trials for political offenses.[23] Protests against the act broke out in April 1919, including two days of rioting in Amritsar, Punjab, which left a several people dead and wounded and an English woman brutally beaten. The government dispatched Indian troops under Brigadier Reginald Dyer to quell the unrest. After posting warnings prohibiting meetings, Dyer ordered his troops to fire on a large gathering in a walled area adjacent to the Sikh Golden Temple. The official report on the massacre put the death toll at 379 people, including children, though Indian sources insist it was much higher. Dyer then marched his troops away, making no effort to aid the wounded. In a move reminiscent of the brutal suppression of the Indian uprising 60 years before, Dyer forced Indians to crawl on their hands and knees past the spot where the English woman had been beaten.

The Amritsar massacre resembled the worst excesses of suppressing the Indian uprising, but the response it evoked in India and even Britain differed dramatically. The British had based their program of gradual devolution on cultivating moderate nationalists while employing repressive measures against radicals. Violence against the Raj had increased in the decade before the Great War. Such extreme repression, directed not against designated agitators, but employed indiscriminately against a group of people, many of whom may have been gathered for a religious festival, turned many moderates into committed nationalists. To Indians of all political persuasions the Amritsar massacre revealed that British rule rested not on idealistic principals but military power. In Britain reactions to the massacre varied. Churchill condemned it in the Commons. The government dispatched a commission that found Dyer at fault for using excessive force, which ended his career. Some British officials in Britain and India, however, hailed him as a hero for preventing another uprising.

Nationalist agitation intensified during the interwar period led by the Indian National Congress and the Muslim League. Both groups had cooperated with the British and their evolutionary approach to granting self-government. By the interwar period, however, the Congress and the League, led respectively by Mahatma Gandhi and Mohammed Ali Jinnah, demanded full independence. Although they would eventually split over the Muslim demand for a separate state, the groups cooperated toward the common goal of getting the British to quit India. London responded to this growing demand with progressive grants of increasing autonomy. Parliament passed the

Government of India Act in 1935. The act created a federated state comprised of provinces Britain ruled directly and states ruled by client princes. The new constitution still left the Indian government subordinate to the British Parliament. Several princes saw it as a dilution of their authority and refused to participate. By the outbreak of the Second World War, the question was no longer if but when India would receive full independence.

FOREIGN AND DEFENSE POLICY

During the interwar period, Britain tried to return to its deep-water strategy. It would maintain naval superiority (at least in European waters) and reduce the size of the army. The enormous debt incurred to fight the war, a postwar recession, and the Great Depression severely limited defense spending. In 1919, the British government decided that defense planning should be based on the ten-year rule, an assumption that the United Kingdom would not fight a major war for a decade. That assumption made sense at the time but renewing it in 1928 did not. When the Nazis came to power in 1933, they began to rearm Germany. Three years later Wehrmacht troops entered the Rhineland in violation of the Versailles Treaty. Neither Britain nor France opposed them. Some in Whitehall believed a rearmed Germany might deter Soviet aggression.

During the interwar period British governments put great store in arms control agreements. In 1922, the Washington Naval Agreement established the ratio of battleships for the United States, the United Kingdom, Japan, France and Italy to 5:5:3:1.67:1.67, respectively, for ten years. The London Naval Conference of 1930 extended the agreement to 1936. A 1927 conference to restrict the number of cruisers failed, as did the 1932–1934 Geneva Conference aimed at reducing land, air, and naval forces.[24]

In addition to limiting armaments, Britain cooperated with its allies to reintegrate Germany into the international system and to reduce its reparations burden. In the 1925 Locarno Agreement, France, Britain, Belgium, and Germany agreed to respect the borders between them and to peacefully arbitrate any difference among them. The pact also demilitarized the Rhineland and pledged the signatories to mutual assistance if they faced aggression.[25] Germany joined the League of Nations in 1926, and the remaining Allied troops left the Rhineland. The 1924 Dawes Plan relieved the economic pressure on Germany caused by crippling reparations stipulated in the Versailles Treaty. The plan staggered reparations payments, gave German a large loan, and required withdrawal of French troops from the Ruhr region.

The Second World War

As the two world wars recede into the past, historians increasingly view them as part of the same struggle for hegemony. The peace treaties ending the First World War helped create conditions that led to the second, particularly the territorial concessions and reparations that fueled German resentment. The Versailles Treaty did not, however, make another world conflict inevitable. Had

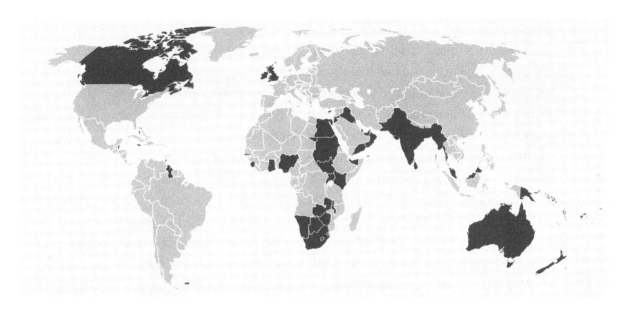

LEAVE THIS TO US SONNY—YOU OUGHT TO BE OUT OF LONDON

MINISTRY OF HEALTH EVACUATION SCHEME

FIGURE 12.8 (a) Map of British Empire, 1921. World War II: (b) Airplane spotter, Battle of Britain; (c) Operation Pied Piper.

it not been for the Great Depression, Hitler and the Nazis would probably never have come to power and war might have been averted.

THE LONG ROAD TO WAR

The British people and their government viewed the prospect of war with fear and loathing. Civilian targets would be vulnerable to aerial bombardment. As Stanley Baldwin warned the

House of Commons in 1932, "the bomber will always get through." Experts' worst case scenarios reckoned that planes could drop more than 750 tons of explosives on Britain daily, killing fifty thousand and injuring one hundred thousand in a protracted bombing campaign. They feared uncontrollable panic would be inevitable and that the widespread collapse of civil institutions would occur. During the Spanish Civil War, bombing of the Basque town of Guernica by German aircraft in the spring of 1937 validated those fears.

While most Britons favored isolationism, some advocated pacifism. On February 9, 1933, the Oxford Union debated the motion, "This house will in no circumstances fight for its King and County."[26] Members were well aware that roughly one-fifth of their fellow alumni a generation or so earlier had been killed in the Great War. The motion was carried by a margin of nearly two to one. The following year, Lord Cecil, president of the (UK) League of Nations Union, organized a national "peace ballot," and over 11.5 million adults responded to the initiative. Announced ahead of the general election of 1935, the ballot demonstrated strong support for the league and its efforts to promote world peace.

While some Britons embraced pacifism, others flirted with totalitarianism. In 1932, former Labour MP Sir Oswald Mosley founded the British Union of Fascists (BUF). Mosley believed fascism better able to deal with the depression than parliamentary democracy. He based his ideology on Benito Mussolini's corporate state. He also expressed admiration for Adolf Hitler, who became chancellor of Germany in 1933. To defend BUF rallies, Mosley created the Black Shirts, who got into violent confrontations with antifascist protestors. At its peak in early 1934, the BUF may have had a membership of fifty thousand, but perhaps only five to ten thousand of these members were active. After a violent meeting at the Olympia Stadium in 1934 and subsequent withdrawal of support from the *Daily Mail*, BUF membership declined precipitously to five thousand by the end of the year. Membership rebounded to about 16,000 by 1936 and 22,500 in 1939.[27] During its peak period of recruitment, the BUF drew support from the middle and working classes, but middle-class membership declined after mid-1934, perhaps because of growing fear of Nazi Germany, the party's open embrace of anti-Semitism, and the violence accompanying its rallies.[28]

The reluctance of British governments, especially that of Neville Chamberlain (1937–1940) to confront German rearmament and even bellicosity must be understood in the broader context of popular attitudes, military realities, and economic exigencies. Chamberlain feared the destructive effects of an air war, contemplated the cost of rearmament amid depression, and considered the reluctance of ordinary Britons to go to war. He may have believed that a rearmed Germany would balance an aggressive Soviet Union. He does not appear to have harbored any sympathy for fascism nor to have been influenced by those in Britain who did. Chamberlain's most infamous act of appeasement, the Munich Pact, which allowed Hitler to seize the Sudetenland in Czechoslovakia, may have been little more than an effort to buy time for Britain to rearm.

FIGURE 12.9 Peace for our time.

Contrary to popular belief promulgated by Churchill's admirers, Britain did not neglect its military during the interwar period. For example, Baldwin's famous dictum that "the bomber will always get through" is easily taken out of context as an expression of resignation or defeatism. In fact, he was making an argument of defense through vigorous offense: The imagined invincibility of the bomber went both ways, and what Baldwin meant was that Britain must acquire a deterrent strike force with the means—and the will—to "kill more women and children more quickly than the enemy" could. The United Kingdom had a small army by continental standards but continued to have the world's highest military expenditure across the 1930s, and obviously the figures were even more impressive when combined with the defense budgets of the Dominions and likely allies in the event of war with a third party. While it is true the production of British military hardware had declined, this was in relative terms only, as compared with other countries (notably Germany and Japan). And this decline, such as it was, was not universal: Britain had a lot of old ships in its fleet but had constructed a million tons of warships since 1928, more than any other power. Having diverted 5 percent of the national income since 1937 to improving the resources of the

RAF, Britain in 1940 still had the greatest capacity for aircraft production. Moreover, Germany and Japan might have been increasing their abilities to sink ships or bomb airfields, but Britain was the only power besides the US with the capacity to catch up at the rebuilding.

Successive governments had also planned for civil defense and maintaining morale. In 1935, the Air Raid Precautions (ARP) Department was formed to direct civil defense preparations at a local level. Its activities expanded when Chamberlain became prime minister in the spring of 1937, and town and local authorities across the country appointed air raid wardens, recruited volunteers for civil defense and emergency services (messengers, rescue parties, first aid teams, etc.), and coordinated with police and fire brigades. The ARP was expanded again under the terms of the Air Raid Precautions Act (1937), which became effective at the start of 1938 and compelled all local authorities to prepare for invasion by sandbagging buildings and constructing public air raid shelters. Air raid wardens were tasked with issuing 38 million gas masks (enough for over four-fifths of the population) at the time of the Munich crisis, and everyone was legally obliged to carry them at all times. Air raid wardens in areas judged especially vulnerable to attacks were also responsible for making available outdoor Anderson shelters and indoor Morrison shelters. Beginning September 1, 1939, the day Germany invaded Poland and two days before Great Britain responded with a declaration of war on Germany, air raid wardens began enforcing total blackouts. At the start of the war some 1.5 million civilians were ready in one capacity or another to serve under the sweeping aegis of the ARP Act.

From 1937 to 1940, volunteers with the ARP and related services were often made the butt of jokes, ridiculed, or worse. Wardens who were particularly attentive to their duties could be pilloried as pompous and self-important busybodies, and members of the Auxiliary Fire Guards were liable to accusations of service dodging or cowardice. In a lighter spirit, one popular quip had it that the motto of the Women's Voluntary Services (established in 1938) was "The women who never say 'no,'" while another suggested the service's initials reflected the composition of its membership: widows, virgins, and spinsters. With the start of the Battle of Britain and the Blitz, however, these groups distinguished themselves by selfless bravery, often leading the way into bombed out and burning structures to deliver aid where it was most needed. For the rest of the war, subsequently all these services were recognized—and revered—as public heroes.

THE OUTBREAK OF WAR IN EUROPE

When German troops marched into Prague in March 1939, violating the terms of the Munich Agreement, even the most blatant political optimists in Britain could no longer deny that war was all but inevitable. The Chamberlin government realized Poland would be next. On August 25, 1939, London signed a formal defense pact with Warsaw. France had been allied to Poland since 1921. Both nations realized that they had little chance of getting material aid to Poland, but they hoped that the threat of war would deter German aggression. Having successfully called the allies' bluff before, however, Hitler felt he had little to fear. He had, furthermore, removed the greatest threat to his plans by singing a nonaggression pact with the Soviet Union on August 23. The two powers pledged not to attack one another for a decade, but secret clauses in the agreement allowed the Soviets to occupy eastern Poland and the Baltic states should Germany go to war with Poland.

On the morning of September 1, 1939, German forces crossed the Polish frontier on the trumped-up pretext that the Poles had attacked first. At 9:00 a.m. on the morning of September 3, the British ambassador in Berlin delivered an ultimatum to the German government: If it did not cease hostilities by 11:00 a.m., a state of war would exist between Germany and the British Empire. When no reply came, Chamberlin went on BBC radio to inform the British public that for the second time in a generation, they were at war with Germany. He prepared them for a long struggle, declaring that "it is the evil things that we shall be fighting against—brute force, bad faith, injustice, oppression and persecution—and against them I am certain that the right will prevail."[29]

Attacked from three sides by German forces from Pomerania, East Prussia, and Slovakia and with the Soviet Union prepared to jump on its back, Poland stood no chance. Resistance collapsed within a month. France, Britain, Belgium, and the Netherlands prepared for the anticipated German attack in the West. French troops manned the Maginot Line along the German border. The British deployed an expeditionary force to the continent to support the French field army as it had done in August 1914. After the conquest of Poland, the Germans redeployed their troops to the western frontier. Before hostilities could commence, however, winter brought an end to the campaigning season. For six months the two sides watched one another warily across the Rhine in what came to be called the "Phony War" or the "Sitzkrieg" (a parody of "Blitzkrieg").

MOBILIZING THE HOME FRONT

At home Britain prepared for a long conflict. In 1914, the Asquith government had tried to wage war while conducting business as usual at home. Going into World War II, the national/conservative government of Neville Chamberlain and the wartime coalition government of Winston Churchill realized that such a limited approach would not be possible. Parliament enacted the Emergency Powers (Defense) Act in response to the Nazi–Soviet Pact, when it became clear that Germany was planning to invade Poland. Initially taking effect for one year, it was reinstated in 1940, for the duration, and periodically strengthened and expanded. The act incorporated over a hundred individual measures to mobilize the country for the war effort and gave the government a wide range of powers to intervene in and regulate every aspect of day-to-day life.

The government brought under its control much of industry, including the transportation infrastructure of docks, railways, and roadways. A critical inclusion in Churchill's coalition government was the trade unionist and Labourite MP, Ernest Bevin, who had been general secretary of the Transport and General Workers Union since 1922, president of the Trade Unions Congress (TUC) in 1937, and, throughout the interwar years, at ideological loggerheads with Churchill on most points. Both men were committed to defeating Nazism, however, and the prime minister invited him to join the government in the capacity of minister of labor and national service. In this role, Bevin persuaded munitions workers to work longer hours, and even to permit unskilled workers to train for skilled jobs. British trade unions would never have made such concessions in peacetime.

The government established a Ministry of Fuel and Power, and its chief priority was managing the coal industry. Its creation was a wartime measure, but the ministry continued until 1970, when it became part of the Department of Trade and Industry. The Ministry of Aircraft Production was designed to respond to the pressures of the Battle of Britain and, among other things, persuaded car manufacturers to turn to the production of aircraft. It did not long survive the war.

FIGURE 12.10 Civilian rationing: A shopkeeper cancels the coupons in a British housewife's ration book in 1943.

Rationing during World War I had been almost an afterthought, and for a while it was merely recommended as a voluntary patriotic duty. With World War II, rationing started earlier, lasted long after the war, and was applied to a far wider range of household necessities. Only those who could demonstrate essential need had access to gasoline, and even then, it was strictly rationed. As a result, trains became more crowded, which—in popular recollection, at any rate—contributed to a spirit of patriotic solidarity. Clothing and even furniture were added to the list of rationed items, giving rise to the spirit (as well as the necessity) of "make do and mend." The Ministry of Food had been discontinued in 1921 but was reinstated in 1939. Households were issued ration books that could be redeemed only at specific shops. The system evolved over time, and points and coupons could be saved or pooled (e.g., for special events such as weddings or Christmas). Families were encouraged to grow gardens and raise rabbits or chickens. Wasting food was a criminal offense. The government even recommended a 5-inch maximum depth for bath water, which was of course hard to enforce.

Ernest Bevin had announced on a radio broadcast that "everyone in the land is a soldier for liberty," and for many this was the literal truth. In April 1939, the government began conscripting young men who were 20 or 21 into the Armed Forces, and in September extended conscription to unmarried men aged 19 (eventually 18) to 41. "Essential workers" were exempt from direct military service but were required to submit to direction of labor to ensure their contribution to the war effort. Women in uniform had been an unusual sight during World War I, but after 1939 they were commonplace. Thousands of young women served with the Women's Royal Naval

Service (WRNS, pronounced "wrens"), the Women's Auxiliary Air Force (WAAF), or some other women's service branch, where they fulfilled essential and often dangerous roles. Volunteerism did not meet the needs of the war effort, however, and ultimately, in December 1941, the National Service Act (no. 2) provided for military conscription of women aged twenty to thirty. As they had done after 1914, many women found jobs in factories, taking the place of men who served in the military, and after 1939, women also provided agricultural labor in the ranks of the Women's Land Army.

FIGURE 12.11 WRNS.

In addition to imposing conscription, the government employed coercive measures against perceived internal threats. Under the terms of the EPA, German nationals living in Britain, homegrown fascists or Axis sympathizers, and other potential "fifth columnists" could be arrested and detained without trial. (For the most part, the official line on conscientious objectors in World War II was considerably more lenient than it had been between 1914 and 1918, although unofficially social stigma and accusations of disloyalty or cowardice persisted.) Newspapers and other media faced censorship again, and the government shut down the (communist) *Daily Worker* for the duration of the Nazi–Soviet Pact. Other papers, such as the *Daily Mirror*, were threatened with closure when their reporting became especially critical of the government or the course and direction of the war.

FALL OF WESTERN EUROPE

The Phony War came to an abrupt end in the spring of 1940. On April 9, Hitler occupied Denmark, which capitulated without resistance, and sent warships into Norwegian ports. The Norwegians resisted, sinking one German cruiser and damaging another at the entrance to Oslo harbor, and the British navy defeated a small German fleet at Narvik Fjord. However, German paratroopers and forces landed by sea quickly overran most of the country. Norwegian troops held out in the north, and the British temporarily recaptured the port of Trondheim at the end of May, but they were too late to save Norway, which surrendered on June 12.

Meanwhile, the French Army supported by the BEF remained on the defensive, awaiting the German onslaught. The Allies assumed that the present war would be like the previous one, with battles fought by massed infantry supported by heavy artillery. France built the system of fortification known as the Maginot Line to protect its eastern frontier, freeing up its field army to forestall an anticipated German advance through Belgium. The bulk of the German forces, however, drove through the Ardennes Forest, outflanking both the Maginot Line and the Anglo-French forces in Belgium.

FIGURE 12.12 Evacuation of Dunkirk.

With French resistance breaking down in the face of Blitzkrieg, the British government decided to evacuate the BEF. On May 23, its commander, Lord John Gort, ordered his troops to fall back on the channel port of Dunkirk. With the Germans poised to capture the town, there seemed little chance of escape. However, a large flotilla of small civilian craft from the English Channel ports, the "little boats," ferried men from the beaches to the transports lying offshore while larger vessels evacuated them from the quay. Overhead the Royal Air Force kept the Luftwaffe at bay. Between May 26 and June 4, the fleet of more than nine hundred ships evacuated almost 340,000 men, most of the BEF, as well as some French and Belgian troops.[30] Most of the one thousand Indian troops serving with the BEF were also evacuated, but they were left out of the narrative of the "miracle of Dunkirk" deliberately promulgated by the Ministry of War to promote the idea of the unbreakable (white) British spirit.[31]

With France defeated, Hitler had no desire to continue the war with the United Kingdom. He hoped to reach an agreement by which Britain recognized German hegemony on the continent in return for being allowed to keep its empire. The idea appears more far-fetched in retrospect than it did at the time. The BEF had escaped, but it had left most of its tanks, artillery, and heavy equipment in France. The RAF had suffered significant losses. In the spring of 1940 neither the United States nor the Soviet Union seemed likely to enter the fray. Foreign Secretary Lord Halifax favored a negotiated settlement and enjoyed considerable support. Churchill, however, vowed to continue the war. When no peace overtures came from London, Hitler ordered his general staff to draw up plans for "Operation Sea Lion," an invasion of the British Isles. Before that operation could proceed, however, the Luftwaffe had to eliminate the RAF.

FROM EUROPEAN TO WORLD WAR

Like its predecessor in 1914, the British Expeditionary Force that deployed to France in late 1939 and early 1940 consisted primarily of troops drawn from the home islands. Now with its back to the wall, the United Kingdom turned once again to its empire for help. London could no longer command the self-governing Dominions to provide assistance. Nonetheless, all but the Irish free state, which chose to remain neutral, enthusiastically supported the war effort. A Royal Canadian Air Force squadron fought in the Battle of Britain, and Canadian infantry waded ashore at Juno beach on D-Day. All told, 690,000 Canadian sailors, soldiers, and airman fought in the Second World War. Australia and New Zealand contributed 413,000 and 128,500 personnel, respectively, most of whom fought the Japanese from Papua New Guinea to Burma. South Africa raised a force of 128,500, whose members fought the Italians in East Africa and the Germans and Italians in North Africa.

British colonies also contributed to the war effort, but soldiers and laborers continued to face racial discrimination. The majority of colonial troops received lower pay than their white counterparts and were commanded by British officers. Residents of African and Caribbean colonies who came to work in Britain faced discrimination in employment and housing, which intensified with the arrival of American soldiers, who often demanded segregation in hotels, restaurants, and dance halls. Many proprietors acquiesced; the British government did little to remedy the situation. British officials were particularly concerned African American soldiers were having sexual relations with British women and sought to educate women and girls about the dangers of miscegenation.[32]

As in the First World War, the largest number of troops came from British India. More than 2.5 million South Asian men fought for the king-emperor. Like their predecessors during WWI, most of these soldiers volunteered for economic gain rather than out of loyalty to the empire.[33] Most South Asian soldiers fought the Japanese, first in Malaya and then in Burma, but some units served in North Africa and Italy. Other colonies contributed 134,000 personnel to the war effort. East and West African troops fought the Japanese in southeast Asia. More than 5,000 West Indian men served in the Royal Airforce, and West Indian women served in the Women's Auxiliary Air Force.[34]

THE BATTLE OF BRITAIN AND THE BLITZ

The most evocative and iconic aspect of the British home front during World War II was undoubtedly the Battle of Britain and the Blitz, and, in anticipation of an air war, the mass evacuation of vulnerable civilian populations. More than a year before Germany invaded Poland, a committee of railway officials, schoolteachers, and police met to plan Operation Pied Piper: the most efficient means of relocating large numbers of passengers (mostly children) from likely targets to the relatively safe countryside. Selected rural households were provided a measure of cash assistance and in return were compelled to receive evacuees. At the start of the war, over a period of 4 days, trains pulled out of major cities, as well as coastal towns in the east and southeast potentially exposed to amphibious invasion, carrying more than a million passengers. (Several thousand others were evacuated overseas to the Dominions, and some others to the US.) This, of course, was the start of the phase that became known as the Phony War (or *Sitzkrieg*), and many evacuees returned to their homes by Christmas 1939. Most were home again before spring 1940.

Operation Pied Piper was implemented again following the fall of France, and this time most evacuees remained in host homes until near the end of the war. The experience was eye-opening all around, as many children (and adults) got their first taste of country living. Conversely, many families of rural Britain were introduced for the first time to the intensity of poverty and ignorance among urban slum dwellers. Evacuation and resettlement brought face-to-face two very different Britains, and the experience raised social awareness and consciousness, laying the groundwork for the acceptance of much of the social reform legislation that followed the war.

The Battle of Britain began in July 1940, overlapping with and giving way to the Blitz. The opening phases of the air war against Britain were not directed specifically against civilian targets, although serious, and lethal, collateral damage was inevitable. Initially, in preparation for a German invasion force, the Luftwaffe sought to destroy airfields and other military installations, industrial sites, and coastal defenses. Churchill responded by ordering RAF bomber command to strike at German cities. Incensed, Hitler directed the Luftwaffe to bomb civilian and commercial targets in the United Kingdom. The aim was to "soften up" the British and weaken civilian resolve.

FIGURE 12.13 Child evacuees with gas masks.

The change in strategy probably took pressure off the RAF and its airfields. The British population suffered terrible losses. The air campaigns destroyed a third of London and killed over forty thousand civilians but failed to break British morale. The calculated targeting of city centers shook the resolve of Britain's remaining appeasers and—in popular and patriotic memory, at any rate—united the home front. (The Luftwaffe also suffered significant losses in aircraft and crews, which hampered its operations in the Soviet Union.)

Those who lived in houses with gardens or sufficient patches of yard could install outdoor Anderson shelters. These were shells made of corrugated steel panels, partially buried underground and covered with dirt, that could theoretically accommodate up to six occupants and could be used as a family-sized bomb shelter. Those without sufficient outdoor space (or adequate cellars) could make do with indoor Morrison shelters, which were essentially 2-foot-high steel cages with meshed sides and mattress bottoms, designed to protect occupants from being crushed as the living compartment around them collapsed from an exploding bomb. The persistence of the nighttime attacks, and the inconvenience of shuffling back and forth, out of doors or indoors, meant that many took up virtually permanent residence in their Anderson shelter during the hours of darkness or simply put small children (or even adults) to bed inside a Morrison shelter.

A Morrison shelter was a sorry consolation prize—after all, fire was a big problem during the Blitz, and a Morrison could become a death trap if a surrounding structure caught fire—but those living in high-density housing did not have even that option. Some could seek refuge in basements (although these had rarely been designed to be bomb-proof), and the government, working with local authorities, provided a number of surface shelters. These were often unsatisfactory, however, and it was not until late in 1942 that eight deep underground shelters, each able to accommodate up to eight thousand occupants, were dug across London. By then, of course, the most intense phase of the German bombing campaign had long ended.

In the meantime, many took the initiative of bedding down underground in the London Tube stations. Authorities opposed such impromptu bivouacking at first, but ultimately conceded, and even provided a measure of very basic amenities. In patriotic hindsight, the iconic experience of spending the night in a Tube station, where the poorest of the poor might (literally) rub shoulders with all but the most highly privileged, was emblematic of communal resolution and high morale, as Britons of all classes came together to muddle through against Hitler. In reality, the inconvenience of queuing up for make-shift public lavatories, and the sounds and smells of living in close quarters with dozens, or hundreds, of strangers, must have been quite different. On top of this, there was always the possibility, on emerging into daylight, of discovering one's home was on fire or was simply a pile of rubble and debris.

Class tensions ran high, and the queen's famous line the morning after Buckingham Palace took nine direct hits from German bombers—that the royal family could now look the East End in the face—was the exception that proved the rule. Those with means could, and often did, flee to the countryside where they lived in so-called "funk holes," far removed from the nightly air raids

FIGURE 12.14 (a) Aldwych Tube station being used as a bomb shelter in 1940.

(b) Firefighters tackling a blaze among ruined buildings after an air raid on London.

on London. Others took refuge in safe (and expensive) basement clubs that operated through the night. Meanwhile the lower middle and working classes were left to face the dangers of the Blitz with inadequate protection.

The Blitz lasted into the spring of 1941. By that time, it was clear that Britain could rebuild and re-outfit at a pace Germany's Luftwaffe could not sustain, and Operation Sea Lion was abandoned. Upward of fifty thousand British civilians had been killed since the previous summer, especially in the intense period of September and October, and at least as many more were seriously injured. Air attacks on London and other cities did not end entirely until the very end of the war. German V-1 and V-2 rockets (essentially first-generation cruise missiles) could be launched from hundreds of miles away, and ten thousand or so civilians were killed between 1941 and 1945.

COURSE OF THE WAR

As Britain endured the Nazi assault from the air it faced an equally deadly threat at sea. The island nation relied on imports of food and raw materials to feed its people and sustain the war effort. The Royal Navy had a decisive advantage in surface warships and swept the seas of German raiders. To sever Britain's lifeline to its trading partners, the German navy turned to submarine warfare. At the height of the Battle of the Atlantic, U-boats were sinking 7 million tons of merchants shipping a year, destroying vessels faster than Britain could build them.[35] The invention of SONAR, long-range patrol planes, and an increasing number of escort vessels, especially after the United States entered the war, eventually turned the tide in favor of the Allies.

For more than a year, British, Commonwealth, and imperial forces fought the Axis alone. The British failed to save Greece, which fell in April 1941, but fared better in North Africa. The 8th Army halted the Germans' advance toward Egypt in late 1942 and began pushing them back across the desert. Axis forces remained on the defensive until being forced out of North Africa by Anglo-American operations from November 1942 to May 1943.

As the situation in Europe deteriorated, London kept a warry eye on its empire in the Pacific. Japan, the third member of the Axis, sought to build an Asian empire and had invaded China in the 1930s. After France and the Netherlands fell to the Germans, Japan occupied their colonies. Following their attack on Pearl Harbor, they seized the Philippines. Hong Kong fell on Christmas Day, 1941, followed by Malaya and Singapore in early 1942. The British fared no better in Burma. Their forces left Rangoon on March 7 and began a fighting withdrawal northward. On May 1, the Japanese captured Mandalay. On May 20, the last British fighting units crossed the border into Imphal, India. Fighting continued for the next two years. The Japanese invaded India in 1944, assisted by the forty thousand–strong Indian National Army comprised of anti-British South Asians, but got no farther than the town of Kohima just inside the border.

VICTORY

After his initial successes, Hitler made two fatal errors. He invaded the Soviet Union, and he declared war on the United States after the Japanese attack on Pearl Harbor. Once the Soviets halted the German advance, an inexorable calculus almost certainly doomed the Axis. The combined resources of the United Kingdom, the United States, and the Soviet Union far exceeded those of Germany, Italy, and Japan. In 1942, Britain alone produced more aircraft than Germany (23,672 to 15,409), and the Allies together produced almost four times the number of planes built by the Axis (101,519 to 26,670).[36] Total allied war production for 1943 amounted to $62.5 billion, Axis production to just $18.3 billion.[37] Hitler had gotten Germany into the war of attrition his generals had warned him he could not win.

The US needed time to build up its forces and so confined its operations to North Africa and Italy before invading France. Operation Overlord took place on June 6, 1944. On D-Day 155,000 American, British, Canadian, and Polish troops hit the beaches of Normandy, and by the end of July 1 million men and 190,000 vehicles had landed.[38] On August 25, Free French forces led the entry into Paris. Another eight months of hard fighting with several setbacks lay ahead, but Germany now faced certain defeat.

The success of Overlord created a new strategic dilemma. As Soviet armies advanced from the east and allied ones from the west, where would they meet? Once the Western Allies reached the borders of the Reich and repelled the last German counterattack in the Battle of the Bulge (December 1944), a dispute arose over the final phase of the war. The commander of British forces, General Bernard Law Montgomery, argued for a deep thrust across the north German plain toward Berlin led by his forces. This plan might have allowed the Allies to reach Berlin ahead of the Soviets. The deep thrust would have been more difficult to achieve and perhaps more costly in lives.[39] On purely military grounds, Supreme Allied Commander and US General Dwight Eisenhower favored an advance across a broader front into the Ruhr valley toward Leipzig.

Beneath the military debate lay divergent political objectives. The United States wanted to end the war in Europe as soon as possible and redeploy troops for the invasion of the Japanese home islands.[40] Churchill, on the other hand, was looking beyond the current conflict to the configuration of postwar Europe. He correctly anticipated the coming struggle between the United States and the USSR and doubted the Soviets would allow democracy in any country they occupied. He wanted the Western Allies to liberate as many countries as possible. President Franklin Roosevelt and his successor Harry Truman did not view this threat with the same urgency. The United States was the dominant alliance partner and the Supreme Allied Commander an American general. Roosevelt allowed Eisenhower to make the decision: The Allied advance would halt at the River Elbe. The Red Army captured Berlin on May 2. Germany surrendered five days later.

THE HUMAN FACE OF WAR

The Second World War did not inspire the literary output that characterized the first.[41] The generation that went to war in 1939 did so with grim determination, not the patriotic euphoria with which their parents and grandparents marched off in 1914. There was no lost generation, no disillusionment, and, so, no coming-of-age novels or haunting memoirs. Wilfred Owen's 1917 poem, "Dulce et Decorum Est," not only depicts the horror of war in graphic detail but repudiates with bitter irony the smug confidence of the prewar world. "If you could hear at every jolt, the blood come gargling from the frost corrupted lungs," he wrote of a poison gas victim,

My friend, you would not tell with such high zest

To children ardent for some desperate glory,

The old Lie: Dulce et decorum est

Pro patria mori [It is sweet and fitting to die for one's country].[42]

Keith Douglas's World War II poem, "Vergissmeinnicht," (Forget-me-not) also captures the horror, sorrow, and pointlessness of war but contains no hint of disillusionment. The poet comes upon the body of a German, finds a photo of his girlfriend, and reflects on what she might feel if she could see the man's decaying corpse:

But she would weep to see today

how on his skin the swart flies move;

the dust upon the paper eye

and the burst stomach like a cave.

For here the lover and killer are mingled

who had one body and one heart.

And death who had the soldier singled

has done the lover mortal hurt.[43]

No Briton living through the Second World War needed to be told that "it is sweet and fitting to die for one's country" was a lie.

If the literature of the two world wars differed markedly, soldiers' letters did not. Like soldiers of the Great War, men described marching, daily tasks, and the places they saw. They wrote of the engagements in which they fought but usually avoided the gory details of death and suffering. They reflected on the simple pleasures of home, to which they longed to return. "At the moment I'm in a fine Red Cross building in a nice town. We get free meals here and a place to read and write," one man wrote his brother. "We had a real bed to sleep in last nite [sic]. Quite a difference from a pup tent."[44] Another described liberating a village in France: "The square was crammed with people—flags appeared at every window and everyone came out dressed in their Sunday best. Cameras clicked incessantly, everyone must shake hands and all the girls had some autograph book or even a piece of paper to have us sign our names."[45] In a particularly moving letter written two days before he was killed in France, Lance Corporal C. P. Ketteridge wrote to the aunt who had raised him:

> In my last battle, things were going hard, and only a handful of our lads came back in one piece. It was at a moment when my last seemed near, that my mind took me away from the battle-field away from mangled human flesh, heroism and death, to you at home and Audrey. … It is only in the face of such trials that value has its real meaning. Value is a small word; few unfortunately ever conceive its real meaning.
>
> I admit myself. I did not know the value of the simple things of life, I do now though.[46]

Soldiers did not see the war as a heroic adventure and seldom spoke of "God, king and country." War was an ordeal to be gotten through.

British people welcomed the end of war with tremendous relief and great expectations. Many of those who sang "Land of Hope and Glory" outside Buckingham Palace had experienced thirty years of conflict and hardship. Their vote for Labour in the July 1945 election was a demand for change. The hope of ordinary Britons for a better quality of life had been too long deferred. The same could be said of the demand for independence among Britain's colonial subjects.

IMAGE CREDITS

Fig. 12.6b: Source: https://commons.wikimedia.org/wiki/File:Civil_Defence_in_Britain-_Indoor_Air_Raid_Shelters,_C_1940_D2030.jpg.

Fig. 12.7: Source: https://commons.wikimedia.org/wiki/File:Easter_Proclamation_of_1916.png.

Fig. 12.8a: Source: https://commons.wikimedia.org/wiki/File:British_Empire_1921.png.

Fig. 12.8b: Source: https://commons.wikimedia.org/wiki/File:Battle_of_britain_air_observer.jpg.

Fig. 12.8c: Source: https://commons.wikimedia.org/wiki/File:Operation_Pied_Piper.jpg.

Fig. 12.9: Source: https://commons.wikimedia.org/wiki/File:MunichAgreement.jpg.

Fig. 12.10: Source: https://commons.wikimedia.org/wiki/File:WWII_Food_Rationing.jpg.

Fig. 12.11: Source: https://commons.wikimedia.org/wiki/File:The_Women%27s_Royal_Naval_Service_during_the_Second_World_War_A15161.jpg.

Fig. 12.12: Source: https://commons.wikimedia.org/wiki/File:The_British_Army_in_the_UK-_Evacuation_From_Dunkirk,_May-June_1940_H1621.jpg.

Fig. 12.13: Source: https://commons.wikimedia.org/wiki/File:Evacuees_in_Montgomeryshire_(4346388594).jpg.

Fig. 12.14a: Source: https://commons.wikimedia.org/wiki/File:The_Home_Front_in_Britain_during_the_Second_World_War_HU44272.jpg.

Fig. 12.14b: Source: https://commons.wikimedia.org/wiki/File:Blitzaftermath.jpg.

CHAPTER 13

Political, Economic, and Social Upheaval

Although significant and far-reaching measures were brought about in response to the outbreak of war in August 1914, the origins of the program of social welfare reform that would mark much of the twentieth century had actually lain a decade earlier, in the legislative measures of the last great Liberal government of 1906. This was itself a product of changes to the ideology of liberalism that had been afoot at least a generation earlier. "Classical" liberalism, it should be remembered, had been a philosophy with broad implications for society and individuals alike. Essentially it was a doctrine of freedom, which, translated to the context of policy, meant limited government involvement in politics and social life. This spirit of classical liberalism had been a big part of British identity and thought throughout the middle two-thirds of the nineteenth century, no matter what party held office. One consequence was that, in contrast to significant reform to the system of representation in the 1830s, in 1867, and in the 1880s, there had been relatively little activity in respect to social reform.

Changing Ideas of Liberalism

Toward the end of the century, however, and especially after the economic slowdown beginning in the 1870s, the ideas of classical liberalism were in retreat. The departure came naturally enough to the Conservatives who increasingly defined themselves (as well as being the party of the moneyed elite) by their commitment to tariffs, expanded imperial commitment, and continued union with Ireland—and it is easy to see all three positions as antithetical to classical liberalism. But the Liberal Party also realized the shortcomings of a traditional laissez-faire outlook and increasingly abandoned it. It was clear that unfettered capitalism—the core concept of classical liberalism—was not perfect. To be sure, no system was better at increasing productivity and generating great wealth. But by and large it failed to deliver the "universal opulence" that Adam Smith had promised in *The Wealth of Nations*. Instead, the new wealth was narrowly concentrated at the top of the economic ladder. At the same time, a series of studies, groundbreaking for their breadth and detail as well as for their sophisticated reliance on statistics, revealed that over one-third of those in London's East End lived in perpetual and abject poverty. A comparable survey of York showed that conditions were not much better elsewhere. Thus liberals replaced emphasis on economic freedom with emphasis on social freedom. Rather than promote equality of opportunity (which often appeared specious in practice), they were increasingly concerned with actual equality, to be realized through policies of collective action that promoted social justice.

Put another way, this new take on liberalism—called, conveniently enough, New Liberalism— called for positive freedom instead of negative freedom. Earlier liberalism had meant freedom *from* regulations, inspections, and taxes; New Liberalism pursued freedom *for* employment security, education, opportunity, and so on—and the state, rather than being excluded or restricted, had a crucial role to play. New Liberalism did not ignore the individual but insisted that the whole of society could be greater than the sum of its parts, and that involvement of the state might be necessary for increasing the liberty of individuals to reach their full potential. This new approach began in the decade before the Great War and intensified in its aftermath.

Reforms to Assist the Young, the Elderly, and Working Families

By the end of 1905, the Conservative government that had been in office for over ten years, first under the Marquess of Salisbury and then his nephew Arthur Balfour, was divided, weak, and unpopular. The prime minister resigned in December but did not seek a dissolution of Parliament: He hoped to catch the minority Liberal opposition off-guard and to use the breathing space to strengthen his own party. The Liberals played their cards skillfully, however. They avoided divisive issues and, in the general election the following month, secured 400 seats in the House of Commons against only 157 Conservative and Unionist MPs, with an additional 83 Irish nationalist and 30 Labour MPs who could in many cases be relied upon to back a Liberal government. Liberals remained in office (albeit with significantly reduced majorities after 1910) for nearly a decade, until they were replaced by a coalition in the first year of World War I. But with an initially commanding majority, as well as over one hundred probable allies among the Irish and Labour ranks, the Liberals were ready to tackle many of the challenging social problems that had gone largely unaddressed by any legislative response for a generation or more.

The spirit of New Liberalism had expanded during the early twentieth century, but it was still far from universally accepted. The older, classical, liberalism—exemplified in the attitude of the Poor Law Amendment Act (or New Poor Law) of the 1830s—cast a long shadow, and therefore the achievements of the Liberal governments of 1906–1915 tended to be piecemeal. Promoters of social reform believed that society had a collective responsibility, through government, to alleviate the chief problems that beset it, including poor health, inferior education, inadequate housing, unemployment, or underemployment. Legislative proposals were designed to address one particular problem at a time. Collectively, these measures sought to assist three broad groups: the young, the old, and the unemployed (or otherwise struggling) working classes.

The School Meals Act (1906) authorized local schools to provide free meals to needy children, and in a proactive step to combat disease and sickness before they became problems, the School Medical Inspections Service (1907) sent doctors and nurses to schools to provide annual checkups and encouraged schools to provide free medical treatment. These two measures, it should be noted, were inspired not so much by an invigorated spirit of reform, but rather in response to the needs of national security: The unsatisfactory physical condition of so many working-class volunteers at the time of the Boer War (1899–1902) had horrified the British public, and the Committee on Physical Deterioration (1904) had already recommended that schools provide meals and medical inspections. Moreover, the new laws only required the inspections. Before they were made mandatory by further reforms, in 1912 and 1914, many schools ignored the recommendations to provide free treatment clinics or free meals.

The Liberals' Education Act (1907) improved on the 1870 Education Act, chiefly by introducing the "free place" system. This required all grammar (i.e., secondary) schools, which were fee paying, to reserve one-quarter to two-fifths of their places for poorer scholarship children who had completed their elementary education (which already was free) and who had successfully completed an entrance examination. The act was especially popular in Wales and among dissenters everywhere since it also reduced Anglican influence in education.

The Children's Act (1908)—also called the Young Persons Act or the Children's Charter—imposed stiff penalties on adults who mistreated youngsters or provided them with alcohol or tobacco. And an important provision of the Prevention of Crime Act (1908) established special juvenile courts for youth offenders who, if convicted, were sent to juvenile detention centers called borstals, rather than incarcerated with adult offenders.

The Liberal government's biggest achievement on behalf of the elderly was the Old Age Pensions Act (1908), which paid a modest weekly allowance to those over seventy, provided a recipient was "of good character" (i.e., without convictions for drunkenness or similar offenses) and did not otherwise have any significant income. The allowance was not large (it was roughly one-quarter the wage of an unskilled laborer), but that was deliberate. The liberal ideal of self-help persisted, and legislators aimed to encourage working families to put something aside for themselves rather than rely on the government for handouts. On the other hand, a pensioner's allowance could be collected at the local post office instead of a workhouse or some other welfare agency, and thus the potential stigma associated with the aid was reduced. And even if the relief was set at a minimum, it still often meant the difference between independence and dignity, and living (and dying) in the union workhouse. The measure was widely popular, and half a million recipients, mostly women, began collecting pensions at the beginning of 1909. Because it was a noncontributory allowance (unlike provisions for the Insurance Acts), the act is often regarded as a major foundation of Britain's social welfare program that would be realized after World War II.

The challenges facing Britain's workers were more varied than those affecting the young and the old, and therefore were addressed by a series of acts in the first several years of the Liberal government. A Conservative act in 1897 had required mine owners to pay compensation to workers injured on the job. The Liberals' Workmen's Compensation Act (1906) expanded the principle in two important respects: First, it applied it not only to miners, but to all workers who earned less than £200 per annum (increasing its coverage from about 900,000 miners to about 6 million workers in various trades); and second, it included workers who were injured or suffered ill health because of conditions at work. The Merchant Shipping Act (1906) improved conditions for sailors by regulating the quality of food rations, as well as improving accommodation onboard ships.

The Trade Disputes Act (1906) essentially reversed the Taff Vale case of 1901, which had decided against organized labor: Unions now were protected against suits for losses or damages incurred by management during strikes. Similarly, the Trade Union Act (1913) reversed the Osborne Judgement of 1909, and gave unions the right to use member dues to support Labour party candidates. The 1906 act had actually been drawn up by the Labour Party but could not have been passed without backing from the majority Liberals. Concerned about the increasing number of Labour victories in by elections, the Liberals supported both acts to attract working-class votes. The rising prominence of Labour was further boosted after the second general election of 1910, when Liberals were exactly tied with Conservative/Unionist MPs, and therefore even more dependent on Labour and Irish support.

A Mines Act (1908) established an eight-hour day for men, marking the first time a British government had involved itself in this way on behalf of adult male workers. The Minimum Wage Act (1912) set up local boards to supervise conditions and to determine regional minimum wages. These measures were significant but fell short of the reforms miners had hoped to achieve.

The Trades Board Act (1909) applied similar measures across a broader spectrum. Boards were established to oversee conditions and to ensure minimum compensation for those employed in the "sweated" industries (e.g., tailors, paper box makers, chain makers, lace makers) who had not been protected by earlier factory acts. In 1910, shop workers were guaranteed, in addition to Sunday, one half-day off each week, although there was nothing to prevent unscrupulous employers from recovering those lost hours through longer workdays. The measures were extended in 1913, to include about 400,000 workers (mostly women and children), and to workers in all low-paid trades and industries in 1918.

The Labour Exchange Act (1909) was designed to assist management and labor alike, by encouraging employers with vacancies to register with regional offices, where those looking for work could easily learn about available openings from a single exchange, without trudging across town (or further) from one employer to another. Participation in the service was voluntary, but effective: By 1913 over four hundred exchanges operated, and by 1914 the network was assisting a million men to find work annually.

Probably the government's greatest—and almost certainly most controversial—social reform project before World War I was the National Insurance Act (1911), designed to assist workers between the ages of 16 and 70 who earned less than £160 per annum. The scheme involved two parts, the first of which required workers to pay 4d. a week (a deduction of probably less than 2 percent for an unskilled worker, or just over 0.5 percent for a skilled worker) into an Insurance Fund. Employers paid a further 2d. and the government contributed 3d. Any participating worker who fell sick was entitled to free medical attention and, if he contracted tuberculosis (which affected the poorer classes especially and was estimated to kill seventy-five thousand annually), he was admitted to a tubercular clinic. If sickness rendered him unable to work, he received 10s. a week for 26 weeks, and thereafter a disability pension of 5s. per week—roughly one-quarter to one-twelfth, and one-eighth to one-sixteenth, his previous wages, respectively. An uninsured worker's wife who had a baby received a maternity grant of 30s. (nearly half her husband's weekly wage if he were employed at the upper end of the £160 range).

The act covered 2.3 million workers under one or both of its parts by 1914 and, unsurprisingly, was criticized from many sides. The Labour Party believed the provisions were inadequate (after all, millions were still left uncovered) and that government and employers ought to contribute more, perhaps the entire share. Workers were also unhappy with the compulsory weekly deduction from their wages and might resent competition to their own workers' insurance programs or friendly societies. Conservatives or classical liberals, on the other hand, complained the measures cost too much, created a sense of entitlement, and rejected earlier emphases on self-help and limited government.

By standards of a later day, the reforms were, to be sure, limited: The Pensions Act was essentially a safety net, did not pay out a lot, and left many elderly people fairly miserable; many of the provisions involving children and schools were merely recommendations and were initially ignored; and the National Insurance Act, which only covered workers in certain fields (and, occasionally, their wives), left dependents and millions of others unprotected. Nevertheless, these measures heralded the expansion of the scope of government, as well as big increases in government expenditure.

Lloyd George and the People's Budget

Expensive though they were, the schemes were generally popular. In this respect, the outlook of David Lloyd George, chancellor of the exchequer after 1908, was crucial. Unlike most earlier holders of the office, who acted on the premise the position was intended to balance budgets and minimize costs, Lloyd George reckoned it his duty to bring about a major redistribution of the national wealth (figure 13.1). The People's Budget (1909) was a case in point. As well as hugely expensive provisions for the construction of the latest Dreadnought battleships, the budget had to pay for the allowances of the Old Age Pensions Act. It met the expenses through various new measures that rested squarely on the shoulders of the well-to-do: taxes on cars, motor fuel, and mining royalties; an increased income tax and high "sin taxes" on alcohol and tobacco; and, most controversial, a 20 percent tax on the increased value of resold land. It also increased "death duties" (inheritance taxes).

The budget was debated from April to November, before being passed by an overwhelming margin in the House of Commons. By convention, the House of Lords did not tamper with money bills, but on this occasion, they vetoed the budget outright. H. H. Asquith, the prime minister, called a general election for January 1910, which he hoped would serve as a de facto referendum in favor of the Liberals' budget and against the House of Lords. But the results were a disappointment for the government, who were narrowly returned to power with only two seats more than the

FIGURE 13.1 David Lloyd George was one of the "New Liberals" who passed welfare legislation.

Conservative opposition. There were 40 Labour MPs, however, who would certainly support the People's Budget, as well as 82 Irish MPs who also agreed to vote with the government in exchange for a new Home Rule Bill and a further bill to revise the relationship between the House of Commons and the Lords, to prevent the latter from permanently vetoing Irish reform measures. This time the House of Lords, probably fearing the outcome of a constitutional struggle with the House of Commons, accepted the budget.

The Parliament Bill

The People's Budget represented the fiscal/economic half of the equation of New Liberalism's aim to reorient British society away from one that catered to and was dominated by the wealthy to one that better suited an increasingly democratic ideal. The political/constitutional half of the equation was advanced in the Parliament Bill (1910), which passed the House of Commons and which the prime minister sent to the House of Lords in November.

Although in step with the Liberal government's overall plan, the particular design of the bill especially satisfied the demands of the Irish MPs, who hoped to prevent the upper house from blocking Home Rule for Ireland, as they had done in 1893. The terms of the bill were threefold. First, the lords could not amend or reject any finance bill the commons had accepted, thus making into formal law a tradition that had been recognized for centuries. Second, although the lords could continue to limit or block non-finance bills, any bill that passed the commons in three successive sessions became law automatically, opposition from the lords notwithstanding. In practical terms, the extent of the ability of the (largely hereditary) House of Lords to check the will of the popularly elected House of Commons was reduced to a delay of two years. Third, the Parliament Bill required a general election every five, instead of every seven, years. The House of Lords (correctly) recognized the measure, especially its first two provisions, as an unprecedented attempt to hobble their place in the constitutional framework.

The new king, George V, was eager to bring an end to damaging partisan strife, but the spirit of compromise he sought broke down, chiefly owing to the intransigence of the Unionists, who wanted the House of Lords to guarantee the security of their position. Irish nationalists and Labour, meanwhile, were adamant in pushing through the reforms and, in this atmosphere, the prime minister called a new election scarcely ten months after the last.

The government fared worse than it had hoped, with Liberals losing their tenuous two-seat advantage, and tying exactly with Conservatives. With Irish and Labour support, the passage of the Parliament Bill through the House of Commons was abundantly secure, but the House of Lords was almost as certain to veto it outright. The only recourse in such a situation was to alter the composition of the upper house. This could only be achieved through the addition of liberal-leaning peers, and the government had secured a pledge from the king, if necessary, to create them.

The only other time in modern history the House of Lords had faced such a threat had been eighty years earlier, in the constitutional crisis leading to passage of the Great Reform Act. Then, the creation of perhaps forty to fifty new peerages would have sufficed. By the early twentieth century—with the intervening expansion of the House of Lords (561 hereditary peers, 4 law lords, 2 archbishops, and 24 bishops) and its transformation to an overwhelmingly conservative body (in large measure owing to the debates on Ireland over the preceding 30–40 years)—the government would require something on the order of four to five hundred new liberal peers. The upper house would become so thoroughly liberal that any future conservative government would likely face difficulty in securing its goals.

This existential threat notwithstanding, the Conservative response in the House of Lords was divided. Despite the risks involved in continuing to stand up to the House of Commons (and the king), some, called "Ditchers," opposed the measure outright and were, it seems, prepared to go down with the ship. Others, however, called "Hedgers," took the more moderate line of a tactical retreat: They preferred accepting a reduced role in the political process to becoming irrelevant. Nearly two-thirds of the peers abstained from voting on the measure, which passed by a margin of only 17 out of 245 cast.

The Demise of the Liberals and the Rise of Labour

On the surface, the spirit of New Liberalism appeared to be riding high on the eve of World War I. In under a decade, the governments of Campbell-Bannerman and Asquith had secured important protections for workers and other vulnerable groups in society; they had changed the expectations of the role of the state in the lives of the people and in business and industry; the People's Budget had shifted the burden of paying for these reforms to the wealthiest landowners and capitalists; and the Parliament Act finally established the political preeminence of the representative House of Commons over the unelected House of Lords.

As it turned out, the Liberal Party's finest hour was also its final hour. In 1906 they had been voted into power with four hundred seats. Even though they lost more than a quarter of that number in the two elections of 1910, they held onto the reins of government until being replaced by a coalition (in which they continued to be numerically dominant) during World War I. They had gone into the war a great governing party and emerged broken and humiliated. In the next general election, scheduled a month after the war, they came in third place, with the number of Liberal MPs reduced to less than 4 percent of the House of Commons. Thereafter Liberal electoral fortunes rallied only once, in the general election of 1923—and even that, finishing again behind Conservatives and Labour, with a mere 9 percent of seats, was an anemic rally. For the rest of the twentieth century, Liberals never held more than a few dozen seats and, in the four elections in the 1950s, they averaged a smidgen over 1 percent. The Liberal Party technically and officially came to an end in 1988, when its tiny remnant merged with the SDP to form the center to center-left Liberal Democrats, but for the past one hundred years, the left-of-center force in British politics, opposed to the right-of-center Conservatives or Tories, has been Labour.

The demise of the Liberal Party has been the subject of considerable historical debate. Some historians believe that the rise of Labour doomed the party. The agreement of 1906 by which the Liberals promised not to contest seats in Labour strongholds in return for a guarantee by Labour not to run against Liberal candidates made possible the election of thirty Labour MPs, a bloc that steadily expanded at the expense of the Liberals. Stuck in the middle of British politics, the argument goes, the Liberals were bound to decline as their share of the electorate gravitated to Labour or the Conservatives. Other historians believe the difficulties of fighting World War I, followed by the coupon election of 1918, destroyed the party. In his effort to preserve his wartime coalition, Lloyd George issued letters of endorsement (coupons) only to those Liberal MPs loyal to him. He thus split the party, which benefited Labour. The Conservatives eventually threw him overboard, by which time the old Liberal Party had been irreparably damaged.

Interwar Years: Initial Economic Boom and Expansion

Instability and paradox were the hallmarks of domestic politics in the UK across the 1920s and 1930s. In under a decade, four men from three parties swapped places as prime minister six times, including two occasions in which governments that were Conservative in all but name were headed by a prime minister who was a Liberal or a Labourite. There were two Labour governments formed with only minority support in the House of Commons, and these governments actually lowered taxes. Indeed, the interwar years in general saw a return by the Conservative Party to its Disraelian tradition of Tory democracy, and its economic and social policies were generally more innovative and progressive than anything Labour had to offer.

This confusing state of affairs was a rude turn of events, however, for the immediate postwar situation appeared to promise prosperity and continuity. David Lloyd George stayed on as prime minister (a position he had held since 1916) in a nominally coalition government that was in reality over 70 percent Conservative/Unionist and of which he was the only important Liberal. There was an initial economic boom and, despite the demobilization of millions of veterans, Britain experienced full employment. These sunny circumstances were due to several factors.

After more than four years of sacrifices, shortages, and a heavy industry geared almost entirely to the war effort, demand for peacetime industrial production increased. Consumers were eager to buy kitchen ranges, household appliances, and even automobiles—items that had been unavailable during the war.

Following the terms of the Representation of the People Act (1918), sometimes called the Fourth Reform Bill, all men over 21, and women over 30 who met other requirements, were enfranchised. Ten years later, following a further measure sometimes called the Equal Franchise Act, adult men and women could vote on the same terms, and the UK had finally achieved a democratic franchise.

The Education Act (1918) made education free and compulsory for all children 5 to 14, and also laid the groundwork for further reforms that, owing to subsequent government economies, were not immediately enacted. A further education report in 1936 recommended more extensive reforms, including increasing the school-leaving age to 15—but most of these measures were not implemented until after World War II. An exception was the provision in schools of subsidized or free milk, which began in 1934.

Another area that experienced significant, but incomplete, improvement in the early interwar years was public housing. Serving in the newly created post of Minister of Health, doctor-turned-politician Christopher Addison helped steer through the Housing and Town Planning Act (1919), which aimed to construct half a million homes in three years. It provided open-ended subsidies to local authorities to construct municipal housing and compelled local authorities with populations over 20,000 to survey lands for new homes. In one light, these measures were a continuation of the spirit of New Liberalism from before the war. In another light, they were belated responses to even earlier concerns raised after the Boer War, but reinforced during World War I, that "you cannot expect to get an A1 population out of C3 homes." Similarly, the "garden city" movement, an effort at systematic zoning that included communities with green spaces, had been launched early in the twentieth century (reformer Ebenezer Howard had founded a company to develop Letchworth in 1903), but really only took off after the war, with the construction of Welwyn beginning in 1920. The government added grants for further development and housing construction in 1922, but by then the economy was beginning to stagnate, and the funds were frozen. In the event, the 1919 act resulted in only slightly more than 200,000 of the promised 500,000 new homes, but even that was important in stimulating the employment of bricklayers, plumbers, electricians, and others involved in building and construction.

The government took advantage of the initially favorable postwar circumstances to introduce an Unemployment Insurance Act (1920) that expanded the scope of the 1911 National Insurance Act. As well as covering veterans, the new policy increased both the contributions (from government, employers, and workers) and the benefits provided, and extended the duration relief was available (yet another Unemployment Insurance Act, in 1927, made the payments potentially indefinite). Arguably this implementation of the "dole" went well beyond the New Liberal conception of the role of the state: Rather than a mere (and limited) safety net, it seemed now the government had accepted the principle of long-term maintenance by the state.

The 1921 measure was introduced in the context of a strong economy and full employment. No one anticipated a massive draw on the Insurance Fund in the near future. In fact, the government expected collection of premiums to generate a surplus for the foreseeable future. But the economic tide turned quickly and, as early as 1921, with over 2 million out of work, the fund had run out of money. The problems were rooted in several factors, including debt to be paid on the loans from the United States, which began immediately after the war, combined with the loss of international markets and worldwide investments. There were also systemic weaknesses in many of Britain's basic industries. The most prominent of these, and probably the most far-reaching, was coal.

Interwar Years: Difficulties in Coal and Other Basic Industries

The extraction of coal had been Britain's most fraught industry before the war. Tensions between labor and management were temporarily held in check by the spirit of domestic truce beginning in August 1914, by government direction of the mines, and by increased demand for production to satisfy the war effort. But the situation deteriorated rapidly after the war as, for several related reasons, demand fell sharply. From a long-term perspective of the whole of the twentieth century, the gradual replacement of coal by oil as a source of power and heat was inevitable. The tendency was especially noteworthy in a British context in the shipping industry, which had earlier been a leading consumer of coal. Similarly, homes and businesses increasingly turned to electricity to provide power, heat, and especially light. Even in cases where coal use continued (e.g., to generate electricity), the overall rate of consumption declined: New boilers and engines were more efficient, smaller homes had less space to heat, and better insulation meant better conservation. These were all positive innovations, of course, except for those—management and miners alike—who depended on steady consumption and high prices.

On top of changes in domestic use and consumption, Britain faced growing challenges from new coal-exporting regions such as Holland, Germany, and Poland. This did not merely mean competition in a field where it had previously been the dominant, and at times sole, player, because Britain now often found itself at distinct disadvantage to these newcomers. Britain may have led the way in industrial development (including coal extraction) in the nineteenth century, but (as was seen in chapter 11) this initial advantage permitted others, who industrialized later, to adapt to changing conditions and demands more easily. New coal exporters in the 1920s adopted the latest and most profitable technologies while avoiding antiquated and costly mistakes.

Similar stories unfolded in Britain's other industries. Shipbuilding had enjoyed an artificial boom during World War I, when German U-boats sank so much of the Allied merchant fleet. But this market, and certainly its breath-taking pace, dried up almost immediately following the war. Much of the traffic that was diverted from British shipping after 1914 was never recovered, compounding the loss to domestic shipbuilding. Meanwhile, there was increased, and typically more efficient and adaptable, competition from the US, Poland, and Japan. The result was widespread unemployment in previously bustling shipyards in the north.

British textiles proved to be yet another casualty of the war. Beforehand, Britain annually imported nearly 2 billion pounds of raw cotton and exported over 5.5 billion yards of cloth. During the war, however, many customers developed or improved their own markets for both domestic consumption and export. India is a good example. Japan and the US increasingly sold cloth to Britain's old clients in Asia and Latin America, respectively. As with coal, so with textiles: New producers were typically competitive and operated more efficient factories that required fewer workers at lower costs. This was good news all around—except, again, for Britain's failing textile manufacturers and (increasingly redundant) workers.

Even Britain's more fledgling industries in the early twentieth century suffered as a result of World War I. The car industry, for instance, had been growing at a promising rate in 1914. But just as British industry shifted almost entirely to meeting wartime needs, Henry Ford began mass production on his fully automated assembly line in Detroit. Under normal circumstances, British industry would quickly have followed the example. As it was, Ford was able to capitalize further on his lead and, by 1920, he had cornered a mass market, even in Britain. Of course, since automobile manufacturing, as well as coal extraction, shipbuilding, and textile production, all required steel, decline in those industries inevitably hurt British steel, which also faced competition from Japan and the US.

The outcome of these combined factors could hardly have been other than a seriously unfavorable balance of trade. While American productivity in manufacturing rose by more than one-fifth between 1913 and 1920, and Japan's by more than three-quarters, Britain's actually fell. British exports declined across the board and, throughout the 1920s, were never as much as 80 percent of their level in early 1914. Meanwhile, to complete this depressing picture, the rate of British imports increased.

Government Responses

The responses of the various governments—coalition, Conservative, or Labour—did not always reflect much considered direction. To meet the extra demands on the Insurance Fund, the government cut spending in other areas (e.g., army and navy, education, health services) and raised taxes. The cuts were known collectively as the Geddes Axe, after businessman Sir Eric Geddes, who advised the Conservative government on the policy. Among other things, spending on the construction of new council housing stopped. Not only did this cancel the wartime aspiration of "homes fit for heroes to live in," it also threw out of work—and onto the dole—those workers employed in building and related trades.

The government also reinstated the Gold Standard in 1925, with the result that British exports became more expensive. This appealed to investors and, under different circumstances, could probably have strengthened the economy generally. But in the 1920s and early 1930s, the effect was to push exports out of reach of potential buyers and therefore reduce British competitiveness overseas. Unemployed families were less likely to afford consumer goods, and thus demand fell at home as well as abroad. The British economy was caught in an unfortunate cycle.

In 1927, another Unemployment Insurance Act lowered the contributions workers and employers paid into the fund but also lowered the benefits paid out to the unemployed. If not exactly robbing Peter to pay Paul, it did not look as though the government had a very clear-sighted or goal-oriented policy in mind. They wanted to appear to be doing something, but this amounted to little more than stop-gap measures of questionable value. Yet another Unemployment Insurance Act (1930) made it easier for the out-of-work to claim benefits and extended those benefits to a wider range of workers so that virtually all families were insured.

The General Strike

The centerpiece of this decade of political uncertainty and economic instability was the General Strike of 1926. Strikes, of course, had been the most forceful tool of the unions for over half a century. Their potency had been curtailed in 1901, with the Taff Vale decision, but restored by the Liberals in 1906 with the Trade Disputes Act. Since unions could again strike with indemnity, they did so. Union membership grew sharply after 1910, and the number and intensity of strikes increased commensurately. Between 1910 and 1912, over 60 million working days were lost, and a series of strikes affected nearly every major industry.[1] Coalminers in Tonypandy, South Wales, were on strike for 10 months beginning in 1910, and troops were sent to the region to disperse strikers and control rioting. There was a brief but intense strike by railway men, who were joined by seamen and dockers, in 1911, and two strikers were killed when the government sent in troops. Twentieth-century Britain's first "Bloody Sunday" occurred on August 13, 1911: Following a summer of strikes and mass organizations in Liverpool, strikers and demonstrators were shot at, and two were killed. The next week, authorities used gunfire against striking protesters in Llanelli, and again two were killed. Miners went on strike for, and achieved, an increased minimum wage in 1912, and Irish transport workers were on strike for eight months in 1913. Strike action and other forms of labor militancy abated for the most part, although not entirely, in the spirit of domestic truce during the war, but resumed afterward. Police called strikes in London, Merseyside, and elsewhere in 1918 and 1919, and in response, the Police Act (1919) transferred control of pay and conditions to the Home Office. There was a further Bloody Sunday, this time in Scotland, in 1919, when police and the military battled strikers in Glasgow.

More fearful was the threat of a sympathetic strike, in which workers with no direct or immediate grievance against their employer went on strike all the same, in a show of solidarity, to aid or support workers striking in a different industry. The summer of agitation and strikes that culminated with the first Bloody Sunday was an example. The Triple Alliance of the three most powerful unions—miners, railway men, and transport workers (including various unions of dockers, seamen, tramway men, and road vehicle workers)—was negotiated in 1914 and brought with it the prospect of the country being ground to a virtual standstill. But the Triple Alliance was unable to coordinate before the war, and for the next four years, like most unions, its constituent parts observed the domestic truce. The resolve of the alliance was finally tested in 1921, when Britain's collieries were returned from state direction (a wartime expedient) to private management. This meant, among other things, a wage reduction—and miners called a strike on April 15. But the commitment of the railway men and transport workers wavered, and they declined to support the unions in a sympathetic strike. The event went down in the annals of organized labor, and especially by miners, as "Black Friday."

Even more devastating than a mere Triple Alliance was the prospect of a wider, or general, strike, in which unions from across the spectrum of working-class labor staged simultaneous strikes. There had been a localized attempt, centered in Glasgow, in 1919, but in the 1920s the possibility of a national general strike seemed increasingly likely.

Once again, the origins lay in the conditions of the coal seams of Yorkshire, Lancashire, Scotland, and Wales. Depressed prices and diminished demand abroad persisted and, since the industry was labor intensive and had hardly modernized over the past several generations—indeed, over 80 percent of Britain's coal was still cut by pickaxes, long after other countries had mechanized—when orders slackened, management's only "solution" was to cut wages or lay off workers. In response to strikes at several mines in 1925, owners had promised a wage hike. On the resumption of the Gold Standard, however, they did an about-face and proceeded with plans to increase hours and reduce wages. The collieries in South Wales and Durham announced a revised workday of 8 instead of 7 hours and a wage reduction of 13 percent—this was less than what British coal miners had been paid at any point since before World War I. The specter of the Triple Alliance rose again, and on July 31, 1925 ("Red Friday"), the government calmed the situation by agreeing to pay a nine-month subsidy to meet the difference of the owners' cuts and creating a commission to investigate. The government also began secretly stockpiling fuel, food, and other essential resources against the possibility of widespread strike action.

The findings of the commission differed very little from those reached by earlier investigations, namely that the coal industry was poorly served by private enterprise. More pointedly, this latest commission, which reported in March 1926, recommended that management go ahead with its proposed wage cuts but drew the line at a lengthened workday. The "compromise" was accepted by neither owners nor unions—whose slogan was "Not a minute on the day, not a penny off the pay"—and both sides waited for the government subsidy to expire at the end of April.

Owners went ahead with plans to cut wages, and a conference of the Trade Union Congress (TUC) met to undertake last-minute negotiations with the government. But Stanley Baldwin, the Conservative prime minister, seemed to have injudiciously lost interest in salvaging the situation: He abandoned an active role in the proceedings and allowed confrontational hotheads such as Winston Churchill to take the lead in representing the government. They delivered the TUC an ultimatum and demanded an unconditional renunciation of a general strike. The TUC felt shocked and betrayed. Most likely they had never expected actually having to resort to organized labor's ultimate weapon, but on May 3, with negotiations evidently at an impasse, they called a General Strike. The next day Britain's coal pits were empty, its factories and foundries silent, and trains, busses, and trams ceased operation. Printers (who, earlier in the week, had refused to run an edition of the *Daily Mail* that criticized the miners and their allies as revolutionaries), engineers, and dockers went on strike as well, in solidarity with the Triple Alliance. Eager to emphasize restraint and wary of giving license to revolutionary expressions, the TUC had arranged for unionized health workers not to participate in any strike.

The government responded swiftly and decisively. A state of emergency was declared and, under the coordination of the Organisation for the Maintenance of Supplies (OMS), headed by Winston Churchill, gas, electrical, and other essential services were not interrupted. Servicemen took on the work of dockers, miners, and postmen, and middle-class volunteers kept lorries, busses, and even trains in motion. Churchill edited *The British Gazette*, a pro-government and often inflammatory propaganda newspaper (the BBC also toed the government line during the General Strike), and used the OMS to seize paper supplies, thus preventing the TUC from distributing its own newspaper, *The British Worker*. The government recruited 226,000 volunteers—mostly drawn from the middle classes—to assist the police, a warship was sent to the Tyne estuary in Newcastle, and the army was called in to escort food supplies brought up to London. No lives were lost during the General Strike, although there was violence: Strikers clashed with police in London and in other cities; busses were tipped over, and some set on fire, in Glasgow; and strikers derailed the *Flying Scotsman* in Northumberland (figure 13.2).

FIGURE 13.2 Troops on guard at a bus station; each bus had a police escort during the strike.

The TUC distanced themselves from violent actions or revolutionary declarations and insisted that the goals of the General Strike were not political but rather simply to achieve economic justice for workers and their families. It did not help their cause, however, when big donations arrived from Russian trades unions (even though the TUC refused the aid and sent it back), and the government arrested nearly four hundred Communists. The prime minister warned that the General Strike threatened Britain with a revolution that aspired to overthrow order and society.

Some textile workers joined the strike rather late in the game, but by then the stamina of the TUC was spent. On only its eighth day, the TUC conceded that the General Strike had failed. Four thousand strikers were prosecuted for violence or incitement to violence, one thousand went to jail, and the government and industry forced most strikers to return to work on May 12. Coal miners were left to their own devices. They continued to hold out, alone, until November, when—cold, hungry, and running short on funds—they returned to their pits at lower wages and for longer hours. They felt betrayed by the Labour Party and the TUC.

Aftermath of the General Strike

The General Strike of 1926 was defeated in part by the strategic preparations of the government that had been underway since the previous summer but also by the enthusiastic moral and practical support the middle classes who had, on earlier occasions, often sympathized with strikes. The course and outcome of the General Strike divided the country and stoked feelings of class antagonism, thus undoing the good feeling that Baldwin's government had aspired to and, thanks to reforms under the ministry of health, delivered. Churches held services of thanksgiving for the restoration of peace and unity, but the tone often identified with law and order and not the strikers. The Catholic Church went so far as to declare unambiguously that the General Strike was "a sin." Baldwin aimed for a conciliatory note in a radio broadcast that appealed to his common refrains of "one nation" and Tory democracy, but this pacific and healing attitude seemed the exception that proved the rule. Other opponents of the General Strike were less diplomatic and practically rubbed in the fact that workers had been forced to accept "unconditional surrender." Winston Churchill had positively enjoyed himself during the eight days of strike—and so had many of the middle-class volunteers. He blithely called it a "war" and, before being reined in by the prime minister, had made unguarded and deliberately incendiary declamations against its participants.

Not content merely to have weathered the strike and sent workers back to their jobs, the government responded with retaliatory legislation that rolled back many of the gains made by labor earlier in the century. A new Trades Disputes Act (1927) amended the terms of its predecessor from 1913 to outlaw sympathetic or general strikes. It also put in doubt the Labour Party's main source of income from union dues. Union membership, which had stood at over 5.5 million before the General Strike (80 percent affiliated with the TUC) fell to under 4.4 million (75 percent affiliated with the TUC) only a few years later.

Depression

Despite the fact that Baldwin's government appeared to have emerged victorious from the aftermath of the General Strike of 1926, and that it was the only government formed that decade to have even approached a natural life of five years, the Conservative Party was, by 1929, deeply unpopular. The prime minister promised very little in the run-up to the general election other than the government's record in office (which, apart from some measures in respect to public housing, secured by Neville Chamberlain as Minister of Health, was frankly uninspiring) and the lackluster advantages of "safety first." It was actually the Liberals, potentially unified behind David Lloyd George following Asquith's death in 1928, who ran on the most ambitious platform, in which they had been advised by John Maynard Keynes, of public works and similar "pump-priming" measures. The Labour Party made only slight nods in the direction of socialism: Their plan differed little from what was proposed by Lloyd George and the liberals and was perhaps most noteworthy for its lack of specificity.

Notwithstanding, and no doubt owing to, the fact that this was the first general election in British history in which all adults over 21 could participate, Labour won the election, albeit with a minority government. But Labour did next to nothing to implement their policies, vague though they had been. In part this was by design: the prime minister, Ramsay MacDonald—whose interests ran more to foreign than domestic policy anyway—was cautious and did not want to risk alienating the middle classes. His approach was to break in the country, gradually, to the idea of a Labour government, and to convince them that there was nothing to fear from it. Indeed, Macdonald aimed to persuade Britain that there could be such a thing as a Labour government.

As it turned out, Labour were unlucky to have stepped into power only a few months before the Wall Street crash, out of which probably no British government could have emerged with a positive record. The widespread suffering and economic disorientation brought about by the Depression perhaps ought to have provided opportunities for Labour to rise to the occasion and establish its credentials as a party of the people. In fact, rather than attempt anything innovative (let alone socialist), Ramsay MacDonald and his chancellor of the exchequer, Philip Snowden, sought refuge in the classical liberal solutions of the previous century. In 1931 they went so far as to slash unemployment and other benefits. This was too much for the TUC and the majority of the Labour Party, and the government resigned.

King George V, however, urged MacDonald to remain at his post as prime minister and see the country through its crisis as leader of a coalition. He agreed, but on condition that there be a general election first, asking for, in MacDonald's words, a "doctor's mandate" from the electorate. What the doctor ordered were conservative measures; the election returned a House of Commons with nearly five hundred Conservative MPs. It was nominally a coalition, but an awkward one, for the Labourite MacDonald stayed on as prime minister. With an overwhelming Conservative majority after 1931, and still well over four hundred conservative members after 1935, when MacDonald was replaced by Baldwin (who was himself succeeded by Chamberlain in 1937), it is unsurprising that many of the responses of the coalition governments of the 1930s in no way departed strikingly from the conservative governments of the 1920s.

In 1932, Britain abandoned the nineteenth-century orthodoxy of free trade and adopted protection. Since World War I it had occasionally been cheaper to import food from overseas than to produce it at home, so the government encouraged domestic agriculture and paid subsidies to the farmers to keep prices low for consumers. To this was added the policy of "imperial preference" for dominion produce, although most likely the scheme served the dominions better than the metropole.

Otherwise, the governments of the 1930s did not attempt any major innovation in its economic or domestic policy. There was occasional further nationalization (e.g., London transport), but for the most part the program was one of "economic management": The government nudged industry along in directions they thought it ought to go, mainly toward amalgamation and rationalization, chiefly through tariff incentives. For example, when the steel industry resisted amalgamation, the government responded with a passive-aggressive stance that permitted the industry to proceed but made it clear it would do so without the advantages of protection. So, steel did what the government wanted and increasingly amalgamated.

The economy gradually improved over the course of the 1930s, but the government probably cannot claim much credit for its policies. Granted, the abandonment of the Gold Standard increased the flow of money in circulation, and the government lowered interest rates, which made it easier for families to pay off debts and encouraged them to buy more goods. The Special Areas Act (1934) was designed to spur the economy by bringing "light" industry to depressed regions (i.e., the so-called special areas), and local councils built half a million new homes, off-setting the earlier impact of the Geddes Axe. For the most part, however, the actual situation was that the economy had reached rock bottom in 1932 or 1933 and had nowhere to go but up. But the process was slow and painful and still had not been completed when World War II broke out. Nevertheless, it is likely at least some of the government's various policies alleviated the people's hardships during the 1930s.

Life "on the Dole"

Millions of British families suffered during much of the interwar years. The early 1930s were the most difficult, but in many ways the period of misery and economic depression reached back to the General Strike of 1926, or even earlier to the widespread miners' strikes of 1921. Workers lost jobs, industry continued to face challenges, and the government was saddled with enormous debt. As we have seen, it is doubtful the renewed commitment to economic protection helped, and the Gold Standard, by artificially inflating the cost of British goods overseas and discouraging exports, positively hurt. The fiscal and personal toll was severe.

The Wall Street crash on October 29, 1929 ("Black Tuesday"), only made matters worse. Americans, who in the 1920s had done much to drive the expanding world economy, stopped buying abroad. Factories in Britain laid off even more workers, and in 1931, the year Labour resigned to be replaced by a de facto Conservative government that was coalition in name only, unemployment stood at over 3 million. The situation was intractable: The government raised the income tax, but high unemployment meant revenue actually declined; more and more families drew on the Unemployment Insurance Fund, while fewer workers (and employers) contributed; and because of the stagnant economy, families purchased less, which tended to thwart recovery.

Given the context, it was unavoidable that the government cut benefits. Legislative changes in 1930 had restored outdoor relief to the able-bodied poor, but the dole paid to an out-of-work married man with two children was cut by almost 10 percent. Furthermore, in 1931, a means test was introduced for those on the dole: Before a family could claim assistance, its wider potential income (or means) had to be assessed, and the inquiry took into account not merely the wages of the head of household, but also the earnings of the whole family, as well as any savings and the value of possessions. On the grounds of a means test, a family's relief from the dole could be reduced or even denied completely. Under the Public Assistance Committees (PACs)—created under the Local Government Act (1929), which abolished the nineteenth-century Boards of Guardians and transferred their functions to county or county borough councils—terms of relief were actually harsher than the Old Age Pensions Act of 1908, which had only considered cash income and not furniture or savings. The passage of yet another Unemployment Insurance Act (1934) applied an even stricter means test. This counted parents, grandparents, and other aged dependents who collected the dole as tenants and therefore sources of income. This could understandably cause strife between husbands and wives, as well as elderly parents or children who were old enough to contribute to a family's income, and unprecedented numbers of British families broke apart in the 1930s, owing to the stresses of long-term unemployment and financial distress.

The situation reached a low point in 1931, when unemployment reached 23 percent, and even among the employed, conditions were harsh. Seebohm Rowntree reported that life had not much improved since the late nineteenth century, and in York 31 percent of the working population continued to live below the poverty line. In other words, they lacked basic necessities, and the dole—contingent on a low means test—did not meet the level Rowntree calculated was required to keep a family healthy. The slightest setback or unexpected expense was likely to spell disaster. There was considerable regional variation and, as in the previous decade, distress was most severe in the older staple industries, and in towns or regions that had supported, and been supported by, a single industry. Regions that were largely or even totally dependent on coal, steel, shipping, or textiles were devastated.

The formerly bustling coal town of Merthyr Tydfil, in South Wales, experienced 45 percent unemployment throughout the 1930s, and at its worst, in 1934, 62 percent of the town was out of work. In Jarrow, in the northeast of England, Palmer's shipyard had previously employed four out of five of the adult male population. Because of the collapse of British shipping, the yard closed, and the men lost their jobs. The nearby coal and steel industries imploded, and Jarrow became known as "the town that was murdered": there was 68 percent unemployment in the middle of the decade. The resultant Jarrow Crusade, in 1936, was the most famous of the "hunger marches" of the interwar period, in which out-of-work men organized and walked to London to demand government action to bring relief and work to depressed areas. Along the way, as they passed through regions less affected by depression, unemployment, and so on, they sought to draw attention to the widespread suffering in South Wales, northern England, central Scotland, and Northern Ireland (figure 13.3).

If unemployment nationally approached one-quarter, and locally was between two-thirds and fourth-fifths, it is obvious there must have been big parts of the country where it was substantially less. And, indeed, in the Midlands and the South, unemployment was around only 6 percent. There was a savage regional divide in the 1930s, and the North (or "outer" Britain, loosely defining an arc in the west and north from Wales through Lancashire to the northeast) continued to

FIGURE 13.3 Jarrow Marchers en route to London.

suffer the consequences of worldwide economic downturn and long-term unemployment. But in the South (or "inner" Britain, those towns and regions inside that arc and closer to London), the situation was not nearly so baleful. Workers could find jobs in the new "light" industries driven by modern technologies. Electricity output in Britain increased six-fold between the wars, creating jobs producing, selling, and servicing a wide range of electrical appliances for the home. There also were advances in chemistry, spurring employment in plastics and synthetic fibers. Because these new industries did not need to be located close to coalfields, their factories were built closer to consumers, in the Midlands and the South. The London suburbs of Cowley and Dagenham grew up as the centers of the British automobile industry, mass producing vehicles made by Morris and Austen, as well as Ford. British-made vehicles were both sold overseas and bought domestically, and although car ownership remained a luxury beyond the reach of most British families until after World War II, the adoption of assembly line production made prices drop across the 1920s and 1930s. Employment opportunities opened in the field of aeronautics, too.

For those who were able to find steady employment—and this amounted to more than three-quarters of the British population—families enjoyed greater comfort and affluence than ever before. Prices fell but wages were about steady, so purchasing power increased and living standards improved. Owing to reliable steamer schedules and refrigeration, exotic and previously unobtainable products from the empire became commonplace. Nearly every town had a cinema by the mid-1930s, and newspapers acquired mass circulations, with many people taking a daily subscription. The *Daily Herald* and the *Daily Express* each had circulations of over 2 million dailies in 1933, and the total sale of national dailies was around 10 million by 1937. Also, on the eve of World War II there were 11 million radios, or "wireless" sets, in Britain, an average of roughly one set per family. There were 3 million new homes built in the 1930s and, with interest rates low, more British families took the plunge and bought a home, filled with consumer items, often through hire purchase, from department stores such as Marks and Spencer or Woolworths, which had first opened in the UK in 1909 and had four hundred branches in 1930 and six hundred in 1934.

Working hours declined overall, and employers increasingly offered paid vacation to employees and their families. After 1938, they were required to by law. Predictably, there was a burst of activity in resort towns along the coasts and elsewhere, and all these developments spurred the economy's "tertiary" industries, or service sector: There was a new demand for travel agents, staff for hotels, and leisure facilities, bankers, insurers, and advertisers, to say nothing of administrators, secretaries, and clerks.

The lifestyle of the majority of those well-off and secure in "inner" Britain in the 1920s and 1930s was worlds apart from those in the coalfields, the shipyards, and the heavy industrial factories of "outer" Britain and served as stark reminders that we ought to be cautious when generalizing about concepts or experiences as vague as class.

The Persistence of Class

Probably more than anywhere else, modern Britain is often reckoned as the epitome of a class-based society. A common explanation for this emphasis on class lies in the fact that many of the associations that internally divided other countries of Europe were not present in Britain. Regional identity, rivalry between "church and chapel," and divisions between industrial and urban as opposed to agricultural and rural, existed but did not undercut "British" identity in a significant way. To be sure, there could be prejudice driven by the national/cultural differences between the English, Scots, and Welsh—and certainly the Irish—but even these tended to be less acute than comparable hostilities derived from perceived ethnic/racial distinctions on the continent. Britain also differed in that it industrialized earliest, with big implications for social and economic concerns. Most notably, the phenomenal wealth that industrialization generated was concentrated unevenly and produced new tensions.

Wealth or income alone, however, could not explain every aspect of British identity. After all, even with universal male suffrage after 1920 and universal adult suffrage after 1928, the interwar electorate, which was overwhelmingly working class, never once voted to the House of Commons a majority Labour Parliament. Perhaps the human face of Disraelian Tory democracy, revived under Baldwin and Chamberlain, accounts in part for the Conservatives' appeal over the Liberal Party (which had never completely shaken off its mantle of condescending bourgeois self-help) but does not explain why the British public had to wait until 1945 for a Labour majority government. Clearly in Britain political inclination was not defined rigidly by perception of class, or vice versa.

If politics did not correlate neatly to class, neither did money simplify matters much—if at all. Even comparatively small groups, such as the middle classes, could be hard to pin down in Britain. Writing in the 1930s of his upbringing earlier in the twentieth century, the heterodox socialist novelist, essayist, and journalist George Orwell placed his own family in the *upper* middle class, a subcategory he defined, in part, by an annual income falling between £300 and £2,000. Indeed, being "not far from the bottom" of that wide range, Orwell self-identified more specifically with the *lower* upper-middle class.[2] If an income of £300 was the bottom of the upper middle class, and the Compensation Act of 1906 had reckoned an income of £200 as falling in the range of the working classes, it seems plausible to imagine families at the top tier of the working classes overlapping with, or even surpassing, those from the bottom rungs of the lower middle, or even the upper lower middle class (figure 13.4).

The categories used in the 1911 Census suggest a similarly ambiguous dynamic. For all the appeal and conceptual convenience of a tidy system of three distinct socioeconomic groups—lower (or working), middle, and upper class—the Census required, to get an accurate picture, not fewer than five. From bottom to top, and based on type of employment, there was "unskilled," "partly skilled," "skilled," "intermediate," and "professional." Presumably the working classes ranged across the bottom three (and probably four), with the middle classes in the top one (and maybe two) tiers. The upper classes continued to command social, economic, and political influence out of proportion to their actual size at this time (perhaps around 1 percent) but for present purposes are less relevant. Often they went into business (and certainly their sons or brothers or cousins did) or married the daughters of professional men, and in the process their interests aligned with those of the upper echelons of the prosperous upper middle classes.

To generalize about the attitudes, aspirations, and outlook of any vast group of people is always fraught with peril. An essential expedient is to think and argue in expansive and inclusive terms (e.g., the middle

FIGURE 13.4 Orwell's press card portrait, 1943.

classes comprising Orwell's lower, upper, and middle-middle classes) or the working classes (comprising suffering families on the dole as well as those gainfully employed) instead of a monolithic middle class or working class. But even this does not clarify Orwell's example of a "naval officer and his grocer[, who] very likely have the same income, but … are not equivalent persons and … would only be on the same side in very large issues such as a war or a general strike—possibly not even then."[3]

Ultimately, therefore, class in early twentieth-century Britain was not so much a question of socioeconomic identity as it was one of sociocultural identity. It was established through a combination of factors, including education, leisure, dress, sport, habits, associations, tastes in newspapers, and so on, and, perhaps most especially, vocabulary and pronunciation. Many of these subtleties, admittedly, reflected access to wealth or lack thereof—but there was always something more.

In any event, the broad trajectory from the late nineteenth century through the first half of the twentieth century was one of upward mobility with increased security and material comfort. There were regional and local interruptions, notably in the late 1920s and early 1930s, but these were blips on the screen. No matter what the criteria—Census categories, government committee findings, income, car or home ownership, self-identification, or anything else—working-class individuals and families became more stable and advanced to the ranks of the middle classes. The transition was gradual, however, and relatively slight: On the eve of World War II, Britain was still roughly seven to three working class to middle class.

IMAGE CREDITS

Fig. 13.1: Source: https://commons.wikimedia.org/wiki/File:David_Lloyd_George.jpg.

Fig. 13.2: Source: https://commons.wikimedia.org/wiki/File:Genral_Strike_1926.jpg.

Fig. 13.3: Source: https://commons.wikimedia.org/wiki/File:Jarrow_Marchers_en_route_to_London_(3084877308).jpg.

Fig. 13.4: Source: https://commons.wikimedia.org/wiki/File:George_Orwell_press_photo.jpg.

CHAPTER 14

Britain in a World Historical Context

On June 18, 1940, with the Battle of France drawing to close and the Battle of Britain about to begin, Winston Churchill addressed the House of Commons to prepare the country for a long, difficult struggle. He ended the speech with one of his most famous lines: "If the British Empire and its Commonwealth lasts a thousand years, men will still say, 'This was their finest hour.'[1] Finest hour or not, however, the empire would last no more than a score of years, and the commonwealth meant to succeed it would fall far short of expectations. By the time Churchill died in 1965, most of the colonies had become independent nations, and the rest were in process of doing so. His biographer William Manchester declared that Britons who lined the streets of London to see Churchill's coffin pass "mourned, not only him and all he had meant, but all that they had been, and no longer were, and would never be again."[2]

No one knows, of course, what the mourners and the curious onlookers really thought. Nostalgia there certainly was, but Churchill died in the middle of a prosperous decade. Good times had finally come to Britain, especially for the working classes. Ordinary Britons probably worried more about the influx of immigrants from former colonies than they did about the loss of those colonies. The people who had lived so long under British rule certainly welcomed freedom to govern themselves, although they would face a host of problems created by imperialism.

Decolonization, however, forms but one chapter in the complex story of Britain's relationship with the world since the Second World War. During this era, Britain developed its "special relationship" with the United States and strengthened ties with Europe. It was a founding member of the North Atlantic Treaty Organization (NATO) but a late comer to the Common Market and an ambivalent member of the European Union (EU). During the first decades of the twenty-first century, Euro-skepticism grew, and in 2016 the United Kingdom voted to leave the EU. On January 31, 2020, its membership formally ended.

From World War to Cold War

In the popular imagination, the Cold War followed fast on the heels of the Second World War. As early as March 1946, Churchill (out of office since the previous July) warned of the looming ideological struggle between East and West. "From Stettin in the Baltic to Trieste in the Adriatic, an iron curtain has descended across the continent [of Europe]," he told an audience at Westminster College in Fulton, Missouri. "Behind that line lie all the capitals of all the ancient states of Central and Eastern Europe."[3] Churchill's prognostications notwithstanding, many in the West hoped for a continuation of the wartime alliance of great powers. The United States did not feel the need to maintain a large military presence in Europe to counter the Soviets and began withdrawing troops soon after Victory in Europe (VE) Day.

The wartime allies did cooperate in the occupation of Germany and Austria. They initially divided Germany into three zones, but at the Yalta Conference in February 1945 Churchill had insisted France also be given a zone. Stalin agreed, provided that Britain and the United States carved the French zone out of their areas of control. In July, the allies met for the final time, although of the big three wartime leaders only Stalin remained. Harry Truman had become president upon the death of Roosevelt in April, and Clement Attlee had replaced Churchill after the July 5 Labour victory. The Potsdam Conference set up an allied commission to govern Germany and arranged for reparations to the Soviets through movement of industrial equipment between zones. The occupation was supposed to be temporary but had no fixed end date.

The allies also placed great hope in a new international organization dedicated to the preservation of peace. Created in June 1945 to replace the League of Nations, the United Nations (UN) sought "to save succeeding generations from the scourge of war, which twice in our lifetime has brought untold sorrow to mankind." The organization had enforcement powers vested in its Security Council, but their use depended on the cooperation of five permanent members (P5), each of whom could veto any decision: the United States, the Soviet Union, France, Britain, and China. The P5 reflected the power structure of the prewar world, but it would soon become clear that Britain and France had fallen out of the first tier of powerful nations. Chinese communists seized power in 1949, but it would take almost 30 years for the council to transfer China's seat from the nationalists exiled to Taiwan to the new government in Beijing.

Relations between the Soviet Union and the Western allies quickly soured. Stalin made clear that he had no intention of allowing free elections in countries occupied by the Red Army. The Soviets set up puppet states in Eastern and Central Europe. Given the communist commitment to world revolution, the United States and its allies understandably worried that the Kremlin would try to expand its influence if not its direct control over states in Western Europe. Documents made available after the collapse of the Soviet Union suggest that security interests, particularly the creation of a buffer zone in Eastern Europe, motivated the Kremlin more than a desire to spread communism. On the other hand, Stalin was an opportunist contemptuous of anything but military strength. He may have had no plans to extend the Soviet sphere, but he certainly would have exploited a power vacuum.

An early sign of the cold wind about to blow across Europe came in Greece. In the aftermath of Axis withdrawal, royalist and communist guerrillas vied for control of the country. British forces backed the royalists and put down an uprising in Athens in December 1944. Following controversial elections, which the communists boycotted, the civil war reignited in 1946. A year later London announced that it could no longer afford to support the Greek government, an admission that its power was declining. The United States stepped into the breach, supplying Greece with military aid and advisors. The Soviet Union and its allies Yugoslavia, Albania, and Bulgaria backed the communist guerrillas. On March 12, 1947, President Truman requested from Congress $400 million in aid for Greece and Turkey and declared that "it must be the policy of the United States to support free peoples who are resisting attempted subjugation by armed minorities or by outside pressures." The Truman Doctrine, as it came to be called, defined the US approach to halting the spread of communism for the next four decades. The war in Greece dragged on for two more years until the communists withdrew in October 1949.

In the meantime, a more dangerous confrontation with the USSR had arisen over Germany. In February 1948, the United States, France, and Britain met in London to discuss merging their occupation zones into a unified state with a new constitution and currency. The Soviets wanted no part of the plan, which would diminish the Kremlin's control over its zone. When the Western allies announced in March their intention to implement the plan in their occupation zones, the Soviets restricted the flow of military supplies to Berlin, the jointly occupied capital deep in the Soviet zone. Ignoring this shot across the bow, the United States, France, and Britain introduced the new currency on June 23. Stalin responded by closing all rail and road routes from the West into the city.

With the blockade in place, the two sides engaged in the first instance of Cold War brinkmanship. The allies did not want to risk a military confrontation by forcing open the land routes into the city. The Soviets were unwilling to start a war by shooting down allied planes flying supplies into Berlin through the narrow air corridor permitted them. Stalin doubted that the allies could supply the city solely by air. That conclusion proved incorrect. Over the next 11 months British, French, and American aircraft flew in 2.3 million tons of supplies per day.[4] The Royal Air Force carried a quarter of the load.[5] Recognizing that its gambit had failed, the Kremlin lifted the blockade in May 1949. Berlin would remain divided for the next 40 years. The allies created the *Bundesrepulik Deutschland* (Federal Republic of Germany), and the Kremlin established the *Deutsche Demokratische Republic* (German Democratic Republic), commonly known as West and East Germany.

FIGURE 14.1 Berlin airlift, 1948.

NATO

The Berlin Crisis established the pattern for the Cold War. The two sides would face each other across a divided Europe, avoiding direct confrontation for fear of a nuclear holocaust. The United States developed an atomic bomb in 1945, the Soviets in 1949. By the mid-1950s, both sides had far more powerful hydrogen bombs. These weapons made the cost of war between the two super powers unacceptably high. The nuclear stalemate did not, however, make conventional forces obsolete. The United States extended its nuclear umbrella over Western Europe, but the allies would have to delay a Soviet attack long enough for the nuclear card to be played. This strategic reality necessitated deployment of a large conventional force in West Germany.

Initially the Soviets held an overwhelming conventional advantage. Unlike the Americans, they had never run down their forces in Europe at the end of the war. Asked to devise a plan for the defense of Western Europe, Supreme Allied Commander Europe general Dwight Eisenhower concluded he could defend the Pyrenes. The Berlin Crisis spurred the Western allies to action.

Britain played a leading role in securing the March 1948 Treaty of Brussels. This defensive pact signed by the United Kingdom, France, and the Benelux countries declared that

> if any of the High Contracting Parties should be the object of an armed attack in Europe, the other High Contracting Parties will, in accordance with the provisions of Article 51 of the Charter of the United Nations, afford the Party so attacked all the military and other aid and assistance in their power.[6]

By themselves the signatories stood no chance against the Soviet Union, but the treaty contained an article that allowed for expansion: "The High Contracting Parties may, by agreement, invite any other State to accede to the present Treaty on conditions to be agreed between them and the State so invited."[7] This clause opened the door for the creation of a broader alliance. A year later the Western European defensive pact became an Atlantic alliance. The United States, Canada, Iceland, Denmark, Norway, Italy, and Portugal joined the members of the Brussels Accord to sign the North Atlantic Treaty in April 1949. The members of NATO agreed that "an armed attack against one or more of them in Europe or North America shall be considered an attack against them all" and that they would come to one another's defense.[8] Lionel Hastings, Lord Ismay, NATO's first Secretary General, quipped that the purpose of the alliance was "to keep the Soviet Union out, the Americans in, and the Germans down."[9] It certainly accomplished the first two objectives. West Germany, however, recovered quickly and thrived. In order to have enough troops to defend Western Europe, the allies rearmed West Germany, creating the *Bundeswehr* (federal military) in 1955, but situated its general staff within the NATO command structure to allay fears of the other members. The Soviets responded to these developments by creating their own alliance, the Warsaw Pact, in 1955. The two alliances would face each other across a divided Europe for the next 34 years.

NATO became a cornerstone of British defense and foreign policy in the postwar world. The alliance required the United Kingdom to bear the expense of a major military deployment in Germany. The United Kingdom also cultivated the "special relationship" with the United States. By positioning itself as America's closest ally in Europe and even supporting US foreign policy farther abroad, Britain played a role in world affairs greater than its actual wealth and power might have allowed. This status would, to some degree, cushion the psychological blow of imperial decline. The United Kingdom made a sizeable troop contribution to UN forces during the Korean Conflict (1950–1953) and the Iraq War (2003), even though the latter did not enjoy popular support in Britain. The United States in turn raised no objections to Britain's war with Argentina over the Falkland Islands in 1982.

The United Kingdom also benefitted enormously from US economic assistance. In his June 1947 speech at Harvard University, Secretary of State George Marshall floated the idea of a massive aid program for European reconstruction. As a condition of this aid, Washington asked European nations to prioritize their needs. British Foreign Secretary Ernest Bevin worked with his French counterpart Georges Bidault to hold a 16-nation conference in Paris to address this issue. Bevin wished Britain to play a leading role in devising the European plan and sought to keep the Soviets from blocking it. He lobbied US under-secretary of state William Clayton unsuccessfully for a separate aid package to deal with the United Kingdom's severe balance of payments crisis. In cooperation with Clayton and Bidault, however, Bevin succeeded in securing agreement for a collective assessment of needs over Soviet objections. Eastern bloc nations would get no American money, but neither could the Soviets obstruct the plan.

Truman signed the Economic Cooperation Act on April 3, 1948, allocating over $13 billion for reconstruction aid, of which Britain got the largest share, $2.7 billion over four years.[10] Bevin had achieved a diplomatic triumph, but unfortunately his government did not spend the aid money wisely. Instead of investing it and the $4 billion it had borrowed from the United States at the end of the war in infrastructure and industrial modernization, the Labour government wasted it in a vein effort to prop up Britain's position as a world power and leader of the sterling zone.[11]

NUCLEAR ARMAMENT

The formation of NATO and redeployment of US troops to Europe reassured Britain but did not alleviate all its security concerns. Washington pledged to defend Western Europe, with nuclear weapons, but no one could be sure whether that pledge would be honored. London wanted direct control of British security. To ensure that control, it decided to acquire its own nuclear arsenal. Although British scientists had contributed to the success of the Manhattan Project, which produced the atomic bombs dropped on Japan, the United States stopped sharing information with the United Kingdom in 1946. The following year Britain launched a plan to acquire its own nuclear weapons. It developed a working atomic bomb in 1952 and a hydrogen bomb in 1957. The British initially relied on manned bombers as a delivery system but transitioned to American-made Polaris submarine-launched ballistic missiles (SLBMs) in the 1960s and Trident SLBMs in the 1990s.

Being a member of the nuclear club did not enhance British military power or diplomatic status. The American arsenal, not the British one, deterred the Soviets. London played virtually no role in the 1962 Cuban Missile Crisis. When President John Kennedy decided to impose a selective blockade on Cuba in response to Soviet deployment of missiles to the island, he did not even send a representative to explain his decision to the British government. He did, however, dispatch envoys to Paris and Bonn (the capital of West Germany). This slight angered the Macmillan government, which, nonetheless, supported Kennedy. Some members of the opposition Labour Party and media commentators, however, questioned the wisdom of Britain's unconditional support for Washington.[12]

Not everyone in United Kingdom agreed with its nuclear weapons program. In 1958, the Campaign for Nuclear Disarmament (CND) formed and held a mass rally in London, followed by marches and demonstrations throughout the country. The movement may have encouraged the British government to sign the 1963 Nuclear Test Ban and 1968 Non-Proliferation Treaties. The CND experienced a revival in the early 1980s in response to the Cruise Missile Crisis. To counter the deployment of Soviet SS20 missiles in Eastern Europe, the administration of US President Ronald Reagan deployed nuclear-tipped intermediate-range cruise

FIGURE 14.2 CND rally.

missiles at sites in Western Europe, including the British airbase at Greenham Commons. Prime Minister Margaret Thatcher, a close Reagan ally, enthusiastically supported the plan, but many Britons did not. Less than a decade after the deployment, however, the Cold War came to an abrupt end.

KOREAN CONFLICT

Whatever strains it underwent in the 1960s, the special relationship had proven sound during its first test a decade earlier. In June 1950, North Korean Forces crossed the 38th parallel and invaded South Korea. The UN Security Council met to discuss the crisis. The Soviet ambassador had absented himself from the meeting to protest the council's refusal to give China's seat to the victorious communists. As a result, he could not veto a resolution condemning the North Korean invasion and authorizing a UN mission to expel it from South Korea.

The United States rushed in troops from occupied Japan to maintain a toehold on the southern tip of the peninsula until reinforcements could arrive from home. Washington also called on Britain to contribute to the UN mission. Engaged in costly rearmament to maintain its contribution to NATO forces in Europe amid postwar austerity and while it was battling a communist insurgency in Malaya, London did not welcome the call to take on another military commitment.

Reliant on US foreign aid, however, it could not afford to turn down a direct American request for help. The United Kingdom contributed more than 90,000 troops to the fight and lost 1,078 of them.[13] The war ended in a ceasefire and return to the prewar boundary between north and south, which persists to this day.

Decolonization

On February 3, 1960, Conservative Prime Minister Harold Macmillan addressed a joint session of the two houses of the Union of South Africa Parliament. "The wind of change is blowing through this continent," he declared, "and, whether we like it or not, this growth of national consciousness is a political fact. We must all accept it as fact, and our national policies must take account of it."[14] The "wind of change" speech has widely been seen as the curtain call of the British Empire, the moment at which the United Kingdom formally acknowledged the inevitable loss of colonial holdings that only 15 years before had spanned almost a quarter of the earth's land surface. Symbolic though it may have been, Macmillan's speech merely acknowledged a process that had been unfolding for some time.

Independence was not a reward Britain granted magnanimously to its subjugated people in thanks for their contribution to defeating the Axis powers, nor was it a paternalistic gesture of recognition that they had "matured" enough for self-government. The demand for independence had been growing since at least the late nineteenth century, and by 1945 it had become irresistible. Continued occupation could be maintained only through military force, which Britain could not afford and which the world would no longer tolerate. The process of decolonization may best be examined by dividing British territories intro three broad categories based on how the transition to independence occurred: South Asia, which is a unique case; possessions that transitioned peacefully; and colonies that gained independence after or as a result of violent conflict.

SOUTH ASIA

As discussed in chapters 8 and 12, nationalism in South Asia began in the nineteenth century and developed steadily during the first half of the twentieth. While moderates initially accepted the idea of autonomy within the British Empire, militant nationalists did not. The grudging slowness with which Britain granted autonomy by degrees combined with repressive measures epitomized by the Amritsar Massacre drew moderates and radicals together around the demand for complete independence. By the outbreak of the Second World War, the question was no longer if but when India would receive full independence.

At the start of hostilities, the Indian National Congress asked Britain for a declaration that India would be granted independence when the war ended. The viceroy flatly refused. Nonetheless, more than two million Indian soldiers served the king/emperor, and 89,000 of them made the ultimate sacrifice.[15] Despite this contribution, the British implemented wartime measures in an arrogant, authoritarian, and inequitable manner. The government provided assistance to Europeans fleeing the Japanese advance while leaving South Asian refugees to fend for themselves. The army requisitioned land, buildings, and vehicles, often with inadequate compensation to the owners. They destroyed boats along the coast to prevent the Japanese using them, thus denying locals their source of income. Badly implemented price controls produced famine in Bengal. Japan's rapid conquest of Malaya, Singapore, and Burma thus exposed Britain's weakness at the same time the government's coercive measures revealed its indifference to Indian suffering.[16]

In response to British intransigence, the Indian National Congress drafted the "quit-India" resolution in April 1942, and the All-India Congress adopted it in August. The resolution declared that Japan's quarrel was with the British Empire, not India, and called on Britain to quit the subcontinent. The resolution backed its demand with the threat of civil disobedience. Considerable evidence suggests that the Congress intended the resolution as a tactic to pressure the government into making concessions.[17] Nonetheless, the British treated it as a security threat and arrested Gandhi and other Congress leaders. The movement never got off the ground, but resentment of the Raj deepened.

Demands for independence intensified with the end of the war. In 1945, the British tried three high-ranking officers of the Indian National Army, which had fought with the Japanese, for treason. All three were convicted, but many Indians considered them heroes fighting for independence. Under popular pressure, the government commuted their sentences. Then in 1946, a large-scale mutiny rocked Royal Navy vessels at Bombay. It seemed that the military the British had created to defend their rule had become a source and purveyor of national identity.[18] Britain could ill afford the cost of governing the Raj in the face of increasing noncooperation and outright resistance. To make matters worse, tensions between Muslims and Hindus were rising, and serious intercommunal violence occurred during 1946–1947. Negotiations among the government, the National Congress, and the Muslim League resulted in a partition plan. Britain announced that it would quit India in June 1948, but the last viceroy, Lord Louis Mountbatten, advanced the date to August 1947. The Raj would be divided into two states: a Hindu majority India and a Muslim majority Pakistan. Both were initially dominions under the British Crown, but India became a republic in 1950 and Pakistan in 1956. Partition sparked mass migration and intercommunal violence that killed more than a million people. British India's remaining territories, Burma and Ceylon (which became Sri Lanka in 1972), received independence in early 1948.

PEACEFUL TRANSITIONS

South Asia had been not only "the jewel in the Crown" but also the lynchpin of empire. Its loss removed the justification for keeping colonies acquired as "inns on the road to India." Indian nationalists, who had gotten the British to leave without a firing a shot, inspired anticolonial movements throughout the empire. Most colonies gained independence without violent conflict.

One individual epitomizes the inspiration Gandhi provided for nationalists. Born in the British colony of Gold Coast in 1909, Kwame Nkrumah was educated in the United States before returning to his homeland in 1949. Inspired by both Gandhi and the American civil rights movement and dissatisfied with the slow pace by which Britain was granting autonomy, he founded the Convention People's Party. Under the motto "Self-government now," the party engaged in strikes

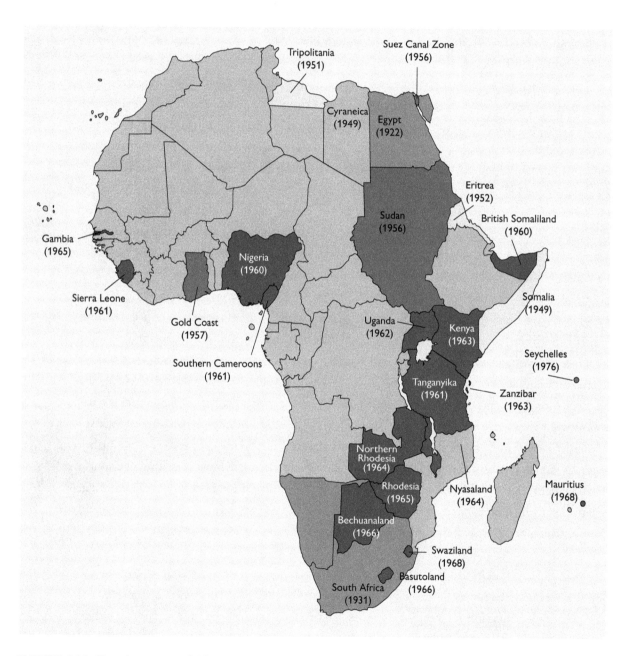

FIGURE 14.3 Decolonization of Africa.

and other forms of noncooperation. The British arrested Nkrumah in January 1950 but released him after his party won the legislative election by a landslide in February 1951. He became the first prime minister of the autonomous Gold Coast and continued to agitate for full independence. On March 6, 1957, Gold Cost and the British colonies of Ashanti, Northern Territories, and British Togoland were merged into the independent state of Ghana with Nkrumah as its first prime minister. Three years later he held a constitutional referendum that transformed Ghana into a republic of which he was elected the first president.

Ghana became the model for other African colonies.[19] Nigeria and British Somaliland became independent in 1960. Sierra Leon, Tanganyika (which later combined with Zanzibar to become Tanzania), and British Cameroon got independence in 1961, and Uganda in 1962. By 1970, Britain's remaining African colonies had achieved independence. In the Caribbean, Jamaica and Trinidad and Tobago became independent in 1962, along with the Pacific island of Samoa the same year.

The remnants of the British Empire in the Middle East, the Caribbean, and Asia lasted a bit longer. Bahrain and Qatar received independence in 1971. The Bahamas stayed until 1973, as did Grenada until 1974. The remaining Caribbean possessions left over the next decade, as did British Honduras (Belize) in 1981, although Britain maintained a military presence in the country until 1994 because of a border dispute with neighboring Honduras. In Asia, Brunei gained independence in 1984, by which time all remaining Asian colonies except Hong Kong had gone. In 1984, the United Kingdom reached an agreement with Beijing on the process for returning Hong Kong to the People's Republic of China in 1997.

A handful of colonies have chosen to remain British Overseas Territories. In 1995, residents of Bermuda opted for that status. British residents of Gibraltar voted overwhelmingly in 2002 to reject joint sovereignty with Spain. In 2013, virtually all residents of the Falkland Islands voted to remain with the United Kingdom. The British Monarch, thus, can still claim to rule "British realms beyond the sea," few though they may be.

WARS OF DECOLONIZATION

While the United Kingdom avoided any long, debilitating conflict like the ones that forced French withdrawal from Indochina and Algeria, not all of its territories transitioned to independence peacefully. The worst conflicts arose in colonies with ethnic divisions. The British faced insurgencies that complicated the process of withdrawal. In some cases, they sided with one faction; in others they left the belligerents to battle it out on their own.

Palestine had been a source of conflict since its inception as a League of Nation's mandate under British trusteeship. The local Arab population resented the influx of Jewish immigrants, which increased dramatically after the Nazis came to power in Germany. The British took three years to suppress an Arab Revolt that ended with the 1939 White Paper, which promised an end to Jewish immigration. The Holocaust made that promise impossible to keep. Dependent on US foreign

FIGURE 14.4 King David Hotel Bombing, Jerusalem, 1946.

aid, Britain acquiesced to American demands that more Jews be allowed to enter Palestine. Other refugees ran the British blockade to enter the mandate. In 1945, Zionist groups launched an insurgency against British rule. After two years of limited conflict in which fewer than 150 British soldiers and police and 50 insurgents died, Britain announced it would turn the mandate over to the UN and withdraw.[20] Zionist leaders proclaimed the establishment of the state of Israel on May 14, 1948, the day before the mandate formally ended. The first Arab-Israeli War ensued.

The British fared better in the Federation of Malaya, where a communist insurgency broke out in 1948. The insurgency remained largely confined to the Chinese minority community while most of the Malay population supported the government. The colonial administration used a combination of reform to address legitimate grievances of Chinese laboring on rubber plantations with forced relocation and limited military action to defeat the insurgents in a 12-year campaign.

By far the bloodiest conflict at the end of empire occurred in the East African colony of Kenya. In 1952, a group known as the "Land and Freedom Army" began attacking white settlers. Desire for land and greater political autonomy spurred the younger generation of the Kikuyu tribe to launch what the British called the Mau Mau Rebellion. During the eight-year insurgency, as many 25,000 Kenyans may have been killed, 100,000 detained without trial, and many tortured.[21] The Kikuyu Home Guard perpetrated some of the worst atrocities, but Britain bore ultimate responsibility for the campaign. In 2013, the British government agreed to pay £20 million compensation to victims. Kenya received independence in 1963.

Violence also broke out on the island of Cyprus. In 1955, a Greek insurgency sough to expel the British and unite the island with Greece proper, against the wishes of its Turkish minority. After defeating the insurgents, Britain granted the island independence in 1960 in return for sovereignty over its military bases there. In 1974, Turkey invaded Cyprus and enforced a partition into Turkish and Greek republics.

SUEZ CRISIS

The accelerated pace of decolonization from the late 1950s owes much to an international incident that laid bare British weakness in the postwar world. Since Britain had gained control of the waterway in the late nineteenth century, the Suez Canal had been the lifeline of empire, the shortest transit route from Britain to East Africa and Asia. Even with the loss of India, many in Whitehall, including Prime Minister Anthony Eden, considered retaining control of it vital to British interests. On July 26, 1956, President Gamal Abdul Nasser of Egypt nationalized the canal. The Egyptian government could now keep the revenue from tolls charged for its use. Eden commenced diplomatic efforts to have it re-internationalized but also prepared to reclaim it by force.

Lacking a strong legal case or UN support for military action, Eden joined the French and the Israelis in an elaborate plot to create a pretext for occupying the canal zone. A confluence of interests drew the plotters together. Britain had strategic and economic interests in the canal. France wanted to get rid of Nasser, who supported insurgents seeking to end French colonial rule in neighboring Algeria, and Israel viewed the presence of Egyptian forces in the Sinai as a threat to its security. From October 22 to 24, 1956, representatives of the three states held a secret meeting at Sevres, France, where they signed a protocol formalizing the plan. The stratagem proposed by the French and agreed to by Eden and the Israelis required Israel to attack the Egyptians in Sinai. The French and British would then demand that both sides withdraw 10 miles from the canal. If they failed to pull back, Anglo-French forces would occupy the canal zone, ostensibly to separate the belligerents, but in reality to seize the canal.[22]

The rouse fooled no one. British and French military preparations to reoccupy the canal zone had begun soon after its nationalization and could not be hidden. Efforts to portray Nasser as a Soviet puppet rather than an Arab nationalist failed. The UN did not support the operation nor did the United States. Israel attacked on October 29, and the British and French announced their intention to separate the belligerents. Air and naval bombardment began on the 31st and lasted until November 6. Troops occupied the northern end of the canal zone during the last 2 days of the operation.

President Dwight Eisenhower rightly feared hostilities might escalate to a major power confrontation. Egypt had received Soviet military aide, and Washington worried that the Kremlin might back its ally more directly. Americans also had no love for the British Empire. The Eisenhower administration blocked an International Monetary Fund loan to Britain and threatened to sell its sterling bonds, which would have led to devaluation of the British pound. London folded under the pressure. The UN deployed its first peacekeeping mission to the Sinai, and Anglo-French forces withdrew from the canal zone. In the face of this humiliating defeat, Eden resigned in disgrace and went into retirement.

The Suez crisis dispelled any remaining illusions about Britain's place in the world. A second-tier power, it could no longer act unilaterally. In all but the most localized foreign policy moves it would

FIGURE 14.5 British paratroopers land in Suez Canal Zone, 1956.

have to consult Washington and defer to the United States as leader of the free world. The crisis also dispelled the notion that Britain needed a large land base to project power east of Suez. It would make one more abortive try to establish a military presence in the region. From 1964 to 1967, British troops backed the government of South Arabia against communist insurgents with the hope of retaining control of the port of Aden with its British Petroleum oil refinery and naval base. They soon got bogged down in a costly counterinsurgency campaign that proved unsustainable and withdrew. Three years later, however, British forces aided the Sultan of Oman in defeating a communist insurgency led from South Yemen. The United Kingdom still maintained economic and political influence in the Middle East but could only be involved directly at the request of a host nation.

RHODESIAN CRISIS

Perhaps the most difficult transition to independence occurred in Southern Rhodesia. Originally called South Zambezia, the colony originated as a fiefdom of the British South Africa company led by Cecil Rhodes, who had gained mineral rights in the territory in 1888. In 1890, the Crown recognized company control, which lasted until 1923 when the British government annexed Southern Rhodesia as a colony with local autonomy following a referendum in favor of self-government rather than incorporation into the Union of South Africa.

Unfortunately, for the governing elite, autonomy meant white minority rule, which they wished to perpetuate into the postcolonial world. The Labour government of Harold Wilson refused to grant independence on terms other than equality for the colony's African population. On November 11, 1965, Southern Rhodesia, under the leadership of its white prime minister Ian Smith, issued a unilateral declaration of independence. Britain chose not to use force against the renegade colony, a decision that seemed hypocritical given its willingness to shed blood in defense of White settlers in Kenya threatened by the Mau Mau but not on behalf of Black Rhodesian's opposing an apartheid government.[23] Britain imposed sanctions against the new Republic of Rhodesia, but these had little effect. A bloody insurgency between the white government and African freedom fighters ensued and lasted until 1979. Following a peace agreement, the Rhodesian Parliament voted to revert to colonial status. Britain reoccupied the country, which it granted independence as the Republic of Zimbabwe in 1980.

THE LEGACY OF EMPIRE

The British Empire died with a whimper rather than a bang. Few Britons and virtually no colonial subjects shed a tear over its demise. The best that can be said of its passing is that with the exception of India and a few counterinsurgency campaigns, transitions from colonies to independent states occurred relatively smoothly and with less loss of life than occurred during the demise of the French empire. The British left behind a cadre of well-educated bureaucrats and professionals capable of governing. Some in Britain insist to this day that the empire served as midwife to a host of new democracies. This claim contains a grain of truth but hides a great lie. The damage colonialism did to Indigenous societies contributed to the instability of the postcolonial era. Many of today's global hotspots have their origin in British colonialism. Then too, imperialism did not completely end with the demise of the empire. British economic, political, and even military influence continued long after the last colonial governors ran down their Union Jacks.

Commonwealth

As the empire declined, some British leaders believed it could be transitioned into a voluntary union of allied states under the British Crown. In the late nineteenth century politicians had begun referring to a "commonwealth" consisting of the semiautonomous dominions, but the first use of the term in a legislative document occurred in the 1921 Anglo-Irish Treaty as part of the oath of allegiance required of Irish Free State MPs. The Statute of Westminster (1931) recognized the "free association of members of the British Commonwealth of Nations," which included the Irish Free State, Canada, Newfoundland (which later became part of Canada), and the Union of South Africa, and acknowledged the sovereignty of their parliaments. New Zealand and Australia formally joined the commonwealth in the 1940s (even though they had long considered themselves members). The statute also asserted that the members would have to approve any change to the law of succession to the British Crown under which they united, a provision that would prove crucial in the succession crisis of 1937. In 1932, the Commonwealth of Nations met for the first time in Ottawa, Canada, to discuss collective economic policy. Members agreed to five years of "imperial preference," a system of free trade or at least reduced tariffs among member nations.

As colonies gained independence, many of them joined the commonwealth as independent states. The London Declaration of 1949 facilitated expansion by removing the adjective "British" from its name and recognizing the British monarch as head of the Commonwealth of Nations but not head of state of each member. The change allowed republics like India to join. That same year, the Republic of Eyre, successor to the Irish Free State, left the commonwealth, followed in 1961 by South Africa, which exited in response to criticism of apartheid. Today the commonwealth has 52 member states.

The commonwealth never lived up to British expectations. Imperial preference did not confer the advantages on the British economy London had hoped. The United Kingdom's trade deficit remained, and the value of the pound continued to decline during the postwar years. Other than staging the Commonwealth Games, the organization has accomplished little. By the 1960s, many in Britain considered that the future of the United Kingdom lay with Europe rather than with an association of former colonies.

International Conflicts

Since the wars of decolonization Britain has been engaged in several international conflicts. Each conflict revealed Britain's limited ability to project power abroad and its dependence on the special relationship with the United States. Throughout the post–World War II era, the United Kingdom steadily reduced the size of its military out of economic necessity. By May 2017, its armed forces consisted of just 138,350 active-duty personnel in all services supported by 58,040 reservists.[24]

The only war Britain fought alone seemed more like an episode from the Victorian era than a modern conflict. On April 2, 1982, the military dictatorship of Argentina invaded the Falkland Islands (which it called the Malvinas) and South Georgia, British Overseas Territories off its southern coast, which Argentines had long considered part of their country. The junta launched the invasion to stir patriotic support for its regime, and the government of Margaret Thatcher responded based on a similar domestic agenda. Occupation of the islands, home to 1,800 British subjects, was certainly a violation of international law, but the affair might have been resolved peacefully. Thatcher, however, eschewed diplomacy and sent an expedition to the South Atlantic. The brief war that followed resulted in the deaths of approximately 655 Argentine and 255 British service personnel and the loss of several ships on both sides. Britain recovered the islands and Thatcher became the "Iron Lady" in the popular imagination. She called a snap (early) election the same year and rode a wave of patriotic populism to a sweeping victory.

A decade later the Iron Lady tried to pull off a similar foreign policy coup. This time Britain joined a 750,000-strong coalition led by the United States to expel Saddam Hussein from Kuwait, which he had invaded in August 1990. As UK troops deployed but before the first shots were fired, however, Thatcher fell from power, ousted by her own Conservative Party. The air campaign against Iraq began on January 17 and the ground assault on February 24. With its superior technology and resources, the coalition overwhelmed the Iraqis, who surrendered on February 28. Britain contributed 43,000 troops plus air and naval assets, the largest contingent of European forces in the coalition but a small percentage of the total military strength, and lost 47 service personnel. Saddam Hussein withdrew from Kuwait but remained in power.

Britain also became embroiled in the wars of Yugoslav succession. The federated state broke apart with the secession of Slovenia, Croatia, and Macedonia in 1991, followed by Bosnia-Herzegovina in early 1992. The multiethnic makeup of Bosnia virtually guaranteed civil war, which broke out in the spring. The United Kingdom contributed more than 3,000 troops to the UN peacekeeping missions in Croatia and Bosnia-Herzegovina from 1992 to 1995. British paratroopers helped lift the siege of Sarajevo in August 1991, and British forces remained to staff the follow-on International Force deployed to enforce the peace settlement.

By 1998, trouble had spread to the once autonomous Serbian province of Kosovo, where insurgents from the minority Albanian population fought a repressive regime in Belgrade. In March 1999, the United States led a 78-day air campaign supported by the Royal Airforce to compel withdrawal of Serbian forces from Kosovo. British troops then participated in NATO's Kosovo Force (KFOR), which provided security in the province.

The 9/11 terrorist attacks once again drew Britain into a war in support of its powerful ally. For the first time in its history, NATO invoked Article 5 of its founding treaty, declaring the al-Qaeda attack on the United States an attack on the alliance as a whole. On October 26, the British government announced that it would contribute 4,200 troops to the coalition invading Afghanistan, where Osama bin Laden (the al-Qaeda leader) had his base of operations. The Afghan capital Kabul fell on November 13, and Kandahar, the last stronghold of the Taliban government, capitulated on December 7. British troops remained in country until 2014 as part of the International Stabilization Force (ISAF), supporting the new Afghan government while combatting al-Qaeda and Taliban insurgents.

Soon after the occupation of Afghanistan, the United States decided to invade Iraq. President George W. Bush and his advisors tried to connect Saddam Hussein to al-Qaeda and argued that he might provide the terrorists with weapons of mass destruction. Most NATO allies were not persuaded, but Britain joined the US-led coalition to invade and occupy the country. The war sparked protests and opposition from members of Prime Minister Tony Blair's own Labour Party. Nonetheless, British land forces occupied Basra during the invasion of March 2003 and remained for the counterinsurgency campaign. The affair proved to be a sad episode. Despite initial braggadocio over their prowess developed during the thirty-year conflict in Northern Ireland, British troops performed poorly. The United Kingdom withdrew its forces in 2009 having lost 179 service personnel. Most British subjects considered those lives to have been wasted.

In retaliation for Britain's participation in these coalitions, al-Qaeda carried out terrorist attacks against the United Kingdom. On July 7, 2005, three terrorists detonated bombs on the London underground while a fourth blew himself up on a bus in the city. Fifty-six people died, including the four terrorists. All four men were British subjects operating under al-Qaeda's instructions. Two weeks later, a second attack on the London underground failed when the terrorists' bombs failed to detonate. In 2007, British intelligence foiled a plot to blow up airliners flying from Heathrow Airport across the Atlantic. The radicalization of all these home-grown terrorists may have stemmed in part from their treatment by white Britons. The attacks definitely increased Islamophobia within the United Kingdom, which in turn may have led to more radicalization and more attacks. On March 22, 2017, a Muslim British man acting on behalf of the Islamic State in Iraq and Syria (ISIS) killed 23 people attending a concert at the Manchester Arena.

INTERVENTION IN LIBYA

Though it was usually drawn into foreign wars by the United States, Britain did sometimes take initiative and request support from Washington. In the spring of 2011, Prime Minister David Cameron and French President Nicolas Sarkozy urged air action in defense of Libyan insurgents trying to overthrow Muammar Gaddafi in an Arab Spring uprising. Britain had good reason to dislike the Libyan dictator. For years he had supported the Provisional Irish Republican Army, and Libyan agents had downed Pan Am Flight 103 over Lockerbie, Scotland, in 1988. The French and British also sought to stop the flow of refugees from Libya to Europe and wished to secure the continued flow of Libyan oil into the world market. In the final analysis, however, Cameron and Sarkozy may have acted out of a desire to show that their countries still mattered on the international stage.[25]

Whatever their motives, the two leaders persuaded the UN to sanction the mission and the administration of President Barack Obama to support it with US military assets. Gaddafi was overthrown and killed, but the rebel victory did not bring stability to Libya. A 2016 House of Commons Foreign Affairs Committee report was scathingly critical of the Cameron government for embarking on the ill-conceived Libyan intervention with no plan for a post-conflict stability mission. As a result, ISIS expanded its influence in North Africa.[26]

The Challenge of European Integration

"We are with Europe, but not of it," Winston Churchill wrote in a February 15, 1930, article for the *Saturday Evening Post*. "We are linked but not combined. We are interested and associated but not absorbed."[27] The future prime minister not only described the prevailing isolationism of interwar

Britain but a long-established popular attitude that would persist into the twenty-first century. Britons had long believed in their country's exceptionalism. The island nation had developed from a kingdom on the periphery of Europe into the epicenter of a global empire. Even after that empire had disappeared the belief that the United Kingdom stood apart remained.

For all its claims of uniqueness, however, Britain had always been intimately involved in continental affairs. It had participated in most of Europe's major wars since 1688. During the heyday of industrialization and empire in the nineteenth century, the continent, not the colonies, provided the largest market for its exports. Britain was also a founding member of NATO, though it has always wanted to keep the organization an Atlantic rather than a purely European alliance. The historic tension between belief in British exceptionalism and the reality of interdependence with continental states virtually guaranteed that the United Kingdom would approach European unity tentatively and with a degree of ambivalence, drawn to the benefits of economic integration but warry of closer political ties.

BRITAIN AND THE COMMON MARKET

What would evolve into the EU began as an effort to integrate the economies of Europe to such an extent that conflict between them would become impossible. The first formal step toward European integration took place in 1951 when the Treaty of Paris created the European Coal and Steel Community (ECSC). France, West Germany, Italy, and the Benelux countries agreed to place their coal and steel industries under a single authority and to create an advisory commission and a consultative assembly, which would evolve into the European Parliament. The members of the ECSC expanded cooperation with the Treaty of Rome in 1957. The treaty set up the European Economic Community (EEC, also known as the Common Market), a customs union committed to removing all tariff barriers between members states over a 12-year period. It also created the European Atomic Energy Community. The treaty promised further integration in the near future, vowing in its preamble "to lay the foundations of an ever-closer union among the peoples of Europe."[28]

At first, Britain not only remained aloof from the process of integration but sought to create an alternative to the Common Market. In 1960, it championed the creation of the European Free Trade Association (EFTA) committed to economic cooperation without the political integration toward which the EEC was moving. With the United Kingdom the only heavy weight among a group of smaller economies (Austria, Denmark, Norway, Sweden, and Switzerland) and the EEC refusing to cooperate with it, the EFTA proved disappointing. Within a year of creating the alternative association, the United Kingdom formally applied for membership in the Common Market. It would soon find its own ambivalence toward the continent matched by continental skepticism toward its commitment to Europe.

British reluctance to join first the ECSC and then the EEC rested on three issues: the commonwealth; the "special relationship" with the United States; and concern about loss of sovereignty.

Commonwealth nations could trade with the United Kingdom on preferential terms, creating the potential for transshipping their goods through Britain to the protected EEC zone to which the EEC objected. As America's closest ally in Europe, the United Kingdom enjoyed influence beyond its real power in NATO and further abroad. London feared a diminution of that stature if it became but one of many states in a federated Europe. Finally, Britons had a strong sense of national sovereignty that they did not wish to compromise. Fear of losing that independence may have been exaggerated, but it was powerful.[29]

Some leaders on the continent had their own doubts about Britain's suitability for membership in the European Union. French president Charles de Gaulle considered Britain different from other members and feared that admitting it to the Common Market would open the door to unwanted American influence. He vetoed Britain's application for membership, first in 1963 and again in 1967. The third time was a charm, however. By the time Britain applied again in 1973, de Gaulle had retired and attitudes in Britain and Europe had changed. Along with Ireland and Denmark, the United Kingdom joined what had become the European Community (EC).

EUROPEAN UNION ACCORDS AND DISCORD

Membership in the EC did not end Euro-skepticism. Britain wanted free movement of goods, labor, and capital within the Common Market, but it remained far less enthusiastic about the continued political evolution of the organization. Conservative prime minister Margaret Thatcher was stridently opposed to further integration. Nonetheless, in 1987 Britain agreed to the Single European Act, which increased the legislative power of the European Parliament and the regulatory authority of the Brussels bureaucracy. However, the Maastricht Accords (also known as the Treaty on European Union) proved far mor contentious. Before the Conservatives would consider ratifying the accord, Prime Minister John Major had to secure an opt-out clause to exempt Britain from the agreement's social provisions. Even then, the House of Commons approved the agreement in 1991 by a narrow margin and only after Major threatened to resign if his own back-benchers failed to get in line. The Maastricht Accords formally created the European Union, established European citizenship, facilitated closer police and judicial cooperation, and laid the groundwork for a common security and foreign policy.

Britain refused to be a party to another epic accord, which went into effect in 1995. Signed in 1985, the Schengen Agreement removed internal borders between five EEC members. With the expansion of the EU since the mid-1990s, the number of countries in the Schengen Zone rose to 26. The United Kingdom had good reason not to open its borders. Embroiled in a long struggle in Northern Ireland, London feared that terrorists could easily enter the United Kingdom from the Republic of Ireland via the continent. The refugee crisis in the second decade of the twenty-first century strengthened Britain's commitment to keeping its borders with other EU members closed.

The United Kingdom also refused to adopt the new EU currency. A 1999 agreement created the Euro, which went into circulation in 2002. As a world banking center, London feared losing control over fiscal policy and being forced to conform to regulations restricting its debt to GDP ratio. The 2007–2008 Greek debt crisis followed by weakness in the Slovene, Italian, and Portuguese economies, left the strong Euro nations on the hook for propping up the weaker ones. Once again, British Euro-skepticism seemed in retrospect to have been well founded. British taxpayers were spared the pain and resentment of their German counterparts who had to subsidize the Greek bail out.

Britain was by no means the sole bastion of Euro-skepticism. After the turn of the new century, an increasing number of EU citizens believed that expansion and integration had gone too far, too fast. The 2004 Rome agreement on a new constitution foundered when France and the Netherlands failed to ratify it. Undaunted the member states signed the Treaty of Lisbon in 2007. The agreement strengthened the European Parliament, made the Charter of Fundamental Rights drafted in 2000 legally binding, and made the president of the European Council an official, full-time position with a 2.5-year term. The treaty also contained a secession clause with a process for a state to leave the EU. By the end of November 2009, all member states had ratified the treaty, which went into effect on December 1, 2009.

BREXIT AND BEYOND

Popular discontent with the EU had been growing in the United Kingdom since the Maastricht Accords. The UK Independence Party, formed in 1993, had little hope of winning seats at Westminster, but it did increasingly well in elections for the European Parliament, coming in third in 2004, second in 2009, and first in 2014. The major political parties could hardly ignore this degree of popular discontent. In 2015, the Conservative Party included a promise to hold a referendum on remaining in the EU in its election manifesto. Following their electoral victory, the Tories passed the European Union Referendum Act. The act stipulated that a referendum be held no later than December 31, 2017, on the question "Should the United Kingdom remain a member of the European Union or leave the European Union?"[30] The government held the referendum on June 23, 2016, and to the shock of opponents and supporters of "Brexit" (short for "British exit") alike, British subjects voted 51.3 to 48.9 percent to leave the EU with a voter turnout of 71.8 percent.[31] On March 29, 2017, Prime Minister Theresa May, who had replaced David Cameron after the Brexit vote, triggered Article 50 of the Lisbon Treaty, formally beginning the process of leaving the union.

Debate over why Britons voted to leave the EU has been as intense and at times as acrimonious as the argument over the referendum itself. The cost of membership, resentment over the Brussels bureaucracy, and objection to excessive regulation have been offered as explanations for the outcome. None of these reasons nor the sum of them, however, explains the demographic patterns

FIGURE 14.6 Anti-Brexit march, London.

of the vote. A majority of people over 45 voted to leave, including 60 percent of those over 65. Younger voters opted overwhelmingly to stay (73 percent of 18–24-year-olds; and 62 percent of 25–34-year-olds). A majority of those working full-time voted to stay in the EU while a majority of the unemployed voted to leave. Most university-educated people voted to stay. Besides age, racial and religious differences among voters were the most striking. A majority of white Britons (53 percent) voted to leave, but 63 percent of Asian Britons and 70 percent of Black Britons voted to stay. A significant majority (58 percent) of those who identified as Christian voted to leave, while seven out of ten Muslims voted to remain.[32]

Attitude surveys provide further insight into the Brexit referendum. The vast majority (81 percent) of those who voted to leave the EU believed multiculturalism was "a force for ill." A similar percentage (80 percent) of this group had the same negative reaction to "social liberalism." An equally large majority (80 percent) of those who voted to leave viewed immigration as a "force for ill" while 71 percent felt the same about globalization, and 74 percent held a negative view of feminism. A third of all those voting to leave identified regaining control over borders and immigration as the principal reason for their vote, while 49 percent said leaving would assure that "decisions about the UK should be taken in the UK."[33]

The data strongly suggest that irrational fears more than rational considerations motivated many of the "no" voters. For example, those who believed the United Kingdom would regain control of immigration and borders were operating under the false assumption that it had been lost in the first place. A 2004 EU directive allows member states to repatriate foreign nationals from other member states who have not found a job within three months. Evidence suggests that the demand for labor, not EU policy, has drawn foreign workers to Britain.[34] A visceral fear of loss of cultural identity in an increasingly diverse Britain bothered many, and overt racism motivated more than a few to vote for parting ways with the EU. To be sure, Britons had legitimate grievances with Brussels, but those differences could have been resolved through negotiations, as they had in the past.

Leaving the EU, however, proved far more complicated than holding a referendum on membership. London and Brussels had to agree on the status of EU citizens working and living in Britain and that of UK subjects in EU countries. British payments to the organization had to be finalized and a new trade agreement negotiated. The land border between Northern Ireland and the Republic of Eyre presented a worrisome challenge. Changing the "soft border," which allowed free movement of people and goods, to a "hard" one with customs and immigration controls could have serious economic and political consequences. There was also concern that Scotland, which had voted 62 to 38 percent to remain in the EU, might opt for independence from the UK.

Theresa May's government reached an agreement on these issues with the EU in November 2018, but hardliners in her own party voted with Labour to defeat the proposal. Efforts to forge a compromise failed, and in May 2019 she announced her resignation, effective June 8. She headed a caretaker government until the Conservatives chose Boris Johnson, a Brexit hardliner, to succeed her on July 24. However, he fared no better in brokering a deal until the general election of December 2019, which gave the Conservatives a clear majority. The United Kingdom formally left the EU on January 31, 2020, beginning an 11-month transition period during which a departure deal had to be reached. On April 27, 2021, the EU Parliament ratified an agreement with the United Kingdom on borders, trade, and security.

CONCLUSION

Few eras in British history have seen such dramatic change as the period 1945 to 2020. Britain lost an empire spanning a quarter of the globe and fell out of the first tier of military powers. To meet its security needs and bolster its status, Britain took a lead role in creating NATO and cultivated the special relationship with the United States, which drew it into conflicts it might otherwise have avoided. The United Kingdom joined the European Economic Community but remained ambivalent toward the organization's evolution into a closer political union. In 2016, the British people voted to leave the EU, ushering in a new era of uncertainty in British foreign policy.

IMAGE CREDITS

Fig. 14.1: Source: https://commons.wikimedia.org/wiki/File:Germans-airlift-1948.jpg.

Fig. 14.2: Source: https://commons.wikimedia.org/wiki/File:CND_rally,_Aberystwyth_(5184388447).jpg.

Fig. 14.3: Source: https://commons.wikimedia.org/wiki/File:British_Decolonisation_in_Africa.png.

Fig. 14.4: Source: https://commons.wikimedia.org/wiki/File:King_David_Hotel_1946.jpg.

Fig. 14.5: Source: https://commons.wikimedia.org/wiki/File:Operation_muskateer.jpg.

Fig. 14.6: Copyright © by Ilovetheeu (CC BY-SA 4.0) at https://commons.wikimedia.org/wiki/File:Anti-Brexit_march,_London,_October_19,_2019_12.jpg.

CHAPTER 15

Society and Politics: Change and Continuity

Much as a routine approach to government had not been up to the task of meeting the day-to-day challenges of the war effort, a return to business as usual after World War II would no longer be acceptable as a domestic settlement. As had occurred during and after World War I, but much more so, the people of the United Kingdom came to realize there were limits to the ethos of free trade liberalism that had, on the surface at least, delivered such high dividends in the Victorian era. Even more so than between 1914 and 1918, Britons living through the period 1939 to 1945 had experienced the power and effectiveness of an involved and interventionist government. If the government in war could coordinate the construction of tanks and airplanes, could not the same government, in peace, oversee the building of new public housing and modern hospitals? Could not the government that had distributed 150,000 Anderson shelters and 38 million gas masks also provide school lunches, eyeglasses, and vaccinations? And could not a government that had organized as daunting an undertaking as Operation Overlord face the challenges of securing sweeping social reform? A government that played a crucial role in defeating the evils of fascism in Europe, Asia, and the Pacific could also rise to the occasion and defeat at home the more subtle evils of want, disease, ignorance, idleness, and squalor that beset too many British families.

Planning a Postwar Britain

This was the sort of stirring imagery adopted by William Beveridge in his 1942 book *Social Insurance and Allied Services*, in which he proposed a wide raft of legislative responses to finally end such domestic evils. Beveridge was a New Liberal of the pre–World War I school of Asquith, Lloyd George, and company, and in many ways his plan simply built on the policies of the Liberal governments of 1906 to 1914. The so-called Beveridge Report attracted much attention and sold 635,000 copies during the war (figure 15.1).

Also popular was a series of pamphlets by Beveridge's brother-in-law, the Christian socialist and London School of Economics Professor R. H. Tawney. In this series, called *Why Britain Fights*, Tawney developed his vision of a reconstructed postwar world. His aim was to convince his readers that World War II was a war worth fighting, and he promised a brighter future and a better Britain at the end of it. If nothing else, there could be no return to the horrors of depression and joblessness that had marked the interwar years (and pretty much any earlier period of British history). Politicians of all major parties acknowledged the need for some sort of program of radical improvement.

FIGURE 15.1 William Beveridge.

If nothing else, the wider population (and electorate) was behind it. We have already seen that it is unrealistic to glamorize the experience of the Blitz or to exaggerate sentiments of solidarity between 1939 and 1945. Nonetheless, the British people could not fail to recognize the effectiveness of collectivity. The experience of evacuees and host families on one hand, or of strangers hunkering for cover in air raid shelters on another, undoubtedly sparked a spirit of civic compassion. This led (at least temporarily) to a necessarily more egalitarian society and a government that was determined (at least to a point) to make sure things stayed that way in the future.

These were tall orders in the best of times, and not least among the wreckage of the Second World War. Then again, several advances in science and technology had been spurred on by the demands of the war and were ready for civilian application with the return of peace. Important strides had been made in the aeronautics industry (especially in the development and enhancement of radar), computing, and in electronics. Similarly, injuries on the battlefield accelerated the progress of sulfa drugs and other new antibiotics. Britain in 1939 had produced only about one-third of the food it consumed; by 1945, thanks to the coordination of the Ministry of Food and the efforts of the Women's Land Army, as well as thousands of individual farmers, the figure had risen to over half. And so long as the United States agreed to share atomic secrets, the reality of nuclear-powered electricity was no longer a distant dream.

Austerity

World War II ended in the summer of 1945, but it would be many years before patterns of everyday life in the British Isles returned to anything approaching normal. Although the UK had avoided

Nazi invasion and occupation between 1940 and 1945 (only the Channel Islands were occupied by the German Army), the material and spiritual toll of five years of fighting was immense. British targets had been bombed relentlessly, in 1940 and 1941 by the Luftwaffe, and in 1944 and 1945 by V-1 and V-2 rockets, and important centers of industry, commerce, and morale—as well as sites crucial to the war effort—were devastated. Over 65,000 civilians had been killed, and probably double that number were injured. Nearly one-third of all homes were damaged, a million were destroyed completely, and in many cases those left standing were derelict relics of the previous century. Hundreds of thousands were homeless. Other aspects of infrastructure took serious beatings as well, and a single sector of transport is probably characteristic of the hardship sustained in Britain by the middle of the twentieth century. Owing in part to fuel rationing and other restrictions, British railroads had done double- and triple-duty during the war, moving troops and matériel, as well as civilians supporting the war effort. There had been relatively little improvement or investment after 1914, however, and virtually none after 1939, so much of the rolling stock and other hardware still in use in 1945 dated to the reign of Queen Victoria.

The state of British finances was, if anything, even more parlous. Having not yet recovered from the drubbing of 1914–1918, Britain had entered World War II on unsteady footing and could not have long sustained any war effort—let alone emerged a victor—without massive infusions of aid from America. This terminated abruptly with the war's end in the summer of 1945, and repayments were scheduled to begin immediately. Overseas investments had been liquidated virtually entirely, however, and, owing to the strains of war, coming on top of the difficult quarter century that had led up to 1939, roughly 25 percent of the national wealth had simply disappeared. Britain was confronted with a massive deficit in balance of payment, and the economist J. M. Keynes warned that without a further US loan (and ideally other accommodations), the country faced "a financial Dunkirk." In other words, Britain would have to retrench severely and settle for a level of prominence in world affairs on par with contemporary postwar France. Britain did receive a US loan (which provided a respite for the short term, but obviously compounded the debt problem over the long term), but it fell short of the $5 billion Keynes had judged necessary. Most of the new loan was exhausted before the end of 1947. The gift of Marshall aid (see chapter 14) was a further lifeline, but Britain, despite having received the overwhelming lion's share of assistance, did not experience an "economic miracle" comparable to France or West Germany.

Instead of rebuilding the war-shattered infrastructure of their own country, Britain's early postwar governments continued to pour millions into the empire, propping up the Sterling Zone and holding at bay the ambitions of the Soviet Union and China. Although Britain pushed into the postwar world with the finances of a loser, it maintained the psychology of a victor and determined to keep up an international program of global prominence and commitment. "De-mobbing" (i.e., demobilization of the armed forces) was widespread, but perhaps less apparent than in other countries of Europe, because of the continued presence of 2 million men in uniform in British fleets and bases in Asia, Africa, Palestine, the Mediterranean, and elsewhere. The adoption of peacetime conscription (called National Service) meant that as late as 1963, about six thousand young men were "called up" every other week. Altogether some 2.5 million were conscripted, with over one thousand dying in Korea and nearly four hundred others in various conflict zones. This was bound to have an impact on an entire generation of young men aged 17 to 21, as well as families and friends of either sex.

The shift from war to peace must also have seemed notional to British civilians. Rationing of food, fuel, and clothing did not end immediately, and in some instances even intensified. A disastrously rainy summer in 1946, followed by one of the coldest winters in recorded history, destroyed first Britain's wheat harvest and then its store of potatoes. Thus consumption of two basic staples—bread and potatoes—which during even the sternest days of the two world wars had never been officially restricted, was rationed in the early postwar years. Other foodstuffs, goods, or commodities simply could not be found in Britain in 1945 or for the next several years.

Unsurprisingly, the decision of the British government to assist the beleaguered inhabitants of West Berlin by sending them food, coal, and gasoline did nothing to relieve the situation at home. Of course, this was in the context of the early days of the Cold War (see chapter 14) which, given the reality of nuclear weapons, seemed an even more ominous specter than the world wars had been. Previously, civilians had made sacrifices and experienced privation on the understanding it was geared toward a noble effort and was "for the duration" only. The unfamiliar and occasionally nebulous nature of the Cold War, by contrast, could mean there was no end in sight. Indeed, in a cruel and ironic twist, it was in March 1948, the very week authorities finally got around to dismantling public air raid shelters that had been constructed to protect against German bombs and rockets, that the home secretary recommended the planning of much bigger shelters, this time in anticipation of a nuclear attack from the Soviet Union.

The decade or so that followed World War II—a decade of hardship, shortages, queues, and limited resources—was labeled by contemporaries and historians alike an age of austerity. The question facing the British public was what sort of government would lead them through it.

The Welfare State

The story of the general election of 1945 is often told as though it were the Conservative Party's to lose and as if Winston Churchill did lose it for his party through unrestrained and unjustified attacks on Labour's proposed scheme for a "New Jerusalem."[1] To be sure, Churchill was popular: His approval ratings across the war years had averaged 78 percent, and in May 1945 were at 83 percent (figure 15.2). But Churchill had led the government as a coalition prime minister, and his personal reputation did not necessarily reflect wider support of the conservative solutions for postwar Britain. Moreover, Churchill's popularity derived from his strengths as a wartime leader, which could be weaknesses in less exceptional times. His first act as prime minister in 1940 had

FIGURE 15.2 Churchill waving the victory sign to the crowd in Whitehall on the day he broadcast to the nation that the war with Germany had been won, May 8, 1945. Ernest Bevin stands to his right.

been to invite Labourites and Liberals to forge a genuine coalition alongside Conservatives. This was a generous and statesmanlike action that rose above petty partisanship. It also allowed him to concentrate almost single-mindedly on his real passion—winning the war—while largely ignoring politics at home for the next five years. With the return of "politics as usual" (or as usual as they could be under the circumstances) in the summer of 1945, the Conservative Party had little sense of direction or aim. As one member of Parliament (MP) had noted the previous fall: "Never was a party so leaderless at the Conservative Party is today."[2] By contrast, the Labour Party had been left to govern at home between 1940 and 1945 and used the opportunity to plan for a postwar Britain—and to win the next general election.[3]

Looking to the past, Labour could, with varying degrees of fairness, condemn Conservatives as the villains of the 1920s, the bungling architects of failure in the 1930s, and, most damningly, the reckless appeasers who had led Britain—and the world—into an exhausting and unnecessary war. Looking to the future, Labour offered an ambitious vision of social welfare and economic reform comprising investment and reorganization and improvement in housing, transport, and education; the extraction, production, and distribution of energy; universal health care, full employment, and more. The British electorate bought what the Labour Party was selling and, in the first general election since 1935, returned to a parliament 393 Labour MPs in a House of Commons of 640 (figure 15.3).

Clement Attlee, who had led the party since 1935 and been deputy to Churchill since 1942, was now prime minister. To set in motion plans for a New Jerusalem, Attlee and his government relied heavily on a proposal drawn up during the war and published in 1942, called *Social Insurance and Allied Services*. Better known as the Beveridge Report, after its author Sir William Beveridge, this was a bold scheme for addressing the social and economic problems besetting the United Kingdom. Beveridge's approach was from the perspective of combatting five great evils: disease, idleness, ignorance, squalor, and want. Earlier efforts to fix such problems had been piecemeal, Beveridge argued, and failed to grasp a big picture. The unsatisfactory legislative responses of the interwar years, for example, found the resources to fund one program by slashing another. To ultimately defeat the five great evils, Beveridge insisted future reform must not be sectional, but rather broad, sweeping, and comprehensive. The services and social security Labour offered after 1945 would provide everyone with the means and ability—as a positive right—to be free from squalor, idleness, and so on.

The scheme was expensive and demanded a collaborative effort from the state and individuals. Costs were to be met in part through a combination of contributions made by workers (through payroll deductions), employers, and the government—a strategy similar to the one proposed by David Lloyd George and other likeminded New Liberals

FIGURE 15.3 Clement Attlee meeting with King George VI in the grounds of Buckingham Palace, following the Labour victory in the 1945 general election.

at the start of the century. Beveridge's plan went further, however: Coverage was now universal, and the assistance offered was more extensive. To meet the difference, the British government would implement a system of nationalization of all major enterprises whose industries were essential to and intimately bound with the public welfare. Labour judged such industries—transport, utilities, coal, iron, steel, and other heavy industries—as services essential to the functioning of the entire economy and, as such, inappropriate in the hands of private interests. The UK already had some experience of a nationalized economy: Radio and electricity had been nationalized between the wars, and the mail much earlier; and coal, transport, and other interests were nationalized in all but name as part of the war effort. Beveridge proposed intensifying the program to include the compulsory purchase by the government of the remaining "commanding heights" of the economy, including the Bank of England. Having compensated owners and shareholders, the government would run these interests in trust for the public; they would garner all the riches, reinvest rationally and without risk (in part because there would be no competition), and use surplus profit to fund the expensive assistance programs.

Nationalization was not merely a means to an end (i.e., a scheme to raise the revenue necessary to fund a comprehensive welfare state). It was part of an aspiration that had been close to the heart of the Labour Party since the beginning and expressed memorably in the most straightforward interpretation of Clause IV of the party's constitution, drawn up in 1918:

> To secure for the workers by hand or by brain the full fruits of their industry and the most equitable distribution thereof that may be possible upon the basis of the common ownership of the means of production, distribution, and exchange, and the best obtainable system of popular administration and control of each industry or service.

Precisely how far Clause IV was intended to go was a perennial source of dispute in Labour circles until the party's constitution was revised in 1995, in the wake of "New" Labour and the leadership of Tony Blair—and whether Britain's Labour Party, in 1918 or in 1945 or at any other point, genuinely qualified as a socialist party has likewise been a topic of intense debate.

Certainly the language of socialism was used, freely by its critics and occasionally by its supporters. Many voters, MPs, and some cabinet members openly avowed themselves and their program to be socialist. Some used the label cautiously, but others were bolder, arguing either that the Labour Party aimed for a uniquely British version of socialism, or even that Britain's postwar welfare state was merely an opening act for what would ultimately blossom into as directed and "scientific" a planned economic system as the Soviet Union. Conservatives did not hesitate to draw such parallels, and Winston Churchill had insisted with vigor that the measure of intervention and control that Labour aimed for was essentially totalitarian and could only be realized with "some form of Gestapo." In any case, what Labour attempted, and achieved, in the years immediately following World War II went further to the left than any British government before or since.

But what motivated Attlee and Beveridge, the chief architect and the practical force behind Britain's postwar welfare state, was not orthodox socialism, at least not as the term is typically understood. Beveridge was a lifelong Liberal, having in fact won a seat for that party, for the first time at the ripe old age of 65, in a 1944 by-election. Attlee shared a similar outlook, although, perhaps with an eye to future ambitions, he had hitched his wagon to the fortunes of the rising Labour Party in 1922, after it was clear the star of the Liberal Party was on the wane. Certainly neither man was a Marxist. Rather they belonged to the mold of conscious-driven nineteenth-century critics of industrialization and its consequences, especially for the poor and downtrodden. Their efforts after World War II built on the accomplishments of the Liberal Party in the decade before World War I. In fact, both had worked for the liberal governments of Campbell-Bannerman and Asquith: Attlee had traveled the country promoting Lloyd George's National Insurance Act, and Beveridge was in many ways the brains behind the system of Labour Exchanges. Now they wanted to take matters a step further—as far, in fact, as their support in the polls and the tenor of the House of Commons would allow them.

An Education Act (1944) had already been secured during the war, establishing a Ministry of Education, making schooling compulsory through age 15 and promising free primary and secondary education, with the possibility of continuation at the university level. Implementation had to wait until after the war, but by 1951, nearly three-quarters of all university students received at least some aid under the terms of the act. The National Health Services Act (1946) was effected in stages through 1948 and drastically reformed the delivery of medical care in Britain. The measures were comprehensive in that they applied to everyone and included virtually everything—services and procedures, prescriptions, even eyeglasses and false teeth—free of charge. The National Insurance Act (1946) was much like earlier acts in the 1910s, '20s, and '30s (a consolidated effort on the part of the state, the employer, and the employee), but once again it went further. Together with the Family Allowance Act (1945) which provided 5 shillings a week for each child, after the oldest, and the National Assistance Act (1948), which removed the final vestige of the nineteenth-century poor laws and aimed to humanize relief granted to those in real need, these laid the foundations of a welfare state that would function in the United Kingdom for more than 30 years. In making available judicious support and assistance—"from the cradle to the grave"—the welfare state aimed to resolve little problems before they became unmanageable disasters. The scheme was undoubtedly expensive, but the rationale was that it would ultimately save money for individuals and families, as well as the state.

Winter of Discontent and the Thatcher Revolution

The welfare state that was launched by Labour after World War II remained largely intact and unchallenged for the next 30 years. At least until the second half of the 1960s, Tories and Labour alike accepted the broad contours of consensus. When controversy did arise, it revolved mostly around practical questions of how to pay for everything, and only occasionally on principled questions of whether the system went too far or not far enough. In most other respects, there was a consensus on full employment through the mechanisms of a mixed economy operating generally in a context of free trade, with public ownership of basic industries and selective but far-reaching intervention or regulation. There was a consensus on a gradual but inevitable retreat from empire, commitment to NATO, and the desirability of joining the European Economic Community (EEC). There was a consensus on the cooperation of management and the state with unions, as a vested and essential piece in the political process, and almost as a separate estate within the realm. Major politicians, as well as the media and civil servants (i.e., the "Establishment") shared these ideas through the 1950s and '60s.

Although it was true that most people living in Britain had, in the words of former prime minister Harold Macmillan, "never had it so good," and in spite—or perhaps because—of the exuberance of the Swinging Sixties and the potential of multiculturalism (chapter 16), there was rising discontent in the late 1960s and especially the early 1970s. Great strides had been made over the past quarter century, many of them owing directly to the welfare state, and although the poverty of the 1970s was nothing compared to the early postwar days of austerity, let alone the years of the Blitz or anything earlier, it was also clear that William Beveridge's "evil of want" had not been destroyed. Furthermore, many of the comprehensive and universal benefits and services that had been promised—and delivered—in the late 1940s and early 1950s had been subsequently curtailed or rolled back. Various factors were responsible, not least that the welfare state by the 1970s had fallen a victim to its own success: The population was rising, people were living longer and healthier lives, and they expected more.

The expectation of full employment lasting indefinitely had never been entertained realistically and, as the 1960s came to a close, its end was in sight. The economy faced decline, especially in manufacturing, and circumstances were exacerbated by the energy crisis in the 1970s. Work was often inefficient (owing in part to shortsighted misuse of Marshall Aid and other misguided policies in early years of the Cold War), inflation was up, production down, and British goods were expensive. In a spirit reminiscent of the 1920s, neither management nor the unions were willing to address these problems in a useful manner. The government declared states of emergency and, to conserve electricity when coal miners went on strike, enacted rolling power outages and went so far as to impose mandatory three-day workweeks. An unavoidable sense that government was not doing much, and in particular failed to deal responsibly with unions, raised the specter of the interwar years. The instability and lack of direction was reflected in the rapid turnovers in government. Continuity of party marked UK governments from 1951 to 1964, and again from 1979 to 1997; in the 15 years in between, however, there were six general elections (two of them a mere eight months apart), and government changed hands five times.

As part of the consensus, British trade unions had been largely accepted as a positive—indeed, essential—part of the industrial, economic, and political landscape for much of the 1950s and 60s. But with the end of full employment, made worse by the energy crisis and government indecision, unions were less of a constructive and vital player and more of a threat and a nuisance. They were intractable, often demanding higher wages for less work, and their tactics were aggressive, relying as often as not on strike action, included unsanctioned, and therefore illegal, "wild cat" strikes. Strikes became more common as the 1970s wore on. With unemployment and inflation at unmanageable levels in 1976, the Labour government was compelled to go to the IMF cap in hand and seek a £2.3 billion bailout. The winter of 1978–79 was Britain's coldest in over 15 years and, with the government having announced a 5 percent cut in wages the previous summer, there were more and more strikes into the new year, often involving vital services: lorry drivers, water works employees, ambulance drivers, and sanitation workers. The strike of Liverpool gravediggers was an unsettling prospect because, with rolling power outages, it was not certain unburied corpses would remain frozen, and authorities considered resorting to dumping bodies at sea. Coming out of this "Winter of Discontent" and with not much improving beside the weather, the UK electorate put into power a conservative government headed by an equally aggressive and intractable Margaret Thatcher (figure 15.4).

Although a great pillar of the modern Conservative Party, Margaret Thatcher introduced a brand of conservatism that had been unknown in Britain since before World War I and that many of her successors in the party have been wary carrying forward. In the judgment of Milton Friedman, an American economist whose ideas had a tremendous impact on her thinking, Thatcher's approach was, in many ways, most in step with classical, or nineteenth-century, liberal thought. She sought to limit the government (its spending, services, involvement, and size); she lowered taxes and was generally friendly to business and free enterprise; and in all this she championed the role and freedom of the individual. This is all true, but simply to cast Margaret Thatcher as a nineteenth-century liberal fails to tell the whole story. She was, after all, a committed monetarist and insisted that the government, to bring down inflation and improve the economy, should act to remove money from circulation. This would require the government to spend less,

FIGURE 15.4 Margaret Thatcher, who won the 1979 general election and became prime minister.

by removing subsidies to industry, reducing social services and welfare, and withdrawing from certain global expenditures. Having achieved this, government could proceed to lowering taxes.

This was bitter medicine, with initially ugly results: Unemployment increased (at the same time the dole was reduced) and, in the short term, inflation actually increased—and the approval ratings of the government suffered accordingly. Thatcher had anticipated this, however, and knew she would need at least a second term in office before the beneficial side of her policies became apparent. It was partially to that end (i.e., offsetting some of the unpopularity it had brought on itself) that the government introduced a policy of selling off council houses to the families who lived in them. No doubt this tack was successful among those who became homeowners for the first time, but the government received another unexpected boost with the outcome of the conflict with Argentina over the Falkland Islands. The Conservative government was also aided by the fact that Labour remained unpopular—linked in the associations of many with the malaise of the 1970s and the darkest days of the Winter of Discontent—as well as internally divided.

In 1983 the Conservative Party won a second term in office. Its share of the popular vote was smaller than in 1979, but its command in the House of Commons was overwhelming. Thereupon Thatcher set her sights on four related goals: humbling the trade unions, undoing nationalization and reintroducing private ownership, and shoring up control of local government. The government had taken steps in the direction of these first two already, when the struggling steel industry was denied subsidies and allowed to fail: As plants shut down, workers lost jobs, and unions lost members. The target Thatcher and her government are most remembered for during these years, however, was the National Union of Mineworkers (NUM). The government's strategy was similar to its handling of the steel industry—simply let inefficient and unprofitable mines close down. The NUM, however, would not go down without a fight. In an attempt to precipitate a crippling energy crisis that would force the government and the National Coal Board to negotiations, over 140,000 miners went on strike for a collective total of 26 million days in 1984–1985. The government had anticipated a severe strike and, as in the case of the General Strike almost sixty years earlier, already begun stockpiling coal. The government also was successful in convincing over 100,000 miners not to strike and used police to break up protests and picket lines at mines that continued operating. In the end, after almost exactly one year of action, most strikers were compelled to return to work. The outcome was pivotal for subsequent industrial relations, marking a big victory for management and a big defeat for the unions.

Privatization followed much the same policy. The government discontinued subsidies, sold off shares, and generally withdrew from the marketplace. As with the privatization of council flats, the program was popular at first, at least in many circles. But Thatcher tried to take the policy as far as her support in parliament would permit—and many thought this was too far. Former prime minister Harold Macmillan, by then Lord Stockton, delivered perhaps the most stinging conservative critique when he complained that the governments of the 1980s were "selling off the family silver." Had she been given free rein—or uncontested support in Parliament—Thatcher would very likely have sold off everything.

On the whole, however, the economy was strong in the run-up to the 1987 general election, and things were looking up for the Conservative Party. Thatcher now took aim at reform in education, housing, and health—areas she believed collectivism was entrenched. And she continued to lower taxes.

But to turn on its head one of Thatcher's own aphorisms—that the problem with socialism is sooner or later the government runs out of other people's money to spend—the problem facing the Conservative government as the 1980s came to a close was that it could only lower taxes and divest itself of nationalized industries for so long before it needed additional sources of revenue. In April 1990, the Conservative government introduced what they called the Community Charge, better known—and derided—as the Poll Tax. This was a regressive or flat tax that substituted local taxes on property with one on individuals. Even by the government's reckoning, the shift adversely affected about seven tax-paying families in ten. Riots and civil disobedience ensued, and the measure was abandoned quickly, being replaced with a council charge in 1993. The prime minister did not last that long, however: she was forced into resignation as leader of the Conservative Party in November 1990.

Margaret Thatcher's run as prime minister was longer than that of any other prime minister since Lord Liverpool in the 1810s and '20s. Her legacy is far-reaching. In 11.5 years, she privatized wide swathes of industry and utilities, including electricity, telecoms, transport, and even water. This reflected her commitment to nineteenth-century liberalism by restoring competition and incentives for hard work and innovation. Thatcher was ultimately successful in lowering inflation (and Conservatives continued to reduce it after John Major succeeded her as prime minister)—but only at the cost of high unemployment. Thatcher succeeded in turning a substantial deficit in 1979 into a surplus by 1990—but in large measure this was accomplished by selling off state-owned interests. UK tax rates, especially income taxes, were slashed drastically across the 1980s (and dropped even further after Thatcher's resignation)—but resources and services dropped correspondingly. Thatcher's policies generally favored big business and financial interests, and undoubtedly many people prospered. But many others were thrown out of work, and many small businesses and city centers, especially in the old industrial north, collapsed.

Thatcher set out to destroy the postwar consensus, and in this she was undoubtedly successful. As she remarked of her government's budget for 1988: It "was the obituary for the doctrine of high taxation[,] the defeat of everything Labour thought was permanent and irreversible in political life[, and] the epitaph for Socialism."[4] It was no mere rhetorical flourish when, asked what was her greatest achievement, Thatcher responded, "Tony Blair and New Labour." As the journalist and British political commentator Peter Riddell commented, a Martian would not have detected any change in the governance of the UK across the second half of the 1990s—Labour's landslide victory in 1997 notwithstanding. By the end of the twentieth century, the Labour Party had, of necessity, redefined itself to such a degree the party of the halcyon days of Attlee and Beveridge was unknown.

Thatcherism by Another Name? Blair and New Labour into the Twenty-first Century

Tony Blair became leader of the Labour Party in 1994, and with a resounding majority in the next general election, in 1997, led the party to its first of an unprecedented three consecutive victories at the polls. He resigned as prime minister in 2007, but Britain continued under Labour rule for another three years. The shifts in the Labour Party, moving it closer to the center of British politics, and closer to policies associated with Margaret Thatcher, are often pinned squarely on Blair and his emphasis on New Labour (the qualifying adjective was adopted in 1994), but actually the process of transformation had been underway a decade earlier. Labour's election manifesto in 1983, in the run-up to the general election of that year, had committed the party to a thoroughly socialist program: abolition of the House of Lords, re-nationalization of industries the Thatcher government had lately privatized, increased personal taxation for the rich, withdrawal from the EEC (in the 1970s and '80s, British attitudes of Euro-skepticism were associated with the left and not the right), unilateral nuclear disarmament (UND), and more. It has been ridiculed as "the longest suicide note in history" and was responsible for Labour's weakest show in the House of Commons since the Great Depression, in 1935.

In response to this stinging defeat, Labour's leader, Neil Kinnock, found it expedient to drop some of the party's more stridently socialist aspirations. The commitment to UND was dropped, and Kinnock promised not to reinstate labor laws that had been scrapped by the Conservative government under Thatcher. The Labour Party in 1986 replaced its former emblem, a red flag, since 1789 a symbol of revolution, with the more staid and sedate red rose—a signal that, in the UK, the party of the left would be thoroughly respectable and not associated with the wild-eyed socialist bogeymen of the continent. Kinnock's successor, John Smith, democratized certain inner workings of the Labour Party, with an intended consequence of reducing the political influence of the labor unions.

It was against this backdrop that Tony Blair rose to prominence in the 1990s. As we have seen, he abandoned in 1995 what many regarded as Labour's heart and soul, officially striking the traditional clause IV from the party constitution. New Labour, the party's (unofficial) new name beginning in 1994, is also chiefly associated with Blair and his tenure. The slogan in full, "New Labour" for a "New Britain," was designed to appeal to a country that had by and large bought what Margaret Thatcher had been selling: a return to market economics and the "classical" liberalism of the nineteenth century. Such an outlook, increasingly labeled "neoliberal," was in step with much of what Britain had been, or tried to be, in the hundred years leading up to 1945. But it was in stark contrast to the period 1945 to 1979. In this interim, the years of consensus, the UK had retreated from many positions of global influence or authority, and at home inequality had been reduced. From the 1980s onward, however, Britain increasingly aimed to resume its place as a world power, and there was a widening gap between the rich and the poor, which 13 years of (New) Labour under Blair and Brown, let alone a further decade of Conservative/Liberal Democrat coalition (2010–2015) or Conservative (after 2015) government would do little to reverse or abate (figure 15.5).

As prime minister, Tony Blair distanced himself and his party from traditional Labour positions. Instead, he explained policy in terms of a "Third Way" (i.e., neither capitalist nor

FIGURE 15.5 New Labour logo.

socialist). Blair did little to undo the de-regulation or roll back the privatization of the Thatcher years and by and large failed to deliver his party's pledge to reduce the value-added tax (VAT), criticized by opponents as a regressive or "stealth" tax. The VAT had stood at 17.5 percent during Thatcher's last year in power and, certain exemptions aside, remained at that level until after Blair's premiership, when it dropped, briefly, to 15 percent.

Tony Blair was notorious for his obsession with "spin," and perhaps a bigger difference between him and Margaret Thatcher was his effort to come across in a warm and fuzzy manner. New Labour under Blair emphasized cooperation and social cohesion ("There is no such thing" as society, Thatcher famously declared in 1987), and although New Labour advanced the rhetoric of social justice, in reality this often meant social mobility (i.e., opportunities for social improvement). The (old) Labour emphasis on equality, from the 1950s and 1960s, was gone.

In matters beyond policy, Tony Blair appropriated something of the executive style of Margaret Thatcher. The personality of a British prime minister has mattered more, and the significance of cabinet and government cohesion less. Blair's careful attention to political spin intensified the tendency, and the character of some of his successors at 10 Downing Street has not lessened it. The new style of governing has been called "presidential," and if nothing else, it has certainly had the effect of making British politics more intelligible to American audiences since the 1980s.

Ireland and the Troubles

The 73 Sinn Féin representatives who had formed the Dáil Éireann in 1918 (chapter 12) issued a declaration of independence from the United Kingdom in 1919 and proclaimed an Irish republic. The difficulty, though, was that the British government in Ireland was still in place, and this led inevitably to conflict. The resulting Irish War of Independence lasted until the summer of 1921, when George V took the lead in orchestrating a truce between Irish revolutionaries and the

British government. A conference met in London that fall and, before the end of the year, negotiations resulted in the Anglo-Irish Treaty. The 26 counties in the south of Ireland were designated a free state within the British Empire, although what exactly this amounted to was infuriatingly vague, and comparisons to Canada (a dominion) did not help. Members of the Dáil continued to swear oaths of allegiance to the Crown, and the Irish Free State was explicitly not a republic—although provision for the office of an elected president possibly blurred the distinction. In effect, the Catholic south had finally achieved Home Rule.

The Treaty of London and effective Home Rule status were as far as the British government was willing to go. But die-hard republicans in Ireland, committed to full independence, insisted Irish negotiators had not pressed hard enough. This time they turned their ire not on the British government nor on symbols of British authority—which, in any case, were largely absent—but rather on those who had signed the treaty and supported the legitimate government it provided for. The consequence was the Irish Civil War, which raged for 11 months across 1922 and 1923. The British government chose to regard the conflict as an Irish affair and stayed out.

From practical perspectives, the situation remained largely unchanged for much of the next half century, although there were big developments at the level of constitutional technicalities. A new constitution in 1937 substituted the Free State label with the new name Éire. This may have closed the door on one area of debate but did not clarify the "republic/not-a-republic" question. The tone and content of the constitution openly appealed to Catholics, cultural or "Celtic" nationalists, and irredentists, and also removed the controversial oath of allegiance to the Crown. The (Irish) Republic of Ireland Act (1948) and the (UK) Ireland Act (1949) formally abolished any remaining links between the British monarch and the government of the Irish state and secured for Ireland unambiguously the distinction of a republic that was independent of the United Kingdom, the British Empire, or British Commonwealth.

None of this affected the six counties with a Protestant majority in Ulster, in the northeast of Ireland, which had themselves acquired what amounted to Home Rule from the (Catholic) Free State. As a province, Ulster remained constitutionally part of the UK (indeed, the Ireland Act of Attlee's government seemed to pull the province even closer to Britain): It was the *Northern Ireland* component of what, after 1921, was called the United Kingdom of Great Britain and Northern Ireland. The Catholic minority in the region was outnumbered by Protestants about two to one. A Protestant hegemony "a Protestant Parliament for a Protestant people"[5]—and Catholics faced institutionalized discrimination in housing, employment, education, and other aspects of everyday life. The situation has been described as a "consensual apartheid,"[6] but it might well be asked to what extent it was consensual from the perspective of the beleaguered Roman Catholic minority. They largely withdrew from public life, in many cases no doubt counting on eventual incorporation, sooner than later, into the (Catholic) south—this, after all, was the aspiration of many in the Free State/Éire/Republic and was affirmed explicitly (if imprecisely) in the 1937 Constitution.

British decline in heavy industry after World War II hit Northern Ireland hard—Ulster was "in a state of industrial free-fall" by the 1960s[7]—and unemployment affected the already straitened Catholic communities worst of all. They found inspiration, however, in contemporary developments in other parts of the world. In 1960, British Prime Minister Harold Macmillan had announced "[t]he wind of change" of third-world nationalism as the weave of the British Empire unraveled on more and more fronts. The civil rights movement in the US was another stimulus to Ulster's Catholic minority to organize in pursuit of just laws and equal opportunity. The Northern Ireland Civil Rights Association united Catholics and sympathetic Protestants to promote reforms at the same time the province's moderate Unionist prime minister, Terrence O'Neill, proposed modest improvements. So far as the plight of Roman Catholics was concerned, O'Neill's thinking was motivated by two linked arguments. His approach was both correct and expedient: On one hand, relieving Catholics of the inconvenient disabilities and discriminatory harassment they lived under was the right thing to do, and on another hand, it ought to reconcile them to future life in Protestant-dominated Ulster. O'Neill also set in motion efforts to improve the economy through modernization and expanded industry, which were intended to assist Protestants and Catholics alike. These programs were welcome in both the Republic and in Great Britain, and the UK prime minster urged O'Neill to step things up.

These were statesmanlike initiatives, designed to address major economic problems across a wide front to improve the conditions of many, regardless of denomination, and they were endorsed by the heads of three interested governments. But Protestant hardliners in Ulster refused to see things in this light. Like their partisan forebears who, half a century earlier, had signed the Solemn League and Covenant to resist Home Rule, extreme Protestants in the 1960s regarded O'Neill's program as a direct attack on their liberties. They were already alarmed at the organization and activities of the Civil Rights Association, and the direction of the government seemed to confirm their worst paranoia. To counter the efforts of the CRA, Protestant extremists formed so-called loyalist organizations. The choice of name harkened back to the bad old days of the Penal Laws and the eighteenth-century Protestant Ascendancy, and blithely ignored the fact that the movement's goals, in defying the elected governments of both Ulster and Westminster, were plainly disloyal. To preserve their privileged place in Northern Ireland and to keep Catholics down, Protestant extremists were prepared to resort to organized violence and terrorism.

The Civil Rights Association and likeminded progressive groups in Northern Ireland organized marches and demonstrations throughout 1968 and 1969, and loyalist organizations staged counter actions. Authorities banned many of the meetings of the CRA but permitted those planned by loyalists to go ahead. Similarly, the government and police clamped down on infractions of the law by Catholic/nationalist groups, while often turning a complaisant eye to comparable violations committed by Protestants and unionists. Catholics also were less likely to benefit from police protection against intimidation or attacks perpetuated by Protestants.

Although the prospect of serious conflict had been brewing in Ulster throughout the second half of the 1960s, it is conventional to identify the Battle of the Bogside, three days of intense rioting and violence in the summer of 1969, as the start of the Troubles. Every year on August 12, militant Protestant groups called the Apprentice Boys (another name summoning past partisanship, this time from the 1690s) marched in provocation alongside or through predominantly Catholic neighborhoods, singing, jeering, and throwing pennies. In 1969, inhabitants of Bogside, a Catholic-majority neighborhood of Londonderry, responded by throwing stones, and ultimately firebombs. Police arrived to try to restore order, but residents had closed off and barricaded Bogside and declared "Free Derry." Confrontation escalated, and the IRA soon provided support, including weapons and ammunitions, to the inhabitants of Bogside. Police were unprepared for action of this intensity, and although they were armed and outfitted with armored vehicles, they were not permitted to use them. They did, however, release over one thousand canisters of tear gas, to disrupt the rioters.

The following day, the Taoiseach (prime minister) of the Republic decried the violence and announced that he was prepared to dispatch the Irish Army to the border to supply field hospitals, a move regarded by unionists as threat of invasion by a foreign power. The day after that, the prime minster of Northern Ireland acknowledged that matters were beyond the control of provincial authorities and requested that the British government send troops into Londonderry to relieve beleaguered police and to pacify the region. This was the Westminster government's first instance of direct intervention, let alone military action, in the north or south of Ireland, since the establishment of the Free State in 1921.

Although the Battle of the Bogside resulted in no deaths—there were over one thousand injuries, however, and many homes and buildings were burned or damaged—it was in other respects the writing on the wall for what would occur in Northern Ireland over the next three decades. The British Army, once in the province, found it difficult to withdraw, and military and police authorities responded to the actions of the IRA, its various splinter groups, and other organizations bent on undermining or ending the British presence in Ireland with arrests, the suspension of habeas corpus, internment, and other practices that were, at best, of questionable lawfulness and, at worst, outright illegal. Home Rule for Northern Ireland was rescinded early in 1972 (the single bloodiest year of the Troubles, which accounted for 480 deaths—over 13 percent of the near 50-year total), two months after the notorious events of January 30th, when peaceful protesters, demonstrating against internment, were attacked by British soldiers: 13 were killed onsite and another died a few months later, and a further 26 were injured. The incident was dubbed immediately "Bloody Sunday," and in the memory of many, is emblematic of the general tenor of the Troubles (figure 15.6). However, about 60 percent of the deaths associated with the Troubles have been perpetrated by republicans, and only about 10 percent by Irish or (mostly) British security forces; a further 30 percent have been the responsibility of loyalist/Protestant groups. Meanwhile, security forces have sustained nearly three times as many deaths as active republicans (and active loyalist deaths amounted to about one in twenty). Over 50 percent of all victims have been civilians, often involved only marginally, if at all, in the politics and rule of the region. The British record in Northern Ireland has hardly been pristine, as Bloody Sunday attests.

FIGURE 15.6 Derry, Ireland, Bloody Sunday 35th-year commemoration.

This is not to say the British government did not attempt positive initiatives across the period. Both Conservative and Labour governments sought to stabilize the region and bring about enduring peace based on a formula of power-sharing between Protestant and Roman Catholic interests and guaranteeing the rights of everyone. The Sunningdale Agreement (1973) emerged from negotiations for a Council of Ireland, which proposed to involve a wide range of representation drawn from both Northern Ireland and the Republic of Ireland. Even though the scope of the council's concerns was quite limited, unionists opposed it on grounds of interference from a foreign power (i.e., the Republic), and meanwhile many republicans pledged to boycott any proceedings that stopped short of complete and immediate unification of the island. Under these circumstances, and against the backdrop of a struggling economy, the Sunningdale Agreement fell apart. The Hillsborough Agreement (1985) also called for a broad-bottomed conference serving a strictly consultative role and confirmed the wisdom of keeping the Republic involved in any decision-making process. Furthermore, it established the principle that there could be no change affecting the status of Northern Ireland without a vote in the province.

Sunningdale and Hillsborough were reasonable and plausible accommodations—in part, admittedly, because they were limited—and under other circumstances might have been expected to lay the groundwork for eventual peace. But extremists on either end of the partisan divide continued to cry foul: Once again, Protestants complained the proposals went too far, and Catholics that they did not go far enough.

It seems likely, however, the real reason the two agreements did not advance very far had to do with matters of wider context, not least the state of the economy. The depths of the Troubles coincided with the oil crisis in the early 1970s, and many continued to struggle with de-industrialization in the mid-1980s. The Republic was hit as well as the UK and, in the UK, Northern Ireland was hit hardest of all. The recession of the late '80s and early '90s did not provide much relief. This emphasis on the importance of the economy is supported by the ultimate success (more or less, and at least in the short term) of the Good Friday Agreement, which owed a lot to Hillsborough and rested on a program broadly similar to Sunningdale—so much so one Ulster politician dubbed it "Sunningdale for slow learners"!

Certainly other factors were present in 1998 that had been absent in 1973 or 1985. Arguably the Labour government of Tony Blair was more willing than the Conservative governments of Edward Heath or Margaret Thatcher to work with the IRA—and vice versa. American involvement, including the involvement of US president Bill Clinton, was another boost to the peace process. But it is also reasonable to draw attention to the uptick in the economy in the UK and in Ireland starting in the 1990s, when the Republic was frequently labeled a "Celtic Tiger." In this context of regional prosperity and a generally sunnier outlook (e.g., the end of the Cold War and piecemeal expansion of the EU), the involved parties were willing to believe positive change might finally be possible. Unfortunately, this emphasis on economic determinism and peace in Northern Ireland also seems to be sustained in light of more recent developments. By 2007 or 2008, the Celtic Tiger had lost much of its roar, and the worldwide economic downturn hit Ireland hard. Conditions deteriorated both in the Republic and in Northern Ireland. For the most part the conflict has been less intense than the bad old days of the Troubles, but much of the optimism of the Good Friday Agreement now seems misplaced.

At the end of the day, the situation in Ireland is unlikely to yield to any easy solution. Historically, the IRA has been nearly as opposed to the republican government in the south as to British rule in the north, and its commitment to thoroughgoing social and economic revolution is bound to be unpopular in an essentially conservative Roman Catholic country. The IRA, as well as mainstream political parties, insist on unifying the north and south. (Protestants in the north, of course, are intent on blocking this.) Despite its rhetorical and grassroots appeal, the Republic is also not necessarily keen to absorb overnight a large and potentially violent Protestant population; well over 1 million Protestants, even balanced by 4.5 million Catholics, must be an immensely destabilizing influence. The United Kingdom, it is safe to say, would like nothing better than to settle the problem. The same is true of all parties of good will in the Republic and in Ulster. For now, the question remains how.

IMAGE CREDITS

CHAPTER 16

Culture, Beliefs, and Ideas

A thick streak of austerity persisted well into the 1950s, and parts of Britain must have resembled the plains of Armageddon rather than any vision of a New Jerusalem. Rationing continued until July 1954, when restrictions were finally lifted on bacon and other meat. Efforts to rebuild bombed-out homes and businesses generally lagged behind need, and condemned buildings and massive craters in public spaces remained familiar features of urban landscapes for a long time to come. The discovery of unexploded live ordnance from German bombs was likewise a source of danger and excitement. As Clement Attlee admitted in 1947, "I have no easy words for the nation. … I cannot say when we will emerge into easier times."[1]

Despite this cloudy backdrop of persisting austerity, there was a determination on the part of the British to find a silver lining and face the future with optimism. The same year the prime minister had delivered his honest if gloomy prediction about postwar life, his deputy, Herbert Morrison, proposed "something jolly" to lift national spirits. The result, in 1951, was the Festival of Britain, which like the Great Exhibition of exactly one hundred years earlier, was designed the celebrate the scientific, industrial, and artistic achievements of the United Kingdom (figure 16.1). On one level, the Festival of Britain must have underscored the depths of austerity, since it showcased a lifestyle of convenience, consumerism, and comfort that was very different from the daily reality experienced by most families and individuals. But at the same time it was a reminder of what could be accomplished in less straitened times.

Swinging Sixties and Permissiveness

Circumstances were assisted in postwar Britain by conditions of full employment (defined by an unemployment rate under 3 percent) at least as late as around 1970. The tensions between labor and management that had plagued the interwar years, with government usually siding with the latter and rarely contributing any constructive angle, were very different from the spirit of the 1950s and '60s, when both Labour and Conservative ministries generally facilitated a mood of conciliatory collaboration with trade unions. With regular income and a realistic prospect of improved financial security, Britons of all classes increasingly bought, and borrowed, more than ever before. Material possessions and household items that had been distant luxuries only a decade or so earlier quickly became essential to an acceptable standard of living.

TVs were one of the earliest signs of consumerism and relative affluence and quickly left an indelible mark. Black-and-white televisions appeared in homes of the well-to-do in the early 1950s, and by the late 1960s, nine in ten households owned a set, increasingly in color. On average, one-quarter of an individual's leisure time by 1970 was absorbed in watching TV. Other amenities spread more slowly, and as late as the early 1970s, one out of six British families did not have sole access to

FIGURE 16.1 The Festival of Britain emblem—the Festival Star—designed by Abram Games, from the cover of the *South Bank Exhibition Guide*, 1951.

a toilet, one in three did not have a washing machine, nearly one in two lived in homes without central heating, and three in five did not have in-house telephone lines. Such limited accommodation seems shocking from today's perspective, but huge strides were made in respect to all these conveniences in the space of only a decade or so and, by the turn of the twenty-first century, they were virtually universal.

The Festival of Britain had emphasized not only the potential for material advances, but also national contributions to the arts and sciences—and, when it came to cultural and intellectual attainments, Britain continued to punch well above its weight in respect to population or wealth. British accomplishments in academics were high, and achievements in science (and not only with application to nuclear physics or missile delivery!) were especially noteworthy. Between 1945 and 1975, researchers and investigators representing the UK accounted for 35 Nobel Prizes in the sciences, and a further 8 in Peace, Literature, and Economics. Only the US, with its much vaster population and resources, produced more laureates across this period (figure 16.2).

The Arts Council encouraged theater, ballet, and other expressions of art by pouring money into various projects that, without funding, would otherwise have been impossible. The coronation of Elizabeth II as queen in late spring 1953 was the first major world event to be televised

FIGURE 16.2 Historic 1953 English runner Roger Bannister, 4Minute Mile, wire photo.

FIGURE 16.3 A ticket for the stands erected of the procession to the abbey through Piccadilly Circus.

and was an opportunity for her subjects to come together and relive some of the patriotism of the war years (figure 16.3). Only days beforehand, Edmund Hilary and his guide Tenzing Norgay had scaled Mount Everest in Nepal. London was the site of the 1948 Olympics (deprecatingly called the Austerity Games), the first summer games since before World War II, and there was excitement and a surge in national pride in 1966, when England hosted—and won—the FIFA

FIGURE 16.4 Elizabeth II presents the Jules Rimet Trophy to England's team captain, Bobby Moore.

World Cup. Many of these events and achievements were broadcast, first via radio and then television, by the superior reporting of the British Broadcasting Company (BBC), which continued to lend a spirit of authority and credibility to a British outlook, in the retreating empire and beyond (figure 16.4).

The US was unrivaled as a cultural force, but there was also a distinct and enviable British label, chiefly centered on London and commemorated in a cover feature of *Time* magazine in 1966. By then it was clear much of the ethos and authority of an earlier day had been replaced by the vibrant enthusiasm of the shops and boutiques of Carnaby Street and Chelsea (figure 16.5). Rock bands such as The Rolling Stones and The Who also had roots in London, although the group most associated with Britain in the 1960s (possibly because it did not remain intact after that decade) was the Beatles, from Liverpool. The first iteration of *Doctor Who* (the pilot episode of the original series aired on November 23, 1963) may not have achieved the conspicuous worldwide success its twenty-first-century reboot would acquire, but enjoyed a modest cult following in its own right. The James Bond franchise, first in the form of Ian Fleming's novels and then in films starring Sean Connery, Roger Moore, and others, spread an image of Britain that was stylish and sophisticated, as well as lethally competent. By the mid-1960s the UK was a busy exporter of film, fashion, music, and more.

As several of these examples suggest, much of this creative exuberance, as well as the culture of consumerism that catered to it, appealed in particular to British youth. Before the second half of the twentieth century, concepts such as adolescence (outside of specific, and technical contexts) or young adulthood would not have made a whole lot of sense. Increasingly, however, styles in dress, music, and leisure activity emerged that set apart teenagers and young adults just as assuredly as the distinctions that separated them from their younger siblings or their parents and grandparents. Family or community got less attention, there was correspondingly more emphasis on

FIGURE 16.5 Carnaby Street, in London's West End, circa 1966.

individuals, and youth took the lead in exploring the potential of this freedom of identity. At the risk of contrasting two very broad generalizations, age, convention, authority, and self-restraint were supplanted by youth, novelty, independence, and self-indulgence.

This shift is often summed up in the concept of permissiveness, although perhaps tolerance is an equally suitable characterization. Contemporaries tended to emphasize the former, whereas today—admittedly, in a culture that is more generally permissive and tolerant—the latter might resonate better.

Changing attitudes and morals were gradually formalized, in fits and starts, in a raft of legal changes beginning in the 1960s. Gambling in the UK was legalized in 1960. The last use of capital punishment was in 1964, and the practice was abolished in most instances a year later. (The death penalty remained officially on the books for certain offenses until 1998, although it was never applied.)

The Abortion Act (1967) decriminalized abortion in Great Britain and made it available under the National Health Service (NHS), although by and large the procedure remained illegal in Northern Ireland more than fifty years later. Beginning January 1, 2019, the Health (Regulation of Termination of Pregnancy) Act made abortion legal, within the first 12 weeks of pregnancy and under certain other specific circumstances, for women in the Republic of Ireland. Beginning in 1961, oral contraception ("the pill") was made available to married women as a service of the NHS, and to unmarried women in 1967.

At the start of the 1960s, there had been about one divorce for every 15 marriages in the United Kingdom.[2] Parliament secured sweeping legislation in respect to divorce before the end of the decade, and the first year it applied, 1972, there was more than one divorce for every five marriages, notwithstanding the highest number of marriages since the beginning of World War II. By the start of the twenty-first century, there were nearly three divorces in the UK for every five marriages. The Equal Pay Act (1970) guaranteed women equal treatment as men in respect to pay and work conditions, but its implementation was imperfect, as demonstrated by the necessity five years later of the Sex Discrimination Act (1975), which protected men and women from discrimination owing to sex or marital status.

As early as 1954, the Conservative government under Winston Churchill summoned the Wolfenden Committee to consider revising the Criminal Law Amendment Act (1885), better known as the Labouchere Amendment, which outlawed homosexual activity between adult males. Part of the committee's recommendation, published in 1957, was that "homosexual behaviour between consenting adults in private … no longer be a criminal offence." By coincidence, the committee first met less than three months after the death, apparently by suicide, of Alan Turing, who had led British code-breaking efforts during World War II and laid the foundation for subsequent advances in theoretical computer science and artificial intelligence. Dr. Turing was gay and prosecuted for "gross indecency" under the aforementioned Labouchere Amendment. In an attempt to "cure" his homosexual tendencies, and to avoid prison, Turing agreed to submit himself to estrogen injection, a process known colloquially as "chemical castration." Turing received a posthumous royal pardon nearly 60 years later, in 2013, and today the Policing and Crime Act (2017) offers automatic and general pardon to men who had been convicted for gay relationships that were no longer criminal offenses (figure 16.6).[3]

The aim of the Wolfenden Committee, however, was not to emancipate gay men, or otherwise advance a progressive agenda. Rather, its purpose was to address failed policies of policing homosexuality and to reduce its public visibility. The parliament of the day, still Conservative (now under Harold Macmillan), rejected the position of the Wolfenden Committee, and the law remained unchanged for another ten years

FIGURE 16.6 Alan Turing, 78 High Street Hampton blue plaque.

before the Sexual Offences Act (1967), secured under a Labour government led by Harold Wilson, finally legalized gay relationships between consenting adults in England and Wales. The same rights and protections were implemented in Scotland and Northern Ireland in 1980 and 1982.

Taken together, these changes marked a significant shift away from traditional patterns of deference and paternalism that had characterized much of British society in the modern period. They coincided with a big drop in the influence of organized religion, reflected in statistics of regular attendance at worship services, as well as occasional markers such as baptisms or marriages in formal religious settings. Numbers dropped precipitately from the 1960s to the early 1970s and entered free fall thereafter.[4]

The change was also evident in the new directions seen in British plays, TV programs, and films in the 1950s and into the 1960s. Dubbed "kitchen sink dramas" because of a generalized setting common to several of them, the antiheroes (or perhaps heroes) of these productions were often young working-class men whose relative affluence and ambition led them to reject the values and lifestyles of their parents' or grandparents' generations but who were nonetheless frustrated in their aspirations to achieve standing in the solid middle class. Playwrights and novelists such as John Osborne (*Look Back in Anger*, 1956) and actors such as Albert Finney (*Saturday Night and Sunday Morning*, 1960) associated with the genre were called Angry Young Men, which aptly captures the mood of disorientation and dissatisfaction that, in reality, must have been vastly more widespread than the idealized imagery of a London high street in the Swinging Sixties.

It would be misleading to locate all these changes in attitudes, morals, values, expectations, and so on after World War II, let alone more specifically in the post-austerity years of the later 1950s or the Swinging Sixties. Owing to the difficult and turbulent first half of the twentieth century, however, it must have occasionally seemed that way to contemporaries. Indeed, with the distortion of hindsight, it can look as though Britain emerged suddenly from the Edwardian era into the 1960s, or from the pages of G. B. Shaw's *Pygmalion* to the B-side of The Beatles' *Abbey Road*. In fact, the disruption was more probably the cumulative and delayed consequences, cultural and economic, of the devastation and displacement of the two world wars, book ending the social and familial stresses of the Depression. It is not too much to say that no comparable stretch of modern British history witnessed as much rapid change as the half century that followed World War II, and to find such thorough social and cultural upheaval across such a short period would probably mean looking to the generations that followed the Black Death in the mid-fourteenth century.

Toward a Multicultural Britain

No society is ever completely homogenous—racially, ethnically, culturally, or otherwise—and modern Britain is no exception. Foreign-born or immigrant elements in the seventeenth and eighteenth centuries, often consisting of diasporic trade communities or on-leave or abandoned sailors, typically congregated around port cities. Many of these newcomers were European in origin, and therefore white, although some would have come from more far-flung homelands. (The observant visitor to Trafalgar Square in London will discern an African sailor, dressed like his fellow British tars and armed with a musket, on the bronze panel of Nelson's Column depicting the admiral's death.) In the nineteenth and early twentieth centuries, immigrants to Britain were increasingly refugees from economic hardship or religious or political persecution, especially in central or eastern Europe. Such immigrants continued to be overwhelmingly white, although often with unfamiliar characteristics or traditions.

Millions of refugees, mostly from central Europe, were displaced at the end of World War II and, partly as an opening move in the Cold War and partly to provide sufficient labor, especially in coal mines and other industries, the British government invited up to two hundred thousand Polish workers to settle permanently in the UK. They were shortly followed by about thirty thousand Italians. Among non-white migrants, pride of place typically goes to the 492 migrants—mostly men, but including women, as well as some families—who completed the 22-day voyage from Kingston, Jamaica, to Tilbury Docks, London, on June 22, 1948. But as we have seen, highly diverse and polyglot communities had been established, decades earlier, in port cities such as London, Bristol, Cardiff, and Liverpool. During the interwar years, such men employed as merchant sailors on British shipping lines—and originally from India, southeast Asia, east Africa, the West Indies, and elsewhere—were often known collectively as "coloured seamen."

In absolute numbers, let alone as percentage of the overall population, their presence was tiny. Their clustering in port cities alarmed traditional white elements of British society, however, leading in 1925 to the Special Restriction Order (SRO), better known as the Coloured Alien Seamen's ordinance. The order, which required "coloured alien seamen" (i.e., non-white sailors) who disembarked from ships in England and Wales to present local police with documentation, was not imposed on their white counterparts. (The burden of proof—in this case, documented evidence of imperial citizenship—rested on the non-white sailors rather than on police or other local authorities and was reminiscent of the Contagious Diseases Acts, which had targeted working-class women, of the previous century.) Moreover, at least in respect to Indians, the order was unnecessary and even of dubious legality, since the Alien Restriction Act and the Alien Order (1919 and 1920, respectively) had clarified the status of Indian sailors in Britain as citizens of the empire and not as aliens. But evidently they were not welcome on the same terms as their white counterparts. The SRO initially operated only in specific port cities, but in 1926 it was extended to apply throughout Britain.[5]

Such laws clearly perceived non-white men to be threats to British identity. They were "the first instance of state-sanctioned race discrimination inside Britain to come to widespread notice"[6] and, as such, they prompted reaction. Indian-born N. J. Upadhyaya founded the Indian Seamen's Union in response to the order and, in 1933, the League of Coloured Peoples was formed to protect non-whites from various harassments ranging from petty inconveniences to legal restrictions or arrest. Other groups that had been formed primarily as social clubs or interest groups, such as the Glasgow Indian Union (GIU), took up the case of dozens of Indians inconvenienced by the SRO in Scotland. The GIU had originally been established, in 1911, as a social club and interest group, but that did not protect it from government surveillance, even before the SRO, in 1923.

It is also worth noting that many of the future leaders of colonial nationalism spent time in Britain in the early part of the twentieth century. Many south Asians associated with the Indian National Congress (founded 1885) had been educated or otherwise procured professional qualifications in Britain, even in the nineteenth century, and this was increasingly true of Africans and West Indians in the twentieth century. Indeed, the Pan-African Conference, which met in London in 1900, led after World War I to five Pan-African Congresses, three of which met in England. Perhaps the most notable of these, the Fifth Pan-African Congress, met in Manchester in 1945 and was attended by future post-independence leaders of Ghana, Kenya, and Malawi.

Even after World War II, most immigrants to the UK remained white. The 1951 Census reported 492,000 Irish-born inhabitants; 387,000 from various parts of Europe, notably Poland, the Soviet Union, or Germany; 136,000 from the United States, Canada, Australia, or Canada; and a comparatively small 111,000 from India.

Irish-born immigrants had jumped to 683,000 by 1961, but migrants from India were in second place—a position they would hold into the twenty-first century. Much of this movement was in the context of Britain's retreat from empire: 42,000 Cypriotes by 1961, 58,000 Kenyans, 136,000 Pakistanis, 171,000 Jamaicans by 1971, 104,000 Bangladeshis by 1991, and, in the first decade of the twenty-first century, close to 400,000 South Africans and Nigerians. According to the 2011 Census, the United Kingdom was home to nearly 1.4 million south Asian-born inhabitants.[7]

Many of these migrants and their families reckoned the odds of steady and remunerative employment to be better in Britain than elsewhere. This made sense: The economies of much of

Africa, south Asia, and the West Indies, whether under colonial or postcolonial regimes, remained in developing stages at midcentury, and conditions of full employment in Britain meant jobs were plentiful, generally with openings and availabilities outstripping the supply of domestic labor. In many cases, migrants probably intended to remain in the UK only for a few years before returning home with savings. Thus it was the prospect of wealth and prosperity that pulled migrants to the UK, and the demands of British industry welcomed this willing influx of labor. Similar factors applied in the case of migrants from war-torn central Europe.

Many big businesses in the UK set up offices abroad and actively recruited. The hotel industry, for example, which had generally had a rough run of the previous three decades, was poised to take advantage of the return to relative stability and prosperity after 1945 but needed to staff its laundry and maintenance services. Newly nationalized interests, such as London Transport, also recruited heavily from the fading empire. With the expectation of universal coverage, Britain's new NHS needed more doctors, nurses, and clerical workers than the private system of care it was supplanting and turned in particular to the West Indies. Engineering firms and textile mills, particularly in the English Midlands and northwest, looked elsewhere and relied especially on immigrants from Asia to take on night shifts, which white workers, who were generally unionized, refused to work.

Although Britain's non-white population was still small after World War II, the racial geography of the country was changing. Whereas previously, pockets of (mostly male) non-whites tended to congregate around specific ports, into the 1950s and 1960s, south Asian and West Indian families increasingly took up residence in inland towns and cities in Britain. Most filled the existing need for labor, but some opened restaurants, shops, or other businesses that catered to ethnic appetites or markets, as well as offered something new to the white population. Not everyone welcomed this change in the feel of Britain, prompting a reaction: the rise—or perhaps more accurately the *articulation*—of racism in the postwar United Kingdom.

Of course, as we have seen, there was racism in Britain after World War I, and doubtless before it. The Cardiff Seamen's Strike, in 1911 had been aimed against the city's non-white population of around 700 (mostly Chinese) and, in 1919, at least three men were killed in several days of riots motivated by racial tension in different parts of England, Scotland, and Wales. A staple allegation was that non-whites competed for scarce jobs and drove down wages, which was particularly ludicrous given the genuine need for labor in the rebuilding of the economy and infrastructure of postwar Britain. Others complained that Blacks contributed to unsanitary and overcrowded conditions, and extended wait times, exacerbated by wartime bombing, for available council housing. Still other complaints were vaguer, alleging Black families eroded a sense of community or otherwise challenged British—and increasingly *English*—identity.

Racist responses in the late 1950s and early '60s ranged from the visceral (e.g., riots and attacks against non-white individuals, neighborhoods, or businesses in London, Nottingham, and elsewhere) to the more formal (e.g., organizations such as the White Defence League and the

Birmingham Immigration Control Association). In 1959, Oswald Mosley former Labour-turned-Fascist MP who had been interned for most of World War II because of his Nazi sympathies, ran for a parliamentary seat that included Notting Hill, site of a week of riots and attacks against the neighborhood's Black West Indian population the previous summer. His platform, as a far-right Union Movement candidate, criticized immigration and promoted repatriation. Mosley finished in last place, winning a little over 8 percent of the votes cast, but the campaign succeeded in normalizing racism and bringing criticism of immigration under a national spotlight.

Such a program could prove effective at winning votes. Conservative candidates in particular played on fears that Blacks kept jobs from whites, contributed to crime and disorder, introduced dangerous diseases from abroad, and were transforming sections of cities and towns into "non-British" enclaves. In 1964 a candidate stood for—and won—what was judged to be a safe seat for the Labour Party on his association with the incendiary slogan "If you want a nigger for a neighbour, vote Liberal or Labour."[8] A new party, the National Front, was formed in 1967, following the merger of smaller right-wing groups including the Racial Preservation Society. Its aimed, among other things, to end non-white immigration and to repatriate those already settled in Britain. Former Conservative cabinet minister Enoch Powell advocated similar positions and, a year later, delivered a notorious speech prophesying rivers of blood in the British heartland if efforts were not taken to stem the tide of non-white immigration into the country. The British National Party was formed 15 years later, on an avowedly white supremacist and anti-immigrant platform that resonated perfectly with Mosley's campaign nearly a quarter century earlier.

Postwar legislation on immigration is reminiscent of government attempts to address problems of poverty and unemployment during the interwar years; rather than any clear or direction-oriented policy, they were a series of knee-jerk responses designed to paper over what were perceived to be the big issues of the day—or, as often as not, to pander to a fickle and frequently prejudiced electorate. First was the Nationality Act (1948), which recognized the wartime contributions of the commonwealth and empire, white and non-white, and responded to the dire need for workers in the UK. The act created a new category—Citizen of the United Kingdom and Colonies, or CUKC for short—that extended equal rights in respect to free migration and unrestricted access to the services of the welfare state. At a stroke, on January 1, 1949, the number of people eligible for a UK passport increased by hundreds of millions. However, beginning in the 1960s and continuing through the 1970s and 1980s, various governments—both Conservative and Labour—were complicit in circumscribing the openness of the 1948 act along racially discriminatory lines designed implicitly to limit non-white entry into the UK.

Restrictions were placed, for example, on unmarried Black men who were, it was alleged, chiefly attracted to the bright lights and short skirts of swinging, affluent Britain. On the other hand, non-white males who were deemed respectable (e.g., those with wives and children or elderly parents) found it easier to acquire visas or gain work permits. At the same time, unmarried non-white women were encouraged to migrate to the UK, on the rationale they would presumably marry unattached men and thus shore up the demographic of single Black males. White migrants from the Commonwealth (e.g., from Australia or Canada) did not face these restrictions, and even migrants from outside the Commonwealth (e.g., from Europe or the United States) sometimes found it easier than non-white citizens of the Commonwealth to live and work in the UK.

Meanwhile, a Race Relations Act (1965) forbade discrimination based on color in respect to employment, housing, or other opportunities or services, and a Race Relations Board was implemented to handle complaints of violations, harassment, and so on. These efforts were not entirely effective, however, and it was necessary, more than a decade later, to form the Commission on Racial Equality (CRE), to investigate continuing violations and combat further discrimination. The CRE also marked the first time a British government identified racial equality, rather than toleration and/or integration, as a goal.

Another sort of diversification that has taken place in the British Isles in the years since World War II reflected not so much an actual change in population or demographics as a shift in identity. In many ways, the century lasting roughly from 1850 to 1950 was the apogee of Britishness, and national categories of English, Scottish, Welsh, and sometimes even Irish were ignored or placed under the comprehensive heading of British. In the nineteenth century this was because of the British Empire, which drew from Scotland and Ireland as much as—indeed, proportionately speaking, more so than—from England and Wales. In the twentieth century, the rigors of two world wars instilled a common sense of patriotism and a common purpose and made it necessary for everyone to pull together. The spread of literacy and national schemes of education tended to erode regional differences, and new technologies such as film and especially radio imposed a de facto English accent on what was regarded as simply British.

After the wars, however, and with the imminent dissolution of the British Empire, Britishness made less and less sense and was increasingly seen to be out of touch and associated with the values and assumptions of an older generation. The rediscovery of unique national identities—or, within the case of England itself, unique regional identities—could be casual and cultural, with emphases on music, traditional life, folk patterns and speech, and the like. But such interests could merge imperceptibly to acquire political motives. A case in point was the theft (although Scottish nationalists might prefer the language of "restoration" or "repatriation") of the Stone of Scone from Westminster Abbey on Christmas Day in 1950. On one level, the action was a waggish prank carried out by four college students between terms. But on another level it was rooted in the reality of dissatisfaction with Scottishness being absorbed in British (which, as often as not, meant English) contexts.

We saw in chapter 13 that the loss of old industries before World War II led to regional unemployment and depression. The trend continued after World War II, often prompting political movements in Scotland and Wales. Economic interest might have pulled toward Labour,[9] but often there was a nationalist response. Plaid Cymru, a Welsh nationalist party, and the Scottish National Party had been formed in the 1920s and 1930s but finally acquired some teeth (i.e., visibility and electoral support) in the late 1960s (figure 16.7). Referenda for home rule were rejected in 1979, but renewed efforts were successful in 1997: Scotland and Wales remained in the United Kingdom and continued to send MPs to Westminster, but certain budgets, worth billions of pounds annually, were handed over to national assemblies. The question of outright withdrawal from the union was revived in Scotland, but when brought to a vote in 2014, the measure failed 55-45.

On the whole, however, Scottish and Welsh political parties have never had much electoral success at a national level, and neither the NF nor the BNP has ever claimed so much as a single seat in the House of Commons. Notwithstanding, they and likeminded third parties (e.g., UKIP) have succeeded since the 1980s in adjusting the tone of political debate in the UK. This shift, along with a broader reawakening of national and regional identities and associations, as well as the uncertainties of globalization, contributed to the spirit that resulted in the Brexit vote in the summer of 2016.

FIGURE 16.7 A Plaid Cymru rally in Machynlleth in 1949 where the "Parliament for Wales in 5 years" campaign was started.

IMAGE CREDITS

PART THREE

Retrospective

On June 18, 2020, Dame Vera Lynn died at her home in England at the age of 103. Her life spanned most of the twentieth century and a good deal of the twenty-first. The daughter of a plumber and a dressmaker, she was in many respects a typical white working-class woman of her generation. However, she lived in extraordinary times, which gave her extraordinary opportunities. Her musical career was already off to a good start when the Second World War catapulted her to stardom. In late 1939, British servicemen voted her "the forces sweetheart" in a *Daily Express* poll. She spent the war entertaining the troops. "We'll Meet Again," the song she popularized, captured the hopes of her generation. When Britain went into lockdown at the beginning of the COVID-19 pandemic, the Queen referenced the song in her address to the nation.

Lynn benefited from increased social mobility and greater gender equality in Britain. She enjoyed a career and a family but faced challenges imposed by society that gave women greater opportunity while offering them little support in balancing the roles of professional and mother. She had only one child, she said, because the demands of performing made it impossible for her care for more. "I was going to be as much of a mother as I could," she wrote in her memoir. "I wasn't going to have any of that nonsense where a nanny produces a spotless infant at around teatime for a kiss and a smile and then whisks her away again to some distant part of the house."[1] Lynn explained her popularity in modest terms. "I think people looked at me as one of them—an ordinary girl from an ordinary family with a voice that you could recognize," she observed. "It's that simple."[2]

Today, Britons have a different notion of what "one of them" looks like. Asked to identify the best female singer in 2020, a new generation chose Leona Lewis.[3] Like Lynn, she came from a working-class family, but unlike her, Lewis is multiracial. If she had been born in 1940, she would not have won a popularity contest in a much less diverse Britain. Indeed, she would probably not have had a musical career at all. Vera Lynn, an icon of the twentieth century, departed a United Kingdom vastly different that the one into which she had been born.

BRITAIN IN A NEW CENTURY

I n this survey, we have tried to present a balanced account of British history within a local, European, and world historical context as it unfolded across more than three hundred years. We have sought to present an unvarnished reconstruction, neither celebratory nor overly critical, of events, people, and movements that shaped a nation, an empire, and the world with which they interacted.

Authors of textbooks such as ours get to pick the point at which their historical narrative begins, to choose a pivotal moment from which change moving forward can reasonably be assessed. They usually do not have the luxury of ending their account on an equally significant date. That fact explains why so many historical surveys either stop abruptly, like a thought in midsentence, or are brought to a cheery conclusion, by writers wanting to end their account on a positive note, as if putting a bow on a package.

Circumstances have spared us the difficulty of deciding when and how to end this history of Britain. The year 2020 was a watershed year like 1688, 1815, 1919, and 1945. The United Kingdom was in the grip of the worst pandemic since the influenza outbreak of 1918–1919, which followed fast on the heels of the Great War. At the end of 2020, Britain formalized its departure from the European Union. The impact of these two momentous events will playout over years and decades, but there are already some indications of the direction change might take.

Many Brexit supporters expected that leaving the EU would reduce or even halt immigration, especially by people of color. Even if that occurs, the United Kingdom will continue to grow more diverse. Demographic projections suggest that by 2061, 35–40 percent of Britons will be non-white.[1] The country will continue to struggle with creating a truly pluralistic society for the foreseeable future.

The Brexit referendum revealed deep divisions within the United Kingdom. While the kingdom as whole voted to leave the EU, polling by country varied dramatically. Of the nearly 66 million people living in the UK in 2016, more than 55 million lived in England, which voted to leave the EU by a margin of 6 percent. In Scotland, however, 62 percent of those who voted wanted to remain. In Northern Ireland, 56 percent voted to stay in the EU, while 53 percent of those in Wales opted to leave, even though Wales has received a great deal of infrastructure and development money from Brussels.[2] The Welsh vote probably resulted from a significant proportion of its electorate fitting the Brexit demographic found elsewhere in the United Kingdom (see chapter 14).[3] Fear over a hard border with the Irish Republic may explain the anti-Brexit vote in Northern Ireland.

The Scottish Brexit vote may be the harbinger of more turmoil to come. Since receiving autonomy in 1999, a minority of Scots have campaigned for full independence. In the 2014 referendum, Scots voted 55–45 percent to stay in the United Kingdom. Brexit may, however, be a game changer. Many Scots who voted against independence also supported EU membership. Pro-independence parties won a majority of seats in the May 2021 Scottish parliamentary elections and are pushing for another referendum on leaving the United Kingdom.

Brexit also revealed divisions by region and generation across the United Kingdom. The more prosperous south voted against Brexit while the North and Midlands (the old rustbelt) along with most rural areas voted for it. Younger voters and those too young to vote at all in the 2016 referendum are unhappy with Brexit, which may affect their ability to work and study on the continent. Whether they will take their anger out against the Conservatives at the polls remains to be seen.

The economic and political consequences of Brexit are more difficult to discern. The United Kingdom reached a trade agreement with the EU on December 24, 2020. That agreement eliminated the threat of tariffs for the near term but imposed borders and customs controls that have already caused serious problems. Fish reportedly rotted on the docks because of new bureaucratic delays in exporting them. A decline in exports is exacerbating an economic slowdown caused by COVID-19.[4]

On the other hand, some foreign companies see an opportunity in Brexit. Nissan has recognized an advantage to the trade deal with the EU and promised to increase production of batteries at its UK plant, which will allow it to avoid EU import duties on parts manufactured in Asia.[5] The decision benefits Britain, but if other manufactures take this approach to skirting EU tariffs, the deal with Brussels could sour.

Britain's relationship with the United States is another variable. Donald Trump liked Boris Johnson and favored Brexit, which he compared to his own "America first" policy. President Joseph Biden is committed to reengaging with America's NATO allies. During his 2021 meeting with Johnson, he reaffirmed the "special relationship."

The impact of COVID-19 has created further uncertainty. It may pass into history with little lasting effect, as did the influenza pandemic of 1918. Preliminary indications, however, suggest that some adjustments to work, family, and social life may be permanent. Even before the lockdowns, more Britons were telecommuting to work than ever before. This trend promises to widen the gap between those with education and technical skills and those without.

All these conclusions are, of course, purely speculative. Expert though historians may be in analyzing the past, when it comes to predicting the future, all that they can do is echo Samuel Beckett's famous quote, "Something is taking its course."

ENDNOTES

INTERPRETING THE BRITISH PAST

1. Ambeth R. Ocampo, *Conversations with Teodoro Andal Agoncillo: Talking History* (Malate, Manila, Philippines: De La Salle University Press, 1995).
2. "Historiography," http://qcpages.qc.cuny.edu/Writing/history/critical/historiography.html.

CHAPTER 1: STRUCTURES AND PATTERNS OF EVERYDAY LIFE

1. E. A. Wrigley, "British Population During the 'Long' Eighteenth Century, 1680–1840," in *The Cambridge Economic History of Modern Britain*, ed. Roderick Floud and Paul Johnson (Cambridge: Cambridge University Press, 2004), 57–95, esp. 57–60; Andrew Hinde, *England's Population: A History since the Domesday Survey* (Oxford: Oxford University Press, 2003), 177–83.
2. Wrigley, 69–75, 83.
3. John D. Ramsbottom, "Women and Family," in *A Companion to Eighteenth-Century Britain*, ed. H. T. Dickinson (Hoboken, NJ: Wiley, 2002), 210–12.
4. Philip Morgan, "British Encounters with African and African Americans, 1600–1780," in *Strangers within the Realm: Cultural Margins of the First British Empire*, ed. Bernard Bailyn and Philip Morgan (Chapel Hill: University of North Carolina Press, 1991), 159; Norma Myers, *Reconstructing the Black Past: Blacks in Britain, 1780–1830* (London: Routledge, 1996), 35. In *Black London: Life before Emancipation* (New Brunswick, NJ: Rutgers University Press, 1995), Gretchen Holbrook Gerzina leaves the realm of quantification to analyze Black cultural presence in England from the sixteenth to the eighteenth centuries.
5. Thomas Robert Malthus, *An Essay on the Principle of Population* (London: J. Johnson, 1798).
6. As quoted in Linda Colley, *Britons: Forging the Nation 1707–1837* (New Haven, CT: Yale University Press, 1992), 289.
7. 1801 Census of Great Britain, *Abstract of the Answers and Returns Made Pursuant to an Act, […] Intitled, "An Act for Taking an Account of the Population of Great Britain, and an Increase or Diminution Thereof"* (London: 1801), https://www.visionofbritain.org.uk/census/GB1801ABS_1/1.
8. Daniel Defoe, *A Review of the State of the British Nation*, VI, 26 (June 25, 1709).
9. Frank O'Gorman, *The Long Eighteenth Century: British Political and Social History, 1688–1832* (London: Edward Arnold, 1997), 272.
10. Douglas Hay, "Property, Authority, and the Criminal Law," in *Albion's Fatal Tree: Crime and Society in Eighteenth-Century England*, ed. E. P. Thompson et al. (New York: Pantheon, 1976), 25 and 56.
11. Reeve Ballard, *The Necessity of Magistracy from the Vices of Mankind. An Assize sermon, preached at Kingston upon Thames, August 16, 1745* (London: H. Pemberton, 1745), 7.
12. Richard Green, *The Benefit of Oaths to Civil Society Consider'd* (London: John and Paul Knapton, 1745), 13.
13. Ballard, *Necessity of Magistracy*, 6.

14. Ian Duncanson, *Historiography, Empire and the Rule of Law: Imagined Constitutions, Remembered Legalities* (New York: Routledge, 2012) and Nasser Hussain, *The Jurisprudence of Emergency: Colonialism and the Rule of Law* (Ann Arbor: University of Michigan Press, 2003).

15. William Blackstone, *Commentaries on the Laws of England*, 4 vols (Chicago: University of Chicago Press, 1979), I: 8.

16. Richard Davenport-Hines, "Shirley, Laurence, Fourth Earl Ferrers (1720–1760)," *Oxford Dictionary of National Biography* (Oxford: Oxford University Press, 2004), http://www.oxforddnb.com/view/article/25432. For more on the insanity defense in criminal trials, see Dana Rabin, *Identity, Crime, and Legal Responsibility in Eighteenth-Century England* (New York: Palgrave, 2004), especially chapter 2.

17. *London Evening Post*, May 6, 1760.

18. Kenneth Morgan, *Slavery and the British Empire: From Africa to America* (Oxford: Oxford University Press, 2007), 111–14.

19. Ruth Paley, "Somerset, James (*b.c.* 1741, *d.* in or after 1772)," *Oxford Dictionary of National Biography*, September 2004, https://www.oxforddnb.com/view/10.1093/ref:odnb/9780198614128.001.0001/odnb-9780198614128-e-70057.

20. Dana Rabin, "'In a Country of Liberty?': Slavery, Villeinage and the Making of Whiteness in the Somerset Case (1772)," *History Workshop Journal* 72 (2011): 5–6.

21. Sarah Minney, "The Search for Dido," *History Today* 55 (2005): 2; Gene Adams, "Dido Elizabeth Belle: A Black Girl at Kenwood," *Camden Historical Review* 12 (1984): 10–14.

22. Thomas Hutchinson, *The Diary and Letters of His Excellency Thomas Hutchinson Esq* (London: S. Low Marston, Searle & Rivington, 1883), 2:276.

23. Susan Kent, *Gender and History* (New York: Palgrave, 2011), 5.

24. Kimberlé Crenshaw, *On Intersectionality: Essential Writings* (New York: The New Press, 2017).

25. Blackstone, *Commentaries*, I: 430.

26. Carole Levin, *The Heart and Stomach of a King: Elizabeth I and the Politics of Sex and Power* (Philadelphia: University of Pennsylvania Press, 1994), 1.

27. Thomas Paine, *The Rights of Man* (London, 1791).

28. Mary Wollstonecraft, *A Vindication of the Rights of Men* (London, 1790).

29. Mary Wollstonecraft, *Thoughts on the Education of Daughters: With Reflections on Female Conduct, in the More Important Duties of Life* (London, 1787), and *A Vindication of the Rights of Woman* (1792).

30. Mary Astell, *Some Reflections upon Marriage, Occasion'd by the Duke & Duchess of Mazarine's Case* (London, 1700), 9.

31. Jacqueline Broad, *The Philosophy of Mary Astell: An Early Modern Theory of Virtue* (Oxford: Oxford University Press, 2015), 127–32.

32. Tanya Evans, "Women, Marriage, and the Family," in *Women's History: Britain, 1700–1850, An Introduction*, ed. Hannah Barker and Elaine Chalus (New York: Routledge, 2005), 66; Douglas James, "Parliamentary Divorce," *Parliamentary History* 31, no. 2 (2012): 169–89.

33. Junko Akamatsu, "Revisiting Ecclesiastical Adultery Cases in Eighteenth-Century England," *Journal of Women's History* 28, no. 1 (2016): 13–16.

34. Leah Leneman, "'Disregarding the Matrimonial Vows': Divorce in Eighteenth and Early Nineteenth-Century Scotland," *Journal of Social History* 30, no. 2 (1996): 468–482.

35. Stella Tillyard, *Aristocrats: Caroline, Emily, Louisa and Sarah Lennox, 1740-1832* (London: Vintage, 1995), 20–34, 76.

36. See Evans, "Women, Marriage, and Family," 62–66 for overview of the debate.

37. Amy M. Froide, *Never Married: Singlewomen in Early Modern England* (Oxford: Oxford University Press, 2007).

38. Evans, "Women, Marriage, and Family," 61.

39. Leonore Davidoff, "The Family in Britain" in *The Cambridge Social History of Britain, 1750–1950*, vol. 2, ed. F. M. L. Thompson (Cambridge: Cambridge University Press, 1990), 90.

40. Margaret Hunt, *The Middling Sort: Commerce, Gender, and the Family in England, 1680–1780* (Berkeley: University of California Press, 1996), 81.

41. Anna Clark, *The Struggle for the Breeches: Gender and the Making of the British Working Class* (Berkeley: University of California Press, 1995).

42. Alannah Tompkins, "Women and Poverty," *Women's History: Britain, 1700–1850, An Introduction*, ed. Hannah Barker and Elaine Chalus (New York: Routledge, 2005), 156.

43. Evans, "Women, Marriage, and Family," 66–67.

44. Tompkins, "Women and Poverty," 153.

45. Olwen Hufton, "Women without Men: Widows and Spinsters in Britain and France in the Eighteenth Century," *Journal of Family History* 9, no. 4 (1985): 367.

46. As quoted in John Beattie, "Hard-Pressed to Make Ends Meet: Women and Crime in Augustan London," in *Women & History: Voices in Early Modern England*, ed. Valerie Frith (Toronto: Coach House Press, 1995), 112–13.

47. Tanya Evans, *Unfortunate Objects: Lone Mothers in Eighteenth-Century London* (New York: Palgrave, 2005).

48. Edward Long, *The History of Jamaica or, General Survey of the Antient and Modern State of that Island* (London: Lowndes, 1774) 2: 276–77.

49. *Susanna Wesley: The Complete Writings*, ed. Charles Wallace (New York: Oxford University Press, 1997).

50. Davidoff, "The Family in Britain," 77; J. H. Plumb, "The New World of Children in Eighteenth-Century England," *Past & Present* 67 (1975): 82–84.

51. http://umich.edu/~ece/student_projects/female_tatler/readership.html.

52. Daniel Defoe, S*A Tour Thro' The Whole Island of Great Britain, Divided into Circuits and Journies* (London: 1726), 2:600–02.

53. Jane Humphries, "Childhood and Child Labour in the British Industrial Revolution," *Economic History Review* 66, no. 2 (2013): 396.

54. Humphries, "Childhood and Child Labour," 395–418.

CHAPTER 2: STRUCTURES AND PATTERNS OF POLITICS

1. Lois G. Schwoerer, "Celebrating the Glorious Revolution, 1689-1989," *Albion* 22, no. 1 (1990): 2.

2. Ibid., 2–8.

3. Steven C. A. Pincus, *England's Glorious Revolution, 1688-89: A Brief History with Documents* (Boston: Bedford/St. Martin's, 2006), 5, 51.

4. Ibid., vii.

5. Ibid., 14–15.

6. Ibid., 37–38.

7. *Bill of Rights* (1689), §9.

8. Frank O'Gorman, *The Long Eighteenth Century: British Political and Social History, 1688–1832* (London: Bloomsbury, 1997), 66.

9. William Blackstone, *Commentaries on the Laws of England*, 4 vols. (Chicago: University of Chicago Press, 1979), I: 156.

10. Ibid., 1:6.

11. *Bill of Rights*, §1.

12. Elaine Chalus and Fiona Montgomery, "Women and Politics," in *Women's History: Britain, 1700–1850*, ed. Hannah Barker and Elaine Chalus (New York: Routledge, 2005), 220.

13. As quoted in John Brewer, *The Sinews of Power: War, Money and the English State, 1688–1783* (Cambridge, MA: Harvard University Press, 1988), epigraph.

14. Roy Porter, *English Society in the Eighteenth Century* (New York; Penguin, 1982), 73–74.

15. Brewer, *The Sinews of Power*, 29, 114–15.

16. *The Massacre of Glenco Being a true narrative of the barbarous murther of the Glenco-Men, in the Highlands of Scotland, by way of military execution, on the 13th of Feb. 1692.* (London: B. Bragg, 1703), 21.

17. Charles Leslie, *The Massacre of Glenco. 13th of February 1692. Being a reprint of a contemporary account of that ruthless butchery* (Edinburgh: E &G Goldsmid, 1885), 14.

18. For more on the Union with Scotland in 1707, see Allan I. Macinnes, *Union and Empire: The Making of the United Kingdom in 1707* (Cambridge: Cambridge University. Press, 2007); T. I. Rae, ed., *The Union of 1707: Its Impact on Scotland* (Glasgow: Blackie & Son Limited, 1974); John Robertson, ed., *A Union for Empire: Political Thought and the British Union of 1707* (Cambridge: Cambridge University Press, 1995), and Christopher Whatley with Derek T. Patrick, *The Scots and the Union* (Edinburgh: Edinburgh University Press, 2006).

19. The British Parliament at Westminster passed the Union with Ireland Act (39 and 40 Geo. III c. 67) which received royal assent on August 1, 1800. For the full text, see *The Statutes at Large, of England and of Great Britain from Magna Carta to the Union of the Kingdoms of Great Britain and Ireland*, ed. John Raithby (London, 1811), 20:395–424.

20. For more on the French Revolution and Ireland, see *Britain and the French Revolution 1789–1815*, ed. H. T. Dickinson (New York: Palgrave MacMillan, 1989), especially Dickinson, "Introduction: The Impact on Britain of the French Revolution and the French Wars, 1789–1815," 1–20 and Marianne Elliott, "Ireland and the French Revolution," 83–102.

21. David Wilkinson, "'How Did They Pass the Union?' Secret Service Expenditure in Ireland, 1799–1804," *History* 82 (1997): 223–51.

22. Theophilus Swift, *Hear Him! Hear Him! In a Letter to the Right Honourable John Foster* (Dublin: J. Stockdale, 1799), 40.

23. Lynn Hunt, *The Family Romance of the French Revolution* (Berkeley: University of California Press, 1992); Joan Landes, *Women and the Public Sphere in the Age of the French Revolution* (Ithaca, NY: Cornell University Press, 1988) and *Visualizing the Nation: Gender, Representation, and Revolution in Eighteenth-Century France* (Ithaca, NY: Cornell University Press, 2001).

24. According to Blackstone, "By marriage, the husband and wife are one person in law: that is, the very being or legal existence of the woman is suspended during the marriage, or at least is incorporated and consolidated into that of the husband: under whose wing, protection, and cover, she performs every thing; and is

therefore called in our law-French a *feme-covert.*" William Blackstone, *Commentaries on the Laws of England,* 4 vols. (Chicago: University of Chicago Press, 1979), I: 430. Amy Erickson, *Women and Property in Early Modern England* (London: Routledge, 1993); Susan Staves, *Married Women's Separate Property in England, 1660–1833* (Cambridge, MA: Harvard University Press, 1990); and Garthine Walker, *Crime, Gender and Social Order in Early Modern England* (Cambridge: Cambridge. University Press, 2003) have shown that the status of *feme covert* was largely a legal fiction; women skirted these restrictions acting as legal agents with and without the help of their male kin in both criminal and civil courts in the early modern period.

25. Most recently, Alvin Jackson's book *The Two Unions: Ireland, Scotland, and the Survival of the United Kingdom, 1707–2007* (Oxford: Oxford University Press, 2012). Macinnes integrates a discussion of Ireland and the comparison with Scotland's union throughout his book *Union and Empire.*

CHAPTER 3: BRITAIN IN A WORLD HISTORICAL CONTEXT

1. P. J. Marshall, "A Nation Defined by Empire, 1755–1776," in *Uniting the Kingdom? The Making of British History,* ed. Alexander Grant and Keith Stringer (New York: Routledge, 1995).

2. David Dickson, *New Foundations: Ireland 1660–1800* (Dublin: Irish Academic Press, 2000), 161.

3. Niklas Frykman, "The Mutiny on the *Hermione*: Warfare, Revolution, and Treason in the Royal Navy," *Journal of Social History* 44 (2010): 169. Frykman details the composition of the *Hermione*. Half of the men were English; a fifth from the British Empire, including Scotland, Wales, Canada, and the British West Indies; a fifth from Ireland; and 10 percent from Prussia, Sweden, Norway, Denmark, the Low Countries, Portugal, Italy, Switzerland, the United States, and the Danish West Indies. Two men were of African descent.

4. Paul Conner "'Maynard' Unmasked: Oglethorpe and Sharp versus the Press Gangs," *Proceedings of the American Philosophical Society* 111 (1967): 199–211.

5. Christopher Magra, "Anti Impressment Riots and the Origins of the Age of Revolution," *International Review of Social History* 58 (2013): 131–51. For more on impressment and resistance to it, see Denver Alexander Brunsman, *The Evil Necessity: British Naval Impressment in the Eighteenth-Century Atlantic World* (Charlottesville: University of Virginia Press, 2013); Robert Burroughs, "Sailors and Slaves: The 'Poor Enslaved Tar' in Naval Reform and Nautical Melodrama," *Journal of Victorian Culture* 16 (2011): 305–22; Keith Mercer, "Northern Exposure: Resistance to Naval Impressment in British North America, 1775–1815," *The Canadian Historical Review* 91 (2010): 199–232; and Nicholas Rogers, *Press Gang: Naval Impressment and its Opponents in Georgian* Britain (London: Hambeldon Continuum, 2008).

6. Nicholas Rogers, "Vagrancy, Impressment and the Regulation of Labour in Eighteenth-Century Britain," *Slavery and Abolition* 15 (1994): 109.

7. William Richardson, *A Mariner of England,* ed. Spencer Childers (London: The Classics, 1908), 292–293. I am grateful to Emma Goldsmith for this reference.

8. Geraint H. Jenkins, *A Concise History of Wales* (Cambridge, UK: Cambridge University Press, 2007), 136; Linda Colley, *Britons: Forging the Nation, 1707–1837* (New Haven, CT: Yale University Press, 1992), 13.

9. Jenkins, 133, 169.

10. Steven Mintz, "Historical Context: Facts about the Slave Trade and Slavery," Gilder Lehrman Institute of American History, https://www.gilderlehrman.org/history-resources/teaching-resource/historical-context-facts-about-slave-trade-and-slavery

11. Dana Rabin, "'In a Country of Liberty?': Slavery, Villeinage and the Making of Whiteness in the Somerset Case (1772)," *History Workshop Journal* 72 (2011): 9.

12. Ibid.

13. The mercantile interpretation of the Anglo-French rivalry is a new departure on the scholarship championed by Daniel A. Baugh, *The International History Review* 20, no. 1 (Mar. 1998): 1–32.

14. David Olusoga, *Black and British: A Forgotten History* (London: Macmillan, 2016), 152.

15. Marianne Elliott, *Partners in Revolution: The United Irishmen and France* (New Haven, CT: Yale University Press, 1982); D. Dickson, Daire Keogh, and Kevin Whelan, eds., *The United Irishmen: Republicanism, radicalism, and rebellion* (Dublin: Lilliput, 1993).

16. Jim Smyth, ed., "Introduction: The 1798 Rebellion and Its Eighteenth-Century Contexts," in *Revolution, Counter-Revolution and Union* (Cambridge, UK: Cambridge University Press, 2001), 14.

17. Ibid., 19.

CHAPTER 4: BELIEFS, IDEAS, ATTITUDES

1. Matthew White, "Poverty in Georgian Britain," British Library, October 14, 2009, https://www.bl.uk/georgian-britain/articles/poverty-in-georgian-britain.

2. John Brewer, *The Pleasures of the Imagination: English Culture in the Eighteenth Century* (New York: Routledge, 1997), 34–35.

3. Ibid., 173.

4. Dana Rabin, *Identity, Crime, and Legal Responsibility in Eighteenth-Century England* (New York: Palgrave Macmillan, 2004).

5. Ibid.

6. Ibid.

7. "Henry Purcell," Virtual Orchestra, http://virtualorchestra.eu/index.php/henry-purcell.

8. "Eighteenth Century Popular Ballads," Eighteenth-Century-Media, November 4, 2012, https://c18media.wordpress.com/2012/11/04/eighteenth-century-popular-ballads/.

9. "Methodist Church," British Broadcasting Company, July 12, 2011, http://www.bbc.co.uk/religion/religions/christianity/subdivisions/methodist_1.shtml.

10. Ibid.

11. Ibid.

12. Linda Colley, *Britons: Forging the Nation, 1707–1837* (New Haven, CT: Yale University Press, 1992), 33.

13. This statute was extended by Anne in 1719 (12 Anne, St. 2, c. 14).

14. Colin Haydon, *Anti-Catholicism in Eighteenth-Century England, c. 1714–1780: A Political and Social Study* (Manchester, UK: Manchester University Press, 1993).

15. On toleration and the Enlightenment, see Martin Fitzpatrick, "Toleration and the Enlightenment Movement," in *Toleration in Enlightenment Europe*, ed. Ole Peter Grell and Roy Porter (Cambridge, UK: Cambridge University Press, 2000), 23–68.

16. Robert Donovan, "The Military Origins of the Roman Catholic Relief Programme of 1778," *The Historical Journal* 28 (1985): 79–102; Karen Stanbridge, "Quebec and the Irish Catholic Relief Act of 1778: An

Institutional Approach," *Journal of Historical Sociology* 16 (2003): 375–404. In "The Catholic Question in the Eighteenth Century," *History Ireland* 1 (1993): 17–21.

17. J. A. Giuseppi, "Early Jewish Holders of Bank of England Stock (1694–1725)," *Miscellanies of the Jewish Historical Society of England* 6 (1962).

18. Dana Rabin, "Seeing Jews and Gypsies in 1753," *Cultural and Social History* 7 (2010): 35–58.

19. Humanus, *Newcastle Courant*, 1792.

20. Horace Walpole, *Horace Walpole's Correspondence*, ed. W. S. Lewis, 48 vols. (New Haven, CT: Yale University Press, 1983), 11: 318.

21. Edmund Burke, *Reflections on the Revolution in France* (Oxford: Oxford University Press, 2009), 16.

22. Ibid., 245–46.

23. Ibid., 221.

24. Ibid., 78.

25. Ibid., 31.

26. Thomas Paine, *Rights of Man, Common Sense, and Other Political Writing* (Oxford, 2009), 117.

27. Ibid., 118.

28. Ibid., 193–94.

29. Ibid., 206.

CHAPTER 5: PEOPLE, PARTIES, AND PATRONAGE

1. Joseph Addison, "Party Patches," *The Spectator*, no. 81, June 2, 1711.

2. As quoted in Frank O'Gorman, *The Long Eighteenth Century: British Political and Social History 1688–1832* (London: Arnold, 1997, 2004), 43.

3. "1708," The History of Parliament, http://www.historyofparliamentonline.org/volume/1690-1715/parliament/1708.

4. *Pasquin to the Queen's Statue*, as quoted in William A. Speck, *Stability and Strife: England, 1714–1760* (Cambridge, MA: Harvard University Press, 1977), 173.

5. Speech by the Lord High Steward, House of Lords, February 22, 1716, in Joel H. Wiener, ed., *Great Britain: The Lion at Home, A Documentary History of Domestic Policy 1689–1973* (New York: Chelsea House, 1983), 1:124–29.

6. John Brewer, *The Sinews of Power: War, Money and the English State, 1688–1783* (New York: Knopf, 1989), 125.

7. O'Gorman, *The Long Eighteenth Century: British Political and Social History. 1688–1832* (London: Bloomsbury, 2016), 74.

8. Roy Porter, *English Society in the Eighteenth Century* (Harmondsworth, UK: Penguin, 1982), 73–74.

9. Lord Wharncliffe and W. Moy Thomas, eds., *The Letters and Works of Lady Mary Wortley Montagu* (London: Cambridge University Press, 1866), 2:37–39.

10. Kathleen Wilson, "Empire, Trade and Popular Politics in Mid-Hanoverian Britain: The Case of Admiral Vernon," *Past & Present* 121 (1988): 74–109.

11. John Wilkes, *North Briton*, no. 45 (London), April 23, 1763.

12. John Wilkes, *English Liberty: Being a Collection of Interesting Tracts from the Year 1762 to 1769. Containing the Private Correspondence, Public Letters, Speeches and Addresses of John Wilkes, Esq., Humbly Dedicated to the King* (London: Gale ECCO, 1769), 83.

13. As quoted in Paul Langford, *A Polite and Commercial People, England 1727–1783* (Oxford: Oxford University Press, 1989), 360.

14. Speech of Earl of Chatham, House of Lords, January 20, 1775, in *Great Britain: Foreign Policy and Span of Empire, 1689–1971, A Documentary History*, ed. Joel H. Wiener (New York: Chelsea House, 1974), 3:2114–19.

15. As quoted in Linda Colley, *Britons: Forging the Nation, 1707–1837* (New Haven, CT: Yale University Press, 1992), 137.

16. As quoted in Langford, *A Polite and Commercial People*, 554.

17. "The General Election of 1754," History of Parliament, http://www.historyofparliamentonline.org/volume/1754-1790/survey/ii-elections.

18. Renata Lana, "Women and Foxite Strategy in the Westminster Election of 1784," *Eighteenth-Century Life* 26, no. 1 (2002): 46–69.

19. Ibid.; Colley, *Britons*, 242–49.

20. As quoted in Boyd Hilton, *A Mad, Bad, and Dangerous People? England, 1783–1846* (Oxford: Oxford University Press, 2008), 61.

21. Porter, *English Society*, 369.

22. As quoted in E. P. Thompson, *The Making of the English Working Class* (New York: Vintage, 1966), 17.

CHAPTER 6: ECONOMIC TRANSFORMATIONS

1. Emma Griffin, *A Short History of the British Industrial Revolution* (London: Palgrave Macmillan, 2010), 11.

2. Boyd Hilton, *A Mad, Bad, and Dangerous People?* (Oxford: Oxford University Press, 2006), 234.

3. Ibid., 250.

4. Eric Evans, *Britain before the Reform Act: Politics and Society 1815–1832*, 2nd ed. (New York: Routledge, 2008), 17.

5. Joyce Burnette, "Agriculture, 1700–1870," in *The Cambridge Economic History of Modern Britain, Vol 1: 1700–1870*, ed. Roderick Floud, Jane Humphries, and Paul Johnson (Cambridge: Cambridge University Press, 2014), 103, 114–15.

6. T. M. Devine, "Scotland," in *The Cambridge Economic History of Modern Britain, Vol. 1*, ed. Roderick Floud and Paul Johnson, (Cambridge: Cambridge University Press, 2003), 401.

7. C. B. Bow, "The 'Final Causes' of Scottish Nationalism: Lord Kames on the Political Economy of Enlightened Husbandry, 1745–82," *Historical Research* 91, no. 252 (2018): 299–300.

8. Devine, "Scotland," 393–95, 398.

9. Ian McBride, *Eighteenth-Century Ireland: The Isle of Slaves* (Dublin: Gill Books, 2009), 106.

10. Roy Porter, *English Society in the Eighteenth Century* (Harmondsworth, UK: Penguin, 1982), 220.

11. Deborah Valenze, *The First Industrial Woman* (Oxford: Oxford University Press, 1995), 32.

12. As quoted in Porter, *English Society*, 229.

13. Burnette, "Agriculture," 97.

14. Robert C. Allen, "Agriculture during the Industrial Revolution, 1700–1850," in *The Cambridge Economic History of Modern Britain, Vol. 1*, ed. Roderick Floud and Paul Johnson (Cambridge: Cambridge University Press, 2003), 99–100.

15. Valenze, *The First Industrial Woman*, 34.

16. *Northampton Mercury*, July 29, 1765, and August 5, 1765.

17. See E. P. Thompson, "The Moral Economy of the English Crowd in the Eighteenth Century," *Past and Present* 50 (1971): 76-136 and *Customs in Common: Studies in Traditional Popular Culture* (New Press, London: 1993).

18. Valenze, *The First Industrial Woman*, 35–36.

19. Devine, "Scotland," 398, 401; Bow, "The 'Final Causes,'" 303–4.

20. Burnette, "Agriculture," 90.

21. Devine, "Scotland," 396, 401.

22. Burnette, "Agriculture," 97.

23. Frances Richardson, "Women Farmers of Snowdonia, 1750–1900," *Rural History* 25, no. 2 (2014): 164.

24. Geraint H. Jenkins, *A Concise History of Wales* (Cambridge: Cambridge University Press, 2007), 139–40.

25. Robert C. Allen and Cormac Ó Gráda, "On the Road Again with Arthur Young: English, Irish, and French Agriculture during the Industrial Revolution," *The Journal of Economic History* 48, no. 1 (1988): 104–8.

26. Jeff Chapman, "The Impact of the Potato," *History Magazine*, http://www.history-magazine.com/potato.html.

27. Steven Pincus, *1688: The First Modern Revolution* (New Haven, CT: Yale University Press, 2009), 6.

28. John Brewer, *The Sinews of Power: War, Money and the English State, 1688–1783* (Cambridge, MA: Harvard University Press, 1990) and P. G. M. Dickson, *The Financial Revolution in England: A Study in the Development of Public Credit, 1688–1756* (New York: Routledge, 1967).

29. Dickson, *The Financial Revolution*, 11.

30. Kenneth Morgan, "Symbiosis: Trade and the British Empire," British Broadcasting Network, February 17, 2011, http://www.bbc.co.uk/history/british/empire_seapower/trade_empire_01.shtml.

31. Ibid.

32. Adam Smith, *An Inquiry into the Nature and Causes of the Wealth of Nations*, https://www.ibiblio.org/ml/libri/s/SmithA_WealthNations_p.pdf.

33. Steven Pincus, "Rethinking Mercantilism: Political Economy, the British Empire, and the Atlantic World in the Seventeenth and Eighteenth Centuries," *The William and Mary Quarterly* 69, no. 1 (January 2012): 3–34. Pincus provides an excellent overview of the historical debate on mercantilism.

34. Jacob Price, as quoted in Natasha Glaisyer, "Networking: Trade and Exchange in the Eighteenth-Century British Empire," *The Historical Journal* 47, no. 2 (June 2004): 464.

35. Ibid., 464–65.

36. John Toland, *Reasons for Naturalizing the Jews in Great Britain and Ireland, on the Same Foot with All Other Nations* (London: The Manuscript Publisher, 1714), 7.

37. Nicholas Rogers, "Confronting the Crime Wave: The Debate over Social Reform and Regulation, 1749–1753," in *Stilling the Grumbling Hive: The Response to Social and Economic Problems in England, 1689–1750*, ed. Lee Davison, Tim Hitchcock, Tim Keirn, and Robert Shoemaker (New York: St. Martin's,1992), 77–98.

38. Maxine Berg, "Consumption in Eighteenth- and Early Nineteenth-Century Britain," in *The Cambridge Economic History of Modern Britain, Vol. 1*, ed. Roderick Floud and Paul Johnson (Cambridge: Cambridge University Press, 2003), 366.

39. Dan Bogart, "The Transport Revolution in Industrialising Britain," in *The Cambridge Economic History of Modern Britain, Vol 1: 1700–1870*, ed. Roderick Floud, Jane Humphries, and Paul Johnson (Cambridge: Cambridge University Press, 2014), 378–79.

40. Porter, *English Society*, 209.

41. Henry Homer, *An Enquiry into the Means of Preserving and Improving the Publick Roads of this Kingdom. With Observations on the Probable Consequences of the Present Plan* (Dublin: Gale Ecco, 1767); as quoted in Porter, *English Society*, 208.

42. Bogart, "The Transport Revolution," 378–81.

43. As quoted in Porter, *English Society*, 208.

44. Paul Langford, *A Polite and Commercial People, England 1727–1783* (Oxford: Oxford University Press, 1992), 391–406.

45. Bogart, "The Transport Revolution," 372–73.

46. Ibid., 374–76; Porter, *English Society*, 224–25.

47. John Brewer, *The Pleasures of the Imagination: English Culture in the Eighteenth Century* (New York: Routledge, 1997), 138–39, 504; Porter, *English Society*, 208, 251–52.

48. Griffin, *A Short History*, 53–56.

49. Ibid., 57–59; Devine, "Scotland," 391, 399.

50. Jenkins, *A Concise History of Wales*, 143.

51. McBride, *Eighteenth-Century Ireland*, 108.

52. Griffin, *A Short History*, 62.

53. Maxine Berg, "Consumption in Eighteenth- and Early Nineteenth-Century Britain," 384–85.

54. Ibid., 378; Sara Horrell, "Consumption, 1700–1870, in *The Cambridge Economic History of Modern Britain, Vol 1: 1700–1870*, ed. Roderick Floud, Jane Humphries, and Paul Johnson (Cambridge: Cambridge University Press, 2014), 241–43.

55. As quoted in Griffin, *A Short History*, 75.

56. Jenkins, *A Concise History of Wales*, 141.

57. Jenkins, *A Concise History of Wales*, 141–42, 183.

58. Chris Evans, *Slave Wales: The Welsh and Atlantic Slavery, 1660–1850* (Cardiff, Wales, UK: Wales University Press, 2010).

59. Griffin, *A Short History*, 147–48, 154, 160–61.

CHAPTER 7: STRUCTURES AND PATTERNS OF EVERYDAY LIFE

1. As quoted in Anna Clark, *The Struggle for the Breeches: Gender and the Making of the British Working Class* (Berkeley: University of California Press, 1995), 171. The following discussion of the Queen Caroline Affair draws heavily on Clark's treatment, 164–174.

2. As quoted in Linda Colley, *Britons: Forging the Nation, 1707–1837* (New Haven, CT: Yale University Press, 1992), 265.

3. As quoted in Jane Robins, *Rebel Queen: How the Trial of Caroline Brought England to the Brink of Revolution* (New York: Pocket Books, 2006), 240.

4. Clark, *The Struggle for the Breeches*, 174.

5. Caroline Norton, *A Voice from the Factories: In Serious Verse* (London: John Murray, 1836).

6. Ellen Johnston, "An Address to My Brother Bards," ll. 47–48, in *Autobiography, Poems and Songs* (Glasgow: William Love, 1867), 139–41; Florence S. Boos, "Ellen Johnston: Autobiographical Writings of 'The Factory Girl,' in *Memoirs of Victorian Working-Class Women: The Hard Way Up* (Cham, Switzerland: Palgrave Macmillan, 2017), 197–222.

7. Johnston, *Autobiography, Poems and Songs*, 3–16, esp. 10–11.

8. Emma Griffin, *Liberty's Dawn: A People's History of the Industrial Revolution* (New Haven, CT: Yale University Press, 2013), 161.

9. Emma Griffin, *A Short History of the British Industrial Revolution* (New York: Palgrave, 2010), 30–33; Shani D'Cruze, "The Family," in *A Companion to Nineteenth-Century Britain*, ed. Chris Williams (Hoboken, NJ: Wiley, 2004), 255–56.

10. Griffin, *A Short History*, 49, 58; D'Cruze, "The Family," 258.

11. "Great Irish Famine," British Broadcasting Company, April 4, 2019, https://www.bbc.co.uk/programmes/m0003rj1.

12. Donald M. MacRaild, *Irish Migrants in Modern Britain, 1750–1922* (New York: Palgrave, 1999), 1, 4–5.

13. E. W. McFarland, "Scotland," in *A Companion to Nineteenth-Century Britain*, ed. Chris Williams (Hoboken, NJ: Wiley, 2004), 507.

14. MacRaild, *Irish Migrants*, 3.

15. Shani D'Cruze, "Women and the Family," in *Women's History: Britain, 1850–1945*, ed. June Purvis (New York: Routledge, 1995), 55–58; Leonore Davidoff, "The Family in Britain," in *The Cambridge Social History of Britain, 1750–1950*, vol. 2, ed. F. M. L. Thompson (Cambridge, UK: Cambridge University Press, 1990), 113; Ginger S. Frost, *Victorian Childhoods* (London: Praeger, 2009), 12.

16. Hilary McD. Beckles, "Freeing Slavery: Gender Paradigms in the Social History of Caribbean Slavery," in *Slavery, Freedom and Gender: The Dynamics of Caribbean Society*, ed. Brian L. Moore et al. (Kingston, Jamaica: University Press of the West Indies, 2001), 201, 218; Diana Paton, "Enslaved Women and Slavery before and after 1807" (2007), https://archives.history.ac.uk/history-in-focus/Slavery/articles/paton.html.

17. "Slave Registers," The National Archives, 2012, https://webarchive.nationalarchives.gov.uk/+/http://yourarchives.nationalarchives.gov.uk/index.php?title=Slave_registers.

18. David Olusoga, *Black and British: A Forgotten History* (London: Pan Books, 2016), 223–28; Paton, "Enslaved Women and Slavery."

19. This discussion of class relies heavily on Martin Hewitt's overview, "Class and the Classes," in *A Companion to Nineteenth-Century Britain*, ed. Chris Williams (Hoboken, NJ: Wiley, 2004), 304–20.

20. As quoted in MacRaild, *Irish Migrants*, 157.

21. Friedrich Engels, *The Condition of the Working Class in England* (Oxford: Oxford University Press, 2000), 161–66.

22. MacRaild, *Irish Migrants*, 5.

23. Ibid., 161.

24. Peter Fryer, *Staying Power: The History of Black People in Britain* (London: Pluto Press, 1984), *262*.

25. Ibid., 263–64.

26. Olusoga, *Black and British*, 246.

27. Caroline Norton, *A Letter to the Queen on Lord Chancellor Cranworth's Marriage and Divorce Bill*, 3rd ed. (London: Longman, Brown, Green, and Longmans, 1855), 8.

28. As quoted in Clark, *The Struggle for the Breeches*, 191. Discussion of the New Poor Law draws heavily on Clark's treatment, 187–96.

29. Alannah Tomkins, "Women and Poverty," in *Women's History: Britain, 1700–1850*, ed. Hannah Barker and Elaine Chalus (New York: Routledge: 2005), 161.

30. D'Cruze, "The Family," 258–59.

31. Testimony of Alexander Dean, June 29, 1832, "Report from the Committee on the Bill to Regulate the Labour of Children . . ." *House of Commons Papers*, vol. 15 (1831–32), 373.

32. Jane Humphries, *Childhood and Child Labour in the British Industrial Revolution* (Cambridge, UK: Cambridge University Press, 2010), 7–11, 177, 208–09, 301–02, 305.

33. Michael Sadler, March 16, 1832, *Hansard Parliamentary Debates*, 3rd Series, vol. 11 (1832), cols. 364, 367.

34. Olusoga, *Black and British*, 229–30.

35. As quoted in Caroline Arscott, "Childhood in Victorian Art," *Journal of Victorian Culture* 9, no. 1 (2004): 97.

36. John Fielden, January 26, 1847, *Hansard Parliamentary Debates*, 3rd Series, vol. 89 (1847), col. 849.

37. Frost, *Victorian Childhoods*, 3.

38. Ibid., 3.

39. Arscott, "Childhood in Victorian Art," 100.

40. Frost, *Victorian Childhoods*, 95; Marah Gubar, "The Victorian Child, c. 1837–1901," Representing Childhood, http://www.representingchildhood.pitt.edu/victorian.htm.

41. Frost, *Victorian Childhoods*, 87.

42. D'Cruze, "The Family," 258.

43. Henry Mayhew, *London Labour and the London Poor*, vol. 1 (London: Griffin, Bohn, and Company, 1861), 468; Arscott, "Childhood in Victorian Art," 97–98.

44. Sally Shuttleworth, "Victorian Childhood," *Journal of Victorian Culture* 9, no. 1 (2004): 108–09.

45. Gillian Sutherland, "Education," in *The Cambridge Social History of Britain, 1750–1950*, vol. 3, ed. F. M. L. Thompson (Cambridge, UK: Cambridge University Press, 1990), 122–24, 146.

46. Jane McDermid, "Women and Education," *Women's History: Britain, 1850–1945*, ed. June Purvis (New York: Routledge, 1995), 117; Sutherland, "Education," 131–32.

47. Ibid., as quoted in 120–21.

48. As quoted in Philip Gardner, in *A Companion to Nineteenth-Century Britain*, ed. Chris Williams (Hoboken, NJ: Wiley, 2004), 354–55.

49. Testimony of Sarah Gooder, March 22, 1841, "Appendix to First Report of the Commissioners Appointed for Inquiring into the Employment and Condition of Children in Mines and Manufactories," *House of Lords Papers*, vol. 20 (1842), 252–53.

50. Sutherland, "Education," 126.

51. Ibid., 127–29.

52. Frost, *Victorian Childhoods*, 37; Gardner, 355–56.

53. Robert Graves, *Good-bye to All That* (New York: Vintage Books, 1929), 20.

54. John Tosh, *Manliness and Masculinities in Nineteenth-Century Britain: Essays on Gender, Family and Empire* (New York: Routledge, 2016), 138.

55. Frost, *Victorian Childhoods*, 46.

56. McDermid, "Women and Education," 108–11.

57. Sutherland, "Education," 154–55; Frost, *Victorian Childhoods*, 53.

58. As quoted in Frost, *Victorian Childhoods*, 14.

59. D'Cruze, "Women and the Family," 69.

60. Ellen Ross, *Love and Toil: Motherhood in Outcast London, 1870–1918* (Oxford: Oxford University Press, 1993), 54–55.

61. D'Cruze, "Women and the Family," 58–60, and "The Family," 258–59.

62. Helen Bosanquet, "Marriage in East London," in *Slum Travelers: Ladies and London Poverty, 1860–1920*, ed. Ellen Ross (Berkeley: University of California Press, 2007), 67, 69–70.

63. As quoted in Clark, *The Struggle for the Breeches*, 257.

64. Ross, *Love and Toil*, 49; D'Cruze, "The Family," 265–66.

65. Clark, *The Struggle for the Breeches*, 259–60.

66. "Sketch of Life in Buildings," in *Slum Travelers: Ladies and London Poverty, 1860–1920*, ed. Ellen Ross (Berkeley: University of California Press, 2007), 44.

67. Ross, *Love and Toil*, 91–92.

68. Graves, *Good-bye to All That*, 14–15.

69. Deborah Valenze, *The First Industrial Woman* (Oxford: Oxford University Press, 1995), 169.

70. D'Cruze, "The Family," 262.

71. Tosh, *Manliness*, 135.

72. Ibid.; John Tosh, *A Man's Place: Masculinity and the Middle-Class Home in Victorian England* (New Haven, CT: Yale University Press, 1999), 16–17.

73. D'Cruze, "The Family," 266.

74. As quoted in Susan Kingsley Kent, *Sex and Suffrage in Britain, 1860–1914* (New York: Routledge, 1987), 28.

75. As quoted in Fryer, *Staying Power*, 246–51. See also Susan Kingsley Kent, *A New History of Britain since 1688* (Oxford: Oxford University Press, 2017), 265.

76. Sarah Grand, "The New Aspect of the Woman Question," *The North American Review* 158 (1894): 271.

CHAPTER 8: BRITAIN IN A WORLD HISTORICAL CONTEXT

1. C. A. Bayly, *Imperial Meridian: The British Empire and the World, 1780–1830* (London: Longman, 1989).

2. Five thousand chests in 1821, eighteen thousand in 1830, thirty thousand in 1835, and forty thousand in 1838–39.

3. Nancy Shoemaker, "A Typology of Colonialism," *Perspectives on History*, October 1, 2015, https://www.historians.org/publications-and-directories/perspectives-on-history/october-2015/a-typology-of-colonialism

4. Quoted in William Rees, "Canada's First Nations," *History Today* 68, no. 9 (September 2018), https://www.historytoday.com/history-matters/canada%E2%80%99s-first-nations.

5. Details on Aborigine demographics and depopulation from John Harris, "Hiding the Bodies: The Myth of the Humane Colonisation of Aboriginal Australia," *Aboriginal History* 23 (2003): 79–104.

6. "Maori Population Decline," New Zealand Wars, http://newzealandwars.co.nz/land-wars/wars/comparing-populations/#:~:text=By%20the%20time%20the%20war,a%20lowest%20point%20of%2039%2C000.

7. Alfred Newman, 1881, quoted in "Story: Taupori Māori – Māori Population Change," https://teara.govt.nz/en/taupori-maori-maori-population-change/page-2#:~:text=In%201856%20physician%20and%20politician%20Dr%20Isaac%20Featherston,peoples%20would%20not%20survive%20European%20conquest%20and%20disease.

8. Charles Callwell, *Small Wars—Their Principles and Practice* (London: His Majesty's Stationary Office, 1906), 40.

9. Rudyard Kipling, "The Ballad of East and West," 1889, http://www.kiplingsociety.co.uk/poems_eastwest.htm.

10. Terry Wilson, "The British Soldier's Dum Dum Bullets," *Military History Journal* 17, no. 2 (December 2016), http://samilitaryhistory.org/vol172tw.html#:~:text=The%20Battle%20of%20Omdurman%2C%20which,but%20effective%2C%20Martini%2DHenry.

11. Christine Kinealy, "At Home with Empire: The Example of Ireland," in *At Home with Empire: Metropolitan Culture and the Imperial World*, eds. Catherine Hall and Sonya Rose (Cambridge: Cambridge University Press, 2006), 85.

12. Ibid.

13. Ibid., 86–87.

14. Christine Kinealy, "Private Donations to Ireland during An Gorta Mór," *Seanchas Ardmhacha: Journal of the Armagh Diocesan Historical Society* 17, no. 2 (1998): 113.

15. Lori Henderson, "The Irish Famine: A Historiographical Review," *Historia* (2005), 138, https://www.eiu.edu/historia/Henderson.pdf.

16. Frank Rynne, "The Great Famine in Nationalist and Land League Propaganda 1879–1882," *Memory(s), Identity(s), Marginality(s) in the Contemporary Western World* 12 (2015), https://journals.openedition.org/mimmoc/1864.

17. Philippa Levine, *The British Empire: Sunrise to Sunset* (New York: Pearson/Longman, 2007), 103–22.

18. Ibid., 95.

19. Troop strengths from Kaushik Roy, "The Beginning of People's War in India," *Economic and Political Weekly* 42, no. 19 (May 12–18, 2007): 1724–25.

20. Ibid., 1721.

21. "The Sepoy Uprising (1857–1858)," http://webs.bcp.org/sites/vcleary/modernworldhistorytextbook/imperialism/section_4/sepoyuprising.html#:~:text=Of%20the%2040%2C000%20Europeans%20living,the%20East%20India%20Company%20altogether.

22. Roy, "People's War in India," 1721.

23. Kate Imy, *Faithful Fighters: Identity and Power in the British Indian Army* (Stanford, CA: Stanford University Press, 2019), 5.

24. Ibid., 18.

25. "Proclamation by the Queen in Council, to the Princes, Chiefs, and People of India," November 1, 1858, https://en.wikisource.org/wiki/Proclamation_by_the_Queen_in_Council,_to_the_princes,_chiefs,_and_people_of_India.

26. Richard Huzzey, "Jamaica's Morant Bay Rebellion: Brutality and Outrage in the British Empire," *History Extra*, December 2015, https://www.historyextra.com/period/victorian/jamaicas-morant-bay-rebellion-brutality-and-outrage-in-the-british-empire/.

27. Kathleen Wilson, *A New Imperial History: Culture, Identity, and Modernity in Britain and the Empire, 1660–1840* (Cambridge, UK: Cambridge University Press, 2004).

28. Thomas Babington Macaulay, "Minute by the Hon'ble T. B. Macaulay, dated the 2nd February 1835," http://www.columbia.edu/itc/mealac/pritchett/00generallinks/macaulay/txt_minute_education_1835.html.

29. Philippa Levine, "'A Multitude of Unchaste Women': Prostitution in the British Empire," *Journal of Women's History* 15 (2004): 159.

30. Ibid., 159–61.

31. David Cannadine, *Ornamentalism: How the British Saw Their Empire* (New York: Oxford University Press, 2001).

32. *Manchester Guardian*, December 31, 1862.

33. Abraham Lincoln to the working men of Manchester, January 19, 1863, *ACWS Archives*, https://acws.co.uk/archives-misc-lincoln_letter.

34. See Eric Hobsbawm, *Industry and Empire* (New York: Penguin, 1968).

35. Fransjohan Pretorius, "The Boer Wars," March 29, 2011, British Broadcasting Company, http://www.bbc.co.uk/history/british/victorians/boer_wars_01.shtml.

36. "Boer Rebels and the Kaiser's Men," The Soldier's Burden, http://www.kaiserscross.com/40184/157701.html#:~:text=During%20the%20Boer%20war%20there,made%20by%20Mauser%20and%20Krupp.&text=A%20German%20Freikorps%20of%20Volunteers,fought%20on%20the%20Boer%20side.

37. Joseph Connell Jr., "The 1912 Ulster Covenant," *History Ireland 20*, no. 5 (September/October 2012), https://www.historyireland.com/20th-century-contemporary-history/the-1912-ulster-covenant-by-joseph-e-a-connell-jr/.

CHAPTER 9: CERTITUDE AND ANXIETY IN AN ERA OF RAPID CHANGE

1. Jeffrey Auerbach, *The Great Exhibition of 1851: A Nation on Display* (New Haven, CT: Yale University Press, 1999).

2. Todd Endelman, *The Jews of Britain, 1656 to 2000* (Berkeley: University of California Press, 2002).

3. "Minute by the Hon'ble T. B. Macaulay, dated the 2nd February 1835," http://www.columbia.edu/itc/mealac/pritchett/00generallinks/macaulay/txt_minute_education_1835.html.

4. Samuel Smiles, *Self Help* (New York: John Lovell Company, 1884) 1.

5. Ibid., 415.

6. John Stuart Mill, *On Liberty*, 1859, https://www.gutenberg.org/files/34901/34901-h/34901-h.htm.

7. Ibid.

8. George Bernard Shaw, *Fabian Essays in Socialism* (London, 1889), https://archive.org/stream/fabianessaysinso00fabirich/fabianessaysinso00fabirich_djvu.txt.

9. Denis Judd, *Empire: The British Imperial Experience from 1765 to the Present* (New York: Basic Books, 1998), 130–153.

10. "Ladies Protest against the Contagious Diseases Acts," *Daily News*, January 1, 1870.

11. Robert Baden-Powell, *Scouting for Boys* (London: Pearson, 1908).

12. Oscar Wilde, *The Picture of Dorien Gray*, preface, https://www.gutenberg.org/files/174/174-h/174-h.htm.

13. "Oscar Wilde," https://www.cmgww.com/historic/wilde/.

14. Emmeline Pankhurst, "Why We Are Militant," 1913, http://historymuse.net/readings/PANKHURST-WhyWeAreMilitant1913.htm.

15. Ibid.

CHAPTER 10: REPRESSION AND REFORM

1. Emmeline Pankhurst, "Why We Are Militant," 1913, http://historymuse.net/readings/PANKHURST-WhyWeAreMilitant1913.htm.

2. Harold Perkins, *The Origins of Modern English Society* (London: Routledge and Keegan Paul, 1972).

3. As quoted in James Sambrook, *William Cobbett* (New York: Routledge, 1973), 85.

4. As quoted in Habeas Corpus Suspension Act 1817, https://en.wikipedia.org/wiki/Habeas_Corpus_Suspension_Act_1817.

5.   As quoted in Robert Poole, "'By the Law or the Sword;' Peterloo Revisited," *History* 91, no. 2 (2006): 254–76.

6.   Henry Hunt, "To the Inhabitants of Manchester" (1819), National Archives, HO 42/192, fol. 19, November 19, 2019, https://media.nationalarchives.gov.uk/index.php/henry-hunts-invitation-people-manchester/.

7.   "List of Persons Killed at St. Petersfield," in *Report of the Metropolitan and Central Committee, Appointed for the Relief of the Manchester Sufferers* (London: William Hone, 1820), 24.

8.   Robert Poole, "The March to Peterloo: Politics and Festivity in Late Georgian England," *Past & Present* 192 (2006): 111.

9.   "Imperial Parliament of Great Britain and Ireland," *Morning Chronicle* (London), August 4, 1832, 1; British Library Learning, "Women's Suffrage Timeline," The British Library, February 6, 2018, https://www.bl.uk/votes-for-women/articles/womens-suffrage-timeline#authorBlock1.

10.   "The National Petition," [July 1838], in G. D. H. Cole and A. W. Filson, *British Working Class Movements: Select Documents, 1789-1873* (London: Palgrave Macmillan, 1965), 354.

11.   "Resisting the Rule of Capital," *Socialist Worker*, May 20, 2000, https://socialistworker.co.uk/art/36020/Resisting+the+rule+of+capital.

12.   "1839 Chartist Petition," UK Parliament, https://www.parliament.uk/about/living-heritage/transformingsociety/electionsvoting/chartists/case-study/the-right-to-vote/the-chartists-and-birmingham/1839-petition/; Dorothy Thompson, *The Chartists: Popular Politics in the Industrial Revolution* (New York: Pantheon Books, 1984), 124, 141; Anna Clark, *The Struggle for the Breeches: Gender and the Making of the British Working Class* (Berkeley: University of California Press, 1995), 228.

13.   Peter Fryer, *Staying Power: The History of Black People in Britain* (London: Pluto Press, 1984), 237–45.

14.   Lord John Russell, "Edinburgh Letter," November 22, 1845, https://victorianweb.org/history/eletter.html.

15.   Robert Peel, Speech on the Repeal of the Corn Laws, May 15, 1846, https://victorianweb.org/history/cornlaws3.html.

16.   Catherine Hall, "Rethinking Imperial Histories: The Reform Act of 1867," *New Left Review*, 208 (1994): 3–29. https://newleftreview.org/issues/i208/articles/catherine-hall-rethinking-imperial-histories-the-reform-act-of-1867.

17.   Caroline Benn, *Keir Hardie: A Biography* (London: Hutchinson, 1997), 28.

18.   Ibid., 96, 98–100.

19.   Quoted in Keith McClelland and Sonya Rose, "Citizenship and Empire, 1867–1928," in *At Home with Empire: Metropolitan Culture and the Imperial World*, ed. Catherine Hall and Sonya O. Rose (Cambridge: Cambridge University Press, 2006), 281.

20.   Katherine Rix, "Before the Vote Was Won: Women and Politics, 1868–1918," History of Parliament (blog), August 29, 2018, https://thehistoryofparliament.wordpress.com/2018/08/29/before-the-vote-was-won-women-and-politics-1868-1918/.

CHAPTER 11: ECONOMY, INDUSTRIALIZATION, AND QUALITY OF LIFE

1.   As quoted in Alexander Charles Ewald, *The Right Hon. Benjamin Disraeli, Earl of Beaconsfield, K. G., and His Times*, vol. II (London: William Mackenzie, 1882), 229.

2.   Benjamin Disraeli, *Sybil, or the Two Nations*, Gutenberg, http://www.gutenberg.org/ebooks/3760.

3.   "The Lancashire Cotton Famine," British Broadcasting Company, May 14, 2015, https://www.bbc.co.uk/programmes/b05tly3f.

4. Friedrich Engels, *The Condition of the Working-Class in England in 1844* (London: Swan Sonnenschein & Co., 1892), 53.

5. Chris Cook and John Stevenson, *The Longman Handbook of Modern British History, 1714–1995*, 3rd ed. (London: Longman, 1996), 264–66.

6. As quoted in *Revised Report of the Proceedings at the Dinner* [of the Political Economy Club] … *Held in Celebration of the Hundredth Year of the Publication of "The Wealth of Nations"* … (London: Longmans, Green, Reader & Dyer, 1876), 68.

7. Cook and Stevenson, *The Longman Handbook*, 206.

PART II RETROSPECTIVE

1. Biographical details from "The Late Mrs. Neves," *New York Times*, April 19, 1903, https://timesmachine.nytimes.com/timesmachine/1903/04/19/101990032.pdf; "The Harvey Family," accessed December 27, 2020, https://web.archive.org/web/20131022135751/http://www.priaulxlibrary.co.uk/priaulx-library-new-details2.asp?ItemID=95; "Margaret Anne Neve," accessed December 27, 2020, https://en.wikipedia.org/wiki/Margaret_Ann_Neve.

CHAPTER 12: BRITAIN IN THE ERA OF WORLD CONFLICT

1. Norman Angell, *The Great Illusion/A Study of the Relation of Military Power to National Advantage* (London: G. P. Putnam's and Sons, 1910), 317.

2. Jens Thiel and Christian Westerhof, "Forced Labour," *International Encyclopedia of the First World War*, 2014, https://encyclopedia.1914-1918-online.net/article/Forced_Labour.

3. "World War I," M. K. Gandhi, https://www.mkgandhi.org/biography/wrldwar1.htm#:~:text=When%20World%20War%20I%20broke,to%20raise%20an%20ambulance%20unit.&text=It%20is%20a%20necessity%20of%20citizenship%20all%20the%20world%20over.%22.

4. "The Conscription Crisis," *Le Canada*, 2001, https://www.cbc.ca/history/EPISCONTENTSE1EP-12CH2PA3LE.html#:~:text=On%20May%2018%2C%201917%2C%20Prime,greater%20than%20in%20French%20Canada.

5. Talat Ahmed, "The British Empire and the First World War: The Colonial Experience," in *International Socialism: A Quarterly Review of Socialist Theory* no. 152 (October 2016), http://isj.org.uk/the-british-empire-and-the-first-world-war-the-colonial-experience/.

6. Claude Markovits, "Making Sense of the War (India)," *International Encyclopedia of the First World War*, 2014, https://encyclopedia.1914-1918-online.net/article/making_sense_of_the_war_india.

7. "Mr. Montagu's Statement," August 6, 1918, https://api.parliament.uk/historic-hansard/commons/1918/aug/06/mr-montagus-statement.

8. Markovits, "Making Sense of the War (India)."

9. "10 Big Myths about World War One Debunked," British Broadcasting Company, February 25, 2014, https://www.bbc.com/news/magazine-25776836.

10. Quotes from Vera Brittain, *A Testament of Youth* (New York: Penguin, 2005).

11. Quotes from Robert Graves, *Good-bye to All That* (New York: Doubleday, 1957).

12. "Trenches: Dodging Damned Great Bombs," National Archives, July 11, 1915, https://www.nationalarchives.gov.uk/education/resources/letters-first-world-war-1915/trenches-dodging-damned-great-bombs/.

13. "Trenches: They Were Mostly Mere Boys," National Archives, May 12, 1915, https://www.nationalarchives.gov.uk/education/resources/letters-first-world-war-1915/trenches-mostly-mere-boys/.

14. "Railhead: We Are Living Very Well," National Archives, October 9, 1915, France. https://www.nationalarchives.gov.uk/education/resources/letters-first-world-war-1915/railhead-living-well/.

15. "Trenches: Had a Game of Football," National Archives, https://www.nationalarchives.gov.uk/education/resources/letters-first-world-war-1915/trenches-game-football/.

16. "Dardanelles: 'An Ever Lasting Nightmare,'" National Archives, June 18, 1915, https://www.nationalarchives.gov.uk/education/resources/letters-first-world-war-1915/dardanelles-everlasting-nightmare/.

17. "Trenches: Up to Our Knees in Water," National Archives, November 10, 1915, https://www.nationalarchives.gov.uk/education/resources/letters-first-world-war-1915/trenches-knees-water/.

18. As quoted in John Keegan, *A History of Warfare* (New York: Random House, 1993), 365.

19. Ibid., 366.

20. W. B. Yeats, "Easter, 1916," February 1998, *The Atlantic*, https://www.theatlantic.com/magazine/archive/1998/02/easter-1916/308483/.

21. Michel A. Kappelmann, "Parallel Campaigns: The British in Mesopotamia, 1914–1920 and the United States in Iraq, 2003–2004," 2012, https://apps.dtic.mil/sti/pdfs/ADA589751.pdf.

22. Durba Ghosh, *Gentlemanly Terrorists: Political Violence and the Colonial State in India, 1919–1947* (Cambridge, UK: Cambridge University Press, 2017).

23. Ibid.

24. "The Ten Year Rule and Disarmament," https://www.nationalarchives.gov.uk/cabinetpapers/themes/10-year-rule-disarmament.htm.

25. "Treaty of Mutual Guarantee between Germany, Belgium, France, Great Britain and Italy; October 16, 1925 (The Locarno Pact)," Yale Law School, https://avalon.law.yale.edu/20th_century/locarno_001.asp.

26. As quoted in in Cameron Smith, *Unfinished Journey: The Lewis Family* (Toronto: Summerhill Press, 1989), 180–81.

27. G. C. Webber, "Patterns of Membership and Support for the British Union of Fascists," *Journal of Contemporary History* 19, no. 4 (1984): 595.

28. Bret Rubin, "The Rise and Fall of British Fascism: Sir Oswald Mosley and the British Union of Fascists," *Intersections* 11, no. 2 (2010): 323–80; Webber's "Patterns of Membership" challenges the ideas that the party declined as much as previously thought and that aversion to anti-Semitism alone explains a decline in middle-class membership.

29. Prime Minister Neville Chamberlain, "Address to the British People," September 3, 1939, https://avalon.law.yale.edu/wwii/gb3.asp.

30. "The Evacuation at Dunkirk, 1940," EyewitnesstoHistory.com, 2008, http://www.eyewitnesstohistory.com/dunkirk.htm.

31. Christopher Woolf and Amulya Shankar, "There Were Indians Troops at Dunkirk Too," *The World*, August 2, 2017, https://www.pri.org/stories/2017-08-02/there-were-indian-troops-dunkirk-too#:~:text=Those%20who%20evacuated%20from%20DunkirkChamberlain,the%20UK%20and%20buried%20there.&text=But%20there%20is%20the%20propaganda,cultivated%20by%20the%20British%20government.

32. Discussion of racism in Britain during World War II is based on Sonya O. Rose, "Race, Empire, and British Wartime National Identity, 1939–1945," *Historical Inquiry* 74, no. 84 (May 2001): 221–37.

33. Maria Abi-Habib, "The Forgotten Colonial Forces of WWII," *New York Times Magazine*, September 1, 2020, https://www.nytimes.com/2020/09/01/magazine/the-forgotten-colonial-forces-of-world-war-ii.html.

34. Statistics on colonial forces and where they served from, "WW2 Peoples War," 2005, British Broadcasting Company, https://www.bbc.co.uk/history/ww2peopleswar/timeline/factfiles/nonflash/a6651218.shtml.

35. John Keegan, *The Second World War* (New York: Penguin, 1989), 106.

36. Paul Kennedy, *The Rise and Fall of the Great Powers: Economic Change and Military Conflict from 1500 to 2000* (New York: Vintage Books, 1989), 354.

37. Ibid., 355.

38. Williamson Murray and Allan Millett, *A War to Be Won: Fighting the Second World War* (Cambridge, MA: Belknap Press, 2000), 424–25.

39. Forrest Pogue, "The Decision to Halt at the Elbe," http://www.history.army.mil/books/70-7_22.htm.

40. Ibid.

41. Peter Kemp, "The Literature of World War II (1939–1945)," https://www.britannica.com/art/English-literature/The-literature-of-World-War-II-1939-45.

42. Wilfred Owen, "Dulce et Decorum Est," Poetry Foundation, 1921, https://www.poetryfoundation.org/poems/46560/dulce-et-decorum-est.

43. Keith Douglas Vergissmeinnicht, All Poetry, https://allpoetry.com/Keith-Douglas.

44. "WW2, the People's War," British Broadcasting Company, May 3, 1943, https://www.bbc.co.uk/history/ww2peopleswar/stories/88/a1958088.shtml.

45. Ibid.

46. Mark Ketteridge, "My Uncle's Last Letter," British Broadcasting Company, June 27, 1944, https://www.bbc.co.uk/history/ww2peopleswar/stories/16/a4035016.shtml. Audrey was the young woman he hoped to marry.

CHAPTER 13: POLITICAL, ECONOMIC, AND SOCIAL UPHEAVAL

1. Chris Cook and John Stevenson, *The Longman Handbook of Modern British History, 1714–1995*, 3rd ed. (London: Longman, 1996), 266–67.

2. George Orwell, *The Road to Wigan Pier* (Gutenberg Australia, 2002), http://gutenberg.net.au/ebooks02/0200391.txt.

3. Ibid.

CHAPTER 14: BRITAIN IN A WORLD HISTORICAL CONTEXT

1. Winston Churchill Speech to Parliament, June 18, 1940, *Hansards Parliamentary Debates*, vol. 362 cc51-64.

2. William Manchester, *The Last Lion. Volume 1: Visions of Glory, 1874-1932* (Boston: Little, Brown, 1983), 39.

3. "Winston Churchill's Iron Curtain Speech," History Guide, March 5, 1946, http://www.historyguide.org/europe/churchill.html.

4. "The Berlin Blockade," Cold War Museum, https://www.history.com/topics/cold-war/berlin-blockade.

5. Charles More, *Britain in the Twentieth Century* (London: Longman, 2007), 2001.

6. "The Brussels Treaty," NATO, March 17, 1948, http://www.nato.int/cps/on/natohq/official_texts_17072.htm.

7. Ibid., Article IX.

8. Ibid.

9. "Lord Ismay," NATO, http://nato.int/cps/en/natohq/declassified_137930.htm.

10. For discussion of Britain's role in shaping the Marshall Plan, see William C. Cromwell, "The Marshall Plan, Britain and the Cold War," *Review of International Studies* 8, no. 4 (October 1982): 233–49.

11. Correlli Barnett, "The Wasting of Britain's Marshall Aid," British Broadcasting Company, March 3, 2011, http://www.bbc.co.uk/history/british/modern/marshall_01.shtml.

12. Discussion of British attitudes during the Cuban Missile Crisis based on H. A. Deweerd, "British Attitudes in the Cuban Crisis," (Santa Monica, CA: Rand Corporation, February 1963), https://www.rand.org/content/dam/rand/pubs/papers/2008/P2709.pdf.

13. "Britain's Forgotten War," British Broadcasting Company, April 20, 2001, http://news.bbc.co.uk/2/hi/uk_news/1285708.stm.

14. Harold Macmillan, "Wind of Change Speech," February 3, 1960, https://web-archives.univ-pau.fr/english/TD2doc1.pdf.

15. Yasmin Khan, "Has India's Contribution to World War 2 Been Ignored?," British Broadcasting Company, June 17, 2015, http://www.bbc.com/news/world-asia-india-33105898.

16. Sudheshna Bhattacharya, "The Making of a Popular Base for the Quit India Movement: The Impact of the Pacific War on the People and the Colonial State in India (1941–42)," *Proceedings of the Indian History Congress* 63 (2002): 694.

17. Jugal Kishore Gupta, "Myths and Realities of the Quit India Movement," *Proceedings of the Indian History Congress* 46 (1985): 577.

18. See Kate Imy, *Faithful Fighters: Identity and Power in the British Indian Army* (Stanford, CA: Stanford University Press, 2019).

19. Daniel Yergin and Joseph Stanislaw, eds., *Commanding Heights: The Battle for the World Economy* (New York: Simon & Schuster, 1998).

20. Casualty figures from Bruce Hoffman, "Why Terrorism Works," *Chronicle of Higher Education*, March 2, 2015, https://www.chronicle.com/article/why-terrorism-works/.

21. "Mau Mau Uprising: Bloody History of Kenya Conflict," British Broadcasting Company, April 7, 2011, https://www.bbc.com/news/uk-12997138.

22. Avi Shlaim, "The Protocol of Sèvres,1956: Anatomy of a War Plot," *International Affairs* 73, no. 3 (1997): 509–30.

23. Margery Perham, "The Rhodesian Crisis: Background," *International Affairs* 42, no.1 (January 1966): 1–13.

24. "UK Armed Forces Monthly Service Personnel Statistics," Ministry of Defence, June 15, 2017, https://www.gov.uk/government/uploads/system/uploads/attachment_data/file/618747/20170501_-_SPS.pdf.

25. Michael Elliott, "Viewpoint: How Libya Became a French and British War," *Time*, March 19, 2011, http://content.time.com/time/world/article/0,8599,2060412,00.html.

26. House of Commons Foreign Affairs Committee, *Libya: Examination of Intervention and Collapse and the UK's Future Policy Options*, HC 119 (London: House of Commons, 2016).

27. Winston Churchill, "The United States of Europe," *Saturday Evening Post*, February 15, 1930.

28. "The Treaty of Rome," March 25, 1957, https://ec.europa.eu/romania/sites/romania/files/tratatul_de_la_roma.pdf.

29. Discussion of British reluctance based on Carol Elder Baumann, "Britain Faces Europe," *Political Science Quarterly* 74, no. 3 (September 1959): 351–71.

30. "European Union Referendum Act," UK Legislation, http://www.legislation.gov.uk/ukpga/2015/36/section/1/enacted.

31. Alex Hunt and Brian Wheeler, "Brexit: What You Need to Know about the UK Leaving the EU," British Broadcasting Company, July 13, 2017, http://www.bbc.com/news/uk-politics-32810887.

32. "How the UK Voted on Brexit and Why—a Refresher," Lord Ashcroft Polls, February 4, 2019, https://lordashcroftpolls.com/2019/02/how-the-uk-voted-on-brexit-and-why-a-refresher/.

33. Ibid.

34. Karan Bilimoria, "Britain Doesn't Need to 'Take Back Control' of Immigration. We Already Have It," *The Guardian*, July 31, 2017, https://www.theguardian.com/commentisfree/2017/jul/31/britain-take-back-control-immigration-eu-directive-brexit.

CHAPTER 15: SOCIETY AND POLITICS: CHANGE AND CONTINUITY

1. Curiously, the expression had most recent currency in the rhetoric of former Conservative prime minister Stanley Baldwin, in 1926, in the aftermath of the General Strike.

2. As quoted in Paul Addison, "Why Churchill Lost in 1945," British Broadcasting Company, February 17, 2011, http://www.bbc.co.uk/history/worldwars/wwtwo/election_01.shtml.

3. The Liberal Party was by no means negligible. Indeed, it was probably liberal voters who determined the outcome of the 1951 general election. It was, however, as we saw in chapter 13, in terminal decline since World War I.

4. "Speech to Conservative Central Council," March 19, 1988, https://www.margaretthatcher.org/document/107200.

5. Mike Cronin, *A History of Ireland* (London and New York: Palgrave, 2001), 209.

6. Ibid., 210.

7. Ibid., 228.

CHAPTER 16: CULTURE, BELIEFS, AND IDEAS

1. As quoted in Tony Rennell, *Daily Mail*, November 20, 2007, https://www.pressreader.com/uk/daily-mail/20071120/281878704024444.

2. "Divorces in England and Wales: 2010," Office of National Statistics, December 8, 2011, https://www.ons.gov.uk/peoplepopulationandcommunity/birthsdeathsandmarriages/divorce/bulletins/divorcesinenglandandwales/2011-12-08.

3. "Policing and Crime Act 2017," Wikipedia, 2020, https://en.m.wikipedia.org/wiki/Policing_and_Crime_Act_2017.

4. Callum G. Brown, *The Death of Christian Britain: Understanding Secularisation, 1800–2000*, 2nd ed. (New York: Routledge: 2009).

5. "Special Restriction (Coloured Alien Seamen) Order (1925)," Open University, http://www.open.ac.uk/researchprojects/makingbritain/content/special-restriction-coloured-alien-seamen-order-1925.

6. Laura Tabili, "The Construction of Racial Difference in Twentieth-Century Britain: The Special Restriction (Coloured Alien Seamen) Order, 1925," *Journal of British Studies* 33 (Jan. 1994): 56.

7. "International Migration," Office for National Statistics, https://www.ons.gov.uk/peoplepopulationandcommunity/populationandmigration/internationalmigration.

8. As quoted in Andrew Geddes, *The Politics of Migration and Immigration in Europe* (London: SAGE, 2003), 34.

9. Depression in Northern Ireland was also severe, but that is another story.

PART III RETROSPECTIVE

1. Vera Lynn, *Some Sunny Day: My Autobiography* (London: HarperCollins UK, 2009), 304.

2. Ibid., 304.

3. "Best British Female Singers," https://www.thetoptens.com/best-british-female-singers/.

BRITAIN IN A NEW CENTURY

1. Nik Lomax et al., "What the UK Population Will Look Like by 2061 under Hard, Soft or No Brexit Scenarios," *The Conversation*, May 30, 2019, https://theconversation.com/what-the-uk-population-will-look-like-by-2061-under-hard-soft-or-no-brexit-scenarios-117475/.

2. Benjamin Mueller, "What Is Brexit? And What Happens Next?," *New York Times*, January 31, 2020, https://www.nytimes.com/interactive/2019/world/europe/what-is-brexit.html.

3. Moya Jones, "Wales and the Brexit Vote," *Revue Française de Civilisation Britannique* XXII-17 (2017), https://journals.openedition.org/rfcb/1387.

4. Luke McGee, "Rotting Fish, Lost Business and Piles of Red Tape. The Reality of Brexit Hits Britain," CNN, January 23, 2021, https://www.cnn.com/2021/01/23/business/brexit-business-intl-gbr/index.html.

5. Costas Pitas, "Nissan to Source More UK Batteries as Part of Brexit Deal 'Opportunity,'" *Reuters*, January 21, 2020, https://www.reuters.com/article/uk-britain-eu-nissan/nissan-to-source-more-uk-batteries-as-part-of-brexit-deal-opportunity-idUKKBN29R016.

BIBLIOGRAPHY

CHAPTER 1: STRUCTURES AND PATTERNS OF EVERYDAY LIFE

Barker, Hannah, and Elaine Chalus. *Women's History: Britain, 1700–1850*. New York: Routledge, 2005.

Chater, Kathleen. *Untold Histories: Black People in England and Wales during the Period of the British Slave Trade, c. 1660–1807*. Manchester: Manchester University Press, 2009.

Clark, Anna. *The Struggle for the Breeches: Gender and the Making of the British Working Class*. Berkeley: University of California Press, 1995.

Davidoff, Leonore, and Catherine Hall. *Family Fortunes: Men and Women of the English Middle Class, 1780–1850*. Chicago: University of Chicago Press, 1987.

Gerzina, Gretchen Holbrook. *Black London: Life before Emancipation*. New Brunswick, NJ: Rutgers University Press, 1995.

Hay, Douglas, and Nicholas Rogers. *Eighteenth-Century English Society*. Oxford: Oxford University Press, 1997.

Hitchcock, Tim. *English Sexualities, 1700–1800*. London: Palgrave Macmillan, 1997.

Hitchcock, Tim. *Down and Out in Eighteenth-Century London*. London: Continuum, 2004.

Hunt, Margaret. *The Middling Sort: Commerce, Gender, and the Family in England, 1680–1780*. Berkeley: University of California Press, 1996.

Johnson, Claudia L., ed. *The Cambridge Companion to Mary Wollstonecraft*. Cambridge: Cambridge University Press, 2002.

Morgan, Kenneth. *Slavery and the British Empire: From Africa to America*. Oxford: Oxford University Press, 2007.

Porter, Roy. *English Society in the Eighteenth Century*. Harmondsworth, UK: Penguin, 1982.

Rabin, Dana. "'In a Country of Liberty?' Slavery, Villeinage and the Making of Whiteness in the Somerset Case (1772)." *History Workshop Journal* 72 (2011): 5–29.

Shoemaker, Robert. *Gender in English Society 1650–1850: The Emergence of Separate Spheres?* London: Routledge, 2014.

Tillyard, Stella. *Aristocrats: Caroline, Emily, Louisa and Sarah Lennox 1740–1832*. London: Chatto & Windus, 1994.

Vickery, Amanda. *Behind Closed Doors: At Home in Georgian England*. New Haven, CT: Yale University Press, 2009.

CHAPTER 2: STRUCTURES AND PATTERNS OF POLITICS

Brewer, John. *The Sinews of Power: War, Money and the English State, 1688–1783*. Cambridge: Cambridge University Press, 1990.

Brown, Michael, Patrick Geoghegan, and James Kelly, eds. *The Irish Act of Union, 1800: Bicentennial Essays.* Dublin: Irish Academic Press, 2003.

Colley, Linda. *Britons: Forging the Nation, 1707–1837.* New Haven, CT: Yale University Press, 1992.

Foster, R. F, *Modern Ireland, 1600–1972.* London: Penguin, 1990.

Jackson, Alvin. *The Two Unions: Ireland, Scotland, and the Survival of the United Kingdom, 1707–2007:* Oxford: Oxford University Press, 2012.

Lenman, Bruce. *The Jacobite Risings in Britain, 1689–1746.* Aberdeen: Scottish Cultural Press, 1980.

Macinnes, Allan I. *Union and Empire: The Making of the United Kingdom in 1707.* Cambridge: Cambridge University Press, 2007.

McBride, Ian. *Eighteenth-Century Ireland: The Isle of Slaves.* Dublin: Gill & MacMillan, 2009.

Pincus, Steven. *England's Glorious Revolution 1688–1689: A Brief History with Documents.* Boston: Bedford/St. Martin's, 2006.

Pincus, Steven. *1688: The First Modern Revolution.* New Haven, CT: Yale University Press, 2009.

Robertson, John, ed. *A Union for Empire: Political Thought and the British Union of 1707.* Cambridge: Cambridge University Press, 1995.

Smyth, Jim, ed. *Revolution, Counter-Revolution and Union: Ireland in the 1790s.* Cambridge: Cambridge University Press, 2000.

Szechi, Daniel. *1715: The Great Jacobite Rebellion.* New Haven, CT: Yale University Press, 2006.

Williams, E. Neville. *The Eighteenth-Century Constitution, 1688–1815.* Ann Arbor: University of Michigan Press, 1960.

CHAPTER 3: BRITAIN IN A WORLD HISTORICAL CONTEXT

Baugh, Daniel. *The Global Seven Years War 1754–1763: Britain and France in a Great Power Contest.* London: Routledge, 2011.

Bayly, C. A. *Imperial Meridian: The British Empire and the World, 1780–1830.* London: Longman, 1989.

Brown, Christopher Leslie. *Moral Capital: Foundations of British Abolitionism.* Chapel Hill: University of North Carolina Press, 2006.

Colley, Linda. *Britons: Forging the Nations, 1707–1837.* New Haven, CT: Yale University Press, 1992.

Dickson, David. *New Foundations: Ireland 1660–1800.* Dublin: Irish Academic Press, 2000.

Dull, John. *The Age of the Ship of the Line: The British and French Navies, 1650–1815.* Omaha: University of Nebraska Press, 2009.

Geggus, David Patrick. *Slavery, War, and Revolution: The British Occupation of Saint Domingue, 1793–1798.* Oxford: Clarendon, 1982.

Fryer, Peter. *Staying Power: The History of Black People in Britain.* Atlantic Highlands, NJ: Open Humanities Press, 2010.

Hibbert, Christopher. *Redcoats and Rebels: The American Revolution through British Eyes.* New York: Norton, 1990.

Jenkins, Geraint H. *A Concise History of Wales.* Cambridge: Cambridge University Press, 2007.

Lawson, Philip. *A Taste for Empire and Glory: Studies in British Overseas Expansion, 1660–1800.* Brookfield, CT: Variorum, 1997.

Lenman, Bruce. *The Jacobite Risings in Britain, 1689–1746.* Aberdeen: Scottish Cultural Press, 1980.

Monod, Paul. K. *Imperial Island: A History of Britain and Its Empire, 1660–1837.* London: Wiley, 2009.

Morgan, Kenneth. *Slavery and the British Empire: From Africa to America.* Oxford: Oxford University Press, 2007.

Olusoga, David. *Black and British: A Forgotten History.* New York: Macmillan, 2016.

Rediker, Marcus. *The Slave Ship. A Human History.* New York: Penguin, 2007.

Stuart, Andrea. *Sugar in the Blood: A Family's Story of Slavery and Empire.* New York: Vintage, 2012.

Thrush, Coll. *Indigenous London: Native Travelers at the Heart of Empire.* New Haven, CT: Yale University Press, 2016.

Wilson, Kathleen. The *Sense of the People: Politics, Culture and Imperialism in England, 1715–1785.* Cambridge: Cambridge University Press, 1995.

CHAPTER 4: BELIEFS, IDEAS, AND ATTITUDES

Bebbington, David W. *Evangelicalism in Modern Britain: A History from the 1730s to the 1980s.* London: Routledge, 1989.

Brewer, John. *The Pleasures of the Imagination: English Culture in the Eighteenth Century.* New York: Farrar, Straus, and Giroux, 1997.

Brown, Christopher Leslie. *Moral Capital: Foundations of British Abolitionism.* Chapel Hill: University of North Carolina Press, 2006.

Butler, Marilyn, ed. *Burke, Paine, Godwin, and the Revolution Controversy.* Cambridge: Cambridge University Press, 1984.

Drayton, Richard. *Nature's Government: Science, Imperial Britain and the 'Improvement' of the World.* New Haven, CT: Yale University Press, 2000.

Girouard, Mark. *Life in the English Country House: A Social and Architectural History.* New Haven, CT: Yale University Press, 1978.

Jacob, Margaret. *The Enlightenment: A Brief History with Documents.* 2nd ed. Boston: Bedford/St. Martin's, 2016.

Katz, David. *The Jews in the History of England, 1485–1850.* Oxford: Clarendon, 1994.

Krikler, Jeremy. "The Zong and the Lord Chief Justice." *History Workshop Journal* 64 (2008): 29–47.

Porter, Roy. *The Creation of the Modern World: The Untold Story of the British Enlightenment.* New York: Norton, 2000.

Taylor, Barbara. *Mary Wollstonecraft and the Feminist Imagination.* Cambridge: Cambridge University Press, 2003.

Yates, Nigel. *Eighteenth-Century Britain: Religion and Politics, 1714–1815.* Harlow, UK: Pearson Education, 2008.

CHAPTER 5: PEOPLES, PARTIES, AND PATRONAGE

Brewer, John. *Party Ideology and Popular Politics at the Accession of George III.* Cambridge: Cambridge University Press, 1976.

Brewer, John. *The Sinews of Power: War, Money and the English State, 1688–1783.* Cambridge: Cambridge University Press, 1990.

Colley, Linda. *Britons: Forging the Nation, 1707–1837*. New Haven, CT: Yale University Press, 1992.

Gould, Eliga H. *The Persistence of Empire: British Political Culture in the Age of the American Revolution*. Chapel Hill: University of North Carolina Press, 2000.

Haywood, Ian and John Seed, eds. *The Gordon Riots: Politics, Culture and Insurrection in Late Eighteenth-Century Britain*. Cambridge: Cambridge University Press, 2012.

Hilton, Boyd. *A Mad, Bad, and Dangerous People? England, 1783–1846*. Oxford: Oxford University Press, 2006.

Hoppit, Julian. *Land of Liberty? England 1689–1727*. Oxford: Oxford University Press, 2000.

Jasanoff, Maya. *Liberty's Exiles. American Loyalists in the Revolutionary World*. New York: Knopf, 2011.

Langford, Paul. *A Polite and Commercial People, England 1727–1783*. Oxford: Oxford University Press, 1989.

O'Gorman, Frank. *The Long Eighteenth Century: British Political and Social History 1688–1832*. London: Arnold, 2004.

Pincus, Steven. *1688, The First Modern Revolution*. New Haven, CT: Yale University Press, 2009.

Thompson, E. P. *The Making of the English Working Class*. London: Vintage, 1963.

Weil, Rachel. *Political Passions: Gender, the Family and Political Argument in England, 1680–1714*. Manchester: Manchester University Press, 2000.

Wilson, Kathleen. *The Sense of the People: Politics, Culture and Imperialism in England, 1715–1785*. Cambridge: Cambridge University Press, 1995.

CHAPTER 6: ECONOMIC TRANSFORMATIONS

Allen, Robert C. *The British Industrial Revolution in Global Perspective*. Cambridge: Cambridge University Press, 2009.

Berg, Maxine. *The Age of Manufactures: Industry, Innovation and Work in Britain, 1700–1820*. London: Routledge, 1994.

Daunton, Martin. *Progress and Poverty: An Economic and Social History of Britain, 1700–1850*. Oxford: Oxford University Press, 1995.

De Vries, Jan. *The Industrious Revolution: Consumer Behavior and the Household Economy, 1650 to the Present*. Cambridge: Cambridge University Press, 2008.

Griffin, Emma. *A Short History of the British Industrial Revolution*. Basingstoke, UK: Palgrave Macmillan, 2010.

Griffin, Emma. *Liberty's Dawn: A People's History of the Industrial Revolution*. New Haven, CT: Yale University Press, 2013.

Paul, Helen J. *The South Sea Bubble: An Economic History of Its Origins and Consequences*. London: Routledge, 2011.

Rogers, Nicholas. *Mayhem: Post-War Crime and Violence in Britain 1748-1753*. New Haven, CT: Yale University Press, 2012.

Statt, Daniel. *Foreigners and Englishmen: The Controversy over Immigration and Population, 1660–1760*. Newark: University of Delaware Press, 1995.

Thompson, E. P. *Customs in Common: Studies in Traditional Popular Culture*. New York: The New Press, 1991.

Valenze, Deborah. *The First Industrial Woman*. New York: Oxford University Press, 1995.

CHAPTER 7: STRUCTURES AND PATTERNS OF EVERYDAY LIFE

Barker, Hannah, and Elaine Chalus, eds. *Women's History: Britain, 1700–1850*. New York: Routledge, 2005.

Cannadine, David. *The Rise and Fall of Class in Britain*. New York: Columbia University Press, 1999.

Clark, Anna. *The Struggle for the Breeches: Gender and the Making of the British Working Class*. Berkeley: University of California Press, 1995.

Davidoff, Leonore, and Catherine Hall. *Family Fortunes: Men and Women of the English Middle Class, 1780–1850*. Chicago: University of Chicago Press, 1987.

Frost, Ginger S. *Victorian Childhoods*. Westport, CT: Praeger, 2009.

Fryer, Peter. *Staying Power: The History of Black People in Britain*. Atlantic Highlands, NJ: Open Humanities Press, 2010.

Griffin, Emma. *Liberty's Dawn: A People's History of the Industrial Revolution*. New Haven, CT: Yale University Press, 2013.

Humphries, Jane. *Childhood and Child Labour in the British Industrial Revolution*. Cambridge: Cambridge University Press, 2010.

Kent, Susan Kingsley. *Sex and Suffrage in Britain, 1860–1914*. Princeton, NJ: Princeton University Press, 1987.

Kinealy, Christine. *This Great Calamity: The Irish Famine 1845–1852*. 2nd ed. Dublin: Gill Books, 2006.

MacRaild, Donald M. *Irish Migrants in Modern Britain, 1750–1922*. New York: St. Martin's, 1999.

Olusoga, David. *Black and British: A Forgotten History*. New York: Macmillan, 2016.

Purvis, June, ed. *Women's History: Britain, 1850–1945*. New York: Routledge, 1995.

Rose, Sonya O. *Limited Livelihoods: Gender and Class in Nineteenth-Century England*. Berkeley: University of California Press, 1993.

Ross, Ellen. *Love and Toil: Motherhood in Outcast London, 1870–1918*. Oxford: Oxford University Press, 1993.

Sanderson, Michael. *Education, Economic Change and Society in England 1780–1870*. 2nd ed. Cambridge: Cambridge University Press, 1995.

Tosh, John. *A Man's Place: Masculinity and the Middle-Class Home in Victorian England*. New Haven, CT: Yale University Press, 1999.

Tosh, John. *Manliness and Masculinities in Nineteenth-Century Britain: Essays on Gender, Family and Empire*. New York: Routledge, 2016.

CHAPTER 8: BRITAIN AND THE WIDER WORLD

Bartlett, Christopher J. *Defence and Diplomacy: Britain and the Great Powers, 1815–1914*. Manchester: Manchester University Press, 1993.

Bayly, Christopher A. *Imperial Meridian: The British Empire and the World, 1780–1830*. London: Longman, 1989.

Cannadine, David. *Ornamentalism: How the British Saw Their Empire*. New York: Oxford, 2001.

Darwin, John. *Unfinished Empire: The Global Expansion of Empire*. London: Bloomsbury, 2013.

Hall, Catherine. *Civilizing Subjects: Metropole and Colony in the English Imagination, 1830–1867*. Chicago: University of Chicago Press, 2002.

Hall, Catherine, and Sonya O. Rose, eds. *At Home with the Empire: Metropolitan Culture and the Imperial World.* Cambridge: Cambridge University Press, 2006.

Hobsbawm, Eric, with Chris Wrigley. *Industry and Empire: The Birth of the Industrial Revolution.* Revised and updated. New York: The New Press, 1999; 1st ed., 1968.

Hyam, Ronald. *Britain's Imperial Century, 1815–1914: A Study of Empire and Expansion.* 2nd ed. London: Palgrave Macmillan, 2016.

Kennedy, Paul. *The Rise and Fall of the Great Powers.* New York: Vintage, 2010.

Levine, Philippa. *Prostitution, Race, and Politics: Policing Venereal Disease in the British Empire.* New York: Routledge, 2003.

Pakenham, Thomas. *The Scramble for Africa: White Man's Conquest of the Dark Continent from 1876 to 1912.* New York: Avon Books, 1992.

Porter, Bernard. *The Absent-Minded Imperialists: Empire, Society, and Culture in Britain.* Oxford: Oxford University Press, 2006.

Thornton, Archibald Paton. *The Imperial Idea and Its Enemies: A Study in Imperial Power.* New York: Doubleday, 1968.

Veracini, Lorenzo. *Settler Colonialism: A Theoretical Overview.* New York: Palgrave Macmillan, 2010.

Wilson, Kathleen. *A New Imperial History: Culture, Identity, and Modernity in Britain and the Empire, 1660–1840.* Cambridge: Cambridge University Press, 2004.

CHAPTER 9: CERTITUDE AND ANXIETY IN AN ERA OF RAPID CHANGE

Auerbach, Jeffrey, and Peter Hoffenberg. *Britain, the Empire, and the World at the Great Exhibition of 1851.* Ashgate, UK: Aldershot, 2008.

Burton, Antoinette. *Burdens of History: British Feminists, Indian Women, and Imperials Culture, 1865–1915.* Chapel Hill: University of North Carolina Press, 1994.

Endelman, Todd M. *The Jews of Britain, 1656 to 2000.* Berkeley: University of California Press, 2002.

Fletcher, Ian Christopher, Laura E. Nym Mayhall, and Philippa Levine, eds. *Women's Suffrage in the British Empire: Citizenship, Nation, and Race.* New York: Routledge, 2000.

Hall, Catherine. *White, Male and Middle Class: Explorations in Feminism and History.* London: Routledge, 1992.

Lambert-Hurley, Siobhan and Sunil Sharma, eds. *Atiya's Journeys: A Muslim Woman from Colonial Bombay to Edwardian Britain.* New Delhi: Oxford University Press, 2010.

Pankhurst, Sylvia. *The Suffragette Movement.* London: Wharton Press, 1931.

Pereiro, James. *Ethos and the Oxford Movement: At the Heart of Tractarianism.* Oxford: Oxford University Press, 2008.

Said, Edward W. *Orientalism.* New York: Pantheon, 1978.

Schwarz, ed. *The Expansion of England: Race, Ethnicity and Cultural History.* London: Routledge, 1996.

Soloway, Richard A. *Demography and Degeneration: Eugenics and the Declining Birth Rate in Twentieth-Century Britain.* Chapel Hill: University of North Carolina Press, 1990.

Taylor, Barbara. *Eve and the New Jerusalem: Socialism and Feminism in the Nineteenth Century.* London: Virago, 1983.

Tosh, John. *A Man's Place: Masculinity and the Middle-Class Home in Victorian England*. New Haven, CT: Yale University Press, 1999.

CHAPTER 10: REPRESSION AND REFORM

Briggs, Asa (ed.). *Chartist Studies*. London: St. Martin's, 1959.

Clark, Anna. *The Struggle for the Breeches: Gender and the Making of the British Working Class*. Berkeley: University of California Press, 1995.

Cowman, Krista. *Women in British Politics, c. 1689–1979*. New York: Palgrave Macmillan, 2010.

Evans, Eric J. *Parliamentary Reform, 1770–1918*. London: Longman, 1999.

Fryer, Peter. *Staying Power: The History of Black People in Britain*. Atlantic Highlands, NJ: Open Humanities Press, 2010.

Gash, Norman. *Politics in the Age of Peel: A Study in the Technique of Parliamentary Representation, 1830–1850*. London: Longman, 1960.

Hall, Catherine, Keith McClelland, and Jane Rendall. *Defining the Victorian Nation: Class, Race, Gender and the British Reform Act of 1867*. Cambridge: Cambridge University Press, 2000.

Hall, Catherine, and Sonya O. Rose, eds. *At Home with the Empire: Metropolitan Culture and the Imperial World*. Cambridge: Cambridge University Press, 2006.

Hawkins, Angus. *Victorian Political Culture: "Habits of Heart and Mind."* Oxford: Oxford University Press, 2015.

Hilton, Boyd. *A Mad, Bad, and Dangerous People? England 1783–1846*. Oxford: Oxford University Press, 2006.

Innes, Joanna, and Arthur Burns, eds. *Rethinking the Age of Reform: Britain 1780–1850*. Cambridge, UK: Cambridge University Press, 2003.

McCord, Norman. *The Anti-Corn Law League*. 2nd ed. London: Urwin University Books, 1968.

Perkin, Harold. *The Origins of Modern English Society*. London: Routledge and Keegan Paul, 1972.

Pickering, Paul, and Alex Tyrrell. *The People's Bread: A History of the Anti-Corn Law League*. London: Leicester University Press, 2000.

Poole, Robert. *Peterloo: An English Uprising*. Oxford: Oxford University Press, 2019.

Pugh, Martin. *The Making of Modern British Politics: 1867–1945*. Hoboken, NJ: Wiley, 2002.

Richardson, Sarah. *The Political Worlds of Women: Gender and Politics in Nineteenth-Century Britain*. New York: Routledge, 2013.

Thompson, Dorothy. *The Chartists: Popular Politics in the Industrial Revolution*. New York: Pantheon, 1984. Reprint London: Breviary Stuff, 2013.

Vernon, James, ed. *Re-Reading the Constitution: New Narratives in the Political History of England's Long Nineteenth Century*. Cambridge: Cambridge University Press, 1996.

CHAPTER 11: ECONOMY, INDUSTRIALIZATION, AND QUALITY OF LIFE

Crafts, N. F. R. "'Some Dimensions of the 'Quality of Life' during the British Industrial Revolution." *Economic History Review* 50, no. 4 (1997): 617–639.

Daunton, Martin J. *House and Home in the Victorian City: Working Class Housing, 1850–1914*. London: E. Arnold, 1983.

Daunton, Martin J. *Progress and Poverty: An Economic and Social History of Britain, 1700–1850*. Oxford: Oxford University Press. 1995.

Griffin, Emma. *Liberty's Dawn: A People's History of the Industrial Revolution*. New Haven, CT: Yale University Press, 2013.

Hamlin, Christopher. *Public Health and Social Justice in the Age of Chadwick, 1800–1854*. Cambridge, UK: Cambridge University Press, 1998.

Hardy, Anne. *The Epidemic Streets: Infectious Disease and the Rise of Preventive Medicine 1856–1900*. Oxford: Clarendon Press, 1993.

Howkins, Alun. *Reshaping Rural England: A Social History, 1850–1925*. London: HarperCollins, 1991.

Perkin, Harold. *The Age of the Railway*. London: Panther Books, 1970.

Reid, Alastair J. *Social Classes and Social Relations in Britain, 1850–1914*. Houndmills, UK: Macmillan Education, 1992.

Reid, D. A. "The Decline of St Monday, 1766–1876." *Past and Present* 71 (1976): 76–101.

Taylor, Arthur J. *The Standard of Living in Britain in the Industrial Revolution*. London: Methuen, 1975.

Thompson, F. M. L. *The Rise of Respectable Society: The Social History of Victorian Britain, 1830–1900*. Cambridge, MA: Harvard University Press, 1988.

Woods, Robert, and John Woodward, eds. *Urban Disease and Mortality in 19th-Century England*. New York: St. Martin's, 1984.

CHAPTER 12: BRITAIN IN AN ERA OF WORLD CONFLICT

Addison, Paul. *The Road to 1945: British Politics and the Second World War*. London: Pimlico, 1994.

Addison, Paul, and Angus Calder, eds. *Time to Kill: The Soldier's Experience of War in the West 1939–1945*. New York: Penguin, 1997.

Barnett, Correlli. "The Audit of War: Britain as an Industrial Society, 1939–45." *Journal of the Royal Society of Arts* 134, no. 5364 (1986): 781–793.

Bourke, Joanna. *Dismembering the Male: Men's Bodies, Britain and the Great War*. London: Reaktion Books, 1996.

Brittain, Vera. *A Testament of Youth*. New York: Penguin, 2005; 1st ed., 1933.

Calder, Angus. *The Myth of the Blitz*. London: J. Cape, 1991.

Connelly, Mark. *We Can Take it! Britain and the Memory of the Second World War*. Harlow, UK: Pearson Longman, 2004.

Donnelly, Mark. *Britain in the Second World War*. New York: Routledge, 1999.

Edgerton, David. *Britain's War Machine: Weapons, Resources and Experts in the Second World War*. Oxford: Oxford University Press, 2011.

Ellis, John. *Eye Deep in Hell: Trench Warfare in World War I*. Baltimore, MD: Johns Hopkins Press, 1976.

Fussell, Paul. *The Great War and Modern Memory*. Oxford: Oxford University Press, 2013.

Graves, Robert. *Good-bye to All That*. New York: Everyman's Library, 2018; 1st ed., 1929.

Gregory, Adrian. *The Last Great War: British Society and the First World War.* Cambridge: Cambridge University Press, 2008.

Gregory, Adrian, and Senia Pašeta, eds. *Ireland and the Great War: A War to Unite Us All?* Manchester: Manchester University Press, 2002.

History of the Second World War. London: Her Majesty's Stationery Office, 1949–1993.

Imy, Kate. *Faithful Fighters: Identity and Power in the British Indian Army.* Palo Alto, CA: Stanford University Press, 2019.

Keegan, John. *The First World War.* New York: Vintage, 2000.

—— *The Second World War.* New York: Penguin, 2005.

Longmate, Norman. *How We Lived Then: A History of Everyday Living during the Second World War.* London: Hutchinson, 1971.

Massie, Robert K. *Castles of Steel: Britain, Germany and the Winning of the Great War at Sea.* New York: Random House, 2003.

Milward, Alan S. *War, Economy and Society, 1939–1945.* Berkeley: University of California Press, 1977.

Murray, Williamson, and Allan Millet. *A War to be Won: Fighting the Second World War.* Cambridge, MA: Belknap, 2000.

Paris, Michael. *Repicturing the Second World War: Representations in Film and Television.* Basingstoke, UK: Palgrave Macmillan, 2007.

Pennell, Catriona. *A Kingdom United: Popular Responses to the Outbreak of the First World War in Britain and Ireland.* Oxford: Oxford University Press, 2012.

Watson, Janet S. K. *Fighting Different Wars: Experience, Memory, and the First World War in Britain.* Cambridge: Cambridge University Press. 2004.

Wrigley, C. J. "The First World War and State Intervention in Industrial Relations." In *A History of British Industrial Relations 1914-1939,* edited by C. J. Wrigley. Vol. 2. Amherst: University of Massachusetts Press, 1987.

CHAPTER 13: POLITICAL, ECONOMIC, AND SOCIAL UPHEAVAL

Carneval, Francesca, and Julie-Marie Strange, eds. *Twentieth-Century Britain: Economic, Cultural and Social Change.* 2nd ed. New York: Pearson Longman, 2007.

Cherry, Gordon Emanuel. *Town Planning in Britain since 1900: The Rise and Fall of the Planning Ideal.* Oxford: Blackwell, 1996.

Daunton, Martin J. *Wealth and Welfare: An Economic and Social History of Britain 1851–1951.* Oxford: Oxford University Press, 2007.

Eichengreen, Barry. *Golden Fetters: The Gold Standard and the Great Depression, 1919–1939.* Oxford: Oxford University Press, 1992.

Garside, W. R. *British Unemployment, 1919–1939: A Study in Public Policy.* Cambridge, UK: Cambridge University Press, 1990.

Hall, Lesley A. *Sex, Gender and Social Change in Britain since 1880*. Houndmills, UK: Macmillan, 2000.

Harris, Alana, and Timothy Willem Jones, eds. *Love and Romance in Britain 1918–1970*. Basingstoke, UK: Palgrave Macmillan, 2015.

Harris, Bernard. *The Origins of the British Welfare State: Society, State, and Social Welfare in England and Wales, 1800–1945*. Basingstoke, UK: Palgrave Macmillan, 2004.

Holt, Richard. *Sport and the British: A Modern History*. Oxford: Oxford University Press, 2009.

Machin, G. I. T. *Churches and Social Issues in Twentieth-Century Britain*. Oxford: Clarendon Press, 1997.

McKibbin, Ross. *Classes and Cultures: England 1918–1951*. Oxford: Oxford University Press, 1998.

Savage, Mike, and Andrew Miles. *The Remaking of the British Working Class, 1840–1940*. London: Routledge, 1994.

Scott, Peter. *The Making of the Modern British Home: The Suburban Semi and Family Life between the Wars*. Oxford: Oxford University Press, 2013.

Sedgwick, John. *Popular Filmgoing in 1930s Britain: A Choice of Pleasures*. Exeter, UK: University of Exeter Press, 2000.

Supple, Barry, et al. *The History of the British Coal Industry*, vols. 3 and 4. Oxford: Oxford University Press, 1984–1987.

White, Jerry. *London in the Twentieth Century: A City and Its People*. London: The Bodley Head, 2001.

CHAPTER 14: BRITAIN IN A WORLD HISTORICAL CONTEXT

Clarke, Harold D., Matthew Goodwin, and Paul Whitely. *Brexit: Why Britain Voted to Leave the European Union*. Cambridge: Cambridge University Press, 2017.

Darwin, John. *The Empire Project: The Rise and Fall of the British World-System, 1830–1970*. Cambridge: Cambridge University Press, 2009.

Dumbrell, John. *A Special Relationship: Anglo-American Relations from the Cold War to Iraq*. London: Red Globe Press, 2006.

Garnett, Mark, Simon Mabon, and Robert Smith. *British Foreign Policy since 1945*. New York: Routledge, 2017.

Gowland, David. *Britain and the European Union*. London: Routledge, 2016.

Greenwood, Sean. *Britain and the Cold War: 1945–1991*. New York: Palgrave, 1999.

Grob-Fitzgibbon, Benjamin. *Continental Drift: Britain and Europe from the End of Empire to the Rise of Euroscepticism*. Cambridge: Cambridge University Press, 2016.

Hogan, Michael J. *The Marshall Plan: America, Britain and the Reconstruction of Western Europe, 1947–1952*. Cambridge: Cambridge University Press, 1989.

Kyle, Keith. *Suez: Britain's End of Empire in the Middle East*. New York: St. Martin's, 1999.

Middlebrook, Martin. *The Falklands War*. Barnsley, UK: Pen and Sword Military, 2012.

More, Charles. *Britain in the Twentieth Century*. London: Longman, 2007.

Stoddart, Kristen. *Losing an Empire and Finding a Role: Britain, the USA, NATO and Nuclear Weapons, 1964–70*. London: Palgrave Macmillan, 2012.

CHAPTER 15: SOCIETY AND POLITICS: CHANGE AND CONTINUITY

Addison, Paul. "British Historians and the Debate over the 'Postwar Consensus.'" In *More Adventures with Britannia: Personalities, Politics, and Culture in Britain*, edited by William Roger Louis. Austin: University of Texas Press, 1998.

Bernstein, George. *The Myth of Decline: The Rise of Britain since 1945*. London: Pimlico, 2004.

Berridge, Virginia. *Health and Society in Britain since 1939*. New York: Cambridge University Press, 1999.

Brown, Callum. *The Death of Christian Britain: Understanding Secularisation 1800–2000*. London: Routledge, 2000.

Burk, Kathleen, ed. *The British Isles since 1945*. Oxford: Oxford University Press, 2003.

Emsley, Clive. *Crime and Society in Twentieth Century England*. London: Routledge, 2011.

Green, E. H. H. "Thatcherism: An Historical Perspective." *Transactions of the Royal Historical Society* 9, no. 6 (1999): 17–42.

Holmes, Colin. *A Tolerant Country? Immigrants, Refugees and Minorities in Britain*. London: Routledge, 1991.

Kynaston, David. *Austerity Britain, 1945–51*. London: Bloomsbury, 2007.

Kynaston, David. *Family Britain, 1951–57*. London: Bloomsbury, 2009.

Marwick, Arthur. *The Sixties: Cultural Transformation in Britain, France, Italy and the United States, c. 1958–c.1974*. Oxford: Oxford University Press, 1998.

Osgerby, Bill. "From the Roaring Twenties to the Swinging Sixties: Continuity and Change in British Youth Culture, 1929-1959." In *What Difference Did the War Make?*, edited by Brian Brivati and Harriet Jones. Leicester, UK: Leicester University Press, 1993.

Reid, Alastair. *United We Stand: A History of Britain's Trade Unions*. London: Penguin, 2004

Rush, Anne Spry. *Bonds of Empire: West Indians and Britishness from Victoria to Decolonization*. Oxford: Oxford University Press, 2011.

Ryan, Deborah S. *The Ideal Home through the 20th Century*. London: Hazar, 1997.

Sandbrook, Dominic. *Never Had It So Good: A History of Britain from Suez to the Beatles*. London: Little, Brown and Company, 2005.

—— *White Heat: A History of Britain in the Swinging Sixties*. London: Little, Brown, 2006.

—— *State of Emergency: The Way We Were: Britain 1970–1974*. London: Allen Lane, 2010.

Thane, Pat, and Tanya Evans. *Sinners? Scroungers? Saints? Unmarried Motherhood in Twentieth-Century England*. Oxford: Oxford University Press, 2012.

Ward, Paul. *Britishness since 1870*. London: Routledge, 2004.

Zweiniger-Bargielowska, Ina. *Austerity in Britain: Rationing, Controls and Consumption 1939–1955*. Oxford: Oxford University Press, 2000.

CHAPTER 16: CULTURE, BELIEFS, AND IDEAS

Brown, Callum G. *The Death of Christian Britain: Understanding Secularisation, 1800–2000*. 2nd ed. New York: Routledge, 2009.

Geddes, Andrew. *The Politics of Migration and Immigration in Europe*. London: SAGE, 2003.

Holmes, Colin. *A Tolerant Country? Immigrants, Refugees and Minorities in Britain*. London: Routledge, 1991.

Marwick, Arthur. *The Sixties: Cultural Transformation in Britain, France, Italy and the United States, c. 1958–c. 1974*. Oxford: Oxford University Press, 1998.

Osgerby, Bill. "From the Roaring Twenties to the Swinging Sixties: Continuity and Change in British Youth Culture, 1929-1959." In *What Difference Did the War Make?*, edited by Brian Brivati and Harriet Jones. Leicester, UK: Leicester University Press, 1993.

Rush, Anne Spry. *Bonds of Empire: West Indians and Britishness from Victoria to Decolonization*. Oxford: Oxford University Press, 2011.

Ryan, Deborah S. *The Ideal Home through the 20th Century*. London: Hazar, 1997.

Sandbrook, Dominic. *Never Had It So Good: A History of Britain from Suez to the Beatles*. London: Little, Brown and Company, 2005.

Sandbrook, Dominic. *State of Emergency: The Way We Were: Britain 1970–1974*. London: Allen Lane, 2010.

Sandbrook, Dominic. *White Heat: A History of Britain in the Swinging Sixties*. London: Little, Brown, 2006.

Tabili, Laura. "The Construction of Racial Difference in Twentieth-Century Britain: The Special Restriction (Coloured Alien Seamen) Order, 1925." *Journal of British Studies* 33 (1994): 54–98.

Thane, Pat, and Tanya Evans. *Sinners? Scroungers? Saints? Unmarried Motherhood in Twentieth-Century England*. Oxford: Oxford University Press, 2012.

Ward, Paul. *Britishness since 1870*. London: Routledge, 2004.

Zweiniger-Bargielowska, Ina. *Austerity in Britain: Rationing, Controls and Consumption 1939–1955*. Oxford: Oxford University Press, 2000.

INDEX

Irish rebellion, 1798, 83–84
Irish Republican Army (IRA), 341, 424, 426
Irish Republican Brotherhood, 291, 339
Irish War of Independence, 421
Islamic State in Iraq and Syria (ISIS), 402
Italian opera, 102

J

Jacobite rebellion, 102
Jacobites, 48, 52, 119, 124
Jacobitism, 119
James Bond franchise, 431
James Duke of Monmouth, 36
James I, 9
James II, 33–34, 36–37, 39, 52, 144
James VIII, 50
James VI of Scotland, 48, 61
Japanese invasion of India, 357
Jarrow Crusade, 1936, 380
Jean le Rond d'Alembert, 96
Jenkins, Captain Robert, 122
Jenkinson, Robert, 272
Jewish immigration, 262, 342
Jewish Naturalization Bill, 107
Jews in Britain, 23, 106–107, 248–249
Johnson, Bartholomew, 170–171
Johnson, John, 13
Johnston, Ellen, 178–179, 202
Jones, Indigo, 86
Joseph II of Austria, 96

K

Kaiser, 235–237
Kant, Emmanuel, 94
Kay, James Phillips, 186
Keats, John, 251
Keble, John, 246
Kennedy, John, 390
Kent, Susan, 16
Ketteridge, C. P., 360
Keynes, John Maynard, 338, 377
Kilmainham Treaty, 292

Kinealy, Christine, 217
King, Gregory, 4–6, 9–10
Kingdom of Ireland, 61
King Lear, 9
King's College London, 198
Kingsley, Charles, 224
Kinnock, Neil, 420
Kipling, Rudyard, 225
Kitchener, Lord Herbert, 330
Knowles, John, 15
Korean conflict, 391–392

L

Labouchere Amendment, 432
Labour Exchange Act (1909), 365
Labour Party, 369, 420–421
Laden, Osama bin, 401
Ladies National Association for the Repeal of the
    Contagious Diseases Acts (LNA), 262–263
Laissez faire economics, 255
Lamb, Charles, 321
Lancashire Cotton Famine, 314
Land Act of 1870, 291
landownership, 62
landscape paintings, 98
Langham Place Group, 204
Last Conquest of Ireland, 217
League of Coloured Peoples, 435
Leighton, Roland, 332
Lennox, Lady Caroline, 21
Leopold II, King, 231
A Letter to the Queen on Lord Chancellor
    Cranworth's Marriage and Divorce Bill, 177
Levine, Philippa, 225
Lewis, George, 38
Lewis, Leona, 441
liberalism, 252, 308–310, 362–363
Liberal Party, 288, 290–294, 296, 362, 368–369,
    383, 415
Liberals' Education Act (1907), 364
Liberals' Workmen's Compensation Act (1906), 365
Liberal Unionists, 292

CPSIA information can be obtained
at www.ICGtesting.com
Printed in the USA
FSHW021225161121
86235FS